Dear readers of this book:

As you read — think about, study, and work with — this book, you will add to knowledge and ideas you already have. You will become increasingly aware of the challenges of teaching and literacy learning today. Your confidence to meet those challenges will be buoyed by new information and strategies that will become part of your own teaching repertoire as you get experience in classrooms.

This book is a resource. As such, it becomes a useful classroom tool. For example, the **Children's Portfolio of Literacy Development** (excerpted on this left page) models both an approach and strategy for dynamic literacy teaching and learning.

Throughout this book, multiple modes of presentation occur to activate it. Moving from exposition, to narrative classroom scenes in action, special emphasis on contextual connections, instructional strategy, bibliographic resource lists, its theme — children's literacy: meaningful learning in context — is deepened.

Become an active participant together with this book, thereby making it more meaningful than we could have ever imagined!

CHILDREN'S LITERACY

Contexts for Meaningful Learning

SHANE TEMPLETON
University of Nevada, Reno

Houghton Mifflin Company   Boston   Toronto
Geneva, Illinois   Palo Alto   Princeton, New Jersey

To my parents, Ruth and Gene

Senior Sponsoring Editor: Loretta Wolozin
Project Editor: Danielle Carbonneau
Production/Design Coordinator: Jennifer Waddell
Senior Manufacturing Coordinator: Marie Barnes
Marketing Manager: Caroline Croley

Cover illustration: ''Dinosaurs with pink/purple blocks'' by Letizia Paolini (Rome, ITALY)
Cover design by Darci Mehall.

Credits can be found on page 645.

Printed in the U.S.A.

Library of Congress Catalog Card Number: 94-76554

ISBN: 0-395-57957-0

123456789-R-99 98 97 96 95

BRIEF CONTENTS

TABLE OF CONTENTS

SPECIAL FEATURES

■ MEANING MAKERS

■ MAKING CONNECTIONS

■ ■ ■ BUILDING YOUR KNOWLEDGE BASE

■ DEVELOPING YOUR INSTRUCTIONAL TOOLKIT

CLASSROOM IN ACTION

PREFACE

In his preface to the second edition of the classic *What Schools Are For* (1979/1994), John Goodlad writes:

> Schools are the only institutions in our nation specifically charged with the two-part mission of enculturating the young in a social and political democracy and introducing them to the organized bodies of knowledge that discipline and enrich our lives as citizens, workers, parents, and individual human beings.

Goodlad observes that schools have traditionally done a better job with the second part of this mission than with the first. At the present time in our history, schools are challenged to do an even *better* job with this second part to make our nation "competitive in the world market." Whatever the benefits and the liabilities of this perspective, we run the risk of losing sight of the importance and responsibility of enculturating our students in the real promise of a social and political democracy. I believe, however, that we *can* genuinely address and lay a very strong foundation in *both* areas, and that we can do so beginning in the primary and intermediate grades—the elementary school. *Literacy*—reading, writing, and all communication skills—will play the pivotal role in this foundation.

We have learned a lot about helping children become functionally and critically literate, but for so many reasons we are not reaching as many children as we could. Through *your* excitement about teaching and your commitment, you will be part of a movement that will change this situation, and that will guide our children towards the truly meaningful goals that Goodlad describes. This text will provide an important part of your foundation in realizing these goals for children.

APPROACH OF THE TEXT

The approach underlying this text is the *authentic reading/integrated literacy* approach. As a process and as a tool, literacy is a part of so much of what we do. It allows us to discover who we are and to come to know about our world and meaningfully engage it. Realizing this, our approach to guiding children to literacy and its uses should rest upon *authentic* reading—authentic purposes for reading authentic texts. Such reading is meaningfully *integrated* with writing and with all areas of the curriculum, those "organized bodies of knowledge and disciplines" to which Goodlad refers.

There are five cornerstones that define the foundation of the *authentic reading/ integrated literacy* approach throughout this text:

■ Focusing on Constructing Meaning as Key
■ Emphasizing the Contexts for Reading
■ Building Upon Children's Developmental Patterns in Literacy
■ Respecting and Encouraging Diversity
■ Using Real Literature

Introduced in Chapter One, the cornerstones pose the following key ideas. First and foremost, reading is a process in which meaning is constructed through a transaction between the reader and the text. Very often this process involves conscious *reflection* on what is being read and how it relates to what one presently knows, and to the values and beliefs one holds. As a *teacher*, you will also be reflective about your own reading and about your teaching; this process of reflection is pervasive and all-important.

Second, reading occurs simultaneously in several different contexts: physical, social, cultural, and psychological. As a teacher, you will need to be aware of these contexts and understand when and how to adjust and adapt your instruction in reading to respond appropriately to them. In the social and psychological contexts, reading is integrated with writing and the other language arts of speaking and listening. Each of these reinforces the other. Children need to think like writers as they read, and think like readers as they write. Learning and sustaining these complementary processes occurs through social interaction with others—talking with them and listening to them. Moreover, our instruction in reading so often occurs within lessons that stress a *larger* context than just the immediate context of the lesson. While these lessons may be one-to-one, small-group, or whole-class, they all relate back to what students do when they are engaged in meaningful, purposeful reading and writing.

Third, our instruction will build upon children's *developmental patterns* in literacy. In order to provide appropriate and timely guidance, it is important that we know what children know about literacy and how they are able to *apply* what they know at different points along a developmental continuum. In general, knowledge about literacy and the ability to apply this knowledge follows a developmental sequence—while children at all levels are able to construct meaning as they read, *how* they do so and the sophistication of the meaning they construct follows a developmental path.

Fourth, our instruction respects and encourages diversity. Effective and meaningful literacy instruction provides the context for incorporating diversity throughout the curriculum. At this time in our history there is much controversy on all sides regarding racial, ethnic, and social diversity and the degree to which it should be acknowledged and incorporated in the classroom. This text celebrates our diversity, presenting throughout suggestions for establishing the environment, selecting the topics, and providing the literature that helps children become aware of diversity and the *promise* it offers to our richly multicultural society.

Fifth, this text emphasizes the use of *real literature* in literacy instruction and throughout the elementary curriculum. There are reasons why real literature has not been used to the extent that it should have been throughout our educational history, but there is little doubt that from this point on literature will remain a cornerstone. Using real literature makes teaching reading both easier and more challenging—easier because, quite simply, children are more motivated to read when what they read is alive with the themes and topics that engage them, expressed through language that is effective and crafted by writers who know children. Real literature makes teaching more challenging—though ultimately more rewarding—because we are engaging children in real *thinking*, challenging them to discover, to explore, to use new ideas. We must understand literature and know how to engage children in it to address different purposes.

The communities in which you will teach will present more challenges than most teachers have faced in years past. *Literacy* may be the most essential tool which, as a teacher, you can offer your students. *What* they will read—and what *you* will read—will be of the utmost importance; as Robert Coles recently observed, ". . . what all of us need who are trying to engage many of our country's pressing and vexing social problems, [is] the wider perspective that literature can provide."

ORGANIZATION OF THE TEXT

Children's Literacy is organized into three major parts: Part One, Building Blocks for Literacy, establishes the theoretical and teaching foundation for children's literacy learning in the primary and intermediate grades. Chapters 1–3 present and elaborate the five cornerstones while providing in-depth examination of the *process* of reading itself and of the developmental characteristics of reading and writing. One entire chapter is devoted to literacy development *before* children begin formal schooling—while offering extensive instructional suggestions applicable to those children who begin formal schooling *without* benefit of certain key literacy experiences.

Part Two, "Literacy Instruction in Action," presents the *authentic reading/integrated literacy* approach in action. It provides an extremely comprehensive walk-through of literacy learning and instruction in the classroom. Chapters 4–9 guide you through setting up a classroom that establishes an optimal environment for immersing children in literacy. Beginning Reading is extensively addressed, and a chapter each is devoted to facilitating children's construction of meaning in narrative and informational materials. The structure, meanings, and moods of *words,* particularly in context, are explored. Because *writing* and reading are in so many ways complementary processes, you will find much in these chapters about children's construction of meaning through their own writing. Part Two concludes with an investigation of the nature and specifics of thematic teaching, showing how literacy infuses your themes and your curriculum, and provides extensive suggestions for development of thematic units as well as describing a progression you may comfortably follow in your own development as a thematic teacher.

Part Three, "Making Choices and Meeting All Needs for Literacy Learning," elaborates on several critical issues that have been mentioned throughout Parts One and Two. Instruction occurs within many contexts, we know, including the *historical* context of literacy instruction. As a nation and society, our instructional legacy will influence your day-to-day instruction, and for this reason we explore it briefly and then turn to a closer examination of the "methods and materials" that have been and continue to be available for literacy instruction. You will examine in much more depth how to *assess* the nature and development of your students' literacy and how to relate this information to your day-to-day instructional decisions. You will explore two critical issues that are addressed every day in your classroom: accommodating the needs of linguistically diverse children and of less-proficient readers and writers.

SPECIAL LEARNING FEATURES OF THE TEXT

A number of special learning features appear throughout the text. These are substantive and organic to text content.

■ *Children's Portfolio of Literacy Development* four color insert presents children's art and writing to show how children learn about their worlds through reading and writing. This feature conveys the rich interconnections that are possible for children among their reading, writing, and artistic experiences. As noted in the introduction to the portfolio, we are coming to understand that art is a major component of children's literacy experiences. I am excited about the works and hope you will find that they are effective examples as you read about different instructional and developmental points throughout the text.

Recurring features are:

■ *Meaning Makers* which focus on meaning construction: what readers do during the *process* of reading; on how classroom teachers are able to make meaning in the context of their classrooms and how they are able to step back to reflect on the meanings they are constructing; and on how you as a student make meaning as you read this text, talk with others in class, write in response to what you are reading, and construct ever richer conceptions of "reading" and how children learn to do it.

■ *Making Connections* that describe how, within an instructional context, strategies and activities can integrate the language arts and help children become aware of and understand this rich network of interrelationships.

■ The *Classroom in Action* vignettes help situate novice readers providing in-depth descriptions of strategies and activities actually being applied in classroom environments.

■ *Developing Your Instructional Toolkits* offer instructional suggestions and materials that can be a rich resource for your teaching.

■ *Building Your Knowledge Base* provides additional information about the children's literature presented throughout the text.

OTHER LEARNING AND STUDY FEATURES

Additional learning and study features include:

- *Focus Questions* at the beginning of each chapter. You should find that, by reading these and thinking about them a bit before you read, your meaning making throughout each chapter is more focused and purposeful.
- Chapter outlines also appear at the beginning of each chapter to help you see, at a glance, how the content of the chapter is organized.
- *Becoming a Reflective Practitioner* features are found at the end of each chapter. The articles and, on occasion, books and book chapters presented here represent the thinking and the work being conducted in the different areas addressed in each chapter. It is difficult to select from the tremendous body of excellent work being done in literacy, but the selections I have made I believe are indeed representative and will help you reflect, question, and if you wish, pursue further.

ANCILLARIES TO ACCOMPANY THE TEXT

Instructor's Resources. This manual combines material that will be useful to both students and instructors who are using CHILDREN'S LITERACY.

Part I contains model syllabi for organizing course materials and activities for either a 10- or 15-week term. This is especially useful for new instructors or those who are using an experiential approach for the first time.

Part II contains Student Study Guide Handouts for each chapter including learning objectives, key terms with definitions, and "Bridging Theory and Practice" activities.

Part III offers chapter-by-chapter Instructor Teaching Aids including extensive annotated outlines, classroom activities, and additional strategies and resources which elaborate on material in the textbook.

Part IV contains a complete set of assessment materials including an ongoing strand of portfolio assessment, multiple choice questions, short essay questions, and essay questions for each chapter.

Computerized Test Generator. The test items contained in the Instructor's Resources are also available in an interactive computerized form upon adoption of the text.

Overhead Transparencies. A set of colorful transparencies is available to each instructor upon adoption of the text. The transparencies feature figures from the text and highlight key content covered in the chapters.

ACKNOWLEDGMENTS

An undertaking as extensive as a text of this type could not have occurred without the support, influence, and ideas from so many, many people. I wish

I could list all of them here. Those who have given so much of their time and have most directly influenced this text include the following:

First, Sandra Madura—the teacher whose classroom and instruction over the years have so closely embodied my own beliefs about what the "ideal" type of classroom ought to look and feel like. I have had the privilege of working collaboratively with Sandra for many years, and I have valued, trusted, and in many instances marveled at her judgment. She read the first draft of this book and responded extensively and insightfully. Realizing how much of her was already in this book, I requested her to become involved in the process of revising several chapters. Not surprisingly, the depth of her involvement in this process and the insights she brought to the text made a significant contribution to the text. Her teaching, reflection, and contributions are most in evidence in the extensive development of thematic units in Chapter 9, the innumerable instructional examples throughout the book, the insights into organization, planning, and implementation. Her extensive knowledge of literature is here as well—including her unique expertise in infusing literature and learning with art, most apparent in our co-authored portfolio insert. Much of Sandra's work is also included in the Instructor's Resources for *Children's Literacy*.

Beth Roberts—former student, presently-valued colleague and friend of many years—accepted the responsibility for preparing the Instructor's Resources for *Children's Literacy*. She created, I believe, an invaluable resource for instructors. Moreover, she did so in a very short time. I am delighted that her gifts as a scholar and teacher are clearly in evidence in this work.

The following reviewers deserve a very special expression of gratitude. Their feedback during successive drafts of the book was invaluable and evidenced a considerable amount of time invested. The book is immeasurably better, I believe, because of their efforts:

Peter Afflerbach, University of Maryland at College Park
Kathy Everts Danielson, University of Nebraska at Omaha
Kate Hathaway, College of New Rochelle
Rita Jensen, Bradley University
Cindy Matthews, Hofstra University
Samuel Miller, University of North Carolina
Sherron Killingsworth Roberts, Iowa State University
Mary Jett Simpson, University of Wisconsin
Laura Smolkin, University of New Mexico
Mary-Claire Tarlow, University of Alaska Southeast
Eileen Walter, Western Washington University
Janice Wilson, University of Alabama

I wish to acknowledge the following teachers and "reflective practitioners" *par excellence* with whom I have worked and from whom I have learned so much; they all have shared their students' work with me over the years, and much of that work appears in this book: Barb Milchak; Ann Urie; Shae Pardini; Wanda Nomura; Marietta Marquis; Claudia Rossi and Diane Olds, who shared their ideas and insights about thematic teaching as well as the "fruits" of those insights; and Damon Palmer, who kindly shared the writing of the "Becoming a Reflective Practitioner" feature.

The following colleagues have, over the years, offered encouragement, support, and countless hours of wonderful talk and argument. I owe a special debt to them for all they have given me: Mary Abouzeid, Diane Barone, Donald Bear, Jim and Carol Beers, Martha Combs, Ron Cramer, Jim Deese, Tom Estes, Linnea Ehri, Tom Gill, Dorsey Hammond, Marcia Invernizzi, Meggin McIntosh, Jim Miller, Darrell Morris, Charles Read, Bob Schlagal, Elizabeth Salzby, Bill Teale, Charlie Temple, Frank Vellutino, Mike Warner, Dave Yaden, Jr., and Jerry Zutell.

Finally, to the incredible people in both the College and School divisions at Houghton Mifflin Company who have supported and encouraged my efforts over the years, the most heartfelt thanks: Loretta Wolozin—an educational visionary in her own right. Loretta talked me into writing one more textbook and has in so many, many ways inspired my efforts; Merryl Maleska Wilbur, the finest developmental editor one could ever hope for and who has been my indispensable companion in this adventure; Danielle Carbonneau, a remarkable production editor who always remained patient and considerate despite my delays; Lisa Mafrici, who has been the linchpin in this project and who has guided so many aspects of this project, including the development of the Instructor's Resources; Janet Edmonds, coordinator of the art insert project, who offered welcome reassurance and encouragement; and the many other people there in Boston who have labored mightily to make this book real. Finally, a very special thanks to those wonderful people from my "early days" with Houghton Mifflin who taught, guided, and encouraged me: Domenica Raciti, Emily Shenk, and Jean Muller.

Once again, my family has been supportive and more than understanding. My children deserve another special acknowledgement for allowing me to use work from *their* early years to help illustrate the developmental literacy continuum. They would want me, I know, to note that they are now much farther along that continuum and are indeed using reading and writing in truly consequential ways.

Shane Templeton

PART ONE

BUILDING BLOCKS

FOR LITERACY

What is the role of "literacy" in our diverse, technological, and rapidly-changing society? In this part, we will explore the tool of literacy and its many uses, and describe the critical role you, the teacher, will play in children's literacy learning. We will present the elements of the reading process—language, thought, prior knowledge, and skills and explore this process as it operates in mature, proficient readers and as it develops in children from the beginning school years through the intermediate grades. We will also focus in depth on the preschool years, describing the emergence of literacy and the support and environments that best encourage this emergence.

CHAPTER ONE

LITERACY LEARNING

AND INSTRUCTION

FOCUS

■ *Why is the ability to read so critically important in our society?*

■ *Why should you reflect on what learning to read was like for you?*

■ *What must children know in order to be able to read?*

■ *In what ways is society becoming increasingly diverse? In such a diverse society, what are the implications for teaching children how to read?*

■ *Are there similarities among children in the ways in which they learn to read?*

■ *Why is the role of authentic literature so important in teaching children to read?*

■ *What is the value of being a "reflective teacher" of reading?*

What *is* "literacy"?

"It's easy to answer that question," we think. "Literacy is the ability to read and write." And this is the basic definition we will apply throughout this book—though as we will come to see, this apparently simple concept is only the surface of a rich and impressive foundation. Before we begin to probe further, though, we should consider for a moment all that our society has come to consider as "literacy":

Literacy can mean knowing about, and knowing how to "do," particular subjects. We speak of math literacy, scientific literacy, and geographical literacy. We talk about being culturally literate, about knowing how to speak and act in a "literate" manner in certain situations, and about being able to "read" features of our environment such as scientific instruments, changes in the weather, and changes in other people's facial expressions, moods, and opinions. And of course we talk about being computer literate, from knowing how to interact with an automatic teller to understanding and using microcomputers for a whole host of purposes.

In this book, however, we will be focusing specifically on the medium of *print.* In fact, in order to acquire and use most other types of literacy, we first must be print literate. We are going to be concerned primarily with the *reading* side of print literacy—although we will be making many connections with *writing,* the other side of print literacy (see Making Connections on page 19). And along the way, I will be pointing out the relationship between print literacy and other types of literacy.

I know it's likely that your primary reason for reading this book and taking a course in the teaching of reading is that you wish to teach children. You most likely have a love for them and a fundamental desire to work with them—to teach them, learn from them, enjoy them. Yet you also are aware that much of what you and your students will engage in—and much of the elementary curriculum—rests upon the foundation of *reading.* So let's think about *your* role in developing children's reading abilities.

As you learn about the teaching of reading and as you apply what you learn, you are going to be thinking carefully about the *process* of reading that occurs when (1) the reader and (2) what the reader reads (3) come together in a particular context or situation. At the same time—this is most important—you will be trying to recapture what it was like to think like an elementary school child!

How *did* you learn to read? Do you even remember? Do you vaguely recall sitting next to or on the lap of what seemed to be a very large adult—who was helping you turn the pages of a book as you listened to and felt their voice tell a story? Can you recall sitting in reading groups and reading aloud? Do you remember what it was like *not* to be able to read? When did your first experiences with reading occur: when you began kindergarten, or in first grade? Were you grouped according to "ability"—in the "high," "middle," or "low" reading group? Were you excited by, bored with, or indifferent to "reading" as a subject throughout elementary school?

As you reflect on these questions, you may recall much about what reading meant to you as a learner and how you were taught to read. As for myself, I can remember not being able to read, and I can remember being in the lowest reading group in first grade. I remember struggling day after day with letters and sounds as I labored to make sense of what Dick, Jane, Sally, and Spot were doing. And I remember what I thought my job was when *I* began to teach children to read: to help them learn how to "sound out" those letters.

How very much more there is to reading than sounding out letters and identifying words! In this book, our exploration of reading instruction will rest on a foundation constructed from five interconnected tenets or cornerstones that underlie what happens when a *reader* and a *text* come together in a particular *context*. We will call this our "authentic reading/integrated literacy" approach to reading instruction. The five cornerstones of this approach not only support the nature and the purpose of reading instruction; they will also be the bedrock of your learning in this book:

1. *Focusing on Constructing Meaning as Key*
2. *Emphasizing the Contexts for Reading*
3. *Building upon Children's Developmental Patterns in Literacy*
4. *Respecting and Encouraging Diversity*
5. *Using Real Literature*

We will probe each of these cornerstones quite deeply later in this chapter. Right at the outset, I would like to help you set up your thinking and reflection about them, however.

■ *Focusing on Constructing Meaning as Key.* In a very fundamental way, reading involves constructing meaning. Constructing or "making" meaning is something people just naturally do. We don't go around letting everything announce to us what it means—quite the contrary, for our brains are designed to construct the meaning of whatever we perceive. So the "meaning" of what we read is not "on" a writing surface to be "lifted off" by us as our eyes move over the print. Rather, the print that we see is one important component that all readers use to *construct meaning* by bringing together what they see on the writing surface with their present knowledge and purposes. In Dewey and Bentley's (1949) and Rosenblatt's (1978) terminology, we "transact" with whatever we are reading. The *transaction* involves the result of the coming together in a particular setting or *context* (classroom, on the job, just before turning out the light at night) of the intended meaning of a text with the meaning that the reader brings to the text.

■ *Emphasizing the Contexts for Reading.* We use the term *context* to refer to whatever surrounds us at a particular point in time. Actually, at any given moment we are in *several* contexts; Cole and Griffin (1987) refer to the notion of "embedded" contexts. Whenever we read, for example, the embedded contexts are these:

Physical: The physical context is *where* we are as we are reading; for example, in a classroom or a kitchen.

Social: The social context strongly affects *what* and *how* we read (Bloome & Egan-Robertson, 1993); that is, are other individuals present and if so, how are they affecting your reading? Are they going to ask you questions? Will you discuss what is being read? Do you comment to one another while reading? What will you be expected to do when you finish your reading: tell what the "meaning" is? identify the tense of the verb? write something?

Cultural: The cultural context potentially reflects several cultures. To an extent, schools are set up in ways that reflect the values, expectations, and language of the mainstream culture. But the values, expectations, and language of nonmainstream cultures are increasingly a part of the classroom; and different cultures often have different expectations about literacy and how it is taught, how it is used, and what it means.

Psychological: The term *psychological context* refers to a particular reader's knowledge, emotions, and attitudes in a particular reading situation.

A context is "meaningful" if it connects with children's experiences and background. In addition, the context is meaningful if it is clearly connected to the rest of what is going on in the learning environment: the other language arts of writing, speaking, and listening, and the other dimensions of the curriculum.

■ *Building upon Children's Developmental Patterns in Literacy.* As we involve children in reading, we should fashion our instruction in light of what we know about their developmental patterns, growth, and interests. What children understand about the *conventions* of printed language, and how children interpret and use what they read, will depend upon their developmental levels. Your knowledge of development will help you avoid the pitfalls of expecting too much or too little of a particular child.

■ *Respecting and Encouraging Diversity.* Reading instruction—in its approaches and materials and in the attitudes conveyed—must respect and encourage our diverse society; it must also allow for diverse response. The concept of "diversity" has always been a variable in the classroom. Traditionally, it has referred to the range of children's abilities and aptitudes that any teacher faces. In recent years it has referred as well to the sociocultural differences that most teachers will find among their students.

All cultural groups have rich language traditions and ways of sharing them. The knowledge of these traditions that many children bring to school is often different from the dominant conception of "reading" and of *what* we read. When we include in our classrooms the literature of diverse groups, we move toward two fundamental goals. First, we ensure that children from "nondominant" cultures see *themselves* in books; this is necessary to sustain a motivation toward and an interest in literacy. Second, we ensure that children, regardless of their sociocultural backgrounds, become aware of other cultures and move toward understanding them. In and of itself this is a positive moral value. Given both the nature of our multicultural society and the need to be aware of issues beyond our own national borders, it is a practical necessity as well.

■ *Using Real Literature.* Reading instruction should be based on authentic literature. Using real books as the basis for instruction builds motivation effectively. Authentic literature can be drawn from all aspects of the curriculum and used as a basis for teaching reading as a tool and for integrating learning with the other language arts and across the curriculum.

THE SPECIAL ROLE OF READING IN OUR LIVES

Eleven-year-old Patrick, a fifth-grader, wrote the following response immediately after reading about the experience of Native Americans in Simon Ortiz's informative and evocative picture book *The People Shall Continue* (1988): "Right now the bloodcells in my body are shoveling out a lump in my throat. This book is a great example of what happened to the Native Americans. A lot of books bring me into the story but this one brought me into the words. . . ." Patrick's experience with that one book became a defining moment in his young life. He already knew the "story" of the fate of Native Americans, as do most elementary children. But in this particular book he heard the story through the voice of that culture, a voice still resonating with hope and pride, and he was touched on a much deeper level.

I asked you earlier to try to remember how you learned to read and what it meant to you. Now, with Patrick's experience in mind, let's reflect on the critical role that reading plays in our lives as adults and in the lives of the children we teach.

The *act* of reading is unique. No other experience will involve us in the same ways reading does. We cannot make as much sense of so much else that we experience, as we can of what we experience through reading—through stepping back and reflecting on what we have read, and through talking with others about our reading. Consider for a moment the nature of this reflective *critical thinking* that reading allows us: the opportunity to engage, to enjoy, to reflect—and to extend our experience and our minds.

There is something about the *language* of books, too, that helps us go beyond ourselves. The language in books so often refers not only to what is and what has been but to what yet *may be*. It is a "what-if" language that represents infinite possibilities. In addition, in this time and place and regardless of where we live, few other experiences can lead us so directly and so often toward becoming "more tolerant, more sensitive, more humane" (Greene, 1972/1980, p. 662).

"But," we occasionally hear, "in an age of multimedia possibilities—interfacing computers with videodiscs, music, text, and so on, the printed word is becoming obsolete—there are newer ways of teaching, not to mention ways of experiencing life." Yes, there are newer ways and there are different ways, but their sum total does not necessarily equal a better way.

There is something unique about the reading experience and the reflection that can accompany it, something that does not occur in quite the same way when, for example, we watch a video. The reasons for this have to do with the psychology of the reading process as well as the nature of whatever other medium we're interacting with. In contrast to watching a television screen, for example, when we are reading a novel, *we* are constructing the story's sights, sounds, and smells, rather than the director or the camera operator of a movie. *We* are controlling the pace of the action; we can go backward and forward at will in the text. And even if we are involved in a quality multimedia instructional experience—alternating, let's say, among reading about Young Sherlock Holmes, viewing scenes, and hearing music from Victorian England on a videodisc—it is during the print presentation that we will usually be in control of the process of reflection and consciously thinking about what it all means.

Margaret Meek explains that in books, we find "the depth and breadth of human experience. . . . Readers are at home in the life of the mind; they live with ideas as well as events and facts. They understand a wider range of feelings by entering into those of other people. *They are free to choose one kind of existence rather than another*" (1983, p. 17; emphasis added). Shirley Brice Heath has observed, "The state of being literate *removes the individual from dependence* on only immediate senses and direct contacts" (1991, p. 4, emphasis added).

It is the same notion of freedom that is particularly compelling in this age of multimedia. Many of the "popular" media—whether large-screen home entertainment centers or Nintendo-type video games—have the opposite effect. They tend to narrow the individual's perception of his or her choices, wishes, and ambitions—at the same time as they give the illusion of freedom. Because of the profound "meaning making" potential of the *process* of reading (Wells, 1986) and the *product* of reading, the medium of print simply offers more options for thinking and for action. As I will emphasize time and again in this text, the *reflection* that the act of reading allows is profoundly important; Maxine Greene once observed that during reading, "reflection is as important as imaginative engagement" (1972/1980, p. 663).

YOUR SPECIAL ROLE IN HELPING CHILDREN LEARN TO READ

Eight-year-old Bianca captured the magic and the meaning of reading when she wrote in her journal, "The important thing about reading is when you first learn how to read you feel so special and grownup. And if you don't ever get to go on a trip or have an adventure and you know how to read you can go on an adventure just by reading. Reading is very important." Bianca's teacher, Sandy Madura, had established the type of environment and instruction that resulted in Bianca's observation. Let's examine directly our special role as teachers in facilitating children's experiences with and feelings toward reading.

At the outset I want to emphasize that you as teacher are (1) a *potent decision-maker* and (2) a *learning facilitator.* Most important, these two critical roles place the students' learning at the center of everything. Margaret Meek captures this idea when she speaks of the significance of how we usher children into literacy:

> The way children are taught to read tells them what adults think literacy
> is. If we want our children to read well, they must themselves have good and
> compelling reasons for doing so . . . so when we help children to read, we
> are also telling them about literacy and society, about the reasons for

reading and about themselves as learners. The view of reading a child accepts is the one his first teacher gives him. (1983, pp. 18–19)

Meek reminds us how magical our initiation into literacy as children must have been and why as teachers we should help create this magic when we teach children how to read—as we make decisions and facilitate their realization of "good and compelling reasons" for reading. I would add only that these reasons need to be sustained *beyond* the child's "first teacher," since children continue to learn about literacy, society, and themselves as learners.

So in an age in which profound societal changes are under way and in which information is doubling every couple of years—with implications for what we teach and how we teach it—there is an urgency as to how you will be helping children learn to read and the reading choices you'll make available to them. This urgency involves but also goes beyond the particular texts the children you teach will be reading: *Do they know what literacy can do for them and do they know how to apply this incredible tool for different purposes?* We can start a list of related but equally important questions:

- Do they know *how* to approach different texts?
- Do they know *how* to set appropriate purposes for reading?
- Do they know *how* to step back and think *critically* about what they are reading—to reflect on it, evaluate it, apply it deliberately to their own lives—and do they know *when* it is important to do this?
- Do they know how to *think about their thinking* as they read—to know when to adjust their purposes, their rate, their strategies?

Learning to read and the reading process itself involve much, much more than simply the "basics," such as how letters stand for sounds. There is a generally prevalent belief, however, that if we just "teach the children the sounds that the letters make, they will learn to read" (Flesch, 1955/1981)—and that that's all there is to it. Quite the contrary: facilitating children's learning to read and learning how to use reading also involves teaching them how to evaluate and apply the meanings they construct as they read in the different types or *genres* of literature: stories, informational books, poems, textbooks, documents, test formats, and so on. It involves teaching children how to think in deeply consequential and meaningful ways about things that are important.

Moss (1990), Cullinan (1988), Norton (1991), and several other children's literature authorities have captured precisely the nature of your role. Joy Moss has observed:

> Children should be given the freedom to choose their own reading material. However, parents and teachers have a responsibility to introduce them to the wide range of books available to them for enjoyment as listeners and readers. The adult serves as a guide, inviting children to explore the world of books and then to develop their own interests and preferences as independent readers . . . I have found that some parts of this world are less likely to be discovered by children on their own than others. (1990, p. 7)

As a teacher, Moss goes on to speak of ". . . my feeling of responsibility to children and my desire to ensure that they do not miss the opportunity to discover their literary heritage'' (1990, p. 7). Bernice Cullinan writes that the extent to which books play a significant role in children's lives ". . . depends entirely upon adults. Adults are responsible for providing books and transmitting the literary heritage . . ." (1977, p. 1).

The literary heritage grows richer with each generation. Why transmit a literary heritage? Because those human values that are best in us are also transmitted, and because ways of understanding ourselves and others are transmitted.

Your special role in helping children acquire, use, and value literacy is illustrated in part by the following vignettes, each of which might not have occurred had not a teacher brought certain children into contact with certain books at a certain, just-right time:

> There is the class of affluent European-American third-graders who identify with Nettie—a well-to-do girl whose family visits the American South before the Civil War in Ann Turner's *Nettie's Trip South*; Nettie's comfortable and secure ideas about the world are thrown into troubled disarray because of what she sees. The class then reads Virginia Hamilton's version of *The People Could Fly* and understands the incredibly strong, moving, ever-hopeful ways in which, through story, slaves in the American South coped with the captivity and the cruelty.

> There is the sixth-grade girl who finds strength and a role model in the character of Harry Crewe (who is actually a girl) in Robin McKinley's fantasy *The Blue Sword* and in Bright Dawn, a young Eskimo girl in Scott O'Dell's *Black Star, Bright Dawn,* who races in the incredibly grueling Iditarod dog-sled race from Anchorage to Nome, Alaska.

> There is the student who, because he moves with his parents from one place to another to pick crops, never settles in with a particular group of children in school. He finds nobility, pride, and purpose when a teacher reads him Florence White's *Cesar Chavez: Man of Courage* and subsequently he pores over the pages, again and again, until the book as well as the man become part of his soul.

You will be helping your students realize that in addition to being a valuable tool that is wielded in many different ways, reading is a unique type of *experience* that generates ideas, feelings, sudden insights, comfort, guideposts, excitement, and an understanding of and bonding with others—most of whom they will never meet.

THE CORNERSTONES OF AN AUTHENTIC READING/INTEGRATED LITERACY APPROACH

Each time readers read a printed message—whether it is a novel, a menu, a poem, a set of directions, or this chapter—they engage in a process that involves an "orchestration" of a number of skills with a reader's knowledge, ideas, attitudes, and levels of cognitive, language, and literacy development (Just & Carpenter, 1987). There is much going on here, and the result of this process is a "meaning" unique to each reader.

How do *developing* readers—the children you will be teaching—"orchestrate" their available knowledge and resources while they themselves are still developing? How do they become mature, skilled readers? Most of the rest of this book will support answers to these two questions. In this section, we will examine the cornerstones for the foundation of your instruction.

We know the special—indeed, *critical*—role you will play in your students' development of literacy. Your decisions and your facilitation of the children's reading development will depend on a number of factors. These include your understanding of the types of skills, information, and cognitive/linguistic abilities *each* of your students has. Knowledge of each student works in tandem with teaching based on the instructional approach we are advocating.

It is time to define specifically the words that occur in the title of our approach and then to see how our five tenets fit as the cornerstones of your literacy instruction in the classroom (see Figure 1.1 below). *Authentic reading* means that students read *real* texts with *real,* student-centered purposes—in contrast to the traditional situation in which students read primarily in "reading programs" and "materials," according to purposes always set by the teacher. *Integrated literacy* refers to how literacy can bring the world of information, experience, and enjoyment integrally into our own lives. Literacy allows a type of involvement with life that is literally unique and special. *Integrated literacy* also refers to the role literacy plays in exploring and understanding the world of the classroom and beyond. As a tool, literacy can be used naturally and effectively as part of different domains—math, the social sciences, natural science, and on and on.

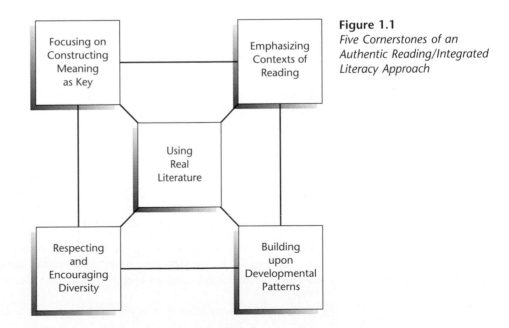

Figure 1.1
Five Cornerstones of an Authentic Reading/Integrated Literacy Approach

Focusing on constructing meaning as key

I will highlight the business of "meaning making," in three ways, throughout this book. First, we will look at how this process works during reading. Second, we will think about how teachers themselves "construct meaning" as they *reflect* on how they are going about teaching literacy. Third, we will reflect on *your* construction of meaning as you read this textbook: I will be involving you in reflecting on *your* "meaning making" as well as on that of the children you will teach. There will be many opportunities, in other words, to be reflective or "mindful" of your own reading and to consider how you can involve children in this type of reflection.

My emphasis on constructing meaning in literacy reflects a broader emphasis throughout education over the past few years on *constructivism* (for example, Barthes, 1970; Moffett, 1968; Piaget, 1970; Polanyi, 1962; Poplin, 1988). *Constructivism* is the term educators have applied to a philosophy and psychology of learning that places the *learner* at the center of the educational enterprise. Learners construct meaning in terms of what they already know; they move from the known to the new. They do not passively receive information "from the outside in." Usually, I will use the term *meaning making* to reflect this constructivist perspective; I feel it brings a more humanistic sense to an important and powerful process.

Reading and the Construction of Meaning   What *is* reading? What does it mean to say that reading is "a process of constructing meaning"?

To answer the questions, we need to operationalize that "process": reading is a process in which (1) readers bring meaning to the text so that (2) they can better approximate the meaning the writer brought to the text (Rosenblatt, 1978; Smith, 1989; Weaver, 1988). As readers, we accomplish this by relating our prior knowledge about language and about the world—the meaning we are bringing to the text—to the processing or "picking up" of the visual, printed information in the text. How effectively we relate our prior knowledge to the writer's intended meaning so that we construct an appropriate meaning depends upon the following factors:

- Our general knowledge and vocabulary; *vocabulary* refers to the words that represent underlying concepts.
- Our knowledge about what is being read: how much do we already know about the topic?
- Our purposes: *why* is this being read?
- Our knowledge about the type of text being read: poems and stories are read differently and for very different purposes than a booklet about using a microwave oven.
- Our interest or degree of engagement with the text.

How efficiently we pick up visual information depends primarily upon our knowledge about the structure of printed words; specifically, how the letters correspond to sounds and to larger meaningful elements (Rayner & Pollatsek, 1989).

All of this—our different types of knowledge and our purposes—in turn depends on the context in which we are reading and on our developmental level as readers.

Louise Rosenblatt refers to this coming together of the reader's meaning with the text's intended meaning as a *transaction;* the meaning that is created is a *new* meaning, one that did not exist before in either the writer's or the reader's mind. This process of transaction is dynamic, because the meaning that is constructed does not wait until we have finished reading but is being created as we move through a text.

Because we understand that reading is a transaction, between a reader and a text, within a context that results in a meaning unique to each reader, much of what a good many people have thought about reading and meaning is turned on its ear. There is no one true or "real" meaning to any piece of writing, regardless of how well the writer may have tried to express an intended meaning. As teachers, it is critical that we understand the implications of this simple fact. We will celebrate the unique insights and understandings of each student. On the other hand, as we will discuss at some length later on, there is also a time when we will want students to converge on as similar a meaning as they can. It all depends on the reader, the text, and the context.

Teachers as Reflective "Meaning Makers"   We have examined your role as a teacher in helping children become literate and in understanding and appreciating the role and meaning of literacy in their lives. What about your *own* "meaning making" in your classroom? You will be a learner right along with your students (Genishi, 1989; Strickland, 1988). It is as important for you as for your students to be reflective and "mindful" of your own learning. This means that you must be able to step back and see the bigger picture and to step back far enough from specific situations that you can be a practical problem-solver.

You will be making meaning in your classroom primarily through your reflection on what you are doing, why you are doing it, and how the children respond (Berliner, 1986; Dewey, 1933; Schon, 1983). This may be particularly challenging when you first begin to teach. It will seem as if there is so much you are trying to stay on top of that to step back, to try to see from a broader perspective what you and your students are doing, is unexpectedly difficult. Yet you will find yourself becoming more and more able to analyze situations and plan instructional and organizational strategies for addressing them. You will be a more practical problem-solver.

You probably are going to discover that over time, you become more analytical about the process of teaching. That is to say, your initial reflections may be rather global ("How well did the two literature discussion groups work while I was doing a minilesson on contextual clues with a third group?"), while your later reflections will probe more intricately the *nature* of students' interactions within their discussion groups ("Yolanda seems to focus primarily on major themes in stories but has some trouble in searching through a story to support her insights when challenged by others . . ."). The breadth and depth of your reflections will correspond to the continuing enlargement of your knowledge base about literacy, its development, and the contexts in which it occurs—and of course about the children you teach.

Your **Construction of Meaning in This Textbook**   We have been talking about "meaning making" at some length. At this point I'll go ahead and state the obvious: of course, you will be making meaning in this textbook as well. I would like you, however, to be able to use your experience with this text as an ongoing means of stepping back to engage in reflection. As a reader, you are bringing *your* meaning to this text—a text that of course represents *my* intended meaning. So there will be an ongoing *transaction* between us. As the writer, I am trying to speak to you as directly as I can, knowing that you will still construct a meaning that will be at least slightly different from the one constructed by the student sitting next to you in class. If I do the best job I can as a writer of this text, however, and you do the best job *you* can as the reader, our transaction will be beneficial and instructive, and will share important common understandings with other readers of the book.

To illustrate and facilitate the three-faceted process of meaning construction, I have included "Meaning Makers" features throughout the book. Each feature has one of these three themes: "The Reader," which focuses on what readers do during the *process* of reading; "The Classroom Teacher," which focuses on how teachers are able to make meaning in the context of their classrooms and step back to reflect on the meanings they are constructing; or "You, the Student," which will focus on *your* process of "meaning making" as you read this text, talk with others in class, write in response to what you are reading, and construct ever-richer conceptions of "reading" and how children learn to read.

Our first Meaning Makers feature focuses on *you,* and we will use this opportunity to suggest that you begin a journal, a learning log, for this text and course.

MEANING MAKERS: You, the Student

Learning Logs

Now would be an excellent time to begin your learning log for this course. Later on we'll be discussing how learning logs can be used by children, but now is an excellent time for you to start your own. The learning log will aid you in reflecting on your learning and on your developing concept of what it means to be a teacher. Over time, it will provide an excellent document of your growth. A colleague of mine, Meggin McIntosh, suggests the following approach.

What do you include in your learning log?

- Brief summaries of what you learn in class and from each chapter in this text.
- New words, ideas, and concepts.
- Profound thoughts that occur to you.
- Wonderings, musings, problems to solve.
- Reflections about the course.
- Questions—answerable and unanswerable.

When should you write in your learning log?

- After class each day.
- As you are preparing/reading/studying for class.
- Any time an insight or question strikes you.

Where should you write in your learning log?

- Anywhere—so keep it with you as much as possible.

Why should you write in your learning log?

- It will record ideas that you might otherwise forget.
- It will be worthwhile for you to read later on in order to note your growth and understanding.
- It will facilitate your learning/problem-solving/writing/reading/discussion in this class.

How should you write in your learning log?

- In single words that express your ideas; in short phrases or sentences; in diagrams, sketches, outlines, and so on. . . . ■

Emphasizing the contexts for reading

There is no "pure" reading process, unaffected by what we know, how we feel and think, and where we are. Reading *always* occurs in a context; and when we teach, we must be aware of this fact and sensitive to it. As adults, we read in contexts that are in part controlled by others (there is, after all, a course you are taking in which a professor has assigned this particular text), but we often have more choice about whether, when, and where we will do our reading. Theoretically children have the same degree of choice, but of course we will be deliberately involving them in reading, thus determining much of the context— though by no means all—in which their reading occurs.

The Physical, Social, Cultural, and Psychological Contexts of Reading   The process of reading does not occur in a vacuum. *Every* time a reader and a text come together, the process occurs in a situation that is determined by several embedded contexts. The nature of the *transaction* between reader and text is determined by the contexts in which the act is occurring. And for every reader, the context for the reading is unique—there is only one relationship between a particular reader and a particular text at a particular point in time. This is why the meaning that each reader constructs, as we said earlier, is truly unique to that reader, different to a larger or a smaller degree than the meanings other readers construct. When I introduced the concept of "contexts" earlier in this chapter, I noted that the immediate act of reading is nested within physical, social, and psychological contexts. Let's examine these now within the elementary classroom.

How about the *physical context*? Does the classroom have a warm, friendly look and feel to it? Does it seem to *invite* children to read? Is there a library corner with *lots* of different books attractively displayed? Are students allowed to snuggle into cozy corners to read if they wish? If reading the same book, can they pair off or cluster in groups of three to read and share? Most of us do not sit rigidly at a desk at home when we are reading a novel; neither should we expect kids to read that way.

The *social context* for reading should also be warm and vibrant. When *we* enjoy a book or find something fascinating in a *National Geographic* magazine, we want to share it with someone else, to tell them about it. So do kids, and they should be allowed to do so. This sharing can set the stage for more deliberate and probing exploration of a book later on. Children will learn much about the process, the meaning, and the purposes of reading in a social context as they talk with others about the meanings they are making and the feelings they are experiencing.

The *cultural context* for reading acknowledges and allows different ways of responding to literacy events, including different interaction patterns among children and between teacher and children. It includes a range of literature in which children from different cultures see themselves and through which all children perceive one another as unique individuals who nevertheless share common bonds.

While we can soon get a feel in a classroom for physical, social, and cultural contexts, we usually have to look harder to determine a particular reader's *psychological context*. There are many factors that determine what readers bring to a text and how they will transact with it. Observing Kerrie, for example, who is squirming in her seat, sighing heavily, and looking up continually from her book, we might infer that she hasn't much prior knowledge about what she's reading or simply isn't interested in the mystery *The Spell of the Sorcerer's Skull* (Bellairs, 1984). Besides, she has said that she doesn't especially care for mysteries. On the other hand, because Kerrie's in sixth grade, she *does* seem to be very interested in Jacob—who is sitting across from her and who seems oblivious of her attentions. But more profoundly, children will learn much when they "dialogue"—converse with themselves—as they read and reflect on what they read. It is part of what *we* experience when we chuckle, feel chills, or get a lump in the throat while reading.

The psychological context also includes "knowledge," which is a very broad domain indeed and includes the reader's knowledge about reading, how it is done, and the skills that it entails. There is much to the knowledge component and we will be probing it in depth in Chapter 2.

In order to highlight the connections among and between reading and other activities, throughout this text we will have a feature titled "Making Connections." This feature will examine the many kinds of contexts that occur and connections that can be made in literacy learning. Often—as seen on page 19—this feature will describe and offer suggestions for strategies, activities, and perspectives that integrate the language arts and help children become aware of and understand this rich network of interrelationships. At other times—as

MAKING CONNECTIONS: *Contexts for Literacy Activity*

The idea of readers constructing unique meanings is easy enough to grasp when thinking about reading a poem or perhaps even a short story. But what about the transaction between a reader and a straightforward, rather dry text, such as reading the directions on a college application form? The transaction between the text and the reader should lead to the same type of information's being written down: name, high school grade-point average, and so on. But this transaction occurs in a context, and any two students may be experiencing significantly different meanings. For example, one may be filling out this particular application just to cover her bases—this institution is good, but not one of the "prestigious" universities she *really* wants to get into. Her parents have donated heavily to one over the years and she knows that may give her an inside track. . . . For the other student, this is the only institution she's applying to, as she is a single parent with a steady job. Her children are in local schools and she does not want to uproot them in a move. She cannot help but feel considerable anxiety as she reads and responds to the application—*so much* is riding on this, she feels.

LEARNING IN CONTEXT: **The ways in which readers engage in and respond to *any* literacy activity depends fundamentally on the contexts in which the activity occurs.**

in the Making Connections feature on page 17, which offers perspective on the nature and meaning of different contexts for literacy activities—a broader sense of context and connection will be explored.

Integration with Writing and the Other Language Arts   As reading can fit more naturally, meaningfully, and enjoyably within the physical, social, and cultural context of the classroom and the psychological context of each child, so too will reading fit more naturally with writing and listening/speaking, the other language arts. In fact, this is a major theme that I will sound throughout this text: in the actual day-to-day world of the classroom, the language arts are usually integrated within our instructional contexts.

As we have seen, a key meaning of *integrated literacy* is that the language arts of reading, writing, speaking, and listening—often used together—often are being taught together. When we read, we often talk about what we're reading; when we write, we are reading what we've written; when we speak, we will usually listen as well. Integration does *not* mean, however, that reading and the other language arts should never be separated to be examined singly or in pairs. You will often teach about just one—such as reading—and then show students how it fits back into a more natural context.

Most children's listening and speaking skills appear to develop and be used very naturally. We should build on these in the classroom, therefore, and use and develop them in the context of focused, meaningful discussion about what is being read. While there's usually no problem in getting children to talk in the classroom (traditionally, many teachers have struggled to control students' talking if not stamp it out), it often *is* a challenge to encourage children to *write*.

We will be talking much about writing in this text. Although there are some obvious differences between the processes of reading and writing, in the final analysis they are quite close (Shanahan & Tierney, 1990). What students learn about reading can help their writing, and what they learn about writing can in turn help them to read. Students learn to read more efficiently and deeply because they are learning how to think like writers; they learn how to write more effectively because they are learning what readers need in order to construct an appropriate meaning. The form and the content of different genres also become models for students as their writing develops from imitation to more original expression within these types.

As a teacher, you will find that you play a very significant role in helping students become aware of this reciprocal relationship between reading and writing. It's a relationship many of them are not likely to discover and apply on their own. To complete the circle, their awareness will occur because of the type of instructional *context* you establish.

Meaningful Instruction Within Lessons That Stress a Larger Context   We know that reading always occurs in a context, and we know that this context can be favorably structured by *you*. So that the context will ensure that children *will* value reading, learn how to apply it as a tool, and *read* widely as well as intensively; there must be an *authenticity* about what we do (Edelsky, 1991). We have already noted that your teaching about reading will tie in naturally with the

MAKING CONNECTIONS: *Reading and Writing Are Two Sides of the Same Coin*

Let's consider just a couple of examples of how reading and writing can be linked:

■ As seven-year-olds "invent" spellings of words when they write, they are *exercising* their knowledge about words by applying "in action" what they know about letters, sounds, and whatever words they already know how to read. This exercise in turn strengthens their ability to identify words when they are reading; identifying words and writing words are two sides of the same literacy coin.

■ In their response journals, students write a letter to a character they are reading about. Students who wish to do so can share, compare, and contrast what they write. This works particularly well when students are reading books in which letters play an important role, such as *Dear Mr. Henshaw* (Cleary, 1983) and *Sarah, Plain and Tall* (MacLachlan, 1985).

■ Students are less likely to copy from encyclopedias and other informational sources when writing reports *if* they

1) first talk about what they already knew regarding their topic, then
2) talk about what they want to find out, then
3) *read* informational books about their topics, and *then*
4) *write. . . .*

■ As children learn more about books and writers, and about themselves as readers and writers, they can develop the ability to read their own writing as someone else might read it. In turn, this ability to read from a different perspective allows them to read from a different perspective what others have written, as well. All this is part of the marvelous power of literacy to remove the individual, as Heath reminds us, from "dependence on only immediate senses and direct contacts" (1991, p. 4). Together, reading and writing—two sides of the literacy coin—can do this for our children.

LEARNING IN CONTEXT: **Knowledge about reading supports growth in writing knowledge—and vice versa. As teachers, we need to ensure that children read *and* write, and that they come to understand that reading and writing *are* "two sides of the same coin."**

other language arts. There will also be a tie to other meaningful contexts, and I'd like to highlight them here.

So many children are not engaged because social and psychological contexts were *not* authentic and did not ring true for them: "If you just sit quietly and keep still and complete your worksheets, you will get extra time at recess" (or a gold star, or a "good citizen" certificate on Friday, and so on). This tactic works for only so long; children will not remain engaged unless there is an authentic, meaningful task. The reading experiences in which you engage your students will ring with authenticity if you are doing the following things:

■ *Using real, authentic literature.*

Example: First-graders read *The Bear's Toothache* (McPhail, 1978) and realize the connection with *their* experiences in going to a dentist or a doctor or a clinic. They discuss their experiences, relate them to the characters in the book, and clearly enjoy the story. As they read it, many children already know most of the words, but they reread the book later with a partner to learn more.

■ *Involving your students in authentic reading situations*—the kind in which children are *actually reading,* not working on a lot of isolated, unrelated tasks. This means that first and foremost, there will be time to read during the class day. These authentic situations also include tasks or activities that clearly relate to what is being read.

Example: Intermediate-grade students are poring over several informational texts on the American Civil War; one of the purposes they keep in mind as they read is to be alert for information about the freeing of the slaves and Lincoln's Emancipation Proclamation. They have learned that the war did not begin with freeing the slaves as the major goal; they have been quite surprised by this discovery and are keenly interested in when the goal of emancipation *did* take hold.

■ *Helping students understand and apply skills that flow directly out of real needs*—needs that the students perceive themselves.

Example: Amanda, a third-grader, writes in her response log that she is really confused about a new character who has suddenly popped up in the book she's been reading. The new character's name is "C-Man." She can't figure out how he fits into the story. Her teacher—also rather confused, because she *knows* there is no such character in this book—asks the student to find where "C-Man" shows up in it. Amanda does so and her teacher realizes what has happened: from time to time, a character says, "C'mon, let's go!" Amanda was not familiar with the written word *C'mon,* so she thought it referred to a new character, "C-*Man*"! Her teacher points this out and then conducts a brief lesson on *contractions* with Amanda and a few other students who also need this information. The students now understand contractions and the process by which they are formed much better because the lesson grew out of an authentic need in an actual reading experience (Barone, 1992).

Building upon children's developmental patterns in literacy

In teaching children how to read, you must begin where the child is; if a child truly is to learn, there is no other place *to* begin. So many of the problems we encounter in working with children are inadvertently of our own making, because we have *not* looked closely enough at where the child is. One of your best guides in determining where and how to begin your instruction with a particular child will be your knowledge of (1) the nature of literacy development specifically, as well as (2) social/emotional, language, and cognitive development more generally.

Although we know that every child is unique, we also have learned that there are some consistent similarities among most children with respect to their literacy development. What they appear to understand about "reading" as a process and their ability to understand and apply skills and strategies develop along a continuum. Their level and degree of response to what they read is also often a function of development.

Your understanding of development will help you interpret and guide children's *thinking* about what they read. Primary grade children may not be able to reflect as abstractly as intermediate children on concepts such as love, goodness and evil, or the meaning and nature of friendship. This does not mean, however, that they cannot deal *at all* with such concepts. They can, and opportunities to do so will arise out of the authentic literature they are reading and discussing. Knowing this, and knowing what is important socially and emotionally to children, helps you do the following:

■ Select books that may engage the students.
■ Set up students' exploration and discussions of what they read.
■ Understand students' interpretations of what they read.
■ Determine the types of questions you ask to help children understand and reflect on the reading they do.

Your understanding of development will help you interpret and guide how children come to understand the *conventions* of print. You will be able to make decisions about what specific knowledge and skills you may talk about directly. You will be able to determine what to teach about word structure, for example, and the interpretation of specific types of punctuation and other characteristics of texts.

Let me offer some examples here to illustrate the value of knowing about literacy development, behaviors that should not surprise or alarm you if you understand this developmental foundation: (1) a first- or second-grade child "knows" the word *them* one day but is stumped by it the next; (2) a fifth-grader who has struggled with reading is still spelling simple words such as *fish, train,* and *sister* as FES, CHRAN, and SESTR, respectively.

As we will see in the next chapter, children's cognitive and linguistic development and their experiences (the opportunities they are exposed to) with print define what they may be able to learn with respect to reading. If you monitor closely your students' development along this continuum of maturation and experience, they will have more efficient, successful, and rewarding experiences with reading.

Respecting and encouraging diversity

That children are diverse is obvious. You will have a range of abilities, interests, motivation levels, and so on, in your classroom. For many years educators have stressed the importance of addressing this diverse range in the classroom. More recently, the range of diversity has come to be considered in terms of *cultural* and *linguistic* diversity.

The many facets of diversity represent potential challenges for literacy instruction. Ours is a culturally diverse and, increasingly, linguistically diverse society.

Today's classrooms need to ac-
commodate and facilitate
learning for children from cul-
turally and linguistically di-
verse backgrounds.

In addition to the many languages now spoken in North America, there are a great many cultures represented as well. By *culture* we mean the values and beliefs of a group of people as well as their art, literature, music, and institutions. Although American English is the native language of many cultures in our society, particular cultures may speak a version of American English—a dialect— that is noticeably different from the standard dialect. All dialects do an equally good job of expressing meaning, but it will be part of your responsibility to help children understand how and when they should use the standard dialect.

In the latter part of the twentieth century, North America has increasingly become home to immigrants from Central and Latin America, the Caribbean, and the Pacific Rim. The cultures and languages of these groups add to an already richly diverse society, one into which people from all over the world have moved for hundreds of years. As a teacher, the challenge to you is clear: Facilitate the acquisition of English as a second language while preparing students for a technologically challenging, information-rich, and rapidly changing society.

In addressing issues of *dialect* with native speakers of English, you can address them nowhere more directly and comprehensively than in the area of reading, upon which so much else in school depends. With children from diverse backgrounds and "mainstream" cultures alike, yours is a marvelous opportunity to facilitate their developing reading competencies that will be appropriate for effective and meaningful functioning in a diverse society. In doing so, however, you will be aware of at least two important points: (1) the functions and meaning of "reading" in different cultures may be different in significant ways from the mainstream perspective of our society, and (2) you will build upon those different functions and meanings, often drawing from them, as you facilitate students' learning the functions and meanings of reading in the mainstream culture.

The notion of "diversity" is complex, because often there is overlap between sociocultural diversity and other societal issues. For example, many families have to move quite frequently—even several times throughout the year, as is the case with migrant workers' families. The children may be transferred to a school across town because it is closer to the parents' new job, or their new school may be in another town entirely. They may never really feel "at home" in any one school, and this of course affects their learning and their literacy development. In many homes the parent simply feels too exhausted at the end of the day to read a bedtime story to a child—a critical experience for preschool children.

At times, teaching children who bring these backgrounds to the classroom may seem overwhelming, but often only because we are thinking of how to place such children in those more "traditional" classrooms in which everyone is supposed to be in his or her seat, working quietly. You will be establishing a different, more accommodating, more successful classroom.

In contrast to classrooms of the past several years, yours will also increasingly incorporate children classified as "special needs" students—children with physical or psychological conditions that can affect (though often not limit) the degree to which they can reach their potential. In years past, these children seldom participated in "regular" classrooms, but they do now—to everyone's benefit. It is becoming quite clear that the cognitive, linguistic, and social development of most special needs students, regardless of disability, occurs more rapidly and is richer when students are mainstreamed in regular classrooms than when such students are placed in special resource classrooms. It is also clear that the normally developing students benefit—their understanding and respect for the way others meet challenges, and their appreciation for the abilities of those special needs students, increase.

There is another group of children with special *literacy* needs; for one reason or another, they have not benefited from the type of instruction to which they have been exposed. They have the potential for reading well, but it has not been realized. For them, we need to adjust our classroom instruction: not by relegating them to the "bottom" reading group, as in years past, but by addressing their literacy needs appropriately at the same time as we continue to involve these children meaningfully in all other aspects of classroom learning and activities. In turn, they contribute significantly to the class; the at-risk child who is a struggling reader can be a compelling storyteller.

Throughout this text, you'll be exploring how to select and involve students in literature that addresses all aspects of diversity. Within our overall belief that all children need to understand both their own culture and the cultures of others, we deliberately set out to include plenty of multicultural literature in our classrooms for these two reasons:

First, children from diverse backgrounds will see *themselves* in these books—and this is where much of the motivation to read and explore originates.

Second, children from all cultures will learn about one another, becoming aware of and understanding different perspectives, values, and attitudes.

As Greene has said, "literature can help us become more tolerant, more sensitive, more humane" (1972, p. 662). For this reason, even if you teach children who come exclusively from the mainstream culture, even if you never have a student whose native language is not English (both of these scenarios are highly unlikely!), you *still* will be presenting literature about diverse cultures. Diversity is a part of the culture of your classroom, every day, not attended to just on Martin Luther King Day or Mexican Independence Day.

There is another significant aspect of diversity: When you open yourself through literature to the collective experiences, knowledge, and opinions of a diverse group of students, you open yourself and your students to a diversity of ideas and interpretations as well. This type of diversity in turn opens up ever-wider awareness, appreciation, and—potentially—acceptance. Purves, Rogers, and Soter have observed that this "diversity in response, rather than being something to frown upon or sigh over, may, in fact, represent just the elusive individualized *engagement* with text that we . . . hope for" (1990, p. 32, emphasis added).

Using real literature

Using real literature for reading instruction is the fifth critical cornerstone of the integrated literacy approach that I encourage for the classroom. A teacher's ultimate aim, then, will be to structure a classroom in which literature and instructional content intertwine. The term *real literature* refers to books that are written for children by writers who *know* children and have a sense of children's perceptions, understandings, interests, and dreams. "Real" literature is *not* necessarily materials written according to formula, in simple words used in simpler sentences, based on a type of "baby talk" for beginning reading that doesn't ring true with the language and the world of kids. (Have you ever actually heard anyone who talks in the language of some materials that are intended for children? *"The dog is up. The dog is down." "I like to play. I like to run."*) While we will explore commendable "simple" reading books later on, those are simple in the way that they *balance* children's interests with meaningful support for the text through effective language, illustrations, and story line—they are *real literature.* Real literature, both fictional and informational, is at the core of our literacy experiences throughout the primary and intermediate grades. Check back to our diagram in Figure 1.1 (page 11) and see how this is graphically demonstrated: Real literature is *literally* at the core of the five cornerstones of our authentic reading/integrated literacy approach.

In years past, many educators have argued for the importance of placing real literature or "trade" books at the heart of reading instruction (Betts, 1936; McKee, 1934; Veatch, 1968). In recent years there has been a reawakening in regard to using children's literature to help students acquire and sustain literacy—instead of using a packaged "program." This reawakening is widespread in schools in the United States and Canada, Great Britain, Australia, and New Zealand (described, for example, by the California Reading Initiative, 1986; Cullinan, 1989; Hornsby, Sukaran, & Parry, 1986; Stewig & Sebesta, 1989). This emphasis stands in sharp contrast to the way "reading" as a subject and as a tool across the curriculum has been taught for a good many years.

And once again, think back to your own experience in elementary school. What did you do during "reading"? If your experience was like most students', you read in a group with your teacher, and you probably followed that up with workbook exercises or worksheets—and much of that "work" may have been only remotely related to the selection. Your teacher's concept of teaching reading may have been something like the following: Learning to read requires mastery of a fairly large number of skills; these skills are sequenced from simple to complex and take several years to acquire. For example, a child begins with simple words and letters and sounds, moves to comprehending simple facts and details, and only much later deals with what the overall story means to him or her, the reader. Your teacher probably used *basal readers* (see Chapter 10), which are reading books with selections that have been created to match specific grade levels.

Somewhat ironically, your teacher probably also would have said that the *purpose* of reading is to enjoy good books, to learn from texts, and to be a lifelong reader. And the hope was always that this would happen as a result of "part-to-whole" instruction. Your success under such instruction was determined in large part by your performance on tests that checked your mastery of specific skills. If you completed the day-to-day work appropriately and well, perhaps you were "rewarded" by being able to read silently in a library book.

If this describes your experience, and if you *truly* enjoy reading today, then as a child you most likely also read outside of class, and in books that truly interested and excited you. If you had a different experience, one in which you were allowed *in school* to read often and widely, and to respond to what you were reading, then you are a very lucky exception. But this is precisely the type of reading experience I am encouraging you to establish for the children you will teach.

In the following four sections we will look at four major reasons for choosing to use real literature as the centerpiece of your instruction: real books are more engaging; real books offer genuine, uncontrived points of departure for skills instruction; real books allow wonderful opportunities for uniting the whole curriculum; and finally, real books provide a dynamic means of implementing our first four cornerstones.

Real Books Build Motivation: That Is, READERS   It is the nature of human beings to make meaning. It is also their nature to question, to seek, to wonder. Children seem to have a million questions. Real books—authentic fiction and nonfiction—provide many answers and many ways to go about questioning, seeking, and wondering. If we make such literature available to children in our classrooms, the books themselves will take care of much of the *motivation* for wanting to read and for wanting to learn. This is especially critical for children who have struggled to learn to read: nothing can be more motivating than the one book that finally "connects" with such a child's interests and feelings.

Consider just a few examples:

Kevin, a third-grader who delights in Jane Yolen's *Commander Toad* series, is writing his own "Admiral Frog" series. As a consequence, he has explored humor, as he has been motivated to read other books.

Letisha, a first-grader captivated by the repetitive rhythms and rhymes of the predictable texts her teacher was reading to the class, learns to "read" several of Eric Carle's delightful books such as *The Very Busy Spider* and *The Very Hungry Caterpillar* after hearing them read aloud several times. Before long she is trying out books that have not been read to her, diligently "having a go" at sounding out unfamiliar words, using clues from the illustrations along with her developing knowledge of letter sounds.

Jamal, a fifth-grader, has been a capable but reluctant reader. His teacher notes that he doesn't seem to "get into" stories at all, no matter how captivating they may be to other students. One day he discovers David Macaulay's *The Way Things Work,* seems to lose himself in it, and begins poring through informational books that discuss the construction or invention of all kinds of buildings, machines, jets and rockets, and more. As the school year progresses, he prides himself on being a "walking encyclopedia" of information.

Maria, a second-grader, is delighted to discover a text in both her own language and English: *Dona Blanca and Other Hispanic Nursery Rhymes and Games* (Schon, 1983). She spends hours going over this book, and one day her teacher discovers her "translating" a picture book from English into Spanish to take home for her parents to read.

Sara, a struggling sixth-grader reading well below her potential, has been captivated by David Weisner's marvelous picture-book fantasy *Tuesday.* She checks out other Weisner books, discovers Chris Van Allsburg—another author/illustrator in the same general vein—and is now devouring such books during sustained silent-reading time.

It is a simple formula: *Real* books will tap children's interests, thereby motivating them to probe further. This motivation from within leads to better readers, writers, *thinkers*.

Real Books Are an Authentic Take-off Point for "Skills" Instruction   The term *skill* refers to the application of specific knowledge and abilities in an appropriate context. For example, a first-grade child looks at the pictures on a page for help in figuring out what an unfamiliar word may be; a fifth-grader looks in a paragraph for a sentence that captures the most important information—or "reads between the lines" to infer this information if it is not explicitly stated. The skills involved in reading—in the efficient application of knowledge in a specific context—are important, and we need to help many students learn them. *How* we go about doing so is critically important.

Traditionally, reading was conceptualized as a process of building one skill upon another until the efficient, completed act was attained; this was usually translated into emphasizing letter sounds first, then whole words, then sentences, and finally entire selections.

In this book we will be looking at skills from quite the opposite perspective. Students' appreciation of skills should grow out of and relate to meaningful experiences with authentic texts. When students experience print through the type of purposeful, interested engagements that they experience in real books, they will be developing the knowledge of what reading is and why we do it that underlies readiness for learning specific skills. Students' understanding and use of skills depends upon an existing understanding of the nature and purposes of literacy.

When and why you teach specific skills depends on your knowledge about your students' development, their individual strengths, and their individual needs. There will be many opportunities throughout this book to learn this "when and why," but just like skill-learning itself, you will have a knowledge base in place before talking about skills instruction.

Real Books Tie the Curriculum Together   As we've already seen, teachers traditionally taught "reading" with a basal reading series that represented a strong skills-based, skills-first model. This was usually done in the morning. When it was time to put away the basals and the accompanying workbooks, the math books came out; later, the science books, the spelling books, the handwriting books, the social studies books. . . . "Reading" in a social studies book, for example, was different from the *subject* of reading—in the kids' perspective, one really had little to do with the other. "Spelling" was something that they did in workbooks and on Friday's test, and it didn't have much to do with what they were learning about words in their reading group.

When we use authentic literature in our classrooms, we have marvelous opportunities to tie together science, social studies, math, word study, art, music, physical education, and dance. These subject areas do not exist of and by themselves out in the real world, with no relationship to any other areas. They interrelate there, and they do so in real books as well.

Nonetheless, the concepts that children explore throughout all the areas of the elementary curriculum are also represented in a very familiar genre: the *textbook*. Textbooks in science, social studies, and so forth are getting better all the time—in terms of format, design, content, and readability (see Chapter 7). While most children find *real* informational books more engaging and motivating, you can nevertheless help your students deal with textbooks, learn how to read them, and learn how to use them to their own best purposes.

Opportunities Exist Within a Single Book   You may begin with specific instances, situations, characters, and then—because students are now motivated—reach out to related lessons, experiences, vocabulary, and so forth, connecting with the rest of the curriculum. Consider these possibilities (there are literally dozens of others) for intermediate-grade students in Jerry Spinelli's *Maniac Magee:*

Science

Let's take nutrition. Compare and contrast the diets of the many different individuals and families Maniac befriends in the book and relate these dietary habits to the individuals' dispositions.

Social Studies

The confrontation between different cultures in this book is as up-front as one can get for a young reading audience.

Consider Maniac versus Mars Bar and the respective cultures they represent.

Consider the war games little Piper and Russell play in anticipation of the final war their father believes will surely come when the blacks invade their apartment.

Consider Maniac's total befuddlement when an elderly black man tells him to "move on now, Whitey" (p. 60) and when the man responds to Maniac's protests with "Never enough, is it, Whitey? Just want more and more. . . . Come on down to see Bojangles. Come on to the zoo. The monkey house" (p. 61).

What do these events have to do with the way we perceive, think about, and behave toward people who are different from us?

Math

Consider spatial relationships; specifically "transformational geometry," which intermediate students are able to grasp and enjoy. Begin exploration of this domain by discussing the episode in which Maniac Magee attacks the famous "Cobble's Knot," the size of a volleyball, with "more contortions, ins and outs, twists and turns and dips and doodles than the brain of Albert Einstein himself. It had defeated all comers for years, including J. J. Thorndike, who grew up to be a magician, and Fingers Halloway, who grew up to be a pickpocket" (p. 69). (Maniac untangled it in a single day. . . .)

Opportunities Exist Within a Theme or Content Area   Branch out into several titles that relate to a particular theme or content area. The concept of "transformation," for example, can be explored through folktales and myths (Moss, 1990) and can include physical transformations as in *Sylvester and the Magic Pebble* (Steig, 1969), as well as internal, attitudinal, and emotional changes or transformations as in *Julian's Glorious Summer* (Cameron, 1987). Scientific processes of transformation can be explored, including the process of *metamorphosis* (how specific rocks are formed). Students can explore mathematical "surface" transformations illustrated by commutative, associative, and distributive properties; and as we have just noted, geometric transformations involving analysis and manipulation of different two- and three-dimensional configurations.

Real Books Provide an Authentic Basis for the Other Cornerstones   The use of real literature can help us make our first four cornerstones of reading really work instructionally within the classroom. Again, Figure 1.1 clearly reflects this possibility. Let's consider each cornerstone in turn:

1. Experiences with different genres and with different purposes for reading help students construct meaning better as well as become *aware of* and able to monitor *how* they construct meaning as they read.
2. Students become aware of different contexts and purposes for reading, including how reading interfaces with listening, speaking, and writing—indeed, with *all* other areas of the elementary curriculum. Literature is a powerful means of developing and applying both critical thinking and the language that represents this thinking.

3. Literature promotes students' development in general and reading ability in particular; it promotes positive human values and healthy emotional growth.
4. Literature helps students explore and understand diversity in all its aspects. In the process, students will become more insightful, more appreciative of themselves and of others.

In closing this discussion of the critically important role of authentic literature in our lives and in the lives of children, I want to leave you with yet another important message: we need to bear in mind that our literacy instruction should be conceived of as more than putting children in touch with good books. *It is important to realize that we cannot assume that just by changing the materials in the classroom—by using real books instead of traditional reading programs—all literacy challenges will be met.* We must also be mindful, in our instruction, of how literacy is used as a tool, about the knowledge that it affords, about the doors that open for the one who possesses it, about the revealing of the "codes" according to which social customs work. We will need to help children see how their experiences with reading will generate knowledge and skills that are applicable in a wider, real-world, everyday context.

■ A CONCLUDING PERSPECTIVE

In this chapter we have looked at what reading is and what it can truly mean to children. So much else in school and so much in society depends upon children's ability to read. In an increasingly diverse society, the ability to read is important for purely practical reasons as well as for the kinds of thinking and action it can facilitate: when children read widely, openly, critically, they are also likely to think widely, openly, and critically. We have conceptualized this instructional orientation as an *"authentic reading/integrated literacy"* approach.

In order to meet the challenge and opportunity of teaching children in a diverse society how to read, you must be a "reflective" teacher, which means that you will be working toward developing the knowledge and skills to be a practical problem-solver in your classroom. You will be able to step back to analyze and address situations appropriately. Your development as such a teacher will be in part a process of continual renewal, rejuvenation, and commitment. This process cannot be otherwise. Why? Because you will *never* stop learning, enjoying, being surprised. The insights of children will amaze and delight you.

In this chapter we have considered the critical role that you, the teacher, play in the facilitation of children's learning to read and their use of literacy. We have elaborated the five tenets that define the cornerstones of your reading instruction:

■ We have seen the centrality of *making meaning* through the transaction of the reader and the text.

- We have seen the influence of different *contexts* on what and how children read.
- We have examined children's *development* as a foundation for your knowing when, what, and how to teach aspects of reading.
- We have considered the implications of *diversity* in your classroom as they affect how you teach reading: sociocultural issues, issues of language and dialect, issues of special needs students.
- We have seen how these first four tenets are realized primarily through the fifth: the use of real literature in your classroom. In addition to being motivating to students, real fictional and informational literature allow you (1) to integrate instruction within the other language arts of listening, speaking, and writing; (2) to integrate instruction across other areas of the curriculum: social studies, science, math, and so forth; (3) to integrate effectively and meaningfully with "where children are coming from"—their own lives, cultures, and developmental perspectives.

It is clear, therefore, that teaching children how to read in the ways and in the classrooms described in this chapter may be the single most important responsibility you have as an elementary-school teacher. Because you will be reflective, critical, and creative with your teaching of reading, your students should be that way in assimilating what they learn. To prosper and grow in peace and in hope, the very society of which they are a part will need both this type of understanding and individuals who will act, with compassion and commitment, on the basis of it.

■ BECOMING A REFLECTIVE PRACTITIONER

Cazden, C. (1988). *Classroom discourse: The language of teaching and learning.* Portsmouth, NH: Heinemann.

A noted authority in language development and language education, Courtney Cazden describes one of the most important factors in any classroom context: The *language* in the classroom. Although she explores classroom language at all levels (elementary through postsecondary), elementary teachers will find most of the book very relevant and interesting. Cazden examines, for example, teacher-student interactions, lesson structures, and student-student interactions. She also addresses issues of diversity in the classroom and how teachers interact with students from different cultural backgrounds.

Heath, S. B. (1982). Protean shapes in literacy events. In D. Tannen (Ed.), *Spoken and written language: Exploring orality and literacy.* Norwood, NJ: Ablex Publishing Company.

"Reading," Shirley Brice Heath reminds us, is "protean"—it is not a constant or fixed phenomenon. It is influenced not only by the reader's skill levels but by context and purpose; by extension, the traditional "school" literacy is but one type of literacy out of many. Heath develops her argument through a concise synthesis of a considerable body of information, including her own extensive research in African American and European American communities in North Carolina. Heath's research and writing has been extremely influential in literacy education, and this chapter is a good introduction to the rest of her work.

Rosenblatt, L. M. (1989). Writing and reading: The transactional theory. In J. M. Mason (Ed.), *Reading and writing connections* (pp. 153–176). Boston: Allyn and Bacon.

Currently influential in reading psychology and education, Louise Rosenblatt's *transactional* theory is explained here as it applies both to reading and writing. Rosenblatt first offers a fine-grained analysis of *how* meaning is constructed during reading, then discusses how the process works in writing. Finally, she compares and contrasts reading and writing—concluding that, within a single individual, these processes are complementary.

Scribner, S. (1984). Literacy in three metaphors. *American Journal of Education, 93,* 6–21.

Addresses problems involved in *defining* literacy. Scribner suggests three metaphors, each of which describes literacy a different way: literacy as *adaptation*—adaptation to existing social and political situations; literacy as *power*—a means toward which individuals can advance in a group or community; and literacy as a *state of grace*—in which the literate individual is presumed to have special virtues. Scribner concludes that "recognition of the multiple meanings and varieties of literacy also argues for a diversity of educational approaches."

■ REFERENCES

Barone, D. (1992). The written responses of young children: Beyond comprehension to story understanding. *New Advocate, 3,* (1), 49–56.

Barthes, R. (1970). Historical discourse. In M. Lane (Ed.), *Introduction to structuralism* (pp. 145–155). New York: Basic Books.

Berliner, D. (1986). In pursuit of the expert pedagogue. *Educational Researcher, 15,* 5–13.

Betts, E. (1936). *The prevention and correction of reading difficulties.* Evanston, IL: Row, Peterson.

Bloome, D., & Egan-Robertson, A. (1993). The social construction of intertextuality in classroom reading and writing lessons. *Reading Research Quarterly, 28,* 304–333.

California Reading Initiative (1986). Sacramento, CA: California State Department of Education.

Cole, M., & Griffin, P. (1987). *Contextual factors in education: Improving science and mathematics education for minorities and women.* Madison, WI: University of Wisconsin, School of Education, Wisconsin Center for Education Research.

Cullinan, B. (1977). Books in the life of the young child. In B. Cullinan and C. Carmichael (Eds.), *Literature and young children.* Urbana, IL: National Council of Teachers of English.

Cullinan, B. (Ed.) (1989). *Children's literature in the reading program.* Newark, DL: International Reading Association.

Dewey, J. (1933). *How we think: A restatement of the relation of reflective thinking to the educative process.* Boston: D. C. Heath.

Dewey, J., & Bentley, A. (1949). *Knowing and the known.* Boston: Beacon Press.

Edelsky, C. (1991). *With literacy and justice for all: Rethinking the social in language and education.* Bristol, PA: Falmer Press.

Flesch, R. (1955). *Why Johnny can't read—and what you can do about it.* New York: Harper and Row.

Flesch, R. (1981). *Why Johnny still can't read. A new look at the scandal in our schools.* New York: Harper and Row.

Genishi, C. (1989). Observing the second language learner: An example of teachers' learning. *Language Arts, 66,* 509–515.

Greene, M. (1972/1980). Review of Louise Rosenblatt's *Literacy as exploration* (pp. 660–664). In M. Wolf, M. K. McQuillan, & E. Radwill (Eds.), *Thought & language/ Language & reading* (Harvard Educational Review Reprint Series No. 14). Cambridge, MA: Harvard Educational Review.

Heath, S. B. (1991). Protean shapes in literacy events. In D. Tannen (Ed.), *Exploring orality and literacy.* Norwood, NJ: Ablex.

Hornsby, D., Sukarna, D., & Parry, J. (1986). *Read on: A conference approach to reading.* Portsmouth, NH: Heinemann.

Just, M., & Carpenter, P. (1987). *The psychology of reading and language comprehension.* Boston: Allyn & Bacon.

McKee, P. (1934). *Reading and literature in the elementary school.* Boston: Houghton Mifflin.

Meek, M. (1983). *Learning to read.* London: The Bodley Head.

Moffett, J. (1968). *Teaching the universe of discourse.* Boston: Houghton Mifflin.

Moss, J. (1990). *Focus on literature: A context for literacy learning.* Katonah, NY: Richard C. Owen.

Norton, D. (1991). *Through the eyes of a child: An introduction to children's literature* (3rd ed.). Columbus, OH: Merrill.

Piaget, J. (1970). *Structuralism.* New York: Basic Books.

Polanyi, M. (1962). *The tacit dimension.* Garden City, NY: Doubleday.

Poplin, M. S. (1988). Holistic/constructivist principles of the teaching/learning process: Implications for the field of learning disabilities. *Journal of Learning Disabilities, 21,* 401–416.

Purves, A., Rogers, T., & Soter, A. O. (1990). *How porcupines make love II: Teaching a response-centered literature curriculum.* New York: Longman.

Rayner, K., & Pollatsek, A. (1989). *The psychology of reading.* Englewood Cliffs, NJ: Prentice-Hall.

Rosenblatt, L. (1978). *The reader, the text, the poem: The transactional theory of the literary work.* Carbondale, IL: Southern Illinois University Press.

Schon, D. (1983). *The reflective practitioner.* New York: Basic Books.

Shanahan, T., & Tierney, R. (1990). Reading-writing connections: The relations among three perspectives. In J. Zutell & S. McCormick (Eds.), *Literacy theory and research: Analysis from multiple paradigms* (39th Yearbook of the National Reading Conference, pp. 13–34). Chicago, IL: National Reading Conference.

Smith, F. (1989). *Understanding reading* (4th ed.). Hillsdale, NJ: Lawrence Erlbaum Associates.

Stewig, J. W., & Sebesta, S. L. (Eds.) (1989). *Using literature in the elementary classroom.* Urbana, IL: National Council of Teachers of English.

Strickland, D. S. (1988). The teacher as researcher: Toward the extended professional. *Language Arts, 65,* 754–764.

Veatch, J. (1968). *Reading in the elementary school.* New York: John Wiley.

Weaver, C. (1988). *Reading process and practice.* Portsmouth, NH: Heinemann.

Wells, Gordon (1986). *The meaning makers: Children learning language and using language to learn.* Portsmouth, NH: Heinemann.

Children's Literature Cited

Bellairs, J. (1984). *The Spell of the Sorcerer's Skull.* Dial.

Carle, E. (1971). *The Very Hungry Caterpillar.* Crowell.

Carle, E. (1985). *The Very Busy Spider.* Putnam.

Cameron, A. (1987). *Julian's Glorious Summer.* Random House.

Cleary, B. (1983). *Dear Mr. Henshaw.* Morrow.

Hamilton, V. (1985). *The People Could Fly.* Knopf.

Macaulay, D. (1986). *The Way Things Work.* Houghton Mifflin.

MacLachlan, P. (1985). *Sarah, Plain and Tall.* Harper & Row.

McKinley, R. (1982). *The Blue Sword.* Greenwillow.

McPhail, D. (1978). *The Bear's Toothache.* Little, Brown.

O'Dell, S. (1989). *Black Star, Bright Dawn.* Houghton Mifflin.

Ortiz, S. (1988). *The People Shall Continue.* Children's Book Press.

Schon, I. (1983). *Dona Blanca and Other Hispanic Nursery Rhymes and Games.* Denison.

Spinelli, J. (1991). *Maniac Magee.* Simon & Schuster.

Steig, W. (1969). *Sylvester and the Magic Pebble.*

Turner, A. (1987). *Nettie's Trip South.* Macmillan.

Weisner, D. (1992). *Tuesday.* Clarion.

White, F. (1973). *Cesar Chavez: Man of Courage.* Garrad.

CHAPTER TWO

THE PROCESS AND DEVELOPMENT OF READING

FOCUS

■ *What are the characteristics of the* content *and the* form *of "texts"?*

■ *Compare and contrast the* contexts *of reading for learners and for proficient readers.*

■ *What categories of* background knowledge *does every individual possess and what is their role in the reading process?*

■ *Describe each of the three models of reading. How is each often translated into reading instruction in the classroom? Which model does* this *text prefer, and why?*

■ *Describe how the "on-line" process of reading occurs in the skilled reader and explain why it is important for you, as a prospective teacher, to understand this process.*

■ *What are the characteristics of literacy development during each of the following* phases: emergent, beginning, transitional, *and* proficient?

Children, like adults, read to explore the world, to escape the confining present, to discover themselves, to become someone else.
    Rebecca Lukens, A Critical Handbook of Children's Literature

When we invite readers' minds to meet books in our classrooms, we invite the messiness of human response—personal prejudices, personal tastes, personal habits, personal experience. But we also invite personal meaning, and the distinct possibility that our kids will grow up to become a different kind of good reader, an adult for whom reading is a logical, satisfying, life-long habit, someone who just plain loves books and reading.
                        Nancie Atwell, In the Middle

And reading itself, as a psycho-physiological process, is almost as good as a miracle. . . . And so to completely analyze what we do when we read would be . . . to describe very many of the most intricate workings of the human mind, as well as to unravel the tangled story of the most remarkable specific performance that civilization has learned in all its history.
        Edmund Huey, The Psychology and Pedagogy of Reading

What is the nature of this liberating process that Rebecca Lukens (1990, p. i) seems to portray? Nancie Atwell goes on to conclude that students who do become good readers will find opening a book like accepting "an invitation to forge and explore new meanings" (1987, p. 154). Edmund Huey, a giant in reading research at the turn of the century, described it as a "psycho-physiological" process (1908, pp. 5, 6). Many contemporary authorities describe reading as a "sociopsycholinguistic" process (Weaver, 1988). They're all correct. Because reading is indeed a "remarkable specific performance," it involves not only "intricate workings of the human mind" but intricate relationships with the environment in which the reading occurs. Thinking about the process of reading, though, should not be as overwhelming as these terms may seem to imply. Today, calling reading a "sociopsycholinguistic" process means simply that reading involves thinking *(psych-)* and language *(linguistic)* and that this process is learned and used within a definite *social* context.

In this chapter, we will examine (1) the major elements of the reading process—texts, contexts, and readers—and how different models of the reading process represent the relationships among them; (2) the reading process "in action"; and (3) the development of reading ability in preschool and elementary children.

MAJOR ELEMENTS OF THE READING PROCESS

Throughout this book, we will be examining the *text*—the nature of what is to be read; the *reader*—the unique experiences, knowledge, and expectations the individual brings to the text; and the *contexts* in which reader and text come together. As we saw in Chapter 1, these three major elements together make up the act of reading, the *reading process*. When the reading process is flowing along smoothly and we are reading efficiently, we are applying our knowledge in general and our knowledge about reading in particular so that we (1) "make meaning" appropriately as we (2) move through the text at a reasonable rate, while we (3) maintain fidelity to the text—that is, to the words the author selected to convey his or her meaning.

Later, we will examine several models of the reading process that attempt to explain how its three major elements combine to accomplish these goals; after that, we will witness the process in action as a proficient reader engages in it. However, for now we will look closely at the nature of each of the three elements—the text, the contexts, and the reader. Understanding the relationships among them should help you make well-founded instructional decisions. Figure 2.1 shows the relationships among these elements and illustrates how your role as a teacher relates to them.

The text: what is to be read

The word *text* used in this sense is very broad in scope: it refers to *any* written form of communication. Much of our instruction revolves around helping children understand what writers say through the form in which they choose to say it. Consider Jeremy, a fourth-grader who asked, "But where's the *ending*?" when he finished the first chapter of his social studies book. Before reading the same chapter, his classmate Sabrina wouldn't look at the questions at the end because, she explained, "That's like cheating!" Jeremy isn't aware of the differences in form between stories and informational texts; Sabrina does not realize that differences in form imply different reading *strategies*. Both children are confused about the relationship between *content* and *form* in a text.

Our best way of looking at texts is in terms of the nature of the written language that composes them. We can describe written language in terms of *content*—*what* the writer wishes to convey—and of *form*—*how* the writer wishes to convey the content. Content and form, the what and the how of the text, influence each other and work together to help the reader construct the intended meaning. Writers make choices regarding what they write, and how they write it, with their intended meaning and their intended audience in mind.

Let's look more closely at what texts express and how they do it.

Content   At its simplest level, *content* reflects the writer's purpose and intended meaning. *What* is the writer trying to say? Is the text supposed to enable someone to assemble a closet organizer, to incite a revolution, or to reflect on the meaning of life at age 21 or 40? Is the message straightforward? Are there several intended meanings?

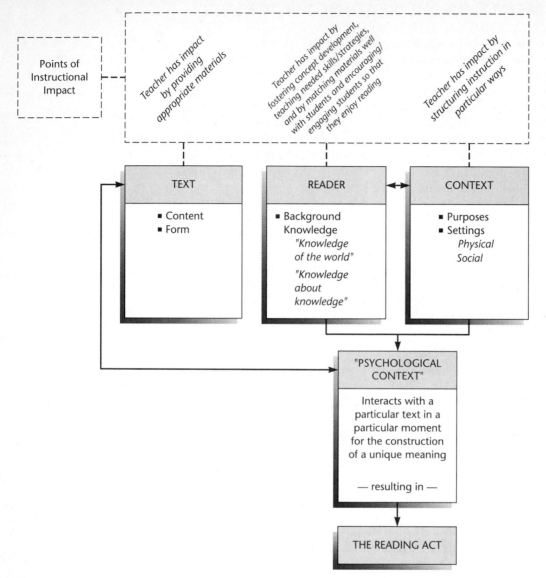

Figure 2.1
Major Elements of the Reading Process and Points of Instructional Impact

"Content" is something a reader can't directly *see* in a text, because (as we've already observed) "meaning" doesn't announce itself. Understanding of intended meaning or content must be constructed through a cooperative effort by both the reader and the text (that is, by the absent writer). Writers' contribution to this effort is reflected in their use of *form—how* they represent their intended meaning for the reader.

Form   At the most concrete level, the form of written language represents information about speech: the words, the sounds within the words, how the words are arranged into phrases and sentences. And in English, this information is presented in a left-to-right, top-to-bottom format. The words and phrases constitute sentences, which in turn constitute paragraphs.

At a more general level, the form or structure of written language reflects either of two basic types of texts: *narrative* and *informational*. In a broad sense, *narrative* texts tell stories and *informational* texts convey information. Depending on their purposes and intentions—the *functions* they wish their texts to serve— writers select one of these forms. Of course, as we'll see later, the reader may be free to read a text while having a fundamentally different purpose in mind than what the writer intended: a story might be read primarily in order to get information, rather than for enjoyment or for insight into the human condition. Usually, however, the two forms or types—narrative and informational—are used differently.

These two primary types of texts are discussed in terms of different *genres*—for example, poems, fiction, plays, biographies, and so forth. We will be exploring different genres in some depth throughout this text. As we'll see, it is important for readers to think about the form and the probable content of what they are going to be reading; this will be a highly significant part of your instruction. For example, you will help intermediate-grade students understand the function of "boxes" in textbooks, guiding them to the realization that such boxes usually highlight and elaborate on important concepts or provide examples. To cite another example: you will help students realize that some narrative genres, such as fables, will explicitly state a moral or a theme, while other narrative genres will not be as direct.

The reader: background knowledge and affect

Each reader brings what we will call his or her body of *background knowledge* to each and every reading experience. Frank Smith has pointed out that because reading involves very broad aspects of human thought and behavior, an understanding of reading cannot be achieved without consideration of "various operating characteristics of the human brain" (1988, p. 3). And because the fundamental purpose of reading is to construct meaning—to understand, to learn, to think—we must look briefly at the resources, the background knowledge, that our brains call upon. Much of each reader's background knowledge, of course, contains much that is unique. Yet there is also much that all readers *share:* the universal principles that structure it. In this section, we will examine individual and common aspects of background knowledge.

Moreover, each reader is equipped with his or her own unique constellation of emotions and attitudes, about him- or herself, about the outside world, and about reading. Our term for this broad constellation is *affect;* and we'll explore affect in depth a little later on.

First, though, let's get a handle on the nature of this broad terrain we refer to as background knowledge. We're going to talk about its two main parts, "knowledge of the world" and "knowledge about knowledge" (see Figure 2.2).

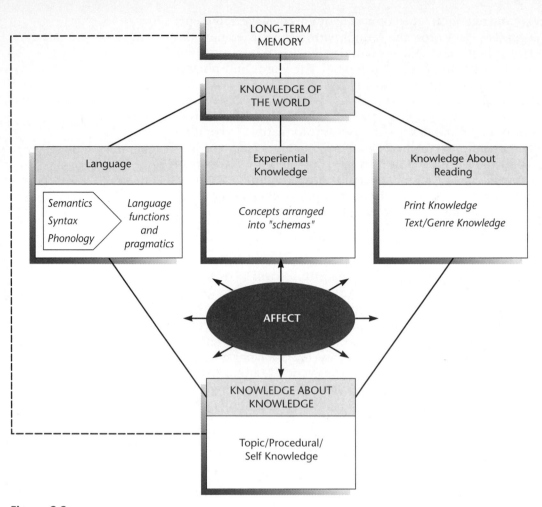

Figure 2.2
The Reader's Background Knowledge and Affect

Knowledge of the World   This knowledge includes three distinct though related categories with a bearing on reading: knowledge about language, experiential knowledge, and knowledge about reading itself.

Knowledge About Language   Linguists and psychologists tell us that language has three components or systems: *semantics*, *syntax*, and *phonology* (Fromkin & Rodman, 1993). Most of the time, these systems operate without our conscious awareness; they are subconscious, or "tacit." (There *is* one aspect of language that frequently can involve a fair degree of conscious attention; linguists refer to this aspect as *pragmatics,* and we'll consider it momentarily.)

Semantics refers to the *meaning* of words and sentences—more specifically, to the ways in which spoken or written language is related to underlying meaning.

Syntax, or "syntactic" knowledge, refers to our ability to arrange words into utterances—into phrases and sentences. Often called "grammatical" knowledge, it tells you, for example, when you should put an adjective before the noun it describes ("the hungry tyrannosaurus" rather than "the tyrannosaurus hungry"). Here are some characteristics of words and word order in English sentences:

■ There are *content* words and *function* words; content words carry the meaning, while function words tell how these meaning-bearing words are related. For example, in the sentence *The pocketbook that you lost was found in a dumpster,* the content words are *pocketbook, you, lost, found,* and *dumpster.* The function words are *The, that, was, in,* and *a.*

■ The *order of words* in English—such as noun, verb, noun—gives information about the subject (the "actor") in a sentence and the object (what is acted on), as well as about *how* the subject acts on the object.

■ Often the order of words or phrases is *inverted* to change meaning in a major or minor way, as in asking a question; for example, *You lost your pocketbook* versus *How did you lose your pocketbook?*

Phonology literally means "study of sound." Linguists also use the term, however, to refer to our knowledge of the sound system of our language: we use this largely tacit or subconscious knowledge whenever we speak. It underlies our pronunciation of the individual sounds ("phonemes") and syllables. It allows us to place a primary or secondary stress or accent on a syllable; it underlies our utterances of whole phrases and sentences—how loudly we speak, our use of rising or falling intonation (contrast the sentences "You *lost* your pocketbook?", "*You* lost your pocketbook?", and "You lost your *pocketbook*?"). Phonology—our knowledge of the sound system of our language—operates almost automatically, serving our thoughts and our intentions.

Although linguists do not consider *pragmatics* one of the three core components of language, it is nevertheless a significant one. Linguists define pragmatics as "the socially appropriate use of language." This "appropriate" use depends on the *context* in which we're speaking: we use a more formal style to make a class presentation; an informal style when talking with friends at lunch. There is a parallel between pragmatic knowledge in oral language and this type of knowledge in reading: readers select appropriate *strategies* on the basis of the *contexts* in which they are reading.

Linguists describing how language is used do so in terms of various *functions* (Halliday, 1975). For example, we use language in order to express what we want, to seek information, to give information, to create imaginary situations, to communicate intimately with another, to get others to do what we want, or to draw attention to ourselves.

Let's summarize the relationships among the systems of language: Our intentions—the *function* we wish our language to perform—determine "the appropriate social rules of language—*pragmatics*—which then influence the selection of words *(semantics)* and the types of sentence structure *(syntax)* and oral expression *(phonology)* used to convey meaning" (Templeton, 1991, p. 42, emphasis added).

Experiential Knowledge   Our experiential knowledge is described in terms of its *concepts* and *schemas,* two components that work together. Psychologists have talked about *conceptual* knowledge for many years; *schema* knowledge is a comparatively recent area of investigation.

Concepts represent our knowledge about "things" in our experience (Carey, 1985; Smith, 1989). When we were young children, these "things" reflected our concrete experiences—chairs, dogs, stoves, and so on. From such a perspective, concepts of such things as love, justice, good, and evil ("badness") are also rooted in concrete experiences—sneaking cookies or calling someone a bad name is "bad" because punishment may follow. As we grew older, the nature of our concepts became more and more abstract: ideas of good and evil, love, and so forth were based on moral and ethical principles, rather than on the consequences of not behaving in certain ways.

Schemas refer to how we psychologically organize concepts in certain ways to interpret and guide our experiences with events, places, and actions (Pearson & Anderson, 1984). For example, you have a schema for "elementary classrooms" and one for "college classrooms"—a set of expectations about what goes on in these different types of classrooms helps you interpret and make sense of what you find there. When you encounter something that is not part of your expectations or schema, either you decide it is a real irregularity or you readjust your schema to include the new information. Bartlett, who coined the term, defined *schema* as "an organisation of past reactions, or of past experiences, which must always be supposed to be operating in well-adapted . . . responses" (1932, p. 201). Taylor and Taylor condense this even further, defining *schema* as "an organized body of knowledge about an event" (1983, p. 322). This organized body of knowledge guides our expectations about what we will experience every time we encounter another instance of a particular type of event.

On the basis of their own concepts and schemas, most readers are able to generate images—mental pictures and sensory associations—as they read. *Imagery* is an important aspect of experiential knowledge, and the ability to generate images during reading powerfully supports effective and efficient reading (Paivio, 1986; Sadowski, Paivio, & Goetz, 1991).

■   **MEANING MAKERS: You, the Student**

How Does Your Own Experiential Knowledge Affect Your Reading?

Eudora Welty, an American novelist from Mississippi, made the following observation: "Whatever our theme in writing, it is old and tried. Whatever our place, it has been visited by the stranger, it will never be new again. It is only the vision that can be new; but that is enough." What does that passage *mean* to you? It probably isn't fair to "break it down," but do give it a try from the perspective of *your* background knowledge. Share your interpretation with a friend; then read the passage again. Do you have a different feeling about it after talking with the friend and then rereading it?

Did the two of you have similar underlying concepts for words such as *theme* and *vision*? Did you engage your "schema" for "what writers do and try to convey" and look for what you felt would be deeper, more symbolic meaning? (What *really* does the stranger in the passage represent?) What may appear to be a thoughtful though straightforward observation, with words that you'd expect would evoke similar concepts in any two readers, may lead to quite different interpretations, depending on the nature and use of each reader's background knowledge. Knowing that this happens for you, remember always that it happens for your students as well. Each "coming together" of child and text results in a unique construction of meaning.

As for the children you will be teaching: occasionally you will discover some blatant differences arising from their background knowledge. Consider the student who read in his history textbook a passage that mentioned the many "toasts" that were drunk to celebrate the completion of the first transcontinental railroad. He was noticeably confused; his underlying concept for the word *toast* did not include drinking, so he was doubly confused: how could anybody "drink" dry toast? And why did *this* toast have an *s* at the end of it? ■

Knowledge About Reading   Here is one of the most crucial areas of your instructional responsibilities—helping students develop knowledge quite specific to the nature and functions of reading. Specifically, children will develop knowledge about *print.* This refers to knowledge about *words* (letter/sound correspondences and spelling patterns—what we call *orthographic* knowledge) and *punctuation.* Orthographic knowledge includes what we have for many years referred to as *phonics*, or letter/sound relationships; it also includes what we have referred to as the *structure of* words—prefixes, suffixes, base words, and so on (Chapter 8). Some authorities use the term *graphophonics* to refer to all the types of correspondence between print and sound (Goodman, 1967; Weaver, 1988). We will explore orthographic knowledge in depth in Chapters 5 and 8.

Children will also learn about the nature and purposes of *texts.* Earlier, we talked about the nature of the text, but more from the perspective of the writer who structures and composes a text. Readers, too, must develop an awareness and understanding of this structure and its influence on the content of the text. As we noted earlier in this chapter, there are two primary types of printed texts or major genres or "discourse structures," as they are referred to by researchers: *narrative* and *informational* (expository). We will examine these types of texts thoroughly in Chapters 7 and 8. For the moment, though, we should point out that narratives follow predictable structures (having beginnings, middles, and ends that gradually disclose how characters solve problems) and that expository texts present information in formats designed to facilitate the "topic" knowledge discussed below.

Knowledge About Knowledge   Each reader has an awareness of how knowledge itself works. When we talk about how this knowledge is engaged in purposeful learning situations, we can use the terms *topic knowledge, procedural knowledge,* and *self-knowledge* (Dillon & Sternberg, 1986). I know; that's quite a few terms, so let's look at the underlying ideas. (Refer to Figure 2.2 on page 40 to help yourself visualize these relationships more clearly.)

Topic knowledge means, quite simply, facts or information about a specific topic or domain of knowledge. The more you know about the topic you're reading about, the more you will comprehend as you read. Still, topic knowledge is not enough, if we are to be truly efficient readers. We need knowledge about *procedures* or "strategies" for reading different types of texts for different purposes. We need *self-knowledge*, awareness of ourselves as readers and learners, in order to realize when to apply specific strategies. We need to "know when we don't know" (self-knowledge), and we need to know what to do about it (procedural knowledge). In recent years, researchers have referred to procedural knowledge and self-knowledge as aspects of *metacognition,* a term that you will encounter frequently. Broadly speaking, metacognition is "thinking about thinking" (Flavell, 1979; Garner, 1987; Metcalfe & Shimamura, 1994). Specific strategies that we will explore later in this text may be termed "metacognitive" strategies—they facilitate self-knowledge and procedural knowledge.

Affect   How we perceive our experiences and how we feel about those experiences has to do with *affect.* Affect will influence our motivation to read, our response to what we read; and often, the sense we make of what we read (Many, 1990; Miall, 1988; Ortony, Clore, & Collins, 1988; Sadowski, Goetz, & Kangiser, 1988). The affective realm includes aspects such as our emotions, our attitudes, our beliefs and values, and our motivation and interest. All of these are operative at some level before, during, and after any reading event.

Authorities refer to an *affective filter* that reflects an individual's motivation and personality (Krashen, 1981; Richard-Amato, 1988). What we experience, how we think about the same experience, and how we feel about that same experience all depend on *affect. Motivation* is important here, because it is involved in *engaging* children in reading as well as in keeping them *sustained* in the effort when the task becomes challenging.

In explaining the problems with reading that so many students experience in school, Athey succinctly notes that "learning may be inadequate for motivational reasons and instruction may be inappropriate because it fails to appeal to the values and interests of the learner" (1985, pp. 527–528). Children will have a stake in their reading and will become better readers if the process is based primarily on interesting and motivating texts.

The contexts: settings and purposes

In Chapter 1, I said that *within a particular context,* reading is the act of processing the visual, printed information in a text and relating it to our prior knowledge about language and about the world. We also saw in Chapter 1 that "context" is really a "plural" idea: *contexts* determine where we read and why we read—the settings and purposes for reading. There is a *physical* context, or *where* the reading is occurring; there is a *social* context that represents the nature of the social interaction that occurs before, during, and after the reading; and there is a *cultural* context, for our cultural background can affect how and

why we read (as we'll explore often throughout this book), and it can determine what children think literacy is, how they think it is used, and how they feel about it.

These contexts are interwoven or "embedded," each influencing the others. Taken together, they create for any reader a particular *psychological* context determining what we read, why we read it, and what we pay attention to when we read. For all of us, children or adults, contexts include three broad domains or purposes for reading (Scribner, 1984; Taylor, 1993):

For Enjoyment   Rosenblatt (1978) has referred to the *aesthetic* purpose of reading; we derive pleasure from much of what we read. Reading is a valued activity in which we can escape the present. This escape, however, is not without purpose; what we find when we "return" is so often personal enlightenment and deeper understanding of the human condition. Enjoyment can be leisurely or it can be the result of a deep probing of a text, as we'll later observe.

To Gain Knowledge   This knowledge can be broad-based, as in learning about economics, or as specific as learning how to conduct an experiment, fill out a loan application, or operate a fork lift. We read newspapers and magazines to learn what's going on in our worlds on a day-to-day basis. In both white-collar and blue-collar jobs, "occupational" reading takes up a significant part of each day (Mikulecky, 1982; Guthrie, Seifert, & Kirsch, 1986) and is bound up with the moment-to-moment business of getting things done.

To Function at Home and as Citizens in the Community and Society   We read to orient ourselves in the practical world of our homes and communities, in order to function effectively as citizens. At home, we may read to make decisions about financial planning. Many reading activities involve communication within and among neighborhoods; religious groups; local social, political, and artistic organizations, and various youth groups.

Contexts of Reading for Learners   Whether during leisure time or in the workplace, adults usually have more choice in the matter of what, where, and when they read than elementary-school children do. Children are required to be in school, so they are more vulnerable to the contexts that influence reading. This is why *we* must carefully think through what we do as teachers and how we do it, how we set up instructional situations and make decisions about reading materials. While we wish to create many opportunities for children to choose what they read, their purposes and contexts for reading are often of necessity structured by us, their teachers. There is good reason for this, however: lifetime habits and attitudes are being established, attitudes that will eventually affect how these children, as adult or proficient readers, will go about setting their own purposes and using the tool of reading effectively and efficiently. By structuring an effective social environment, we can help children experience and learn from so much of their reading and the activities that spring from it. They will experience, in fact, something like what Winnie-the-Pooh sagely observed, that ". . . when you are a Bear of Very Little Brain, and you Think of Things, you find sometimes that a Thing which seemed very Thingish inside you is quite different when it gets out into the open and has other people looking at it" (1928, p. 102).

Contexts of Reading for Mature Readers   The ability to read has always been valued in our society because it has been equated in Western culture, rightly or wrongly, with being an educated person. We do hope, of course, that with our help all children *will* mature into young adults who want to read, and not just because their eventual workplaces will require it, but because each of them has become—as Atwell expresses it—"an adult for whom reading is a logical, satisfying, life-long habit, someone who just plain loves books and reading."

But there *is* the practical reality of the workplace. Over the past several decades, literacy demands in both professional and blue-collar workplaces have in fact increased. Rarely will someone say, "Read this memo *now*" or "Read this set of instructions *now*," but employees must read job-related materials and respond appropriately to what they have read. The workplace is where contexts require literacy to be used most often as a *tool* to get things done. Beginning in the elementary grades, we can give children a strong start toward understanding and using reading as a tool throughout their lives. Whether the contexts determine adult reading to be for enjoyment, to gain knowledge, or to accomplish goals in the home or the community, today's students will gain the effective literacy tools for tomorrow's needs.

■   MEANING MAKERS: You, the Student

Your Own Purposes for Reading

Before reading further, try the following activity. In your learning log, brainstorm a list of the reading situations you have engaged in recently.

Think broadly! Afterward, compare your list with a friend's and talk with him or her about the different *purposes* your different reading situations involved. ■

The elements come together in a particular reader's psychological context

It is critical to remember that at any given moment, the context of *a* particular reader with *a* particular text is a *unique* context. While a reading experience may occur in school, on the job, or at home, there will always be the specific context of a reader's mind in contact with the world of the text a writer presents. In other words, the meaning you, as the reader, make at any one time or place may be different from the meaning you make at another time or place.

Let me share an example of this "uniqueness." Did you ever go back and read a "required" book from a high school or college English class—and discover that this second experience was *very* different from the first? One that I remember in particular is Somerset Maugham's *Of Human Bondage*, a required text in a freshman English class I took. Although I did enjoy and "get into" it the first time, I remember how exasperated I was with the main character: why *was* he always making poor decisions? His plight seemed to me so easy to avoid. . . . From the perspective of a good many years later, and upon my second experience with the book, I still think the main character made some bad decisions; but I understand now that very few choices are as cut-and-dried as I once assumed, and I'm a little more tolerant and understanding of the main character's predicaments. By virtue simply of *living*, in other words, I brought to this second reading much more—and very different—prior knowledge. Clifton Fadiman captured this phenomenon in what he wrote about classics; it is applicable to any good book that you revisit: "When you reread a classic you do not see more in the book than you did before; you see more in you than was there before."

Remember, though, that this "uniqueness" of any reading context is always going on; it needn't take years between reading experiences to realize it. To reiterate: each reading experience *is* unique; the meaning that a child makes when reading in the classroom is a fluid entity, because the relationships among the various contexts are themselves fluid, never static, and always shifting to various degrees.

THE ELEMENTS INTERACT: MODELS OF THE READING PROCESS

You already know that *both* reader and text contribute to efficient reading. The real issue is the *degree* to which the reader and the text contribute in any particular context. Is the flow of information or the "meaning" coming primarily from the text? from the reader? from somewhere in between?

Over the years, reading theorists and researchers have elaborated different models to explain their positions about the balance of elements and about how elements work one with the other. A good model will try to explain as much of the process of reading as possible. I will try to do so on the basis of what we have learned from the best research on what happens when we read. Three different models of the reading process are commonly referred to as the "bottom-up," the "top-down," and the "interactive/transactional" models. It is important to realize that these are theoretical models and do not speak *directly* to instruction. However, a particular stance on this issue—whether it is yours, your fellow teachers', or your administrator's—can powerfully affect what you are encouraged to do in your classroom and can have an impact on how you go about teaching reading.

Debates about how to go about teaching literacy are usually framed in either/or terms, both within the educational community and without, and these debates usually result in efforts to affect directly what goes on in your classroom. The instructional implications of the bottom-up model have predominated in American schools, but we are beginning to see more and more classrooms reflecting the top-down model. You will need to be aware of the strengths as well as the shortcomings of each model; and in actuality, the relevant aspects of each come together in the context of the classroom that reflects the *interactive/transactional* model—which is the model we'll explore last in this section.

Figure 2.3 graphically represents the relationship between reader and text that each model of the reading process implies. Let's look briefly at each model, and then I will elaborate on implications that can be drawn from the models. I'll be paying special attention to the model that gives equal attention to the role of the reader *and* that of the text—the model that guides our orientation in this text.

Figure 2.3
Flow of Information in Reading: Three Models

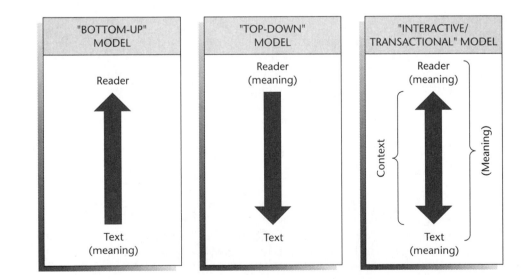

Reading as a "bottom-up" process

This model assumes that the *text* is "in control" and that readers automatically take up information from the page (Gough, 1972; Massaro, 1975). In the bottom-up model, information is processed linearly, in a sequence of stages. The process is initiated when the reader takes up visual information from the page, and this information is processed with little or no influence from the reader's knowledge of the world or from the ongoing context itself.

The process gets under way with letter identification. Readers look at just about every word in a left-to-right fashion, letter by letter, converting letters to sounds, and this results in the identification of each word. There is no influence of surrounding context on this identification process. Once a word is identified, its meaning is added to the meanings of the other words in the sentence in a linear fashion—word by word, phrase by phrase—until the total meaning of a sentence is built up according to syntactic and semantic rules. As the meaning of each sentence is constructed this way, it is added to the cumulative meaning of previous sentences throughout the text. Inferences and interpretations occur but depend on what is coming into the brain from the text, not on what is already in the brain from background knowledge.

In the bottom-up model, the reader is clearly "controlled" by the print because there is no room for conscious strategies to be brought to bear on the text. The process will proceed automatically, as just described. Of course, the information that the reader needs in order to identify words and assemble their cumulative meanings into sentences resides in the reader's head, but this information can operate only on what comes up "from below"—off the page. Incidentally, the bottom-up model has been referred to as the "common sense" model of reading, since it is probably the concept of the reading process that the "person in the street" entertains (Weaver, 1988). Most people do seem to believe that the meaning is "on the page" and that the reader must "get" it—for this reason, this model has also been referred to as the "outside-in" model (Smith, 1975).

Instructional Implications of the Bottom-Up Model By looking at the nature of reading instruction in a classroom over several days, we can usually infer the model of the reading process that a teacher holds—even if the teacher has not necessarily thought about employing a particular model of reading. Let's first consider here the implications of the bottom-up model for instruction; then, after each of the other model presentations, we can look at the instructional implications for those models.

When the bottom-up model is the dominant belief system, the *text* is seen as in control. Instruction will usually emphasize strategies that focus exclusively on figuring out the text, most often in a sequential-skills, part-to-whole instructional format with lots of practice. Practices that are typically associated with the bottom-up model are the following:

■ Children are grouped according to ability levels; traditionally, there have been three groups: high, middle, and low. The teacher meets with each group every day.

■ Instruction is based on a published basal reading program that includes attention to all the reading "skills" (see Chapter 10).

■ There is direct skills instruction every day for each reading group, with follow-up practice during "seatwork" time. This practice most often is in the form of workbook pages, dittos, or copies made from black-line masters.

■ Children read out loud from a selection in the basal reading book during reading group time; and prior to the reading, the teacher usually introduces and works with new words that will appear in the selection. The selection usually is read in a "round robin" format, with the children taking turns reading aloud, proceeding around a circle. (Teachers who follow this format explain that round-robin reading allows practice in word recognition, reinforces learning of new words, and also helps the teacher see how well the children are doing with their reading.)

■ Teachers ask questions to check whether the children are comprehending what they are reading. The questions focus almost exclusively on the text, with few attempts to connect to students' individual interpretations or understandings.

■ In the intermediate grades, round-robin reading is common during science and social studies sessions. Students take turns reading paragraphs from the textbook ("This way, I know the students will have gone over the material at least once," teachers often explain).

■ Writing is taught apart from reading. Conventions and correctness are emphasized. Models are usually provided, most often from selections in the basal reader or an English language arts textbook. The teacher assigns the topics.

You can see that the bottom-up model does not seem to translate into an approach that has much room for children's choices and interests in reading and writing. Because of this, the teacher spends a good deal of time keeping students "on task," because many of the tasks are tedious in and of themselves when done day after day. Children are expected to be quiet most of the time, attending to their work. This in turn means that management and motivation are continual challenges for the teacher.

Because the bottom-up model places primary emphasis on learning the parts of the reading process, it gives relatively little attention to *why* we read in the first place: to enjoy, to learn, to share information in a social context. Because such overemphasis on skills is not inherently motivating, the teacher often must work to keep students in control and on task.

Reading as a "top-down" process

Writers, after all, do want to communicate. This is obvious enough—and this understanding led to the "common sense" view of reading as a "bottom-up" process. But what about those doing the reading—the *readers*? Do they simply lift the intended meaning off the page, reconstructing *exactly* what the writer intended? We now understand that of course they don't—and this realization led to the top-down model of reading. The top-down model assumes that the *reader* is primarily "in control" of all levels of processing and that the process begins with the reader's general knowledge of the world and of language. This knowledge is used to guess, predict, or make hypotheses about the possible meaning of what will be coming next in the text. Kenneth Goodman characterized this top-down model of reading as a "psycholinguistic guessing game" in which the page is "sampled" only as much as is necessary to confirm the reader's predictions or guesses about the hypothesized meaning (Goodman, 1967; Smith, 1971, 1988). In contrast to the bottom-up model, in the top-down model readers are actively relying on their own resources and only incidentally relying on the text. The perceptual image of the print—the letters and words that are sampled—is influenced by the reader's hypothesis about what he or she *expects* to be on the page, an anticipation that in turn is based on top-down semantic and syntactic knowledge. The whole process, in other words, is based on what the reader expects or tacitly predicts will come next in the reading. As Weaver describes, ". . . it is the reader's schemas, expectations, and reading strategies that determine how the parts will be perceived and what meanings will be assigned to them" (1988, p. 38). Another term for this model, Frank Smith has suggested, is the "inside-out" model.

According to the top-down model, when readers misidentify words or "miscue" (Goodman & Goodman, 1977), they will continue reading *if* they are still "making sense." If they realize that something is not quite right, however, they usually will go back and locate the word or words that were miscued and identify them correctly in light of the subsequent information.

Instructional Implications of the Top-Down Model The *reader* is in control, and instruction usually reflects students' interests and emphasizes strategies that help readers do two things: first, consider what *they* already know about what they will be reading; and second, organize and adjust what they do. Typically, instruction proceeds like this:

■ Children are *not* grouped according to reading ability. They spend a lot of time reading independently, and the teacher often meets with them in small groups organized according to interest rather than reading skill. These groups meet with the teacher every two or three days. On occasion, the teacher meets with students in individual conferences.

■ Instruction in specific skills is avoided.

■ Children apply their developing knowledge about skills to real texts, not in isolated "practice" tasks that do not relate directly to real reading.

■ There is no round-robin oral reading. Students *do* read aloud, but in meaningful contexts and from real texts—and this oral reading usually is *re*reading. For example, a child will go back to a section of a story and read to the group the part that supports her interpretation. This allows the teacher a more authentic assessment of the child's reading ability. The teacher may also, during an individual conference, have the child read a favorite part aloud; this, too, provides important information.

■ Students read for their own purposes. Questions are generated from their own reading, not by the teacher.

■ Writing is taught along with reading, and vice versa. Writing topics always arise out of the children's interests. Models come from authentic literature and from other students. There is much demonstration, by the teacher and by students, of the process of writing: how to go about it, what kinds of thinking one does along with it. The student's intended meaning is stressed first, with conventions and correctness addressed later on—both developmentally and during the writing of a particular composition.

As you can see, because the top-down model places so much emphasis on authentic literature and contexts, explicit attention to skills may be neglected—from the nature of word structure to how reading can be used as a tool. For example, although skills are supposed to be taught and applied in a more natural context, occasionally it may be beneficial to provide "practice" in a more contrived context to ensure that both the student and the teacher know that the student can indeed apply the skill.

Reading as an "interactive/transactional" process

As we have seen, over the years considerable attention has been given to "where the meaning is" during reading. Certainly, writers usually intend what they write to evoke certain thoughts, ideas, and interpretations in the reader. Still, they cannot control *every* thought and reaction a reader might have. Recent research investigating the process of reading has helped us blend aspects of the bottom-up and top-down models and provided support for an *interactive/ transactional* model. I believe that the strengths and shortcomings of the nature and instructional implications of the bottom-up and top-down models are adequately accounted for in this model. Partly for this reason, I'll spend more time with the *interactive/transactional* model. I also prefer it because I believe it better represents what we now understand about what goes on during reading: therefore, this model appropriately represents the elements our instruction should address.

In contrast to the bottom-up model, we now understand that background knowledge *does* influence the meaning and interpretations a reader constructs; meaning is not automatically "assembled" with no contribution by the reader (Pearson & Anderson, 1984). In contrast to the top-down model, we now understand that readers *do* look at almost every word as they read and that they *do* pick up the actual orthographic or spelling features of the words, rather than operating on what they *expect* to be there (Perfetti, 1991; Rayner, 1976; Rayner & Pollatsek, 1989). As readers, then, we construct our meaning partly on the basis of the information supplied in the text—information that begins at the level of the word. I've always liked the description of the text as a blueprint for constructing meaning (Adams, 1980). Using this blueprint, as readers *we* construct a richer, actual meaning based in turn on our background knowledge—which, as we've seen, includes knowledge about the type of text we are reading and the type of topic or subject the writer is addressing.

The meaning that we make when we read arises from the top-down features of our background knowledge and the bottom-up features of the text—the text being what the writer has given us in his or her absence. As we saw in Chapter

1, some theorists have referred to this exchange or coming-together of reader and text—and the resultant meaning that is constructed—as a *transaction*, a term suggesting that meanings are exchanged and a new meaning created (Rosenblatt, 1978). Bringing *your* meaning together with the intended meaning of the *text* yields this "third meaning," unique to the text and you, which did not exist prior to your interaction with the text.

The *interactive/transactional* model, in other words, helps us understand how the process of reading results in a *new* meaning, based on contributions from the text—the intended meaning of the writer—and contributions of the reader, the meanings he or she brings to the text from background knowledge.

In the interactive/transactional model, readers do look at almost every word as they read. Once identified, the words are integrated with top-down syntactic and semantic knowledge, and there is an ongoing interaction between these bottom-up word-identification processes and top-down general knowledge processes as meaning is constructed. We'll soon look at how this process actually works during proficient reading.

You should know that I have taken the liberty of combining two perspectives on the reading process—interactive and transactional—that are usually discussed separately. For our purposes, however, I believe they are actually quite similar. The interactive model has developed out of research by cognitive psychologists (for example, Just & Carpenter, 1980; McClelland, 1986; Rumelhart, 1977; Stanovich, 1980), while the transactional model has developed out of the thinking of teachers of literature (for example, Rosenblatt, 1978, 1983, 1989). While the interactive model emphasizes the intended meaning of the text coming together with the meaning that the reader brings to the text, the transactional perspective helps us understand the importance of the *new* meaning that results from this coming-together. In addition—perhaps because the transactional view was developed by those working with students who were reading and interpreting texts in instructional settings—the transactional view emphasizes the importance of *context* in a model of the reading process (see, for example, Weaver, 1988). Context determines the nature of the meanings that will be made.

Instructional Implications of the Interactive/Transactional Model   This model strikes an instructional balance between the advantages of both the bottom-up and the top-down models. The model acknowledges that *both* text and reader play important roles in the construction of meaning. The interactive/transactional perspective recognizes that it is important to learn about the characteristics and features of texts, from word level on up through the overall macrostructure level, *and* that explicit, teacher-guided instruction may be necessary for much of this learning. The interactive/transactional perspective recognizes, too, the importance of accessing the *reader's* prior knowledge, background, and affect—and likewise recognizes the teacher's role in helping readers become aware of how they can access and apply their background knowledge. Typically:

■ Children read independently and in groups. Depending on students' needs and interests, they may be grouped heterogeneously or homogeneously.

■ Teachers guide and facilitate. They also engage in direct-teaching, which means that they explicitly address areas of need by discussing, modeling, and walking students through appropriate activities and strategies.

■ Students are guided toward understanding how to identify and read for their *own* purposes. But the teacher also plays a role in extending students' own perspectives so as to help them consider meaningful questions that otherwise they would not consider, to let them consider points of view of which they have not been aware—in other words, to *challenge* and *extend* students' learning in consequential ways.

■ As with the top-down perspective, *writing* is taught along with reading, and vice versa. While topics may arise at first from children's own immediate interests, they come to include topics that they may not have addressed on their own. Teachers knowledgeably create areas of interest that will stretch children's minds as they explore those areas through reading and writing. For example, the mandated "history of the state" curriculum that is most often taught in fourth grade is rarely *inherently* interesting to children. A knowledgeable teacher, however, can create excitement and interest through giving an effective introduction to this area of study, then allowing students to choose, for research and writing, specific topics that connect with their own interests.

THE READING PROCESS IN ACTION: HOW PROFICIENT READERS READ

In this section, we will examine the process of reading as it occurs in proficient readers. My purpose in exploring the process of mature reading is twofold. First, by looking at what mature readers do—at what's really going on for us as we read—we can understand and appreciate the nature and complexity of the reading process. Second, we can better understand and appreciate just *why* we need to give instructional attention to different aspects of the process, as children move toward mature, proficient reading. As teachers, this should help us with our overall understanding of our own reading, of our students' reading, and of literacy in general. We will shortly be looking at the reading process from a *developmental* perspective, but it is the model of mature reading that helps us keep the overall focus and goal of our instruction in mind. By the way, you may find it interesting to reflect here on your *own* process of reading—how much of this model will you find you've figured out through an introspective analysis of your own reading? How much will you realize you weren't aware of?

We will look first at the components of the process—the different types of memory involved and how visual information is input to the brain—and then consider how these components work together in the actual process of reading. As we move through the specifics of these components, please refer to Figure 2.4; it should help keep the overall process in focus.

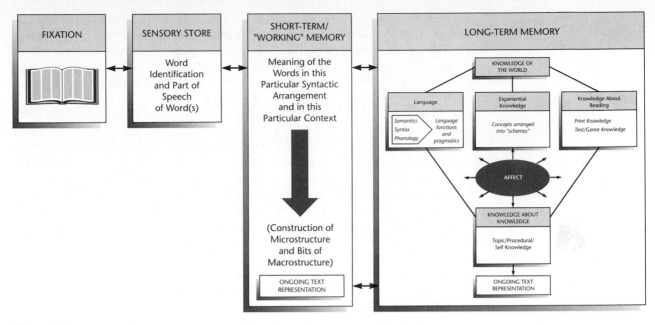

Figure 2.4
The Process of Reading

Memory

How are we able to take in information and remember it? Why do we seem to assimilate certain types of information easily, yet easily forget other types? It has to do with the ways our brains have been set up; and when it comes to *memory*, psychologists tell us, our brains seem to operate as if there were three "types" of memory (Klatzky, 1984; Wyer & Srull, 1989): the *sensory store; short-term memory;* and *long-term memory.* Let's consider each in turn.

Our *sensory store* very briefly holds visual information picked up by our eyes, holds it only until that visual information is identified. In the case of *reading,* this visual information usually consists of individual letters or words. Indeed, information is identified so rapidly from the sensory store that what takes place is often referred to as "automatic" processing. It is with the sensory store that the processing of visual, printed information in a text occurs. This identified, processed information is then sent on to what psychologists call *short-term memory.*

Short-term memory (or "working memory," as it's often called) includes what you are paying attention to at any particular instant in time. In the case of reading, this would be the words that you have just now identified. Short-term memory works to interpret the meaning of those identified words in the particular context and syntactic structure in which they occur. This process of interpretation is guided not only by the "bottom-up" process of word identification but also by the "top-down" input from *long-term memory*—by relating this information to our background knowledge about language and about the world. As Figure 2.4 shows, short-term memory carries part of the "ongoing text representation," which consists of the *microstructure* and a few "bits" of the macrostructure.

As you've probably noticed on many occasions (specifically, when you were trying to memorize something), short-term memory's capacity is limited. It can hold or "work on" only a certain number of items of information at a time, usually no more than seven or eight. As we'll see later on, these "items" can range from single letters to "chunks" of information—for example, remembering the *thirteen* separate letter units *IBMJFKAIDSIRS* becomes manageable if these units are chunked into only *four* larger recognizable units: *IBM - JFK - AIDS - IRS*. The support for such strategies also comes from long-term memory, which recognizes these as meaningful units. As we'll see a little later, this limitation on short-term memory has implications for beginning readers as well.

Long-term memory also is referred to as "prior knowledge" or "background knowledge" (the term I'll use here); it includes both "knowledge of the world" and "knowledge about knowledge"—really, *everything* that you know. This knowledge includes the information defined previously, in the section dealing with language and print. When we are reading, this background knowledge includes knowledge about the topic as well as knowledge about the type of selection or *genre* (we'll talk more about this in Chapters 6 and 7). It also includes *self-knowledge* and *procedural knowledge;* that is, our awareness of ourselves as learners and our awareness of the strategies we use.

Visual input

During reading, your brain tells your eyes where to look. The brain directs the eyes to "jump" from one place to another. This "jump" is termed a *saccade* (pronounced suhKAWD). When your eyes stop after a saccade, this is a *fixation.* Contrary to our intuitive impressions, our eyes are moving—engaged in saccadic (suhKAYdik) movement—only about five percent of the time during reading; our eyes are spent in fixations the rest of the time.

Have you noticed, while reading, that from time to time your eyes jump backward in the printed text? When you look back at something you read earlier, you are making what's called a *regression*. Regressions are, in fact, quite normal in mature as well as developing readers. Usually we aren't aware of them. They occur when we are reading along and suddenly something doesn't make sense; we usually go back to find the source of the confusion, which most often is a word misread or misinterpreted the first time and which subsequently did not fit the meaning we were constructing. At other times, we simply enjoy *re*reading something, in which case too we make a regression.

How it all comes together to form *the reading process*

Your visual system and your memory are busily at work during reading—but what, precisely, is the result of their efforts? They are helping construct a *text representation*, which includes lower-level or *microstructure* information as well as higher-level or *macrostructure* information about what you're reading (Brown & Day, 1983; Kintsch & vanDijk, 1978; Meyer & Rice, 1984). As you read, you construct your understanding of the text at these two levels. Microstructure processing refers to the word-by-word, phrase-by-phrase, and sentence-by-sentence meaning that is constructed. Macrostructure processing refers to the global structures that are constructed. This higher-order level includes information about the *episodes* and *theme* of the text (if it is a story; see Chapter 6) or about the organizational structure of the text (if it is expository; see Chapter 7).

Now we can plug in all the components of the reading process in our second-by-second, step-by-step analysis. At this point it should help to refer once again to Figure 2.4. You will recognize a significant part of this figure from earlier in this chapter: the right-hand box that represents long-term memory, or your background knowledge. Now we'll see how long-term memory fits with the other aspects of memory as you read.

1. As you move through a text, you operate during each fixation beginning with the information that is in your *sensory store*. During the fixation, what your brain "sees" includes the beginning of a fixated word and about six to eight letters to the right of your fixation. As your eyes move over the print in each successive fixation, you must identify the words appropriately and understand their meaning in this particular context. At this level, you will process almost all the words on the page. While information is in your sensory store, you will identify each word, as it is fixated, almost automatically and in a fraction of a second. Psychologists believe that the syntactic role of a word (noun, verb, adjective, and so forth) probably is tacitly identified at this time.

2. Your brain will next work primarily to construct the lower-level microstructure. As this happens, you will hear a "voice" in your head; this is what psychologists refer to as "inner speech," and it helps keep the information identified from the sensory store available for the comprehension processes in both working memory and long-term memory to operate on. (Proficient readers do not "sound out" words on the page to identify them; but once identified, some or all of the sounds in these words are automatically "played" in the brain and probably support meaning construction.) During this work on the microstructure, your brain is integrating the identity of each word that is processed, integrating it into the ongoing "text representation" being constructed in your working memory. This is done by constructing the underlying relationships among the concepts that the words represent, first within a particular sentence (syntactic knowledge) and then between that sentence and other sentences. The relationships within a sentence are between words and between groups of words (when a sentence contains phrases or clauses).

3. The product of your comprehension at the microstructure level interacts with, and is influenced by, long-term memory. Long-term memory is constructing the macrostructure—the global or "top-level" text representation. Some of this structure is maintained in short-term memory, but a fuller, more elaborate representation is being constructed in long-term memory.

Precisely *how* this macrostructure is constructed is very hazy, and psychologists are still hard at work trying to determine what the "units" of meaning at these levels really are. But it is clear that as you continue to read, the overall text representation that you construct becomes more elaborated while at the same time, it helps guide your construction of meaning at the microstructure level. In short, you have an ongoing back-and-forth, interactive relationship between your long-term memory and your working memory. You'll recall from our earlier discussion about experiential knowledge that this construction of meaning will include *imagery:* the abstract text representation that your brain is constructing includes, and is supported by, images constructed by your prior knowledge with input from the text. In addition, *affect* is brought to bear: your general emotional state as you are reading, as well as your emotional response *to* what you are reading. And of course there are the different experiences you may have with the *same* text at different points in time, as I did with Maugham's *Of Human Bondage.*

■ **MEANING MAKERS: You, the Student and You, the Classroom Teacher**

The Complexities of Comprehension

Let's consider how and why the process of constructing meaning can be so complex:

What we comprehend when we read is based on information that is literally stated "right there" in the passage and on information that is *implied* in the passage. Not only is much information implicit; the communicator is absent. Thus, a reader must be able to apply skills and knowledge appropriately to the text without recourse to the person who wrote that text. In other words, in order to construct meaning appropriately, a reader must know how to reconstruct and interpret a message that may have been stated indirectly in the first place and that is being presented by someone who is no longer there. To illustrate, here are two examples:

Let's start with the notion of "main idea"—a common label in reading instruction, referring to the most important information in a text. Sometimes the most important point of a paragraph, for example, can leap right out—it may be stated in a topic sentence. At other times, the main idea may be *implied*—much of the information given seems important, but the *most* important aspect of all may be left to the reader to capture in a "gist"-type statement. To use an old metaphor, you would have to "read between the lines" to *infer* the main idea or most important point. For example, read the following paragraph:

> Sally wanted to be the very best in her class at everything. She practiced her multiplication facts. She tried to read more books than anyone else. She even did homework on weekends!

What is the most important information in this paragraph? You would probably agree that the first sentence offers it; that sentence expresses the "main idea." On the other hand, consider *this* paragraph:

> Sally practiced her multiplication facts. She tried to read more books than anyone else. She even did homework on weekends!

That main idea is *not* stated explicitly. You must use the information given to *infer* the main idea, obviously a more demanding task than simply identifying it when it is explicitly stated. In fact, if you asked three different people, you might get three different notions of what the main idea is, depending on the nature of *their* experiential knowledge (Sally is a good student; Sally is an overachiever; Sally is competitive . . .). If you are uncertain about how to infer the main idea, *then* you will need instruction from someone who can model how that is done—how he or she uses information that is present, to reason through to the "main idea."

The boundary between what is explicit in reading comprehension and what must be inferred (read between the lines)—or even figured out by calling on information "beyond" the text—is not always so cut-and-dried. In order to appreciate this, read the following paragraph excerpted from a 1985 newspaper. Then we'll discuss the questions that follow, deciding whether the answers are explicitly, implicitly, or only partially in the text.

> The wreckage of the *Titanic,* the "unsinkable" victim of one of history's most storied ocean disasters, has been found 13,000 feet below the surface of the North Atlantic, a joint U.S.-French expedition announced Monday. The *Titanic,* which carried a glittering array of American and British socialites and a fortune in gems when it collided with an iceberg 73 years ago on its ill-fated maiden voyage from Southampton, England, to New York, was identified early Monday, its wreckage lying on the ocean bottom at an undisclosed location off Newfoundland, according to expedition officials.

1. At what depth was the *Titanic* found?
2. Was the *Titanic* on its first voyage?
3. Was the *Titanic* found near Newfoundland?
4. In what year did the *Titanic* sink?
5. Had the *Titanic* already crossed the ocean when it sank?
6. How was the fate of the *Titanic* similar to that of the *Lusitania*?

First, if you're wondering: none of the answers to these questions are *explicitly* given in the excerpt. None are "right there"—although at first it may appear as if some of them are.

Questions 1, 2, and 3 are similar in that they require the reader to make a connection between words in the text and the wording of the questions. Question 1 asks, "At what depth . . . ?" and the article does say, "13,000 feet below the surface"; no mention is made of "depth," so the reader must make a connection between "below the surface" and "depth." Question 2 asks about the "first voyage," and the passage mentions a "maiden voyage"; again, the reader must draw a connection between "maiden voyage" and "first voyage." Question 3 asks about the *Titanic*'s being found "near Newfoundland," and the passage says "off Newfoundland."

Do you see what is going on with these first three questions? If we didn't think much about them, we might say the answers to them are *explicit*, "right there" in front of us. But our *brains* have had to make these subtle little connections, these tiny little inferential leaps, in order for us to process and understand.

Questions 4, 5, and 6 give you some information to work with; but in contrast to the first three questions, you need consciously to "plug in" some information that is not given in the text. In the case of question 4, you need to remember that the article was published in 1985 and then subtract 73 from 1985, to be able to answer the question. Similarly, with question 5 you need to call upon your knowledge of geography *or* know where to go to get the additional information you need. Question 6 requires you to compare information about the fate of the *Titanic*, given in the passage, with the fate of the *Lusitania*, which (unless you already know it) you must go elsewhere to research.

The reason why we often must pay careful attention to finely tuned distinctions among different types of meaning construction, such as the differences between the first three question types, the fourth question, and the last two question types, has to do with students and with instruction. There are students who will have difficulty "reading between the lines" in some material, while *you* may believe the information is "right there," explicitly expressed, because it seems so obvious to you. Often it is not nearly as obvious to the students. And most will need help in determining when not all the information they are seeking is in the text and must be sought elsewhere.

I hope our little exercise with these two examples has helped you become aware of the complexities inherent in defining, identifying, and eventually teaching aspects of comprehension or meaning construction. Later in this text, you will learn how to teach comprehension strategies to students. ■

THE DEVELOPMENT OF READING

We already know that children differ from one another. This variability is evident in the nature of their experiences and in the sense they make of those experiences. It is apparent in *how* children use their knowledge and in the attitudes they have toward what they know. But we also have discovered—comparing across children—that the learning of basic processes such as how to talk or how to read follow strikingly similar developmental paths (Juel, 1991).

Children are set up to make meaning. Their knowledge is not received passively from the environment; instead, it is constructed as children interact with others in the context of a social environment. Researchers have noted this phenomenon for decades in the case of oral language development. Young children say things that they could not possibly have heard an adult say, and yet there is logic to their utterances: "Allgone doggie"; "I *wented* to Todd's house." What young children seem to be doing is "testing hypotheses" about how oral language works. They then get feedback from the social environment and, in time, will modify what they say and try out other hypotheses (perhaps "I *goed* to Todd's house"!). All of this is largely subconscious, of course—children do not "test hypotheses" in the deliberate sense that scientists do. Because oral language development is the foundation of all later literacy learning, we will look first at children's language development.

Next, we will turn our attention to children's development of reading from the preschool through the intermediate school years. We will also look at children's *writing* development as it relates to and reveals specific insights into what they know about reading.

As we have emphasized, all literacy development occurs within the embedded contexts of home, school, and community. The individual learner's cognitive and language resources interact with written language in a broad social and cultural context.

Marie Clay (1979) has referred to the development of reading as the "patterning of complex behavior"; Bussis et al. (1985) have referred to it as the "orchestration" of a set of simpler skills. This patterning or orchestration requires a good deal of time in which to develop.

The development of reading from the preschool years through the elementary grades is a marvelously complex though fascinating phenomenon. Table 2.1 presents in broad strokes the picture to which I'll be adding detail throughout the book as we address readers' developmental reading behaviors and their

For this child—as for other children—literacy develops in the embedded contexts of home, school, and community.

TABLE 2.1 Reading: A Developmental Overview

	Emergent Reading (Birth–6 Years of Age)	Beginning Reading (5–8 Years of Age)	Transitional Reading (6–11 Years of Age)	Mature/Proficient Reading (10 Years of Age and Up)
Text-level knowledge	• A beginning concept of what a "story" is, and in some cultures, beginning concepts about simple rhymes and nursery rhymes	• A more elaborate concept of "story" as well as a beginning awareness of expository or "informational" texts; children will begin consciously to differentiate between these two types of texts	• Better able to adjust prior knowledge to expository material	• In-depth knowledge of organization of expository material
	• Aspects of the sound and content of "book talk"—the language of books (primarily narratives) is different from that of everyday speech	• Responding to what is read: Able to recall "what happened"	• Responding to what is read: summarizing, analyzing, generalizing	• Critical analysis of and generalization from what is read; includes in-depth knowledge of elements of stories and poems
Word-level knowledge	• Prerequisite understandings about the nature of reading, including many important conventions of print such as the fact that it stands for speech and is "read" left-to-right and top-to-bottom	• A "concept of word in print" (voice-to-print match) • Phonemic awareness: sensitive to phonemic structure of words		• Knowledge of word structure includes awareness and understanding of word bases/roots and prefixes/suffixes as well as the ways in which these elements combine to form the meaning of words
		• "Alphabetic" concept of how print works (sounds are matched to letters, left-to-right)	• "Pattern" concept of how groups of letters form units within words to represent sound	
		• More rapid acquisition of sight vocabulary	• Very rapid growth of sight vocabulary	• Vocabulary of content-related words develops rapidly
Reading behaviors	• "Pretend" reading at first; picture somehow "contains" the story	• Characteristics of oral reading: word-by-word, "out loud"	• Toward fluency/expression—read with more expression, more "naturally," rate increases	• Flexible, strategic reading based on purpose
	• Later, print "tells" the story and children point to it as they "read" a memorized text		• Silent reading begins to take over	• Silent, fluent reading

knowledge about texts and words. I will consider the development of reading from preschool through sixth grade in terms of four developmental phases: (1) emergent literacy, (2) beginning reading, (3) transitional reading, and (4) mature or proficient reading.

The samples of children's *writing* that I have included should help demonstrate what these young writers know at each developmental phase about the nature of written language. While our focus here is primarily on reading development, it is important that you know what role writing development and writing instruction will play in reading development (recall our discussion of the relationships between writing and reading in Chapter 1). For our purposes in this chapter, I will be sharing the samples of writing because they so graphically reveal to us what children are learning about many aspects of reading: that is, children's developing knowledge about words and print conventions such as sentences, punctuation, and paragraphs; their increased knowledge about different genres; their sensitivity to style (how language can be used most effectively to convey particular meanings and feelings); and so on.

Throughout this section, we will be looking at the course of development that characterizes most children, and we will describe it in terms of most children's apparent capabilities within a particular age and grade span. Some children move through this developmental sequence quite rapidly (Bissex, 1980); others may not exhibit such behaviors and understandings until they begin to learn to read as adults. As we examine this continuum of development, we will notice how children continue to "test hypotheses" throughout their schooling. Actually, this is a lifelong pursuit. We, as reflective practitioners, are all "hypothesis testers"—but *consciously;* and how much time and effort we invest in trying out our understandings depends, in school and in life, on whether and how we have learned to "take risks" and be bold with our learning.

Oral language development as the basis of literacy

Children the world over acquire most of their language competence by the time they are about five years of age. This happens regardless of where they grow up, what language is spoken around them, or how others interact with them. The striking aspect about language development is that it seems to occur so *naturally*, without explicit instruction (Pinker, 1989).

During their first year of life, infants do a great deal of *babbling*, trying out a whole range of sounds. Their babbling becomes more "focused" in a few months, involving many of the sounds the infants hear around them and having many of the "up and down," or rising and falling, speech contours of the language they hear. By the time they are a year old, most children have begun using single, real words to express meaning, and they continue to do so for several more months. At approximately eighteen months to two years of age, they are using two words together and doing so in an interesting fashion, with utterances such as "More dirty" and "Here pretty." This is marvelous evidence, as we've noted, of children's natural tendency to "test hypotheses" about how language works. They certainly have not heard an adult say anything like "Here pretty"; so rather than imitating the word order spoken around them,

Ideas and actions do not emerge in a vacuum. The models of the reading process that we discussed earlier grew out of developments in fields related to education in general and reading in particular: primarily, the fields of linguistics, psychology, and—more recently—psycholinguistics, sociolinguistics, and cognitive science (the computer simulation of human information processing).

Because learning a language is such an incredible feat and children seem to accomplish most of the task by the age of five, many educators have drawn a parallel between learning to speak and learning to read. From the child's point of view, *is* learning to read just like learning to talk? No; although there are important parallels, there also are many dissimilarities. If talking and reading were similar, all kids would in fact learn to read and read well. But the fact remains that while almost all normally developing children learn to talk, not all children learn to read. Kids *not* immersed in a rich oral language environment nevertheless learn to talk, while many children immersed in a rich literacy environment do *not* learn to read. Table 2.2 graphically represents this situation.

We are usually in an extremely rich communication context when we are using oral language, and there are many, many contextual cues that work just about automatically to support our hearing and interpreting spoken words. The context of the printed page is not as rich contextually, nor does it as automatically support picking up the words; this is why we point out to children what context *is* available in printed texts—the pictures, the layout, the title and headings, the nature of printed words, and so forth.

Because of the rich contexts for oral language, children learning to listen and speak do not have to analyze consciously the "parts" of oral language. It is not necessary to know at a conscious level how to blend the sounds of language together in order to speak, nor how to break them apart in order to listen. On the other hand, it *is* necessary to know at a conscious level how the "parts" of written language work, in order to read and write. The important parts that require analysis are *words*, of course; and investigators are discovering that children must learn about the structure of words in order to advance in learning to read, as well as in order to read skillfully.

Do children pick up on word structure as naturally as they pick up on the sounds of their language when they are learning to talk? Some appear to do so, but most children require conscious and direct attention to how words work. We will explore *how* we can help children do this, in as interesting and motivating a manner as possible, in Chapter 5.

TABLE 2.2 A Comparison—Learning to Talk and Learning to Read		
	Oral Language Development	**Reading Development**
Exposure	Necessary and sufficient	Necessary but not sufficient
Rich immersion	Important but not mandatory	Necessary
Focused attention to specifics	Not necessary	Necessary

LEARNING IN CONTEXT: Context can powerfully support oral and written language development, but appropriate instruction *within* facilitative contexts is necessary for reading to develop.

they are using that information as best they can to generate their own ideas about how the grammar of the language works. Sometime during their third year most children move into what has been termed the "telegraphic" period. Their utterances grow longer and are "telegraphic" in that function words are usually left out, as are any inflectional endings such as those that form plurals or the past tense: "Gavin sit down car"; "No eat cookie." Over the course of another couple of years, the grammar that children are constructing becomes considerably more complex. Their vocabulary grows tremendously, and they develop a whole range of syntactic or sentence structures—including question structure—that they use to express their meaning.

Language-learning carries important implications for reading instruction. Most have to do with a meaningful and supportive context, as we have seen in Chapter 1 and earlier in this chapter. Language-learning is strongly supported by the context that renders it meaningful, and this should also be the case with learning to read. On the other hand, children in situations where not much interaction with adults occurs do acquire language—even in cultures where children are discouraged from talking much with adults. Learning language is innate, and the drive to learn it is "preprogrammed" biologically (Lenneberg, 1967; Luria, 1975). This raises an interesting and important issue, one that we address in the "Making Connections" box that follows: children who do not receive rich and motivating support in their interaction with print do *not* usually learn to read very well. Learning to read is not innate. Reading must be directly taught and learned.

Emergent literacy

While researchers have believed for quite some time that young children are "meaning makers" and hypothesis-testers with respect to learning oral language, it was not until the last twenty years or so that most researchers realized that young children attempt to "make meaning" with respect to *written* language as well. Children try out hypotheses about how print represents the world, they play with print just for the fun of it, and they interact with others in the process of figuring out how written language works and how it is used. Also, until the past twenty years or so, most educators didn't consider seriously what these children were actually doing. There was a prevailing belief that "real" learning about reading began when the children started school; and as for writing, well . . . the belief was that children couldn't write about anything until they had learned to read!

Now we know differently. Preschool children *do* construct powerful under-standings about reading and written language. Perhaps the most striking aspect about reading development during this time is that so much of it is *tacit* or below the level of conscious awareness. Children are like very active sponges; they learn a great deal about the nature and purpose of printed language by observing, by asking questions, and by acting on written language (Harste, Burke, & Woodward, 1984; Teale & Sulzby, 1986; Yaden & Templeton, 1986). The "actions" they perform on written language include their own attempts at *writing*.

Preschool children, to become literate individuals, need to be around books, and they need to be read to by a literate person. This should begin early on. Children will gradually learn that many books tell stories; and though at first they'll probably believe that the story is somehow in the illustrations, eventually they will attend to the print. They will, quite naturally, learn by memory a number of favorite stories and "read" them back while turning the pages of the book. This is a time when proud parents proclaim that their preschooler is *"really* reading!" As we will explore in Chapter 3, these memorized texts play a critical role in the child's learning about the specifics of print—about words, letters, and sounds.

In the preschool years or emergent literacy phase, most children develop a concept of what a story is. They begin to learn about how books "work" in that books have a "different-sounding" language than everyday conversational speech. They learn about what print can do—label things, tell about things, help people do things. They will learn to distinguish writing from drawing. They learn about conventions of print, something of how it "works" on the page to represent what can be said. They remember favorite texts and "read" them many times over, and they eventually take on unfamiliar texts and "read" what they think those texts say. They experiment with letters and letterlike characters. The following effort by a five-year-old reveals some of this experimentation.

Although we cannot be too sure about what the large loops and curves represent, we definitely can identify some letters *(P, B, R, M, S, A)* and a letterlike character or two. Oftentimes a child will attribute a message to this experimentation, either during the actual writing or afterward. Such writings may be an occasion for the child to run up to you and demand that you "read what it

Figure 2.5
Child's Art Showing Experimentation with Letters

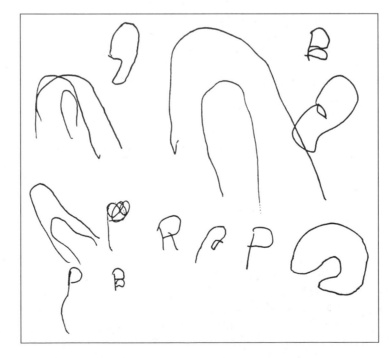

says"! (A coping strategy I have found useful is telling the child, "I'd like *you* to read it to *me*!" More often than not, a child will comply.)

Toward the end of the emergent literacy phase, something occurs that helps signal you as a teacher that a child is moving into the next phase of beginning reading. Children begin to understand the *word* as a unit, the relationship between the written representation of a word and its spoken counterpart, and some of the *sounds* within single words. These understandings are guided by adults who help direct a child's attention to words, letters, and sounds, and (as we will explore in Chapter 3), if you teach kindergarten or first grade, you will be playing a significant role here.

Before children can consistently identify one word after another in a line of print (an ability that develops considerably during the next phase of beginning reading), they have to have an understanding of what a word in print *is* (Morris, 1983). The task is conceptually more demanding than you may think, because "words" in speech all run together, and a young child can't really tell where one ends and another begins. We can infer that children have developed this concept when they demonstrate the understanding that in print, *words are groups of letters that have spaces on both ends*. Once this concept is acquired, children are able to be more analytical about the nature of written words and how letters correspond to spoken language. Their ability to think consciously about the phonemes or sounds that make up words—their *phonemic awareness*— will soon allow them to identify all the sounds within a word. They have moved into the phase termed *beginning reading*.

Beginning reading

First, I need to make an important observation about the term *beginning reading*. Because the term is so commonly associated with what happens starting sometime during the first grade year, I use it to refer to this particular phase. A more appropriate term might be beginning *conventional* reading, since so much knowledge about reading develops prior to this phase. For brevity's sake, however, I will continue to use this shorter term.

Although many at the beginning of their first-grade year are emergent readers, most children will move into the beginning-reading phase sometime during this year—and many will move into the following *transitional* phase as well. During the beginning-reading phase, children will develop a richer understanding or more elaborated "schema" for stories, though they also spend a good deal of time just trying to figure out what the words on the page *are*. Children at the beginning-reading phase have to allot much conscious attention to figuring out words, and that makes the whole reading process move along slowly. Still, they usually can recall what they have read and reflect more critically on its meaning—for example, talking about characters' motivations, comparing one story with another.

When do we know that a child has moved into the beginning-reading phase? Reliable benchmarks are (as we have just seen) the awareness of a printed word as a unit and the awareness of some sounds within the word. These awarenesses represent *qualitative* differences in the ways children interact with print (Juel,

1991; Perfetti, 1991); such children will be "glued" to the print in a way that earlier, they were not (Chall, 1983). They are not comfortable with simply inventing whatever they think the text *should* say. They want to construct exactly the words that the text presents to them.

During the beginning-reading phase, children will develop their store of *sight words* (also referred to as "sight vocabulary" or "instant recognition words") much more rapidly than during the emergent literacy phase. A child's sight vocabulary consists of words she can identify immediately when she sees them in print, either in context or in isolation.

When children read during this phase, you are likely to notice that they read *out loud*. Among other things, hearing themselves *say* what they are looking at helps support word identification and comprehension. This oral reading will usually be in a monotone, fairly slow and choppy; it's often described as word-by-word reading. The children are likely to keep their place with a forefinger, pointing to each word while pronouncing it—what Marie Clay has called "voice pointing" (1979).

In the beginning-reading phase, children's knowledge about words is of an "alphabetic" nature. Sounds are matched to letters in a left-to-right sequence. Early in this phase, as they read and try to figure out the identity of an unknown word, they will do so primarily on the basis of the beginning consonant, the preceding context, and any accompanying pictures. A little later, they will try both beginning and ending consonants. Eventually, they will apply their developing knowledge about vowels to scanning unknown words in a left-to-right, letter-by-letter fashion (Ehri, 1991, 1993, 1994; Frith, 1985; Reitsma, 1983). As they build their sight vocabulary, they will gradually become aware of similar spellings across words and will use this awareness to figure out an unknown word—*tray* might be identified by combining knowledge about *truck* and *say*.

The word-identification strategies that children consciously use at this phase, however, depend both on their developing knowledge about words and on what teachers are modeling (Vellutino & Scanlon, 1991). While underlying knowledge about word structure may be similar across children at the same developmental point, their *application* of that knowledge depends on the nature of instruction. Most children seem to benefit most from instruction in which teachers (1) model the use of context as well as (2) give attention to the nature and use of phonics, or letter-sound correspondences (Stanovich, 1994). This dual emphasis on both context and word structure will lay the groundwork for students' ability to develop flexible and productive word identification strategies, as opposed to relying exclusively on context or phonics.

As we've mentioned, children experiment with their developing knowledge about the forms and functions of written language as they *write*. In fact, much of what we can learn about what children know about written language—words and texts—arises from their written efforts. Let's take a look at a child's composition so that we can examine what he knows (see Figure 2.6). Loren is at an early point in the beginning-reading phase.

WEnI WFtto the hoGpito lAahPI WusO munhsoLP
ButmymomWusBErLEDAmeⁿtJ andI wuⁿsAsBⁿg
Agutⁿte Bear

Loren

Figure 2.6
Beginning Reader: Early First Grade

When I went to the hospital I was zero months old but my mom was barely damaged and I was as big as a teddy bear.

Loren wrote his little description in November of his first grade year in response to his teacher's question about experiences any of the children may have had in hospitals. He makes some delightful observations about when he was born—his only "experience" in a hospital—including comparing his size with that of a teddy bear's. Loren has been read to a lot; he already has a concept of word in print, even though he has not included spaces between the words as he writes (not uncommon among children at this point). We can infer he has this understanding, however, because he is sensitive to almost every sound within a word, using a letter to stand for each sound, and such sensitivity is not this fine-grained unless children have a concept of word in print. He is inventing his spellings primarily according to the sounds of letters (Beers & Henderson, 1977; Henderson, 1990; Read, 1985; Templeton & Bear, 1992), although he *has* spelled a few words correctly—those words that are in his sight vocabulary. We'll examine this phenomenon of "invented spelling" in some depth in Chapter 5.

Transitional reading

Most children during their second- and third-grade years will be in the transitional-reading phase. This is a time for consolidating knowledge about words and texts, a time of lots of reading, rereading, and writing. It is "transitional" in the sense that it is a rather lengthy bridge between the beginning-reading phase and the proficient phase (where reading develops into a well-honed tool that can be applied purposefully to a wide range of tasks and a wide range of materials).

Transitional readers are moving nicely toward balancing word identification with comprehension, really thinking about the meaning they are constructing as they read—recalling, interpreting, and reflecting on it. They can more easily summarize, analyze, and generalize from what they read (Barone, 1989). Their increasing knowledge about reading in general and about word structure allows them to expand their sight vocabulary at a dramatically accelerated pace.

Transitional readers are absorbing complex information about how words are put together: specifically, about the *patterns* of letters within single syllables and how these patterns represent sound. For example, they understand that the letter *a* in *plate* stands for a "long *a*" sound (it "says its name") because of the letter pattern in which the *a* occurs: that is, the *a* is followed by a single consonant and a silent *e*. Children build up an understanding of the connections among letters in a pattern and gradually come to think of each pattern as a unit. They will now read a word such as *cake* by processing the beginning of the word (*c*) and then the rest of the word (*ake*) as a unit. We will examine this type of word knowledge in some depth in Chapter 5. Most important, at this phase you are helping students develop a *flexible* approach to figuring out words. If, for instance, a second-grader comes across the unknown word *glove* and tries pronouncing it with a "long *o*" sound because of the vowel pattern (yielding *glowv*, which doesn't sound like any word he's ever heard before), he won't be stumped; he can use the context (*She put the magic glove back on her hand before visiting the wizard . . .*) or think of a word he knows with a similar pattern *(love)*.

Children at the transitional phase are learning much about the nuances of stories and about the structure and language of expository texts. Their more efficient perception of words during the reading process lets them read more rapidly and therefore to dedicate more attention to thinking about what they are reading. Though still "choppy" at times, their reading is more fluent and they usually read silently, to themselves. And of course their experiences allow them to bring a richer and more elaborated "knowledge of the world," or prior knowledge, to what they read and to what they *think* about what they have read.

I've included an expository composition, written in the fall by a second-grader, to help bring transitional-phase children to life (see Figure 2.7).

In his note to his father, Jason attempts to address and resolve a fairly serious problem that apparently was not effectively addressed face-to-face. In certain contexts, written language can accomplish what oral language perhaps cannot, and Jason is aware of this. His note shows us he has learned some basics about the format of a letter and that within this format, he has learned how to sequence the points he wants to make. Notice that most of the words he uses are spelled correctly and that his invented spellings are logical: long vowel sounds are

Figure 2.7
*Jason, Transitional Reader,
Early Second Grade*

Dear daddy,

    I promes I will peck up well too night. On the weekends I will help out. I allwase try to help out, but sumtimes I gofe. Can we buy icecreme after denner?

I was not tring to say that you were mad at me I was only tring to apolageise to you. You know that I love you very much! I want thank you for leting me yose the tiperiter.

If we can't buy icecreme let's pop popcorn. I watcht little house on the prary.

    I love you,

    love Jason.

I promise I will pick up well tonight. On the weekends I will help out. I always try to help out, but sometimes I goof. Can we buy ice cream after dinner? I was not trying to say that you were mad at me. I was only trying to apologize to you. You know that I love you very much! I want [to] thank you for letting me use the typewriter. If we can't buy ice cream let's pop popcorn. I watched "Little House on the Prairie."

spelled by pattern (ALLW<u>ASE</u> = *always*; T<u>I</u>PERITER = *typewriter*; ICECR<u>EME</u> = *ice cream*).

Achieving proficient reading

Sometime during the intermediate grades (4 through 6, ages 9–13), children move beyond the "transitional" phase into the next phase of reading development. The proficient-reading (mature reading) phase represents their ability to bring their advancing knowledge and skills to bear on the process of reading.

During the intermediate years, children experience their last significant spurt of brain growth (Lenneberg, 1967). Therefore, they have the *potential* to exercise some rather striking powers of reasoning. They are able to see the world anew and to reflect on it in ways previously unavailable to them. And of course this reasoning can be applied to their reading. Rayner and Pollatsek observed that "skilled readers are all doing pretty much the same thing . . . the basic way in which information is initially encoded and processed is quite similar for all skilled readers" (1991, p. 460). While this is true, note that the emphasis in this quote is on "initial" encoding or picking up visual information on the page; what mature readers do *afterward* with this information may vary widely— what they think about it and how they use it. So although there is considerable *potential* in upper elementary children, we teachers still have much work to do in helping students realize and apply it.

Proficient readers at the upper elementary grades are able to read widely and in depth. Depending on their purposes for reading, they are capable of applying different strategies to different types of texts. If interested in a particular topic or area, they can quite readily learn a lot more about it than you or I may ever know. As Figure 2.6 shows, they are capable of understanding both the structure and the content of different genres to a considerable degree; Brian reveals his understanding of the form of an expository text in his rough draft. As they learn more about specific content areas such as mathematics and geography, they learn the vocabulary associated with each area. Many of these words are more complex in structure, and most students are capable of examining these words (1) specifically, to understand their meaning and (2) more generally, to understand how word elements such as prefixes, suffixes, and base words all combine to form the words and indicate their meanings.

Brian, a fourth-grader, has written a rough draft about planes that reveals his interest in gleaning (and displaying) as much information as he can about different types of planes and their characteristics (see Figure 2.8). Because he is comparing old planes with new, he has picked up an understanding—consciously or not—of what we term a "comparison/contrast" pattern in exposi-

Figure 2.8
Rough Draft of Fourth-Graders' Expository Text

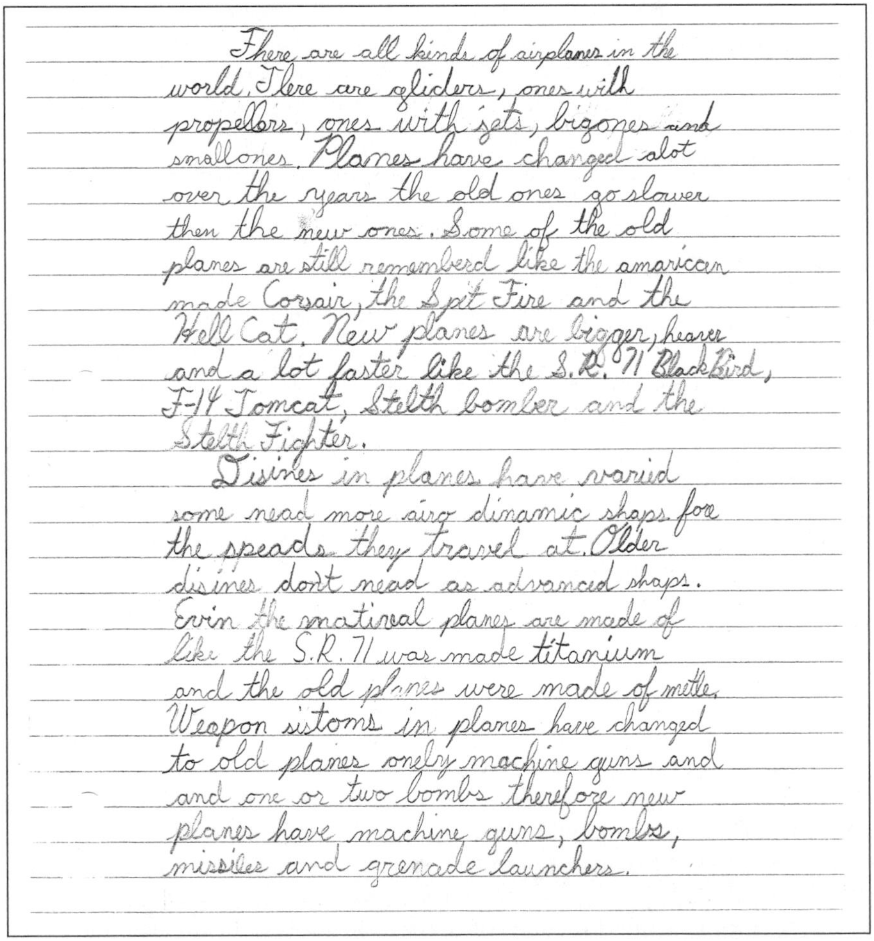

There are all kinds of airplanes in the world. There are gliders, ones with propellers, ones with jets, big ones and small ones. Planes have changed alot over the years the old ones go slower then the new ones. Some of the old planes are still rememberd like the amarican made Corsair, the Spit Fire and the Hell Cat. New planes are bigger, heaver and a lot faster like the S.R. 71 Black Bird, F-14 Tomcat, Stelth bomber and the Stelth Fighter.
Disines in planes have varied some need more airo dinamic shaps for the speads they travel at. Older disines don't need as advanced shaps. Evin the matireal planes are made of like the S.R. 71 was made titanium and the old planes were made of mettle. Weapon sistoms in planes have changed to old planes onely machine guns and and one or two bombs therefoge new planes have machine guns, bombs, missiles and grenade launchers.

tory writing. His invented spellings, such as DISINES, SISTOMS, DINAMIC, and MATIREAL, are all logical, reflecting how he is sounding them out. Not too long ago some teachers (and most parents) would have had fits about such spelling "errors" at the upper elementary grade level, but because this is a rough draft, Brian's teacher really isn't concerned at this point. If Brian were held "accountable" for correct spelling in *all* his writing, he wouldn't take risks in his writing (or his reading, for that matter), and we wouldn't see such richness of detail or the content-specific vocabulary. Such "errors" help us discover what we might focus on instructionally further down the road—they give us clues, for example, about Brian's level of word knowledge—but they should never blind us to the content and the effort of a student's writing or reading.

■ A CONCLUDING PERSPECTIVE

We have covered a good deal of basic and essential information in this chapter. We have explored reading from two major perspectives: the *process* of reading and the *development* of reading. The reading process involves a *reader* and a *text* in a particular *context*. The text presents information or content in a particular format; this text is read in an environment that represents several embedded contexts, which in turn determine in large part how the reader will read that text. As for the reader, he or she brings a rich network of background knowledge to every reading event. This background knowledge includes knowledge of the world—language knowledge, experiential knowledge, and specific knowledge about reading—and knowledge about knowledge itself, which includes the ability to reflect on one's own learning and to apply different strategies for knowledge acquisition. The experience of reading *any* text is colored by the reader's *affect:* motivation, interests, values, beliefs, attitudes, emotions.

Researchers and educators have described different *models* of the reading process. These models differ according to the degree of contributions of the reader and text to the meaning that results from the reading process. The *bottom-up* model has the text in control; the *top-down* model has the reader in control; and the *interactive/transactional* model recognizes the equal contributions of both reader and text. Discussions about models of reading are more than academic exercises, because all teachers, whether aware of it or not, have a model of the reading process that guides their instruction—what and how they attempt to teach about reading. We then explored in some depth the well-tuned process of mature reading, *proficient reading.* Proficient reading provides a glimpse of the goal toward which elementary students are moving, even as it allows *us* to see how the various elements are orchestrated so as to construct meaning efficiently.

By examining the *development* of reading, we are better able to understand children's orchestration of knowledge and skills as they move toward proficient reading. Because of this understanding, we can facilitate and respond appropriately to this development. There appear to be four distinct phases of reading development, each characterized by qualitatively different ways in which readers' brains process textual information: emergent literacy, beginning reading, transitional reading, and mature or proficient reading. While most students move into the proficient phase in the late elementary years, they will continue to extend and refine their reading abilities. In this sense, we really cannot say that there is an end point to proficient reading; readers simply become more skilled in applying their proficient reading abilities.

■ BECOMING A REFLECTIVE PRACTITIONER

Ehri, L. C. (1993). How English orthography influences phonological knowledge as children learn to read and spell. In R. J. Scholes (Ed.), *Literacy and language analysis* (pp. 21–33). Hillsdale, NJ: Erlbaum.

Ehri's research into the acquisition of reading and spelling skills for emergent readers emphasizes and supports the dominance of the role that grapheme/phoneme relationships contribute to this process. The section headed "Learning to Spell" demonstrates the developmental process through which the acquisition of spelling (literacy) goes, and how important phonemic awareness is in this process.

Goodman, K. S., & Goodman, Y. M. (1977). Learning about psycholinguistic processes by analyzing oral reading. *Harvard Educational Review, 47,* 317–333.

This borders on being the quintessential article on the psycholinguistic nature of oral reading mistakes or miscues. Actually, the Goodmans demonstrate and explain that these miscues really aren't mistakes, but rather insights into the reading processes and strategies employed by readers. This article also points out how important and vital prior knowledge is and the importance of being able to use that knowledge to predict during the reading process.

Juel, C. (1991). Beginning reading. In R. Barr, M. L. Kamil, P. Mosenthal, & P. D. Pearson (Eds.), *Handbook of reading research: Volume II* (pp. 759–788). New York: Longman.

After a brief discussion of the whole language approach to reading acquisition, the author offers a detailed and thorough examination of the "stage" or developmental model of reading acquisition. She not only responds to some of the more common arguments against the developmental approach to reading, but also demonstrates how children move through these different stages.

Kintsch, W., & vanDijk, T. (1978). Toward a model of text comprehension and production. *Psychological Review, 85,* 363–394.

If you are able to sort through the technical jargon in this article, then you should find a terrific amount of information regarding the reading comprehension process. The authors do a good job of showing the connection between short-term memory and prior knowledge, as well as the reader's interaction with the text in order to extract information from and comprehend what is being used. They go into quite a bit of detail to demonstrate the process of extracting meaning from text by building knowledge from the preceding text, and of the importance of prior knowledge, or schema, to unfamiliar text in which the reader may need to construct or infer his or her own meaning in order to make sense of the written passage.

Meyer, B. J., & Rice, G. E. (1984). The structure of text. In P. D. Pearson et al. (Eds.), *The handbook of reading research.* New York: Longman.

Meyer and Rice take a good look at the relationship between the structure of text and the importance it plays in comprehension. This is a worthwhile chapter to look into in order to get a grasp of the components of text analysis and the interaction among them. The story grammar approach to text analysis is discussed, as well as the most common prose analysis systems. An important aspect of this chapter is that it reminds us that there may not be only one right way to analyze text; rather, it depends upon what purpose is expected and upon the text itself.

Rumelhart, D. E. (1977). Toward an interactive model of reading. In S. Dornic (Ed.), *Attention and performance VI*. Hillsdale, NJ: Erlbaum.

This article has become the classic reference for interactive theories of reading. Rumelhart was the first researcher to present a model that incorporated in such explicit and comprehensive detail the nature and role of the background knowledge of the reader in the reading process. You may wish to skip the sections in which the mathematics that explain how the model works are presented; the balance of the article, however, is quite informative and fairly comprehensible.

Stanovich, K. (1994). Romance and reality. *The Reading Teacher, 47,* 280–291.

With his colleague, Richard West, Keith Stanovich has conducted some of the best research into word recognition processes during reading. He has also investigated at length the nature of reading disability—we'll explore this aspect later in the book. In this article, Stanovich summarizes the nature of his research in these two areas. Read the part of this article with the heading ''Research I Have Done That Not Everyone Likes''—he addresses aspects of the reading process that deal most directly with the nature and role of word recognition in the process of reading for both novice and skilled readers.

■ REFERENCES

Adams, M. (1980). Failures to comprehend and levels of processing in reading. In R. Spiro, B. Bruce, & W. Brewer (Eds.), *Theoretical issues in reading comprehension* (pp. 87–112). Hillsdale, NJ: Lawrence Erlbaum Associates.

Anderson, R., & Pearson, P. (1984). A schema-theoretic view of reading. In P. Pearson, R. Barr, M. Kamil, & P. Mosenthal (Eds.), *The handbook of reading research* (pp. 255–291). New York: Longman.

Athey, I. (1985). Reading research in the affective domain. In H. Singer & R. Ruddell (Eds.), *Theoretical models and processes of reading* (3rd ed., pp. 527–558). Newark, DE: International Reading Association.

Atwell, N. (1987). *In the middle: Writing, reading, and learning with adolescents.* Upper Montclair, NJ: Boynton/Cook.

Barone, D. (1989). *Young children's written responses to literature: Exploring the relationship between written response and orthographic knowledge.* Unpublished doctoral dissertation, University of Nevada, Reno.

Bartlett, F. (1932). *Remembering.* New York: Macmillan.

Beers, J. & Henderson, E. (1977). A study of developing orthographic concepts among first graders. *Research in the Teaching of English, 11,* 133–148.

Bissex, G. (1980). GYNS AT WRK: A child learns to write and read. Cambridge, MA: Harvard University Press.

Brown, A., & Day, J. (1983). *Macrorules for summarizing texts: The development of expertise.* Urbana-Champagne: Center for the Study of Reading, University of Illinois.

Bussis, A., Chittenden, E., Amarel, M., & Klausner, E. (1985). *Inquiry into meaning: An investigation of learning to read.* Hillsdale, NJ: Lawrence Erlbaum Associates.

Carey, S. (1985). *Conceptual change in childhood.* Cambridge, MA: MIT Press.

Dillon, R., & Sternberg, R. (Eds.). (1986). *Cognition and Instruction.* Orlando, FL: Academic Press.

Chall, J. (1983). *Learning to read.* New York: Macmillan.

Clay, M. (1979). *Reading: The patterning of complex behaviour.* Auckland: Heinemann.

Ehri, L. (1991). Development of the ability to read words. In R. Barr, M. Kamil, P. Mosenthal, & P. Pearson (Eds.), *Handbook of reading research* (Vol. II, pp. 383–417). New York: Longman.

Ehri, L. (1993). How English orthography influences phonological knowledge as children learn to read and spell. In R. Scholes (Ed.), *Literacy and language analysis* (pp. 21–43). Hillsdale, NJ: Lawrence Erlbaum Associates.

Ehri, L. (1994). Development of the ability to read words: Update. In R. Ruddell, M. Ruddell, & H. Singer (Eds.), *Theoretical models and processes of reading* (4th ed., pp. 323–358). Newark, DE: International Reading Association.

Flavell, J. (1979). Metacognition and cognitive monitoring: A new area of cognitive developmental inquiry. *American Psychologist, 34,* 906–911.

Frith, U. (1985). Beneath the surface of developmental dyslexia. In K. Patterson, J. Marshall, & M. Coltheart (Eds.), *Surface dyslexia: Neuropsychological and cognitive studies of phonological reading* (pp. 301–330). London: Lawrence Erlbaum Associates.

Fromkin, V., & Rodman, R. (1993). *An introduction to language* (5th ed.). Fort Worth, TX: Harcourt Brace Jovanovich.

Garner, R. (1987). *Metacognition and reading comprehension.* Norwood, NJ: Ablex.

Goodman, K. (1967). Reading: A psycholinguistic guessing game. *Journal of the Reading Specialist, 6,* 126–135.

Goodman, K., & Goodman, Y. (1977). Learning about psycholinguistic processes by analyzing oral reading. *Harvard Educational Review, 47,* 317–333.

Gough, P. (1972). One second of reading. In J. Kavanagh & I. Mattingly (Eds.), *Language by ear and by eye.* Cambridge, MA: MIT Press.

Guthrie, J., Seifert, M., & Kirsch, I. (1986). Effects of education, occupation, and setting on reading practices. *American Educational Research Journal, 23,* 151–160.

Halliday, M. (1975). *Learning how to mean.* London: Elsevier.

Harste, J., Woodward, V., & Burke, C. (1984). *Language stories and literacy lessons.* Portsmouth, NH: Heinemann.

Henderson, E. (1990). *Teaching spelling* (2nd ed.). Boston: Houghton Mifflin.

Huey, E. (1908/1968). *The psychology and pedagogy of reading.* Cambridge, MA: MIT Press.

Juel, C. (1991). Beginning reading. In R. Barr, M. Kamil, P. Mosenthal, & P. Pearson (Eds.), *Handbook of reading research* (Vol. II, pp. 759–788). New York: Longman.

Just, M., & Carpenter, P. (1980). A theory of reading: From eye fixations to comprehension. *Psychological Review, 87*, 329–354.

Kintsch, W., & vanDijk, T. (1978). Toward a model of text comprehension and production. *Psychological Review, 87*, 363–394.

Klatzky, R. (1984). *Memory and awareness: An information-processing perspective.* New York: W. H. Freeman.

Krashen, S. (1982). *Principles and practices in second language acquisition.* London: Pergamon.

Lenneberg, E. (1967). *The biological foundations of language.* New York: John Wiley.

Lukens, R. (1990). *A critical handbook of children's literature* (4th ed.). Glenview, IL: Scott, Foresman/Little, Brown.

Luria, A. (1975). *The working brain.* New York: Basic Books.

Many, J. (1990). The effect of reader stance on students' personal understanding of literature. In S. McCormick & J. Zutell (Eds.), *Literacy theory and research: Analyses from multiple paradigms* (pp. 51–63). Thirty-ninth yearbook of the National Reading Conference. Chicago, IL: National Reading Conference.

Massaro, D. (1975). *Understanding language: An information-processing analysis of speech perception, reading, and psycholinguistics.* New York: Academic Press.

McClelland, J. (1986). The programmable blackboard model of reading. In J. McClelland, D. Rumelhart, and the PDP Research Group (Eds.), *Parallel distributed processing: Explorations in the microstructure of cognition* (Vol. 2). Cambridge, MA: MIT Press.

Metcalfe, J., & Shimamura, A. (Eds.). (1994). *Metacognition: Knowing about knowing.* Cambridge, MA: MIT Press.

Meyer, B., & Rice, G. (1984). The structure of text. In P. Pearson, R. Barr, M. Kamil, & P. Mosenthal (Eds.), *The handbook of reading research* (pp. 319–351). New York: Longman.

Miall, D. (1988). Affect and narrative: A model of response to stories. *Poetics, 17*, 259–272.

Milne, A. (1928). The house at Pooh Corner. New York: E. P. Dutton.

Mikulecky, L. (1982). Job literacy: The relationship between school preparation and workplace actuality. *Reading Research Quarterly, 17*, 400–419.

Morris, D. (1983). Concept of word and phoneme awareness in the beginning reader. *Research in the Teaching of English, 17*, 359–373.

Ortony, A., Clore, G., & Collins, A. (1988). *The cognitive structure of emotions.* New York: Cambridge University Press.

Paivio, A. (1986). *Mental representations: A dual coding approach.* New York: Oxford University Press.

Perfetti, C. (1992). The representation problem in reading acquisition. In P. Gough, L. Ehri, & R. Treiman (Eds.), *Reading acquisition* (pp. 145–174). Hillsdale, NJ: Lawrence Erlbaum Associates.

Pinker, S. (1989). Language acquisition. In M. Posner (Ed.), *Foundations of cognitive science* (pp. 359–399). Cambridge, MA: MIT Press.

Rayner, K., (1976). Developmental changes in word recognition strategies. *Journal of Educational Psychology, 68*, 323–329.

Rayner, K., & Pollatsek, A. (1991). *The psychology of reading*. Englewood Cliffs, NJ: Prentice-Hall.

Read, C. (1985). *Children's creative spellings*. London: Routledge Kegan-Paul.

Reitsma, P. (1983). Printed word learning in beginning readers. *Journal of Experimental Child Psychology, 36*, 321–329.

Richard-Amato, P. (1988). *Making it happen: Interaction in the second language classroom*. New York: Longman.

Rosenblatt, L. (1978). *The reader, the text, the poem: The transactional theory of the literacy work*. Carbondale, IL: Southern Illinois University Press.

Rosenblatt, L. (1983). *Literature as exploration* (4th ed.). New York: Modern Language Association.

Rosenblatt, L. (1989). Writing and reading: The transactional theory. In J. Mason (Ed.), *Reading and writing connections* (pp. 153–176). Boston: Allyn and Bacon.

Rumelhart, D. (1977). Toward an interactive model of reading. In S. Dornic (Ed.), *Attention and performance VI*. Hillsdale, NJ: Lawrence Erlbaum Associates.

Sadowski, M., Goetz, E., & Kangiser, I. (1988). Imagination in story reading: Relationships between imagery, affect, and structured importance. *Reading Research Quarterly, 23*, 320–336.

Sadowski, M., Paivio, A., & Goetz, E. (1991). Commentary: A critique of schema theory in reading and a dual coding alternative. *Reading Research Quarterly, 26*, 463–481.

Scribner, S. (1984). Literacy in three metaphors. *The American Journal of Education, 93*, 6–21.

Smith, F. (1971). *Understanding reading*. New York: Holt, Rinehart, and Winston.

Smith, F. (1975). *Comprehension and learning*. New York: Holt, Rinehart, and Winston.

Smith, F. (1988). *Understanding reading* (4th ed.). Hillsdale, NJ: Lawrence Erlbaum Associates.

Smith, E. (1989). Concepts and induction. In M. Posner (Ed.), *Foundations of cognitive science* (pp. 501–526). Cambridge, MA: MIT Press.

Stanovich, K. (1980). Toward an interactive-compensatory model of individual differences in the development of reading fluency. *Reading Research Quarterly, 16*, 32–71.

Stanovich, K. (1991). Word recognition: Changing perspectives. In R. Barr, M. Kamil, P. Mosenthal, & P. Pearson (Eds.), *Handbook of reading research* (Vol. II, pp. 418–452). New York: Longman.

Stanovich, K. (1994). Romance and reality. *The Reading Teacher, 47*, 280–291.

Taylor, D. (1993). *From the child's point of view*. Portsmouth, NH: Heinemann.

Taylor, I., & Taylor, M. (1983). *The psychology of reading*. New York: Academic Press.

Teale, W., & Sulzby, E. (Eds.). (1986). *Emergent literacy: Writing and reading*. Norwood, NJ: Ablex.

Templeton, S. (1991). *Teaching the integrated language arts*. Boston: Houghton Mifflin.

Templeton, S., & Bear, D. (Eds.). (1992). *Development of orthographic knowledge and the foundations of literacy: A Memorial Festschrift for Edmund H. Henderson.* Hillsdale, NJ: Lawrence Erlbaum Associates.

Vellutino, F., & Scanlon, D. (1991). The effects of instructional bias on word identification. In L. Rieben & C. Perfetti (Eds.), *Learning to read: Basic research and its implications* (pp. 189–203). Hillsdale, NJ: Lawrence Erlbaum Associates.

Weaver, C. (1988). *Reading process and practice.* Portsmouth, NH: Heinemann.

Wyer, R., & Srull, J. (1989). *Memory and cognition in its social context.* Hillsdale, NJ: Lawrence Erlbaum Associates.

Yaden, D., Jr., & Templeton, S. (Eds.). (1986). *Metalinguistic awareness and beginning literacy: Conceptualizing what it means to learn to read and write.* Portsmouth, NH: Heinemann.

CHAPTER THREE

EMERGENT LITERACY

FOCUS

- As they move through the emergent literacy phase, what sense do young children make of the functions and nature of print?

- How does the home impact young children's concepts of literacy?

- What can children learn about "stories" and "informational" texts—and why is this knowledge important?

- What is metalinguistic awareness? What aspects of it are important in the later phase of emergent literacy?

- Why is reading to young children important? How do we read to toddlers and older preschoolers?

- How can teachers of young children facilitate emerging understandings about the nature and purpose of print? Specifically, how can language experience activities and shared book activities facilitate literacy development?

- What are the nature and the importance of young children's writing, in the development of concepts about literacy?

When they are three to six years old, before starting formal schooling and while beginning their kindergarten and first-grade years, young children are learning that their world is represented symbolically through pictures, music, movement—and of course language. Part of this discovery involves probing into the world of print and the processes of reading and writing. The children's unfolding interest in these areas emerges and develops through stimulating contact with lots of print material and writing supplies, as well as through much active involvement with play, art, music, dance, creative dramatics, and games.

> I consider the period from age two to age six or seven a fascinating period of human development. In my view, in fact, it harbors more of the secrets and power of human growth than any other comparable phase of growth. The first instances of symbolic competence are mastered. Habits of body and mind are set. Artistry and creativity in general are unleashed—or blocked—at this time. (Gardner, 1991, p. 82)

As we hurry to usher children into the world of literacy, all too often we give little attention to "unleashing" their artistry and creativity—a most highly valued facet of the more general symbolic competence Gardner describes. In such a context, we realize next the importance of affording preschool children as much opportunity as possible to actively examine their world—closely, intently, systematically (Egan, 1987)—without their being rushed into a premature preoccupation with "formal" instruction in reading and writing. Unfortunately many books and commercial programs encourage parents to attempt formal instruction, when in fact a considerable amount of knowledge about print and the processes of reading and writing can develop *in*formally and naturally. Referring to Piaget's perspective on development, Carol Chomsky noted: "Children have real understanding only of that which they invent themselves, and each time we try to teach them something too quickly, we keep them from reinventing it for themselves" (1974, pp. 13–14).

While much of my focus in this chapter will be on the preschool years, it is important to keep in mind that the information is particularly relevant for kindergarten and first-grade children as well. We'll also be considering the many children—from kindergartners through those entering the intermediate grades, who may enter school with few or no literacy experiences. It is, obviously, necessary for you as an elementary educator to be knowledgeable about the characteristics and the facilitation of emergent literacy. Your first teaching assignment may be at the primary level, in which case you'll find that the many ideas, strategies, and activities presented in this chapter are directly applicable to your immediate situation. However, if you are teaching at a higher level, you may have students who have no more literacy experience than a kindergartner or first-grader. Although your students may be older, what you know about emergent literacy and the beginning stages of reading will mold your instructional focus with these children. You will need to know not only what terrain the children already have traveled but also what terrain still needs to be covered. Most important, as your students move along the developmental continuum of literacy, you will need to be able to see how your instruction fits into the larger educational landscape.

In this chapter, we will survey the wondrous panorama that the preschool and kindergarten years offer. What children do and the meanings they "make," as they emerge as readers and writers, provide some enchanting and engaging visions. We will explore this territory by following a logical progression of children's emerging literacy. After elaborating on the distinction between the traditional concept of "readiness" for reading and the newer concept of "emerging" literacy, we will talk about the young child's developing *oral* language competence as a foundation for literacy. Next, we will address initial concepts of literacy and the development of print awareness, for once young children derive an understanding of what reading and writing are, they will develop an evolving perception of what print *is* and of the different functions it serves.

The balance of the chapter will address the many ways in which we can involve young children in experiencing and examining literacy—its features and its functions. There is a significant role for parents here, and I will offer you some suggestions for involving parents in this critical and exciting adventure.

Before we begin, I'd like to establish my approach in this chapter. There is considerable *overlap* among the developing literacy concepts in young children. When we read to preschool children, for example, we help them learn something about the nature and structure of stories at the same time that their attention can be directed to the squiggles on a page and they learn something about print as well. As another example, consider that as young children write, they are learning something about the features of letters—which in turn helps them when they "read." Of necessity, however, our discussion in this chapter will address such concepts in a more linear fashion. Nevertheless, I have arranged the topics in the sequence that comes closest to the apparent developmental sequence of *awareness* and *beginning understanding* that children follow: they find themselves surrounded by an environment that includes pictures as well as print; they notice this global medium first, before they become aware of the different functions that the visual medium serves. For this reason, we will be looking first at how children develop an awareness and understanding of *print* before we examine the development of awareness and understanding of the functions or purposes that print can serve.

THE EMERGENCE OF LITERACY: NO LONGER STEPS, BUT A CONTINUUM

For many years, the big question in reading education was "When is a child *ready* to read?" Since at least the 1960s the question of "readiness" for reading has been researched and debated. Most recently, the whole issue has been reconceptualized (Sulzby & Teale, 1991), and you don't hear as much discussion of "readiness"—finding that exact point at which a child suddenly is ready to read. Rather, we have come to realize that children progress along a developmental continuum that reveals their gradual, or *emerging,* construction of knowledge about reading and writing. Termed *emergent literacy,* this development is defined as "the reading and writing behaviors that precede and develop into conventional literacy" (Sulzby, 1989); in other words, those behaviors that come before and are necessary for the development of the conventional literacy we spent some time discussing in Chapter 1.

As we'll see in this chapter, children are engaged in "reading" as well as writing from a very young age. There is no single point where we can say, "Okay! Sarah's ready to be exposed to books now!" We *can,* however, talk about the point at which young children have enough prior knowledge about reading and print to enable them to explore, explicitly and systematically, how print corresponds to spoken language; this will be the onset of the Beginning "Conventional" reading phase (see Chapter 5).

Conceptualizing reading in terms of a developmental continuum built on experiences with real, authentic literature is not the same as conceptualizing it in terms of a series of steps in which the task is laid out in a programmatic fashion. When reading is viewed on a developmental continuum, young children spend much time being read to, looking at books and other print material, coloring and drawing, and retelling familiar stories. All this goes on in a very comfortable environment where adults and children are talking and reacting in a lively exchange. The alternate point of view, one that sees reading as a narrow sequence of tasks to be mastered, will involve children in structured pencil-and-paper activities before they have even realized that what we say can be written down; that the marks on a page can be spoken; and that when we translate the marks into sounds that make words, we do so in a systematic fashion. The steps for completing a task are organized by the adult, with the child moving up a step each time a task is adequately completed. The feeling of the environment is one of trying to come up with the correct answer, not one of chatty interaction and experimentation.

In the last chapter, we saw that people read for three major purposes: to enjoy, to gain knowledge, and to function in the community. Emergent readers can develop an *intuitive* sense of these purposes for reading, through their supported and independent interactions with print. Because so much about the nature and purposes of reading and writing is learned in the preschool, kindergarten, and first-grade years, our job as educators is to provide an environment that will allow children's awareness of print and its functions to emerge naturally.

YOUNG CHILDREN BUILD INITIAL CONCEPTS OF READING AND WRITING AND DEVELOP PRINT AWARENESS

Most of a young child's world exists in three dimensions. Young children physically manipulate an object to become familiar with its characteristics: for example, they gain an understanding of *round* by holding and playing with objects that are round. Similarly, they begin building awareness of how books are put together by turning the pages of cloth or cardboard books or plastic tub-books. (And in doing so, they see pictures and drawings of familiar objects and animals—chair, spoon, table, dog, cat, bird.) These "beginning" books also feature children their own age engaged in activities that they understand and most likely have experienced directly themselves—playing ball, swinging, digging in a sandbox.

Very young children exhibit much joy and enthusiasm at having these books read to them again and again. Through this repeated exposure, they become increasingly aware of how the world can be represented in two-dimensional forms, as in the drawings and pictures in their books. This awareness comes early, when they are still in the crib. When they first turn a cloth book over, they may appear to be surprised: if the picture on the book's front cover is of a pig looking right at them, they expect that when they turn the book over, they'll see—you guessed it—the backside of the pig!

Simultaneously, as the young child turns the pages of a favorite book, he or she will commonly receive verbal encouragement from a loving adult who explains what's in the book, as well as how to hold the book and turn the pages. We point to the pictures, name the objects on each page, and of course read the words aloud. As children grow in their own verbal abilities, they chatter back to us in a verbal exchange that enhances their ability to use language. A child responds to the adult's comments, identifies the pictures on the page, and mimics the words he or she has heard read over and over again. Although young children's understanding of the pictorial representation of real-world objects and events develops before their understanding of the function of print, pictures and drawings provide a powerful context for understanding print; *environmental print* such as labels, signs, logos, and so forth often appears in the company of pictures.

As we examine directly young children's awakening to the world of literacy, keep in mind the overlap I mentioned earlier in regard to the onset and elaboration of many concepts we will discuss. For our own understanding of these concepts and how they develop, we do have to separate them and present them in a linear fashion. While the young child is immersed in the totality of the literacy experience—talk, print, pictures, books, songs, and television—there are still certain concepts that appear and coalesce at different points along the developmental continuum; children appear to become *aware* of different aspects of literacy in a certain order.

Oral language is the base

Oral language serves as a foundation for learning about reading and writing (Snow, 1983). Print "encodes" spoken or *aural* language in a *visual* medium; but before understanding *how* this is done, children must have a fairly firm grounding in the spoken medium. Children's developing syntactic, semantic, and phonological systems resonate with their environment, and *visual* representation of information, in pictures and in print, is an integral part of this environment. Parents and others help direct young children's attention to aspects of this environment by labeling and commenting on objects and events.

Parents, in fact, should be encouraged to talk with their children as much as possible. This furthers the degree of the child's language development, and it points out and elaborates important aspects of a child's environment. While petting the family dog with a parent, for instance, the child learns about "doggie" concepts and the terms that represent them *(wagging tail, hangy slurpy tongue, spotted tummy)*. In a very big way, language helps differentiate and define the culture to which the child belongs, so it is important that young children *examine* their environment—and talk about it with others.

Also, in our society, most parents are concerned about how to prepare their children for what these young students will encounter when they begin school. Children are best prepared by being encouraged to examine their world and learn how it can be described through language. Because much of that world

MAKING CONNECTIONS: *Literacy Experiences of Children from "Mainstream" and "Nonmainstream" Backgrounds*

In writing about the importance of preschool literacy experiences as a foundation for successful literacy experiences in school, Marilyn Jaeger Adams noted how since her son was six weeks old,

> . . . we have spent 30 to 45 minutes reading to him each day. By the time he reaches first grade at age six and a quarter, that will amount to 1,000 to 1,700 hours of storybook reading—one on one, with his face in the books. He will also have spent more than 1,000 hours watching "Sesame Street." And he will have spent at least as many hours fooling around with magnetic letters on the refrigerator, writing, participating in reading/writing/language activities in preschool, playing word and "spelling" games in the car, on the computer, with us, with his sister, with his friends, and by himself, and on and on. (1990, p. 85)

American schools, and specifically the first-grade curriculum, have traditionally operated as though all children's preschool experiences have included these elements. However, Adams also noted:

> It is easy to imagine children who have no magnetic letters on their refrigerators, no home computer with word and letter games, no reading classmates in preschool, and no ready supply of paper, pencils, and crayons lying around the house for their use. It is equally easy to imagine children whose television, if they have one, is preoccupied with programs that are less directed to scholastic readiness of preschoolers than is "Sesame Street." (p. 86).

In our society, we usually categorize children who fit this second scenario as "at-risk." If we interpret Adams's observations without further investigation, we are seeing only one side of our challenge as elementary educators. Yes, it *is* important that children who have not had the types of literacy experiences

that many "mainstream" home environments provide be immersed in just these types of experiences. There are several programs that involve nonmainstream parents of preschool children in reading to their children, for example; many of these programs provide little books, appropriate in vocabulary and predictability, that can be shared with children (e.g., McCormick and Mason, 1986).

As I briefly noted in Chapter 1, however, this does *not* mean that children from nonmainstream backgrounds have not had *any* literacy experiences, or that whatever experiences they have had are not as worthwhile as those of mainstream children's. They have had experiences with literacy, but their experiences have usually been centered around different types of texts than those that mainstream children experience and that commonly are emphasized in kindergarten and first grade classrooms (Heath, 1983; Pellegrini, 1990; Taylor & Strickland, 1989). Rather than centering around stories, concept books, and bedtime read-alouds, the literacy events of nonmainstream children have primarily centered around expository materials such as grocery coupons, newspapers, or community event calendars. Discussions occur during the actual "hands on" use of the materials and are steeped in practicality. Perhaps a family is sitting at the kitchen table after supper. One parent reads the newspaper, commenting on the latest headline, a change in the weather, and tomorrow's school lunch menu, while the other parent looks through the mail, responding simultaneously to the ongoing conversation; each has a child in his or her lap. Similarly, at the grocery store, a preschooler is in the infant seat in a shopping cart. The child holds a stack of coupons; with the parent's assistance the child sorts through the coupons each time they locate an item from their grocery list. In

involves print, their experiences with print should take place in situations rich in oral language.

In this context I cannot emphasize too much the critical importance of *reading to young children*—and not just stories, but from informational books

Literacy Experiences of Children from "Mainstream" and "Nonmainstream" Backgrounds

continued

both of these scenarios, the parents talk about the materials with their children; they point to pictures and print; they make comments and ask questions (Pellegrini et al., 1990). These efforts are important and need to be acknowledged, applauded, and encouraged.

It is unfortunate that the term *at-risk* is all too commonly applied without question to children from nonmainstream backgrounds. The term brands such children negatively and discounts or even ignores outright the understanding of literacy they bring to the classroom. As elementary educators, we can avoid this mistaken perception as we work to change appropriately how reading is "traditionally" learned in our classrooms.

Part of our change will involve the following tactics or procedures. In addition to continuing to present, discuss, and explore narratives, we will also present, discuss, and explore expository texts—printed matter on food containers and menus; newspapers; and so forth. We can use these materials in the classroom when we reenact favorite story events, plan group snacks, search for spelling patterns, or write advertisements for class-composed books. It is important that we do so, and our modeling will connect with the experiences of allegedly at-risk chil-

dren in our classroom. Taylor and Strickland (1989) emphasize that we should pay close attention to the types and uses of literacies that occur within families and if possible, get out into the communities in which we teach; this is especially important if the communities are different from those in which we grew up. We should also show or describe in the classroom examples of literacy from the community; these can include posters announcing upcoming theater events, street signs, labeling tags on newly planted trees, and the ever-familiar advertisements for stores and services. We could bring community members into the classroom to discuss how they use literacy in their lives, and we can take our students on field trips to nearby businesses and community centers. This type of communication can draw interest in literacy from areas you may not have foreseen: for example, children will discover that landscapers read blueprints, blacksmiths write reports for veterinarians, and the office assistants in insurance agencies review doctors' summaries. There are many possible applications of neighborhood and parental involvement. As we tie the real world in with the children's classroom experiences, children become aware of a greater need to become skilled readers and writers.

LEARNING IN CONTEXT: "Literacy" occurs in almost all families; though young children may experience different literacy events, all of these instances are important and should be developed when children begin formal schooling.

Young Children Build Initial Concepts of Reading and Writing and Develop Print Awareness 87

and other types of print formats (see the "Making Connections" feature on pages 86–87 and the section about reading to preschool children, beginning on page 105). This situation provides the opportunity for much interaction between adult and child.

Interestingly, while oral language in a sense provides a foundation for learning about written language, written language can do the same for oral language. During the preschool years, experiences with *written* language specifically, and symbolic representation more generally, can provide a context for expanding and elaborating *oral* language (Chomsky, 1972; Galda et al., 1989; Olson, 1984; Whitehurst et al., 1988). The child models the verbal exchange he or she has experienced many times before: the kind initiated when an adult points to an object in an illustration and asks, "What's this?" or "What does *this* do?"; and similarly, when the child initiates an inquiry, pointing to the bear in the book or the shoe in the Sunday paper and asking what's going on. With the first response, the back-and-forth exchange begins.

All such instances provide opportunities for expansion and elaboration of thought and language. More talk occurs; and often, new terms are used, all in a meaningful, natural context. We recognize the value of these experiences when we hear the syntax, vocabulary, and style of "book language" incorporated into a child's own speech (deVilliers and deVilliers, 1978); having just heard the phrase "millions and billions and trillions of cats" in Wanda Gag's *Millions of Cats,* five-year-old Janelle delights us when she chants, "Millions and billions and trillions of *ants* . . ." while studying a swarming anthill in her backyard.

Initial concepts of reading and writing

Let's consider the following two vignettes:

> Tonisha, age two and a half, observes her father sitting motionless, reading the newspaper. Grabbing a section of the paper, she imitates him, sitting quietly. She can't take it for long, however—absolutely nothing is going on! But being two years old, she doesn't puzzle over this seemingly worthless activity for long. Throwing the paper down, she goes and picks up a favorite cardboard book and begins "reading" it, jabbing at the pictures with her fingers and talking to it in a singsong way, sounding uncannily like someone reading a book aloud.
>
> Four-year-old Bryan runs up to you, proudly clutching a pageful of scribbles. "Read it!" he crows, thrusting the page toward you. Not wishing to disappoint him, and perhaps feeling a little awkward in trying to get out of "reading" it, you reply instead: "Bryan, I'd really like *you* to read it to *me!*" And to your amazement and delight he does, rambling on about some man who would not stop laughing. As he "reads" his scribbles, you can tell a difference in his voice; it rises and falls more noticeably than in everyday conversation. He is clearly "reading" in a "reading voice" that he has heard from an adult who reads to him frequently.

Young children like Tonisha and Bryan have already learned much about reading and writing, not in a conventional sense, of course, but in the sense of what must be known in order for conventional literacy to develop later on.

Very young children will play with their cardboard books (many years ago there were only "cloth" books—resilient, but likely to get soggy and difficult to manipulate!). Their first response to a cardboard book may be to do with it what they do with most other objects—stick it in their mouths, suck on it, and flail around with it. If they see *you* turning the pages, though, and "talking" to it, they will do the same. And the "backside of the pig" phenomenon reveals that this may be their first realization that books work differently than the rest of the world (Henderson, 1979; Snow & Goldfield, 1983). They will soon learn where the front and back of a book are and how to turn the pages from front to back. They will learn to "read" pictures first, looking at the left-hand page and then at the right-hand page.

For such young children, "reading" is an engaging routine, much like a ritual. Initially, it does not appear to be keyed in any systematic fashion to the print on a flat surface; rather, it is a ritualized procedure in which certain behaviors occur in the presence of flat surfaces with pictures and squiggles on them. It will remain a mysterious event, however, unless a literate voice is part of the associated behaviors. Moreover, when we read aloud to young children, we *sound* a bit different than we do in casual conversation. You have only to listen to yourself as you begin to read to a young child; the words "Once upon a time," for example, carry a livelier tone as your voice rises and dips in a fashion that helps draw the young listener into the world of the book. Of course, the other side of so many of these experiences is *writing*. Children see adults inscribing forms and checks, making lists, and so on, and notice that the adults are not drawing pictures; the marks being made are clearly different from pictures. It will be some time before young children differentiate drawing from writing

As this preschool child "reads" in the company of her stuffed animals, she continues to learn enough about reading and writing for conventional literacy to develop later on.

in their own productions (see the "Emergent Writing" section beginning on page 116), but they need to continue to see adults engaged in real-world application of writing.

As we will soon discuss, when *children* first make marks that they indicate are not pictures but represent writing, they don't seem to realize that this different kind of graphic representation corresponds to speech; the different marks simply are there and exist as entities by themselves. Children seem to accept this status for writing. Over a long period of time, however, during which children are read to and pay closer attention to print in books and in the environment, *and* as they continue to "write," they will evidence understanding that *somehow* writing corresponds to speech—as Bryan does (page 88) when he "reads" his squiggles. The evolution of this understanding is fascinating and merits the further attention given to it in the section on emergent writing (pages 116–121).

Rudimentary print awareness: learning what print *is* and *does*

So many of the concepts about print and literacy in general are all part of the fundamental understanding of what print *is* and of what it *does*—how its form and function work in meaningful ways. Young children develop a global sense of how print "makes meaning" when they see it in use; think again about a trip to the grocery store. The mother or father may comment on products on the shelves, reading labels as they are pointed to, reading price tabs on the shelves underneath the products, reading signs that indicate specials. Parents may point to the large signs over the produce section, the seafood section, the housewares section. Payment may be made with a checkbook, cash, credit card, or food stamps; each way allows children to see print used functionally to get things done. For the young child, the meaning of print is in the context in which it occurs—a concept you are quite familiar with by now. The squiggles of print are associated with real-world objects, events, and actions. At first they are not analyzed carefully; they occur globally in a context. The three-year-old who on her thirtieth trip to the market points to the "Seafood" sign and "reads" it is seeing that agglomeration of print as quite different from what you or I would see.

As viewed by a preschool child, the awareness that printed language can be broken down into words—and the words broken down into sounds, the sounds then becoming spoken language—is not nearly as straightforward as it seems. Through consistent exposure to print during the preschool years, which involves interaction with older, literate individuals and opportunities for independent exploration with print, children gradually gain an awareness that print connects to the real world; that it is somehow different and distinct from drawing; and that it can stand for spoken language (Clay, 1979; Hall, 1987; Holdaway, 1979; Rowe, 1990; Strickland & Morrow, 1989; Sulzby & Teale, 1991; Teale & Sulzby, 1986).

Investigators of emergent literacy have identified, as essential for young children to develop, the following awarenesses about print. We will consider each in turn:

- Print has to do with the real world.
- Print is different from drawing.
- Print can stand for spoken language.
- Print has *directionality.*
- Print occurs in different places.
- *Letters* are important building blocks of print.

In the paragraphs that follow, we'll look closely at each of the six points listed above.

Print Has to Do with the Real World   Context is a powerful support to children in figuring out what print corresponds to and "says" in their day-to-day environment. They learn to expect that print on or near doors may say "Exit" and that print around food will label food. They don't expect the exit sign to say "Produce" or the produce sign to say "Exit." They expect the print they find on the tag attached to a stuffed animal to say something about that animal. Print "appears at the beginnings and ends of . . . television shows (that is how you know they are over) and on the ads in between (that is when you are afraid they are over)" (Adams, 1990, p. 334). Almost literally, print *is* everywhere! I recall how my firstborn son, barely three years old, astounded a gathering of adults by pointing to the letters on a car while proudly stating, "Volvo!" (the car was, indeed, a Volvo). Somehow, for some reason, that print configuration had captured his attention previously; he had asked what it said; and he remembered the answer. Quite pleased with the reaction he now received, he ran over to another car, pointed to the word *Chevrolet,* and just as proudly announced, "Volvo!" It is true that with an adult to help out, "By the time they are two or three, many children can identify signs, labels, and logos they see in their homes and communities" (Teale & Sulzby, 1989, p. 3).

Print Is Different from Drawing   Children learn that print is different from drawing—it "means" differently than picturelike graphics do and refers to the real world in a different way. Children will begin to differentiate writing from pictures in their own graphic creations as well. They may continue, however, to switch the words *writing* and *drawing* for quite some time. They may say that they are going to "draw" a story or "write" a picture. But early in their development we can see evidence of their dawning understanding of the difference between the two modes of representation. Figure 3.1 shows peoplelike figures along with letterlike characters. Emilio Ferreiro (1984; 1990) found that for many children, there is a progression in their understanding of the function of print and that this parallels their attention to print when they are being read to (see Figure 3.1). At first their letterlike characters are in the pictures just because they've seen these kinds of marks along with pictures in the real world. Later, these characters "go with" the pictures and can name something in them. Often, children will "write" the name of something—say, a dog—and the length or size of their writing will correspond to the relative size of the dog they are

Figure 3.1
Child's Writing: Mix of Shapes and Letters

Left: (Writing that "goes with" the drawing)
Right: (Writing that is based on the size of the object "written about")

(Dog)   (Horse)

writing about! If it is a big dog, they will write with large characters; if it is a small dog, with small letters (see Figure 3.1).

Print Has Directionality   As children interact with adults in the context of reading, and as they experiment with writing, they are developing significant concepts about how those "squiggles" operate. One of the earliest of these concepts is the *directionality* of print: in English, as well as in most other Western writing systems, print flows in a left-to-right direction with a return sweep to the next line, and the lines run from top-to-bottom. A child learns about directionality while watching an adult write and as an adult slides a finger along under a line of print while reading aloud.

Print Can Stand for Spoken Language   As children learn that print is a part of and refers to their environment, they gradually learn "where it comes from" and thus what it represents: it stands for speech. Understanding *how* it stands for spoken language will take some time. As Ferreiro has shown, young children first think print goes along with what it refers to, and later that it corresponds in some way to the *physical* characteristics of what it refers to (recall the example of the dog). Eventually they understand that the length of the squiggles has something to do with the length of the utterance. They have moved from "print represents reality" to "print represents speech, which represents reality."

Print Occurs in Different Places   As mentioned previously, print can be found in many different environments: in shop windows, on the marquees of movie theaters, in newspapers, magazines, and storybooks, not to mention on containers, cars, trains, buses, and pieces of artwork. Print appears everywhere we look. It is important to remember though, that young children may not extract meaning from the print they see around them or value it, unless someone else calls their attention to it. Words upon buildings, for instance, appear as part of the architecture (though perhaps beautiful in their own right), blend with other architectural features, and do not stand out as having extended meaning as print—unless someone reads them.

Print Is Made Up of Building Blocks (Letters)   Thus far, we have been talking about children's experiences with print—its many forms and functions—in a fairly global fashion. Such exposure and experience are necessary before children

A critical element in children's understanding of print is the role that their printed *name* plays (Clay, 1975; Ferreiro, 1986; Ferreiro & Teberosky, 1982). For most children, their written names become a benchmark for so much other learning. Their names in print stand for the real world—stand for what can be said and for the fact that they, the children, somehow "exist" on paper, apart from their actual selves. Later they will learn the names of the letters that are in their names and will begin to understand what a "word" is in print and what is meant by the "beginning," "middle," and "end" of a word. In addition, this knowledge will spur their interest in and attention to the alphabet, as well as facilitate their beginning awareness of letter/sound associations.

Jason, at age three and a half, has "signed" his piece of art; if we were to look at the rest of his "writing," it would be primarily a jumble of letterlike characters. For the moment, he has learned his written name the same way he learns a logo: these are lines and curves arranged in a certain way, and when we see them we respond, "Jason." His name, however, will become a standard of real letters and of real words, a standard that some time later will define most of his written attempts.

LEARNING IN CONTEXT: The child's written name is the benchmark from which so many other understandings about the nature and function of print will develop.

can learn about letters, the building blocks of print. But it is of course critical for children to learn about letters and to learn letter names, to lay the groundwork for understanding what words are, how words are put together, and letter/sound relationships. Before children can really get down to the business of learning printed words and moving successfully into conventional reading, they have to look at and examine a number of letters and learn something about how they work, both in and out of natural text. In order to begin to acquire a sight vocabulary of words they can identify regardless of context and size, they need to become acquainted with the building blocks—the letters (Clay, 1975; Ehri, 1994; Ferreiro, 1984; Lomax & McGee, 1987; Mason, 1980; McCormick & Mason, 1986).

Children learn about the *distinctive features* of letters—such as closure, curvature, line segments, and angularity—and how these features combine to differentiate one letter from another (Gibson, 1970). Each individual letter will need to be examined: to learn what an A is, children have to look closely at examples of A and learn how it is different from an H, say, and how a B is different from a P, and how an M is different from a W. They'll need to learn that letters that appear dissimilar are actually the same letter (capital and lower-case D and d, A and a, and so on) not to mention recognizing as the same letter different printed versions such as "ɑ" and "a" and "ɡ" and "g".

Children learn about the features and the identities of letters through comparison and contrast. To get an idea of how challenging this must be for young children, think about the letters *b, d, p,* and *q*. Visually they are similar—made up of the same types of curves and lines—but *how* these curves and lines are put together is different—and crucial. Think about it: any other item in the real world keeps its identity when you change its position. On its side, upside down, or twirling in the air, a chair is still a chair. When you change the orientation of *b,* however, you change its identity: upside-down, it is a *p;* backward, it is a *d;* upside-down and backward, it is a *q*.

METALINGUISTIC AWARENESS DEVELOPS IN A CONTEXT OF USING LANGUAGE, READING, AND WRITING

In order for children to advance beyond the emergent phase and understand how print works in a conventional sense, they need to become aware of sounds, letters, and words. This awareness is part of the more general type of *metalinguistic* awareness (Downing & Valtin, 1985; Tunmer, Pratt, & Herriman, 1984; Yaden & Templeton, 1986). To be metalinguistically aware means that one can move *beyond* the message or meaning that the language conveys (from the Greek prefix *meta-* meaning "beyond," and *linguistics,* or "language") and think consciously about the nature and characteristics of language itself. One can treat language as an *object.*

The foundations of metalinguistic awareness, this ability to think about language as an object, are established during the emergent phase. They best occur through children's experiences with texts in *authentic, meaningful* contexts. Such contexts include (1) being read to one-to-one and engaging in shared book experiences, (2) language experience activities, and (3) writing. We're about to look closely at the development and facilitation of children's metalinguistic or conscious awareness of sounds, letters, and words in print. These are three fundamental metalinguistic concepts that children must develop in order to advance in beginning conventional literacy. Let's briefly define each of these concepts and then discuss them more fully.

Phonemic awareness is the ability to attend to specific segments of sound within a syllable, segments that we defined as *phonemes* in Chapter 2. For our purposes we will say that children are developing phonemic awareness when they can attend to aspects of sounds smaller than a syllable.

Letter-name knowledge refers to children's ability (1) to understand that letters are important features of print and represent speech and (2) to identify several letters by their names.

A *concept of word* refers to the ability to match a printed word with its spoken counterpart. We all, of course, use words when we speak, but our speech flows along without the equivalent of the spaces that are between words in print. In print the words are delineated by spaces, and these spaces define where a particular word begins and ends.

Developing awareness of individual sound elements: phonemic awareness

Children's dawning awareness of sounds smaller than a syllable probably begins with their sensitivity to *rhyme* (Bradley & Bryant, 1985). Rhyming words facilitate this sensitivity in two ways. First, rhyming words stand out because they are part of language structures that are rhythmic and because the words sound similar. Second, in order to tell simple rhyming words apart, a child has to note their only distinguishing feature: while the rhyming words sound as if they *end* the same way, they also sound as if they *begin* differently. The beginning sound is "highlighted" therefore, and children gradually begin to attend to it. This constitutes children's beginning conscious analysis of a word according to its component sound parts: the beginning element (usually a consonant) and the rest of the word (the vowel and what follows it) (Henderson, 1981; Goswami, 1991). This conscious analysis is the dawning of phonemic awareness.

How can we help young children become aware of rhyme? Most children seem drawn to it naturally, as well as to the language play it encourages. This is why nursery rhymes have been so important over the years. They are often nonsensical, playful, and therefore engaging to young children. Their rhythm and their rhyme, particularly when supported by music, facilitate memorization and become a means of drawing children's attention to *sound* apart from meaning. It really doesn't matter if children have never before heard of a tuffet—what Miss Muffet sat on; the *sound* pulls them in and directs attention to itself, and this is what is so valuable in the rhymes and rhythms of early childhood. So we should read young children nursery rhymes and other books that are built around rhyme. We don't need to talk to them much about the characteristics of specific rhyming words; the children will be tacitly picking up on them. We may, however, play rhyming games with the children's names, using real words as well as nonsense words ("James Fames," "Letisha Bonisha," "Carlos Marlos," "Tiffany Miffany" [McGee & Richgels, 1990]).

Increasing awareness of print and of individual print elements

We have already seen how, when young children have developed rudimentary print awareness, they understand its nature and function—what print is and what it does. This rudimentary understanding allows children to examine the *form* of print; and at this level, form has to do with *how* print goes about representing spoken language.

Developing Letter-Name Knowledge   You already know that children will learn a lot about the features of letters through their interaction with adults in the company of print and through their own explorations with writing (Clay, 1975; Ferreiro, 1984). Yet these activities alone will not teach all the names of the letters in the alphabet. At some point, explicit teaching of letter names is usually necessary for most children—especially for any who have *not* learned them already in the home. *Sesame Street,* by the way, has rendered a very great service in this regard. Although it may appear obvious *why* ensuring that children know letter names is so necessary, we need to be explicit about the issue. Letters are indeed the building blocks of print, but *why* they are may not be so obvious to children. Learning to identify letters helps young children focus more precisely on the features of *words,* so they have more clues with which to remember those individual words. Letters help define what words *are* (see "Developing Your Instructional Toolkit" below). And learning about letters and their names is in fact an excellent facilitator of phonemic awareness (Holdaway, 1986; Ehri & Wilce, 1987); they are a *visual* representation or "placeholder" for sound.

Remember that such directed instruction should occur in a rich literacy classroom environment in which children are immersed in lots of different texts as well as writing. How do you know when a child is ready for more directed instruction? He or she will be able to write his or her name and will, not surprisingly, seem to be more interested in and intrigued by alphabet books (see the "Alphabet Books" list below); you also will often see lots of letterlike features in the child's writing.

■   BUILDING YOUR KNOWLEDGE BASE

■   **Alphabet Books**

■   Baskin, L. (1972). *Hosies' Alphabet.* Viking Press.

Bayer, J. (1984). *A, My Name Is Alice.* Dial.

■   Bruna, D. (1967). *B Is for Bear.* Macmillan.

Drucker, M. (1992). *A Jewish Holiday ABC.* Harcourt Brace Jovanovich.

Ehlert, L. (1989). *Eating the Alphabet: Fruits and Vegetables from A to Z*. Harcourt.

Feelings, M. (1974). *Jambo Means Hello: Swahili Alphabet Book*. Dial.

Hague, K. (1984). *Alphabears: An ABC book*. Holt, Rinehart, & Winston.

Hoban, T. (1982) *A, B, See!* Greenwillow.

Hoban, T. (1987). *26 letters and 99 cents*. Greenwillow.

Hubbard, W. (1990). *C Is for Curious: An ABC of Feelings*. Chronicle Books.

Ipear, D. (1964). *I Love an Anteater with an A*. Alfred A. Knopf.

Kellogg, S. (1987). *Aster Aardvark's Alphabet Adventures*. Morrow.

Kitchen, B. (1984). *Animal Alphabet*. Dial.

Lobel, A., & Lobel, A. (1981). *On Market Street*. Greenwillow.

Lyon, G. E. (1989). *ABCedar: An Alphabet of Trees*. Orchard Books.

Magee, D., & Newman, R. (1990). *All Aboard ABC*. Cobblehill.

McNab, N. (1989). *A–Z of Australian Wildlife*. Lamont Publishing.

Pallotta, J. (1986) *The Icky Bug Alphabet Book*. Charlesbridge Publishing.

Rice, J. (1990). *Cowboy Alphabet*. Pelican Publishing.

Zabar, A. (1990). *Alphabet Soup*. Stewart, Tabor & Chang

We hear a lot of discussion about teaching preschool children the *sounds* that letters stand for. For example, as the letter *a* is presented and children are told, "This is the letter *a*," they are also told that it makes the ă sound (as in *cat*). As the letter *b* is presented, children are told that it makes the sound *buh*. In reality, this type of presentation usually is not as helpful to young children as we might imagine. Think of how much information we actually are presenting to them if we do this (and how overwhelming it all may be). Knowing what is involved in just learning about features of letters, visual letter shapes, and the names of letters, you can recognize the potential difficulty in trying to teach "sounds" on top of all that—for when children learn that the letter *a*, in addition to having a name and standing for the sound of its name (*a* as in *cake*), can also stand for other sounds such as the *a* in *cat*, and that *c* stands for an *s* sound or a *k* sound, and so forth—they can indeed be overwhelmed.

Most preschool and kindergarten children benefit more if we teach only letter names in the beginning. They will use this knowledge to invent their own spellings, and your time is far better spent than it would be if you also tried to teach them sounds (Adams, 1990). Of course if a child happens to inquire about a letter's having more than one sound, you may mention that some letters do; but this incidental information is far more helpful and far less challenging than trying to combine, for every letter taught, its name with its sound or sounds. Teachers can help older preschoolers (and any kindergarten and first grade children who need such assistance) to learn the names of the letters through the following activities.

◼◼◼ DEVELOPING YOUR INSTRUCTIONAL TOOLKIT

Learning the Names of the Letters

1. Post a large alphabet strip prominently in the classroom—where all the children can see it. Also post one at child level, so that the children can practice tracing the letters when they wish.

2. Focus on one letter at a time. You may find that it is easier for many preschoolers and kindergartners if you begin with upper-case (capital) letters rather than with both upper- and lower-case. Usually, though, if children are interested at all in letters and seem to be attending to them, they can learn upper- and lower-case letters concurrently.

3. When you introduce a letter, show the children how you print it. This presentation is not a penmanship lesson; you are just showing them *how* you make a particular letter (of course, you are also modeling this when you are doing Language Experience [see page 112], but that context is different—you would not be explicitly highlighting letters *per se*). Have the letters available on paper or on laminated cards, so that the children can trace them, if they like, before writing them.

4. Use concrete, manipulable representations of letters, such as magnetic letters and LinkLetters®. Magnetic letters are excellent for use with all preschool children; LinkLetters® are better for older preschoolers because the children must be able to connect one letter to another like doing a simple jigsaw puzzle. Children may use these letters, of course, to form their names as well as any and all other "messages" they wish. One of the advantages of these letters is that they are "ready-made"; children have to recognize only the letter they wish to use, as opposed to generating it from memory.

5. Make letters with clay and Playdoh® and construct letters using noodles and paste or other materials. Children should work in pairs or in small groups or individually, under your guidance, so that someone will always be repeating the name of the letter, ensuring that it becomes associated with the shape.

6. Sing the alphabet song. Children eventually know it by heart; and even though they may think for some time that L-M-N-O-P ("ellemenopee") is *one* letter, the aural support of this timeless ditty makes it easier later to match letters to their specific names. As you sing, it is helpful to point to the letters on the alphabet strip (sing slowly; then when you hit "L-M-N-O-P," you won't feel frantic).

7. When a specific letter is targeted, write on the board those children's names that begin with that letter. Children can underline the first letter of their names, and the names will remain on the board for as long as you are focusing on that particular letter.

8. Associate a keyword and a picture with the letter. The *keyword* is a word, such as *bat,* with which children can associate the letter they are learning. The keyword begins with the targeted letter and should be accompanied by a picture of a bat (your choice: a baseball bat or the mammal). A more concrete association is to

Figure 3.2
Associating a Keyword with a Letter

incorporate letter, picture, and keyword in one presentation (Ehri, Deffner, & Wilce, 1984; Harrison & McKee, 1971).

Note that guidelines 7 and 8 in the list are obviously incorporating the teaching of letter *names* with the *sounds* that those letters stand for. There are two important points I'd like to make about this:

> *First,* don't be concerned if many preschool or kindergarten children seem to have difficulty understanding this type of match-up—of the letter *b,* for example, with "things that *begin* with the letter *b.*" Such children are not developmentally there yet. Because of all the attention to one specific letter, though, they usually *will* learn the name of that letter, which is your main objective.

> *Second,* with children who (1) are clearly interested in and enjoying literacy-related activities and (2) have been attending to print and can identify a few words in their environment, you may expect that they will understand the relationship between letters and beginning sounds; these types of activities can be excellent springboards for directly examining beginning consonants. We will explore this type of word analysis in Chapter 5.

> The basic issue to keep in mind is that letter names need to be learned, of course, but that letter/sound relationships (phonics) should not be initiated too soon—that is, not before a child has much understanding of the basic functions, forms, and some of the features of print.

MEANING MAKERS ■

Learning About Letters and Groups of Letters

Let's put letter-learning in a broad perspective so we can appreciate its importance for children. First, as they are learning about the distinctive features that comprise letters and about the identities of individual letters, the task of identifying a *particular* letter involves careful examination and requires consideration of all its parts or distinctive features. Later, children are so familiar with a particular letter that the "parts" or features appear to them to form a single *pattern,* the letter itself, so they are able to identify the letter almost automatically.

Later still, children's ability to identify letters automatically, together with their other knowledge about print, including context, allows them to look at a written word and apply a more efficient level of analysis in order to identify it: a *letter-by-letter* analysis. Earlier they would have been overwhelmed by a jumble of lines, angles, and spaces. And later still in their development, as children come to know a lot about how words are constructed from individual letters, they will be able to group letters into single patterns that aid in identification: *-ate,* for example, will be identified as a single pattern, and just as rapidly as a single letter. When you think about it, this is an astounding accomplishment! It's a process of one understanding's flowing into the other; that is, the "parts" are at first a random set of distinctive features that becomes identified as a *pattern,* which in turn becomes known as a letter. Once children have this ability, *these* parts—a larger set of letters as opposed to individual distinctive features—become identified as a pattern within a word. (How children develop this knowledge will be examined more extensively in Chapter 5.)

To give yourself a more concrete sense of the task young children confront in learning letter patterns and within-word patterns, try the following activity. You will be working with "letters" and with "words" that are constructed with these letters. First, study the following letters and the sounds they represent in the left hand columns. When you feel you have memorized them, cover the letters; then look at the "words" to the right and try to identify them.

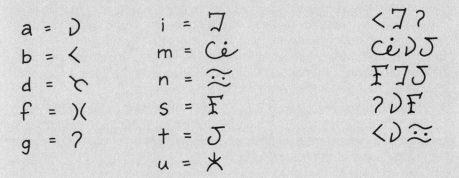

Given enough experience with those letters and words, you would eventually "pick up" as a unit the within-word pattern in the following words:

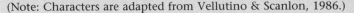

(Note: Characters are adapted from Vellutino & Scanlon, 1986.)

Young children of course do not learn "nonsense" words such as these, but they *are* confronted with an array of visual configurations they will be learning about. The entire enterprise of learning about features of letters, letter names, and how letters are grouped within words best occurs in rich learning environments where the children are seeing print in all the usual places and are learning about letters and playing with them. ■

Developing Word Awareness   Much of what we have already discussed will facilitate children's developing word awareness. In the case of literacy, word awareness is more specifically referred to as a *concept of word in print*—the realization that in print, a word is a printed unit, a group of letters, bound by spaces at both ends (Clay, 1991; Morris, 1980, 1992; Roberts, 1992). Morris (1983) underscored the importance of this awareness when he observed that unless children "develop a stable concept of word, until they can focus on individual words within a line of text, they will be unable to develop a sight vocabulary or attend to the orthographic patterns of words in text" (p. 116)—those developments that characterize the Beginning Reading phase.

Phonemes and the letters that represent them are organized systematically within the unit we call "word." As children are listening, looking, and gradually learning about the "pieces" of print and sound, they are seeing natural text. They see single words used as labels; they see lines of print pointed at by a literate adult. They learn to write their names; they learn to identify and write some letters. Gradually, all this information is being assimilated and will result in the dawning realization that *words* are the elements that "organize" sounds and letters; words are the frame within which letters and sounds match up. Once children grasp the nature and boundaries of that frame, they can attend to what's inside it—in this case, the *order* of the sounds within the word. They understand where the beginning of the word is and where the word ends. As they attempt to write the word, they can hold it in mind as they sound their way through it. Once they've dealt with the beginning sound and selected a letter that makes that sound, they move to the next sound they hear, select a letter, and so on. Until they know what in some sense a "word" is, however, it is difficult to do those things—to attempt to think about "beginnings," "endings," and so forth.

While very young children can "learn" to identify a few words, they do not have a concept of word in print. They usually depend heavily on the context in which a word occurs—the logo on a soft-drink can is used to identify *Pepsi,* for example—because they are not yet able to use all the letters as a clue to identification. As they begin to learn about letters, however, and continue to be immersed in print and have their attention directed toward it, they will use a word's first letter and general configuration to remember it. *Turkey,* for example, is identified by the first letter and the general shape (a line that reaches up in the middle of the word and a line or "tail" that reaches down at the end). As children look over a printed version of a memorized text, however, this knowledge will help them home in on the "word" as an individual unit in print, corresponding to a spoken unit (Morris, 1992).

◼ DEVELOPING YOUR INSTRUCTIONAL TOOLKIT

Developing a "Concept of Word" in Print

Here are some specific guidelines and activities for helping children develop a concept of word in print.

1. Make sure that children are able to hear and see favorite texts read over and over, including their own language experience dictations. Over time, as children scan these memorized texts, they will begin to attend to particular words and remember them. This "memorization" is critically important.

2. Keep in mind that children need to see words—and to have their attention directed toward words—in all their contexts: in environmental print; used as labels in the classroom environment (the word *wastebasket* can be taped to the wastebasket; the word *clock,* underneath the clock on the wall, and so forth), and in books.

3. Remember that we usually *point* to printed words when we talk to children about them and read them in the environment, on labels, in a storybook.

4. Comment about features of words when appropriate: "Oh, look—this word [pointing to *pig* in a big book] *begins* just like Paul's name!" or "Isn't this something? The word *candy* rhymes with *Sandy,* doesn't it?" or "Can you find the word *happy* somewhere else on this page?" or "Look how the words *bommy knocker* are printed so much larger at the end of the book than in the beginning."

EMERGENT READING

Reading aloud to children and exposing them to stories and books is essential. This section will highlight the critical value and ways of reading aloud to children and the interpersonal, collaborative nature of a read-aloud experience.

The first major discussion will describe unstructured immersion in books and stories. As children grow in their literacy experience and enter formal schooling programs, both teachers and parents become more structured in their presentation of print and what it means. Thus, the second major section that follows focuses on the adjustments that are made when we begin to edge children into more organized reading experiences. You will learn what teachers can do to encourage the development of emergent reading, and what concepts are enhanced through these guided environments and directed lessons.

Immersion in stories and books

For children to begin to think about books and stories, they first must see and hear them. Daily, consistent exposure to books makes children curious about them. When they snuggle into listening to a story, whether in a parent's lap or in a beanbag chair with classmates, we want the experience to be so rewarding that they will ask for it to be repeated again and again. As the hours spent reading and listening to stories increase, so will a child's background knowledge of how books are put together, how print works, and how stories develop.

Development of the Concept of Story and of Storybook Reading Why are young children—and we ourselves—drawn to stories? Why do they entrance us? Their appeal and their purpose were probably laid down in the human subconscious eons ago. Our distant ancestors huddled around fires in caves and told stories to help themselves understand and cope with their world, with lives of hunting, gathering, and dealing with natural phenomena such as storms, lightning, and the occasional earthquake. The stories offered *explanations* for phenomena that frightened and confounded; stories soothed, they offered resolutions to problems, and they nurtured growing and tenuous children and societies (Campbell, 1966).

Stories continue to play a profound role in our lives. "They seem comfortable because they tell us about things we know in some sense—perhaps tacitly, perhaps consciously. They help us rediscover or reinvent our reality and thereby understand it more deeply and meaningfully" (Templeton, 1991, p. 342). Stories will help children with the many unknowns and myriad mysteries that loom in early childhood. Anne Dyson suggests that although young children may not be able to articulate their thinking about abstract themes such as "existence" and "good and evil," such themes can be experienced meaningfully in the context of story (Dyson, 1990). Let's explore how children's concepts about stories and storybooks usually develop.

We've discussed how children are exposed to the environmental print that surrounds them at all times. They see things done in the context of print and develop beginning ideas about what "reading" is and what print does. A critical aspect of this emergent phase is exposure to *stories* and to books that contain them. Such exposure helps children develop what we call a "concept of story"—a sense of how stories are structured and what they can represent. For example, in most stories there are characters who become involved in some type of problem or situation that requires a resolution; there is a beginning, middle, and end to this encapsulated slice of life. Children come to expect this beginning/middle/end and the problem/resolution type of structure. This schema, or expectation, for how stories work guides children's "meaning making" when they hear stories. Many cultures continue to make storytelling part of ongoing family and community interaction (Heath, 1983), and stories once told only within private cultural settings are now being preserved in print. Most prevalent of these are Native American and African-American folktales. As our population diversifies, so do the availabilities and variety of books published specifically for young children.

As we saw in Chapter 2, children learn to differentiate between narrative and informational genres—texts that tell stories and texts that present information. In addition, they learn that there are different examples or formats of each of these genres. Fairy tales are different from nursery rhymes; concept books are different from "how to" books. These understandings, like other concepts about print, are rudimentary at first, but they help children eventually become aware of the different purposes or functions that print can serve: print can entertain us as well as give us information.

Moreover, the *language* in books is so often different from the everyday, conversational language with which we usually engage young children. Book language has to carry more of the story, to sketch in more of the context, simply because the world it is suggesting is not encircling the children as they read. The language in the book has to give them more information about how to construct that world in their heads. In addition to developing understandings about reading, storybook reading advances children's development in writing, in thinking, and in *feeling* in an emotional sense, as well as in talking and listening. Storybook reading comes into play, and powerfully, in another way: when adults ask children about the feelings of characters in a story or about what they think "the author is trying to tell us," they are gently inviting children to stretch and extend their own worlds by relating those worlds to those of others (Wellington Department of Education, 1985). Young children usually have some difficulty considering another person's point of view; Piaget termed this "egocentrism" (Piaget & Inhelder, 1969).

Researchers have studied the development of young children's concepts about stories as represented in storybooks. In studying children from ages two through five, Sulzby (1985), Yaden, McGee, and others (Yaden & McGee, 1984; Yaden, Smolkin, & Conlon, 1988) have detected some general trends.

At first, children's efforts depend heavily on the *pictures;* there is a "picture-dependent" sequence of development:

- Each picture stands on its own, rather than as part of a whole.
- Children understand that the sequence of pictures corresponds to the sequence of what is happening in the story; when they "pretend read," there is a mixture of language that sounds like oral reading and language that is more informal or conversational.
- Children have naturally memorized the storybook; they "pretend read" either a verbatim recall of the story or a very close verbatim recall.

When these things happen, children are attending to the print, and they realize that those squiggly little characters somehow "contain" the language:

- Children initially may refuse to "read," since they understand that they don't know what the print says, in the sense of their being able to identify words
- Soon children *are* able to pick out parts of the print and read it correctly; they may "fill in" the rest.

Children ask a great many questions about the stories that are read to them. Earlier in development, these questions primarily have to do with the pictures; later, they focus on the story's meaning and eventually on the significance of unfamiliar words.

In general, storybook reading first facilitates development of preschool children's ability to construct meaning in the context of a book, rather than their knowledge about aspects of print (Yaden et al., 1989; Wells, 1987). Understanding of how stories "work"—a sense of their structure—in turn "provides an inner model of the rhythms and patterns of written language" (Yaden et al., p. 208). The cadence of language used within a story can often extend that story's meaning; the ups and downs of how the words sound can tell us about a character's emotions, cultural background, age, and so forth. Patterns within the sentences may let the reader know whether the words are written as poetry or as prose, as a riddle or a recipe, as a song or a slogan. And as we'll see in Chapter 5, children's construction of knowledge about specific aspects of print—words and their structure—is powerfully dependent on and supported by these rhythms and patterns.

Reading to Preschoolers   I cannot state it too often: reading to preschool children is probably the most important and facilitative thing we can do for their reading development. Simply expressed, ". . . reading aloud to young children *teaches* them about reading" (Teale & Sulzby, 1989, p. 7). You've just read about the understandings that develop when children are read to, so let's examine the finer points involved in sharing books with children, points appropriate for both parents and teachers of preschoolers. *How* we read to preschoolers seems to change with their age; they are usually the ones who cause the changing dynamics.

Adults who interact with preschoolers seem to use their story-readings to construct *with* the child what the book "means" (Cochran-Smith, 1984). There is conversation about what is going on in the book: questions, comments, elaborations, giggles—a whole gamut of interactions—surface.

Reading to Infants and Toddlers   So many of the books we share with infants and toddlers up to three years of age are picture books and wordless books. These are excellent props for social interaction and language-learning. Booksharing

Reading to children and discussing what is going on in the books is probably the most important contribution parents can make to their children's reading development.

After studying many situations in which parents were reading to their children, Taylor & Strickland (1986) found that, regardless of ethnic, educational, and socioeconomic background, most parents "often expand and extend the content of the stories in natural and meaningful ways. Parents seem to sense when such expansions are necessary, or when an unembellished reading is the best way to share a particular story" (Taylor & Strickland, 1989, p. 30). The context of these story-reading experiences is usually—though not always!—a cuddly one. Bedtime is popular for booksharing, and usually more manageable for parents. Still, regardless of the time, when children want to be read to, they usually will come to the parent with a book and a demand to be read to.

Two of my children followed the scenario parents dream of. As I read to them they were usually plopped in my lap or cuddled next to me, their attention riveted on the book. They were interested, wanted to see the pictures, made comments, and asked questions about what was being read. For our middle child, however, this was decidedly not the case! He was not a "cuddler" during our reading and in fact displayed little overt interest in whatever was being read to him. I eventually learned, however, that even as he was roaming about the room, appearing to be engrossed in other activities, he was still paying a good deal of attention to what I was reading. As I sat on the floor, reading aloud, he would toddle over from time to time to have a peek at the pictures, then toddle off to get back to his blocks or whatever. I got used to this, and learned not to take it personally! So you can reassure parents who worry about their children's *not* appearing to take an interest in books that they should continue to read aloud, probably on the floor, and that very often this in itself will tempt the "active" child to come on over for a look.

Parents learn early on that children enjoy having a favorite book read to them over and over. We should indulge children in this, but also not be reluctant to introduce another book we feel they would enjoy. The advantages of reading the same book repeatedly are many. Children come to remember the story and will "read" it on their own, using pictures as clues. But we also have the opportunity to talk about what is going on in the book, from a number of different angles, and this is important, too. Remember that for young children, these stories and rhymes are like friends, and no one wishes to leave friends after only one visit!

LEARNING IN CONTEXT: **As teachers, we cannot emphasize too strongly to parents the values of their reading to their children—whether their children are "cuddlers" or "wanderers" during reading time.**

can be like any other type of play for very young children. At first, they don't realize that what we are saying has much to do with the book. Before long, though, we can engage the children in talk about the book. We behave as though the infant or toddler answered a question we posed, for example. In her research on reading to very young children, Ninio (1980) found that parents seemed to use three strategies or routines when sharing books with their very young children. There is the "name" routine, in which parents name something in a picture for the child after getting the child to attend to it. The "where" routine involves asking the child where something is in a picture, and the "what" routine elicits the name of something in a picture from the child. In any of these routines, parents usually expand on what the child has done or said to reinforce their response (see also Resnick, 1987).

Reading to Older Preschoolers As young children grow and change in development, we adjust our manner of interaction to accommodate their needs. Teale and Sulzby offer an excellent overview of what we should do when we read to older preschoolers, three to six years old, including kindergartners:

> . . . engage the children in discussion about what is being read. Talk about the characters and their motivations and responses, make predictions and then listen to confirm or disconfirm them, draw inferences, discuss the themes of books, link information in books to real life experiences, examine the author's use of language, and draw connections among various books. (1989, p. 7)

That may sound like a lot for a three- or four-year-old, but you will find that since most children of this age like to chat, a reading session will move quickly, bouncing back and forth easily between text and talk. Most often a child will let you know when he or she has had enough talk and wants to get on with the story. Following are guidelines for presenting and sharing storybooks with older preschoolers, guidelines appropriate for one-to-one as well as small group situations:

Before reading storybooks: While displaying the cover, briefly talk about the book. Ask children what they think the book might be about; predictions can be made based on the title or illustrations or both. You might briefly discuss the type of story; for example, whether it's a fable or a fairy tale. You may discuss the main characters and where the story takes place. You might tell a little about the author and the illustrator, but always be sensitive to how well the children are attending before continuing with an "introduction." All this can provide a purpose or purposes for listening—such as making predictions.

During the reading of storybooks: Read with expression! (We'll discuss this aspect further in Chapter 6.) Ask the children whether their predictions or ideas about what they thought would happen in the story are following that pattern. Then have them make further predictions. In addition, you might ask questions that help them understand what unfamiliar words may mean, what unfamiliar concepts are, and how characters are feeling and thinking in the story (Mason, Peterman, & Kerr, 1989).

After the reading of storybooks: Go over the order of events in the story with the children. Ask questions about the setting, what the main problem (or conflict) was, how the character or characters tried to solve the problem, and how it eventually was solved—the outcome of the story. Help the children to relate what happened in the story to their own lives. It's unwise to belabor this follow-up discussion, though. If you're not getting cohesive responses, do a bit of rereading to help the children redirect their thoughts to the story at hand; then move on. Additional story readings will offer other opportunities for concept development.

For decades, most adults have thought that young children would learn to read better if given mainly narrative materials. It was assumed that informational materials would not be of as much interest. However, recent investigations have affirmed what sensitive teachers have known for a long time: young children find informational books just as engaging as narratives—and sometimes more so (Pappas, 1990). Following are guidelines for sharing informational books with older preschoolers (adapted from Mason, Peterman, & Kerr, 1989).

Before reading informational books: Through discussion based on the cover picture, find out what children know about the topic; then relate this to what is in the book. As with storybook reading, set purposes for listening—again, as much as possible, these should reflect children's ideas or *predictions* about what they believe they may learn from the book.

During the reading of informational books: Elaborate as necessary on the information, explaining it to the children. Use illustrations as much as possible; question the children from time to time to make sure they are understanding most of the text.

After the reading of informational books: There should be a back-and-forth questioning between you and the children; you ask questions about the text and they should feel free to ask as well. Whenever possible, follow-up activities or projects should extend ideas and new concepts encountered in the text.

Children who have had these types of experiences will usually enjoy spending time with books and will pore over a favorite book countless times, reciting it from memory. As they learn a few words by sight and learn something about letters, they enjoy tackling new texts on their own, relying on this budding information but relying more strongly on the illustrations and what they *think* the text says.

■ **BUILDING YOUR KNOWLEDGE BASE**

Books for Three- Through Six-Year Olds

"Concept" or Informational Books

Aliki. (1985). *My Visit to the Dinosaurs.* Crowell.

Bang, M. (1983). *Ten, nine, eight.* Greenwillow.

Carle, E. (1969). *The Very Hungry Caterpillar.* Philomel/Putnam.

Crews, D. (1978). *Freight Train.* Greenwillow.

Hoban, T. (I'm suggesting a whole bundle of books here; Hoban is a marvelous photographer who clearly captures the concepts she is presenting.): All are published by Greenwillow. *Is It Red? Is It Yellow? Is It Blue?; I Read Symbols; I Read Signs; I Walk and Read; Dots, Spots, Speckles, and Stripes; Is It Larger? Is It Smaller?*

Feelings, M., & Feelings, T. (1976). *Moja means one.* Viking.

Gibbons, G. (1986). *Up Goes the Skyscraper.* Four Winds.

Kitchen, B. (1987). *Animal Numbers*. Dial.

Rockwell, A. *I Like the Library*. Dutton.

Rockwell, A. & H. (1979). *The Supermarket*. Macmillan.

Wildsmith, B. (1984). *Brian Wildsmith's one, two, three*. Oxford University Press.

Storybooks

dePaola, T. (1981). *The Comic Adventures of Old Mother Hubbard and Her Dog*. Harcourt, Brace, Jovanovich.

Dr. Seuss (T. Geisel). *The Cat in the Hat*. Random House.

Galdone, P. (1968). *Henny Penny*. Clarion.

Galdone, P. (1981). *The Three Billy Goats Gruff*. Clarion.

Lobel, A. *Frog and Toad Are Friends*. Harper & Row.

Martin, B. (1967). *Brown Bear, Brown Bear, What Do You See?* Henry Holt and Company.

Minarek, E. (1957). *Little Bear*. Harper. (Minarek wrote several other books based on this particular bear family.)

Sendak, M. (1963). *Where the Wild Things Are*. Harper.

Slobodkina, E. (1947). *Caps for Sale*. Scott, Foresman.

Planned experiences to facilitate reading

As children grow in familiarity with books and stories, teachers may wish to direct children's attention more specifically to the many aspects of print, while continuing to capitalize on their strength to make meaning of the world around them. This can be done in the contexts of the Shared Book Experience and the Language Experience Approach activities. Let's examine these more closely.

Predictable Texts and the Group "Shared Book" Experience We now know very well that young children need adult support in their early efforts to learn about the nature of print and how it corresponds to speech. Along with all the other ways in which you can facilitate this development, the role of *predictable texts* is extremely important. Texts can be "predictable" in many ways, as Heald-Taylor pointed out: Predictability exists through "strong rhythm and rhyme, repeated patterns, refrains, logical sequences, supportive illustrations, and traditional story structures" (1987, p. 6). In actuality, we can say that "predictability" as a concept can apply to almost any type of text, for any level of reader; once you understand how stories work, for example, this knowledge will help you understand a particular story as you read and predict what may be happening later on. You will most often encounter the notion of "predictability," however, as applying to texts intended for emergent and beginning readers.

The term *shared book experience* is used to refer to the ways in which predictable texts are presented to emergent and beginning readers (Holdaway, 1979; Slaughter, 1993). Following are the basic procedures for a shared book experience for emergent readers; in Chapter 5 we'll look at shared book experiences for children who have moved into the beginning conventional reading phase:

1. Use a "big book"—usually about 24" tall and 18" wide—a predictable text that is placed on an easel. ("Big books" are available through educational publishers such as Scholastic, the Wright Group, or Rigby Education). Its story length most often follows the traditional sixteen-page format. You first introduce the book and talk about it with the children. Keeping in mind your students' prior knowledge about books and their "world" in general, read the title of the book aloud and ask the children what they think a book titled (for example) *In a Dark, Dark Wood* might be about and why (see Figure 3.3).

2. Next, you can read the book to the children, "modeling" reading behavior by pointing to each word as you go, moving from left to right and top to bottom. Read as naturally and engagingly as you can, using a lighthearted voice for a silly text and a more mysterious, spooky-type voice for a text like Joy Cowley's *In a Dark, Dark Wood.*

As the children catch on to the rhythmic patterns and words in the book, they may join in; this is terrific and should be encouraged. Your voice will usually continue to "lead" the reading, though, and should be clearly heard. Just as when reading to a child one-to-one, you may stop—ever so briefly—at appropriate points during the reading to ask the children what they think is going to happen next, and why.

3. Discuss the story with the children. Did what they expected to happen actually occur? Why or why not? Heald-Taylor suggests asking two or three questions such as these: Was there a "problem" in the story? If so, how was it solved? You may also ask how the children liked the story, and if appropriate, whether *they* ever experienced anything like what happened in the story.

4. Reread the book *with* the children. Invite them to read with you, if they are not naturally doing it on their own. Again, point to the words as you read. This repetition is extremely effective. It reinforces children's memory of the text and allows children who as yet don't know much about print to feel they are involved (and those who are reluctant to try reading along will still *hear* the story several times). You will find that these rereadings will be an ongoing means of assessment of whether and how children's emergent concepts about print and about reading are developing.

Reread the story several times over the next couple of days. It is helpful to have the children attend to different aspects during a rereading. For example, on one occasion you may ask them to think about how the pictures help tell the story along with the print. On the next reading, you might ask if they know people who are like those in the story. Yet another time, you will be pointing out certain letters, and words that begin with those letters.

5. Some related activities should usually be tied to the shared reading experience. In addition to your encouraging the children to read the "little book" copies of this story, these activities may include:

- Making illustrations.
- Dramatizing the story.
- Dictating stories or parts of stories patterned on the shared book. The language and content can be quite similar or can vary ("In a dark dark wood there was a dark dark skateboard . . ."). We will explore how you can "take dictation" from children in the next section, on the Language Experience Approach.
- Listening to a tape of the story at the Listening Center. Some tapes that accompany published series include sound effects and music.
- Creating a patterned story together. On an overhead transparency, write sentences from the story but leave certain words out; the children will fill these gaps in. For example, "In a dark, dark _____, there was a dark dark _____" or "In a _____ wood, there was a _____ path."
- Word study. Children can find particular words in the story, and you can talk about words that are similar to a target word—"Find the word that begins like *stop* . . . , that rhymes with *Mark* . . . ," and so forth. (See the section on developing metalinguistic awareness, pages 94–102).
- When copies of little books to accompany the big book are not available for the children to go over on their own, the teacher or helper or aide can from time to time make individual copies for the children, with the text on each page; the children can color in or illustrate each page.

Shared book experiences and related activities will provide one of the best ways in which individual written words can be remembered. It is important to emphasize, however, that the children should not be expected to learn as a sight word *every* word that appears in a predictable book—this is not our main objective.

Several publishers market big books with accompanying multiple copies of

In a dark, dark wood,   there was a dark, dark path.

Figure 3.3
The Beginning of In a Dark, Dark Wood

little books. The series are sequenced according to length and complexity and provide excellent supporting illustrations. You should be wary, however: many other publishers are simply taking regular-size books, "blowing them up," and calling them Big Books. Unlike the types of books we have been exploring here, these books have not been constructed with predictability in mind. In the United States and Canada, for example, "genuine" Big Books are published by Scholastic; Troll Associates; Wright Group; Children's Press; Ginn & Company; in Australia and New Zealand see Shortland Publications and Rigby Education (the latter are also available in the United States and Canada). Also examine the recent literature-based reading programs published by major educational publishers such as Houghton Mifflin; Macmillan; and Scott, Foresman—in contrast to the beginning books in reading series of the past, these include the format and principles of predictable texts in the kindergarten and first-grade programs (see also Chapter 10).

The Language Experience Approach   The Language Experience Approach (LEA) or simply "Language Experience" is the label that has been applied to an approach that directly models how print works, at the same time as it demonstrates that what children can say can be written down and read (Hall, 1981; Stauffer, 1970). We will explore LEA in much greater depth in Chapter 5, as it facilitates beginning conventional reading, but we should look at the "basics" here because the approach is such a valuable means for demonstrating the nature of print and of literacy, as well as of encouraging children's expansion and application of oral language competencies.

In the Language Experience Approach, both children's *language* and their *experience* are represented in writing. Acting as scribes, teachers write down what children say about a particular experience—such as a teacher's demonstration of an acoustic (wooden) guitar. After writing down what many children contribute, the teacher reads this "dictation" back to the class. A number of activities can follow the initial dictation, to support children's learning about print. Sentences can be reread, particular words located, and a store of sight words from these dictations gradually built up. These sight words in turn can become a core collection of words to be examined later on for purposes of learning about word structure.

Just as with predictable texts, LEA models for children the features and the functions of print. In contrast to predictable texts, though, it is more natural in the sense that it is based on the *children's* experiences and the children's language. It is therefore highly motivating and attention-sustaining—important criteria when working with very young children in a group.

Let's make explicit why LEA works so effectively with young children:

As with predictable texts, it helps "model" how print works, developing print awareness and a concept of word in print.

LEA is highly motivating.

LEA shows children that what they say can be written down and "reproduced" orally each time it is read, exactly as they said it. They are also learning this about language in books, of course—the print "says" the same thing each time it is read—but LEA shows them directly where authorship begins: with what *they* say!

LEA is a natural way of helping children build their sight-word vocabularies (an issue we will explore in greater depth in Chapter 5).

Experiencing the Stimulus In demonstrating her guitar, for example, the teacher strums a few chords and asks the children to describe how the instrument sounds, what its parts look like, and what function each part has. The teacher and the children gradually name the parts and use descriptive words about them. Just about any stimulus would lend itself to this type of examination. By questioning, the teacher models *how* to question—how to *think* about experiences we have with our world and the things in it. This is not idle chitchat, by any means; while teacher and children are having fun in the context of a motivating experience, there is direction and purpose in the teacher's facilitation of the children's thinking and talking.

Writing a Group-Dictated Experience Chart The second phase of this experience is the "dictation" phase. The teacher elicits comments from the children about whatever has been experienced. Usually she or he will focus the children's thinking on what they have already noted in their discussion, but if new ideas come out, that's fine. The teacher writes the children's comments in large print, perhaps on a pad of chartpaper propped on an easel, and begins by eliciting and writing a title such as, "The Guitar," pronouncing each word while writing it. The teacher then continues, asking questions about the children's experiences and writing exactly what each child contributes. While writing each word, the teacher pronounces it in a natural fashion. And each time a child contributes, the teacher writes the child's name and what the child said *(Erin said, "It's got a neck and pegs")* until a list of statements is on the chart.

Let's pause and look at what is being modeled:

- Children see that what they or other children say can be written down exactly as it is said.
- The teacher has modeled *how print "works":* left to right, top to bottom.
- Children realize that the end of a line is not necessarily the end of what is said.
- Each word is pronounced as it is being written; this helps children develop a concept of word in print.
- Children see letter formation "in action."
- Children see additional features of printed language: periods, commas, quotation marks, apostrophes, capital and lower-case letters.

If the text becomes too long—more than one page—it becomes more difficult for the children to remember. Recall that *memory* for text is extremely important in the early stages. If any children seem discouraged because they wished to contribute and could not, the teacher can reassure them that there will be many other opportunities to contribute—either another dictation about the guitar or something else.

The reason for preceding each child's contribution with the child's name is that because most children will learn to recognize their name in print, they can use this knowledge to locate their sentences on the chart. Each child's sentence is begun on a separate line so that children can find their names more easily. Later on, the teacher can write a continuous text.

The teacher reads the group-dictated experience chart aloud, with as much natural expression as possible, pointing to each word as she reads it. She uses a pointer rather than her hand, so that she does not inadvertently block any child's view of the chart. (Depending on the particular children a teacher is working with, it may be necessary to read a chart a second time.)

Next, it's time for the children to join in the reading, so the teacher again reads the chart as naturally as possible, "leading" the children with her voice. If they seem to be taking off on their own, however, she can lower her voice so that the children are in the lead. The chart should be choral-read this way a second time, and if necessary, a third time.

Finding Out What Children Know About Print Dictation activities provide teachers the opportunity to see how particular children are developing understandings about reading in general, and print and words in particular. The teacher asks volunteers to come to the chart and find their names, "read" their responses, or point to a particular word in a response.

Children who did not dictate a sentence are of course free to locate another's sentence and "read" it. For most first-graders a fifteen- to twenty-minute session is possible; this includes the "stimulus" and the accompanying discussion as well as the dictation writing and reading, and the short time during which the teacher is finding out about the children's print knowledge.

Always an excellent follow-up to the dictated experience chart is having the children illustrate the experience—in this case, of course, a guitar, or perhaps the teacher holding the guitar. The guitar would be placed so that all the children could see it, and as they draw their pictures, the teacher would walk around and write the word *guitar* on their papers. That is one word everyone would know by the end of the day.

Throughout this whole experience and dictation, the teacher would have been learning about the pupils in her class. In addition to noting who felt comfortable contributing to the statements on the chart and who volunteered to come up to the chart, she would notice those who were "with" her the whole time, easily sustaining their attention. And she would notice those who began to "fade" after a few minutes. She does not make final decisions about smaller instructional groupings, but she does begin her own "data collection" process so that she can understand and respond more appropriately to her pupils.

On another day, the teacher can *temporarily* split her class into two groups, but there is nothing sacred about two groups; it could as easily be three or four. Each group could include children who contributed on the first day, but the teacher would plan to have one group include those who participated and several other children who seemed to be attentive; the other group would include children who did not contribute and/or may not have been attending as closely on the first day. In each group, she could probe further and learn more about the children. With fewer children in the group, those who did not contribute the first day may feel more comfortable in doing so on the second day—and they may dictate their own chart about the guitar.

For the group of children who did not contribute the first day, the teacher again brings out her guitar to get the discussion going. She may spend most of her time with these children just talking, bringing out their language, directing their attention, thoughts, and words to the guitar and its different features. But these children will probably be ready before the time goes by to dictate their own experience chart. This will also be a good time, by the way, to read a predictable book to this group.

For the group of children that includes those who contributed yesterday to the story, the teacher will probe more deeply into their knowledge about print and about reading. She first rereads the dictated account, then choral reads it with the children. She then asks different children to read different sentences and locate different words. Remember, all the children in this group—not just those who contributed—can participate in this. She can also probe for which children have constructed a concept of word in print (see below) because, just as with a favorite poem or predictable book, the dictated experience chart is becoming a memorized text. The teacher will query to determine which children can 1) point to words as they say the words, and 2) locate particular words in a sentence. If children can in fact locate words, *how* do they do it? The teacher will observe to see whether they can immediately point to the word she asks them to locate, or whether they return to the beginning of the sentence and read up to the target word, using context to help their identification.

Based on her assessment about which children have a concept of word in print, the teacher will also be thinking about which words these children might be able to identify if they see them out of the context of the dictation tomorrow—if they can do so, these words will become part of these children's sight vocabulary. In Chapter 5 we will examine the procedure for harvesting sight words from Language Experience dictations.

The teacher engages the other group in rereading their dictated chart. She may probe to see which children can identify their names and other selected words. And again, this is a good time to read a predictable text with this group.

You may be as flexible as you feel you need to be with the "dictation cycle" of dictating, rereading, and dictating again. One group, for example, may be able to dictate charts and reliably identify words out of context every two days; another group may need to spend all week exploring a chart. You should place charts in conspicuous, easy-to-reach places in the room so that children can visit them often; you will see them "reading" the chart with a pointer, just as you do, and playing "teacher" as they ask another child to find a particular word or read a particular part of the chart.

You may also run off copies of the chart and paste them in individual books for each child; each group dictated account can be illustrated again in the book, numbered, and the children are excited as they see the book is growing and developing with each additional account.

You're probably already thinking of possible extensions of LEA: For example, the steps to a science experiment can be dictated and written down; a list of supplies or things to do can be dictated; the classroom "rules" can be generated and written down within an LEA-type format. Important objects and centers in the classroom can be named and labeled. What is common to each of these applications is the fact that language and experience are linked in meaningful contexts for children learning to read.

EMERGENT WRITING

We could have been discussing young children's writing throughout this chapter; but because of its importance in facilitating emergent concepts about print and about reading, it deserves its own section. All the understandings about print—its features and its functions—are reinforced through writing.

In this final portion of the chapter, we will take a look at children's emergent writing. Young children learn to write just as they learn to read—by watching others write and by having opportunities to produce print on their own, as well as by spending much time surrounded by adults who help them construct meaning during authentic reading and writing experiences. Young writers, when supported and prompted to put crayon, marker, pencil, or paintbrush to paper, can create marvelously interesting and expressive compositions. But in order for children to freely communicate their ideas on paper, they must know that what they produce will be accepted and valued. Therefore, our job as classroom teachers is to ensure that an environment exists where children are willing to take risks.

As we guide children in their literacy growth, we need to incorporate daily planned experiences that bring reading and writing together. Scheduling structured classroom time for young preschool children to write and share their work will be essential to expanding the risk-taking environment that invites expression with print. In the sections that follow, I will make suggestions and give examples for encouraging young children to write, all of which will blend and mingle naturally with those made previously for the development of emergent reading.

Encouraging risk-taking by young writers

When children are allowed and encouraged to write, they will usually attempt to re-create the kinds of print and visual displays they see in their environment—including, of course, books. Their developing understandings of the conventions and features of print are exercised and reinforced through their explorations with writing. Their ability to reflect on language as an object—that is, to be metalinguistically aware—develops through their early writing attempts.

We need to encourage the same *degree* of risk-taking with writing as we do with reading. Just as young children will often invent the text they believe goes along with the pictures in a book as they "pretend read," they will invent their writing; this free abandon is valuable and necessary. And it is worth noting that "most children make essentially the same discoveries about [writing], in the same order" (Temple et al., 1993, p. 2).

The nature and complexity of any particular composition by an emergent writer depends on the task he or she has set. For example, when a child is writing a "story," her writing often looks like ~~~~~~~~; when she labels her drawings, the writing usually will include recognizable letters and, late in the emergent phase, invented spellings. It is not until most children are well into first grade that invented spelling attempts consistently occur (Teale & Sulzby, 1989). When invented spellings do occur, however, they can be an excellent indicator of the degree of a child's phonemic awareness. For example, the child who writes *ILKDGSNKTS* ("I like dogs and cats") is able to attend primarily to individual consonant sounds within a syllable.

The "graphics" that children create follow a developmental path that in broad strokes evolves from random scribbles to more finely differentiated marks that look like letters. Along the way, children develop tacit understandings about the principles that govern the physical appearance of writing. In her research, Marie Clay (1975) has identified some of these; Figure 3.4 gives examples.

Flexibility principle: The features that make up *letters* can be flexibly combined to create new letters.

Recurring principle: A limited number of letters (or drawings, for that matter) recur over and over.

Generativity principle: Letters can be combined in different ways to generate different-looking text.

In Figure 3.4 you can see how a child is flexibly experimenting with the features of letters. Some of his letters are actual letters but others are not, though they *could* be; and part of what children learn is of course the narrowing-down of possible letters to only those that we use in English. The recurring principle is nicely illustrated in picture and in print; it is almost as if children have noticed that print and pictures usually "fill up" a page, and they are going to do the same! So they fill up the space, using a particular drawing or a limited number of the letters that they *do* know. Eventually, children learn that letters are used in different combinations or patterns. The children may be quite uncertain about what "words" in print are, but they *have* noticed that letters can be arranged in various ways.

Children's characters and letters—the print—will begin to match up to spoken language more systematically. For so many children this correspondence first begins at the *syllable* level: a five-year-old will explain to you that the letters *IYSC* say "I want some candy!" Obviously, the children are matching up one letter with one syllable. Later still, they will write primarily in *consonant* letters, using few vowel letters: "I want some candy" may now be written as *IWNTSMKNDE.*

All this experimentation, play, and "hypothesis-testing" with print lays an extremely important foundation for children's learning about the actual letters that we use to write and the names of those letters. It is no accident that children who have been allowed to play with writing this way usually learn the alphabet and the letter names more quickly than children who have had few or no such

MMMOOO
MMMOOO
MMMOOO
MMMOOO
MMMOOO

EMDAVB

AMASESSAMA

Figure 3.4
Principles of Writing That Young Children Learn

experiences. Even more important, though, these children usually learn to read and write conventionally much more easily than other children do. We'll explore the implications of this a little later.

Children learn about the features and the principles of writing through copying and tracing and by generating their own characters (Clay, 1975; Ferreiro & Teberosky, 1982; Goodman, 1990). If we provide them with a printed version of their names, they will often trace over them. Copying is a bit more demanding, but children seem to enjoy doing it; many of them will spend a considerable amount of time copying the print they see around them in their preschool or kindergarten classroom. And (as we have already seen) if we allow and encourage them to do so, they will spend a lot of time simply generating or inventing their own characters.

By studying preschool children's writing and looking at what adults do in responding to these writings, one finding emerges as extremely significant: when adults respond to children's writing as if it is "real" writing, as if it really does "say something," this shows respect and value for what the children have done. With this atmosphere of acceptance consistently available, young children will enjoy writing and will engage spontaneously in writing activities.

Planned experiences to facilitate writing

If children are to become comfortable with expressing their thoughts on paper, they must have practice in doing it. Awakening their interest in books and

A writing center is a must in the preschool or kindergarten classroom. It is a place where materials are available and stored, as well as a work space for the children. The following materials should be available:

■ All kinds of writing materials—different-colored markers, pencils (thin as well as fat but not too sharp), colored chalk, crayons
■ Sharpeners for crayons and pencils, scissors, tape, glue, stapler
■ Magnetic letters, Linkletters®, letter blocks, Play-doh®

■ All different kinds of paper, including scrap paper (newsprint and large-size computer paper from businesses and schools—one side will be printed on, but the other side is always blank). Also, old wallpaper samples are great; often they are bound in a sample book and are easily cut out. They are excellent for decorative art work to embellish a "composition" in collage style, and they work very well as covers for journals and little books the children create and use.

LEARNING IN CONTEXT: **Writing should be natural and enjoyable for young children, but we must provide appropriate space and materials to allow natural expression to occur.**

reading requires that children be involved in hearing stories read to them as well as in retelling and "reading" familiar stories themselves. The same holds true for writing. Young children will naturally model adult writing behavior in a supportive environment. With kindergartners and first-graders, you will want to enhance their development in communicating their ideas through print, by immersing them in opportunities to write.

Within the dynamic, interactive type of language and literacy climate I'll be describing throughout this textbook, the possibilities for writing activities are almost limitless. I would like to share several with you now. Although I have in mind primarily a classroom setting, many of these suggestions apply to the home environment as well and may be offered to parents. I would like to make another useful instructional point here: while many of these activities will benefit a good number of preschool children, some or all may not be appropriate for other preschoolers until they are well into their first-grade year. This may be due to their place along the developmental literacy continuum or due to their social development; they may not be able to remain focused and to work collaboratively with others for longer periods of time.

Extending Writing into the Shared-Book Experience and Language Experience Approach Once children have had plenty of opportunities sharing books with the process described on pages 110–112, you can use the predictable text to model alternate versions of the patterned language. The example above uses the text from Joy Cowley's *In a Dark, Dark Wood.* In this case, you can begin by using the patterned language to fashion a similar story with a new setting. Instead of using *dark, dark wood,* ask children to offer suggestions for an alternate location: garden, playground, bakery, stable. Once you have decided on a location, move to finding a descriptive word that will complement the setting: *flowery, flowery garden; friendly, friendly playground; dusty, dusty stable.* You can then move on to three or four objects that would naturally be part of that setting. A small group of first-graders wrote:

> In a green, green garden, there was a green, green plant. On that green, green plant grew some green, green leaves. On the green, green leaves crawled a green, green caterpillar. On the green, green caterpillar were dark, dark spots. The green, green caterpillar crawled up the green, green plant to a red, red flower. And when the green, green caterpillar reached the red, red flower . . . BOO! . . . out popped a bee.

The group composed the story orally while the teacher recorded their words in Language Experience fashion on chart paper, stopping occasionally to reread portions of the original book. As the children were composing, they found the need to make some changes in sentence sequencing and verb choice, as well as the conclusion. The adjustments they made added to the flow and meaning of their story, thus involving them in decision-making about how to change the pattern to meet the needs of their own composition. This story can be reread from the chart, or it can be typed in small-book form, with each child illustrating his or her own copy. Group composing in this manner provides a model for how to go about writing a story based on a story the children already know.

As young students' knowledge of print grows, you can prepare for each child a one- or two-page small book typed with just a skeleton framework of words on each page. Then children can each create a *dark, dark wood* story by writing an individual version of the text. For example, the first page might look like this:

> In a ＿＿＿, ＿＿＿ ＿＿＿ there was a ＿＿＿, ＿＿＿ ＿＿＿.

Together, you and a student can complete the story. Children make their best attempts at spelling the words they want to use in their own stories. You may opt to print below the child's writing so that both of you will remember what was written, but this isn't necessary. The child can illustrate the small book and share it with several other classmates, taking it home that day to be shared with a family member. The quickness with which small books like this can be created gives children a great sense of accomplishment. They are eager and responsive to composing books that they can then read.

Other extensions to having children compose in the Language Experience fashion can include having them write their reactions to classroom activities. This works particularly well for field trips and classroom guests. You can create a class chart on the day of the event. On the days following the activity, you can prepare individual small books where you have printed the beginning words of each sentence, or you might prepare one sheet for each child, to be compiled into a class book. The children complete their own books or sheets individually, personalizing the pages with their own illustrations and any additional sentences or words they wish to include. In this way you can create your own repetitive texts. Once the class books have been read several times in whole-class or small-group settings, most of the children will have memorized the text; and even though the book may be quite long and some of the invented spelling a bit difficult to make out, the children can read it without hesitation, given the book's repetitive phrasing along with the pictures to help. A text of that nature would look something like this:

page 1: On our field trip we saw _____.

page 2: We saw _____.

page 3: We saw _____.

page 4: We saw _____.

final page: We liked _____ the best.

Journals   Although we want to give children opportunities to construct their own books at a writing center, preparing bound journals for each child, with enough paper for daily entries for a week or so, will help give students a sense of permanency about their writing. Journals of this nature are nothing more than six to ten sheets of unlined paper stapled between pages of colored construction paper. Many teachers glue an alphabet chart to the inside cover, for easy reference when children can't remember what a particular letter looks like. On the pages of a journal, students can write whatever they want to. Very young children's first journals will most likely be collections of drawings accompanied by dictated stories.

When first introducing journals to a group of kindergartners or first-graders, you will need to impress upon them the value of using each page to keep ideas and thoughts, tell stories and make drawings—the main focus being on using each page to its best advantage. Most teachers limit children to one page per day. If this is not made clear to the young writer, he or she will quickly put a line on each page of the journal and announce that it is all done. Once children have the concept that they can use the space to write and draw anything they wish, you will begin to see them saving ideas to record in their journals. As time progresses, they will look back and revisit previously composed pieces, add to the text and drawings, or continue with similar or extended topics. Even though they may not be able to reread what they have written, they will joyously look back over their work; fortunately the drawings usually provide a clue and will send the child into a retelling of what the page is about.

■ A CONCLUDING PERSPECTIVE

In this chapter, we have seen how print is inescapably present in young children's worlds. They can learn from the environmental print that surrounds them. They can learn from the storybooks read to them—from the comments on stories and print and from the questions and language growth that occur in the context of booksharing. They can learn much from the functional roles that they see literacy serving in people's day-to-day lives. As a consequence of all these types of experiences, young children can construct a solid intuitive understanding of the nature and functions of reading and writing.

Over time, young children begin to make distinctions between drawing and print or writing. Gradually, they realize that print doesn't just "hang around" with pictures but somehow refers to something else. They begin to differentiate among letters and to develop the understanding that letters are very important elements in print. Eventually they will begin to understand that these letters can stand not for concrete objects themselves, but for speech. This emergent ability to step back and attend to the *sounds* of language apart from the *meaning* is part of *metalinguistic awareness*. This dawning awareness is critical because it forms the foundation for children's later understanding of individual sounds within *words,* as well as of the concept of a "word" itself. Once children can match words in print to the stream of speech, they are able to attend consciously to *every* sound in a word. This degree of *phonemic awareness* is necessary in order for children to learn to read in a conventional sense, attending to how language and ideas are conventionally represented in print.

All these understandings may develop *when literate adults are interacting with the child in the context of print.* Young children need literate adults to help them negotiate the medium of print. Moreover, these understandings can develop through more deliberate efforts to show children how reading "works." As teachers, we model the conventions, features, and nature of the reading process through "shared book" experiences and the Language Experience Approach. We also read to children, and through our comments and questions begin to involve them in understanding and reflecting on what is being read.

We have seen how *writing* can reveal children's emerging understandings about how print "works." As a meaningful activity, writing is extremely potent in helping children develop and exercise their concepts and understandings about the function and features of print. So to the classic question with which we began this chapter, "When is a child 'ready' to read?" we can answer, "*All* the time."

Now, having explored the richness of children's construction of emerging literacy knowledge, it's time to turn our attention to setting up the environment in which conventional reading will develop.

■ BECOMING A REFLECTIVE PRACTITIONER

Egan, K. (1987). Literacy and the oral foundations of education. *Harvard Educational Review, 57,* 445–472.

Kieran Egan has been quite influential in the area of early childhood education. This article presents ideas about children and curriculum that Egan has explored more extensively in his subsequent work, but it provides a foundation for this work and conveniently does so in the space of one article. Egan examines the nature and function of oral language in nonliterate communities and compares it with the potential of preschool children's language in literate societies. He argues for increased understanding of this potential and suggests how we can build a curriculum for young children that is strongly grounded in their language and their experience. Such a curriculum will more naturally help children with the transition from "orality" to literacy.

Hiebert, E. (1986). Issues related to home influences on young children's print-related development. In D. Yaden, Jr., S. Templeton (Eds.), *Metalinguistic awareness and beginning literacy: Conceptualizing what it means to read and write* (pp. 145–158). Portsmouth, NH: Heinemann Educational Books.

In her research, Elfrieda Hiebert has for many years addressed issues related to early literacy development. This chapter provides an excellent foundation in this area; Hiebert explores issues (such as the nature of different types of parent/child interactions during literacy events and the characteristics of home intervention programs) that in subsequent years have been intensively investigated both by her and by several other researchers.

McCormick, C., & Mason, J. (1986). Intervention procedures for increasing pre-school children's interest in and knowledge about reading. In W. Teale & E. Sulzby (Eds.), *Emergent literacy: Writing and reading* (pp. 90–115). Norwood, NJ: Ablex.

Jana Mason and Christine McCormick have been involved in both basic and applied research into the nature of young children's emergent/beginning literacy and the effects of different types of literacy interventions. Much of their work is directed at families outside the mainstream. While they have continued their investigations in this area since this publication, this particular chapter is representative of their work and presents an excellent overview of the problems to be addressed and the characteristics of successful efforts to meet these challenges.

Morris, D. (1993). The relationship between children's concept of word in text and phoneme awareness in learning to read: A longitudinal study. *Research in the Teaching of English, 27,* 133–154.

Elaborating on Marie Clay's conception of the voice-to-print match, Darrell Morris's research exploring *concept of word in text* has helped us understand more precisely *how* this match develops. In previous studies, Morris has found that emergent readers' knowledge of beginning consonants helped them locate printed words in text, which then helped them become aware of individual phonemes. This particular study reviews that work and demonstrates that these earlier hypotheses hold true within the *same* children throughout their kindergarten year. Moreover, Morris found that once children were aware of both consonant and vowel phonemes within words, their word recognition abilities developed more rapidly.

Sulzby, E. (1985). Children's emergent reading of favorite storybooks: A developmental study. *Reading Research Quarterly, 20,* 458–481.

Sulzby traces the development of two-, three-, and four-year olds as well as kindergarten children's attention to and understanding of different features of storybooks. While there is variability of some type from one child to the next, in general young children seem to follow a developmental pattern in which they attend first to the pictures and gradually over time realize that print exists and that *it* somehow conveys meaning; this development is strongly dependent on literate adults interacting with them and discussing the book.

Yaden, D., Jr., Smolkin, L., & Conlon, A. (1989). Preschoolers' questions about pictures, print convention, and story text during reading aloud at home. *Reading Research Quarterly, 24,* 188–214.

This article provides an excellent example of the more "naturalistic" studies that yield insights based on extensive observation of young children engaging in "literacy events" with adults. Yaden and his colleagues intensively examined the types of questions preschoolers ages three to five asked during readaloud sessions in the home. The range of questions these children asked was considerable: they asked about characters, events, motives, word meanings, features of print, and the nature of reading—just to highlight a few question types. Interestingly, the article concludes that parent/

child interaction during readalouds may influence comprehension processes more than it does print awareness.

■ REFERENCES

Adams, M. (1990). *Beginning to read: Thinking and learning about print.* Cambridge, MA: MIT Press.

Bradley, L., & Bryant, P. (1985). *Rhyme and reason in reading and spelling.* Ann Arbor, MI: University of Michigan Press.

Campbell, J. (1966). *The hero with 1,000 faces.* Princeton, NJ: Princeton University Press.

Chomsky, C. (1972). Stages in language development and reading exposure. *Harvard Educational Review, 42,* 1–33.

Chomsky, C. (1974). Invented spelling in first grade. Harvard Graduate School of Education. Mimeographed. Cited in G. Bissex, (1980), *GNYS AT WRK: A child learns to write and read* (p. 203). Cambridge, MA: Harvard University Press.

Clay, M. (1975). *What did I write? Beginning writing behavior.* Exeter, NH: Heinemann.

Clay, M. (1991). *Becoming literate: The construction of inner control.* Portsmouth, NH: Heinemann.

Cochran-Smith, M. (1984). *The making of a reader.* Norwood, NJ: Ablex.

deVilliers, J., & deVilliers, P. (1978). *Language acquisition.* Cambridge: Harvard University Press.

Downing, J., & Valtin, R. (Eds.). (1985). *Language awareness and learning to read.* New York: Springer-Verlag.

Dyson, A. (1990). The role of stories in the social imagination of childhood and beyond. *New Advocate, 3,* 179–195.

Egan, K. (1987). Literacy and the oral foundations of education. *Harvard Educational Review, 57,* 445–472.

Ehri, L., & Wilce, L. (1987). Does learning to spell help beginners learn to read words? *Reading Research Quarterly, 22,* 47–65.

Ehri, L. (1994). Development of the ability to read words: Update. In R. Ruddell, M. Ruddell, & H. Singer (Eds.), *Theoretical models and processes of reading* (4th Ed.) (pp. 328–358). Newark, DE: International Reading Association.

Ehri, L., Deffner, N., & Wilce, L. (1984). Pictorial mnemonics for phonics. *Journal of Educational Psychology, 76,* 880–893.

Ferreiro, E. (1984). The underlying logic of literacy development. In H. Goelman, A. Oberg, & F. Smith (Eds.), *Awakening to literacy.* Portsmouth, NH: Heinemann.

Ferreiro, E. (1986). The interplay between information and assimilation in beginning literacy. In W. Teale & E. Sulzby (Eds.), *Emergent literacy: Writing and reading* (pp. 15–49). Norwood, NJ: Ablex.

Ferreiro, E. (1990). Literacy development: Psychogenesis. In Y. Goodman (Ed.), *How children construct literacy: Piagetian perspectives* (pp. 12–25). Newark, DE: International Reading Association.

Ferreiro, E., & Teberosky, A. (1982). *Literacy before schooling.* Exeter, NH: Heinemann Educational Books.

Galda, L., et al. (1989). A short-term longitudinal study of preschoolers' emergent literacy. *Research in the Teaching of English, 23,* 292–309.

Gardner, H. (1991). *The unschooled mind.* New York: Basic Books.

Gibson, E. (1970). The ontogeny of reading. *American Psychologist, 25,* 136–145.

Goodman, Y. (Ed.). (1990). *How children construct literacy: Piagetian perspectives.* Newark, DE: International Reading Association.

Goswami, U., & Bryant, P. (1991). Rhyme, analogy, and children's reading. In P. Gough, L. Ehri, & R. Treiman (Eds.), *Reading Acquisition* (pp. 49–63). Hillsdale, NJ: Lawrence Erlbaum Associates.

Hall, M. (1981). Teaching reading as a language experience (3rd ed.). Columbus, OH: Merrill.

Harrison, L., & McKee, P. (1971). *Getting ready to read.* Boston: Houghton Mifflin.

Heald-Taylor, G. (1987). Predictable literature selections and activities for language arts instruction. *The Reading Teacher, 41,* 6–12.

Heath, S. (1983). *Ways with words.* Cambridge: Cambridge University Press.

Henderson, E. (1979). *The cloth book and the beginnings of literacy.* Unpublished manuscript, University of Virginia.

Henderson, E. (1981). *Learning to read and spell.* DeKalb, IL: Northern Illinois University Press.

Hiebert, E. (1986). Issues related to home influences on young children's print-related development. In D. Yaden, Jr., & S. Templeton (Eds.), *Metalinguistic awareness and beginning literacy: Conceptualizing what it means to read and write* (pp. 145–158). Portsmouth, NH: Heinemann.

Holdaway, D. (1979). *The foundations of literacy.* Sydney, AUS: Ashton Scholastic.

Holdaway, D. (1986). The visual face of experience and language: A metalinguistic excursion. In D. Yaden, Jr., & S. Templeton (Eds.), *Metalinguistic awareness and beginning reading: Conceptualizing what it means to read and write* (pp. 79–97). Portsmouth, NH: Heinemann.

Kaisen, J. (1987). SSR/Booktime: Kindergarten and first grade sustained silent reading. *Reading Teacher, 40,* 532–536.

Lomax, R., & McGee, L. (1987). Young children's concepts about print and reading: Toward a model of word reading acquisition. *Reading Research Quarterly, 22,* 237–256.

Martinez, M., & Teale, W. (1988). The ins and outs of a kindergarten writing program. *Reading Teacher, 41,* 568–573.

Mason, J. (1980). When *do* children begin to read: An exploration of four-year-old children's letter and word reading competencies. *Reading Research Quarterly, 15,* 203–227.

Mason, J., Peterman, C., & Kerr, B. (1989). Reading to kindergarten children. In D. Strickland & L. Morrow (Eds.), *Emerging literacy: Young children learn to read and write.* Newark, DE: International Reading Association.

McCormick, C., & Mason, J. (1986). Intervention procedures for increasing preschool children's interest in and knowledge about reading. In W. Teale & E. Sulzby (Eds.), *Emergent literacy: Writing and reading* (pp. 90–115). Norwood, NJ: Ablex.

McGee, L., & Richgels, D. (1990). *Literacy's beginnings.* Boston: Allyn & Bacon.

Miller, J. (1990). Three-year-olds in their reading corner. *Young Children, 46,* 51–54.

Morris, D. (1980). Beginning readers' concept of word. In E. Henderson and J. Beers (Eds.), *Developmental and cognitive aspects of learning to spell: A reflection of word knowledge* (pp. 97–111). Newark, DE: International Reading Association.

Morris, D. (1983). Concept of word and phoneme awareness in the beginning reader. *Research in the Teaching of English, 17,* 359–373.

Morris, D. (1992). Concept of word: A pivotal understanding in the learning to read process. In S. Templeton & D. Bear (Eds.), *Development of orthographic knowledge and the foundations of literacy: A memorial festschrift for Edmund Henderson* (53–77). Hillsdale, NJ: Erlbaum.

Ninio, A. (1980). Picture book reading in mother-infant dyads belonging to two subgroups in Israel. *Child Development, 51,* 587–590.

Olson, D. (1984) See, Jumping! In H. Goelman, A. Oberg, & F. Smith (Eds.), *Awakening to literacy.* Portsmouth, NH: Heinemann.

Pappas, C. (1990, April). Young children's discourse strategies in using the story and information book genres: An analysis of kindergartners' understandings of co-referentiality and co-classification. Paper presented at the World Congress of Applied Linguistics, Thessalonika, Greece.

Pellegrini, A. (1990). Joint reading between Black Head Start Children and their mothers. *Child Development, 61,* 443–453.

Piaget, J., & Inhelder, B. (1969). *The language and thought of the child.* New York: Basic Books.

Pikulski, J., & Cooper, J. (1991). *Houghton Mifflin Literature Experience.* Boston: Houghton Mifflin Company.

Reading in junior classes (1985). Wellington, NZ: Department of Education.

Resnick, M. (1987). Mothers reading to infants: A new observational tool. *Reading Teacher, 40,* 892.

Roberts, B. (1992). The evolution of the young child's concept of *word* as a unit of spoken and written language. *Reading Research Quarterly, 27,* 124–138.

Rowe, D. (1990, December). Author/audience interaction in the preschool: The role of social interaction in literacy learning. *Journal of Reading Behavior, 7,* 311–349.

Smolkin, L., Yaden, D., Jr., & Conlon, A. (1988). An exploratory examination of the effect of print salience in picture books on preschoolers' questions and comments. Paper presented at the annual meeting of the National Reading Conference, Tucson, AZ.

Slaughter, J. (1993). Beyond storybooks: Young children and the shared book experience. Newark, DE: International Reading Association.

Snow, C. (1983). Literacy and language: Relationships during the preschool years. *Harvard Educational Review, 53,* 165–189.

Snow, C., Dubber, C., & DeBlauw, A. (1982). Routines in mother-child interaction. In L. Feagans & D. Farran (Eds.), *The language of children reared in poverty* (pp. 53–72). New York: Academic Press.

Snow, C., & Goldfield, B. (1983). Turn the page, please: Situation-specific language acquisition. *Journal of Child Language, 10,* 551–569.

Stauffer, R. (1970). *The language experience approach to the teaching of reading.* New York: Harper & Row.

Strickland, D., & Morrow, L. (Eds.). (1989). *Emerging literacy: Young children learn to read and write*. Newark, DE: International Reading Association.

Sulzby, E. (1989). Assessment of writing and of children's language while writing. In L. Morrow & J. Smith (Eds.), *The role of assessment and measurement in early literacy instruction* (pp. 83–109). Englewood Cliffs, NJ: Prentice-Hall.

Sulzby, E., & Teale, W. (1991). Emergent literacy. In R. Barr, M. Kamil, P., Mosenthal, & P. Pearson (Eds.), *Handbook of reading research* (Vol. 2), (pp. 727–757). New York: Longman.

Taylor, D., & Dorsey-Gaines, C. (1988). *Growing up literate: Learning from innercity families*. Portsmouth, NH: Heinemann.

Taylor, D., & Strickland, D. (1986). Family literacy: Myths and magic. In M. Sampson (Ed.), *The pursuit of literacy: Early reading and writing*. Dubuque, IA: Kendall-Hunt.

Taylor, D., & Strickland, D. (1989). Learning from families: Implications for educators and policy. In J. Allen & J. Mason (Eds.), *Risk makers risk takers risk breakers: Reducing the risks for young literacy learners* (pp. 251–276). Portsmouth, NH: Heinemann.

Teale, W., & Sulzby, E. (Eds.). (1986). *Emergent literacy: Writing and reading*. Norwood, NJ: Ablex.

Teale, W., & Sulzby, E. (1989). Emergent literacy: New perspectives. In D. Strickland and L. Morrow (Eds.), *Emerging literacy: Young children learn to read and write*. Newark, DE: International Reading Association.

Temple, C., Nathan, R., Temple, F., & Burns, N. (1993). *The beginnings of writing* (3rd ed.). Boston: Allyn & Bacon.

Templeton, S. (1991). *Teaching the integrated language arts*. Boston: Houghton Mifflin.

Tunmer, W., Pratt, C., & Herriman, M. (Eds.). (1984). *Language awareness in children*. New York: Springer-Verlag.

Vellutino, F., & Scanlon, D. (1986). Linguistic coding and metalinguistic awareness. In D. Yaden, Jr., & S. Templeton (Eds.), *Metalinguistic awareness and beginning literacy: Conceptualizing what it means to read and write* (pp. 115–141). Portsmouth, NH: Heinemann.

Wells, G. (1987). Apprenticeship in literacy. *Interchange, 18,* 109–123.

Whitehurst, G., Falco, F., Lonigan, C., Fischel, J., Debaryshe, B., Valdez-Menchaca, M., & Caulfield, M. (1988). Accelerating language development through picture book reading. *Developmental Psychology, 24,* 552–559.

Yaden, D., & McGee, L. (1984). Reading as a meaning-seeking activity: What children's questions reveal. In J. Niles & L. Harris (Eds.), *Changing perspectives on research in reading/language processing and instruction* (pp. 101–109). Rochester, NY: National Reading Conference.

Yaden, D., Jr., Smolkin, L., & Conlon, A. (1989). Preschoolers' questions about pictures, print convention, and story text during reading aloud at home. *Reading Research Quarterly, 24,* 188–214.

Yaden, D., Jr., & Templeton, S. (1986). Introduction: Metalinguistic awareness: An Etymology. In D. Yaden, Jr., & S. Templeton (Eds.), *Metalinguistic awareness and beginning reading: Conceptualizing what it means to read and write* (pp. 3–10). Portsmouth, NH: Heinemann.

PART TWO

LITERACY

INSTRUCTION

IN ACTION

*When children begin to read in a conventional sense, and on
throughout the elementary school years, how do we facilitate
their processes of constructing meaning? In this part, we
describe ways you can arrange your classroom to optimize
children's interaction and growth in literacy. We extend what
you learned about emergent literacy into beginning
conventional reading development and instruction. We focus
on narratives and informational reading, address intermediate
children's exploration of words and their structure and
conclude by looking at thematic units.*

CHAPTER FOUR

ORGANIZING, ASSESSING, AND GROUPING FOR READING INSTRUCTION

FOCUS

■ *How can you best arrange your classroom and organize and allot your time?*

■ *How can you help the children develop a sense of "ownership" of their classroom and of their learning?*

■ *How can initial and ongoing informal assessment be used in making instructional decisions?*

■ *Why is it important to have children work in both heterogeneous and homogeneous small groups?*

■ *What are some of the management issues involved in working with several small groups at a time?*

■ *How do the factors of classroom organization and grouping children for instruction work together in the collaborative interactive classroom?*

THE COLLABORATIVE INTERACTIVE CLASSROOM: OVERALL CLIMATE

ORGANIZING THE CLASSROOM FOR INSTRUCTION
Organizing the Physical Environment • Organizing Classroom Time for Instruction
• MAKING CONNECTIONS: Getting to Know Your Students Before You "Know"
Them • MAKING CONNECTIONS: Getting to Know Your Peer Teachers and the Staff
• MAKING CONNECTIONS: How Integrated Instruction Affects Your Planning and
Scheduling

GROUPING FOR INSTRUCTION
Taking a New Look at Grouping • Defining a Variety of Small Groups • Forming,
Unforming, and Re-forming Groups • Managing Groups in the Classroom • BUILDING
YOUR KNOWLEDGE BASE: Resource Books for Setting Up a Collaborative Classroom
• MAKING CONNECTIONS: Preventing Discipline Problems: A Dialogue Between Denise
Jackson and Brian Sable • Other Instructional Settings

A CONCLUDING PERSPECTIVE

BECOMING A REFLECTIVE PRACTITIONER

REFERENCES

Those of us who have written within a community of writers and read within a community of readers know that these communities have a different feel. They have a sense of intimacy and of adventure.
                        Lucy McCormick Calkins, Living Between the Lines

Classrooms where children understand the purpose of their work and have a sense of attachment and responsibility to their own and their classmates' learning will have the special "feel," or aura, that conveys the warmth of belonging. Learning is going to occur best when students are *motivated* and guided by a classroom organization that fosters productive, social interaction. The way we teachers organize a classroom environment is intended to work in conjunction with our understanding of both the reading process and the social nature of learning. As you create a classroom environment that will help children construct meaning in a purposeful context, while you also are carefully accounting for their developmental needs and diverse backgrounds, you will need to consider the following four factors.

Use of curricular objectives to provide a framework for planning and organizing instruction

Opportunities for students to have audiences outside their own classroom

Ways for small-group work and peer collaboration to advance and support learning

Use of initial and ongoing assessment practices that guide instructional choices

How to implement these factors is what we'll be discussing in this chapter. We'll first look at the materials and supplies most likely to be at hand, as well as at those you will probably need to gather. Then we will examine what you'll need to accomplish before the school year begins and later, as the school days move along, in regard to setting up a physical environment that will encourage children's interaction and collaboration. Finally, the chapter will deal with organizing, managing, and structuring small groups. We will appraise the use of various kinds of groups within a cooperative learning environment. You will see *how* group work can be initiated and sustained—because much, if not most, of what the children will be doing will be accomplished by them as members of a bustling, interactive learning community.

THE COLLABORATIVE INTERACTIVE CLASSROOM: OVERALL CLIMATE

The overall atmosphere of the collaborative interactive classroom encourages talk and welcomes individual opinions. Here, children work individually and in a variety of groupings. In this type of classroom, each child's family culture is honored, instructional techniques embrace students' diversity, and teacher and students make decisions together about literacy events.

Upon entering this type of classroom, you are likely to see children working all over the room: at tables, behind bookshelves, or in clusters on a carpet area. Denise Jackson's multigrade classroom is such a place. The class's current integrated language arts unit is centered around Ezra Jack Keats's writing and illustrations. Denise has gathered a group of beginning readers at a table to enjoy rereadings of *Over in the Meadow* and *A Snowy Day*. While Denise works with her small group, the rest of the children engage in several different independent activities. Three boys are clustered behind the sink area with their writers' workshop files. Each has stapled several sheets of paper together to make a small book. Together they have decided to write about several characters that appear throughout Keats's stories, and they are chattering about their compositions. Matthew, Si-Yi, and Wang have chosen to model their writing after *Regards to the Man in the Moon*.

Matthew tells his partners, "Let's send the kids on another outer-space adventure! We can change the design of the bathtub spaceship to include turbo engines so they can get past the meteor field. What do you think?"

Si-Yi responds, "I can help a little. I'll make a list of things the kids could take, like paper and pencils and crayons and markers. They will need those things so they can remember what they saw."

Wang holds up his drawing of the kids' bathtub spaceship and adds, "You guys can do the story and I'll draw the pictures. I'll listen and you tell me what you write, so I'll know what to draw."

In the library corner Tessa, a third-grader, and Selina, a first-grader, snuggle together in the beanbag chair. They're holding a copy of Ezra Jack Keats's *Apt. 3* between them. They read aloud, stopping to make intermittent comments about the dark colors Keats has chosen and how the colors make them feel as if they too are in the apartment building. Several other children listen to a recording of Keats's *John Henry: An American Legend*. At desks, pairs of children read, discuss, and respond to *Peter's Chair*, *Goggles*, and *Whistle for Willie*. As follow-up activities, some are working on story maps; others are creating collage illustrations; still others are composing personal written responses. As small-group work time is completed, the children gather on the carpet to give an oral synopsis of the work they have completed that morning, as well as to share suggestions for tomorrow's work time. The session closes with Denise reading aloud *A Letter to Amy*.

The first-, second-, and third-graders in Denise Jackson's classroom are working within a strongly organized framework. They each have a clear idea of responsibility to themselves and to the other students. This isn't a quiet classroom, yet the noise level is not high enough to cause distraction. During the scheduled time for small-group work, the children know they have a choice of projects that must be in final form by the end of the week. They also are aware that they will be moving in and out of several different small groups. For this unit of study on Ezra Jack Keats, Denise has chosen to have her students work in assigned groups as well as in self-selected interest groups.

This brief discussion of Denise Jackson's classroom and her topic of study, the work of Ezra Jack Keats, can help us understand the ideas behind integrated, collaborative, and interactive learning. As we picture the surroundings and atmosphere in which Denise's students live and learn during their time at school, you know that the activities she structures for her students would not be possible without open space for children to cluster in, writing and art supplies, a substantial selection of children's literature, and tables for small groups.

The physical arrangement of Denise's classroom functions in concert with the literacy activities. Her students talk with one another; compose and create their own stories; read, discuss, and then respond with both written work and visual production. By providing choices of highly social, interactive activities, Denise gives her young students opportunities to use their time productively. The topics of classroom organization and small-group selection are indeed critical issues, ones that will set the stage for your entire instructional year.

ORGANIZING THE CLASSROOM FOR INSTRUCTION

Since the classroom is a home for the children during their school hours, it needs to be a place where they'll feel comfortable and safe. The arrangement of desks and chairs contributes to the type of atmosphere that prevails: desks in rows will give a different "feel" than desks arranged in clusters. A good physical environment will simulate a community setting that supports interaction and communication.

Children love to feel a sense of "ownership" in the classroom—that it is *their* community, that it reflects who they are and what they do, and that they have a stake in how it functions. And once they acquire this sense of ownership, they begin to understand the importance of their role as decision-makers and risk takers (Hansen, 1987). You *can* retain control in the classroom, yet help children develop this sense of ownership and community—but this all depends on how you go about it.

Let's look again at Denise Jackson's classroom—in particular, at how she has combined the organization of the physical environment with the formatting of instructional time. She has had to allow for her own preparation time in gathering books and other materials, in addition to anticipating what supplies her students will need to carry out their projects. It's now evident to us that decisions about instructional time, the environmental setup, curriculum choices, student input, and classroom atmosphere should merge to present an organized whole, the collaborative interactive classroom.

Organizing the physical environment

When we consider the actual hands-on organizing of a classroom physical environment, the two most obvious needs are to gather materials and to arrange the furniture and the work areas. Let's first think about some specific materials that help make a collaborative interactive classroom run smoothly.

Gathering and Assembling Materials   Many schools have set procedures for distributing supplies to each teacher. Some school systems will give you money for the year and ask you to order your learning materials and other supplies, while other school systems simply provide what the officials think you need. Upon arrival in my very first classroom, I was taken aback by its bareness. There were two tables—one of them stacked with basal readers and math books, twenty-five desks and chairs, and one bookshelf. This tends to be a common experience for most beginning teachers.

To start, you will want to set up a "central supply" area with some or all of the following items: pencils, markers, glue, a variety of writing and construction paper, paper clips, scissors, staplers, tape, and erasers, in addition to wallpaper scraps, yarn, fabric, and a variety of other craft items. Having a central area where supplies are easily accessible will make project work more manageable, especially when the small items are readily available.

Next, you will need to make sure you have an updated globe or world map, a map of your state, and a local city map. Children will enjoy using them to locate story settings, visitors' hometowns, and authors' birthplaces. You would also find it helpful to have an overhead projector, tape recorder, cassette or record player, and large writing easel. A computer or two in the classroom would be ideal, but some schools house their computers in one main lab. No matter what materials you have or can assemble, you should think carefully about their use and placement.

Books and Learning Materials   Since the children will be reading and writing within an integrated instructional framework, the books and other learning materials you collect will be directly related to whatever topics you investigate. Trade books (books that are not considered textbooks) will be of utmost importance as the mainstay of your reading program. Therefore, you will need to collect them from as many different sources as necessary. For example, if you are going to begin the school year with a study of "seeds," you will need to check with your school, city, or county librarians in order to borrow single or multiple copies of trade books—both fiction and nonfiction—that support your topic.

If you have been doing planning with other teachers at your grade level—or with those who share your orientation to integrated reading and writing programs—you might consider sharing books and project ideas. If your school is using a published reading program, it may offer stories and poems that complement a particular cross-curricular topic of study; and depending on their availability, you can also cross-reference science and social studies texts for additional reading material. These sources can provide you with whole-class or small-group sets of stories or informational texts. With the trend toward putting authentic literature in the classroom, most published reading programs include well-known stories in their entirety.

If you are teaching in a multigrade classroom, you will have access to three grade levels of materials. In addition, you can talk with your school librarian about audiotapes, videocassettes, and learning games that can round out a topic of study. Subscriptions to magazines like *Ranger Rick, Zoobook,* and *World* can supplement your reading instruction; their short informational articles are accompanied by incredibly beautiful photographs and drawings. (They're sure to be favorites of the children during silent reading time.) And don't forget an assortment of dictionaries. It is helpful to have one large unabridged dictionary, in addition to several copies of smaller, paperback ones.

Additional Supplies   Besides the instructional materials provided at your school, you can use all kinds of additional "stuff." You may, in fact, need to become a pack rat—if you're not one already! Especially during the summer before your first year of teaching, try to collect a variety of useful learning materials, from pizza wheels for games to carpet squares to travel brochures to magazines. Don't hesitate to tell store managers you are a teacher—they will usually give you as many discarded or discontinued items as they can; and when there are "specials" (say, spiral notebooks and pocket folders, limit six to a customer) they just may let *you* buy more. (I even try to purchase by the case.) Print shops, carpet retailers, and home improvement stores are happy to have you take boxes of scrap paper, wallpaper books, carpet squares, and broken bags of soil off their hands. The local newspaper will often donate end rolls of newsprint to teachers, and don't forget to check with the local book distributor for books that have been refused for minor damage. For convenience, many teachers have large boxes labeled "Science," "Social studies," "Math," and so forth—for any materials that conceivably could be used in these areas.

Arranging the Classroom   Let's begin with the scenario you may already be envisioning: it's your first year of teaching, the school year begins in a few days, and you're standing in an empty classroom. The decisions you make about arranging the room will depend on your philosophy of teaching as well as on the day-to-day "nitty-gritty" of accommodating children.

Traditionally, desks were placed in rows so that the children wouldn't be tempted to talk. Teachers did not want students sharing information; working together to arrive at a collective answer was considered "cheating." At times this picture strikes us as something from the Dark Ages—violating the very nature of children, and greatly at odds with the way the "real world" operates. (Adults in the workplace, for example, most often work *cooperatively,* whether they're fitting ceiling beams or brainstorming marketing strategies. And even when we are struggling to learn something on our own—whether we happen to be writing a poem or riding a horse—it makes all the difference in the world if a peer, another student, is close by to provide helpful feedback about our attempts.)

You're free now, of course, to arrange your students' desks in ways that allow them to talk with one another. And the children you teach will be engaged in ongoing processes and projects that will involve them in working *cooperatively* toward common group and individual goals (Johnson and Johnson, 1975; Slavin, 1980, 1986; Torbe & Medway, 1981). Your room arrangement will reflect the type of social interaction you want to establish and maintain—and to achieve this, there are basic functional guidelines to observe. Evertson and his colleagues (1989) offer these four considerations:

1. High-traffic areas should be free of congestion.
2. The teacher should be able to see all students easily.
3. Frequently used materials and supplies should be readily accessible.
4. Students should be able to see all presentations and displays without difficulty.

These general guidelines allow many possibilities for arranging the classroom. Because classrooms are always a bit smaller than we'd like, a teacher definitely needs to plan space-allotment as wisely as possible.

Figure 4.1 illustrates two classroom layouts that will work for either primary or intermediate grades (grades four, five, and six). Let's examine their features.

Library Corner. Stacking bins and shelving, low enough for everyone to reach, will let you store books and magazines, as well as display them. You might group your books (science topics, folktales, and so forth) and place colored dots on each, corresponding to a shelf label. A beanbag chair or a small sofa, throw rugs, and large fluffy pillows will invite children to "snuggle up" with a book.

Carpet Area. An open carpet area can be a convenient place for whole-group instruction and discussion, small-group project work, student or guest presentations, author's chair, or sharing circle. You may want to have a large easel with chart paper close at hand to use in appropriate learning situations.

Supplies and Instructional Materials. Smaller items, as mentioned earlier (page 135) are best kept in a central area. Students may take turns monitoring them to make sure they'll be replenished and kept in order. It's advisable to locate paints, clay, and other messy products close to the sink.

Display Tables. These can feature exhibits, allow you to put flat items at eye level, and provide extra work areas. They should be placed away from major traffic paths, preferably against a wall.

Storage Areas. Designate one shelf area of baskets or bins marked with pictures or labels as the place to turn in and store work. All projects can then be found in one common area, already sorted by subject or group.

Bulletin Boards. Let most of them be student-created indicators of current topics of study, classroom interests, and communication among the children. Displaying student work reinforces their feelings of ownership and community. And when teacher-designed bulletin boards contain interesting reading with colorful illustrations—whether the material is commercially, teacher-, or child-produced—students always enjoy "reading the walls."

Computer Area. Like display tables, the computer area ought to be out of main traffic but in a space large enough to allow two or three children to work together. (We'll explore computers' role in literacy extensively in Chapter 10.) For now, keep in mind that computers, whether housed in the classroom or in a lab, will play a role in room organization and curriculum planning.

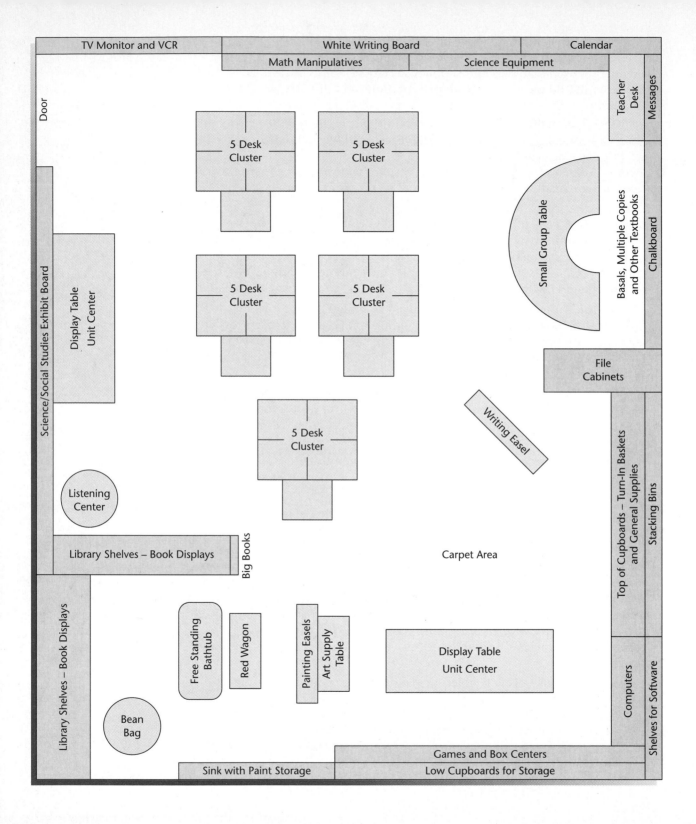

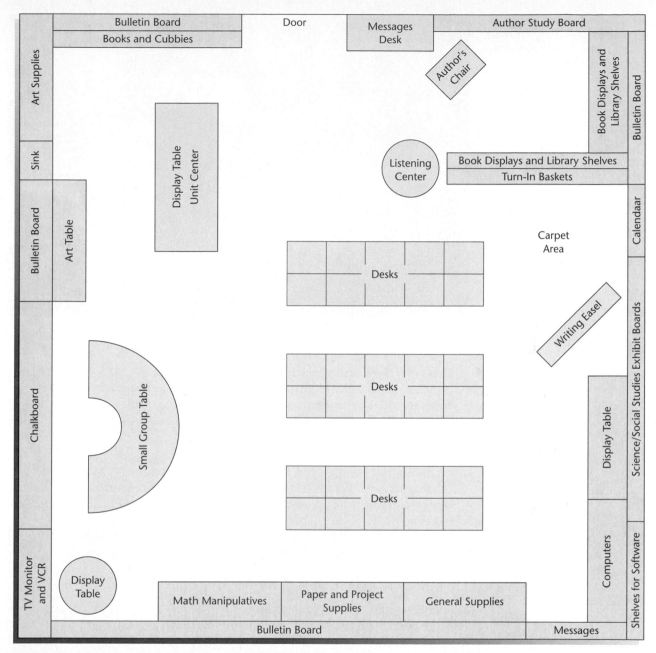

Figure 4.1
Two Classroom Diagrams

In this carefully arranged classroom, children are able to read their books comfortably in the Library Corner.

Desks or Tables. In the classroom diagrams (pages 138 and 139), desks are arranged so that the children face one another, a cluster arrangement that facilitates collaborative interaction. If you use tables, plan to keep each group's supplies and books together, perhaps in small tubs in the center of each table.

Centers. Often called "learning centers," these designated areas present activities that children can be involved with individually, in pairs, or in small groups. Some teachers don't allot particular learning areas, but offer children a list of activity choices that reinforce and extend understandings and skills. Still other teachers arrange very open-ended centers—blocks, painting easels, writing table—that change only in regard to the unit of study and the children's method of orchestrating their activity.

Organizing classroom time for instruction

Now that you know how your classroom will be physically arranged, let's move ahead to organizing your time and designing yearly, weekly, and daily plans. Your own and your school district's expectations for learning, along with your students' particular needs, strengths, and interests, directly determine what types of activities will go on in your classroom. So, we'll first take a look at establishing instructional goals; next, we will decide how these goals can be translated into practical plans and schedules.

Identifying Content and Skills to Be Taught and Establishing Goals   Obviously, curricular expectations must be combined with student needs. On the basis of the school district's objectives for your assigned grade level, you will have the challenge of introducing your students to required content material while interweaving the skills that will move them along the literacy continuum. Your knowledge of the range of developmental needs in your classroom will help you decide which skills to introduce to the entire class, which to support by small-group instruction, and which attend to the smaller details that only a few students are ready to learn.

Curricular Expectations As a professional educator, you are required to work with your school district's mandated curriculum as the framework from which you determine what major topics and concepts to teach. The mandated curriculum also will provide you with baselines and minimum competencies for each grade level.

As soon as you know which grade you have been assigned, take the district's curriculum guides and, if appropriate for your grade, the teacher's edition for each content area—social studies, math, science, and so forth—and lay them all out on the floor, to get an overview of your entire grade-level curriculum and to familiarize yourself with the objectives and major concepts you will be expected to cover. If you plan to develop cross-curricular thematic units (see Chapter 9), begin thinking about possible connections between reading and social studies, for example; what themes suggest themselves to you? Can you use traditional stories from a particular part of the world? Then make a chart or a time line to give yourself a sense of *what* you can cover *when,* and for *how long.* Decide what books, projects, and related skills you would like to include and plot them out on the chart. This not only will give you a general idea of how a thematic unit will run; it also allows you to foresee and predict trouble spots that might require extra time.

If your district is using a published reading or literature program, you probably will be expected to use it (see Chapter 10). *How* you choose to use your basal reading program—or literature-based language arts series—will depend on your goals for instruction, the school administrators' expectations, and your own comfort level in either staying with or venturing beyond the structure that a published program offers. Your choices are many. You may choose to follow the recommendations suggested by the publisher, reading the stories in the order in which they are presented, matching particular stories to specific subskills. You can also follow district requirements by pinpointing selections that align with mandated curriculum objectives.

Other ways of getting the most mileage from a published reading program include, for example, selecting stories by genre or author, or by integrating several stories or informational selections with particular content areas such as science, social studies, music, or sports. Many literature-based series are now arranged by theme, which could provide a starting point for sketching a yearly overview. Making connections across curricular areas takes a great deal of pre-planning. As you become more experienced, you will develop a well-rounded manner of approaching integrated instruction: first selecting, say, a science or social studies topic such as trees, then collecting trade books, content-area texts, and stories from published programs that fit your needs. With this type of organization, trade books are the major source of reading material, the published reading program becomes one more resource for bringing quality literature into the classroom, and most of your instructional time is spent working with materials that reflect one unifying theme (in this case, trees).

The organizational strategy you choose will depend on what materials are available to you, how comfortable you are with the goals and objectives of your grade level, your working knowledge of children's reading and writing development, and your growing ability to create meaningful literacy experiences for your students. Whether or not you organize your instruction according to thematic units, you are likely to find yourself with transition time between topics of study. You may want to use that time to read those trade books and basal stories that reinforce specific grade level objectives—such as using commas in a series, providing antonyms, correcting subject/verb agreement, identifying the subject and predicate in a sentence, or using punctuation within quotation marks. Although some of these topics will come up naturally during writing conferences or reading discussions, some will not; therefore, you will need to introduce them directly, as well as provide opportunities for using these skills in a meaningful context.

Your Own Students' Needs, Strengths, and Interests   You'll need to begin students at a level at which they can function comfortably. This may or may *not* match with grade level expectations. We'll talk about initial and ongoing assessment as we move through this chapter. In addition, Chapter 11 will give you detailed guidelines for assessing students. At this point, my main objective is to explain that it will be necessary for you to adjust your instruction to what the children can do when they walk through the door, not only on the first day of school but every day thereafter.

Gathering information about your students acquaints you with their word knowledge, reading levels, and comprehension abilities; and it guides you in setting up special-needs and achievement groups. Eventually, you will be setting up a daily routine for keeping track of each child's progress; then you can adjust instruction as necessary. Informal observations of learning behavior and consistently kept running records of your students' reading (Clay, 1979) will become essential for charting progress. However, it is ongoing assessment of your students' reading and writing and close observation of behavior that drives your decisions as to what your students need to learn and that therefore affects your overall planning and scheduling.

It is a good idea to set up for each child a file that will contain your notes, samples of the child's work (both teacher- and student-selected), running records of the child's reading progress, and self-evaluations and comments each child has made about his or her own learning. This file or "portfolio" of collected work will then become an *expression* of what a child has learned (see Chapter 11). The writing students do during the first few days of school will provide a wealth of information about how they put thought and words together to communicate, so this is an excellent starter item for each child's portfolio. We will be extending these ideas in Chapter 11.

During the very first week of school, you can select activities that you know will be successful for all your students: writing stories above themselves, drawing illustrations, producing a bar graph of their favorite games, and so forth, will help give you an idea of where these children are on the developmental

How can you get to know children "before you 'know' them"? That is, how can you obtain information about them that will help you plan for them, begin probing their interests, and get your school year under way more smoothly?

I suggest that you first write a letter to each student and a letter to his or her parents or guardian. Using a word processor would allow you to write one letter of each kind, then personalize it by inserting the child's or adult's name. Figure 4.2 illustrates a letter of this type. In your letter to each child, ask for a letter in reply. Ask the child to tell you about him or herself in an uncorrected first draft. This gives you information about him or her and provides you with a writing sample as well. You can also request the children to draw you a picture—preferably of themselves.

Ask first-graders to try to write *two* things by themselves. In your letter to parents of first-graders, ask them to take down a little bit of dictation from their child (see Chapter 5); you can include simple instructions.

In your parent letter, briefly share your teaching philosophy, your expectations, and some of what the children will be doing throughout the year. And—this is important—ask the parents to write to *you*. Ask them what their child is like, what they would like him or her to learn and why, and whether there are any health or other physical concerns they would like you to be aware of. It is also an excellent opportunity for you to give dates and times when you'll be working in your classroom before school begins. One word of caution: parents and children will want to talk, so be sure to schedule visits for a time when you'll be doing something that can be interrupted—such as putting name tags on desks or stapling up bulletin board paper. Invite the parents

to come by with their child. This is an excellent, nonthreatening introduction for all of you. When parents and children *do* come by, chat with them—and if they have the time, invite them to help out right then and there if they wish.

There is an additional way to obtain information about your students before you meet them, but it should be used judiciously. *Cumulative files*—the kind that follow the children from one year to the next—usually contain background data such as address, phone number, birthplace, parents' occupations, schools previously attended, and health records, along with test scores, past report cards, and perhaps notification of special services received. Should you look at cumulative files? Some educators have felt that a file might contain potentially biasing information that could predispose the teacher to respond in a negative fashion to that child. In recent years, though, there has been considerably less such information in the files. The real problem several years ago were the comments some teachers wrote about students' behavior and learning potential; the comments would follow students year after year, so they never had a "clean slate." Nowadays, the cumulative files primarily contain testing information and "flags" for special services or unusual health conditions; for example, a child may be a diabetic, or may need to lip-read what the teacher says, work with the speech therapist, or report to the school nurse for daily medication.

My suggestion, therefore, is definitely to look at the cumulative file, primarily for the reasons just mentioned. You need to have this information about a child, and you also need to know who else besides you, the classroom teacher, will be responsible for him or her.

LEARNING IN CONTEXT: Important connections with children and their homes can be established *before* school begins.

Evergreen Elementary School
755 Pine Drive
Cedar, NV 89674
Date

Dear Parents,

My name is Brian Sable; I will be your child's teacher during the next school year. Together we will work to guide your child's academic and social development. For this collaboration to begin, I will need your help. You see, I believe that you know your child better than anyone else; you have insights about his or her likes and dislikes and strengths and difficulties, as well as knowledge of special health concerns and influential changes that have taken place in your lives. To begin our partnership, I would like you to send me a short letter telling me about your child: What are your expectations for this coming year? What would you most like me to know?

To help us get better acquainted, I am inviting you and your child to stop by the classroom anytime between 1:00 and 3:00 P.M. on the Friday before school begins. You can take a look around, chat with me, and maybe see old friends, as well as take care of any unfinished registration forms.

The children and I will begin our school year with a look at who we are, where we've come from, and what we can teach one another. I will be asking your child to share a special talent that has been passed down from an older family member.

I know that within the next few days you may be shopping for school supplies. Below you will find a short list of items we will be using on a regular basis:

1. large box of tissues
2. 4 oz. bottle of white glue
3. glue stick
4. eraser
5. pencils
6. markers

Please feel free to call me or to drop by the classroom if you have any questions. I look forward to meeting you soon.

Sincerely,

Brian Sable
Fifth Grade Teacher

This letter is based on materials shared with me by Barbara Milchak of Elizabeth Lenz Elementary School, Reno, Nevada.

continuum. Also, choose activities that will allow you time to watch and note social behaviors, interests, attention spans, and self-concepts.

As the year progresses, you will be looking at journal entries and word study notebooks to determine whether a child is ready to move on in word study or if he or she needs additional exposure to a particular vowel pattern. You will listen, as children read to you and to each other, to discern whether one more day of rereading is necessary before going on to another story. The point I'm making is that throughout the year you will spend much time interacting with and observing your students, and much time in sessions of reviewing, reading, and responding to their written projects. This will help you understand how they think and absorb knowledge—so that you can plan for, guide, and keep records of their learning, records of what they have learned and of goals to be attained.

Planning and Scheduling We will look first at your macro-level planning (yearly basis) and next at your micro-level planning and scheduling (weekly and daily). Finally, we will look in some detail at the kind of schedule you might set up for a very special time of year—the first week of school.

Plan for the Year I am suggesting that you begin by plotting out a tentative yearly plan where you identify major concepts and units of study for your grade level and the scope and sequence of material to be learned. It may seem a little overwhelming to realize that before the children even arrive, you should map out a tentative plan for the year. This is also where working with a like-minded, more experienced teacher can be extremely helpful. Because you have only a very partial sense of your students at the time you do your planning, this yearly plan is not engraved in stone; it can be modified along the way. This type of advance planning will also allow you to order materials well in advance, such as films and videodiscs, that will be helpful down the line.

As you are making your unit plans, the types of projects you undertake may depend on the time of the year. You will need to address certain units of study early in the school year to build background knowledge for more complex information to come. And to help students function as a cohesive unit, we need to show them how, then give them time to "settle in" with one another. By December your students will have a broader understanding of how the classroom functions, and you can focus on more complex content material.

Setting Up Your Daily and Weekly Schedules The week becomes the important short-term unit for planning. Realistically, what can you accomplish between Monday and Friday? You will need to determine your time blocks within each day; these may vary a little from day to day, but they should be quite predictable most of the time. This predictability is comforting to students, especially for those who are learning English as a second language, and ultimately allows students more freedom with their learning than a plan that changes constantly.

	SEPT.	OCT.	NOV./DEC.	JAN.	FEB.	MARCH	APRIL	MAY/JUNE
WRITING	Beginning Journals / Selected Topics (Prewriting)	Lead Sentences / Capitals, Periods / Giving Positive Response	Word Choices / Capitals Other than Beginning of Sentence / Plurals	Using Feedback to Improve Story / Subj./Predicate / Revising	How Stories Begin / Sources of Story Collecting / Back to Response Groups	Oral Story Telling / Mapping a Story for Sharing	Use of Punctuation / Dialogue / Subj./Verb Agreement / Editing	Pulling All Together / Lead Sentences / Paragraphing / etc.
READING	Beginning/Middle/End	Setting/Repetition	Plot — Biography / Journey Stories	Characterization	Point of View	Info Text vs. Story	Theme	Style
READING	Family Stories & Nonfiction Family Books — Cultural	Native American Stories	Map Books / Streets / Atlas	European Folktales / Fact Books on Castles	Asian Folktales / Body/Health Books	African Folktales / Zoo Books	Environmental Awareness Stories / Dino Books	Space Stories / Space Fact Books
AUTHOR STUDY	Vera Williams / Cynthia Rylant	Paul Goble / Jane Yolen	Eric Carle / Ezra Jack Keats	Paul Galdone / James Marshall	Ed Young / Allen Say	Verna Aardema / Leo & Diane Dillon	Bill Peet / Brian Wildsmith	Joanna Cole / Seymour Simon
ART	Watercolor / Pencil Drawing / Still Life	Watercolor / Landscape	Collage / Mixed Media	Crayon / Black Line Drawing	Watercolor / Oil Pastels	Mosaic / Pottery	Mural / Tempra	Cartoon vs. Photography
SCIENCE	Animal Families	Living with Animals	Seasonal Changes	Cells / Germs / Disease	Body Systems	Soils / Habitat Regions	Rocks and Minerals / Fossils	Solar System / Solid/Liquid/Gas / Space Travel
SOCIAL STUDIES	Family	Community / North American Continent	Mapping	Europe / Shelters / Different Kinds of Homes	Asia / Healthy Eating / First Aid	Africa / Animal—Pop-up Books / Reports / Human Interaction	Man's Use of Rocks & Minerals / Dinosaur Posters	Transportation
MATH	Addition / Sorting / Classifying	Subtraction / Place Value	Measuring / Advanced Add. and Sub.	Geometry / Multiplication	Volume / Area / Perimeter / Graphing	Basic Functions +/−/× / Mixed Applications / Word Problems	Data Collection / Multistep Word Problems / Division	Symmetry / Congruency / Fractions

First, fill in lunch, recess, and any special classes such as music and library; then plan your major instructional blocks in reading, writing, and math. If you are using an integrated theme for your reading and writing, you can extend that topic into the afternoon science and social studies time for experiments, videos, whole-class bulletin board creations, or related outdoor games. For example, if your thematic unit centers around North America, students can spend

MAKING CONNECTIONS: *Getting to Know Your Peer Teachers and the Staff*

Get to know the staff! Don't ever hesitate to introduce yourself to other teachers at your school. Get to know them. Give them a sense of who you are; offer your strengths and approach them for help when you need another point of view.

I can't overemphasize the importance of talking, thinking, and planning with other teachers. The way your day usually is set up, however, can work mightily against doing this! Unless you are in a team-teaching situation, you see other teachers only briefly throughout the day. Despite the scheduling difficulties, it *is* extremely important for you to find a way to plan with another teacher, one who more or less shares your philosophy of teaching. Preferably, this will be someone in your own school, and it *is* helpful if both of you are teaching at the same grade level. This combination of minds can be incredibly helpful and supportive—even when together, you are setting out your curriculum guides

and textbooks on the floor to get a "general overview" of the school year.

Though it may be a struggle, you simply *must* carve out the time for talking, thinking, and planning! I know several teachers who meet for breakfast early on Friday mornings (knowing they can sleep in on Saturday makes getting up early more palatable). Others meet one evening every other week; some meet one afternoon on a weekend. Despite the inconvenience, they do find that the payoff is immeasurable.

Spend some time, too, in getting to know the school secretary, the librarian, the custodian, and the lunchroom staff. Many teachers bring these individuals into their classrooms to meet the children. If you can in some way make them working members of your classroom, you will discover their paramount importance in running the school. Having them "in your corner" does afford definite benefits.

LEARNING IN CONTEXT: **Your classroom is a community, but it, in turn, is part of the larger school community—it is important to fit comfortably within that context.**

their morning time reading and responding to Native American folktales, knowing that in the afternoon they will be watching a video about the major mountain ranges of North America and beginning a three-dimensional map of the continent.

You may need to work out different schedules for different units of study. Some projects may override your regular routine, especially if you are planning for presentations to be given on a specific date. Denise Jackson's multilevel class

MAKING CONNECTIONS: *How Integrated Instruction Affects Your Planning and Scheduling*

Teachers who believe in integrated instruction will usually view their classroom schedule quite differently than will teachers who schedule the day with a time slot for each subject. An integrated approach calls for large blocks of work time that blend the language arts, and eventually several subjects into a unified whole. I have found that children as young as first-graders need more than the traditional twenty-minute work period. You may be wondering if first-graders *can* pay attention for longer than twenty minutes. Maybe not on the first day of school; but as you progress through the year, your students gain confidence in their reading and writing abilities and are exposed to longer and longer work periods with a selection of whole group, small group, and independent activities. So you are bound to discover, eventually, that you can barely get started in twenty minutes.

If you are going to ask your students to read well-developed stories, discuss those stories, and then write about them, you must, of course, allow them as much time as it takes to read and reread, talk and compose—a process that will take even a first-grade student at least *forty* minutes. Upper-grade students will need even longer stretches of time. Cooperative response projects will require extended sessions for brainstorming, decision-making, project organization, gathering of materials, production time, revisions, final publication, and presentations. You may find that an hour a day devoted to overlapping topics in reading, writing, English, and spelling may not feel like enough time.

A more traditional approach to teaching will have children stopping and starting a different subject every twenty to thirty minutes. The textbook is shut, and the worksheet is completed so as to go on to the basal story or the comprehension exercise. There may be some valuable teaching and learning going on within each of these sessions; however, the learning is segmented and disjointed with no unifying elements. The integrated approach to teaching and learning, on the other hand, will see the same subjects taught but with a vision that connects and overlaps the knowledge in one area in a way that guides the understanding of the next. For you to do this type of teaching and learning, you will need more than a thirty-minute work session. And that brings us right back to planning for a collaborative integrated classroom. The most concise answer to the question of how to plan for one lies in the amount of thoughtful anticipating and scheduling devoted to building that type of learning environment.

LEARNING IN CONTEXT: **Not only children's learning, but your *teaching* as well, flows more naturally when literacy and content are integrated.**

wrote and illustrated hardcover books about their birth stories to be presented to their parents at the close of a unit on growing and changing family life. Once the project was under way, the class devoted every work session to progressing through the authoring cycle. They had to compose interview questions for their parents, organize the information they gathered, write first drafts, share in response groups, revise their stories, and make "dummy" books of what they wanted the final product to look like, as well as pool ideas for illustrating the story text and designing the book jacket. Denise found it best to present minilessons each morning and afternoon, then work with children in twos and threes for ten-minute intervals. This way, she was able to meet with every child each day, while the children themselves formed free-flowing small groups when necessary. Although the class's usual routine had changed, it was replaced by a new short-term schedule that held *some* predictability. After the presentation day had passed, Denise and her students took a week to get back into the habits of their old schedule before starting a new unit.

Figures 4.4 and 4.5 show daily schedules for a primary classroom and an upper elementary classroom, respectively.

Regardless of whether you teach at the primary or the intermediate level, some recommendations apply throughout the whole school year. For example, reading instruction should be integrated with all subject areas, so that—literally—all day long, you will be teaching about reading. You will also have large blocks of time during which children will be reading and writing (Atwell, 1987); they need this time to immerse themselves in all the myriad activities and projects involving reading and writing. A predictable schedule will not only ensure you enough time to plan instructional periods on specific topics and

9:00	Journal Writing and Record-Keeping
9:15	Calendar
9:20	Read-Alouds with Discussion: One previously-read book, child-selected One book not previously read, teacher-selected
10:00	Word Study
10:15	Recess
10:30	Reading: Whole group, small groups, and individual work
11:30	Writers' Workshop (including English minilessons)
12:00	Lunch and Recess
12:45	Read-Aloud: Chapter book
1:00	Sustained Silent Reading
1:15	Math
2:00	Science and Social Studies
2:45	Community Sharing Time: Response to the day
3:00	Dismissal

Figure 4.4
Primary Classroom Daily Schedule

Figure 4.5
Upper Elementary Classroom Daily Schedule

9:00	Journal Writing and Record-Keeping
9:15	Silent Reading and Reading Conferences
9:45	Reading: Literature discussion groups
10:45	Unit Projects: Small-group work (includes science and social studies topics)
11:45	Lunch and Recess
12:30	Read-Aloud
12:45	Math
1:45	Recess
2:00	Writers' Workshop (including English mini-lessons)
2:45	Evaluation of the day: Goals for tomorrow
3:00	Dismissal

skills; it also will guarantee your students extended work periods they can depend on. Earlier I promised a detailed plan for the first week of school. Figure 4.6 presents such a plan for the intermediate grades.

GROUPING FOR INSTRUCTION

As you set up your classroom schedule and plan your lessons, you will need to consider a variety of group configurations. Think back to Denise Jackson's

Small-group instruction is one of a variety of group configurations for you to consider as you set up your classroom and plan your lessons.

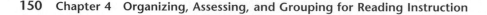

MONDAY	TUESDAY	WEDNESDAY	THURSDAY	FRIDAY
9:00 Desks; Pledge; Record Keeping	9:00 Pledge; Journal (I read comments, write back); Record Keeping	9:00 Pledge; Journal; Record Keeping	9:00 Pledge; Journal; Record Keeping	9:00 Pledge; Journal; Record Keeping
9:15 Scavenger Hunt	9:15 Computers	9:15 Media Center	9:15 Music	9:15 Observation and drawing of body lesson with partner – Focus on hand of partner – Describe distinguishing features of partner's hand – Brainstorm descriptor that will be specific and not generic – What words won't work? Extend to arm – Make comparison and size estimates – How many hands in an arm? How many hands tall, etc? Draw from math lesson done on Wednesday Move to gesture drawing; have one student stand up front. Use loose big ovals to sketch out general body proportions – Where do elbows come in relation to waist, etc? Pair again to pose for each other and sketch
9:45 Paper Bag Princess – R. Munsch Discussion – Shallow – Superficial Pairs: Cartoon Response Focus – 3 pictures with dialogue or caption – Examples of Prince's shallow behavior Sharing of cartoons – Arrange on sideboard	9:45 Review classroom rules made yesterday; Name poem partner – Cluster ideas of when you give to others – Minilesson on descriptive words and powerful nouns 5 – Saturated, strong A – Animated, allowances M – Mindfulness, mystery Small group sharing of poems; model procedure and positive response: One thing liked and a favorite used... – tell why.	9:45 3 stories from basal Topic – Personal Reflection "Louella's Song" – Greenfield "Making Room for Uncle Joe" – Litchfield "Chasing After Annie" – Sharmat Begin dialogue journals – Journal lead – Model entries with Think-aloud from a reread of Paper Bag Princess Pair for reading basal stories Circulate to listen and guide	9:45 Sustained silent reading	
10:45 Silent Reading – Circulate to read with children; Take notes		10:00 Byrd Baylor rereading – Guess Who My Favorite Person Is Focus on senses – connect with illustrations Use text as model for creating individual poems – Do one whole class, then partners – Each pair produces a poem Watercolor painting to extend poem's feeling		
11:00 Diagnostic Spelling Inventory	11:00 Community Circle "I Like My Neighbor" game	10:45 Discuss dialogue journal writing		
11:15 Community Circle – Set guidelines for group sharing – Topic – One thing like about school... – Avoid exact repetitions		11:00 Community Circle Favorite Foods	11:00 Poem sharing in small group – Pairs join with another pair; review procedure for response	11:00 Record in journal observations made of partner – Distinguishing features hadn't noticed before – Stress uniqueness
11:30 Lunch	11:30 Lunch	11:30 Lunch	11:30 Lunch	11:30 Lunch
12:15 Read-aloud – Intro author study – Byrd Baylor – Give some biographical material Guess Who My Favorite Person Is (Guided Listening-Thinking Activity) Final discussion focus for pairs: Compose list of at least 5 things we need to do to be good friends to each other. Share lists/use board to record ideas. Use colored chalk to web ideas together. Discuss umbrella terms for each large category – Fashion into classroom rules.	12:15 Read-aloud – Hawk I'm Your Brother – B. Baylor biographical material – Begin chart of stylistic characteristics of Baylor's books	12:15 Read-aloud – continue Be A Perfect Person in Just Three Days	12:15 Finish watercolor	12:15 Read-aloud – Be A Perfect Person In Just Three Days
	12:45 Review fire drill procedure – Do earthquake drill	12:35 Whole class – Math – End of book test from previous year; pull heterogeneous groups Content Guided Reading-Thinking Activity: Science book – Use "Weather" passage	12:30 Read-aloud – Be A Perfect Person In Just Three Days	12:45 Sustained silent reading
1:15 Class Graph: What we missed about school – Friends, projects, special programs, other – Use Post-It notes – Oral observation	1:00 What do you want to learn this year – Interests – In 3's with chart paper; assign writer; topic keeper; time watcher; Practice giving compliments – 15 min. Join with another 3 to share thoughts and charts. Review small group format from morning. Pull small groups for Guided Reading-Thinking Activity; use basal, p. 430, "Louella's Song"	1:30 Silent reading	1:00 Pull children individually to hear, read, and begin running record of oral reading while pairs working with math facts +/–/x/÷ with card game – Continue math logs – Show how to set up – Play and record math equations created with game	1:15 Venn diagram pairs of two Byrd Baylor books – Do one whole class to model discussions and process
1:45 Outdoor game: Partner tag. Practice fire drill exit; Go over playground rules	2:00 Read-aloud – Begin chapter book Be a Perfect Person In Just Three Days	2:00 Body measuring – Who is a square?; graph results – Make graph observations	2:00 Writers' Workshop Intro: Minilesson on collecting ideas; 15 min. writing alone; 15 min. may choose to work with someone	2:00 Share Venn diagram with another pair
2:30 Journal – Feelings about first day of school – What do you need?	2:20 Design and decorate writers' workshop folders with images that reflect self – Magazines, crayon, markers, paper cutouts			2:15 P.E. – Hook-Up Tag
2:50 Clean-up	2:50 Clean-up	2:50 Clean-up	2:50 Clean-up	2:50 Clean-up
3:00 Dismissal	3:00 Dismissal	3:00 Dismissal	3:00 Dismissal	3:00 Dismissal

Figure 4.6
Plan Book for the First Week of School: Intermediate Grades

classroom, described earlier in this chapter. Denise chose to assign a group of beginning readers for a shared reading experience, while the rest of her students worked together in various interest groups or response groups. Another teacher's plans for the first week of school might have the students working not only in pairs, but also in small groups of three or four. Both teachers will have grouped their students for specific purposes.

As we saw earlier in this chapter, many of your instructional decisions will be based upon your initial assessments of students' academic and social abilities. The information you collect at the beginning of the school year will help you provide realistically and efficiently for their reading needs and interests. Specifically, you will be able to determine at what levels and in what ways they are attempting to construct meaning as they read, where they are in their developing knowledge about printed words, and how they can be grouped for particular instructional objectives according to what they already know about reading. This in turn will allow you to facilitate meaningful, consequential literacy events that connect with your children's imaginations and life experiences. As the year proceeds, your grouping decisions will be influenced by the students' developmental progress and increased skills.

Taking a new look at grouping

During the past twenty years, educators across the country have been working to parallel classroom learning with real-world experiences. Beginning in the mid–1970s, the cooperative learning techniques endorsed by Johnson and Johnson and others have helped teachers' progression from the exclusive use of traditional ability grouping and have caused teachers to consider the benefits of alternate, more flexible methods of grouping—groupings that are much more supportive of life away from the classroom. In addition, research suggests that having children work in a variety of small-group settings far outweighs keeping them exclusively in rigid ability groups (Allington, 1991; Barr 1989). I don't mean to suggest that you will *never* want to group your students by ability; many occasions will arise where ability grouping will provide the most appropriate setting for your instruction.

The make-up of a group will depend first and foremost on the group's purpose; there will be times when you will want to mix better-developed readers with less-well-developed ones for creative story-response activities, "author of the month" story analysis, or research projects. At other times, several children of similar reading ability can meet with you in a small group for purposes of word study or to experience a Guided Reading-Thinking Activity with a selection at their instructional level (see Chapter 6). Still other academic and social circumstances will present themselves where you will group children by expressed interest or surfacing needs or for the sharing of content information. Without a doubt, grouping children for instruction no longer carries the assumed meaning of "ability." Teachers have found worthwhile alternatives in cooperative and flexible grouping patterns (Flood et al., 1992).

Defining a variety of small groups

The heterogeneous or homogeneous groupings you choose will depend upon your instructional objectives. You will want the groupings you select, much like the time schedules you devise, to enhance and benefit the overall collaborative climate within the classroom. Therefore, whether the work you do within your small groups concerns direct instruction with content reading material or a loosely structured literature response group, the interaction you orchestrate should strengthen students' belief that learning is reinforced if it is done with others. Logically, this makes sense: if you are working with fewer students on aspects of reading that your assessment has shown they can address, you'll be able to spend more time interacting with each child—and in a facilitative social context.

The reasons for incorporating small groups within your classroom are many. We will appraise their advantages and disadvantages as we examine different forms of groupings.

Ability Groups   Every classroom is composed of children with a range of developmental needs and abilities; therefore, you will need to customize particular lessons for specific groups of students. For example, students of one reading level can benefit greatly from small-group discussions on plot, characterization, setting, or point of view, when these are done with material at their instructional or independent reading level. To provide optimal opportunities for each child to participate in both the reading and the discussion, grouping children with similar reading abilities can have instructional advantages. We know that reading ability is relative, and that how well a student interacts with a particular text depends on a number of factors. Perhaps this complexity explains the rather stunning estimate that 50 to 60 percent of students in the elementary grades work with inappropriate instructional materials (Shake, 1989).

If we believe children need practice reading to become better readers, it only makes sense to have part of their day include time spent with other children at similar reading levels, examining stories that extend and develop their fluency, word knowledge, and comprehension. Guiding children along the developmental continuum often calls for direct instruction in a homogeneous group (Routman, 1991). Au (1993) concurs that circumstances will arise where we do need to place children in ability reading groups; but she cautions us to take particular care to ensure that the instruction received by children at an earlier phase of reading development is of the same quality as instruction given to children whose development is farther along. This is especially true for students from diverse backgrounds.

Cooperative Learning Groups   Cooperative learning groups are those that focus on the social interaction of a group's dynamics. The group's social nature and the role each child takes within the group determine its interactive patterns. Generally, students interact with one another in three distinct ways: cooperatively, individually, or competitively (Kohn, 1986). In recent years, teachers have been taking steps to encourage more cooperative behavior among students by structuring group work that de-emphasizes competition. Cohen (1986) cites research supporting the premise that the more children are exposed to cooperatively structured experiences and instructed in collaborative behaviors, the more likely they are to exhibit prosocial behaviors. The effectiveness of these groups, Au (1993) reminds us—especially for children from diverse backgrounds—will depend on the teacher's providing systematic small-group instruction accompanied by independent collaborative peer interaction. This type of interaction adjusts social expectations to the cultural background of the children involved.

For cooperative learning groups to work effectively, teachers need to set guidelines to help students depend on one another in a positive, supportive manner and to ensure that every participant's contributions will be valued and rewarded. When these things happen, children will learn more (Johnson & Johnson, 1975). As you prepare for cooperative groups, it is important to have clear expectations and to include no more than five students in each group, to have a balance of achievement, language ability, gender, and ethnicity (Cohen, 1986). I have found it best to begin cooperative work with *pairs* of children. As the students gain skill in working with each other, I begin to form groups.

Johnson and Johnson (1975) and Cohen (1986) describe the basic cooperative group as a small group of four to five children in which each child has a specific role. Children are assigned roles that focus on their academic and social competencies. One child is assigned to read, another to record information, yet another to facilitate discussion. Other roles might include keeping track of time, gathering materials, giving positive feedback, or posing questions. The roles you select for children will change, depending on the task to be completed. As children become proficient at taking on assigned roles within structured, cooperative groups, you may find they can work with less teacher direction.

Sharan (1980) refers to this more open group organization as *group investigation.* With this method, students take full responsibility for organizing the members of their group. The students within each group decide what topic they want to investigate, who will take responsibility for locating specific information and materials, and what role each child will take to ensure that the group is a functioning unit. *Group investigation* assumes that students have had much successful practice in working in many different kinds of small groups for a variety of purposes. This type of group organization is particularly appropriate for multilevel classes whose members have been together for several years and are well versed in the group dynamics of their classroom. Let's examine several other ways of forming cooperative groups.

Peer Tutoring   Peer tutoring most often pairs two children of different ages or abilities in a given area, to assist each other in completing an independent task. For instance, you may want to pair a non-English speaker with a child who has some knowledge of his partner's native language; in a multigrade classroom, it would be appropriate to assign incoming students to those who are knowledgeable in the workings of the classroom procedures. Ideally, you will want to instruct children as soon as possible in the procedures for working with another child, so that you will be free to gather small groups for direct instruction. Beginning the year by pairing children during independent work periods lays the foundation for more complex groupings to come. Although you will want to continue to pair children throughout the year, pairing done during the first month of school will ensure that classroom procedures and cooperative social patterns are instilled early on.

Student Teams Achievement Divisions *Student team achievement divisions (STAD)* (Slavin, 1978, 1983) can be formed to study material that has been presented previously and in another setting. Each team stays with the material until it feels all its members can be successful when tested on the information. Before the groups begin, the teacher has prepared an exam and informs students of the standards he or she has set for each team. Teams are then rewarded for meeting the predetermined standards. This type of arrangement works well with material that can be learned through rote memory. Learning story sequences or the spelling of unusual science terms might be appropriate for this type of grouping. One difficulty I have observed when using this technique is that teams may become excessively competitive with each other. This, however, can be overcome by setting whole-class goals and rewards along with those established for each team.

Jigsaw Groups The *jigsaw approach* (Slavin, 1986; Tierney, Readence, & Dishner, 1990) requires students to become experts on pieces of information contained within a larger topic. Children are grouped according to the information they would like to have or that you have determined is appropriate. This technique works well with content information, such as a social studies chapter covering the causes of the Civil War. To use the jigsaw approach, you would divide the chapter into sections and prepare focus questions for each section. Groups would then use the questions as a guide for becoming conversant speakers on their assigned portions of the chapter. When each "expert" group feels confident enough to share, the initial groups disband and new groups are formed, using one student from each of the original groups. Information is then shared and groups are quizzed and rewarded.

You will find this grouping technique to be particularly advantageous for covering large, complex pieces of informational text. You can be selective about what information is given to which students and how the children are then regrouped to provide for the best sharing experience. Lower-ability students often flourish with the jigsaw approach because it provides them with opportunities to impart information in a leadership role. A more extensive discussion of the jigsaw approach can be found in Chapter 7.

Flexible Groups Within the integrated classroom, flexible groups are those formed on the basis of the unit of study, skill needs, and special events within the classroom. Their arrangements can be quite structured, or you may allow them to come about informally.

Interest Groups Once your students have had opportunities to expand their knowledge base through their experiences with integrated instruction and thematic unit study, they can benefit from working in groups based on similar interests. These types of groups often develop naturally during the course of the day or from regularly scheduled work sessions: During a writers' workshop, one child may discover several others who would like to compose a book about special trees; children may gather with ideas for designing thank-you notes for guest speakers. As the teacher, you may have more deliberate reasons for organizing interest groups; one such possibility is the literature response group. Recalling Denise Jackson's classroom once again, we remember that her students had a choice of reading one of three Ezra Jack Keats titles. The selections the children made determined whom they would work with during that particular seatwork session. Interest groups are usually short-lived and work to accomplish short-term goals.

Project and Research Groups Project and research groups will most likely become a major part of your thematic studies and your extensions to literature. Although project and research groups often form out of interest, there are more expansive enterprises taken on by two or more children to demonstrate explicitly their learning and understanding of, for example, a particular short story or a content area. Often the demonstrations are culminating or closure presentations of a unit, done orally, in writing, with dramatic representation, or through visual arts. Groups arranged for these purposes usually remain intact for several weeks or for the duration of a unit of study. You may want to begin this type of work by having each group complete a similar project or investigate related topics, so that you can provide guided instruction on how to complete the assignment. As children build a repertoire of possible culminating activities, they will have experience to draw on when making future decisions about similar work. Throughout the remainder of this book, you will be learning about the specifics for engaging your students in extensive reading and writing activities of this nature.

Skill or Needs Groups Generally speaking, skill or needs groups address issues that arise as children read and write together. As you are responding to their journals, you may discover a few children who repeatedly neglect to capitalize the first word of each sentence. Since there are only two or three children who seem to be having difficulty with this particular skill, it won't be necessary to organize a whole-group lesson on the topic. For the sake of time, you simply call the three children together and present a minilesson on capitalization. Other circumstances of this nature may develop during your writers' workshop sessions. As you circulate among your students, you may notice that several are having difficulty finding a topic, while others are struggling to create strong lead sentences for their stories. Gathering children with specific needs for short sessions of direct instruction provides the guided support students require to advance their learning; this is particularly true for children from nonmainstream backgrounds (Au, 1993). Although skill or needs groups may appear similar to ability groups, they are in fact quite different because you are not basing your decision to group children on their overall reading ability, but rather on specific difficulties that cross reading levels—for example, use of punctuation, summarizing, paragraph writing, using guide words in the dictionary.

Friendship Groups Most teachers I know will fashion loosely structured friendship groups to facilitate and reinforce positive social interaction among their students. These groups encourage full inclusion of all students as members of their learning community. They provide, for example, opportunities for practice in giving positive feedback, in brainstorming alternatives for behavior when difficulties between students occur, and in offering supportive assistance. Once your other cooperative groups are well under way, friendship groups usually meet only intermittently; however, you may find that your students enjoy the sharing and wish to have a regular schedule for meeting.

Forming, unforming, and re-forming groups

In order to form groups of any kind, you as the teacher must become familiar with the interests, needs, and achievement levels of your students. You will spend the first several weeks of every school year compiling this information. The assessment process, as we have mentioned before, will of course continue as your students grow and learn. At this point, we will cover some of the basics (the finer details of assessment and evaluation will follow in Chapter 11) of how the data you collect will affect your planning as you form and re-form ability groups, cooperative groups, and flexible groups, for instructional purposes.

Once you have made your students feel at home in the classroom and have taken careful note of their initial reactions to you and to the literacy experiences you have offered them thus far, and have noted as well their socialization skills with one another, you can begin to work with them individually and in small groups to pinpoint where their reading abilities lie. The information you gather will be invaluable and will serve as the basis for many of your grouping decisions.

Ability Groups Exactly how *do* you decide to group children by their reading ability? While there will be many literacy activities that you will do with your whole class or with heterogeneously grouped children, there will be many other times when you will want to meet with small groups of students of similar reading levels. And as you are aware, the information you gained from initial assessments gives you a very solid basis for making decisions about forming these small groups to facilitate your students' development as readers.

Administering an informal reading inventory (procedures for this are explained in Chapter 11) will help you determine each student's independent, instructional, and frustration reading levels. Educators have found the concept of a student's "reading levels" useful, particularly if the concept is used with caution (Betts, 1946; Stauffer, 1969; Pikulski & Shanahan, 1982; Lipson & Wixson, 1991). Simply described, reading levels are referred to as *independent, instructional,* and *frustrational.* You will find the notion of reading levels useful in planning your direct instruction in both comprehension and word knowledge. As you listen to your students' oral reading, you will get further insight into their construction of meaning and their word-recognition strategies. During this process, you will begin the first of many running records for each student's ongoing assessment file. While word-recognition miscues may support your findings on a Qualitative Inventory of Word Knowledge (also discussed in Chapter 11), children's retellings of what they have read, along with their responses to your questions, give you some insight into how they are attempting to construct meaning as they read. Students who are overrelying on one particular strategy and need to develop others may be brought together in a small group for your direct instruction and modeling of processes.

As we will explore further in Chapters 5, 6, and 9, you'll rely on what you know about your students' *reading levels* when assigning them to small literature discussion groups of five or six. These groups will focus on an "extended" text (see Chapter 6) related to a common theme that the class is pursuing. Your understanding of your students' levels will also help you select appropriate "readable" books for their recreational reading—books they'll be reading merely for pleasure during Sustained Silent Reading (SSR) and at home. Your students simply *must* do lots of reading that is within their comfort zone.

There will be variability in your students' *word knowledge.* You naturally would not expect a second-grade child spelling *bad* for *bed, driv* for *drive,* and *chran* for *train* to benefit from a lesson on long vowel patterns in the same way as a child (in the same grade) spelling *drieve* for *drive, trane* for *train,* and *flote* for *float.* (See Chapter 5.) The first child doesn't yet know enough about words to understand such a lesson, while the second child most certainly *would* benefit because she is already experimenting with such patterns in her invented spellings. These children, obviously, should be in different small groups for word study, so that they can examine, explore, and talk about words with other students whose word knowledge is similar to their own. As a child begins to show consistent written evidence of having assimilated particular spelling patterns, the group with whom this student works can be changed on the basis of his or her expanded awareness.

Cooperative Learning Groups   How do you go about forming cooperative learning groups? Careful assessment of your students' social and academic abilities guides your placement of individual students within cooperative groups. *Balance* within a group can determine its success or failure: for example, placing *all* struggling readers within a group whose goal is to read and compare two different versions of a fairy tale will surely fail. If, however, you place more competent readers with struggling readers and assign each a role he or she can fill competently, you will secure the group's success. Heterogeneous grouping that supports natural diversity among children can make even the most challenging material available to all (Cohen, 1986).

When you form cooperative groups, Cohen (1986) suggests, the students should be "mixed as to academic achievement, sex, and any other status characteristic such as race or ethnicity" (p. 61). With this objective in mind, she offers the following guidelines when setting up cooperative groups (pp. 53–71):

- Carefully consider the goals of the task.
- Write out all instructions.
- Assign no more than four to five students to a group.
- Select at least one resource person for each group.
- Place children who are academically advanced, developmentally delayed, or socially or linguistically problematic in groups where at least one other child can support their special needs.
- Post group assignments.
- Select specific roles for every student within each group.

- Provide space for each group to work in comfortably.
- Provide a central area for supplies.
- Set reasonable time limits for completing a task.
- Schedule sharing time to provide feedback on group process and the work completed.

As you begin this procedure, careful observation of your students' strengths will guide your placements. A firm knowledge of your students' abilities is necessary for your cooperative groups to be successful.

Flexible Groups   The organization of flexible groups and the way in which you manage them depends heavily on student interest and specific need. How students respond to a *reading attitudes and interests* probe can be used, as Norton points out, "to help students find recreational reading that interests them, group students for research and interest projects, and stimulate additional interests" (Norton, 1991, p. 105).

We know you can gain a lot of information about the children in your classroom just by observing their responses to and their choices about the books and literacy activities they select throughout the year. You may also gather information about their attitudes and interests more systematically by conducting attitude surveys or by obtaining written responses to specific questions. Most basal programs or literature-based series now provide teachers with interest inventories. Several questions may be addressed at one time, or each question may be a prompt for a journal entry during the first few days of school. Let's look at this more "informal" probe first.

Several researchers who have investigated student attitudes toward reading agree that certain questions usually seem to "work" in eliciting honest responses from most students (Estes, 1971; McKenna & Kear, 1990; Lipson & Wixson, 1991). Ideally, you would ask each student these questions individually, but they work well enough when you're eliciting responses from small groups, or—with older students—from the whole class. Following is a list of questions adapted from Lipson & Wixson that tap the most important information about interests, attitudes, preferences, and motivation (p. 108):

1. Of all the things you do after school or in the summer, which do you like best?
2. Do you have any hobbies or collections?
3. Do you like to read? Why or why not?
4. What's the easiest thing about reading, for you?
5. What's the hardest thing about reading?
6. What are some titles of books you've enjoyed?
7. Who is the best reader you know? What does he or she do that makes him or her such a good reader?
8. Have you ever had a teacher who made reading fun and exciting? Tell me about him or her.
9. What are some of the reasons why people read?

McKenna and Kear (1990) provide a survey of students' attitudes about reading that may be used for all elementary grades. It is easy to administer and score, and it yields information about students' attitudes toward both *academic* and *recreational* reading. By using a response sheet that has four different pictures of the cartoon character Garfield the cat (the pictures represent attitudes ranging from "very happy" to "very upset"), students indicate their reactions to twenty questions about reading. Examples of the questions are: "How do you feel when you read a book in school during free time?", "How do you feel about getting a book for a present?", "How do you feel about reading instead of playing?", "How do you feel when the teacher asks you questions about what you read?", and "How do you feel when you read out loud in class?"

Regardless of how you collect information about students' attitudes toward reading, you will find this information very helpful as a baseline. Toward the end of the school year you can ask the same questions again, and the students' responses should reassure you of the value and success of involving them in literature-based reading. In addition, you may want to have them reflect on the projects and research topics they have been involved with throughout the year. What stands out in their minds as their most memorable experiences will help you plan your units of study for the following year.

Managing groups in the classroom

Now that you have the hows and whys of grouping students, you face the challenge of managing them. Issues of *management* and *discipline* top every beginning teacher's list of concerns. First: how can you manage a classroom on an overall basis when you have several groups operating simultaneously? Second: what are some particular challenges that your students will be confronting—and that you'll need to help them handle—within a given group? And finally, what disciplinary and behavioral issues confront all teachers—and can you avoid or prevent them? What are some reasonable consequences for students if problems do develop despite your best planning?

Managing Multiple Groups Simultaneously   As you have noted in reading this chapter, substantial segments of classroom time are blocked out for group work. Whether the children are grouped heterogeneously or homogeneously, several small groups will be working at one time. For this process to run smoothly, your students must know what is required of them and have the skills to follow through on those responsibilities. Providing children with interesting, engaging activities with a focus that either works through a process or addresses a short-term goal will be your first concern. Your next is being sure your students have had enough guided practice in completing reading and writing activities independently or in pairs, before you begin organizing groups.

During the first few weeks of school, your job will be to circulate among your students, helping them problem-solve when they get "stuck." Where they can seek help when you are not available can be role-played during a class meeting. Assigning children "study buddies" can alleviate the problem of students coming to you with "What do I do now?" With a partner, children can review the directions they have been given and act independently of the teacher to move themselves along during work time. Giving students permission to choose among several reading and writing activities builds confidence and encourages commitment to their own behavior and performance (Routman, 1991). The opportunities for choice must, of course, be guided, so that you are sure the children are making healthy decisions about their own literacy learning.

When you do begin to call small groups together consistently, instructional time will be lost if you are constantly interrupted by children who are supposed to be working elsewhere in the room. Therefore, you first must be sure that the material students are reading is at their independent level and that they have clear instructions as to what is expected of them both socially and academically. Second, you must make clear that there is another child each can go to for help. Third, you'll need to offer an alternate list of productive choices in case for some reason they cannot continue without you or have completed their required work. Choices usually include activities like centers, independent story writing, word study games, and silent reading. Fourth, you'll want to set aside time for the whole class to process how their work sessions are progressing. In a classroom meeting format, students can brainstorm ideas for adjusting their behavior so that everyone's time will be spent productively. This "talk time" may need to take place only periodically throughout the week, once your students have gained self-monitoring and decision-making skills.

Let's also consider how many groups you can meet with comfortably during an hour (or hour and a half). If you organize three homogeneous reading groups, you won't be able to meet with each group *every* day and still have time to interact with and monitor students who are working independently. More capable readers may need to meet with you only once a week; on other days they are reading and writing by themselves and assembling in literature response groups. Other groups might need to see you every day for ten-minute mini-lessons: children from culturally diverse backgrounds, for instance, and children learning English as a second language (Au, 1993).

Handling Intra-Group Dynamics   The guidelines you establish for small-group experiences are supposed to work in tandem with your emphasis on collaboration and interaction. Much of students' comfort and ease when operating within a particular group dynamic will depend on the training and practice time you provide beginning group work with a highly academic focus. Cohen (1986) reminds us that students may have little previous experience with working in small groups, and therefore may have to learn how to work collaboratively and cooperatively with one another:

> Assigning group tasks involves a major change in traditional classroom norms. Now the student is supposed to depend on other students. Now students are responsible not only for their own behavior but for group behavior and for the product of group efforts. Instead of listening to the teacher they must listen to other students. In order for the group to work smoothly they must learn to ask for other people's opinions, to give other people a chance to talk, and to make brief, sensible contributions to the group effort. These are . . . new norms that are useful to teach before the start of groupwork. (p. 35)

■ **Resource Books for Setting Up a Collaborative Classroom**

■ *Circles of Learning,* by David W. Johnson and Roger T. Johnson et al. (1986). Interaction Book Company, Cooperative Learning Center, University of Minnesota, Minneapolis, Minnesota 55455.

Designing Groupwork, by Elizabeth Cohen (1986).Teachers College Press, 1234 Amsterdam Avenue, New York, NY 10027.

The Collaborative Classroom, by Susan Hill and Tim Hill (1990). Heinemann Educational Books, Inc., 70 Court Street, Portsmouth, NH 03081.

Cooperative Learning: Resources for Teachers #202, by Spencer Kagan

Cooperative Learning and Language Arts: A Multi-Structural Approach #602, by Jeanne Stone. Resources for Teachers, 27134 Paseo Espada #202, San Juan Capistrano, CA 92675.

Student Team Learning: An Overview and Practical Guide, by Robert E. Slavin (1988). NEA Professional Library, The Johns Hopkins Team Learning Project, Center for Social Organization of Schools, Johns Hopkins University, 3505 North Charles Street, Baltimore, MD 21218.

Tribes, by Jeanne Gibbs. Center Source Publications, 305 Tesconi Circle, Santa Rosa, CA 95401.

■ ■ ■

The cultural background of students within each small group will influence how these children react to one another and to their teacher. In general, though, children will benefit greatly from small-group work that gives them time and opportunity to hear other points of view, as well as to express their own.

Au (1993) speaks specifically to the issue that a teacher cannot always respond in his or her traditional dominant role to a group, but instead must adjust a style of interaction to incorporate and validate children's home culture. For example,

> . . . both African American and European American students from working class communities had difficulty seeing that teachers intended their indirect requests to serve as direct commands . . . [w]hile many students from mainstream backgrounds automatically regard teachers as authority figures, many students from diverse backgrounds do not share this perception. Instead students from diverse backgrounds may expect teachers to earn their respect by behaving in an authoritative manner. (pp. 81, 82)

Behavior, Discipline, Choices, and Consequences   It is wise to spend the first few weeks of school establishing "norms" of behavior. You can begin with a discussion of possible classroom rules. (You will certainly need to have a few pre-set procedures for pencil sharpening, bathroom use, hallway behavior, and movement within the room.) You can follow with a brainstorming session on the kinds of behavior your students believe are necessary for a safe, productive, and "kind" classroom. Students can then categorize these ideas. Allowing students to participate in the formulation of rules and to have some say about the consequences for stepping beyond them helps build the collaborative environment.

Time devoted to decision-making where children are able to collect and voice ideas freely, consider alternative choices for getting along together, and offer input about the subjects they study does limit the amount of inappropriate behavior that may occur. Yet there *will* be times when even though you've carefully walked through every direction, practiced and discussed each child's responsibility, matched tasks to be completed with each child's independent and instructional level, and carefully mapped out a time schedule, several children or the entire class may become disruptive. When the entire class is having difficulty, you will find it helpful to stop the activity, review your directions, focus on the trouble spots, and then try again. If one or two small groups are struggling to complete their assignments, reviewing the task to be completed and redefining each child's responsibilities will help redirect the group. If one child continues to be disruptive and uncompromising, you might have him or her work independently, but only as a last resort after several attempts by the child's group members and you to include the child in the activity.

Once an activity or work block is completed, it is helpful to schedule some follow-up discussion time to identify what went well for each group, what trouble areas they experienced, and what their options are for solving problems. The first month of group work will require much "processing" time. Role-playing or talking-through the workings of a successful group will assist children greatly in being able to identify and perform collaborative behavior.

Until group work is second nature to your students, your role will be that of a troubleshooter. You'll need to visit each group to offer guidance in task behavior as well as to answer questions. Then, as group work becomes a routine experience in your classroom, you can spend more of your time as a participating member of particular groups.

It is at this very time that you will have to rely on your classroom rules to provide consequences for inappropriate behavior. (I have always found that two warnings or reminders of what behavior needs to occur are the limit.) If there are substantial rewards for remaining in a group, being removed from it will have a significant effect. Most teachers will first ask a child to work away from a group but within hearing distance, so he or she can benefit from the discussion going on. Sometimes a short break of this nature is all that's necessary to redirect a child's attention. Several minutes of "think" time enables him or her to rejoin the group without causing any further trouble. If, however, a child continues to be disruptive, he or she will need an alternate work space. Having several quiet study areas in the room can give disruptive children an accepted place for completing their work. If these areas are available to everyone, being set apart in this way will have less impact on a child's self-esteem.

Talking with other teachers about devising lessons, selecting appropriate reading material, and redirecting your instructions to meet your students' needs will go a long way toward preventing disciplinary problems in your classroom. As you and your colleagues discuss the timing involved in a smoothly run work session, you will also most likely address how each of you deals with "off-task" behavior. Hearing how others deal with students' inappropriate behavior can help you foresee potential problems (and can give you a frame of reference as to when to simply blame the barometric pressure or the phase of the moon!).

MAKING CONNECTIONS: *Preventing Discipline Problems*

A Dialogue Between Denise Jackson and Brian Sable

After school one day, Denise Jackson wanders into Brian Sable's room. It's January, and the children in her multilevel first-, second-, and third-grade class have decided they would like to investigate North America through self-selected topics.

Denise: Okay, Brian; help me out. My kids want to compile information about North America. I was thrilled to see their excitement, so I want to be sure to plan ahead and have their time spent as productively as possible. Some, of course, will get themselves into reading material that's too difficult for them. Then you know what happens: they begin fooling around and don't get anything done.

Brian: Well, first off, you're going to have to plan for a substantial amount of time for this. You'll have to plan your minilessons around finding information in different kinds of sources: encyclopedias, magazines, newspapers, and so forth. I think they'll probably need more individual guidance, since they'll all be searching for different information. Maybe you should pair them so that they'll have someone to keep them focused. And you're also going to have to set up some kind of network system so that when they come across facts about someone else's topic, they'll have a means of sharing.

Denise: Let me think. Could we set up info mailboxes for each child? I could put out a basket of paper strips so the kids can jot down the book and page numbers where they find their information. Then they could drop the slips into the boxes. I'll have to prepare for the mailboxes ahead of time, or we'll have reference slips all over the place. And I'll

have to schedule time for them to "pick up their mail," or interruptions will come all day long.

Brian: But you've got to get them into the reading first. What are you going to do with those beginning readers who still read word by word? They're the ones who'll get silly on you. Not to mention some of those older boys who have trouble staying focused.

Denise: Well, I have some choices here. I could keep the little ones together in one group so as to keep close tabs on the books they use to find their information. Or I could pair them with more capable readers, those older boys you mentioned; and with some guidance done with the whole class, as well as small-group instruction, they could decide who would be responsible for what. I suppose I'll have to go to more structured direct instruction on reading content material. Then I can gradually move to self-monitored sessions, once everyone has a topic and some background on searching for information. That should take care of those older boys. They do best when they have the leadership role within a group.

Brian: Maybe you'll want to group the kids in threes instead of pairs; that way, if one child is absent, you don't have a beginning reader without any support.

Denise: Good idea. I'm probably best with the heterogeneous groups on this. I can still pull ability groups or needs groups when we come down to the individual compositions. With this type of large endeavor, each of the kids will want his or her own

Other instructional settings

We have discussed several different ways of grouping your students for instruction. When they are not working in small groups, either they'll be assembled together as a whole class or they'll be working individually; each way has its place within the elementary school curriculum.

Preventing Discipline Problems   **continued**

completed project. And anyway, I want everyone to work through the process of reading and writing factual text. We'll have to start by brainstorming possible topics. Then I can ask the librarian to help the kids locate a selection of books that will apply to the majority of us. After we've all done some general reading, we can narrow down the specifics of what they'd like to cover and how they'd like to present the information: make books, posters, maybe puppet shows. I do think that for *this* project, we're going to have to come up with one or two choices for the format so that I don't get stretched too thin and end up feeling frazzled.

Brian: You're going to have to think ahead about those few kids you have who are always wandering around the room. What are you going to do when they won't stay with the younger ones? And don't forget how you're always telling me about that one kid who races ahead in his work and has the whole assignment done before the first-grader even has his name on his paper.

Denise: You're right. I may need to give some kids the choice of working independently on this one. If my intuition is right, that particular child will probably want to work on a topic that no one else is interested in. Having to do all the work himself will be a good experience for him. He'll realize what an easier job the others have.

Brian: But what if they act up? How about consequences for, well, unproductive behavior?

Denise: Suppose I work for the positive and set up a special lunch group for those who keep their groups running smoothly. Each day we can post daily expectations for work to be completed. The groups can keep a "task" chart and check off each child's accomplishments. . . . Then every two days, each group that has *everything* done can eat with me at the picnic tables. The ones who haven't completed their work will then have a required recess study session. I suppose we ought to have a classroom meeting about this before we start. I'll present the ideas you and I've just talked about. I know the kids will have other suggestions for taking care of on-task as well as off-task behavior.

Brian: They always do. This is going to work out great. Let me know how you're doing.

Denise: Thanks for helping me work some of this out. I know I'll be back once we're in the thick of things.

LEARNING IN CONTEXT: **Planning ahead and thinking through instruction ensures better organization and management—as well as fewer discipline problems.**

Whole-Class Instruction As you arrange your daily schedule and make your weekly plans, you will need to organize time when your class can meet as one group. Socially, assembling children together for whole-class instruction will provide the broader setting for building a strong feeling of community—individuals reading and writing, learning and sharing together to create one tightly woven citizenry.

Academically, whole-class instruction can provide opportunities to introduce units of study, gather ideas for extension activities, demonstrate strategies, conduct Guided Listening-Thinking Activities, or give minilessons. It is often during whole-class instruction that we read aloud to children, model how to "think through" a story, and organize for project groups. The chapters that follow will provide you with the background for implementing effective whole-class instructional practices. You'll be using whole-class instruction to teach and review procedures for completing small-group and individual assignments, and this will give your class the time to think and respond to one another's needs collectively. And while you will balance your whole-class instruction with small-group learning, it's during whole-class instruction that you and your students will be able to monitor and reflect upon the day's work.

Individual Instruction In between small-group and whole-class instruction, you will also need to find time to meet with children individually. Most teachers, working within an integrated framework, try to meet with each child at least once a week. You may find it most convenient to embed individual instruction in your writers' workshop conferences—time you set aside to have each child discuss his or her writing with you. During the writing process, children will need time to share compositions in progress. The nature of the instruction that takes place during these conferences will depend on the developmental level of the student and at which point in the "authoring cycle" the student is working.

In addition to writing conferences, you may also want to arrange time for reading conferences. During your individual sessions, after you've shared responses to the book, you can focus your instruction on areas of story structure, author's style, and word analysis. Your time with each child will be short; children *can* often benefit as much, if not more, from similar lessons conducted in a small-group setting. This will be a judgment call based on your knowledge of each child's needs. For emergent and beginning readers, though, you will definitely want to plan a time, however brief, when the two of you can read and write together. That way, you can model the conventions of print in a close, intimate setting.

Other circumstances calling for individual instruction will occur when you have children with exceptional educational, emotional, or social needs. Some may come to you with *individual education plans* that can be fulfilled only through one-on-one contact with you or another teacher. (This subject will be extensively addressed in Chapter 12.) Still other children will show substantial developmental delays and require intensive individual instruction to help them acquire and maintain a functioning status within the classroom. Regardless of the circumstances under which you plan for individual instruction, your decisions will continue to be based on initial and ongoing assessment of your students' developmental needs.

■ A CONCLUDING PERSPECTIVE

We have glimpsed the most important factors in establishing and managing the physical and social organization of your classroom. I hope I have in fact answered some important questions you had about these issues and that I have succeeded in defining some of the "essentials" that go into creating a collaborative interactive classroom. But in doing so, I have probably also caused you to think of additional questions. That is, the questions you are asking now have to do with the "fine-tuning" of these issues: How do you know which books to select for your library corner? How do students know when and which learning centers to go to? The answers will come as you begin the actual process of customizing your instruction to meet your students' needs. So for now, you have learned how to transform an empty classroom into a learning environment in which both you and the children you teach will have an honest and compelling stake in what is read, written about, learned, and enjoyed.

This collaborative interactive classroom, this learning environment, will develop in large part because of your knowledge of your students and of the homes from which they come. The whole-class, small-group, and individual instruction you organize will extend and nurture your students' strengths so that they will feel like confident and valued members of a learning community. The environment you establish will have focus and vision because you will have spent time examining and organizing the curriculum in such a way that its content crosses subject areas and engages student interest.

Beginning with the next chapter, "Developing Beginning Reading," we'll answer those many new questions you have been generating. The answers will build your knowledge base about teaching reading in an authentic reading environment that interconnects with all areas of the curriculum. By the time you reach the end of the book, you will be well on your way toward confidently answering this fundamental question about teaching, the question often put to you by parents, other teachers, administrators: just *why* are you doing what you do?

■ BECOMING A REFLECTIVE PRACTITIONER

Allington, R.L. (1991). Children who find learning to read difficult: School responses to diversity. In E. Hiebert (Ed.), *Literacy for a diverse society: Perspectives, practices, and policies* (pp. 237–252). New York: Teachers College Press.
This chapter presents a good overview of the issues surrounding struggling readers and diversity. It portrays how teachers can respond in various situations to children from diverse backgrounds. Allington's previous research, which underlies part of his presentation here, has addressed the differential responses of teachers to students classified as "poor" or "good" readers. Traditionally, teachers have focused on skills and "sounding out" strategies for poor readers, while emphasizing "reading for meaning" with the better readers. *All* children should perceive the literacy environment as well as the act of reading as meaningful, and teachers can send this message through the ways in which they interact in literacy contexts with their students.

Atwell, N. (1987). *In the middle: Writing, reading, and learning with adolescents.* Montclair, NJ: Boynton/Cook.
This book has become a classic of sorts. It offers information about how to set up and sustain both a *reading workshop* and a *writing workshop* in the classroom. Although it

is concerned primarily with middle school students, almost all of it is appropriate for intermediate students. I am recommending it here because the "mechanics" of organizing and scheduling are particularly relevant to this chapter.

Cohen, E. (1994). Restructuring the classroom: Conditions for productive small groups. *Review of Educational Research, 64,* 1–35.

Elizabeth Cohen is well known for her work in helping teachers establish productive learning environments. I refer to and recommend her book, *Designing Groupwork,* in this chapter. In this article, Cohen reviews research that explores the "fine-tuning" of small group learning situations. Cohen explains that, depending on the nature of the learning task, either informal or more formal, guided small-group interaction may be desirable. Issues of "status" within groups also depend on the nature of the tasks the group undertakes.

■ REFERENCES

Allington, R. (1991). Children who find learning to read difficult: School responses to diversity. In E. Hiebert (Ed.), *Literacy for a diverse society: Perspectives, practices, and policies* (pp. 237–252). New York: Teachers College Press.

Atwell, N. (1987). *In the middle: Writing, reading, and learning with adolescents.* Montclair, NJ: Boynton/Cook.

Au, K. (1993). *Literacy instruction in multicultural settings.* Fort Worth, TX: Harcourt Brace Jovanovich.

Barr, R. (1989). The social organization of literacy instruction. In S. McCormick and J. Zutell (Eds.), *Cognitive and social perspectives for literacy research and instruction,* Thirty-eighth Yearbook of the National Reading Conference (pp. 19–33). Chicago, IL: National Reading Conference.

Betts, E. (1946). *Foundations of reading instruction.* New York: American Book Company.

Calkins, L. (1991). *Living between the lines.* Portsmouth, NH: Heinemann.

Clay, M. (1979). *The early detection of reading difficulties.* Exeter, NH: Heinemann.

Cohen, E. (1986). *Designing groupwork.* New York: Teachers College Press.

Estes, T. (1971). A scale to measure attitudes toward reading. *Journal of Reading, 15,* 135–138.

Evertson, C., Emmer, E., Clements, B., Sanford, J., & Worsham, M. (1989). *Classroom management for elementary teachers.* Englewood Cliffs, NJ: Prentice-Hall.

Flood, J., Lapp, D., Flood, S., & Nagel, G. (1992). Am I allowed to group? Using flexible patterns for effective instruction. *Reading Teacher, 45,* 608–616.

Hansen, J. (1987). *When writers read.* Portsmouth, NH: Heinemann.

Johnson, D., & Johnson, R. (1975). *Learning together and alone: Cooperation, competition, and individualization.* Englewood Cliffs, NJ: Prentice-Hall.

Kohn, A. (1986). How to succeed without even vying. *Psychology Today, 20,* 22–28.

Lipson, M., & Wixson, K. (1991). *Assessment and instruction of reading disability: An interactive approach.* New York: HarperCollins.

McKenna, M., & Kear, D. (1990). Measuring attitude toward reading: A new tool for teachers. *Reading Teacher, 43,* 626–639.

Norton, D. (1991). *The impact of literature-based reading instruction.* Columbus, OH: Merrill.

Pikulski, J., & Shanahan, T. (Eds.). (1982). *Approaches to the informal evaluation of reading.* Newark, DE: International Reading Association.

Routman, R. (1991). *Invitations.* Portsmouth, NH: Heinemann.

Shake, M. (1989). Grouping and pacing with basal materials. In P. Winograd, K. Wixson, & M. Lipson (Eds.), *Improving basal reading instruction* (pp. 62–85). New York: Teachers College Press.

Sharan, S. (1980). Cooperative learning in small groups: Recent methods and effects on achievement, attitudes, and ethnic relations. *Review of Educational Research, 50,* 241–271.

Slavin, R. (1986). Learning together. *American Educator, 10,* 6–13.

Slavin, R. (1980). Cooperative learning. *Review of Educational Research, 50,* 315–342.

Stauffer, R. (1969). *Directing reading maturity as a cognitive process.* New York: Harper and Row.

Tierney, R., Readence, J., & Dishner, E. (1990). *Reading strategies and practices* (3rd ed.). Boston: Allyn & Bacon.

Torbe, M., & Medway, P. (1981). *The climate for learning.* Montclair, NJ: Boynton/ Cook.

Children's Literature Cited

Bash, B. (1989). *Tree of life: The world of the African baobab.* Sierra Club.

Baylor, B. (1976). *Hawk, I'm your brother.* Macmillan.

Baylor, B. (1992). *Guess who my favorite person is?* Macmillan.

Cherry, L. (1990). *The great kapok tree: A tale of the Amazon rain forest.* Harcourt Brace Jovanovich.

Ehlert, L. (1991). *Red leaf, yellow leaf.* Harcourt Brace Jovanovich.

Keats, E. J. (1962). *The snowy day.* Viking.

Keats, E. J. (1964). *Whistle for Willie.* Viking Children's Books.

Keats, E. J. (1967). *Peter's chair.* Harper & Row.

Keats, E. J. (1968). *Letter to Amy.* HarperCollins.

Keats, E. J. (1971). *Apt. 3.* Macmillan.

Keats, E. J. (1971). *Over in the meadow.* Scholastic.

Keats, E. J. (1987). *Goggles.* Macmillan.

Keats, E. J. (1987). *John Henry: An American legend.* Knopf Books.

Keats, E. J. (1987). *Regards to the man in the moon.* Macmillan.

Keats, E. J. (1988). *Hi cat.* Macmillan.

Manes, S. (1982). *Be a perfect person in just three days.* Bantam.

McNulty, F. (1986). *The lady and the spider.* HarperTrophy.

CHAPTER FIVE

DEVELOPING
BEGINNING
READING

FOCUS

■ *Why should we continue to read to children during the beginning-reading phase?*

■ *What are the sources of "predictability" in predictable texts, and how do they support the beginning reader?*

■ *How does the Language Experience Approach facilitate children's learning about reading?*

■ *What are sight words? What is their role in instruction about word identification?*

■ *How can beginning readers' concept development be an integral part of their beginning-reading experiences?*

■ *What activities will guide young students in their ability to "make meaning" from the texts they read?*

■ *Explain why* writing *supports learning to read—and vice versa.*

■ *How can we combine children's learning about word structure with their applying this knowledge through word-identification strategies?*

> . . . even at their orneriest, consonants were fun. Vowels were
> something else. He didn't like them, and they didn't like him . . .
> you could go through twenty words without bumping into some of
> the shyer consonants, but it seemed as if you couldn't tiptoe past a
> syllable without waking up a vowel. Consonants, you knew pretty
> much where they stood, but you could never trust a vowel.
>
> *Jerry Spinelli,* Maniac Magee

> "Jem, that damn lady says Atticus's been teaching me to read and
> for him to stop it—"
> "Don't worry, Scout," Jem comforted me. "Our teacher says Miss
> Caroline's introducing a new way of teaching [reading]. She learned
> about it in college. . . . It's the Dewey Decimal System."
>
> *Harper Lee,* To Kill a Mockingbird

Throughout the decades, and for all kinds of reasons, perhaps no area in education has been more controversial than the teaching of beginning reading. As Jerry Spinelli engagingly portrays in *Maniac Magee,* the relationship between letters and sounds can be a problem for many people. And as for the *methodology* of teaching beginning reading, Harper Lee humorously captures the eternal hope that the one "true" way to teach *all* children to read may yet be found.

In both psychology and education, there is much beneficial information about the beginning-reading phase, but there also has been a great deal of mysticism. Much research has been conducted in an effort to determine the "best way" to teach beginning reading, but what it all comes down to is this: a teacher who knows what children need to learn and who motivates and engages them in *wanting* to explore the worlds in print and learn how that print is put together—a teacher who immerses the children in stories, information, and words, helping them think and grow in ways that depend critically on reading. So while children will learn how they can bring their own background experience and their own understanding of the world to every encounter they have with written language, they will also be learning what print is and how it represents spoken language.

In this chapter, we will be looking at critical elements of instruction. They are based on a solid theoretical and teaching foundation and assume that the kinds of experiences discussed in Chapter 3 have occurred: children have been immersed in print and are aware that it is used to communicate and to inform. If children have not had early literacy experiences, this exposure (and a certain amount of play) with print must occur before formal reading instruction can begin. Before we wade more deeply into the chapter, let's examine the critical elements of reading instruction.

WHAT DO WE MEAN BY "BEGINNING READING"?

We have been referring to "beginning reading" often, up to this point. Now, however, it is time to plunge into this area with all the comprehensiveness it needs and deserves. Therefore, this section will explore all the implications of beginning reading, through four related themes:

- Messages we wish to impart about reading
- Tracing a developmental flow
- Tracing an instructional flow
- Relating beginning writing to beginning reading

Messages we wish to impart about reading

By the end of the first month or two of first grade, what messages about "reading" do we wish our students to have received? We hope that the children are the beneficiaries of *our* cornerstones, or tenets, of instruction as laid out in Chapter 1—so let's look at our beginning-reading instruction from the *children's* perspective.

- "Reading" is *real* reading—it is done with books and other types of texts for enjoyment and for information.

- Reading involves losing yourself every now and then in the book you are looking at. Whether you are lost in the world of a story or in the intricacies of examining the details in a diagram, you are finding in books some very interesting *other* worlds, and you are learning something about them.

- Reading is making meaning, especially when you think ahead to what will happen later on in a story and then are delighted or surprised at how things turn out.

- Because of these first three fulfilling experiences, you believe that reading is *fun;* that books are, indeed, friends—pleasurable to encounter on first acquaintance and on subsequent visits as well.

- An important part of your experiences has to do with coming to understand how print works and being able to say the words that the page holds—to release them and feel your control over them. This is truly empowerment of the first order, and many of your successful experiences with discovering how to know what those words probably are have been arranged and supported by your teacher.

Recall from Chapter 1 what Margaret Meek observed about beginning reading; it bears repeating in this context:

> The way children are taught to read tells them what adults think literacy is . . . so when we help children to read, we are also telling them about literacy and society, about the reasons for reading and about themselves as learners. The view of reading a child accepts is the one his first teacher gives him. (1983, pp. 18–19)

Tracing a developmental flow

In our society the term *beginning reading* is commonly taken to refer to *instruction* with all its connotations of different methods or approaches. Traditionally, the aim of beginning-reading instruction has been to help children acquire a sight vocabulary that includes the words most frequently occurring in print and to help them acquire "decoding" or word-identification skills through phonics instruction, thus enabling them to identify unknown words in print. This is a laudable aim and one that we embrace wholeheartedly. The problem was that all too often, the pursuit of this aim obscured just about everything else that had to do with "reading." Children who had developed the concepts associated with emergent literacy became bored; children who had not developed those concepts became frustrated; and all too often (in the interest of teaching children *how* to read) such instruction inadvertently removed the *desire* to read. We'll look into this phenomenon more in Chapter 10.

In this chapter, I am using the term *beginning reading* in two ways: first, as a label for a developmental phase; and second, as signifying an orientation to the instruction that occurs over the course of the early grades, primarily the first and second grades. I want to point out a potential point of confusion stemming from the use of the term in this dual sense. The two meanings do work well together for first grade, where most children are in fact "beginning readers" developmentally. However, at some point in second grade, most children will be in the "transitional" phase of literacy development. With this duality understood, we can continue using *beginning reading* as a term because it will allow us to demonstrate developmental trends across several chapters. We began with emergent literacy in Chapter 3 (preschool through kindergarten and beginning first grade). This chapter will address instructional issues for grades 1 and 2; Chapters 6 and 7 will overlap developmentally with transitional readers in grade 3 and move toward mature, proficient reading for students in grade 4 and beyond.

Let's consider, for a moment, beginning reading as it has been developmentally defined—the phase most first-graders will be in at some time during the year and that some second-graders will still be in. (As we observed earlier, the label *beginning reading* actually does not capture the competencies that children at this level have developed. *Beginning conventional reading* would be more precise, but in the interests of brevity I will continue to use the shorter and more common label.) We find two complementary processes going on during this beginning-reading phase. First, when compared to the emergent phase, children in the beginning-reading phase have acquired sufficient knowledge to allow them to explore deliberately and in more depth the nature and functions of print. They are really focusing in on print to learn about it and how it works, and they are focusing on words and the relationships between letters and sounds. Most children's attention to these aspects is so pronounced that this phase has been described as one in which the children are "glued" to the print (Chall, 1983; Juel, 1991). Second, this is a time of empowerment, of feeling that a world of books can be explored, because the ability to crack the code—to understand conventional letter/sound relationships—affords a child the opportunity to discover what is *really* there in the print, to construct and understand messages that others truly intended to convey. Once children begin to exhibit these behaviors, we can say that they are in the beginning-reading phase.

A balanced instructional environment will allow these complementary processes to develop. As we saw earlier, an environment weighted too heavily toward the "print" aspects will rarely lead to sustained enjoyment and excitement with reading. An environment weighted too heavily toward simple immersion in texts without appropriate and timely attention to the print will lead to frustration when children do not develop the knowledge that enables them to explore new texts.

Following is a brief review of the observable developmental characteristics of the beginning-reading phase (you may wish to refer back to the developmental chart on page 62 in Chapter 2 and review the discussion there).

- Children have a *concept of word in print,* which means that they can match a printed word in a line of text to a spoken word. Early in this phase they usually point to each word as they are reading it.
- Children know the names of most if not all letters of the alphabet.
- Children are able to tell how many sounds are in a word and can represent each with a letter as they "invent" the spelling of a word.
- Children's reading is usually "out loud"; reading of unfamiliar texts is word-by-word and may be "choppy."

Tracing an instructional flow

The five messages about reading we want first-grade children to receive early in the year define our instructional goals for the whole year, if not beyond. Within the instructional environment that will develop these goals, we will be focusing deliberately on specific areas. Aspects of each area may be emphasized throughout this phase; other aspects will be emphasized at different times. This chapter is set up to reflect these emphases. As you read and study the chapter, notice the two fundamental characteristics of the instructional flow:

First, we support children early on but gradually relinquish a certain amount of control as they acquire more knowledge and more strategies for applying that knowledge.

Second, we emphasize meaning first and meaning throughout as we clearly maintain our focus on constructing meaning. Our examination of words, of how they work, and of how this knowledge is applied in reading will be embedded within this emphasis.

Here are the major areas we will be addressing:

- Reading aloud to children in a regular classroom setting, involving them more deeply in the read-aloud, and—for beginning readers—extending the "shared-book experience" that we introduced with emergent readers
- Extending the Language Experience Approach beyond the initial "group dictation" stage appropriate for emergent readers

- Building and maintaining children's sight vocabulary, words they identify immediately in print
- Supporting children in their more focused efforts to make meaning, as we deliberately explore different types of texts and expand conceptual/ vocabulary knowledge
- Employing *writing* as a means of learning about print as well as of developing ways of thinking about and dealing with the world
- Identifying words—helping children learn about word structure and how to apply that knowledge in their reading
- Encouraging children's reaching beyond to take those first steps into reading books comfortably on their own

Within this overall flow, it is important to realize that on occasion there are overlaps in which some instructional activities simultaneously address different emphases, and that because children will be at different developmental points with different strengths and needs, there will be individual situations you will need to address. We addressed the logistics of accommodating these needs in Chapter 4, and we will be addressing this issue throughout the rest of this text.

Figure 5.1 highlights the flow of instruction during the beginning-reading phase. Chapters 6 and 7 will pick up this instructional flow and emphasize the intermediate grades and later developmental phases. Notice how *constructing meaning* is both a unifying thread throughout all phases and an ultimate goal.

Relating beginning writing to beginning reading

There has been a revolution over the past few years in the way educators have thought about *writing* and its role in the literacy development of primary-grade children. We have already addressed the *development* of writing in young children, and at this point we will consider how we can address its role instructionally. We'll see that writing relates to reading in a number of fundamental ways:

- Writing helps children think of themselves as authors; this "thinking like a writer" permits a deeper, reverberating understanding of what *reading* text is all about.
- Writing in *response* to reading fosters deeper reflection on and understanding of what has been read.
- Writing allows children the opportunity to exercise their developing knowledge about words and other conventions of print and about the purposes and genres of different kinds of texts.

Children at this phase of development may appear to labor over every word, and sometimes every sound. But this is a labor that children can undertake willingly because it can be incredibly rewarding and self-motivating. Each word that a child puzzles through to represent on the paper is truly a creation that can be understood by another, and that is powerful incentive indeed.

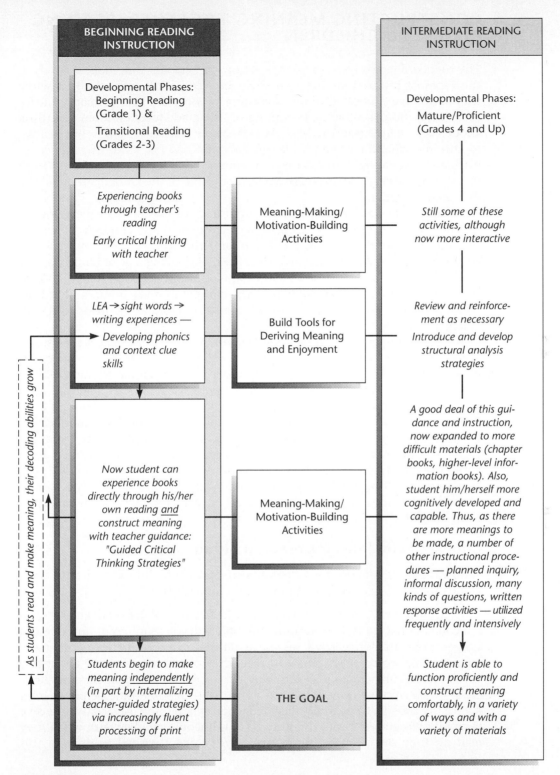

Figure 5.1
Instructional Flow in Beginning Reading

CONSTRUCTING MEANING TOGETHER: READING ALOUD TO CHILDREN

The roots of literacy lie in social interaction. In Chapter 3 we looked closely at the types of interactions that can occur between adults and children while they're sharing a book. Children's concept of story emerges primarily out of such interaction, and by the beginning of first grade most children can think about stories and respond to them. As a classroom teacher, you must be sensitive to children who, for whatever reason, have not had the kinds of experiences discussed in Chapter 3; to ensure your students' literacy success you will need to infuse these very activities into the daily routine of the kindergarten and the first-grade experience.

We can appreciate the impact and importance of our role as readers of texts to children if we are aware of this simple fact: for so many children, *we* will be the only literate adults reading to them, and this *teacher's* voice may be the only voice that models for children the sound of the language of books—a very special "sound" indeed, as we saw in Chapter 3. In this section we will look at the how-to's of reading to children in the context of a classroom and at how you can extend and elaborate the type of read-aloud format we introduced with emergent readers.

For beginning readers, "read-aloud" experiences are *extensions* of the "story-book reading" we discussed in Chapter 3 for older preschoolers who are emergent readers (p. 103). The two kinds of experiences are similar in that children talk about what is read, make predictions about what may happen and then follow up on those predictions, and relate what is going on in a book to their own lives and to other books they have experienced. The big difference for beginning readers is that their discussions can have more depth than younger children's, for by this point in their development the beginning readers have had more life experience, and they know more about how books "work." Also bear in mind, though, that there are many times during which you should simply read to the children with little if any discussion; allow them simply to hear and enjoy the language and the story as it washes over them.

General guidelines for reading aloud

Following are guidelines for what *you* can do before, during, and after read-alouds for your class (adapted from Templeton, 1991b):

1. *Read the book yourself before you read it to the children.* Reread or at least skim it if you have not read it in some time. Not only will you be more comfortable and simply do a better job, you will see ahead of time any problematic or potentially embarrassing words or references. (I recently violated my own rule about this when I read Faulkner's "A Rose for Emily" to my reading/language arts methods class. It is a riveting story, but I had not read it for some time before sharing it with my class. So I was mildly flustered when I encountered a racially offensive term I had forgotten was in the story—a word people can deal with when they read on their own, but definitely not a word that I wished to utter in this

particular context. I "edited" Faulkner's phrase, but it was clear to my students, I'm afraid, that I was momentarily thrown . . .)

2. *At the beginning of the year, read shorter, more attention-grabbing selections; then work into longer ones later on.* This will be highly dependent on your grade level. If you are teaching an intermediate grade, you may be able to begin the year with a longer picture book that will take several days to read, working your way into chapter books by the end of the first month of school. With primary children, you may need to start with highly engaging picture books and remain with this genre for several months, including longer stories as your students become accustomed to blocks of time devoted to listening.

3. *Read books that you enjoy.* It is difficult to force personal enjoyment of a book, much less to try to convey that enjoyment to children. If you are attuned to your students you will usually make good selections. Do *not,* however, continue reading a book that you adore but that doesn't seem to hold the students' interest. This is particularly important to remember when reading longer stories and chapter books.

4. *Set aside a particular time each day for reading to the children.* This is a special time, one that they'll eagerly anticipate. Some teachers set this time apart by sitting in a special chair or even wearing an unusual hat while reading.

5. *Allow time for students to settle down and be attentive before beginning reading.* The "mood" cannot arise spontaneously, so students need to be receptive—and they will more likely be so if you allow this time *and,* of course, if the story or book is eagerly anticipated. You'll also need to remember that the children should all be listening, not engaged in some other activity. This should definitely *not* be a time during which students complete unfinished work; they should be clearly tuned in to the reading. They need to *hear* and attend to the language, to think and feel about what is happening, to build images in their mind's eye.

6. *Sit or move in a way that allows you to project your voice effectively to all the children and that lets them all see any pictures you show.* In the primary grades, children can usually be up at the front of the room with you, seated in a semicircle or large cluster. When they remain in their seats, however (and this certainly pertains to older students), many teachers prefer to walk around when reading picture books so that when they show the pictures, all the children will have a chance to see them up close.

7. *Read slowly.* Most of us have the tendency to speed up when we are reading before a group. We need to be conscious of when to slow down, because our listeners need time to imagine and visualize what is happening (and how and why it happens) and to appreciate, reflect on, and *savor* the words they hear.

8. *Read a variety of stories and chapter books over the course of the school year.* If you're reading a longer selection, stop at a suspenseful place. This will surely help on the following day when you're waiting for the children to settle down before the read-aloud.

9. *Most of the time, allow for response and reaction to what has been read.* There are many levels of responding to a read-aloud, from the discussion of general impressions to more probing questions and reflections. As we'll see later on, these response sessions can be a very important part of your literature-based

units. Beware, though, of falling into the habit of "interpreting" the selection for the children, for this could teach the children that *you* are supposed to be the source of the "true" meaning of a book. (It is a different matter, however, to *guide* them in responding to the selection.)

10. *You'll need to practice!* You're already familiar with your mirror, so start there—practice in front of it. This will help you feel more comfortable looking up now and then to engage your students' eyes. Your next step is to practice with one of your own classmates and then before a small group of supportive friends.

■ BUILDING YOUR KNOWLEDGE BASE

■ Read-Aloud Books Appropriate for Beginning Readers

The following books work exceptionally well as read-alouds for beginning readers because of their content, their language, or both:

Aardema, V. (1978). *Why mosquitoes buzz in people's ears: A West African tale.* Dial Books.

Allard, H. (1974). *The Stupids step out.* Houghton Mifflin.

dePaola, T. (1975). *Strega Nona.* Prentice-Hall.

Erickson, R. (1974). *A toad for Tuesday.* Lothrop, Lee and Shepard.

Fisher, R. (Ed.) (1986). *Ghosts galore: Haunting verse.* Faber and Faber.

Freeman, D. (1968). *Corduroy.* Viking.

Gag, W. (1928). *Millions of cats.* Coward, McCann and Geoghegan.

Heide, F. (1971). *The shrinking of Treehorn.* Holiday House.

Kennedy, R. (1975). *The contests at Cowlick.* Little, Brown.

Lobel, A. (1985). *Frog and Toad are friends.* Harper and Row.

Michels, B., & White, B. (1983). *Apples on a stick: The folklore tales of black children.* Coward, McCann and Geoghegan/Putnam

Milne, A. A. (1926). *Winnie the Pooh.* Methuen.

McCloskey, R. (1976). *Make way for ducklings.* Penguin.

Pinkwater, J. (1983). *The cloud horse.* Lothrop, Lee and Shepard.

Potter, B. *The tale of Peter Rabbit.* Frederick Warne.

Sendak, M. (1984). *Where the wild things are.* Harper and Row.

Steig, W. (1969). *Sylvester and the magic pebble.* Simon and Schuster.

Viorst, J. (1975). *Alexander who used to be rich last Sunday.* Atheneum/Macmillan.

Waber, B. (1975). *The house on East 88th Street.* Houghton Mifflin.

Waber, B. (1975). *Ira sleeps over.* Houghton Mifflin.

Williams, V. (1982). *A chair for my mother.* Greenwillow.

Zolotow, C. (1972). *William's doll.* Harper and Row.

Listening-thinking activities

There are many ways for us to involve children in read-aloud experiences in which they are actively engaged in listening, thinking, and discussing. To get a handle on good practices, I will present listening-thinking activities within the context of two excellent procedures, the Guided Listening-Thinking Activity and the shared-book experience.

Guided Listening-Thinking Activity The Guided Listening-Thinking Activity (GLTA) is a read-aloud *with a more focused interaction* with the children. It builds on the foundation established with storybook reading (see p. 103, Chapter 3). In storybook reading with emergent readers, an adult familiarizes the children with storybooks and stories in general, including simple elements of stories such as who the characters are and the order of events. When children have those basic concepts—when they are beginning readers—then the Guided Listening-Thinking Activity is very appropriate. Because beginning readers (in contrast to emergent readers) know more about books and stories and so forth, you can help them become more *aware* of how they are interacting with a story and help them become more *thoughtful* about the story and what the author is sharing with them. Even though you are reading to them, they are more focused and "in control" of this interaction than emergent readers usually are. And most important, the GLTA allows beginning readers the opportunity to enjoy and reflect on stories that they might not yet be able to read on their own— usually because of the number of unfamiliar words in the text.

The GLTA strategy helps children become aware of what they already know about the content of a book or story to be read, and it helps them engage the "known" as they relate it to the "new." You should know, by the way, that the basic format of the GLTA will apply when children eventually are *reading* stories on their own (we'll address that later in this chapter and again in Chapters 6 and 7).

Here are the basic steps of the Guided Listening-Thinking Activity. The procedure remains pretty much the same when used with older students.

1. Select an appropriate book to share. Of course, with first-graders the book will very often be a picture book.
2. After reading the title of the book to the students and showing them the first picture or two, ask, "What do you think this story might be about?"
3. Read to a predetermined stopping place. This should be a point in the story where the plot or action rises to a "peak." Ask the students, "*Now* what do you think?" This helps them relate the predictions they first made to what they have learned from the story, and those predictions now can be confirmed, rejected, or revised. Occasionally ask the students "Why?" or "Why not?" after a prediction. When you're ready to resume reading, say something like, "Well, let's listen now and find out!"
4. After the reading, you may ask several questions based on the children's reaction to the book. For example, you can ask them where in the story they realized that such-and-such was happening . . . and how do they think so-and-so felt about it—thereby getting them to think back to the

story and use information to support an idea. You may ask whether *they* have had similar experiences or how they felt about what happened.

It is important that you remain flexible with the procedure for the Guided Listening-Thinking Activity. For example, you don't need to ask children to justify their predictions every time; just often enough that they will get used to thinking about the reasons for their ideas and used to justifying their opinions.

The Shared-Book Experience   The shared-book experience, which we first introduced in Chapter 3, is similar to the Guided Listening-Thinking Activity in many ways. Most notably, both experiences involve children within a comfortable and facilitative social context in a meaningful interaction with a story—the children are actively listening, thinking, and discussing. On the other hand, there are some significant differences between these two types of activities because of their different literacy objectives.

The GLTA is primarily a *listening* experience. The shared-book experience involves not only listening to the text but looking at the print and joining in with the reading of the text. Slaughter (1993) pointed out the sequenced, logical nature of the shared-book experience: "Children first become familiar with an entire story; teachers then use this familiarity to help students attend gradually to smaller segments of text—sentences first, then phrases and words within sentences, and finally letters within words" (p. 7).

The shared-book experience involves the use of a predictable-text Big Book (see Chapter 3, p. 110). McGee and Richgels observed that ". . . informal talking with children about what people do when they read can be very helpful . . . Big Books merely make that kind of talk available for more than one child at a time" (1989, p. 286). Big Books allow participation in the shared reading

The shared-book experience involves a predictable-text Big Book such as the one this teacher is sharing with the children in her classroom.

because children can clearly see the print and pictures in the enlarged format. Because of the predictability of these texts, children can catch on to their rhythm, cadence, and pattern and "choral read" them. And since children are able to memorize these texts comfortably, they may even learn to identify most or all of the words in the book in a short period of time. The accompanying "regular-size" versions of the Big Books can then be enjoyed and examined independently or in small groups with you.

While for emergent readers the shared-book experience allows the modeling of more global functions and features of books for beginning readers, the shared-book experience can be extended in the following ways for beginning readers (Combs, 1987; McGee & Richgels, 1989; Slaughter, 1993):

Children can be involved in a more elaborate interaction with the Big Book than they may have been during the emergent phase. For example, you may provide more informative introductions and more extensive questions, help the children with inferences (more about this later), more deliberately tie the book content to background knowledge by helping the children examine what they already know and make adjustments in their thinking, and so on.

You can write down predictions the children make, involve them in a deeper or more extended response to the book, focus more deliberately on words and sounds.

As with the Guided Listening-Thinking Activity, you may wish to stop at predictable places to check predictions and make further ones. You can demonstrate how to use the text to corroborate or check information—for example, pointing to sentences or words or places on the page where information can be found.

Although most of your questioning will spring from the children's predictions and responses, you can feel free to check children's understanding of specific information. For example, after reading the book *The Greedy Goat* (Bolton, 1986), you might ask a question or two about which animal came first, second, or third to try to help the old lady after the goat locked her out of her house; you could probe to check whether students recall what the goat ate and how much of it he ate ("all of the rice pudding, to the very last grain").

Your *re*readings of the book with the children can be more probing, looking at supportive or contradictory information as well as at language that has stimulated the children's imaginations. For example, in *When the King Rides By* (Mahy, 1986), a predictable text that follows a cumulative pattern (people, animals, and things are added to the crowd as the King rides by), a child may ask, "What's a *mouse*-hold?" after hearing

Oh, what a fuss when the king rides by:
Rockets dance in the starry sky,
Mice in their mouse-hold wonder why,
The people throw their hats up high . . .

This is an opportunity for another child or you to ask if "mouse-hold" reminds anyone of another word. . . . You can query, "Have you ever heard of a . . . *house*hold? What is that? Is that a clue to *mouse*-hold? What might a mouse-hold be like? Do we get any ideas from the illustration? Does *mouse-hold* seem like a funny word to you? Why do you think the author used *mouse-hold* instead of maybe *hole* or *home?*" Such discussion gets children thinking about language and how different words have different effects and can give us different or more elaborate pictures in our minds (recall the importance of imagery in supporting students' comprehension of texts).

Many *informational* books are now published in Big Book format, and they lend themselves very nicely to shared-book experiences. For example, *Animal Clues* (Drew, 1987) has marvelous close-up photographs of parts of different creatures, accompanied by written clues:

Here is my eye [close-up of the eye]
and here are my claws [close-up].
I live near your house. I am a . . . [turn the page]
lizard [photograph of the *whole* lizard].

This format obviously leads to excellent predictions from the children during the initial reading, and the photographs provide opportunities for discussion about different characteristics of the creatures during rereadings and follow-up discussions.

Segments of the text may be reread by several children *together* as well as by individual children. Depending on the story, certain children can read what different characters say (the lines spoken by the different animals in *The Greedy Goat,* for example).

To give them a feeling of reading with fluency in a text that they cannot read on their own with ease, you can have the children read a line or lines in "echo" fashion immediately after you read them. This may be done first in the whole group, with children echo-reading individually as they become comfortable with doing so. Echo-reading will be particularly important for the second-language learners in your classroom. You may need to read with these children one-on-one to be sure they feel comfortable sharing and that they are following the text appropriately, for words can easily become confused.

BUILDING A STORE OF KNOWN WORDS: SIGHT VOCABULARY

What is sight vocabulary and why is it so important?

A *sight word* is a printed word that a reader is able to identify immediately. *Sight vocabulary* is the term commonly used to refer to all the printed words that a particular reader is able to identify immediately by sight. We want to develop beginning readers' sight vocabularies so that their encounters with printed materials will be more comfortable; when they can identify most words automatically, they can construct meaning more comfortably and efficiently as they read. If beginning readers spend the majority of their time trying to figure out most of the words they encounter, reading becomes more of a labor than a reward. There is an important link between sight vocabulary and reading fluency: a child's reading fluency increases in part because his sight vocabulary expands each time he reads a familiar text. The more he reads, the more fluent he becomes, and the larger his sight vocabulary grows. In this way the beginning reader builds the experience in reading that in turn builds the foundation for more proficient reading later on. Such reading is possible because mature, proficient readers possess large sight vocabularies.

Many of the words that beginning readers need to learn are words that occur often in print—so often that they account for most of the words that appear in most texts. These are words such as *the, of, where, that, then,* and *to—function words* that "glue" ideas or content words together. Out of context, function words do not carry much meaning. In addition, many cannot be figured out by using letter/sound knowledge. Therefore, function words need to be learned *in context*. Repetitive pattern books where function words appear again and again in a predictable fashion can provide one type of meaningful context; environmental print is another. It is obvious that reading would be slowed significantly if a child had to stop every time she encountered one of these words to try to figure it out; it's better that she recognize the function word automatically.

Because of the importance of these high-frequency words, over the years a number of word lists have appeared that give words most frequently occurring in written English (for example, Dolch, 1936; Fry, 1980; Johnson, 1976; Kucera & Francis, 1982). These lists are helpful as a reference, informing teachers about the words that children at different grade levels are likely to encounter. However, these lists are often *mis*used, albeit with the best of intentions. For example, many teachers have attempted to teach these words in isolation, out of context, or in contrived sentences that are not part of meaningful, authentic reading experiences. Worse yet, easily confused words such as *the, these, then, that, there* and *when, where,* and *what* are often put on flash cards and children drilled on them. Ironically, all such attempts to "teach" these words out of meaningful context are the *least* effective means of doing so. Because the words usually have no concrete meaning and no real-world referent, they are by nature more abstract. Beginning readers encountering them out of context have next to no meaningful associations with them (Johnson & Pearson, 1982). As we just pointed out, such words are *best* learned in meaningful printed contexts; because they occur so often in print, children are likely to learn them more comfortably.

Besides function words, beginning readers will also develop a storehouse of sight words which, though not high-frequency words, are sight words nonetheless because they hold special meaning for the child. These include words such as *elephant, jump rope, pizza,* or *Suburban*. Other commonly used words that can be visualized or physically experienced or encountered will also become part of a child's sight vocabulary. Words of this nature might include, for example, *bed, bike, tree, pencil, bed, sister, table, car, grass, sink*—and so many of these words *are* spelled more "regularly." They can and should be used as the basis for beginning phonics instruction.

While sight words should always be *learned* within a meaningful context, most beginning readers will also need to *examine* their sight words outside a connected text situation. For this reason, sight words are at first written on cards that the children can keep in "word banks" (see below). Together with lots of reading, this practice of collecting words and then reviewing and examining them ensures that the children's memory for the words—as well as their developing understanding about phonics and word structure—can be reinforced regularly (Brady & Shankweiler, 1991; Gough, Ehri, & Treiman, 1992; Reiben & Perfetti, 1991).

Early sources of sight words

We have already seen that emergent readers are capable of remembering a few words and "reading" them. Because beginning readers know more about words as printed entities and because they know more about the relationships between letters and sounds, they are able to build up a sight vocabulary more rapidly than emergent children. These sight words are learned first in meaningful contexts—that is, in the real world as well as in engaging printed materials—so it is worth spending some time here describing the sorts of contexts and experiences that facilitate children's acquisition of sight words.

Environmental Print, Basic Concepts, and Personal Names Because the real world contains all kinds of environmental print—and therefore all kinds of opportunities for learning words—we take advantage of this and build on it in the classroom. If you can, bring in signs and labels (or copies of them) from the community and the home and talk about what they mean. You will thereby establish a strong foundation for children's learning those words. The immediate environment of the classroom offers all kinds of possibilities: you can put up signs and labels identifying important objects and supplies: CLOCK, WASTEBASKET, COATS, PAPER, LIBRARY CORNER. You can also use print related to topics the children will be learning about: *Calendar* (and the words for the months and days), *Our School, Pets,* and so forth.

We also saw in Chapter 3 that personal names are powerful facilitators of knowledge about print and reading. Certainly a child's own name is critical in this regard; but for kindergartners and first-graders their classmates' printed names are also a valuable source. Children's individual "cubbies" are labeled with their names, and lists of the names of children who are monitors/helpers for the week can be kept prominently in view and read over by the teacher to the whole class.

As you move into the school year and children are encountering new words that are a part of their ongoing reading, writing, and content learning, these words may be printed on large cards and placed on a "word wall" (Cunningham, 1991). You may wish to be selective, including only the most important or most frequently used words so that the wall won't become overrun with words, thus losing its effectiveness.

You will also find that "concept books" that are appropriate for emergent readers (see Chapter 3), books designed to develop basic concepts such as time, sequence, color, and so forth, become excellent sources of sight words. Because children now understand the concept represented in the book, they can easily pair the accompanying printed word with the illustration and after a few exposures come to know the word as a sight word. As an example, look at Bruce McMillan's *Here a Chick, There a Chick* (1983) in Figure 5.2. Through contrasting the pictures on the facing pages, children can remember the different words *stand* and *sit*. Words that do not have a straightforward concrete referent (and thus are often difficult to learn at first) can be presented very effectively in concept books. Children will, for instance, very much enjoy Donald Crews's *Freight Train* (1978) and Linda Banacheck's *Snake In, Snake Out* (1978), in which prepositions such as *through, under,* and *into* are presented; adjectives are treated nicely in Bruce McMillan's *Super Super Superwords* (1983). Because they are such an excellent source for learning sight words, concept books should be a part of your library corner (see below). Your ESL children, who understand the pictured concepts in their native language, can simultaneously learn the spoken and written English equivalents from these types of books (see Chapter 12).

The Language Experience Approach The Language Experience Approach should be a part of the kindergarten classroom and definitely should be used with most beginning first-graders. It is an extremely important component of the total literacy environment in the classroom.

Just as with predictable texts, LEA models for children the features and the functions of print. In contrast to predictable texts, however, LEA is more natural in the sense that it is based on the children's experiences and the children's

Stand

Sit

Figure 5.2
Early Sight Words

language. Because of this, it is also highly motivating and attention-sustaining—important criteria when working with small children in a group.

We covered the "basics" of the Language Experience Approach in Chapter 3, in the context of helping children understand basic conventions of reading and of print. We are going to elaborate and extend LEA in this chapter because it is such an essential and effective instructional component for moving children into conventional beginning reading. In this section, we will explore its effectiveness in helping children develop their sight-word vocabularies. A later section will discuss its effect on their *meaning* vocabularies.

Harvesting Sight Words from Group Dictations   Children can harvest sight words from group-dictated stories composed according to the format described in Chapter 3 (Stauffer, 1980). Teachers can check to see which words children *know* as sight words—that is, which words they immediately identify outside the context of the dictation—after a group dictation has been read and enjoyed for a couple of days.

How do you know which words to check for a particular child? Here are two reliable criteria. If a child has been able to remember and reread a sentence she or another child contributed to the dictation, as well as identify particular words when asked, you can check her on those particular words. When you first begin doing this, there may be only one or two words you will check with each child, but that's fine; it is better to ensure success for each child than to check several words and have a child be unable to recall most of them. You will rapidly get a good sense of each child, however, and of how many words he or she might acquire from a single group dictation.

The procedure is straightforward. Print the words on separate cards (for example, 3 × 5 cards cut into fourths) and ask each child to identify particular words you believe he or she will know. On the basis of the group dictation about the guitar we presented in Chapter 3, for example, you would show the word card for *yucky* to a child as you say, "Georgia, can you tell me what this word is?" If Georgia is correct—as you expect she will be—you hand her the word card as you say, "Terrific, Georgia! This is *your* word. . . ." It is important to underscore the importance of the word *belonging* to the child, the sense of "ownership" so compellingly described by Ashton-Warner (1963). You would go on to try *violin* with Annie, *strings* with Mark, *sound* with Jeanine, and so forth.

The Process of Taking Individual Dictations   When children are able to identify words from a group-dictated experience chart on a regular basis, they are usually ready to move into *individual* dictations. Teachers take individual dications from just a few children on most days; it would be quite difficult, as you can imagine, to try to take dictations from all or most children on a single day. You may also enlist the assistance of aides, parents, adult volunteers from the community, and older students.

When do you begin individual dictations? When a child is regularly and easily remembering selected words from the group dictation, she can benefit from individual dictations. These dictations may be written in the sturdy-covered composition book in which group stories have been copied (see Chapter 3) or whatever book format works for you and the children. As with these group accounts, children's individual dictations will be numbered and illustrated. As you will notice, the underlying format for individual dictations is very similar to the one for group dictations, but the children will be harvesting more words as sight words from each dictation.

Day One   A stimulus is discussed as a group. Next, children individually dictate a composition to the teacher, an aide, an adult volunteer, or an upper-elementary student. This dictation will *not* be as long as the group-dictated charts—primarily for the practical reason that it won't take as long to write down. In addition, though, a child's memory for the dictations will not be overly challenged by a longer dictation. A rule of thumb is to limit the dictation to about three sentences.

After taking the dictation, the teacher reads it back to the child. The teacher and student next choral-read the dictation, and the child returns to her seat with two important tasks. First, the dictation will be reread and the child will underline *once* each word that she knows. Second, the child will draw an accompanying illustration for the dictation.

Day Two   This is a brief session. The teacher will reread the dictation with each child and may check words here and there in the dictation by masking surrounding words. Then the child returns to her seat with this task: each word that the child believes she *still* knows will be underlined again; but if there is a word that the child thought she knew on Day One but does not know now, she will draw three small diagonal lines through the underlining.

Day Three   The teacher checks to determine which words from the dictation the child can immediately identify—a process I will describe in a moment. In addition, for each word the child knew on Day Two but cannot immediately identify on Day Three, the teacher shows the child how to take the word and check it in the dictation by sliding the word card along under each word in the dictation until the "match" is found. Our purpose here is to emphasize the role of *context* in facilitating word identification.

Individual dictations provide a rich source of sight words as well as opportunities for rereading, thus building fluency. They are a strong component of children's beginning-literacy experiences.

Harvesting Sight Words from Individual Dictations   Here is a way to help children harvest sight words from their individual dictations. On Day Two of the individual-dictation cycle, the teacher will look over the child's dictation. She will write on a word card each word that the child underlined twice—these are the words the teacher believes the child definitely knows.

On day three, sitting next to the child, the teacher shows each word one at a time. She asks simply, "What is *this* word?" If the child immediately identifies the word, the teacher responds "Good!" and places it to the side. She continues in the same fashion with each remaining word. If the child does *not* immediately identify a word, the teacher will cut it off and place it in a separate pile from the known words. The key here is *immediate identification*. If the child hesitates at all when the teacher exposes a word, that word must be considered not known, for reasons we will examine shortly.

Figure 5.3
Back of Word Card for Word Bank

The words that the child immediately identifies will be "deposited" in the child's *word bank,* which is simply a collection of all the child's known words. Before depositing them, however, the child should turn each little word card over and write his or her initials and the number of the dictation from which the word came (see Figure 5.3). This information will come in handy whenever the identity of a word is forgotten, because the child can quickly turn to the dictation in which it occurred. The initials provide for easy identification of the word card's owner, which is invaluable when word banks are spilled or, more often, when word cards are used in word games (see Figure 5.3).

At some point you may want the children to write their own word cards; these would carry the words they know on Day Two. This is particularly helpful if you cannot get to each child on Day Three, the day when you normally would check the words. Once the child has written the words, they can be put in an envelope until you can check the words with the child, at which time they can go into the permanent word bank. Writing the word cards will give the children the opportunity to check the words, look back to the relevant text if they have forgotten a word, and be more likely to know the word "for keeps" by the time you do your checking.

Having described individual dictations in general and harvesting sight words from them in particular, I should mention at this point my "dictum" from Chapter 4: as a novice teacher, you may find that attempting to orchestrate an individual-dictation cycle is a bit much at first. This is okay, as long as you make sure that sight words are coming from a wide range of other sources. I do encourage you, however, to set individual dictations as a goal, because they will be a rich source of words that children may not otherwise encounter in their literacy exploits.

■ BUILDING YOUR KNOWLEDGE BASE
The Language Experience Approach

Ashton-Warner, S. (1963). *Teacher.* New York: Simon & Schuster.

Hall, M. (1980). *Teaching reading as a language experience.* Columbus, OH: Merrill.

Henderson, E. (1981). *Learning to read and spell: The child's knowledge of words.* DeKalb, IL: Northern Illinois University Press.

Nessel, D., & Jones, M. B. (1981). *The language-experience approach to reading.* New York: Teachers College Press.

Stauffer, R. (1980). *The language experience approach to the teaching of reading* (2nd ed.). New York: Harper and Row.

Predictable Texts and the Shared-Book Experience. Predictable books are an excellent source of sight words. Their repetition of words and phrases provides a natural reinforcement for learning. After a book has been read, reread, and discussed, you can return to it with the students and check their memory of specific words. Recall from Chapter 3 that children's ability to locate specific words in a sentence follows a beginning/end/middle sequence. At first they can point to and identify words at the beginning of the sentence, then at the end of the sentence, and eventually somewhere in the middle. Because they have a concept of words and know about letters and their function, beginning readers at first can identify words this way relatively easily. It may take a few exposures to the words, though, before beginning readers can identify the words out of the natural context in which they occur—the best test of whether a word is a sight word for a particular child.

Recall from our discussion above the sequence you can follow when presenting and discussing a predictable text with a group of children. After the children have read the text two or three times, you can focus on specific aspects or features of the text—in this case, words that the children might acquire as sight words. There are two ways you may help them with this acquisition. First, after you have checked certain words with students in the context of rereading the text, you may write the words on individual cards in order to check to see whether the children know these words on the following day. Word processors are wonderful timesavers for this. You can input a list of words, print out however many copies you need, and then have the children check their knowledge with you. Known words are harvested for the word bank (see the next section). The second possible approach to harvesting sight words from predictable texts is just like the procedure for individually dictated stories and is less of a scattergun approach. You can print a copy of one or two pages from the predictable text and have the students each underline the words they think they know. Then follow the usual step of preparing word cards for those words and then checking them with the child on the following day. When you believe that a child does know a word or words from a predictable text, check them just as you do with words from dictations: have the word printed on a card and check the word with the child. If the word is identified immediately, praise the child, and give her the card to deposit in her word bank.

Working with sight words: word banks

The more that children look at words, the more they'll remember them and learn about their structure. We have already seen how important it is for children to read and reread familiar texts, and this of course helps with word learning. I cannot overestimate the importance, however, of children keeping their own collection of sight words and reading them and examining them on a regular basis. Such attention to words "in their own right" pays powerful dividends in terms of remembering printed words and learning about their structure; both memory and structure facilitate reading and writing.

A note about word banks: We've already noted that they are depositories for known words. Word banks can be just about any type of small container such as a margarine tub; 3 × 5 plastic file-card boxes usually work best, and their alphabetical divisions will be useful when the children have so many words that alphabetizing them becomes more efficient—an excellent way to learn about alphabetical order.

"Personal" Books for Children

In Chapter 3 we talked about giving each child a copy of a group-dictated chart. In this chapter, we have discussed how children may keep their own individual dictations and their own individual copies of excerpts from predictable books. In addition, children are learning lyrics to simple songs and words to simple poems and may be keeping their own copies of them. You may wish to assemble all these selections into one book, a "personal book," for each student. As each selection is added, number it. As sight words are acquired from each selection, students can put their initials and the number of the selection from which the word came on the back of the word card, as we discussed above. Word cards can be stored in an envelope stapled to the inside of each "personal book." In addition to being readily available sources for checking sight words, these personal books are concrete possessions for each child, a constant reassurance of texts that they know, representing what they have learned.

LEARNING IN CONTEXT: *Personal books* are invaluable possessions for children—they provide their own reasons for being reread and are a concrete affirmation to children of what they can read.

Word banks will be a ready source of known words for word study (see next section), so *only* words immediately identified should go into them. Because of the use to which the words will be put, children should review their word-bank words on the average of once a day, either singly or with a partner. Any words that are forgotten should be checked in the story from which they came. The teacher or another adult should check each child on his or her word-bank words about once a week; any words not immediately identified should be taken out.

As word-bank acquisitions grow, the need for filing the words alphabetically becomes apparent. An envelope for each letter can be placed in the word bank behind the appropriate alphabetical divider; upper- and lower-case forms may both be written on the envelope.

An excellent way of keeping the *home* current on the children's word-bank acquisitions is to staple a list of the word-bank words to the inside cover of each student's work folder that goes home each week. The children can read their words for their parents. Either the teacher or an aide, a parent or an adult volunteer, or an older student can keep the lists up to date.

What about the children who are still doing the group experience charts with you? They will be acquiring sight words at a slower rate, but you can and certainly should adapt their word-bank acquisitions to include a word or two for those students; when these children's developing knowledge supports more rapid sight-word acquisition, they, too, will move into individually dictated stories.

For how long should a child maintain a word bank? The *idea* of a personalized depository of words is attractive; so theoretically, kids can keep maintaining word banks for a long time, well into second grade or even beyond. The important question, though, is "How long do I have to put *every* word I know in the Word Bank?" Though children's needs vary, you will find that by about the time a child has 75–100 words in a word bank, the rate of acquisition of new sight words will really take off, and it will become unwieldy for you to keep putting all of them in the bank. On the other hand, some children acquire their words at a slow but steady pace, so you may keep putting all *their* known words in the bank until they reach at least a hundred or more.

I will be elaborating on several activities you can do with sight words from the word bank as we continue through this chapter. For the moment, though, let me list just a few to give you an idea of the possibilities (Templeton, 1991b):

- Categorizing Words: Sight words may be sorted in many different ways in order to highlight the different types of structural and semantic information the words represent.
- Card Games: When you are using word-bank words in your phonics instruction, games such as "Go Fish" can involve children in applying their knowledge.
- Sentence Construction: Children enjoy creating sentences by arranging their word-bank word cards. Children often enjoy writing down each sentence after it has been constructed, before moving to constructing the next sentence.

A final word. While managing these word banks may at first seem like a lot of work for *you,* the payoff for beginning readers is invaluable. We cannot overestimate the value and importance of the feeling of ownership that children have with respect to these words. The developing knowledge about them that will grow out of children's examining and playing with these words—using them as a source for developing word knowledge—will be invaluable as well.

CONSTRUCTING MEANING: EXPERIENCES ON THE WAY TO INDEPENDENCE

There will come a time when your beginning readers are able to move beyond reliance primarily on their *memory* and your support to sustain their reading of a text. They will be better able to orchestrate the relationships among their knowledge of "reading" as a process, about words and about genres, and they will have developed a substantial sight vocabulary. All this will allow them to read new material that is at a comfortable level and to think about it as actively and in the same way as they did during the Guided Listening-Thinking Activities. Now, as *they* read—in contrast to listening to *you* read, or watching as you modeled and they joined in—they can rely more on their *anticipation* of what is going to be happening in a story and on their *purpose* for reading (Bussis et al., 1985; Henderson, 1981). In this section, we will examine four means through which you can further develop your students' growing proficiency: (1) guiding students through text and encouraging their efforts at constructing meaning, especially through the Guided Reading-Thinking Activity; (2) deliberately and thoroughly introducing books to students; (3) building students' ever-increasing concept vocabulary; and (4) providing a great deal of time for students to simply *read*.

Reading with students to make meaning

You have been getting the children to anticipate or predict all along through Listening-Thinking Activities and shared reading; but because of the children's reading knowledge, they are now able to rely more on their *own* resources as they read. They don't have to give as much attention to figuring out what the print "says" as they read, so they can allocate more of their cognitive resources to thinking *as* they read.

At this point, you can begin guiding students through *their* reading of a story, since you don't have to support their efforts simply to move through the print as much as you did earlier. You will help usher them into the possibilities of "critical" reading, the general orientation to reading that best draws upon the reader's background knowledge and harnesses it to the reader's purpose. In other words, we know that children in first and second grade can indeed think critically about their lives—we have engaged them in thinking critically about things we have read *to* them; we are now helping them apply this ability when *they* are reading.

So we begin here, with beginning readers in the developmental sense, by addressing the "essence" of all effective prereading, during-reading, and post-reading strategies for readers at this and every successive phase of development: speculating, searching, and evaluating. Specifically, these three processes are realized through predicting, inferring, and making connections during reading—making connections within the text and between the text and the reader's background knowledge—and through learning to ask good questions. When we begin this "critical" type of reading with young children, we are laying a very strong foundation for their problem-solving skills in general. In other words, some powerful understandings and abilities will be developed and exercised through the way we engage children in reading, and these can reach beyond "reading" itself to many other areas.

You'll be continuing to meet frequently with small groups of children and guide their reading experience, facilitating the children's anticipation and their thinking about what they are reading, involving them in important talk about their reading, and discussing how they are going about it. In this process, which we will begin to examine in a moment, you will have a good many opportunities to look closely and observe how children are going about their thinking as they read. In addition, you will be able to monitor how they are applying, within an authentic literacy context, what they are learning; when you see the need for some immediate direct-teaching, you can offer it. Finally, the very process through which you guide your students is a process that in time, *they* will internalize and use as they read independently.

The guided reading-thinking activity

Many years ago the noted reading educator Russell Stauffer criticized a widely used instructional strategy known as the Directed Reading Activity (DRA) because he believed it was too teacher-controlled, producing passive readers who did not actively think and anticipate as they read (1969). The DRA was in fact quite rigid; teachers carefully walked students through the reading of a story, asking all kinds of questions. Stauffer noted, only partially tongue-in-cheek, that what was missing from this strategy was "thinking," so he proposed what he termed the Directed Reading-*Thinking* Activity (DRTA). The term *Directed* still sounds a bit too controlling; we might prefer "Guided" Reading-Thinking Activity instead, so that is what I'll use from here on. Regardless of the label, however, the process that the activity entails represents an approach to reading stories that initially does involve the teacher in giving more direct guidance, but with time this guidance may become less pronounced. Eventually, we hope, the children will have internalized this process whenever they read on their own. The Guided Reading-Thinking Activity will always be a very effective format for involving students in the social aspect of critically reading and discussing a story.

Not coincidentally, the format is very similar to that for the Guided Listening-Thinking Activity we discussed earlier, except of course that the *students* are now doing the reading, rather than you. (You may wish to refer back to page 181, where we discussed the GLTA.)

(You may wish to refer back to page 181, where we discussed the GLTA.)

■ ■ ■ ■ ■

CLASSROOM IN ACTION

Conducting a Guided Reading-Thinking Activity

In the Guided Reading-Thinking Activity, each child has a copy of the story to be read. It can be either a little book or an appropriate selection from a basal or literature-based reading series.

To illustrate the Guided Reading-Thinking Activity, we'll use the story "Fix-It," by David McPhail, from the first-grade level of a literature-based series (Houghton Mifflin, 1993). The story is quite short but lends itself nicely to the Guided Reading-Thinking Activity. Here's a nutshell synopsis: Emma, a little bear, finds out that the television doesn't work. Her mother and father can't fix it, so they call the "fix-it" man. By this time Emma is quite upset, so her parents try to "fix" her with various amusements. Nothing works—until her mother reads her a book. Emma gets wrapped up in the experience, wanting to read the book again and again. Meanwhile, the fix-it man fails in his efforts, and only later does the father bear notice that the television simply wasn't plugged in all along! By this time, though, Emma is reading to her doll, Millie, and is "too busy" to watch TV.

Wanda Nomura, a first-grade teacher, begins the activity by having the children look only at the title page (see Figure 5.4):

"By looking at the picture and reading the title, what do you think this story might be about? Michael?"

"The TV's broke and the little girl wants her dad to fix it."

"Good! What other ideas do you have? Marcie?"

Figure 5.4
Title Page for "Fix-It"

FIX-IT

by David McPhail

"She wants to stay up late to watch TV but it's broke."

"All right! Why do you think she wants to stay up late, Marcie?"

"'Cause she's got her pajamas on."

And just as with the Guided Listening-Thinking Activity, this is how you usually can start the Guided Reading-Thinking Activity. The children use both picture and title clues to predict, and occasionally you ask a child why he or she made a certain prediction.

Wanda continues by telling the children to read the first two pages of the story and to look up at her when they've finished. She then picks up the discussion:

"Well, now . . . do we know if the television is broken? . . . Yes, we do! How do we know that? Donna?"

"It says so! And it says she asked her mom to fix it."

"Good. . . . *Now* what do you think will happen? Stephen?"

"Her dad will try but he won't be able to fix it."

"Oh! Why do you think so?"

"'Cause in the first picture, her dad looked confused!"

After a couple of more predictions, Wanda tells the children to read the next two pages to "find out what happens," and then look up at her again when they are through. This is where the children read that Emma's father couldn't fix it and called the fix-it man, and that "He tried to fix the TV. Emma's mother and father tried to fix Emma."

Wanda continues: "*Now* what do you think? Yes, Karen?"

"It's not gonna work and Emma will start being bad."

"Her mom and dad will give her candy to be nice," another child offers. Wanda asks why she thinks so, and the child responds, "Because she's really crying and her mom and dad look like they're fed up!"

"So that's *one* way her mother and father might try to 'fix' Emma! What other things might they do to try to fix her?"

The children make a few more predictions; then Wanda tells them to read the next four pages and look up when they've finished. The parents try three tactics with Emma; none of them work. On the third page, her mother reads her a book—and then rereads it three times at Emma's request. The page ends with Emma saying, "Now *I'll* read to Millie," and going to her room. The fourth page reveals that the TV has simply been unplugged, so Emma's father "fixes" it. When he calls to Emma, however, she doesn't come out of her room.

Wanda asks the children whether the things they *thought* Emma's parents would do actually happened. During this discussion one of the children asks, "Who's *Millie?*" Another child responds that Millie is Emma's doll.

"How'd you know that?" Wanda asks.

"Because the picture showed Emma going to her room and holding Millie and the book!"

After a very brief discussion, Wanda asks the children why they think Emma isn't coming out of her room. In unison they respond that it's because she's enjoying reading to Millie. Wanda suggests, "Let's find out!" and lets them read the last page, which confirms their prediction.

Wanda has required the children first to predict, then to "check" their predictions after they've read. She asks them *how* they know what they now know, and this redirects the children to the text and the pictures. When one child isn't sure about something, Wanda realizes that another student may be helpful in explaining how she solved the uncertainty—as was the case with the question about Millie.

Follow-up discussion will allow the children to discuss the overall story, and together with Wanda, they may ask additional questions. There are many possibilities for discussion. For example, Danny comments, "Hey, this is really weird—she has a human for a doll!" It's not a *real* human, of course, but Danny has noticed a clever bit of subtle humor by McPhail; the illustration could have depicted a "bear"-doll instead! Such insights benefit *all* the children, as of course do the comments, predictions, explanations, and occasional disagreements that arise from the group. Learning is a social phenomenon, and in addition to learning about how to read and how to think while reading, children are being helped to use books as prompts for all kinds of important learning, discussion, and critical thinking.

Follow-up is also a time for checking on specific skills. For example, Wanda asked the children to turn to page 48 and read to themselves the first sentence on the page ("One morning Emma got up early to watch television"). She then asks, "What is the last word in that sentence. . . . How did you know?" This requires the students to think consciously about *how* they used picture clues as well as contextual clues from the text to read that word.

Let's consider again what Wanda has been doing. While she has guided or directed the pace of the reading and selected the stopping points, she has not controlled or limited children's thinking and interpretation. She has determined where to stop on the basis of points where predictions are most likely to follow productively. She has taken comments by the children as cues to what they know and what they need to know, and she has decided how to respond—with an explanation by her or by turning it back to the students and relying on one of them to explain it, thus benefiting all.

■ ■ ■ ■ ■

Introducing and presenting books to children

Good introductions of new books are an important aspect of supporting children in making the move from teacher-supported reading, as in shared-book experiences, to reading on their own, whether in the context of a group or independently. When children are well on their way toward acquiring a larger sight vocabulary and are moving along with individually dictated experience stories, we can help them read, *on their own* and without a prior reading by us, books that are appropriate for them. Often it helps if we set the stage to aid them in doing this, which entails introducing the book effectively. As Marie Clay has pointed out, "A good introduction makes the new text more accessible to the reader," and she goes on to say that this introduction "creates a scaffold within which children can complete a first reading of a whole story" (1991, p. 265).

Introductions for these independent readings are more elaborate than those for shared reading experiences. In addition to discussing what a book might be about, teachers may go through the book one page at a time, talking with the children about the illustrations and commenting on what seems to be going on in the story. If the teacher sees an unfamiliar term or phrase, he or she will include it in the discussion. And the teacher may need to present new knowledge or clarify a potentially confusing part of the text.

Earlier I have referred to Marie Clay's description of learning to read as a "patterning of complex behavior." She relates this phenomenon to the importance of providing supportive introductions when she notes, "If learning to read involves bringing many complex behaviours together as the reader problem-solves his or her way through a story, then *introductions provide the teacher with many opportunities to model important reading behaviours . . .*" (1991a, p. 271, emphasis added). These behaviors include both relating new information in the book to known information and *knowing* that one is doing so. In our terminology about knowledge, this is an excellent example of how *topic knowledge, procedural knowledge,* and *self knowledge* can all be engaged—even at the very beginning of conventional reading.

Building concept vocabulary

Through oral communication and literature, language is growing all the time. During the primary years we do not teach "vocabulary" as deliberately as we usually do in later years. Children seem quite naturally to add new words to their speaking/listening vocabularies, and at a pretty good pace (Lorge & Chall, 1963; Johnson & Pearson, 1982). But it is also true that children quite clearly benefit from experiences that involve them in examining their world more closely and more expansively, and with the new concepts that emerge through these explorations come new words to label the concepts.

Building concept vocabulary is an integral part of the learning process. This development will strongly support children's meaning construction as they read, as well as allow them increased enjoyment from their reading experiences. Experiences and the language that accompanies those experiences are the heart of the growth of concept vocabulary. In this section, we will address different means of developing and enriching new concepts in primary-age children, and we will consider the value of authentic literature as a source of new concepts and new words.

Sharing   The value of children's sharing through oral language with small groups or with the whole class really cannot be overestimated. When young children bring to class something that is important to them—a keepsake, a souvenir from a trip, photos—or when they talk about an important event in their lives, there are opportunities for conceptual growth and for learning the new terms that represent it. One ten-minute sharing session I was privileged to sit in on recently in a primary classroom generated the terms *geode*, *barnacles*, *razor clams*, *saguaro*, and *fossil*. The context for this generation was exciting:

When children share through oral language, they have opportunities for conceptual growth and for learning new terms.

the teacher asked appropriate and timely questions, but the children themselves frequently provided appropriate new terms and elaborations. Let's consider three illustrative examples:

> One little boy reached into the sack he was clutching and pulled out a wooden carving. "This is a *saguaro*," he announced proudly. As he held it for the other children seated in the circle to see, it became clear to the teacher that the child had said all he planned to say about the carving. "Boys and girls," the teacher began, "what do you think a saguaro is?" "A cactus?" one child hesitantly suggested. The teacher turned to the child who was holding the carving and asked, "Daniel, *is* a saguaro a type of cactus?" After he nodded, she asked him, "How is a saguaro like other types of cactus . . . how is it different?" This led into a brief discussion about sizes, shapes, types of needles, and so forth—and ended with the teacher's telling the children that when you're talking about more than one cactus, you say cact*i* rather than cactus*es*. They all laughed at this, saying it sounded funny; but because of the context in which it was presented, you can be sure that they remembered this plural form from that point on.

> The little girl who pulled her object out of a bag had just announced, "I got some shells here." The first one she pulled out appeared to the teacher to be a type of clam, so she asked, "Tessa, what is that called?" "A *clam*," she replied. Another child said, "That's a *razor* clam!" The teacher asked, "Zack, how do you know that?" and Zack proceeded to point out sharp edges, which the children then looked at very closely as Tessa ran her finger gingerly over the edges of the shell.

> Terese had been clutching a small stuffed animal during sharing time. The teacher asked her to hold it out so everyone could see it. She thrust it out at arm's length. Knowing how shy Terese was, the teacher asked her simply what type of animal it was. "Harry," Terese softly said. "Oh, Harry's a lovely name for such a cute animal, Terese, but what *kind* of animal is Harry?" "Otter," Terese responded. Knowing that these two responses were as much as Terese would probably contribute in a group—but knowing also that Terese was a little girl who did know a lot about animals—the teacher asked her to show the group the interesting way that otters often ate. Terese turned Harry on his back and placed his front legs across his abdomen. That was enough of a clue for another child to say, "Oh, I remember seeing on TV when they go on their back how they use a rock to crack open clams to eat!"
>   In this little exchange, some of the children learned a new word, *otter*. While the rest of the children already knew what an otter was, however, there still was vocabulary development going on. Why? Because their concept of an otter was elaborated to include the interesting way otters eat—a bit of knowledge that would surely lead to further exploration about otters (the teacher would soon add several books about otters to the library corner).

As young children share specific objects and talk about something that has happened to them, you may model types of questions and appropriate listening-questioning behavior, as the teacher in these examples demonstrated. Questions can direct the children's attention to the specific uses, features, and importance of an object and to the sequence, meaning, and importance of an event they are sharing.

The Language Experience Approach   Let's examine the now familiar format of the Language Experience Approach. An excellent means by which *sight* vocabulary can be developed, the LEA can be used to develop new *concept* vocabulary as well.

Animals are usually an excellent focus. They are "right there," concrete, inherently interesting and engaging. For these reasons you can use them to help children notice different features and behaviors, followed by your supplying the corresponding label or term. In the following vignette, one of the children has brought to class her pet *axolotl* (pronounced "ACKsuhLOTul"), a type of salamander. The axolotl is in a small aquarium.

> "Girls and boys, Amy has brought her very special pet to share with us today. Amy, can you tell us something about your pet?" Amy tells her classmates that her pet's name is "Chuckles" and that he is an axolotl. As in any sharing situation, you can ask questions about where Amy got her pet, how she cares for it, how old it is, and so forth. Then you can help children focus on its various features:
>
> "Boys and girls, Chuckles seems to be floating there in the water. Amy, does he ever climb out of the water? He does? Kids, when you look at Chuckles, what do you see that could give you a clue about his being able to live on land as well as in the water?" You can then use the terms *salamander* and *amphibian* as you talk about one type of animal that can live both in and out of water. Amy could also be asked if she had owned Chuckles since he was a baby—if she had, she could talk about how he lived entirely in the water when young but comes out now that he's an adult. You might point out the difference in size between the animal's front and *hind* legs, then have the children look at the tail and tell you why they think it is shaped as it is.
>
> After you have talked about the axolotl with the children and helped direct their attention to important features, while introducing and using the appropriate terms, turn to a large piece of chart paper and cluster what has been generated in the discussion:
>
> "Let's write down some of the things we noticed about Chuckles. We can also write down the new words that have to do with an axolotl." (See Figure 5.5 for part of the cluster that was generated.)

As each bit of information is added, you can comment again on its importance and what it means—for example, the term *amphibian*. You may then do either of two things: proceed to take a group dictation on the axolotl, or allow the children to write about him on their own—descriptions, stories, journal entries, illustrations, all are possibilities.

The essence of instructional situations such as these is that (1) the learning of concepts is embedded in concrete experiences that generate children's language as well as (2) provide opportunities for introducing new words to label new understandings and awarenesses. You have pointed out features to be labeled, provided the new labels or elaborated on existing ones, and reinforced

Figure 5.5
"Chuckles" Cluster

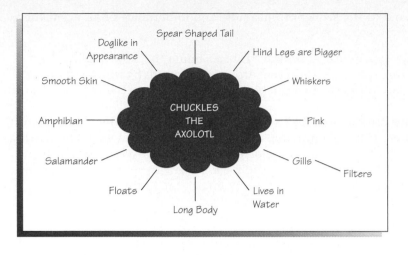

these by writing down the terms in a visually effective manner. Most children will retain the new words in their oral language, and many will recognize them in print as well.

Books   At the beginning-reading phase, children can learn some new words that represent new concepts when reading on their own, but it will be through your read-alouds that they will experience most of the new words that occur in books. Read-alouds are marvelous opportunities for introducing and elaborating on concepts in a comfortable manner, and you can elaborate as necessary about the terms. Many informational books have recently been published that are directed at primary-age children and effectively present words that represent new concepts. In addition, many excellent books have recently been published in Big Book format so that the pictorial context and the language are clearly evident.

Time in the library corner

Children need independent time *in school* to read, read, read. Whether this time is spent literally "in the library corner" or at their desks, under a table, or wherever they are comfortable, children must have the opportunity *every day* to read independently. The concept of independent reading time has had a number of labels over the years, the most common ones being Sustained Silent Reading (SSR), Sustained Quiet Uninterrupted Reading Time (SQUIRT), and Drop Everything and Read (DEAR). Most often, the books that children read during this independent reading time are those that are within their independent or instructional "comfort zone," as we first noted in Chapter 4. This zone is important because it represents the books with which children can easily construct meaning, getting the feel of what efficient reading is like.

We usually need to show children how to select books that are within that comfort zone, books that they can comfortably read. For many years children have been encouraged to "try a book on for size" using the "five-finger rule"

(Chall, 1953): as they read a page in a book, they raise one finger for each unknown word they run into; if they use up all five fingers on a single page, the book is probably going to be tough going—unless, of course, they are *really* interested in it and want to persevere. But it is of great importance for children to read a lot at their independent level and to learn how to handle books that are at their instructional level (see Chapter 4 and also Chapter 12). Books at their independent level help them develop fluency and are confidence-builders. Books at their instructional level help them exercise their developing skills in applying word-identification knowledge and in actively thinking about the meaning they are constructing. Ohlhausen and Jepsen (1992) offer an engaging strategy they term the "Goldilocks" strategy; it helps children determine, on their own, which books will work for them. In this strategy, you use the terms *too hard, too easy,* and *just right*—an obvious spin-off from Goldilocks's sampling the bears' porridge that was "too hot," "too cold," and "just right." "Too easy" books are ones children have read many times before and in which they know almost all the words. "Just right" books are ones they haven't yet read and which deal with a topic they think they know something about; in addition, there are few unknown words on a page. "Too hard" books contain many unknown words, and it is difficult for children to figure out what's going on.

You will probably find it helpful to arrange the shelves in your library corner into sections that reflect different genres and characteristics. For example, your categories might be poetry books, stories with people, stories with animals, concept books, science books, and other types of informational texts. During the very first week of school, gather all the children around you in the library corner and talk briefly about the different categories, showing a couple examples of each. Talk with the children about the fact that you will be reading many of these different books to them throughout the year. Tell them that this way of grouping the books will help *them* when they are looking for books to read; that they should first think of what they are interested in and then look through the books on that particular shelf or section of a shelf. Together with your (later) discussion that will focus more specifically on the differences among different types of texts, such conversation about books explicitly helps children develop, from the very beginning of their formal schooling, schemas for different genres, different ways of using language, and the complementary roles of illustrations and photographs in texts.

WRITING AS A WAY INTO READING

For beginning readers, writing can be a way into reading in at least three respects. *First,* from the very outset, frequent writing can help children think of *themselves* as authors. They will be "publishing," or making available to others, books that will be placed in the library corner and on occasion in the school's media center as well. "Thinking like a writer" will gradually lay the foundation for *reading* like a writer—an invaluable perspective that will help children develop a certain kinship with texts, thereby becoming better able to construct meaning (Hansen, 1987). *Second,* writing affords children the opportunity to "exercise" their developing knowledge about print, such as letter/sound relationships, and their developing knowledge about the different purposes and genres of written texts. *Third,* writing in response to a particular piece they have read affords readers a deeper way to reflect on it and understand it. Although we will focus here on all the aforementioned ways that writing can build stronger readers, the "flip side" is also true: frequent reading and growing familiarity with reading make better writers. Keep this angle in mind as well, as you are reading this section.

As we observed in the last chapter, the primary years can be a time of tremendous excitement and discovery in writing and reading. They can also be the years in which the desire to write and read, along with attitudes toward writing and reading, are negatively set—possibly forever. In years past, the usual first-grade writing curriculum consisted primarily of handwriting—learning proper letter formation and copying short pieces, such as poems, from the board. "Story" writing began at the end of first grade for some and in second grade for most, and the common expectation was that spelling would be correct. In other words, when children were allowed to write, they were expected to perform well in all areas: content, neatness of handwriting, and correct spelling. These are, of course, very heavy demands. In spite of these experiences, some children loved to write, but most did not.

Children *will* write if they perceive a purpose for writing and if they believe that writing is an enjoyable activity. Just as you help children understand the nature and purposes of reading through the classroom environment you establish and the informal and more direct experiences with reading you allow, so will you establish a classroom environment for writing in which you convey the feeling that writing in your classroom is natural, expected, and fun. In addition, you will model how to get started and what writers might think about as they write. In such environments, children will seldom want for something to write about, but some children may still be reluctant to try their hand because they "don't know how to spell."

You will probably need to model how the children can begin. At these early stages, you are not concerned with the quality of what they write; you simply want them to begin writing. Matters of form and substance will be addressed some time later. Here is how you can usher children—singly or in a group—into writing, into "inventing" their own spelling:

Embed the eventual writing in a meaningful, enjoyable context. Such a context might be your exploration and discussion of a concrete experience such as the axolotl (above), or it might be a read-aloud. For example, after reading Karen Davis's *Star Light, Star Bright* to the class, you could have them draw a picture of a special star that they would like to wish upon, a wish they might like to make, or anything else that they thought about or were reminded of as they listened to the story. Drawing will then lead into writing: tell them they can write something about their star (or whatever they drew), and show them how:

"Boys and girls, because you know the names of the letters of the alphabet and you already know how to read many words, you can write down anything you want to say. Here, let's see how.

"Maya, tell us about your picture—you drew something that you *wish* you could have? A hippopotamus? Oh, my! What a wonderful wish! *And* what a wonderful word! Let's write it. What's the first sound you hear? . . . What letter do you think stands for that sound? What's the *next* sound you hear? . . . What letter stands for *that* sound?" Continue in this fashion until the word is sounded and written out. In this case, you might wind up with something like HEPAPOTAMIS. When you finish the word, say something like, "Fantastic! You did a super job of sounding out *hippopotamus*. Now, when you are writing on your own, you can write down any word you want just by sounding it out like that." Should a child ask, "Is that right?" you respond, "You know, you'll see it spelled differently in books, but I really like how *you* sounded it out!" This type of response acknowledges what the children already know—they will probably see different spellings in print, but it is fine to make their best attempts, getting close to the word.

We will examine the nature and implications of children's invented spelling later in this section. For now, know that for reluctant writers this type of exchange will get the writing going; you may have to model this several times for a very few students, but most will soon internalize this process.

Journal writing: exploring the self and the world

Journal writing has been a popular means of encouraging and sustaining students' writing (see, for example, Fulwiler, 1987; Barone, 1990, 1992), and a number of different formats for writing in journals have been suggested over the past few years. It is important to know that beginning and transitional readers and writers can benefit from journal writing as much as older children. Journals provide children an opportunity to express themselves in writing in whatever way they can, as they reflect on themselves, their reading, and their worlds in general. We often think of journals as spiral-bound notebooks; but while these may be fine for older students, younger ones often enjoy journals that they have made themselves: sheets of writing paper with construction-paper covers (or some type of fabric such as wallpaper samples) that can be stapled together.

Journals are a comfortable "way into writing" for beginning readers and writers. The children are not expected to write extended pieces but simply to get a few thoughts down. Figure 5.6, written on Monday by a transitional reader/writer (second grade), reveals what he experienced over the weekend.

Journals can function in a learning-log capacity. Figure 5.7 shows the entry by first-grader Eric in October. He has recorded his observations about some seeds that are nestled underneath a moistened paper towel in a clear plastic cup on his desk.

Second-grader Adrienne used her journal one day to respond to the book *A Kiss for Little Bear,* by Else Minarik (1968). A common type of response for beginning readers before they have had much opportunity to discuss books more deeply is a "retelling" response (see Chapter 6), and as we see in Figure 5.8, this is what Adrienne has partially done. Though not a more personal response, a retelling is nonetheless valuable; for both before and during her writing, Adrienne had to think back through what had happened in the book, thus reinforcing her concept of story structure and her recall of important events.

Figure 5.6
*Transitional Reader/Writer's
Journal Entry*

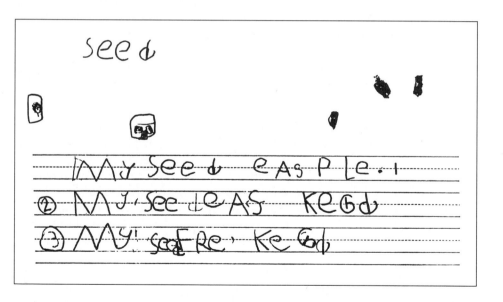

My Dad's wedding day. There was
much excitement. I had to get a
hair cut. After the wedding there
was much recovering. The reason
there was too much punch and rock
and roll.

Figure 5.7
Journal as "Learning Log"

My seeds are peeled.
My seeds are crinkled.
My seeds are crinkled.

The journal entries of Eric and Adrienne illustrate how writing is, for children,
a powerful way into reading. The content of the entries mirrors the purposes
and functions of different types of texts. As they write, we can see these children
actively at work *constructing* their schemas for different texts. Eric is learning
that certain texts *describe* the world, and this knowledge will, over time, help

Figure 5.8
Journal as "Response Log"

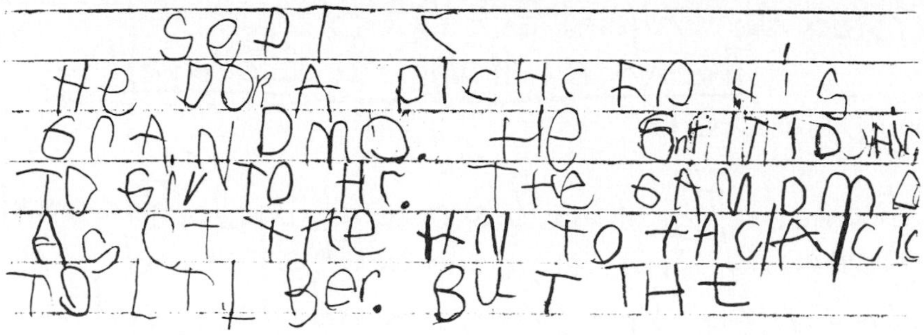

SePT
HE DDR A PICHCFO HIS
GRANDMD. HE SMT IT TO HM
TO GIV TO HE. THE SANDMA
ASCT THE HN TO TACAICIC
TO LTI BER. BUT THE

Sept. 7 He drew a picture for his Grandma. He sent it to hen to give to her. The Grandma asked the hen to take a kiss to little bear. But the

him construct more and more images and understandings as he reads informational texts. Adrienne's recall of events is building a deeper foundation for story structure, one that will extend far beyond *A Kiss for Little Bear* to support her reading of many, many other stories.

There is no strict demarcation between the types of writing that beginning readers and writers do in their journals and the writing they do in other contexts—we see lists, descriptions, brief narratives, and so on. Journals often are simply a more comfortable way of getting thoughts and writing going, as well as of exercising knowledge about the form and functions of written language. In subsequent chapters, we will look at the uses of journals again.

Stories and information: telling and showing

As the preceding journal entries imply, when beginning readers and writers are *immersed* in reading and writing, they try out what they are learning about written language and all that it represents. Many children spontaneously begin writing their own stories or "informational" texts; other children do not respond so readily. At the beginning phase, though, our primary objective should be to initiate and sustain children's writing, regardless of what forms it might take.

Experiencing lots of narratives and lots of informational books provides the foundation for children's composing these types of texts. In turn, the process of composing helps children reflect on the form and the content of different types of texts so the process is creating more active and more critical readers. It is a cyclical process, in other words, that gets kids thinking like writers and writing like readers. And as the few examples in this section will illustrate, children's reading and writing grows from interesting and meaningful— oftentimes *deeply* meaningful—topics and concerns.

Children can be initiated into the idea of composing stories through *group* composition activities. These often begin with retellings of favorite stories and informational books through group dictations. Retellings can be expressed through storyboards (see part of one for Eric Carle's *The Hungry Caterpillar* in Figure 5.9), by using a favorite book as a "frame" for creating a simple story

Tessa Lee   Agust 30, 1993.
The verey Hungry Caterpillar.
by: Eric Carle.

Ounce Ther was a egg and' The next morning The egg hachet and he was very hungry and he atte a aplle and tow peres and 3 plum s and 4 stroderys 5 orenjes The mext week he atte cake pickol e chees slaomy lollypop cheryy cake I like Thispart case av The food

Once there was a egg and the next morning the egg hatched and he was very hungry and he ate a apple and two pears and three plums and four strawberries five oranges. The next week he ate cake pickle cheese salami lollypop cherry cake. I like this part 'cause of the food.

of one's own (see Chapter 3), and so on. Similarly, children can learn about informational texts as they talk about and then write about the life cycle of a particular type of butterfly. They may list the important aspects of that life cycle, and this group listing becomes an informational composition that will be beneficial for someone who doesn't know about that type of butterfly.

Group composing places little demand on any individual student, and this is important. Too often our expectations for children's writing have inadvertently required them to take care of *all* the aspects of a composition, from matters of form and legibility to matters of information, sense of audience, decisions about what to include, and on and on. On the other hand, when we immerse children in excellent examples of narrative and informational texts and help them compose first as a group, we are taking that first important step toward effectively helping them become more responsible as individuals for their writing. In the process, they are reflecting on what they know about how stories and informational texts work; this reflection in turn supports their *reading* of such texts.

As we help children elaborate their understanding of story structures, we will see this knowledge reflected in the stories they compose on their own. This is evident in the excerpt from one book in a "series" that Kirstin, a transitional reader/writer, wrote beginning in second grade (see Figure 5.10). Influenced by the notion of several books focusing on the same characters, Kirstin wrote a series of "Buster" books, in which Buster the dog figured prominently. Each of her "Buster" books was structured in a straightforward beginning/middle/end

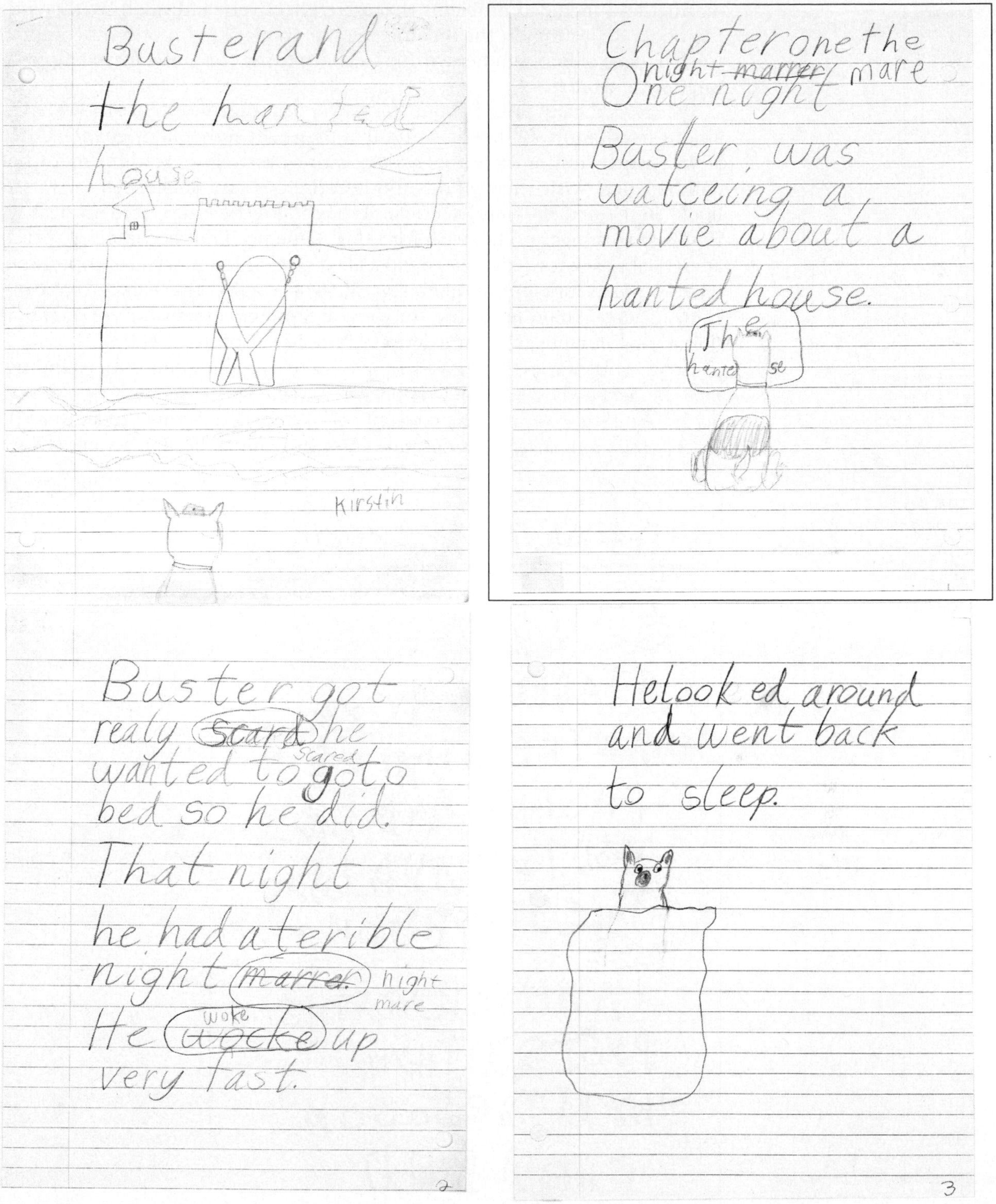

Buster and
the hanted
house.

Kirstin

Chapter one the
night marrer mare
One night
Buster, was
watceing a
movie about a
hanted house.

The hanted house

Buster got
realy scard he
scared
wanted to got o
bed so he did.
That night
he had a terible
night marrer night
mare
He woke up
woke
very fast.

He look ed around
and went back
to sleep.

2

3

Figure 5.10
First Four Pages from Buster and the Haunted House, *Written by a Transitional Reader/Writer*

manner and included problems that were effectively addressed by the end of the book. Reflecting on the reading she was doing, Kirstin often incorporated the language of books in her writing—certain turns of phrase, for example, and interesting words.

We have already talked about the power and meaning that stories have in all our lives, and we'll be revisiting this theme in subsequent chapters. But it is well worth noting here that *writing* stories as well as reading them helps children deal with their worlds, both conscious and subconscious. Kirstin's book, *Buster and the Haunted House,* brought together her need to deal with frightening things and her wish for a dog. (One need not become very psychoanalytical to acknowledge that almost all young children need to work through whatever fears lurk within them, regardless of whether the fears are concrete— from an actual "haunted house" movie—or represent expressions of their developing subconscious [see, for example, Temple & Collins, 1992].)

Just as with stories, when we help children elaborate their understanding of *informational* texts, we see them apply this knowledge in their writing (see Figure 5.11). Jason's exposure to the concept of *sequence* in a number of simple "how to" books is reflected in his description of how his father built a bookcase for

Figure 5.11
Beginning Reader/Writer's Informational Composition

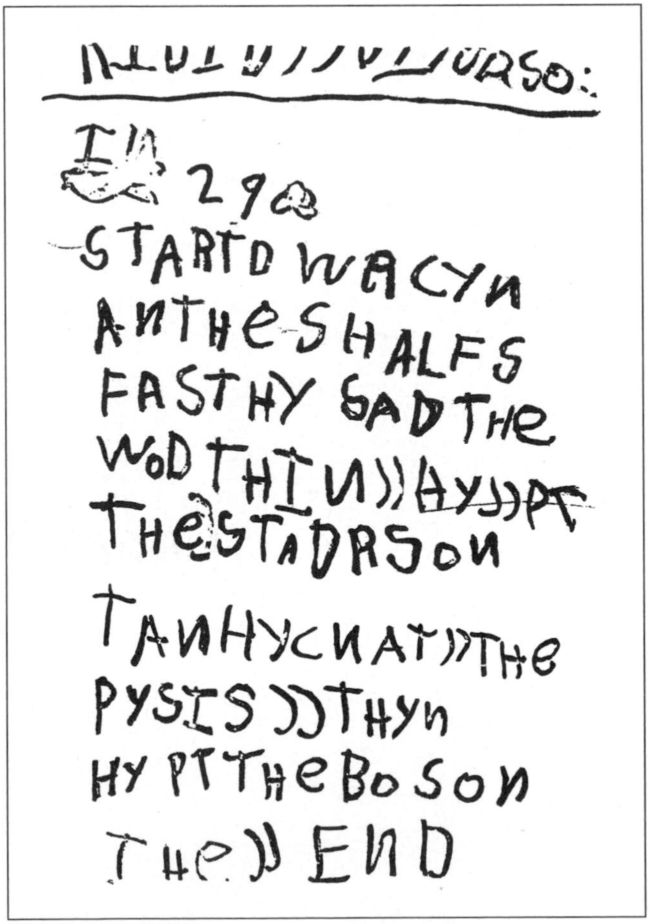

On the 29th Shane T. started working on the shelfs. First he sawed the wood. Then he put the standards on. Then he cut the pieces. Then he put the boards on. The End

Jason's room. Note the stance that Jason, a kindergartner, takes as a writer of informational text: Rather than writing something like "my dad," he uses his father's first name and the first letter of his surname!

Other forms, other awarenesses

As several writing authorities have pointed out, children write in *many* forms, not just stories and descriptive expository pieces (Dyson, 1991; Newkirk, 1989). If we allow and support young children's writing, we will likely see all types of writing: letters, lists, poems, persuasive pieces, and so forth. At the beginning-reading phase these written efforts

- help significantly to build initial schemas for the macrostructure of different types of texts;
- help children become aware of different functions of these texts;
- provide authentic contexts in which children can exercise what they know about conventions of writing and of word structure.

Simply put, because children have a purpose in selecting a particular form in which to write, all their knowledge about print and about what texts do is exercised in one of the most meaningfully rich contexts possible.

Beginning readers and writers may try out their developing sense of "text." This is what Jason has done in Figure 5.12. Having seen in a book a diagram

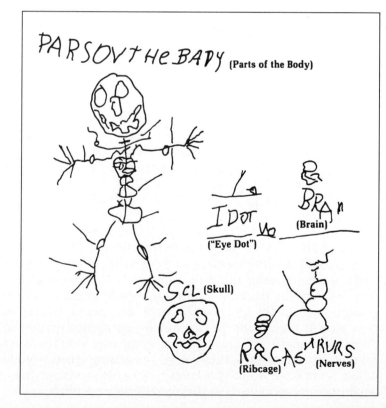

Figure 5.12
Beginning Reader/Writer's Diagram Showing Developing Sense of "Text"

showing the parts of the human body, Jason has composed his own diagram—even titling it "PARSOVTHEBADY" ("Parts of the Body"). Jason's diagram constructs his understanding of one of the many ways in which informational texts can literally "show us" the nature of the world. Notice his invented spellings in the labels of the parts.

Invented spellings

Years ago a journal article appeared that not only generated a lot of excitement but became a battle cry for many early literacy educators: Carol Chomsky's "Write First, Read Later" (1971) related how a preschool child became engaged in creating words, first with movable letters and later in writing. It was a startling but exciting thought: young children could figure out or "invent" the spellings of words before they could read. Although appearing quite strange to adults, these spellings were logical in their own way. Equally striking was the suggestion that children who "invented" their spelling in their early writing attempts seemed to pick up the letter/sound conventions of written words without much difficulty and were off and running in their development as beginning readers.

We now understand that the relationship between reading and writing is not as sequential as the title of Chomsky's article suggested. Instead, there is more of a reciprocal relationship between early writing and reading (Templeton & Thomas, 1984). While young children's developing knowledge about writing does feed their developing knowledge about reading, it is also true that reading feeds knowledge about writing. The point that was not lost about invented spelling, however, is that if children are allowed to try to figure out or spell the sounds they hear in the stream of speech, they will indeed be much more likely to succeed early in beginning conventional literacy. And the practical, day-to-day message to you as a teacher is that children's invented spellings will give you invaluable clues as to what they know about words and what you can help them attend to.

In Chapter 3 we looked at some of the invented spellings of children who were in the latter part of the emergent literacy phase. We saw that such children could "encode" what they wanted to say if they knew the names of several if not most of the letters of the alphabet. In the *beginning-reading* phase, we find that children often spell several of their sight words correctly and invent the spellings of remaining words. At these levels invented spelling is a strong foundation for learning the conventional letter/sound relationships in English (Freppon & Dahl, 1991), and for learning the nature and purposes of word-identification routines (Templeton, 1991a). At the *transitional* phase, we see children's invented spellings reflecting the type of word knowledge that allows more efficient and fluent reading as well as writing.

As we consider the types of invented spellings we see in first- and second-graders, I will briefly note how they provide clues for your subsequent instruction. We will discuss fully the *nature* of this instruction in the next major section, "Word Identification." I would like to emphasize here that as children work to get their thoughts down, they will be "exercising" their word knowledge to its fullest, reinforcing words they know how to read and applying their knowledge of consonants and vowels as they invent their spellings.

Alphabetic Spellings   Recall from Chapter 2 that children who are beginning readers are learning about words in a strictly left-to-right, letter-by-letter fashion; that's how they expect letters and sounds to match up. When beginning readers write, we see this conceptualization of words reflected in their invented spellings. Figure 5.13 is a representative example from Melissa, a beginning reader:

Figure 5.13
Alphabetic Invented Spelling

I like sitting under my favorite tree

Melissa's description shows how she's using names of the letters in the alphabet to guide her attempts, which is very characteristic of children's invented spelling when they can match a letter with each consonant and vowel sound they hear. Notice that she has applied her knowledge of consonants quite well; she has even represented the /tr/ sound conventionally, with the blend *tr*.

Melissa spells long vowel sounds according to the name of the letter that stands for each particular sound: ī is spelled with *i,* ā with *a,* and ē with *e.* (For further discussion of long and short vowels, see the next section, "Word Identification".) Melissa's spelling of short vowel sounds, while more complicated perhaps for *us* to understand, is not complicated for *her* and follows the same "letter name" strategy that works for long vowels. In fact, it takes quite a bit longer to describe this process than it does for Melissa to apply it: unlike the long vowels, each of which has a sound like the name of a letter of the alphabet, the sound of a short vowel does not have a corresponding letter in the alphabet whose name is that sound; there is no letter, for instance, whose name sounds like the ă in *cat.* So Melissa uses a letter whose name contains the sound of the short vowel. She has spelled the short *i* sound (ĭ) in *sitting* with the letter *e* because the *name* of the letter *e* includes the short *i* sound (Read, 1970, 1975; Beers & Henderson, 1977). To get a sense of Melissa's thinking, try slowing the way you pronounce *e*: do you notice how your pronunciation of it begins with a short *i* sound, then sort of glides into the long *e* sound? Next, consider how Melissa spelled the short *u* sound in *under*. She selected the letter *i* because it contains the sound she needs; again, try slowing your pronunciation of *i*: do you notice how you begin with a short *u* (ŭ) sound and glide into the *i* sound? What is so striking about children's strategies at this phase is that they figure out how to represent these sounds with little if any awareness of how they are going about it. If you ask Melissa why she used the letter *i* to spell the "uh" sound, she would probably simply say, "I sounded it out!"

What does Melissa's word knowledge as evidenced in her invented spellings tell us about where we might go with instruction? She clearly understands her beginning consonants and is attending to vowel sounds. She has not yet realized how the short vowel sounds are represented in English, though she may well be reading many words with conventional spellings, so we should point out these conventional short-vowel correspondences and help her explore them.

As children progress through the beginning-reading phase, they will come to spell many of their sight words conventionally, and knowledge of the conventional spelling of many of these sight words will in turn influence their invented spellings. An example of this phenomenon is first-grader Jeff's journal entry at the end of the school year (Figure 5.14), when he is writing in response to the prompt "What would you teach first-graders next year?":

Figure 5.14
Conventional Spellings Influence Invented Spellings

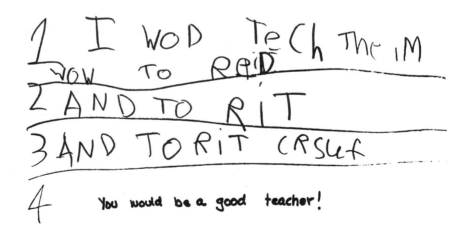

I would teach them how to read
and to write and to write cursive

First of all, notice the conventionally spelled words *how, to,* and *and.* Jeff knows something about how short vowels are conventionally spelled, and he uses this knowledge as he sounds out *them;* in fact, we can almost see the interplay between his visual memory for this word (he knows it by sight when reading) and how he is sounding it out: he inserts the letter *i* because he hears a short *i* sound as he says the word slowly in order to spell it. The letter *e* remains, however—evidence of his visual memory for this sight word. The vowel sound in *would* is not straightforwardly long or short; although we cannot be certain how Jeff decided to use the letter *o,* we can be pretty sure that he probably applied his knowledge of the sight words *would* or *wood,* both of which contain the letter *o.* Given that Jeff appears to understand conventional short-vowel spellings but is not spelling long vowel sounds conventionally, we might try exploring a simple long-vowel pattern with him (see next section); but if he seems to have difficulty understanding how it works, we should drop back and play with short vowel patterns a little more—all the while making sure that he is continuing to read, read, read, and write, write, write. He will then benefit from exploration of the more abstract long-vowel patterns.

How can you be reasonably sure that your students will be able to explore those more abstract long-vowel patterns? They will begin to include in their invented spellings letters that do not themselves represent sounds. When you see this on a regular basis in a child's writing, you know that he or she has moved into the *transitional* phase of reading and writing. Let's examine children's invented spellings at that point.

Within-Word Pattern Spellings   We can continue to use the term invented spelling for students who have technically moved beyond the *beginning-reading* phase and are now in the *transitional* phase, because they are still inventing spellings for words they do not know in a conventional sense.

After you have examined a number of young children's invented spellings, you will be able to differentiate quickly between those of beginning readers and writers and those of transitional readers and writers—in fact, you will have a more precise sense of *where* a child is within a phase of development (Bear & Barone, 1989; Bear et al., in press). Right now, your best indicator in determining where a child is (for purposes of determining the most appropriate type of word study—see next section) is a look at how a child is inventing the spelling of long vowels. Are "silent" letters included in the vowel spelling? In other words, is the child attempting to spell according to *pattern* rather than *sound*? In Jeff's invented spellings of *write* (RIT) and *read* (RED), he was spelling according to letter *sounds.* The invented spellings in Eldon's journal entry at the beginning of his second-grade year (Figure 5.15) reveal that he is attending to *pattern.* Notice, for example, his spelling of the long *u* sound in *school:* SCOOLE. Even though Eldon has correctly represented the $\overline{oo}$ sound, he has added a "silent" *e,* which of course often indicates a long vowel sound. He is testing a generalization based on a common vowel *pattern.* He has done the same thing in his spelling of *piece:* PECE—the "silent" *e* indicates a long vowel. Notice also that the proportion of conventionally spelled words in Eldon's entire composition: it is higher than for beginning readers/alphabetic spellers. In terms of word study, Eldon's invented spellings indicate that he could benefit from examining less-frequent long vowel patterns (as in *sch<u>oo</u>l* and *p<u>ie</u>ce*) as well as different ways in which particular sounds can be represented, depending on their position within the word (*<u>kn</u>ow; sti<u>tch</u>es*).

Later in the transitional phase of development, within-word pattern knowledge is characterized by certain features evident in the following observations.

Figure 5.15
Within-Word Invented Spelling

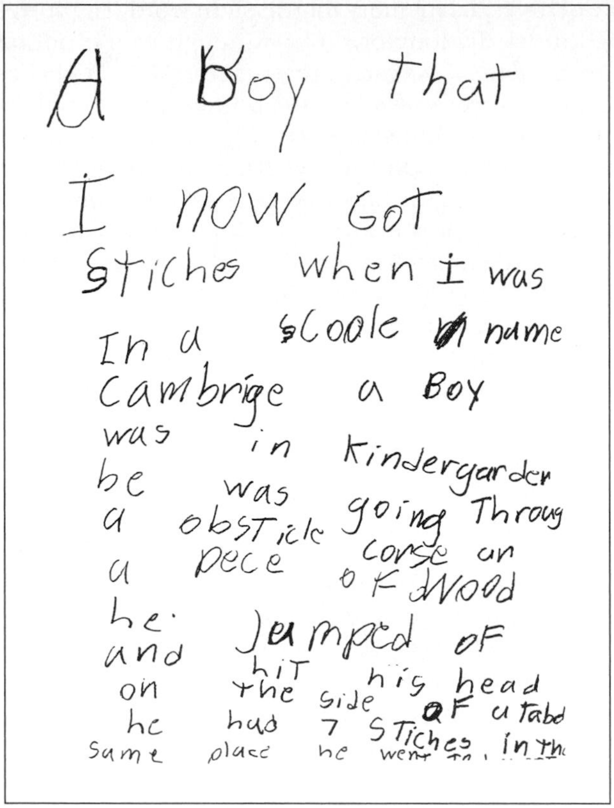

A boy that I know got stitches when I was in a school named Cambridge a boy was in kindergarten he was going through a obstacle course and a piece of wood he jumped off and hit his head on the side of a table he had 7 stitches in the same place he went to hospital.

Second-grader Ryan wrote them after a walk across a university campus during the fall (Figure 5.16).

Ryan is still inventing his spellings according to *pattern,* but now he can apply more knowledge about words. For example, notice his spelling of the verb *leave* in the fourth line (LEVE), and his spelling of the noun *leaves* in the last line (LEAVS). In both instances he has a "silent" letter in the vowel pattern, but he has used a different pattern for the long *e* sound. It seems as if Ryan realizes that in English, we usually spell differently words that sound the same when the words *mean* different things (Templeton, 1991a). These words are called *homophones* ("same sound"; we'll talk more about these in Chapter 8). Invented spellings of *diphthongs* (see below) will usually include two letters: FAWND (but note NOSY for *noisy*). Invented spellings for words of more than one syllable almost always have a vowel in every syllable: BISIKLS, CELLEKSHON.

For purposes of word study, Ryan's knowledge of words as revealed in the number of correctly spelled words and in his invented spellings suggests that he would benefit from exploring further:

Vowel spellings, through comparison and contrast (see below); at this point, some children benefit from exploring the influence of sound *and* meaning on the spelling/structure of words.

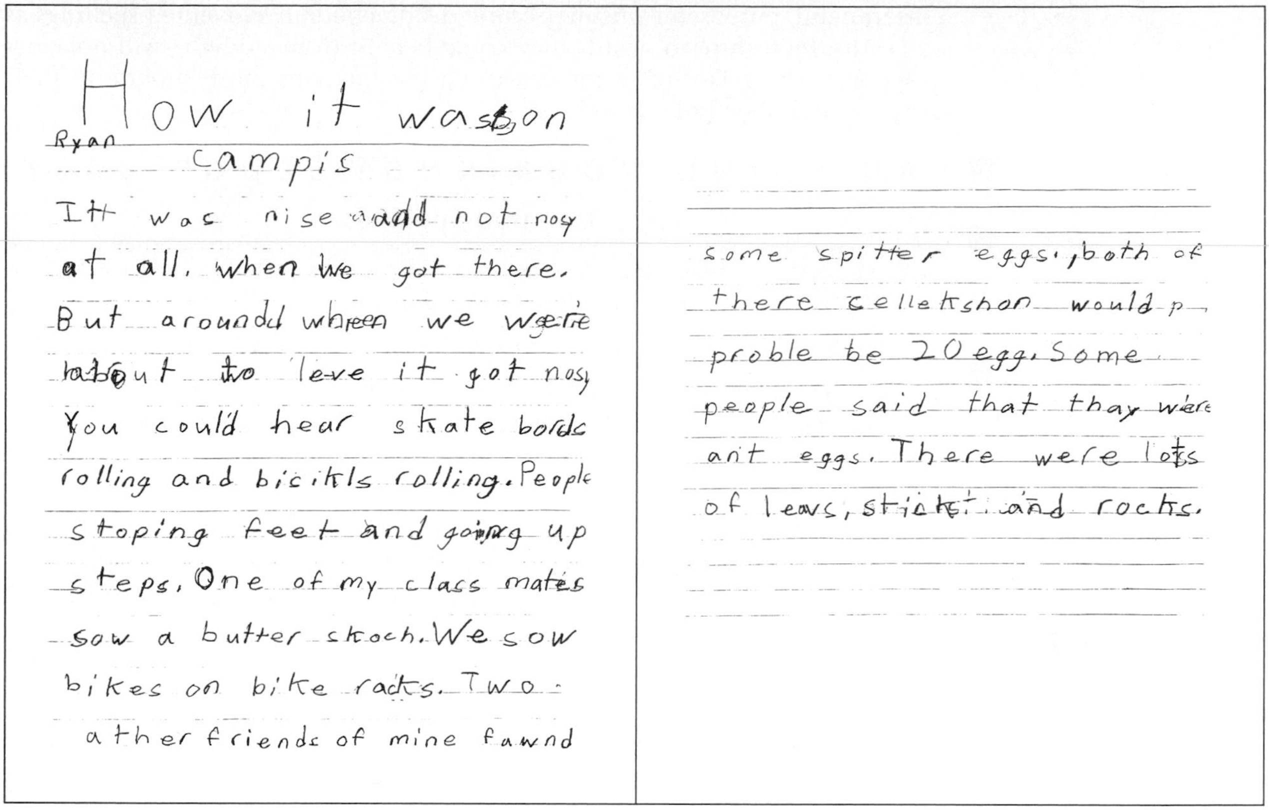

Ryan

How it was on campis

It was nise and not noy at all. when we got there. But around when we were about to leve it got nosy You could hear skate bords rolling and bicikls rolling. People stoping feet and going up steps. One of my class mates sow a butter skoch. We sow bikes on bike racks. Two ather friends of mine fawnd some spitter eggs, both of there sellekshon would probe be 20 egg. Some people said that thay were ant eggs. There were lots of leavs, sticks and rocks.

Figure 5.16
Later Within-Word Invented Spelling

It was nice and not noisy at all when we got there. But around when we were about to leave it got noisy. You could hear skate boards rolling and bicycles rolling. People stomping feet and going up steps. One of my classmates saw a butterscotch. We saw bikes on bike racks. Two other friends of mine found some spider eggs. Both of their selections would probably be 20 eggs. Some people said that they were ant eggs. There were lots of leaves, sticks and rocks.

Some diphthong patterns (such as *oi* and *ou* as in ar*ou*nd); Ryan may need only to note that he can remember *found* on the basis of his knowledge of *about* and *around.*

Some "*r*-influenced" vowel patterns (BORD).

Two-syllable words (SPITTER).

I would like to close this discussion of invented spelling by making two key points. First, when parents or other teachers question you about "bad habits" being formed through invented spellings, know that you are on very strong ground. The research clearly demonstrates that children who are allowed to write freely, inventing their spellings, usually develop into good readers, writers, *and* spellers. Allowing children to invent ways of spelling words is allowing them to exercise their word knowledge in the best manner, by trying it out in meaningful, purposeful writing. Second, using children's invented spellings as a key to the features of words they could benefit from studying will not only support their *spelling* of words in writing but, perhaps most important, their *word identification* skills as well.

■ **B U I L D I N G   Y O U R   K N O W L E D G E   B A S E**

■ **Invented Spellings**

■ For teachers, the following references contain some of the best descriptions to date of the logic underlying invented spellings:

■ Henderson, E. (1990). *Teaching spelling* (2nd ed.). Boston: Houghton Mifflin.

■ Bear, D., Invernizzi, M., & Templeton, S. (1994). *Words their way: Developmental phonics, vocabulary, and spelling, K–8.* Columbus, OH: Merrill/Prentice-Hall.

■ Gentry, J., & Gillet, J. (1992). *Teaching kids to spell.* Portsmouth, NH: Heinemann.

■ Temple, C., Nathan, R., Temple, F., & Burris, N. (1993). *The beginnings of writing* (3rd ed.). Boston: Allyn & Bacon. [See in particular Chapter 4.]

■ ■ ■

WORD IDENTIFICATION

You should begin your phonics instruction by giving appropriate guidance. *When* and *what* you teach depends directly on your students; many of them will figure out letter/sound correspondences on their own, while many others will seem to require more direct support and/or more "walking through" and modeling.

Beginning readers have many sources to draw upon as they develop their abilities to figure out what texts "say." While they are increasingly able to identify most words in the texts they are reading, they will still be encountering words they don't immediately recognize. It is imperative that we help them become aware of and learn to use the sources available to them. These sources include the children's own developing knowledge about words—how letters conventionally represent sounds, the surrounding context of a sentence, the page (including pictures), and the whole text. And sometimes, when even these sources do not yield the identity of a word, other children can help out.

Word knowledge is a critical factor underlying efficient reading. Readers must learn to identify most of the words they encounter in their reading, rapidly and with minimal effort. For most children the ability to do this has two sources. First, there should be lots of reading and lots of *re*reading of favorite texts in which words are encountered again and again in meaningful contexts and in which appropriate opportunities to apply strategies for figuring out unknown words are available. Second, children should have the opportunity to examine words, comparing and contrasting them, so as to note and understand how words are put together. This type of examination will also underlie children's ability to write and spell efficiently. Your guidance in both of these areas should ensure that the development of word-identification abilities in children leads to a deeper understanding of "words" in general—their meanings and their structures.

In this section we will address the terminology of word identification, the general sequence according to which children appear to learn about word structure best, and basic instructional principles and tasks for learning about word structure and for applying this knowledge in meaningful contexts. The variety of ways in which you will facilitate your students' thought about words will help them make essential connections among words' sound, structure, and meaning.

Defining the balanced role of phonics instruction

The term *phonics* refers to the study of the relationships between sounds and letters within single syllables. It is a critically important aspect of learning to read; although as we've already noted, the term unfortunately has become burdened with negative connotations. Because of the intensive instructional focus on phonics in years past and the often dull and repetitive phonics exercises so many children had to endure, many educators de-emphasize the importance and the role of learning conventional letter/sound relationships. This "great debate" (see Chapter 10) will probably continue to rage; but in the meantime, you should be reassured that many children need guidance in understanding letter/sound relationships and in learning how to apply that understanding in meaningful reading. The important issue here is *balance*. Phonics will be a means to an end—constructing meaning—not an end in itself.

Table 5.1 presents the important phonic terms and gives illustrative examples of each.

A sequence of phonics for word identification

I would like to make three points here before we examine the specifics of instruction:

First, depending on what a particular child needs, you'll want to emphasize letter/sound activities more or less, but always within the broader context of meaningful reading and writing. As you will see, there are enjoyable and meaningful ways in which we can help those children who need more guidance in this area to think about letter/sound relationships.

Second, always use known words—sight words—when you first introduce a correspondence. Whether the words for a lesson are written on the chalkboard or come from the children's word banks, you should always work from the *known* to the *new*. This makes certain that children are working from their *strengths*, the words they know, rather than from words they do not know (Barnes, 1989).

Third, notice that children will experience and "play around with" phonic elements and patterns before they study them explicitly, using the terminology of phonics.

TABLE 5.1   Concepts and Terminology: Phonics

Consonants

A *consonant* sound is produced by obstructing the flow of air in some fashion somewhere between your throat and your lips. For example, the sound at the beginning of *come* is made by shutting off the flow of air far back in the mouth; the sound at the beginning of *tip* is made by interrupting the flow of air by touching the tongue on the ridge just behind your upper front teeth. The sound at the end of *push* is made not by shutting off the flow of air but by forcing it through a very narrow opening. Letters that stand for these sounds are often simply referred to as "consonants" as well.

Vowels

A *vowel* sound is produced by keeping the flow of air from the throat *un*obstructed. The different vowel sounds that we are able to produce are made by changing the shape of our vocal tract and placement of the tongue. The common terms *long* and *short* refer to the length or duration of the vowel sound, although technically this distinction does not always hold: there are some so-called "short" vowels (the *a* in *have,* for example) that are longer than so-called "long" vowels. It is unnecessary to make this fine distinction for children, however; we discuss long vowels with them in terms of "Does the vowel say its name?" If it does, then it is long; if not, then it is probably short. You can begin using these terms and definitions with children when they are experimenting with both consonant and vowel letters in their invented spellings. Within a single syllable, the *phonogram* is the vowel and what follows.

Single consonants	*Consonant digraphs*	*Consonant blends/ clusters*	*Short vowel phonograms*	*Long vowel phonograms*
These are single sounds represented by single letters. Examples: *b, m, r, s.*	A consonant digraph is an element that uses two consonant letters to stand for one sound. Examples: *ch, th, ph, sh.* Notice also that with consonant digraphs you cannot "break them apart" to hear the sound represented by each individual letter—*ph* has an /f/ sound; it is not the result of combining a /p/ and an /h/ sound.	A consonant blend or "cluster" is an element in which each consonant letter retains the sound it would have if it occurred by itself. Examples: *bl, sn, fr, str.*	Examples of short vowel phonograms are *-ag, -itch, -ump.*	Examples of the most common forms of long-vowel phonograms are referred to as "VCe" (vowel + consonant + silent *e: -ate, -ime, -oke*) and phonograms that include "vowel digraphs," or two vowel letters occurring together (*-ait, -oam, -eat*).

Table 5.2 presents a suggested sequence of phonic elements. Not all possible correspondences are represented here, but I have included those that lay the foundation for children's understanding of the basic consonant and vowel patterns. The sequence follows a developmental course that reflects the order

Learning About Consonants

Letter names

Beginning single consonants

b	m	r	s
t	g	p	n
h	f	d	c
l	j	k	w
y	z	v	q

Learning About Short Vowels

Teach concept of short vowel phonograms, or "patterns" (the term we use with the children) following this sequence: short *a*, short *i*, short *o*, short *u*, short *e*. The fundamental pattern is the "CVC" phonogram:

CVC: -at -ad
 -it -ig
 -op -ot
 -ut -un

Beginning consonant digraphs

ch sh th wh

Beginning consonant blends

bl	cl	fl			
br	cr	dr	fr	gr	tr
sm	sp	st	sn		

Learning About Long Vowels

Teach concept of long vowel phonograms, or "patterns":

CV: go, me, my
VCe: -ake -ame *VV:* -ee- -ay -ai-
 -ike -ide
 -oke -ope

in which children conceptually deal with word structure: simple alphabetic principles first, more complex within-word pattern principles second (Ehri, 1993; Templeton & Bear, 1992). The watchword here is *flexibility*—the important point is *not* that you cover every correspondence, but that you follow *in general* the alphabetic, within-word, and structural developmental sequence. If you follow this sequence when it is developmentally appropriate for children, *and* if the study is embedded within lots of appropriate reading and writing, your students benefit by learning strategies for identifying words in their reading and learning about the structure of words.

Not all children will need to attend explicitly to each element or category, but this suggested sequence can serve as a reference for your instruction. You will find that many children may skip some elements, while others may need to study more examples of particular elements. Also, you should know that not all elements in one category should necessarily be covered before moving to the next: for example, short vowels needn't all be studied before children can start looking at some consonant digraphs and blends. Note that different correspondences, within the same category, that may be examined at the same time (for example, the beginning consonants *b, m, r,* and *s*) are listed in groups, although you should always be alert to some children's need to examine a smaller number first.

Here is the basic two-step framework for your explicit examination of letter/sound relationships:

1. Involve the children in *examining* words that illustrate the correspondence you are targeting;
2. Involve the children in *applying* understanding of the correspondence to new words in text.

As we'll discuss shortly, a prominent feature of your word exploration will be the *sound chart* that is prominently displayed in your classroom. You will often refer to this sound chart when you talk about letter/sound correspondences with the children. Figure 5.17 demonstrates some possible sound-chart illustrations for consonants and vowels.

Learning About Beginning Single Consonants A necessary note before we begin looking at how to help children explore letter/sound correspondences: starting off by attending to beginning single consonants will work quite well *if* it is clear that the children have the prerequisite knowledge mentioned above. If they do, they understand the concept of a single sound and they understand the concept of the *beginning* of a word—all because the teacher has been exposing them to predictable literature through Big Books, has been doing LEA dictations with them, and has been encouraging them to write.

We begin explicit examination of letter/sound relationships with beginning single consonants because children are developmentally ready to examine these

Figure 5.17
Partial Sound Chart for Letter/Sound Correspondences

before middle or ending correspondences. They know most if not all the names of the letters of the alphabet (see Chapter 3), and they will find that there is much more consistency in these relationships (words that begin with *b*, for example, will have the same sound at the beginning).

Children are ready to examine beginning single consonants explicitly when they know several sight words; while they may not be able to identify many other words out of context, they can usually locate them in a familiar dictation or a predictable text by returning to the beginning of the line and reading up to the word (see Chapter 3, p. 101). And though they may not have a firm concept of word in print, their continuing acquisition of sight words, together with their developing knowledge about beginning single consonants, will soon lead to this concept.

Examining the Correspondence Let's assume that this is the first time you're involving the children in examining beginning consonants. You will be working with *b* and with *m*. Gather around you, in the circle or small-group area, a small group of children you believe need to explore beginning single consonants. Select words that all of these children know; write them in random order on the chalkboard: *big, ball, man, bike, my, bump, milk, bag, mop, mud.* Children can respond either individually or as a group, as the following suggested presentation illustrates:

> "Boys and girls, today we're going to be listening for the sound we hear at the beginning of *bat* [point to the picture of the baseball bat on the sound chart] and the sound that we hear at the beginning of *moon* [point to the picture of the moon on the sound chart].
>
> "We're going to put our listening ears on [showing how to do this]: cup your hands behind your ears like this." This will help the children attend better to *their* pronunciation of words (not the teacher's), especially important when a teacher is working with children who speak a variant dialect. "Now we're going to listen to the sound that we hear at the beginning of *bat* [puts picture of the bat where it can be clearly seen] and see if we hear this sound at the beginning of the names for these other pictures. Here is a picture of a *ball*. Be sure your listening ears are on and say these two words: *bat . . . ball.* Do they sound as if they begin the same way? Good! Let's see about this one . . . Here is a picture of a *bike*. Say these two words and see if they begin the same way: *bat . . . bike.* Do they sound as if they begin the same way? Good! Here's another one. This is a picture of a *fork*. Do these two words sound as if they begin the same way? *Bat . . . fork.* Good! They *don't* sound as if they begin the same way."

The pictures offer a concrete referent for thinking about a sound, but you may find that the children catch on quickly and can attend to the pronunciation very nicely on their own. You may also combine auditory discrimination alone with an "every pupil response" format (Cunningham, 1991). Pass out a card with a smiley face on one side and a frowny face on the other. Explain to the children, "When I say a word that sounds as if it begins like *bat,* show me your smiley face; but if I say a word that does *not* sound as if it begins like *bat,* show me your frowny face. Listen to these two words: *bat / big . . .* Good! Now, how about these: *bat / Bill . . . bat / sun . . . bat / top. . . ."* Continue in this fashion. The "every pupil response" format that the smiley face cards allow involves all the children, even those who may be a little uncertain.

Next, write the *b* words in a column:

bat
big
ball
bike
bump
bag

Ask the children, "What is the same about *all* these words?" When the children respond that they all begin with the letter *b*, ask, "What can we say, then, about words that begin with *b*?" You are leading the children toward the generalization that if a word begins with *b*, it begins like *bat;* this generalization is reinforced by the key word and picture—*bat*—on the sound chart.

Now go through this same procedure with words that begin like *moon:* "*moon / milk . . . moon / bat . . . moon / mop. . . .*"

When ready, tell children to go through their word banks or the packet of sight words you have given each child, to find words that begin with the letter *b* or the letter *m*. Show them how to arrange the words in the appropriate column and how to check each word with the key word and picture on the sound chart. If one of their words is *bangles,* for example, show them how to match the beginning letter of *bangles* with the beginning letter of *bat* on the sound chart, holding the word card directly under the key word. As you do so, say, "*Bangles* and *bat* both begin with the letter *b.*"

Children can do this activity first with you in a small group, then with each other at their desks. They should each have a small copy of the sound chart to use at their desks, or you may provide charts when you meet with a small group.

Applying the Correspondence   It is important that the children have the opportunity to apply their understanding of a particular correspondence in a meaningful context as often as possible. This will allow them to apply their knowledge of the correspondence with context clues, to try to identify a word. A meaningful application for the *b* and *m* lesson, for example, could involve the book *The Hungry Giant* (Cowley, 1990), which is published in a Big Book format. You would display the two pages on which the giant is roaring about wanting some butter:

"I want some butter!" roared the giant.
"Get me some butter, or I'll hit you with my bommy-knocker."
So the people ran and ran and got the giant some butter.

You have assumed that the children will be uncertain about the word *butter.* You can ask them, "What might this word be [pointing to *butter* in the first line]?" If they don't know, you can point out: "You already know something about it . . . it begins just like *bat,* doesn't it? So let's use the rest of the sentences and other clues on these two pages to figure out what this word is. . . . The giant has been wanting things to eat, hasn't he? Then whatever this word is must have something to do with eating. . . . Let's read these two pages and see how we can use our clues.'' (Butter is pictured on the right-hand page; and you already will have identified *bommy-knocker* on previous pages). After the children identify the word *butter,* you can tell them explicitly, ''If you don't know a word when you're reading, you can use the beginning sound *and* the rest of the words and the pictures to get important clues.''

Learning About Short Vowels   Just as with their study of beginning consonants, children will begin with *known* words.

Examining the Correspondence   Your procedure is the same as with beginning single consonants. First, have the children listen for the sound they hear in the middle of *cap* when you pair it with words such as *bag, cape, sat, fan, game.* (Notice how you are providing a fairly *obvious* contrast between vowel sounds here—long *a* does not sound like short *a*. If a child seems to be confusing the letter with the sound in this discrimination task, however, use different long vowels, in examples such as *bike* and *hope*.)

Second, just as you did with beginning single consonants, write the ''short *a*'' words in a column:

man
sat
bag
sad
hat
trap

Now you can ask, ''Do we hear the *same sound* in the middle of each of these words? . . . What letter stands for this sound? . . . Good! Do you see any other vowel letters in these words? When you see just one *a* in the middle of a word, what sound do you think it will stand for? Good! The sound that we hear in the middle of words like *man* and *sat* is the short *a* sound. That sound is usually written with one letter.''

Applying the Correspondence   Reproduce a page from a book that includes several words with ''short *a*'' patterns; discuss these words with the children. For example, display the following page from *The Fat Cat* (Kent, 1971), an adaptation of a Danish folktale in which a cat eats a bowl of gruel he was supposed to be guarding and moves on to gobble up everyone in sight until he runs into the woodcutter (who helps everyone escape):

When the old woman came back,
she said to the cat, ''Now what
has happened to the gruel?''

Read the first line with the children, pausing at the word *back*. If they hesitate, remind them that they know something about the sound in the middle; using their knowledge of the context, the beginning sound, and the middle sound, what might the word be? Continue reading and pause at *what;* ask the children about the word and if they don't mention that the *a* doesn't have the ''short *a*'' sound, you may do so. This is the opportunity to point out that what they know about ''short *a*'' will not *always* work, but most of the time it will. Read on, pointing out that *has* follows the pattern. Pause before *happened* and ask the children if the *meaning* helps them. If necessary, cover all but the initial *hap* in *happened* and ask them to try saying *that;* then read to the end of the line. Ask them if the meaning, together with the beginning sounds in *happened* (point to the word), give a clue. . . .

And so it goes. Always try to balance attention to the pattern you are examining with a discussion about how that knowledge can be used during reading. Point out that—as with *happened*—even with longer words, knowing how to pronounce part of a word may often, together with context, be all the help they need.

Another way to introduce the short-*a* letter/sound correspondence is to ask the children to search through their word banks in the following manner:

■ Have them look through for one-syllable words; by now, the children have been sensitive to syllables for quite some time. Then have them sort all the single-syllable words into two piles, words that have only one vowel and words with two or more. Next, ask the children to collect only those with the single (vowel) letter *a* in them; these can then be examined as you talk directly about the short *a* pattern.

■ Show the children the key word on the Vowel Sound Chart *(cat)* and tell them that this word has the short *a* pattern. Then ask them to sort through the words they've selected, to pronounce each, and to compare it to the vowel sound they hear in *cat.* (Some children are *over*analytical at this point, and they'll note subtle differences between the vowel sound in *fan* and that in *cat.* The important issue here, though, is that they *are* attending to the middle sound and are noting how it is represented in their own word-bank words.) Make a list of these words from one or two contributions from each child.

You may have children who need additional exploration use picture cards, as you did with beginning consonants. You may use pictures of objects whose names contain either a short *a* or a long *a* sound; for example a *cap* and a *rake.* Remind the students, "Listen for the sound that you hear *in the middle.* Do we hear the same sound *in the middle?*" Over time, continue with whichever remaining short vowels *(i, o, u, e)* may need to be addressed.

Learning About Consonant Blends (Clusters) and Digraphs Consonant blends and digraphs are usually introduced and examined explicitly after two or three short vowel patterns have been explored. Key words and pictures can be added to the Sound Chart for these, and you will introduce and talk about them just as you did for beginning single consonants.

Examining the Correspondence For blends, have children contrast words such as *cap* and *clap, bend* and *blend, dive* and *drive;* for digraphs, contrast words such as *cat* and *chat, sack* and *shack.* For both blends and digraphs, you are helping the children discriminate between beginning sounds that they would have earlier grouped together; now, they can clearly attend to the difference between a beginning single consonant and beginning consonant blend or digraph, and can learn these correspondences.

Applying the Correspondence   As before, point out words in a natural text that illustrate different blends and digraphs. Often, as in the following case, it can be a book you have read aloud to the class. As an example, consider the following excerpts from *The First Song Ever Sung* (Melmud, 1992), a beautiful, lyrical story in which a young boy asks different people and animals what they think was the first song ever sung.

> *"What was the first song ever sung?" said the little boy to his grandmother.*
> *"The first song ever sung was a spinning song, a weaving song, a magic thread*
> *and thimble song," said the grandmother to the little boy.*
>
> *"What was the first song ever sung?" said the little boy to the minnows in the*
> *brook.*
> *"The first song ever sung was a ripple song, a splash song, a pebble song, a flash*
> *song," said the minnows to the little boy.*

There are many possibilities throughout this book. On these two pages alone, you could point out the beginning blends in *sp*inning, *thr*ead, *gr*andmother, *br*ook, *spl*ash, and *fl*ash as well as the beginning digraphs in *wh*at, *th*e, and *th*imble. You might mention to the students how the author has used these words so that we get a *feel* and a *picture* in our heads. This will also help highlight the *sounds* that the clusters represent: "Boys and girls, when I hear the words of the minnows—*ripple, splash, flash*—I can almost feel their world in the water, and I can see in my imagination how they are darting about underwater." Such occasional comments help children develop a sense of why authors use certain words, and they provide a richer foundation for children's remembering particular letter/sound correspondences as well.

Learning About Long Vowels   Long vowel sounds can be represented by several different spelling patterns. For each long vowel correspondence you study, introduce the most common patterns first—the less frequent patterns will be phased in later on. The most common pattern, and the one that we usually begin with, is the VC*e* pattern (vowel-consonant-silent *e*). Following we consider the procedure for exploring this pattern for long *i:*

Examining the Correspondence   Write the known words *bit, hid,* and *slid* on the board. After asking different children to read the words, write the known words *bite, hide,* and *slide* in an adjacent column:

    bit   bite
    hid   hide
    slid   slide

Now ask the children, "What's the difference between the vowel sound in the words in this column (pointing to *bit,* etc.) and *this* column (pointing to *bite,* etc.)? Does the vowel sound change? . . . What is different about the *spelling* of the words in this column (the *bite* column) from the words in this column (the *bit* column)?"

As you can see, you are guiding your students toward the realization that the final *e* makes the vowel a "long" vowel. (You would already have introduced this pattern with long *a,* so the children will probably be quicker to pick up on this.) At this point, you could have the children go through their word banks or examine word cards you have provided in order to find words that fit this pattern. If some students observe that this "long" pattern also applies to *a*, so much the better—the search can be expanded to include long *a* and long *i* words that follow the VC*e* pattern (see Developing Your Instructional Tool Kit).

Applying the Correspondence   As illustrated with beginning consonants and short vowel patterns, show children in a natural context how the knowledge of the VC*e* pattern, together with context, can be applied to unfamiliar words.

■■■ DEVELOPING YOUR INSTRUCTIONAL TOOLKIT

Word Sorts

"Word Sorts" are an instructional/learning technique that involves students in actively comparing and contrasting words as they sort or categorize them into groups. Regarding word sorts, Gillet and Temple pointed out that "instead of presenting generalizations directly, we can help students to form and verbalize their *own* generalizations about how words work" (1990, p. 255).

Word Sorts work best when students have manipulable word cards to sort, either from their own word banks or provided by the teacher. Depending on how you as teacher set them up, the "sorts" can reinforce students' learning or lead to initial new understandings. Sorts may be "closed," when you determine the categories into which students will sort words, or they may be "open," when students determine what their categories are. We will explore "open" sorts in more depth in Chapter 8; let's examine a "closed" word sort here.

■ The understanding of short vowel patterns vs. long discussed above can be developed in the context of a "closed" word sort. The *students* will sort selected sight words into two categories. Each category will be represented by a picture clue and a spelling pattern clue. For example, one category is labeled by the picture of a hat and the word *hat;* the other is represented by a picture of a lake and the word *lake.* Different phonograms are represented, but their spelling follows either the short *a* CVC pattern (for example, *bag, ran, fat, ham*) or the long-*a* VCe pattern (for example, *game, plate, plane, cage, grape,* and so forth).

Students are asked to sort these words into either of two categories; if they aren't sure where a particular word goes, they may place it in a "leftover" category. They are not told that one category is "short *a*" and the other is "long *a*"—that is part of the understanding we will want *them* to come to. When they have finished sorting the words, ask them to look over each category and think about *why* they sorted them the way they did. The students' responses determine how you will follow up with your questioning. For example, in this instance some responses might be "Because one is short *a* and the other is long *a*." You could ask, "How do you know?"—thereby getting them to examine the structure of the words. If they say, "Some words end in *e* and the others don't," you could respond, "What does that tell you about the sound you hear in the middle of each word?" If they answer, "All the words in this group [indicating the CVC words] have three letters," you could say, "That's true; but now, listen to the sound you hear in the middle of each of those words. . . ."

■ When children are able to do this type of sorting with ease, you may augment the task by adding the *ai* pattern, as in p<u>ai</u>l. Each long vowel pattern that is examined will be approached this way, with the first discrimination being made between the short and the long sound, and the next discrimination being made between the most frequent pattern (such as <u>a</u>C<u>e</u>) and the other patterns for that sound.

■ For children who are well into the beginning-reading phase or the transitional phase, this "closed" sort task may be very effectively supplemented by tasks in which the children hunt for and collect other words that follow a particular pattern or patterns. These words can be written down on a sheet of paper and brought back for group discussion or entered in a "word book" or "word notebook." Let's look at this notebook more closely.

The notebook (it can be part of students' journals) can be set up as follows. First, for each vowel there can be a page on which words are written in either a "long" or a "short" column. As students acquire more experience and learning, these columns can then be subdivided by spelling pattern. These subdivisions will grow and will become more differentiated. Eventually, any categorizations are possible; but regarding word structure, children will be adding categories for the different sounds of consonants (hard and soft *c* and *g,* for example), as well as for ways in which plurals are formed and inflectional endings added. The possibilities go on and on.

In time, children will examine the "*r*-influenced" vowel patterns as well, as in c<u>ar</u> and f<u>ur</u>, and the way in which they are studied may, yet again, follow this same procedure!

MEANING MAKERS ■

How Phonics Knowledge, Context, and Meaning Can Work Together in Beginning Reading

Throughout this section on word identification, I have suggested we do a "two-step" in presenting different phonics correspondences to children. First, we help children *examine* the correspondence, and then we show them how to *apply* this knowledge in real texts. This second *application* step includes an emphasis on the role of *context* as an important aspect of word identification in beginning reading. Our goal is to help children realize that phonics knowledge will often yield an approximate pronunciation which, together with context clues, reveals the word's identity. In helping them in this manner to become *flexible* in their approach to identifying words, we are providing them with a strategy that draws upon and integrates phonics, context clues, and the overall meaning that the children are constructing as they read. We state this strategy explicitly:

"If you don't know a word when you're reading, you can use the beginning sound [or word part, such as vowel pattern] and the rest of the words and pictures to get important clues."

The "rest of the words" can include (1) the sentence in which the word occurs as well as (2) the preceding text up to that point and (3) the children's overall understanding as they are reading.

One example of this strategy includes sharing with the children the simple process of saying to themselves the word *blank,* then reading to the end of the sentence, using the context together with what they know about words. For instance, a teacher might show the sentence *Katie went to the store to get some cookies* and model how to figure out the word *went,* which she believes the children do not know. She reads the sentence as "Katie *blank* to the store to get some cookies," telling the students that whenever they run into a word that they can't figure out right away, they can say "blank" to themselves, read to the end of the sentence, and then use the context and what they know about words. The teacher then can point to *went* and say, "You know, very often we can figure out a word by thinking of *another* word we know that is like the one we don't know. We all have learned the word *tent* [writing it on the board]. Look at *tent* and see if it gives you a clue to *this* word [pointing to *went*]." If the children don't pick up on the clue, the teacher can underline the *-ent* in *tent,* then cover the *w* in *went:* "What does *-ent* say in *tent?* Good . . . now put the *w* on the beginning and what do you have? Good! Now let's read the whole sentence, using *went.* . . . It makes sense, doesn't it?" ■

Some closing thoughts on phonics instruction

Now that we've gone through the most important features in the sequence of phonics instruction, I'd like to make a point that a good many educators have missed: While this systematic and careful study of words helps reinforce children's acquisition of sight words and develops their strategies for identifying unfamiliar words during reading, keep in mind that the main purpose I am encouraging in exploring words is to help children learn how words "work." That is, children are learning words not as isolated visual configurations unrelated to one another, but rather as elements that are constructed according to *patterns.* You and I can describe these patterns using the shorthand of CVC, CVC*e,* CCVCC, and so forth, but children are getting a "feel" for these patterns, and at a higher level, their brains are learning to examine and categorize words this way. To illustrate: is it easier to learn the words *bag/tag; hitch/catch;* and *cake/bike* as unrelated words or is it easier to learn them because they share structural and sound similarities?

For years, the raging controversy in beginning-reading instruction has been whether or not to teach phonics. This issue has evolved into debates about "how much" and "what kind" of phonics (Adams, 1990). Many educators say "*not* much" because they are concerned that a stronger endorsement of phonics

Do Children Have Different "Styles" for Approaching Print?

I have been emphasizing, throughout these chapters, children's developmental progression in understanding words, sounds, and letters. This understanding constitutes a critical knowledge base about the nature of print. It underlies the efficiency with which children acquire sight words, and during actual reading it underlies their ability to recognize known words and figure out unknown ones.

As long as children are reading texts in which they can recognize most of the words rather quickly, we usually will not notice any striking differences in how they are going about their reading. When children are attempting to negotiate texts that contain many words they do not know immediately, however, we may notice differences among some children. These differences have to do with how the children are applying their knowledge as they attempt to deal with text that is challenging because of the number of unknown words it contains. Some children will freely skip unknown words and on occasion entire phrases, making up the words they think "belong." Other children will stop at an unknown word and spend as much as a minute trying to figure it out—sometimes out loud, sometimes

without a sound. (In fact, many adults have the same tendencies when reading difficult text: some try to speed up and "fill in" meaning, while others will plod along very systematically, working deliberately on each new word, trying to pry out the meaning of each difficult sentence.) These "style" differences in approaching challenging texts suggest for us as teachers three imperatives.

First, work to ensure that *most* of the time, children are reading materials in which they know most of the words.

Second, realize that it is important for children to try out their developing knowledge in challenging texts of their own choosing. In such instances, usually allow them their individual "styles" in working through unfamiliar words.

Third, because we are involving them in lots of different literacy experiences, both informal and directed, children will eventually have a rich enough knowledge base to be able to coordinate knowledge about context with knowledge about word structure, in order to identify unknown words. (This is why it is so crucial for you to teach about the nature of words and texts *and* to model how to figure out words.)

LEARNING IN CONTEXT: Some children may stick to a single strategy when trying to figure out unknown words in print. While being sensitive to this, we can still help them understand how to coordinate *several* sources of information in solving the riddle of an unknown word's identity.

instruction will lead to the same dull and boring worksheets of the past. And there is no question that some individuals have made an "icon" of phonics instruction and have suggested that intensive phonics instruction is the only way to teach children.

The reality lies in between the extremes. Children need to learn about printed words and their structure. They need to because this knowledge will help them identify unknown words they encounter in their reading *and* because this knowledge ultimately makes reading and writing more efficient.

CONSTRUCTING MEANING INDEPENDENTLY

The beginning-reading phase and the move into the transitional phase are delicate times for the learner. We need to support children's reading efforts just enough: not too much, not too little. This will best lead to increasing independence in reading. We can think of the independence in two ways: we can realize that on their own, children look through books, though they don't necessarily read them—and we can think of independence in terms of those books that beginning readers are able, on their own, to read *conventionally*, constructing appropriate meaning while recognizing most if not all of the words.

We have discussed earlier how we can help children determine for themselves which books are "just right." Children need to have the opportunity to read these "just right" books, and many, many books written for beginning readers and early transitional readers are very appropriate for independent reading; some of these I've listed below. The very fact of reading a *whole* book can be thrilling and motivating in itself to young readers. This ability to select and become engaged with appropriate texts is an important foundation for their *metacognitive awareness*.

Beginning readers need to have the opportunity to read and *re*read books independently. They should have free access to the classroom's library corner (see Chapter 4). Favorite books that you have shared with them or read to them should be prominently displayed in the library corner. Kids can then enjoy them individually and with others, for the library corner should be a place where children can chat and share with one another. Children also have the opportunity during Sustained Silent Reading to read independently; and when you have individual reading conferences with the children, they can share with you a book or books that they have read on their own (see Chapter 11).

In addition to (1) the many age-appropriate books you can have in your library corner and (2) the sequenced books such as those in the *Story Box* (Wright Group) and *Bookshelf* (Scholastic) collections, you will find that (3) "series" books also are excellent for children to read on their own. These books are often simple "chapter books," collections of stories based on the same character or characters, or a whole "book-length" story. You will be able to build your own personal stock of these series books, as well as of other titles, through bonus points from book clubs (for example, Scholastic, Trumpet, Troll, and so forth), which you are awarded when you send in your children's monthly book club order and which allow you to obtain additional copies free of charge. In addition, browse through the annual catalogues of the major publishers of children's paperback books for good buys (for example, Dell, Scholastic, and Bantam). While these catalogues do not give the same degree of comprehensive information about each book as do most of the guides to children's literature (see Chapter 9), you'll recognize many of the titles and be introduced to many more. Basic information about each book is included, along with the price; you can use part of your instructional budget (see your principal) to purchase sets of books. In catalogue descriptions (and on the back of each book) you will find information about age or grade designations that can help put you "in the ballpark" in determining appropriateness.

Following are series books for beginning readers and transitional readers:

"Series" Books for Beginning Readers

Barbara Baker, *Digby and Kate* (a dog and cat) and *Digby and Kate Again.* Dutton.

Lobel, Arnold. "Frog and Toad" series. Harper.

Else Minarik (illus. by Maurice Sendak), "Little Bear" series. Trumpet Club.

Miriam Cohen (illus. by Lillian Hoban), "Jim and His Friends" series. Dell.

James Marshall, "George and Martha" series. Houghton Mifflin.

Cynthia Rylant, "Henry and Mudge" series (Mudge is a large dog). Bradbury.

"Series" Books for Transitional Readers

Bernice Chardiet and Grace Maccarone, "School Friends" series. Scholastic.

Russell and Francis Hoban, *Bedtime for Frances,* and others. Harper & Row.

Patricia Reilly Giff, "The Kids of the Polk Street School" series. Dell.

Suzy Kline, "Horrible Harry" series. Putnam.

Jean Marzollo, "Kids on the Block" series. Scholastic (chapter books).

Barbara Ann Porte, "Harry" books. Scholastic.

Marjorie Sharmat, "Nate the Great" series. Dell.

You should know that some scholars are critical of referring to these types of books as "children's literature." They would argue that the books are not representative of the truly consequential, well-written literature to which children should be exposed. This will probably always be an issue, but I will reiterate my reason for recommending series such as these: the authors *do* know and understand kids, and the popularity of these books attests to the fact that they are reaching kids. And after all, one of our primary objectives is to motivate kids to read. Because these books are ones that they can read independently— thus giving them practice in reading on their own—I do not hesitate to recommend them. And remember that you will also be sharing many other books with your students through read-alouds and group discussion (see Chapter 6), providing a well-rounded literature experience.

■ A CONCLUDING PERSPECTIVE

The beginning conventional reading phase is a delicate though fascinating period. As teachers, we must be especially sensitive to our students so as to provide just the right amount of support—and independence—as we provide models of how books and the language of books work. We balance immersion in print with analysis of print. In this chapter, we have explored the major components of effective beginning reading:

- Modeling through read-alouds and Guided Listening-Thinking Activities
- Shared reading and predictable texts
- Language Experience Activities
- The acquisition of sight vocabulary and the examination of sight words to discover patterns as part of flexible word-identification strategies
- Guided reading of selected texts
- Ongoing concept development
- Beginning writing

And forgive me for again being redundant; but lest we get overly analytical with the specifics of beginning reading, I must draw our discussion to a close with a wide-angle view of the classroom. Not all of what we've been discussing will work in a regimented classroom boiling with unrealistic expectations for seven-year-olds. At the very best, such classrooms produce a few children who can read but choose not to. *Your* beginning-reading classroom, on the other hand, should facilitate literacy learning in children who are learning not only how print works but who will come to understand the meaning, the marvelous potential, of literacy in their lives.

■ BECOMING A REFLECTIVE PRACTITIONER: CHAPTER 5

Barone, D. (1990). The written responses of young children: Beyond comprehension to story understanding. *The New Advocate, 3,* 1, 49–56.

Diane Barone was one of a handful of researchers in the 1980s who closely examined beginning readers' written responses to their reading. Her data come from the primary classroom in which she taught; she discovered that young children are capable of more insightful understandings of what they read than they generally are given credit for. While providing important insights from research, this article is a comfortable "read," offering clear implications for classroom practice.

Clay, M. (1991). Introducing a new storybook to young readers. *Reading Teacher, 45,* 264–273.

Marie Clay is one of the most respected researchers and teachers in the area of emergent and beginning literacy. Her insight into how children become readers has influenced teachers in Australia, her native New Zealand, North America, and Great Britain. Don't be fooled by the title of this article—in the process of describing in excellent detail how to introduce a new storybook, Clay discusses many critical features of her work, synthesizing within a few pages much of what she has written in a number of books and articles over the past three decades.

Henderson, E. H. (1981). *Learning to read and spell: The child's knowledge of words.* DeKalb, IL: Northern Illinois University Press.

A master clinician, Edmund Henderson was also one of a very few educators in the late 1960s and early 1970s who closely examined how children invented their spellings and related these insights to young children's reading and writing. He describes these insights and their implications for instruction in this volume. You'll find the chapters that address beginning reading instruction particularly helpful. Henderson provides a comprehensive walk-through of guided reading lessons and beginning word study.

Read, C. (1971). Preschool children's knowledge of English phonology. *Harvard Educational Review, 41*, 1–41.

This has become a classic piece in the literature on children's invented spelling. With Carol Chomsky, Charles Read conducted the first investigations of young children's attempts to spell. This is the first published article that explored this phenomenon in depth. A linguist by training, Read provided the key that unlocked the rationale behind children's invented spelling and helped us "decode" what the children were writing. While somewhat technical in many places, the article is engaging when it explores specific invented spellings of young children.

■ REFERENCES

Adams, M. (1990). *Beginning to read: Thinking and learning about print*. Cambridge, MA: MIT Press.

Ashton-Warner, S. (1963). *Teacher*. New York: Simon & Schuster.

Barnes, W. G. W. (1989). Word sorting: The cultivation of rules for spelling in English. *Reading Psychology, 10*, 293–307.

Barone, D. (1990). The written responses of young children: Beyond comprehension to story understanding. *The New Advocate, 3*(1), 49–56.

Barone, D. (1992). "That reminds me of": Using dialogue journals with young students. In C. Temple & P. Collins (Eds.), *Stories and readers: New perspectives on literature in the elementary classroom* (pp. 85–102). Norwood, MA: Christopher-Gordon.

Bear, D., & Barone, D. (1989). Using children's spellings to group for word study and directed reading in the primary classroom. *Reading Psychology, 10*, 275–292.

Bear, D., Invernizzi, M., & Templeton, S. (in press). *Words their way: Developmental phonics, vocabulary, and spelling, K–8*. Columbus, OH: Merrill/Prentice-Hall.

Beers, J. & Henderson, E. (1977). A study of developing orthographic concepts among first graders. *Research in the Teaching of English, 11*, 133–148.

Brady, S. & Shankweiler, D. (Eds.). (1991). *Phonological processes in literacy: A tribute to Isabelle Y. Liberman*. Hillsdale, NJ: Lawrence Erlbaum Associates.

Bussis, A., Chittenden, E., Amarel, M., & Klausner, E. (1985). *Inquiry into meaning: An investigation of learning to read*. Hillsdale, NJ: Lawrence Erlbaum Associates.

Chall, J. (1953). Ask him to try on the book for fit. *The Reading Teacher, 7*, 83–88.

Chall, J. (1983). *Stages of reading development*. New York: McGraw-Hill.

Chomsky, C. (1971). Write first, read later. *Childhood Education, 47*, 269–299.

Clay, M. (1991a). Introducing a new storybook to young readers. *Reading Teacher, 45*, 264–273.

Clay, M. (1991b). *Becoming literate: The construction of inner control*. Auckland, New Zealand: Heinemann.

Combs, M. (1987). Modeling the reading process with enlarged texts. *Reading Teacher, 40*, 422–426.

Cunningham, P. (1991). *Phonics they use*. New York: HarperCollins.

Dolch, E. (1936). Basic sight vocabulary. *Elementary School Journal,* 36, 456–460.

Dyson, A. (1989). *Multiple worlds of child writers.* New York: Teachers College Press.

Ehri, L.C. (1993). How English orthography influences phonological knowledge as children learn to read and spell. In R. J. Scholes (Ed.), *Literacy and language analysis* (pp. 21–43). Hillsdale, NJ: Lawrence Erlbaum Associates.

Freppon, P., & Dahl, K. (1991). Learning about phonics in a whole language classroom. *Language Arts, 68,* 190–197.

Fry, E. (1980). The new instant word list. *Reading Teacher, 34,* 284–289.

Fulwiler, T. (Ed.). (1987). *The journal book.* Portsmouth, NH: Boynton-Cook.

Gentry, J., & Gillet, J. (1992). *Teaching kids to spell.* Portsmouth, NH: Heinemann.

Gillet, J., & Temple, C. (1990). *Understanding reading problems* (3rd ed.). New York: HarperCollins.

Gough, P., Ehri, L., & Treiman, R. (Eds.) (1992). *Reading acquisition.* Hillsdale, NJ: Lawrence Erlbaum Associates.

Hansen, J. (1987). *When writers read.* Portsmouth, NH: Heinemann.

Henderson, E. (1981). *Learning to read and spell: The child's knowledge of words.* DeKalb, IL: Northern Illinois University Press.

Henderson, E. (1990). *Teaching spelling* (2nd ed.). Boston: Houghton Mifflin.

Houghton Mifflin Literature Experience (1993). Boston: Houghton Mifflin.

Johnson, D. (1976). *Johnson basic sight vocabulary test manual.* Lexington, MA: Ginn.

Johnson, D., & Pearson, P. (1982). *Teaching reading vocabulary* (2nd ed.). New York: Holt, Rinehart, & Winston.

Juel, C. (1991). Beginning reading. In R. Barr, M. L. Kamil, P. Rosenthal, & P. D. Pearson (Eds.). *Handbook of reading research: Volume II* (pp. 759–788). New York: Longman.

Kucera, H., & Francis, W. N. (1982). *Frequency analysis of English usage: Lexicon and grammar.* Boston: Houghton Mifflin.

Lee, H. (1960). *To kill a mockingbird.* Philadelphia: Lippincott.

Lorge, I., & Chall, J. (1963). Estimating the size of vocabularies of children and adults: An analysis of methodological issues. *Journal of Experimental Education, 32,* 147–157.

McGee, L., & Richgels, D. (1989). *Literacy's beginnings.* Boston: Allyn & Bacon.

Meek, M. (1983). *Learning to read.* London: The Bodley Head.

Newkirk, T. (1989). *More than stories: The range of children's writing.* Portsmouth, NH: Heinemann.

Ohlausen, M., & Jepsen, M. (1992). Somebody's been choosing my books but I can make my own choices now! *The New Advocate, 5,* 36.

Read, C. (1971). Preschool children's knowledge of English phonology. *Harvard Educational Review, 41,* 1–41.

Read, C. (1975). *Children's categorization of speech sounds in English.* Urbana, IL: National Council of Teachers of English.

Reiben, L., & Perfetti, C. (1991). *Learning to read: Basic research and its implications.* Hillsdale, NJ: Lawrence Erlbaum Associates.

Slaughter, J. P. (1993). *Beyond storybooks: Young children and the shared book experience.* Newark, DE: International Reading Association.

Stauffer, R. (1969). *Directing reading maturity as a cognitive process.* New York: Harper and Row.

Stauffer, R. (1980). *The language experience approach to the teaching of reading* (2nd ed.). New York: Harper and Row.

Templeton, S. (1991a). Teaching and learning the English spelling system: Reconceptualizing method and purpose. *Elementary School Journal, 92,* 185–201.

Templeton, S. (1991b). *Teaching the integrated language arts.* Boston: Houghton Mifflin.

Templeton, S., & Bear, D. (Eds.). (1992). *Development of orthographic knowledge and the foundations of literacy: A memorial Festschrift for Edmund H. Henderson.* Hillsdale, NJ: Lawrence Erlbaum Associates.

Templeton, S., & Thomas, P. W. (1984). Performance and reflection: Young children's concept of "word." *Journal of Educational Research, 27,* 139–146.

Children's Literature Cited

Banachek, L. (1978). *Snake in, snake out.* New York: Crowell.

Bolton, F. (1986). *The greedy goat.* New York: Scholastic.

Cowley, J. (1990). *The hungry giant.* Bothel, WA: Wright Group.

Crews, D. (1978). *Freight train.* New York: Greenwillow.

Drew (1987). *Animal clues.*

Kent, J. (1971). *The fat cat.* Scholastic.

Mahy, M. (1986). *When the king rides by.* Bothel, WA: Wright Group.

McMillan, B. (1983). *Here a chick, there a chick.* New York: Lothrop, Lee, and Shepard.

McMillan, B. (1983). *Super super superwords.* New York: Lothrop, Lee, and Shepard.

Minarik, E. (1968). *A kiss for little bear.* New York: HarperCollins Children's Books.

Spinelli, J. (1990). *Maniac Magee.* Boston: Little, Brown.

CHAPTER SIX

CONSTRUCTING MEANING IN NARRATIVES

UNDERSTANDING AND DEFINING TYPES OF LITERATURE

Fiction and Poetry • Formats for Fictional Narratives • Elements of Narration
• BUILDING YOUR KNOWLEDGE BASE: Books to Develop Awareness of Elements of
Narration • MEANING MAKERS: You, the Classroom Teacher—Why Stories?

OVERVIEW OF TEACHING THE CONSTRUCTION OF MEANING IN NARRATIVES

What Students Can Gain from Learning to Read Narratives • Instructional Experiences
• MAKING CONNECTIONS: How to Organize All This?

INSTRUCTIONAL "BRIDGE" EXPERIENCES: GUIDING STUDENTS TOWARD INTERNALIZATION

Guided Critical-Thinking Activities • CLASSROOM IN ACTION: Conducting a Limited
Guided Reading-Thinking Activity •Direct Teaching of Skills and Strategies
• CLASSROOM IN ACTION: Modeling Making Predictions • CLASSROOM IN ACTION:
Modeling Rereading for Sense

ASKING GOOD QUESTIONS

Our Purposes for Questioning • Levels of Information and Types of Questions
• MEANING MAKERS: The Reader and the Classroom Teacher—Exemplar Questions for
Narratives

INSTRUCTIONAL EXPERIENCES: STUDENTS LEARN TO INTERNALIZE THROUGH DOING

Intensive Reading • MAKING CONNECTIONS: Literature Groups and Intensive Reading
• MAKING CONNECTIONS: Different Abilities, Backgrounds, and Perspectives
• DEVELOPING YOUR INSTRUCTIONAL TOOLKIT: Uncovering the Structures of Stories
• Extensive Reading • MEANING MAKERS: The Reader: Value of Rereading—from
Fluency to Deeper Insights • Constructing Meaning Through Writing • MEANING
MAKERS: You, the Student—A Perspective on Writing

READING POETRY

Reading Poetry Aloud to Children • Students Reading and Responding to Poetry
• Learning Different Forms

A CONCLUDING PERSPECTIVE

BECOMING A REFLECTIVE PRACTITIONER

REFERENCES

Novels and stories are renderings of life; they can not only keep us company, but admonish us, point us in new directions, or give us the courage to stay a given course. They can offer us kinsmen, kinswomen, comrades, advisers—offer us other eyes through which we might see, other ears with which we might make soundings.

Robert Coles, The Call of Stories

As they are told and retold, stories have the function of wrestling with the ultimately inexplicable chaos of reality around us. They give it form, and in shaping and reshaping the form, they help us gain control over it.

Alan Jabbour, National Folklife Center

With this chapter, we begin exploring in depth the "what, why, and how" of the understandings children construct when they come together with texts. We start with fictional narratives—stories, chapter books—and poems, because those types of literature most directly help children (and us) gain control, see beauty, and achieve understanding in the "chaos of reality."

First, however, an important comment about the titles of this chapter and the next: a time-traveling teacher from the 1950s or 1960s, skimming the table of contents of this book, would be perplexed. "Where," she or he would most likely ask, "are the chapters on reading comprehension"? They are here, of course—this chapter and the next, most specifically—but the chapter titles reflect a significant change in *how* we talk about readers, texts, and understandings. As we have seen already in *this* text, the process of "making meaning" is a collaborative process between reader and text. Each brings a type of "meaning" to the act of reading, and a *new* meaning is thereby created. The reader must construct the meaning that arises from a transaction with the text. The teacher from the middle of the twentieth century would probably have a very different view of the reading act: that the reader must "get" the meaning that is "in" the text. Thirty to forty years ago, little attention was being paid to the reader's prior knowledge and its role in understanding what was read. I am emphasizing the *construction* of meaning, in these two chapters, to underscore the *active* nature of readers' transactions with texts.

Of course, *we* have a role in this process of construction. And as we have seen up to this point, the role includes helping children understand initially how print represents spoken language. It also includes bringing the children into the company of good books and getting them to talk, write, and think about those books. We are primary facilitators in this process:

We will help guide children's choices.

We will challenge students through important questions, and in so doing help them internalize both the process of questioning and the types of questions that may be asked.

We will teach, through modeling, whatever specific skills the students may need in their "construction" process.

By understanding the nature of narratives, we can further the role they play in our students' lives. Let's begin, then, by considering how stories are put together.

UNDERSTANDING AND DEFINING TYPES OF LITERATURE

Fiction and poetry

Fictional narratives include novels and short stories. Poems include lyric poetry and ballads and other story-poems. Figure 6.1 shows some relationships between the two literary forms. Throughout most of this chapter, we will be focusing primarily on fiction; we will discuss poetry in some detail in the final section. Keep in mind as you read this chapter, however, that many of the approaches and responses we will be discussing in regard to stories may apply to some types of poems equally well.

Formats for fictional narratives

Short Stories When we hear the phrases "It was a dark and stormy night" and "Once upon a time," why do we know what's coming up? Quite simply, we have a *schema* for stories—an organized body of knowledge about how stories

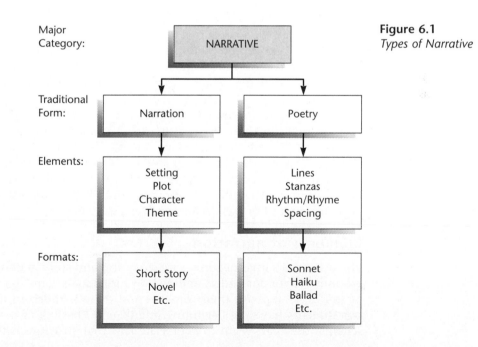

Figure 6.1
Types of Narrative

"work." This knowledge about story structure is part of the prior knowledge we all bring to the stories that we hear or read (see Chapter 2). If young children have opportunities to hear stories, they will develop a tacit understanding—a schema—for these structures.

Research into children's understanding of story structure began in earnest several years ago; in fact, many researchers attempted to determine whether children develop a "grammar" for stories just as they develop a "grammar" for sentences (see, for example, Mandler, 1984; Mandler & Johnson, 1977; Stein & Glenn, 1977; Templeton, Cain, & Miller, 1981; Thorndyke, 1977). That is, stories may have certain structural features that are arranged in certain ways according to tacit "rules" of story grammar—just as the elements of sentences (words, phrases, clauses) are arranged in certain ways according to sentence grammar. Researchers tried to identify what these basic story features might be; in essence, the features reflected our more traditional conceptions of a beginning, a middle, and an end. Each of these features in turn must contain certain others: Beginnings should introduce the main character(s) and include the setting and some type of "initiating event" or problem. Middles should include one or more "episodes" or events that represent the character's attempts at resolving the problem introduced at the beginning. The end includes the resolution of the problem. Stories the world over, in different cultures, reflect this basic structure (Campbell, 1967; Gee, 1989). They may differ with respect to how characters are described, how they behave, the nature of the problems they encounter, and so forth, but the basic structure is inevitably there.

Chapter Books   Not only *short stories* but book-length narratives follow certain basic structures. Each chapter becomes an episode; there are minor problems and solutions within each episode; overall, there are major themes and plots that extend across the whole book; and usually the book ends with a final resolution. Readers are required to construct and maintain in long-term memory an ongoing text representation that will support understanding adequately. Often chapters have titles; sometimes they do not. Readers develop an understanding of what the chapter titles tell, and why the boundaries of chapters occur where they do.

Sometimes stories and chapter books are "*un*grammatical," and that's when they do their best job of surprising us. A class of third-graders, for example, may have a difficult time accepting the way E. B. White's *Stuart Little* ends; this will lead to a lengthy discussion about how authors choose to close stories. So we have to analyze basic narrative structure in short stories and in chapter books, not only to understand typical stories but to understand what is going on when an author has decided to break the rules.

Elements of narration

The researchers investigating story structures and story grammars have laid the groundwork for our understanding how individuals come to grasp the structure of stories, along with their content. And there is much to understand: Once our students have the beginning/middle/end "basics" of a story grammar or schema, they can begin to appreciate *how* that structure is fleshed out by an author and start to relate this fuller entity to their own lives. They can learn about the elements of narration referred to as *characterization, setting, plot, theme, point of view,* and *style.*

Our overriding objective in teaching about elements of narration is to involve readers more deeply and meaningfully in stories. These elements should not be considered ends in themselves, but rather *means* by which readers are pulled into narratives. These elements also become part of the vocabulary with which readers are able to discuss stories, writing, and their own response to and understanding of narratives.

Peterson and Eeds point out that "awareness of literary elements and of their function in a story nurtures the development of children's ability to respond imaginatively to a text . . ." (1990, p. 25). And beyond this imaginative response, the awareness helps children come to understand much about life, about thought, and about themselves. If this sounds a bit overstated, I hope it will appear less so as we learn more about how stories work and how children can transact with them. As we'll see a little later in this chapter, through involving our students in reading and in discussing what they read, we will be setting the stage for children's developing understanding of the six elements. We can then build on this "experiential" foundation by talking about these elements explicitly. In this section, we will describe each type of story element. Later in the chapter, a few activities for developing and extending awareness of them will be presented.

Characterization How does the author *develop* characters? Characters can be "flat," simply *there,* without any real fleshing-out; or they can be "rounded," with many different facets—like real people (Lukens, 1990). Good characterization does more than simply help the reader form a mental image of a character. Because characters can be stand-ins for ourselves when we read, they must be believable. Authors fully describe their "rounded" characters—how they think, speak, and act, as well as how others think, speak, and act in relation to them.

Setting The *setting* of a narrative is the physical, geographical, and historical context in which the story will unfold. The setting orients the reader in place and time; it can be a mere backdrop or it can be integral, playing a significant role in the development of the narrative—for example, working to support or to foil the main character. A setting can take us away from our own experience or shelter us within what we know to be safe. By itself, setting can channel a character's reaction. Often mentioned in the context of discussing settings is *mood,* the emotional context the author develops, partly through the way in which he or she develops the setting. The author's description dictates the mood of a story and is meant to affect readers accordingly.

In an engaging description of setting with a powerful evocation of mood, Natalie Babbitt begins her remarkable book *Tuck Everlasting* with this prologue:

> *The first week of August hangs at the very top of summer, the top of the live-long year, like the highest seat of a Ferris wheel when it pauses in its turning. The weeks that come before are only a climb from balmy spring, and those that follow a drop to the chill of autumn, but the first week of August is motionless, and hot. It is curiously silent, too, with blank white dawns and glaring noons, and*

sunsets smeared with too much color. Often at night there is lightning, but it quivers all alone. There is no thunder, no relieving rain. These are strange and breathless days, the dog days, when people are led to do things they are sure to be sorry for after.

Plot   What happens in a story? In a nutshell, this is what *plot* is all about. In addition, plot has to do with *how* things happen—the pace and type of action, the number of episodes and whether and how they are resolved, the buildup of anticipation or suspense. Plot involves *conflict* of some type. This conflict may be any one or a combination of the following types: (1) between persons, as in *The Pain and the Great One,* by Judy Blume; (2) between a person and nature, as in *Black Star, Bright Morning,* by Scott O'Dell; (3) within a person, as in *Bridge to Terabithia,* by Katherine Paterson, and *Ira Sleeps Over,* by Bernard Waber; (4) between a person and society, as in *NightJohn,* by Gary Paulsen, and *Harriet the Spy,* by Gail Fitzhugh.

Theme   Theme is what the reader discovers the story is *really* about: not what happened (plot), but the underlying message or messages the reader feels the author has subtly whispered or even shouted forcefully. In a story, boys and girls may meet strange beings and challenges during a journey, for example, but they will return as men and women—or at least much wiser and humbler than before. How all this happens is the plot; the real *meaning* of the journey, however, is the theme. Themes can be grandiose: life versus death; youth versus maturity. Themes can be more mundane: look before you leap; if you try to please everyone you'll please no one.

For intermediate students, Elizabeth George Speare's *The Witch of Blackbird Pond* (1958) represents a number of themes: prejudice; the dark side of blindly following a trend; the realization that people who make us unhappy or uncomfortable may have our best interests at heart or even have riches to share with us; persons with physical handicaps should not be viewed mainly in terms of this surface factor.

Point of View   This term refers to the perspective from which we see what happens in a particular story. Are we viewing the story through the main character's eyes? If that character is the narrator—an "I" who is describing the events—we get a *first person* point of view, as with Bright Morning in Scott O'Dell's *Sing Down the Moon.* If we view the events through the eyes of someone who can see all the action and knows what's going on in every character's mind, the point of view is *omniscient* or "all-knowing," as in *Charlotte's Web.* Understanding point of view is important for children because they will come to consider others' perspectives in real life.

Style   Style is an author's use of language—the distinctive or special way in which he or she uses language to communicate or talk with us. A writer's style may include *imagery* (descriptions appealing to our senses), *figurative language* (personification, hyperbole, similes and metaphors, idioms), devices of sound (such as *rhyme* and *alliteration*), and *symbolism* (anything that operates on two levels, literal and suggested). Some or all of these aspects may intersect and overlap. In Chapter 8, we will look closely at them as we explore learning about word meanings. Traditionally, style is not an "element" of stories, but very often it is considered part of what infuses a story and makes it "work."

Consider Scott O'Dell's style in his moving and uplifting tale of Bright Morning, a Navaho girl whose story is set in the 1860s during a massive, forced resettling of the Navahos by the Anglos. Though fairly short, O'Dell's descriptive sentences take us into Bright Morning's thoughts and character on the second page of *Sing Down the Moon.*

> *The day the waters came was a wonderful day. I heard the first sounds of their coming while I lay awake in the night. At first it was a whisper, like a wind among the dry stalks of our cornfield. After a while it was a sound like the feet of warriors dancing. Then it was a roar that shook the earth. I could hardly wait until the sun rose. (1970, p. 2)*

O'Dell's straightforward sentences move us forward in anticipation while he presents precise, vivid images through metaphors and similes ("At first it *was* a whisper, *like* a wind. . . . Then it *was* a roar that shook the earth").

BUILDING YOUR KNOWLEDGE BASE ■

Books to Develop Awareness of Elements of Narration

Books for Exploration of Character

Primary

Bunting, E. (1989). *The Wednesday surprise.* Clarion.

Turner, A. *Nettie's trip south.* Macmillan.

White, E. B. (1952). *Charlotte's web.* Harper.

Intermediate

MacLachlan, P. (1986). *Sarah, plain and tall.* Harper.

Paterson, K. (1978). *The great Gilly Hopkins.* New York: Crowell.

Spinelli, J. (1990). *Maniac Magee.* Little, Brown.

Books for Exploration of Setting

Primary

Aardema, V. (1979). *The riddle of the drum: A tale from Tizapan, Mexico.* Four Winds.

Scheer, J. (1964). *Rain makes applesauce.* Holiday.

Sendak, M. (1963). *Where the wild things are.* Harper.

Intermediate

Hamilton, V. (1990). *Cousins.* Putnam.

Jagendorf, M. A., & Boggs, R. S. (1960). *The king of the mountains: A treasury of Latin American folk stories.* Copp, Clark.

Paulsen, G. (1987). *Hatchet.* Bradbury.

Books for Exploration of Plot

Primary

Gag, W. (1956). *Millions of cats.* Coward.

Galdone, P. (1972). *The three bears.* Seabury.

Peterson, R. "The Littles" series. Scholastic.

Intermediate

Burnford, S. (1961). *The incredible journey.* Little, Brown.

Taylor, M. (1976). *Role of thunder, hear my cry.* New York: Dial.

Books for Exploration of Theme

Primary

Grifalconi, A. (1987). *Darkness and the butterfly.* Boston: Little, Brown.

Lobel, A. (1980). *Fables.* Harper.

Piper, W. (1954). *The little engine that could.* Platt.

Williams, M. (1958). *The velveteen rabbit.* Doubleday.

Intermediate

Armstrong, W. (1969). *Sounder.* Harper.

Baylor, B. (1976). *Hawk, I'm your brother.* Scribner's.

Uchida, Y. (1978). *Journey home.* Atheneum.

Voight, C. (1981). *Homecoming.* Atheneum.

Yolen, J. (1981). *The acorn quest.* Crowell.

Books for Exploration of Point of View

Primary

Aardema, V. (1988). *Oh, Kojo! How could you!* Dial.

LeGuin, U. (1988). *Catwings.* Watts.

Mayer, M. (1974). *Frog goes to dinner.* Dial.

Wood, A. (1985). *King Bidgood's in the bathtub.* Harcourt.

Intermediate

Byars, B. (1989). *Bingo Brown and the language of love.* Viking.

George, J. C. (1959). *My side of the mountain.* Dutton.

Jukes, M. (1984). *Like Jake and me.* Knopf.

O'Dell, S. (1960). *Island of the blue dolphins.* Houghton Mifflin.

Books for Exploration of Style

Primary

Aardema, V. (1981). *Bringing the rain to Kapiti Plain.* Dial.

dePaola, T. (1978). *Clown of god.* Harcourt, Brace, Jovanovich.

dePaola, T. (1990). *Little Grunt and the big egg.* Holiday House.

Ehlert, L. (1991). *Red leaf yellow leaf.* Harcourt Brace Jovanovich.

Lionni, L. (1969). *Alexander and the wind-up mouse.* Pantheon.

Rylant, C. (1982). *When I was young in the mountains.* Dutton.

Intermediate

Frank, R. (1986) *No hero for the Kaiser.* Lothrop, Lee & Shepard.

Lawson, R. (1944). *Rabbit Hill.* Viking.

Speare, E. G. (1958). The *witch of Blackbird Pond.* Houghton Mifflin.

MEANING MAKERS: You, the Classroom Teacher

Why Stories?

Not long ago a friend of mine was challenged while on a cross-country flight. The man in the seat next to her was an executive for a thriving corporation. When he learned that my friend was an English teacher, he said something like this:

"You know, I don't know why you people spend so much time having kids read stories when they're having so much trouble just being able to read and write simple stuff. You people need to teach them how to read and follow directions, fill out forms correctly, and express themselves simply and clearly in writing. Face it—how often in everyday life do people sit down and read stories? It's time you people got real! You know what I tell my sixth-grader? I tell him not to pay any attention to that 'interpretation' crap from his teachers."

Although this gentleman's point of view was very baldly expressed, he does represent a common point of view: Many people believe that literacy should be practical and that while stories are certainly good, we should not be spending a lot of time on them. After reading this far in this chapter, where do *you* stand on the issue—and why? ■

OVERVIEW OF TEACHING THE CONSTRUCTION OF MEANING IN NARRATIVES

There are many compelling reasons for immersing children in the reading of narratives, and there are many ways to facilitate that immersion. In this section, I will provide first a major overview of our rationale and our instructional activities. The balance of the chapter will offer in-depth elaboration of this overview. We will begin by re-examining the Instructional Flow (Figure 6.2) that was originally presented in Chapter 5. This time, focus on the right-hand column, noting how our intermediate grade instruction focusing on

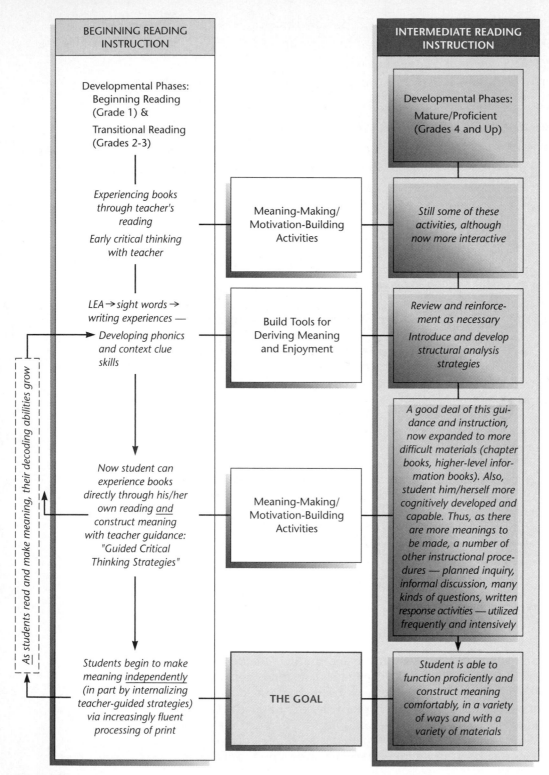

Figure 6.2
Instructional Flow in Beginning Reading

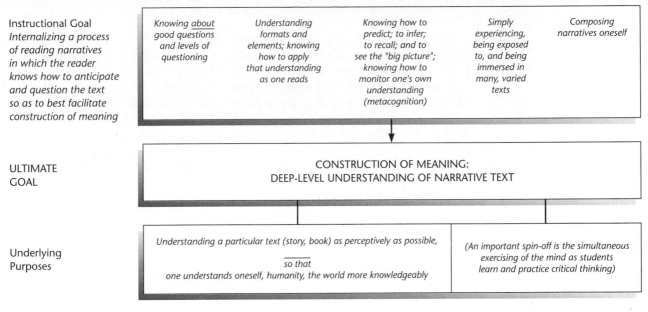

Figure 6.3
Perspective on Constructing Meaning in Narratives

constructing meaning picks right up from that of Beginning Reading. Also note the increasingly significant role that constructing meaning plays in all instruction.

With your students, you will be reading many narratives, as thoroughly and as consciously as possible. As Figure 6.3 illustrates, the underlying purpose of such deep reading is understanding oneself and one's world. Yet not every narrative should be read so deliberately. While the ultimate goal is "deep-level understanding," many avenues toward that goal can be traveled, and they may reach additional destinations. *Which* avenues will be traveled depends on our *instructional* goal, in which *questioning* plays such an important role. Much of the reading of narratives will be *intensive*. Over time, students will internalize many aspects of such an active and perceptive stance, aspects that they will absorb at a subconscious level and that will play a subtle role whenever the students read narratives, including those read for recreation and those that they compose themselves.

During and after the transitional-reading phase, we involve our students in narratives in which we set up progressively more *reflective, analytical* experiences. Our purpose in doing this is twofold:

First, we wish to provide students with a means of approaching stories as *active* readers, on their own, anticipating keenly what will be happening and why.

Second, we want to provide students with the opportunity to engage in increasingly intensive and meaningful reflection on their experiences with narratives and to support and guide them as they do so.

Children also need opportunities not only to experience story reading *independently* but also to *talk* with one another about stories they are reading, apart from our involvement. The enjoyment they experience through these freer interactions supports the *aesthetic* types of response to narratives that is so crucial to developing an ongoing desire to read (Rosenblatt, 1982; Zarillo, 1991). To illustrate our first purpose stated above, let's think for a moment about our own reading. If we are really enjoying a particular novel, we want to share that excitement with a friend. If the friend happens to be reading the same novel, we'll probably wind up in an animated discussion about what's happening in the book, how the characters are dealing with the events, and what each of us thinks about the whole matter. We are *not* as likely, though, to talk about symbolism or other literary elements.

On another occasion, however, we may re-examine that novel from a different, more analytical, perspective—our second goal stated above. That perspective will let us see much more, notice aspects that hadn't struck us earlier—thus making our whole experience of the book and the world to which it refers even more satisfying and enlightening. This is the type of experience we want our students to have.

What students can gain from learning to read narratives

I stated in the preceding section that children's understanding of story elements helps them understand much about themselves, about others, and about their own world. Why is this so? Why *do* stories have the types of elements we've just discussed? Why are these elements found in stories the world over? Stories are about what it means to seek, to struggle to overcome obstacles and challenges, to gain knowledge and acquire wisdom. "Useful stories," William Kittredge has observed, "are radical in that they help us see freshly. That's what stories are for, to help us see for ourselves as we go about the continual business of reinventing ourselves" (p. 9, 1992).

Children can listen to or read fairy tales such as "Hansel and Gretel" and "Cinderella" and remain drawn to them, without anyone's asking them to think about what the stories "mean." But unless we play a role in facilitating which stories they read and how they experience their reading of stories, children might miss the potential for understanding and realizing *why* they resonate with such tales: these stories are teaching them about the world and about their own place in it, about the reality and threat of evil, about the victory of good over evil. As with us, stories teach children about the inevitable gray areas—times when they encounter ambiguity or uncertainty and try to come to grips with it. Along these lines, for example, consider Jane Yolen's postscript to *The Devil's Arithmetic,* her gripping novel about the Holocaust. She reaffirms the power, meaning, and *role* of stories in children's lives in the face of unfathomable experiences and realizations:

Fiction cannot recite the numbing numbers, but it can be that witness, that memory. A storyteller can attempt to tell the human tale, can make a galaxy out of the chaos, can point to the fact that some people survived even as most people died. And can remind us that the swallows still sing around the smokestacks.

And eventually, children will learn that the end of one story is merely the beginning of another.

There is another reason for involving children deeply in stories, a reason not often discussed in recent decades: because stories are *guides* to ways of living, they offer ways of *coping* as well. This is a fundamental message to all children. For many of our children who are now "at risk," these guides may be more important than ever. Even when the values of the home are strong, the values of the street may, sadly, win out—even for eight- and nine-year-olds. And there is no guarantee that children from "comfortable" and "safe" neighborhoods will have a better-developed value system simply because of where they live.

A great deal may be missing from many children's lives. Through the guidance of a knowledgeable and caring teacher, however, stories may help children lead tolerable, meaningful lives in what for many of them may be very trying and challenging situations.

Instructional experiences

We have examined the nature of narratives and discussed their importance in children's lives. We're ready to explore the activities and strategies through which we will involve students in "meaning making" in narratives. At times we will guide them quite deliberately; at other times we will let them, by and large, guide themselves. Toward this end we as teachers may be more obvious guides early in the school year, less obvious ones as students grow accustomed to the freedom of inquiry and exploration allowed by their developing skills and the overall literacy environment we have set up. Intertwined with these experiences with narratives will be (1) our direct teaching of needed skills, information, and strategies, along with (2) our modeling of different types of questions. The two objectives often overlap, but I am keeping "questioning" separate and will discuss it in a separate section because of its central importance to students' guided reading. As we'll see, our goal will be to help students internalize both our *process of questioning* and the *types of questions* we pose. As Figure 6.3 demonstrates, internalized questioning and meaning construction are inextricable.

Refer for a moment to Figure 6.4, "Classroom Reading Experiences: Narratives." This chart represents the relationships among different contexts, types, and goals of reading. It should be a helpful map and reference point as we discuss the different ways in which we can involve our students in experiencing narratives. Its underlying organization reflects (1) the *context* in which any reading experience occurs and the *teacher's role* within that context, as well as (2) the *type* of reading experience.

We will begin our examination in the following three sections. In the first, we will consider the range and flow of instruction, from guidance to internaliza-

	"BRIDGE" EXPERIENCES	INTENSIVE READING	
		Core Selections	Extended Selections
TYPE OF READING MATERIAL	Most typically, short stories selected by teacher	Typically, whole books selected by teacher as essential experiences for all students	Typically, whole books self-selected by groups or individuals from a set provided by teacher
READING MODE	Guided by teacher	Either as read-alouds with partner, or by self	Read individually in context of theme exploration
INSTRUCTIONAL METHODS/ PROCEDURES	Guided Critical-Thinking Activities: Guided Reading-Thinking Activity and exploration of elements of narratives	Informal discussion; planned inquiry; written response activities, GLTA read-alouds, cooperatively grouped	Informal discussion; planned inquiry; written response activities
		Supplemented by "literature expansion" activities	
OCCURS	Early in term, before thematic teaching under way	Once the initial "bridge" phase has occurred, all year long	
INSTRUCTIONAL SETTING/FORMAT	Usually, small groups made up of students of similar reading abilities	Sometimes whole class; sometimes small groups (formed by teacher and/or students); sometimes partners; sometimes individuals	Small groups based on interest or reading level
LEVEL/KIND OF TEACHER MANAGEMENT	Direct, strong leadership with modeling	From moderately strong (choose/assign book; lead or moderate discussion) to light (monitor/guide response activities)	Light: provide book recommendations; lead or moderate discussion with planned questions; monitor/guide response activities
THEMATIC UNIT CONTEXT	Not related to any particular theme	Central relationship: each seen as a selection that (1) so embodies the basic theme(s)-at-hand that it should be experienced by everyone in the class or (2) is so important in and of itself that it can become the springboard for the theme itself	Of key importance in theme exploration — each literally "extends" the theme embodied by the core selection
RELATIONSHIP TO WRITING	Model the narrative structure and elements that students can apply and explore in their own writing	Provides springboard for written response activities and is enchanced by original writings and writing-process work	
RELATIONSHIP TO DIRECT TEACHING OF SKILLS AND STRATEGIES	Excellent opportunity for minilessons in skills/strategies as needs become apparent and/or are planned and structured by teacher	Whenever "teachable moments" regarding the need for a particular skill or strategy emerge	
REASON FOR USE	Provide link and steppingstone to more intensive reading experiences (from primary to intermediate grades and also within intermediate grades)	Provide deep, critical probing of the "critical content" at the center of a thematic unit	Provide deep, critical probing of issues related to a thematic unit
SPECIFIC GOALS	Assessment/observation opportunities for teacher; enabling students to begin internalizing critical-thinking and modeling strategies	Book or selection itself being known/experienced Book or selection enhancing and elaborating knowledge of theme-at-hand Thinking engaged in, during this kind of intensive inquiry, becoming an internalized model for all deep reading	

Figure 6.4

Classroom Reading Experiences: Narratives

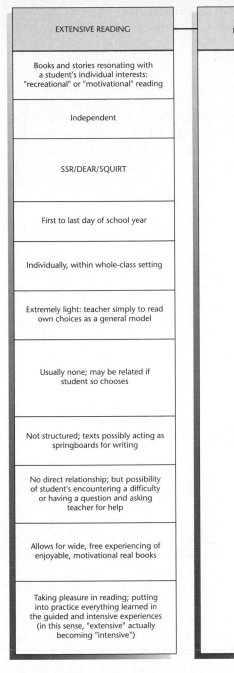

EXTENSIVE READING	GOALS Later Literacy Experiences Outside the Classroom
Books and stories resonating with a student's individual interests: "recreational" or "motivational" reading	
Independent	
SSR/DEAR/SQUIRT	
First to last day of school year	Ultimately, the goal is that guided/intensive and extensive reading become "one"; the student/adult reads widely, frequently, and by choice, books that are of interest and reads them deeply and critically, with perception, empathy, and understanding.
Individually, within whole-class setting	
Extremely light: teacher simply to read own choices as a general model	
Usually none; may be related if student so chooses	
Not structured; texts possibly acting as springboards for writing	
No direct relationship; but possibility of student's encountering a difficulty or having a question and asking teacher for help	
Allows for wide, free experiencing of enjoyable, motivational real books	
Taking pleasure in reading; putting into practice everything learned in the guided and intensive experiences (in this sense, "extensive" actually becoming "intensive")	

tion; in the next, we'll consider the types of approaches to text from *intensive* to *extensive* reading; in the third section, we will discuss the *core/extended/recreational* continuum of reading experiences—that is, the determination of *which* texts are read intensively or extensively.

Range and Flow of Instruction: From Guidance to Internalization   Starting with beginning and transitional readers and elaborated through guided and modeled reading experiences, we will release control and power to our students as they internalize *strategies* and a *process of questioning*. As you examine the map in Figure 6.4, bear in mind that it is in effect picking up from the underlying flow we established in Chapter 5: the gradual empowering of students as readers via the internalization of what are at first guided and modeled reading experiences but later become student-driven experiences.

Kinds of Approaches to the Text: Intensive and Extensive   We will be encouraging our students to approach their reading both *extensively* and *intensively*. *Intensive reading* involves a deliberate kind of reading, rereading, discussing, thinking, and writing. While we should not destroy stories, for children, by mercilessly pulling them apart, children *should* seek deliberately after meaning in many of the narratives—stories and books—that they read. It is our job to help them construct the understanding that comes from bringing their personal meaning *to* the story as they make meaning *from* the story. This process of consciously thinking about "what it means," and why, is what intensive reading is all about. *Extensive reading* is of critical importance. As we first noted in Chapter 1, this is the wide and free type of reading that students do independently. The extensive reading may be related to a theme, but often is not; these are books and stories that resonate with students' individual interests. In our classrooms, extensive reading usually occurs during Sustained Silent Reading time.

Kinds of Materials: Core, Extended, and Recreational   Educators have conceptualized intensive and extensive reading in terms of *core, extended,* and *recreational* or *motivational* selections. This perspective assumes that students will be reading selections that are linked together in one or more ways: by author, theme, genre, curriculum, and so forth. In Chapter 9 we will explore in some depth *how* to go about arranging these linkages by developing literature-based units; here, I will provide much of the foundational information we'll need in the meantime.

   Core works are works of "compelling intellectual, social, or moral content" (California State Department of Education, 1986, p. ix). Core works are read *intensively*. Usually we have one core selection, presented either through a read-aloud by the teacher or in a partner situation (for students who are unable to read it on their own), and the whole class is involved in response to and discussion of the selection. Occasionally we may decide to have a small set of core selections, each read and discussed by a different group of students; in essence, this format is like the way we address the reading of extended texts (see below) and allows for cross-group comparisons. Core works are discussed, reread, and responded to in writing. They represent central themes, issues, or topics we explore over several days or weeks.

In Chapter 4, we looked at some general organizational and management guidelines, and we will tie everything together in Chapter 9 when we explore the specifics of organizing thematic units. For now, though, you may be wondering how to keep straight in a classroom different activities with different types of reading and different types of texts. It is quite doable, however, as we'll see later on. In the meantime, keep in mind the following general instructional flow, and know that we will be examining it in depth before long:

Early in the year, try getting under way with Guided Reading-Thinking Activities and literature discussion groups. Later on, you can begin one-to-one reading conferences with the students (you'll find more about this in Chapter 11) and meet with children individually on the average of once every two to three weeks—some children need that attention more often; others, less. This sequence sets the format for the students, and they will subsequently be getting a lot from one another as they read and discuss their narratives.

In this type of environment, children begin to read several different books at any one time; they've got different chapter books going (some read intensively, others read extensively), informational books, a stack of picture books in the bathroom at home, and so forth.

Just like adults, children need a break from their "weightier" reading. In an intermediate class, for example, you may have for the kids a box of "lighter" books that includes picture books and easy-to-read books (students finish *Bridge to Terabithia,* for example, then read *Nate the Great* for a break). This is analogous to reading a romance novel on the beach during vacation: we know the books that help us grow, but it *is* fun just to relax and effortlessly read a steamy potboiler or some other book that doesn't require much effort.

LEARNING IN CONTEXT: We can organize our instruction to engage children in deeply meaningful experiences with books as well as in the lighter yet enjoyable works—the same experiences, in other words, in which *we* are engaged.

Extended works have the same characteristics as core works in terms of content and value. Also referred to as "text sets," they relate to the central themes, issues, or topics expressed in the core work. The only real difference between them and most core works is that extended selections are read not by the entire class but by smaller groups or individuals. Like the core works, extended works are also usually read *intensively:* The teacher will discuss them with a small group, for example; children who each are reading different extended works will discuss a book with the teacher or with other students in terms of how the book relates to and expresses the common theme, issue, or topic that underlies all the extended texts.

Recreational or *motivational selections* may or may not relate to the content of the core and extended texts. They are selections that children read individually for pleasure and enjoyment. They fall into the *extensive reading* category, for they are rarely discussed or responded to in any depth—other than by a child's mentioning to others, for example, "This is a really good book that you would enjoy reading" (just as we would comment to a friend about a book that *we* particularly enjoy).

INSTRUCTIONAL "BRIDGE" EXPERIENCES: GUIDING STUDENTS TOWARD INTERNALIZATION

We know that children can be very good critical thinkers. As they develop into more independent readers in second grade and beyond, they are better able to think critically more often *as* they read. In this section, we will examine a few ways in which we can help children cross that "bridge" from beginning and early-transitional reading into more critical reading. Our objective is to continue appropriate support of students in their reading as we help them learn to use reading as a tool with which they will think more discerningly, carefully, and divergently. With such continued experiences with reading, they will come to internalize this critical stance.

"Bridge" experiences serve another important function. We can use them whenever we see that students need more support in their experiences with texts. Bridge experiences are not jettisoned later on when it seems as if students are capable of reading a lot on their own. We may use these experiences less with such students; but there will always be a situation, a topic, a theme, or a text that requires us to step in and provide the appropriate amount of support.

As children develop more independence as readers in the second grade and beyond, they move from beginning and early transitional reading into more critical reading.

The bridge experiences I will present here deal with two different means of approaching critical reading. First, we will revisit the Guided Reading-Thinking Activity first introduced in Chapter 5. We will see how it can "grow" with the students' increasing reading skills, continuing to serve as a way through which students see reading as a problem-solving, active, and reflective experience. Next, we will explore ways in which we can directly present specific skills and strategies that help students construct meaning more efficiently.

Guided critical-thinking activities

In this section, we will explore how we can more directly help students internalize a critical stance toward narratives. There are a number of different instructional activities through which we can guide and engage students with texts, but I would like to focus specifically and in some detail on one widely used instructional format.

The Guided Reading-Thinking Activity The format of the Guided Reading-Thinking Activity allows us to help students tap into prior knowledge about the content of the story to be read and to make predictions about what might occur in the story. It is a cyclical process of "predict, read, prove or revise."

The GRTA allows the teacher to monitor, in a group, how students' comprehension/understanding is developing. It also allows the teacher to see how students are applying reading knowledge to support their thinking. On the basis of this monitoring, teachers can point out how to analyze, think about, and support or revise responses in the group. The GRTA format allows a meaningful context for modeling and teaching some specific skills as well (Davidson & Wilkerson, 1988; Bear & Invernizzi, 1984; Gill & Bear, 1988). Before reading further, you may wish to refer back briefly to the feature that describes a GRTA with first-grade children.

The Guided Reading-Thinking Activity acts both as a bridge *to* intensive reading (see below) and as a periodic engagement *during* intensive reading. It is a bridge to "deeper" reading because we are modeling some of the types of questions that are asked during intensive reading of a text, and we are helping students internalize a *strategy* for reading narratives, one that they will employ as they read other texts intensively. Because of this, and because it is more directed and more manageable, we will conduct more Guided Reading-Thinking Activities earlier in the year than we will later in the year when our students are involved with intensive and extensive reading—and when we have become comfortable with orchestrating this type of literacy environment.

We do not spend as much time, however, with a story read in the GRTA format as we usually do with a selection that is read *intensively*. We can do GRTAs throughout a thematic unit with certain stories at the same time as we are intensively reading "core" and "extended" texts. It is an excellent activity to intersperse throughout the other types of reading and responding activities that the students will be doing. We can employ it with particularly challenging stories that will involve the students in an exciting discussion as they move through these texts.

There are several specific stages to a GRTA, and we will now consider each.

Before We Meet with the Students   When we form groups for GRTAs, we usually group together children of similar reading abilities. Although most of our reading activities will not involve this *homogeneous* arrangement, it works well for GRTAs because (1) the students' reading *rates* will usually be similar, and (2) we can address similar skills needs as a follow-up to the reading (see below).

Which stories should we use for the GRTA? When first getting GRTAs under way, we should select stories that we believe will *immediately* engage the children. We know the students' interests and abilities, and this will guide our selection. For example, Cynthia Rylant's *Every Living Thing* and Gary Soto's *Baseball in April* work well for intermediate students. (Stories that are, on the surface, "dull" in the kids' eyes—but potentially winners in ours—may be read later on, if we wish.) Books we use for this purpose—pupil texts from a reading series or an anthology—should be kept on a shelf in the reading circle corner. This is so that they will not be in general circulation with books from the library center. Students will not have read the stories inadvertently (or deliberately), thereby putting a crimp in the prediction phase. Explain to the students *why* these are the only books in the entire room that they may not have access to on a regular basis; most students will honor this rationale.

Once we have selected a story, we will determine *where* and *how often* in the story we want the students to stop in their reading. These points will vary in number, depending on the story and our purposes. Initially, we may stop two or three times; later, perhaps only once. These stopping points should always be suspenseful, points at which the readers are left hanging. That's when children's ideas and rationale will be closest to the surface, ready to be tapped.

Before the Reading   When we meet with the students, we first establish background. We ask them, "What do you know about . . . ?" Then we read the title with the students, have them look at any pictures on the first page or two, and then ask, "What do you think a story called [supplying the title] might be about?" We write down some of their predictions while asking, "Why do you think so?" or have each student write down a prediction.

In narratives, we rarely "preteach" new words—a common practice in years past—because we want the students to use context and to apply their developing knowledge about words, whether phonics or structural analysis, in a meaningful situation. On occasion we may need to preteach a word (see Chapter 8) *if and only if* the word is crucial to the overall understanding of the story *and* there is little if any support from context *and* we are fairly certain that the students' word knowledge is not sufficient for figuring the word out. (As we might expect, this situation does not happen too often.) A lot of times stories will contain *names* of people and places that come from other languages. While it is fun and instructive to talk about these different pronunciations, it is usually *not* effective to spend a lot of time doing this prior to reading. It could be an excellent follow-up activity. We pronounce the name of the main character for the students, for example, but then tell them not to worry about pronouncing the rest of the names and we'll all talk about them later.

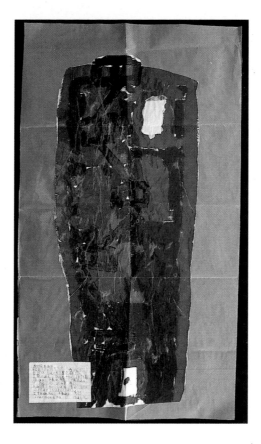

WHAT IS THIS PORTFOLIO?

This is a special portfolio that we have developed to show you how children come to learn about and reflect on their worlds through their reading and writing. Through their literacy experiences *we* come to know, understand, and better facilitate their growth. We are also coming to realize that an indispensable component of children's literacy experience is another kind of symbolic experience: art. When the eminent child psychiatrist Robert Coles was a young intern, the poet and physician William Carlos Williams advised him, "Ask your children to draw pictures. That way you'll really be told about their lives."

In this portfolio, you will see the work of three children who offer us glimpses into their lives and how they view their worlds. Our purpose in sharing these children's work is to illustrate the rich interconnections that exist among their literacy development, their expressive creations that grow out of and lead into their literacy experiences, and the tools and the contexts we offer them as they become skilled learners. You will see evidence of the communicative potential of children and the nature of literacy development in a rich learning environment.

The children whose art and writing you see over the next few pages are students from the Early Learning Center in the College of Education at the University of Nevada, Reno. The children from this multiage primary classroom represent a variety of ethnic and socio-economic backgrounds and developmental levels. Their teacher, Sandra Madura, follows the *authentic reading/integrated literacy* approach presented in this text. Within this framework the students' literacy experiences are enriched through discussion, writing, and the art they create. Sandra encourages her students to respond to their reading through writing and creating art. We hope that this visual exploration of reading, writing, and illustrating will convey the wonderful diversity of children and of the meanings they construct.

NICHOLAS, ADRIENNE, AND TESSA

A few words about each of the children whose art and writing you see in these pages:

* **NICHOLAS** is seven years old and in first grade. He was born in the Philippines and arrived in the United States at the age of nine months when he was adopted by an American family. Nicholas is playful and outspoken; he is always eager to experiment.

NICHOLAS #3

2

❋ **ADRIENNE** is a second grader; she was seven when the school year began. Reading and writing do not come easily for Adrienne. She is a quiet, thoughtful child who usually needs twice as much time to develop her ideas and to complete her work as her classmates.

❋ Our third grader is **TESSA**; she is eight years old. Tessa talks her way through most new projects, spending every spare minute orally revising her work. She is extremely independent; however, she is very willing to model or expand the ideas of others.

We present children from the primary grades because the most dramatic jumps, changes, and signs of growth come as children move from the *emergent* phase through *beginning reading* and on into the *transitional* phase. Toward the end of the transitional phase, children are well on their way to becoming mature readers when the milestones in their literacy development are more ones of refinement rather than leaps. The work you see here spans the developmental literacy continuum from the late *emergent* phase through the *transitional* phase.

At the beginning of the school year Nicholas is at the late *emergent* phase; by the end of the year he is in the late *beginning reading* phase. Adrienne is in the middle of the *beginning reading* phase when school begins and by the end of the year is in the middle of the *transitional* phase. Tessa begins in the middle of the *transitional* phase and ends in the early *mature/proficient* phase.

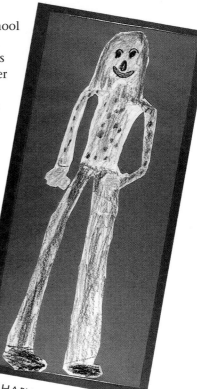

HAPY HAPY ME ME

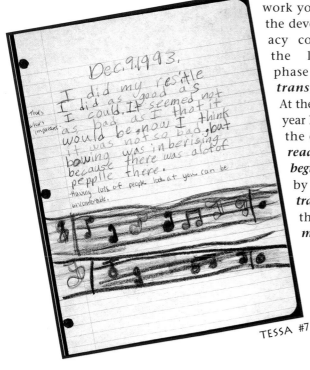

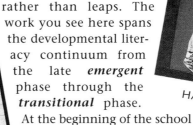

TESSA #7

3

WHAT IS LITERACY FOR CHILDREN?

There are many kinds of **literacy**. In this book we focus primarily on **print** literacy, and we see that there are different contexts and different strategies for engaging children with print. Once engaged, children talk about and reflect on particular texts, relating them to their own world and purposes. This is apparent, for example, in Adrienne's conclusion that the blind man in Ezra Jack Keats's *Apt. 3* "sees with his heart." We see how the children appropriate the structure and the language of text in order to extend and elaborate their ideas, their reflections, and their problem solving; note how Tessa takes on a satirical tone in her journal entry (#13) modeled after Jon Szieszka's *The True Story of the Three Little Pigs*.

We can see how children reflect on themselves as learners, as readers, as writers, as artists; often their reflections occur "along the way," quite naturally, as they think about their daily projects and about their learning environment. Other times these reflections are in response to the teacher's inquiries. For example, toward the end of the year Adrienne writes that "I sound out words and practice reading if it's sad or happy if it's exciting or boring to me"; about **writing**, Adrienne writes that "It can get very exciting. I use very expressive words."

TESSA #13

ADRIENNE #12

4

Tessa Lee May 20, 1994.

Reading

I learned that when you read and you do not know what a word is, you look at the word that you just read then you look at the word that is after the word that you do not know what it says and you think of what word would fit there.

When I read I use the things I know about reading and I use those to find out what it says.

The things that are important in storys to me are humor, and meaning, and things that your readers like.

I still need to learn other word and how to spell them and there meaning.

TESSA #15

Tessa Lee May 20, 1994

Writing

I didn't know that there were so meany ways to write in cersive and printing.

When I write I write what my dreames are and what I am thinking and what I like.

I need to learn diffrent tecneaces like italien, fancy cersive, or fancy printing.

I think we study athores and illustrates to find how ather people do there art and there storys.

TESSA #16

Nov. 15. 1993.

Writing

Writing is a good thing. I could not write you about writing. If people did not write books how would we learne. We write all the time. I think writing is fun. I think I do good at writing in cersive and it is fun. It might be to you to write you can lerne by doing it.

TESSA #6

Tessa, a year older, observes that "When I read I use the things I know about reading and I use those to find out what it says. The things that are important in stories to me are humor, and meaning, and things that your readers like...When I write I write what my dreams are and what I am thinking and what I like." Note that in November (#6) Tessa commented, almost as an afterthought, that "you can lerne" by writing—an awareness so many children never realize.

WORK ITSELF AND DEVELOPMENTAL POINTS

When you first look at these young children's written productions, you may notice the increasing growth in the "surface" aspects of their writing—those conventions such as spelling, punctuation, legibility, and so forth. Closer inspection, however, reveals *growth* in sophistication of thought, insight, and expression, as well as the growing sophistication of the children's transactions with the texts they read. It is important to note that quite often, as Adrienne's work reflects, these more *qualitative* aspects of writing develop in spite of lack of significant growth in some of the conventions.

These growth trends are apparent in the children's artwork as well. The jerky lines, strokes, and asymmetry in younger children's efforts—as in Nicholas's drawing of a building on campus (#10)—develop into the smoother, symmetrical, and organized arrangements of older children, as in the branches and blossoms in Tessa's still life (#10).

NICHOLAS #10

TESSA #10: THE FLOWOR'S IN BLOOM

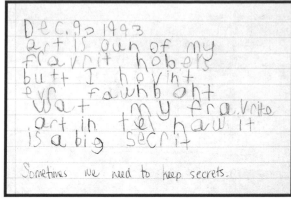

ADRIENNE #3

NICHOLAS #1

Importantly, children construct **patterns** in what they observe, and they apply this awareness in their writing, reading, and art. These patterns are discernible within words, stories, the arrangement of print on a page, and the representation of the visual world in two-dimensional space. Their awareness is reflected in their increasing **precision** as well—precision in story development, precision in visual representation. Contrast Adrienne's arrangement of her writing on the page (#3) with that of Nicholas (#1); contrast Tessa's arrangement and precision in her autumn scene (#3) with Adrienne's (#1). Adrienne strikingly expresses this tendency toward pattern when she writes, "I use my imagination to put shapes together and out of that make a beautiful picture" (#12 on page 4).

TESSA #3: THE BRANCHIES IN COLOR

ADRIENNE #1: FERY FORIST

NICHOLAS #7

We see the children's growing knowledge about words through their *invented spelling*; we see their developing sense of *narrative* and *informational text* and how it works; we see their growth of *"voice"* as they present definite styles. These voices and styles grow out of the transactions among the children's personalities, their world knowledge, and the texts they read. For example, notice how Tessa's journal entries become narratives, stories she composes.

The work of *beginning readers* and writers is slow and deliberate but every bit as meaningful and *purposeful* as that of children farther along in development. For example, Leo Lionni's *Nicholas Where Have You Been?* was one of Nicholas's favorites because he and the main character have the same name. While his response to the book is a straightforward retelling of part of the story—characteristic of beginning readers—note the event Nicholas chose to retell: The main character is alone and then plucked up and placed in a secure situation where others want him to stay.

Adrienne shows us how, in brief phrases and extended writing alike, that *transitional readers and writers* are able to articulate the increasing sophistication of their thoughts and their emotions. Note, for example, the titles of some of her artwork: **"Ranbowe of My Amajnashin," "The Fase in My Mynd," "Fery Forist."** We see Adrienne's sensitivity in her response to *The Little Wood Duck* by Brian Wildsmith, and we get the feeling that she is proud not only of the little duck but of herself as well.

It is important to note that all three children *"went beyond"* the worlds in the texts, relating the texts to their worlds. For Nicholas, his response to Brian Wildsmith is very personal—the cat made him sleepy, too—whereas the worlds of Adrienne and Tessa exist beyond themselves, and they are aware of and concerned about these worlds.

ADRIENNE #6

NICHOLAS #13

9

A CLOSER LOOK AT GROWTH AND LEARNING

In order to look more closely at developmental trends, let's take a selective "tour" of Nicholas's, Adrienne's, and Tessa's work.

The tendency toward a *rigidity of line* and *texture* in Nicholas's work is still apparent later in the year, though Nicholas is clearly developing as an artist. In his self-portrait, **"My bad hair day"** (#11), he is modeling his work after Michael Marchenko, illustrator of so many of Robert Munsch's books. Note the lines defining the eyes and nose and the stiffness of the crayon strokes. In addition, there is still *asymmetry*—one eye, for example, is bigger than the other; the shading is darker around the eyes and nose. In his **"Flower of My Lif"** (#8; painted in December and titled in April), note the "slapping on" of additional color onto the vase. Note also that in his background wash, Nicholas's lines curve upward into the stem, though he *intended* for them to be straight across. He drew the opening of the vase first, not leaving space for the stem that would later be painted—just as in writing, the concept of *planning* is significant here. Planning is also an issue in **"My Body"** (#16)—the drawing of his tank top covers the left side of his body, but note what happens on the right side.

NICHOLAS #11: MY BAD HAIR DAY

NICHOLAS #16: MY BODY

NICHOLAS #8: THE FLOWER OF MY LIF

NICHOLAS #20

NICHOLAS #21

Toward the end of the year, when Nicholas is reading much of Don and Audrey Wood's work, his art is more refined. He copied the picture you see here (#20 and 21), but he is maintaining the **proportionality** of the legs under the body; this skill is not completely refined because his attempt with the arms is not as successful. Do note, though, the **symmetry** of the ears, eyes, and the **evenness of line** in the eyes that is not apparent in the facial features of his self-portrait (#16). He has attempted to capture the texture of the fur in his picture of the mouse; his coloring is blended as opposed to the earlier jerkiness, which characterized his need simply to fill up space. Also, later in the year he captured **texture** through his painting, as is apparent in his work modeled after Brian Wildsmith (#13)—note also the **balance** he creates between the tail feathers and the heavy beak, the legs under the body—this pelican is not going to topple over!

NICHOLAS #13

ADRIENNE #1: FERY FORIST

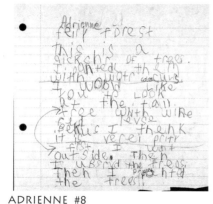

ADRIENNE #8

In a rough draft describing her **"Fery Forist"** (#1), Adrienne asked the reader to note her "wine-red levse"; she has clearly learned something about water colors here. With the orange tree, she used a slightly damp brush; when she was unhappy with the result, she began to use a *wetter* brush and discovered the true potential of water colors!

In his comment on his collage in response to Keats, Nicholas is focusing on *art* more than on content—the medium rather than the message. This preoccupation is not unusual at this level—children are often observed to focus on the conventions or medium of their writing as well. Adrienne's collage in response to Keats (**"Ranbowe of My Amajnashin,"** #2), is **more abstract**—beyond a cityscape. Notice also how she represents appendages and proportionality; in contrast to Nicholas's response to Ezra Jack Keats, the arms of her figure are rounded, in balance. The arms in Nicholas's collage are short, stubby, and square. In Tessa's **"Ezra Jack Keats Life"** (#5), we see the "stepping beyond" the straightforward perspective, looking *from behind* at the two figures as they walk away from us, the woman with hands clasped behind her back as she talks to the man.

THE BLUE WROLD

ADRIENNE #2: RANBOWE
OF MY AMAJNASHIN

TESSA #5: EZRA JACK KEATS LIFE

FASE IN MY MYND

ADRIENNE #10

Adrienne's **"Fase in My Mynd"** reveals more control in the evenness of the watercolor on the page. She uses varying shapes to *conceptualize* specific facial features—triangles, rectangles, ovals; diagonal, horizontal and vertical lines. Her **"Fase"** is of her neighbor, whose head was slightly turned—thus the *asymmetry* of jaw. Note her untitled still life of iris (#10), where she overlaps the long angular leaves and petals; we have a sense of *three-dimensionality*, in contrast with the two-dimensional nature of Nicholas's work.

As we look at Tessa's artwork, let's first compare **"The Branchies in Color"** (#3) done in the fall of the year, with her **"Flowor's in Bloom,"** painted in March. Note the

TESSA #3: THE BRANCHIES IN COLOR

THE FLOWOR'S IN BLOOM

13

TESSA #9

harmonious arrangement of the blossoms and stems compared with her earlier work in which there is no *relationship* among the leaves and seeds. In **"Flowor's in Bloom"** there is. Indeed she has not painted what is actually there, but arranged the blossoms, stems, and overlapped them on the page. Notice the *planning* and preparation that is apparent in her rough draft (#9).

As in her writing, we see Tessa's sense of *humor* in her **"Funky old grany"** (#8) in which she portrays herself as a spirited older woman. Using the cartooning techniques of Michael Marchenko, she colors with smooth, even strokes. She selects colors strong in contrast: the dark red of the mouth stands out against the light skin tones, adding to the comedy of the portrait. She shows an ability to portray personality with this granny's goofy smile and a partially-hidden raised eyebrow. Again, we see Tessa's sense of humor in her comment about King Bidgood staying in the bathtub so long: "he must be a prune by now (#18)." Yet she chooses to draw the very "proper" lady-in-waiting, who stands in disapproval of the King's behavior (#17). Finally, we see the visual humor in Tessa's depiction of a "gumberoo" from Steven Kellogg's version of *Paul Bunyan;* her gumberoo looks nothing like Kellogg's, but she has definitely captured the weird yet humorous "flavor" of these creatures (#19).

TESSA #8: FUNKY OLD GRANY

14

TESSA #18

TESSA #17

TESSA #19

A PERSPECTIVE ON LITERACY TRANSACTIONS

In the spring, the classroom prepared their "art show." This was an opportunity for the children not only to share with family and community but to reflect on the creative work they had done throughout the year. They selected their personal favorites, explained their choices, and through their autobiographies—written primarily in third person—provided a brief overview of themselves as individuals and as readers, writers, and artists. *Developmentally*, note how Nicholas's autobiography is very **"here-and-now" oriented**, while Adrienne and Tessa reveal their **expanding perspectives**. For example, Nicholas writes that "I like art because you can do collages I like collages because I like glueing and cutting out." Adrienne is projecting ahead, writing that her next piece is "a unicorn on a distant hill." She reveals her most traumatic experience, while in the same thought showing us how remarkably strong and *resilient* the young can be; Adrienne's father died when she was six, which leads her to comment "That was the worst day of my life but I will always remember the good days I had with him." Recall that Adrienne works slowly, but the *quality* of her insights and observations reaffirm the importance of providing the rich contexts and many opportunities for these reflections to occur and develop. Tessa's warm and secure childhood emerges through her playfulness while her growing sophistication is expressed through her wish, "I hope to have a peaceful world."

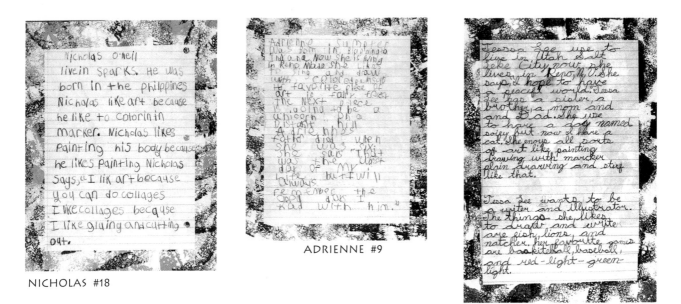

NICHOLAS #18

ADRIENNE #9

TESSA #12

As we guide children through learning about the nature and purpose of our symbol systems, we will often talk directly about these systems and their uses—we guide children through stories, we present certain stories to them, we *guide* them in their writing, and we talk about what is going on in their writing. We guide them in their art, pointing out how pictures are put together, talking about color and form. We establish a *cycle* in which exploration and discussion through reading and writing infuse exploration and discussion in art, which in turn infuses the reading and writing. Significantly, we are guiding children towards knowledge of texts, words, shapes, *patterns* so that they may ultimately use this knowledge as a tool for exploring, discovering, and moving beyond themselves into new worlds.

During the Reading This is where the "predict/read/prove" cycle is applied in earnest. At each stopping point we ask the students, "*Now* what do you think? Let's check our predictions. . . . Did [such and such] happen? Why [or why not]? Can you prove it from what you've read? What in the story suggested that?" In this way, predictions are confirmed up to this point, rejected, or modified. If we are writing down the students' predictions, we will make these changes on the chart paper or chalkboard: we add and modify some predictions and cross out or erase those that the group feels cannot be supported.

Throughout this predict/read/prove cycle, we avoid using the terms *right* and *wrong* in referring to the predictions. It may appear to be a small matter, but students—particularly at the intermediate grades—are usually so locked into the "right/wrong" syndrome that it shuts down quality thinking even as it contributes to an overly competitive learning environment.

Even with students who are similar in reading behaviors, some will reach the stopping point before others. How do we handle this? We may tell them beforehand that if others are still reading when they have finished, they may think about their predictions. If they have been writing their own predictions, they may check and change or modify them—write down what they think *now* is going to happen. This is also an important opportunity for us to check process and skills: In a whisper, we ask a student about his or her prediction and do a one-on-one "Why-do-you-think-so?" check. We may also check on students' application of specific skills: ask a student if there were any words he or she didn't know, and what he or she did to try to figure them out. When we first begin doing GRTAs, this whispering may momentarily distract the other readers; very quickly, however, they will get used to it. And remember, we may need to remind certain students that this is *not* a race to see who can get to the stopping point first.

After the Reading As soon as we finish, there is usually a definite sense of closure—whether with satisfaction or surprise—based on the outcome of the story. This allows for a final check on predictions and a referring back to the story for support and confirmation. Students may then discuss their overall impressions of the story. Did they like it? Why or why not? What parts? How did they respond to different characters? Would they have ended it differently? If the story were to be continued, what might happen?

Then it is our turn to ask a few questions that will help pull together important aspects of the narrative. Although we may not be ready to present the labels just yet, our questions may direct the students' thinking toward *theme, conflict,* and so forth. These questions are usually of the "critical thinking" type (see next section). We will also follow up on how well students applied specific skills. What did they do in figuring out a potentially confusing bit of text? How did they figure out a word they'd never seen before (remember, we did not preteach new words)? This allows us or other students to explain and model application of a particular strategy or skill.

Because we've already seen how a GRTA is used with first-graders (Chapter 5), let's look at one with older students, a group of fourth-graders. The teacher we'll be looking in on has selected *The Shrinking of Treehorn,* by Florence Heide, from a literature-based reading series (the publisher of the series has reprinted it in its entirety in the student anthology; see Figure 6.5). The short book is a modern fantasy, but a rather peculiar and humorous one. Edward Gorey contributed wonderful illustrations that are humorous in their own right. The tale deals with a boy, Treehorn, who discovers he is shrinking. The humor in the story comes from the fact that no one else seems to be alarmed—a little concerned, perhaps, but nothing more. His father at one point thinks Treehorn is doing it on purpose, but when he realizes that Treehorn *is* in fact shrinking, the following exchange between father and mother occurs:

> *"Look Emily, Treehorn is shrinking. He's much smaller than he used to be."*
> *"Oh, dear," said Treehorn's mother. "First it was the cake, and now it's this. Everything happens at once."*

Amusing little incidents occur; the teacher sees Treehorn in the hall trying to reach the water fountain by jumping up and down. She tells him, "Just because you're shrinking, it does not mean you have special privileges." She sends him to the principal, who thinks that Treehorn is *shirking* rather than *shrinking* and gives him an irrelevant lecture. Eventually, Treehorn returns to his normal size when he plays a board game called "The *BIG* Game for Kids to Grow On." The

Figure 6.5
Title Page from The Shrinking of Treehorn

story concludes with his turning green, but he doesn't say anything and no one seems to notice.

Now let's look in on our model teacher and examine how she goes about presenting this story.

Guided Reading-Thinking Activity with *The Shrinking of Treehorn.*

Before Reading: The teacher explains that this is a modern fantasy, and has the students read the title. After discussing what it might be like if *they* were to shrink, she asks the students to read the first page and look up when they've finished. [This is one of many variations on the basic GRTA format; predictions need not *always* be made before any part of the story is read.]

During Reading: The teacher asks the students, "Well, what do you think is going to happen now that Treehorn has discovered that he's shrinking?" The students suggest that perhaps no one will notice. "Why?" the teacher asks. A student responds that Treehorn's mother seems more concerned that her cake hasn't risen. Another student predicts that not only will Treehorn keep shrinking, but whenever he says something, the *print* in the book will get even smaller [a clever technique the author has employed]. The teacher sets up the next phase of the reading by telling the students to "read on" to the bottom of the page and see if in fact anyone *is* going to notice Treehorn's shrinking and whatever else may happen.

At the next stopping place, the students observe that yes, Treehorn's parents have noticed. "What's going to happen now?" the teacher prods. One student says that Treehorn might be punished, since his father thinks he's doing it on purpose!

And so the GRTA proceeds. There are two additional stopping points, selected (as you now know) because they occur at more suspenseful points in the story.

After the Story: After the story is completed, the teacher asks some additional questions:

■ "What struck you as funny in the story, and why?" Her purpose here is to get the students to explore aspects of *humor*—the juxtaposition of peculiar occurrences with normal events.

■ "What were some ordinary things that happened that also struck you as being funny?" Once a student replied that he couldn't stop laughing at the point when Treehorn saw the "BIG Game to Grow On" under the bed and "walked under the bed" to look at it. The boy tried to explain why this really got to him: "I mean, it's so *plain!* It's just like the author said, 'He walked across the street' but instead he just 'walked under the bed' and I pictured this tiny little guy just kind of strolling under the bed, not having to stoop down or anything. . . ." The boy's teacher pointed out that many readers might not have noticed this and gotten the same mental picture of tiny little Treehorn strolling under his bed.

■ Picking up on an underlying theme in the story, the teacher asks the students: "Do you ever have the impression that people are not really paying much attention to you when you're trying to tell them something important?" While this was, of course, a primary source of the humor in *The Shrinking of Treehorn,* it is a very real—and common—experience in kids' everyday lives. This leads to an excellent discussion.

■ The teacher winds up the discussion by asking if the students had difficulty figuring out or understanding any of the words in the story. It turns out that *privileges* is problematic; the teacher talks about context clues—there are excellent ones in the surrounding sentences—and then asks the students what they think the word means. This would also be an opportunity to find out if there were any confusing parts in the story—transitions, comments, and so forth. If so, the teacher could follow up on the next day with an appropriate minilesson (see below). Often, however, students themselves are quite good at helping one another clear up points of confusion—and this is an ideal context in which this peer help can occur.

■ ■ ■ ■ ■

Direct teaching of skills and strategies

Before exploring the role of direct teaching, let's define what we mean by *skills* and *strategies.* In general usage the term *skill* is employed more broadly than it is in education. We usually refer to the *skill* of carpentry, the *skill* of writing, the *skill* of hang gliding, and so forth. *Skill* in these instances refers to all the knowledge and behavior that underlie a complex act.

In education, and more specifically in literacy, the term *skill* is used much more narrowly: it refers to each specific component or bit of information employed in accomplishing the broader act of reading. "Reading," then, is not a specific *skill* but an orchestration of a large number of component *skills.* Many literacy skills are learned without conscious effort; many others are learned *through* conscious and deliberate effort and become "automated" with more experience and knowledge for applying them.

As we read, we usually orchestrate the skills we need without conscious effort or attention (Bussis, Chittenden, Klausner, and Amarel, 1985). Quite often, though, we either (1) need to read a text with a particular purpose in mind or (2) encounter some roadblocks while we are reading—whenever we realize something isn't making sense. This is where *strategies* come in. In each instance, we'll apply a particular *strategy* that will address our difficulty appropriately. A *strategy* is a plan of action in which we take certain deliberate steps to address a particular need; we consciously attend to those skills that will help us best in a particular reading situation. Here are two examples:

■ Most of the time, we are not consciously aware of our word-identification skills (knowledge of letter/sound correspondences, use of context, how plurals are represented, and so forth); but when we encounter an unfamiliar word, we use the *strategy* of applying our knowledge about context and word structure.

■ When we realize something doesn't make sense, we need to know how far back in the text to go to start applying a conscious *strategy* of thinking about our knowledge of particular words or ways in which sentences are put together. Then we can rethink what is going on in the text.

We speak of the importance of *strategic* reading. Depending on the task or the challenge, when students know how to use their reading skills *strategically*, they are empowered to control their own reading—*they* can set the agenda for approaching, interpreting, and learning from a text; and they know what to do when they hit rough spots.

Minilessons and Modeling   What exactly is a "minilesson"? When we perceive a need our students have or when we anticipate such a need, we can direct the students' attention explicitly to what is going on and "demonstrate" or talk about a particular skill or strategy. Cambourne (1987) uses the term *demonstrate* because we are in effect demonstrating how *we,* as knowledgeable readers, figure something out. This demonstration or *modeling* occurs in the instructional context of the *minilesson* (Atwell, 1987; Au, 1993). *Minilesson* is the term currently applied to direct teaching that occurs in an authentic literacy context: we teach a particular skill to particular students when we perceive that those students need that skill. Our modeling in the context of the minilesson is directly demonstrating to students what they can do when they realize that

1. their sense-making has somehow been disrupted during reading (*self-knowledge*); and
2. they can apply a strategy for doing something about it (*procedural* or "strategic" knowledge).

Children vary in the degree to which they need different skills explicitly addressed. For example, more frequent and explicit direct instruction may initially be necessary for children who, for whatever reason, have been struggling with reading, as well as for children from diverse cultural and linguistic backgrounds. Very often, therefore, we need to teach about a strategy or skill *directly,* and we may need to teach or demonstrate it *often* before students feel competent to try it out with us looking on as well as on their own, when they apply their budding understanding (Holdaway, 1986; Routman, 1991). These demonstrations and "gradual release of control" characterize a model of direct or explicit teaching (see, for example, Brown, Campione, & Day, 1981; Pearson, 1984). Direct teaching has the following four traits:

■ A description of the skill, detailing its purpose and how it is applied in an authentic context
■ Demonstrating the skill through teacher modeling
■ Practice under the guidance of the teacher
■ Independent practice

Before we discuss further how we can apply the minilesson format, though, let's review how we know when our students need help—how we identify the aspects of reading they may be finding difficult. The key is in our interactions with them on the basis of the reading they are doing, and these interactions encompass discussion, rereading, and response journals. In a more authentic reading context, we will be much more able to monitor how well our students are applying the reading strategies and skills they have been learning and which new strategies and skills they may be ready to acquire. If we tried to teach directly all the types of skills involved in reading, there would never be time to actually *read*. Because we know about children, the reading process, and the nature of texts, we are able to spot areas of difficulty and help directly with whatever the child needs. Once we know what the needed skill is, we share *our* knowledge about how *we* use that skill.

Let me add a cautionary note. So much of what we *think* children need is based on their efforts to deal with texts they have not freely chosen to read or that are at their *frustrational* level. We should most often use independent-level or instructional-level materials for our explicit teaching. Only after students understand the skill or strategy we are teaching should we have them try it out with a more challenging text that will "stretch" them. The concept of *scaffolding* (Cazden, 1988) is useful here. As the term suggests, we support readers in their attempts to apply a skill, and we help fill in the gaps in their repertoires. Irwin speaks of scaffolding as "reducing the size of the task to a manageable amount and controlling the frustration level of the learner" (Irwin, 1992, p. 2).

Now that we have discussed at some length the *what* and the *how* of direct teaching, let's also examine the *when* of such instruction.

Many teachers plan for this more explicit instruction at the beginning of the reading/writing block; others, toward the end. And of course there may be a "teachable moment" anywhere along the way, with one or more students. As already noted, you can also provide direct teaching to conclude a GRTA session. (Remember that when we do *any* direct instruction, we already know the areas in which children need help. We'll explore this matter extensively in Chapter 12).

So many of our minilessons will help our students learn and understand what to do when the reading gets tough or when they encounter momentary difficulty—when they realize they are not "making sense." We help them understand that they may need to step back and figure out what the problem might be. In many cases the difficulty may be overcome by simply reading on to get an overall sense of what's happening (Atwell, 1987; Smith, 1988). If sense is still not being made, however, then it is appropriate to go back and "fix up." Quite often we find that the problem is at the *microstructure* level. In Chapter 2 we described how readers construct a "microstructure" of a text as they read. This microstructure represents the syntactic and semantic relationships within a sentence and the connections between senten-ces—the logical relationships among lower-order bits of information. Often, students need help in figuring out how some of these connections, or links, function. Following is a classroom illustration of a minilesson focused on one aspect of microstructure with which students often have difficulty: deter-mining the referent for a particular pronoun.

The following classroom scenario illustrates the use of modeling within a minilesson. It involves a "macro-level" strategy for actively anticipating what might be occurring in a story. For a number of reasons, some children hesitate to risk predicting or anticipating what may lie ahead in a story. If this hesitancy continues even after we have made sure that a student is comfortable in the social context in which the reading is being done, the reason may be that he or she is uncertain as to *how* to make predictions—that is, whether to draw on personal experience, the text, or what?

"You know, you predict just about all the time, even though you may not be aware of it. For example, when you watch television, your brain is working right along, thinking to itself things like 'Hmm . . . what might happen next? I think Octavian is going to avoid running into those creatures and try to trap them instead. . . .' You're using clues from the program you're watching, and you're using what you know about those kinds of programs in general.

"It's the same with a story you're reading. For example, when I look at Chris Van Allsburg's *The Polar Express* [holding it so that students can see the front of the book], I'm already thinking about what this book might be about. I'm looking at the picture on the cover of the book—a locomotive engine going through a snowy night—and at the first picture in the book [turning to the page]—a boy in bed at night looking out his window. I'm thinking that somehow, this boy might see the train and even get on it. When I'm reading the first few lines and they're telling about Christmas Eve many years ago, I think 'Oh, I bet this is a train that goes to the North Pole,' because I know what the North Pole has to do with Christmas, and the title of the book has the word *polar* in it. . . .

"So you see, even though I haven't read more than the title, looked at two illustrations, and read a few lines, I can come up with ideas. How am I able to do this? I think about what I already know about trains and about holidays and even about the kinds of things I sometimes think about when *I* look out a window at night. Each time *you* start reading, you should rely on what *you* already know, so you can think about what might happen."

Your next step is to walk students through a story, encouraging them to use both their own knowledge and clues from the story to make predictions. Ask different students to explain why they made certain predictions; remember, *students'* explanations provide quite powerful models as well.

■ ■ ■ ■ ■

ASKING GOOD QUESTIONS

Knowing how, when, where, and why to ask good questions is one of the most important aspects of teaching. I am addressing "questioning" head-on at this point in the chapter because, first, it will help us reflect on much that we have been reading up to this point about helping students do better in constructing meaning as they read. As we saw in Figure 6.1, the kind of *critical inquiry* we

The teacher refers students to the following two sentences written on the board:

The games were a lot of fun. They enjoyed playing them.

After asking the students to read the sentences, he or she proceeds as follows:

"Was anyone puzzled at first when you read these two sentences? What happened, do you think? The word *they* threw you off, right? What do you suppose made that happen? [Upon reflection, students often will identify the source of the problem. If they don't, we may explain as follows.] Our first thought when most of us read *they* was that it referred to the games. But when we continue reading the second sentence, it seems strange to say that the games enjoyed playing themselves! So we realize that *they* refers to people rather than to the word *games*.

"When you suddenly realize that something isn't making sense, a good strategy is to go back and *re*read—read again—a couple of sentences before whatever you're having trouble with. Usually you will discover that the problem was like the one we had here—and you can find the word or words that threw you off.

"By the way, if *you* were the writer of these sentences, how would you word them instead? . . ." [This question is an effective tie-in to writing, of course, and helps reinforce the importance of the reciprocal relationship between reading and writing.]

■ ■ ■ ■ ■

want readers to establish with a text takes the form or shape of questions they continually ask themselves as they read. *Inquiring* minds literally know how to ask questions. Second, effective questions that we ask of our students in the contexts of the ongoing extensive and intensive reading they will be doing are at the core of effective instruction.

I'd like to establish a perspective before we explore questioning. We need to be aware that questions can deal with the *product* of reading or with the *process* of reading (Durkin, 1981; Irwin, 1991). Questions that address *product* are focused on the *result* of the meaning that is constructed during reading. Questions that address *process* focus on *how* readers go about answering questions based on their reading. For example, here is a "product" question based on the preceding paragraph: "What is one of the most critical aspects of teaching?" And here is a "process" question based on the same paragraph: "How did you determine the author's purpose for addressing questioning at this point in the chapter?"

As we'll soon see, we need to make sure we are focusing appropriately on process throughout our interactions with students. This is necessary because we need to help students understand how to respond to a question in terms of (1) determining exactly what the question is asking, (2) the degree to which the question relies on information explicitly or implicitly stated in a text, and (3) bringing their prior knowledge to bear in responding to a question.

Questions of course are also a part of our ongoing instruction. They help us determine how well our objectives are being addressed, and they help us respond moment-by-moment to our *students'* understanding and process. In the past, many teachers wound up asking questions focused on factual, literal recall because those questions are easier to ask (Gambrell, 1987) and because the teachers wanted to check whether students had in fact read the material assigned to them. This is a far, far cry from the role that questions *should* play in facilitating thinking and learning. If, in our own teaching experiences, we have not been in the habit of responding to or asking questions that serve a nobler function than simply "checking," we probably need to work at generating *good* questions.

Perhaps the hardest adjustment for many of us to make is learning how to truly *listen* to students as they talk about what they read. This is particularly challenging when we first begin teaching, because of all the other things we are trying to attend to. But we *will* get better if we make the effort—and it's only by really *listening* to what students are saying that we can ask good questions and, just as important, provide effective and appropriate *feedback* (Weber & Shake, 1988).

There—we have our perspective established. Let's begin our exploration of questioning.

Our purposes for questioning

Bearing in mind that questioning may be based on product and process, refer again to Figure 6.3. Let's consider the following three fundamental purposes for asking questions:

■ *As Models for Students' Internalizing.* We want to *model* how to ask good questions. Internalizing good questions is a student's means of generating frameworks for ongoing "meaning making"—at the micro and the macro levels and beyond. Our ultimate goal is for students to generate their own questions, their own "wonderings," as they read independently.

■ *To Focus Students' Internalizing.* We want to facilitate and focus students' questioning and thinking strategies, particularly in regard to thinking more critically. Moffett and Wagner (1991) suggest that we can do this by asking for *clarification* ("Is this what you meant?"), *elaboration,* in which we ask students to consider additional information or perspectives ("How else might this problem be solved?"), and *qualification* ("Would this work in *every* situation?" "Would Jake have behaved the same way if he'd been living during the time of the Nat Turner rebellion?").

There is another way in which we can help focus students' internalization, especially in regard to focusing on specific information in a text. Often *we* know the answer to a question (and the students know we know), but we want to help them understand that we're helping *them* through the process of discovering the answer. (Note that we don't want students to misinterpret our purpose here as simply playing "Guess what's in Teacher's head.")

■ *To Gain Information.* We are genuinely interested in what students are thinking, so we probe further; we need to assess the degree to which their meaning construction corresponds to the author's probable intention (this is more of an issue with expository texts; see Chapter 7).

Levels of information and types of questions

Students need to understand the *sources* of responses to questions as well as the *process* of determining what different questions require. To help them do this, we explore with them the relationship among the text, the reader, and the questions in a particular instructional context (Pearson & Johnson, 1978; Raphael, 1986; Raphael & Pearson, 1982). Can you recall our exercise in Chapter 2 where we read the newspaper account of the *Titanic* and responded to questions? That exercise highlighted the distinction between information that is *explicit*—"right there" on the page—and information that is *implicit*—the kind we have to piece together from information already given. We also experienced how information of course comes from the reader's *background knowledge* as well. Background knowledge can help both to fill in the information that is implied in the text and to elaborate and go beyond the text, making personal connections and associations with the text (Irwin, 1991). While primary-grade students can absorb some of these distinctions, the procedure usually isn't necessary or really beneficial for many students until they are at least in third grade.

Raphael (1986) has described an approach that does a good job of helping students understand these "Question/Answer Relationships," or "QARs," as she calls them. Let's examine her procedure more closely.

First, we explain that the information students obtain during their reading, and in response to questions based on that reading, is of two main types: "in the book" and "in my head."

"In the book" information can be "right there"—the book actually states the information in one or two sentences—or it can involve the reader's putting it together. The latter kind of information is not expressed directly in the book, but readers can figure it out by relating or putting together information from different places in the text. By using terms such as *right there* and *putting it together,* we help children understand what *we* often refer to as *literal* and *inferential* comprehension: "reading the lines," if you will, and "reading *between* the lines."

"In my head" information is also of two kinds: "author and me" and "on my own." "Author and me" information is the kind that readers can obtain from some given by the author and some not included by the author, but in the reader's head. "On my own" information cannot be derived from cooperation between the text and the reader; the reader must go outside the text to find it or may already possess it—perhaps even be able to answer a reading-based question without reading the text. To facilitate our explanation for our students, we can display these diagrams:

If we feel it's necessary, we can immediately follow up on our minilesson about QARs with opportunities for the students to apply what we've just been discussing. We give them a passage and questions and have them work collaboratively or individually to determine answers and how they derived them. And they're going to observe that what is "author and me" for one student may be "on my own" for another.

MEANING MAKERS: The Reader and the Classroom Teacher

Exemplar Questions for Narratives

The following questions, identified according to the story element each most *closely* corresponds to, are examples of the kinds of thought-provoking, process-oriented questions you will be developing. These questions work because they involve students in identifying and pulling together information, usually relating it to their own prior knowledge in order to interpret it most effectively.

Characterization

- If you could be any character in this book, who would you be? Why?
- Which characters seemed like real people? *How* did the author make them seem like real people? Did you feel you were really inside them—feeling, thinking, and seeing the way they did?

Setting

- If the story had taken place in a different setting, would that have changed the plot? If so, how?
- What words or phrases did the author use to make you feel you were really in the story? How did the author put you in a certain mood right away?

Plot

- Sometimes stories leave you with the feeling that there is more to tell. Did this story do that? What else do you think might happen?
- What kinds of people and events were working against the main character? How were they affecting him or her?

Theme

- What do you feel is the most important word, phrase, sentence, passage, or paragraph in this story? Explain why it is so important.
- Why do you think the author wrote this story? Explain your view.

Style

- How did the language of the story work for you?
- (If students have read several different authors' worksin the same genre): How does their style seem the same? How is it different?

Point of View

- Why did the author have _____ tell the story?
- Did the point of view switch back and forth? Why?

A good overall question is:

- Would this story make a good TV show or series? Why or why not? ■

INSTRUCTIONAL EXPERIENCES: STUDENTS LEARN TO INTERNALIZE THROUGH DOING

After and along with numerous guided or "bridge" experiences, students are becoming more and more proficient at internalizing critical-thinking questions and strategies. They are moving along the spectrum of instructional experiences (refer again to Figure 6.3). This section will focus on the kinds of literacy—both reading and writing—experiences and opportunities we want to offer to foster students' growing sense of independence and internalization. These experiences will include both *intensive* and *extensive* reading and writing activities.

Intensive reading

Informal discussion and *planned inquiry* are the two phases into which I have divided our move toward intensive reading of the "core" and "extended" texts that we discussed at the beginning of this chapter. *Informal discussion* gets us involved with our students in an ongoing discussion, over several days, about a lengthier story or book. The context for in-depth discussion and critical interpretation and understanding is established. *Planned inquiry* involves "deep" reading, the critical inquiry that will touch the more profound issues in our students' lives through the medium of the book. We usually will be using books, rather than short stories, because this will foster the ". . . immersion and distancing" that will truly engage, inform, and stretch our students (Lovell, 1992, p. 30). We will also examine a third instructional avenue to allowing students opportunities for intensive reading experiences: Writing in response to reading, especially writing in response journals.

Informal Discussion   You are an active and *almost* equal participant during informal discussion. You are a participant in that you contribute to the discussion in the group. You are "first among equals," however, in that you will still *subtly* direct the general course, if not the specifics, of the discussion—to keep it from wandering too far afield, away from the book.

To prepare for the informal discussion, you'll need to do the following things:

- Read the story or chapter in a book.
- Determine how much of a "chunk" will be read at a time by the students (usually, a single chapter); write down for your own reference three or four key events, in each chapter, that can serve as a check on the whole group's understanding.)
- Prepare questions that you believe will facilitate productive discussion (see above).
- Have the students read.
- When they'll be comfortable doing so, have the students write their responses in their response journals before gathering to discuss the reading with the group (see below).
- Engage the students in discussing the reading and allow a range of individual responses.
- Allow other opportunities for responding to the reading in many different ways.

More specifically, Susan Hepler (1992) suggests the following:

- Sit in a circle, rather than having children face you.
- Allow children to share initial comments and reactions *before* you ask your prepared question or questions. This initial sharing allows the children to "check" what they have understood about the story thus far. Aspects that were unclear to one child can be explained by another, and this will give you insights into specific strategy lessons you may need to teach—for example, if it becomes apparent that occasionally a student is being thrown off course by the use of flashbacks or by a changing point of view.
- Always be prepared to go with the flow of the children's observations. Adjust, as necessary, or omit questions *you* may have prepared, depending on this direction. This is a delicate process at which you'll become more adept the more you engage children in such discussions. It is not, of course, an "anything goes" free-for-all; the objective is to maintain the children's focus on meaningful inquiry and on justifying their interpretations on the basis of what is being read.

Student choice is an important part of this environment in which books are discussed. You will set the stage for these small groups by giving a brief booktalk about four or five books—"extended" titles. Hepler comments that "adult readers in the classroom dignify titles by their attention and actually help readers develop a wider literary scope" (1992, p. 71). In your booktalk you tell a little bit about each book: background about the author or illustrator, other books the students may have read by the same author, the type of genre, a little bit about the main character or the plot—whatever you believe may be *most* enticing about the book. Then the children sign up to read and discuss a particular book. If a lot of students want to read one particular book, Samway and her colleagues

Literature Groups and Intensive Reading

I'd like to comment on terminology and the context in which *informal discussion* and *planned inquiry* occur. As we read about involving children in literature, we encounter quite a few terms used to refer to similar instructional situations: *grand conversations, literature circles, literature study circles, literature groups, reading response groups,* and so on. All these descriptions refer to the same undertaking—*intensive* reading of stories and chapter books. Watkins and Davis (1988) note that

> The literature study group program does more than add another title to a list of books read or another segment to the bookworm elongating itself around the room. Children are asked to slow down, move back and forth between their lives and the text life, to consider meaning embedded in characterization, mood, pattern, ordering of time, circumstance of setting, even conventions of print. In other words, they are encouraged to participate in higher order thinking—anything

that helps them live through the literature experience, learn from it, and value it (p. 61).

One variation of such literature groups is literature "share groups" (Hansen, 1987), which often are heterogeneous groups of three or four children and in which students are reading different books or stories. With the teacher sitting in, each child summarizes what he or she is reading, reads a favorite or representative part, and then asks for comments and questions. Each student is an "expert" on the book, and the other students are asking real questions out of a genuine desire to know. The teacher can guide the discussion at first, through modeling a summary of the book she is reading and the responses to students' questions, but will very soon turn matters over to the students. She will also be modeling appropriate "response"-type behavior. Literature share groups become excellent "booktalk" formats, a forum for getting other students interested in and excited about reading other books.

LEARNING IN CONTEXT: **Sharing and exploring books in the social context of the literature group expands children's awareness of possible meanings and potentially engaging texts.**

(1991) suggest, you might have a lottery. (This won't happen as often as you might think. Besides, the book they "didn't get" can of course be read recreationally and be taken home).

Students do become adept at discussing books on their own. You can provide thought-provoking questions for a group just before they meet; the questions will be addressed *after* the students have initially checked with each other about "what's happened so far" in the text.

Planned Inquiry   On the surface, planned inquiry *appears* very similar to our informal discussions. The big difference is in the way *we* prepare for it and in the extent to which we explore a selection with our students. We will usually spend more time formulating our questions for planned inquiry; let's see why.

Plecha (1992) has referred to this type of inquiry reading as one in which

Different Abilities, Backgrounds, and Perspectives

You may be wondering: aren't there some major problems when a teacher is bringing together students with different reading abilities or from significantly different backgrounds to discuss the *same* book? Moreover, some of these students may be learning English as a second language.

There *are* adjustments you have to make, but there should *not* be problems. In Chapter 12, we'll explore more extensively how you can make many of the adjustments, but here I would like to underscore the value of making the adjustments and bringing students together. If you have students from diverse backgrounds in your classroom, you have a truly exciting opportunity to break down barriers that may have been erected by the *adult* communities in which those students live. You will find that whether or not you bring up an issue through a thoughtfully phrased question, the students will wind up talking about issues that touch them deeply and that all too often work to keep them apart from one another, failing to communicate or even to understand. The *book* becomes the context for addressing these critical and important issues, and you will find it a much more natural and authentic context for addressing them.

■ Be sensitive to the communication patterns of different minority cultures; at first, these patterns may not follow the predominant taking-turns pattern where one student finishes, another picks up, and so forth. Rather, comments may overlap or appear unfocused—but ultimately, meaning is being made. For example, many African-American students follow a "topic associating" rather than a "topic specific" pattern (Au, 1992; Heath, 1983). In discussing a part of a story, they may draw associations with many examples in their own lives; this is desirable unless the teacher is expecting a "topic specific" response addressing the situation at hand, a response that is "sticking to the topic." Unless the teacher is clear about this expectation, teacher and student will not connect. Many Native American students think it inappropriate to look directly at the teacher when speaking or being spoken to, and there are some topics they believe are "taboo" to discuss, so the teacher should not expect contributions from a student in such a situation (see, for example, Sleeter and Grant, 1994).

■ Allow more "wait time"; Cazden (1988) indicates that increasing wait time to three seconds dramatically affects the involvement of students and the quality of their responses.

Purves and Monson (1984) pull this issue together for us beautifully: "Our experience, what we have done, what we have seen, what we have read, separate us. At the same time, the text brings us together and gives us the chance to explore how we resemble each other and how we differ from each other" (p. 8).

LEARNING IN CONTEXT: Through the use of literature as a vehicle for discussion and response, children come to see their commonalities and differences in a more genuine light, leading ultimately to *understanding.*

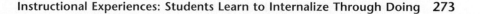

"fundamental questions of meaning . . . present a challenge to the under-standing of *both* children and adults" (p. 105, emphasis added). *We* wish to pursue the questions as much as the children do, so this will be an exciting, surprising, eye-opening quest for us as well as for them. The questions will relate specifically to the text at hand; they're not of the "generic" variety we might pose in informal discussions or in response to a "recreational" book a child is reading. Instead, such questions will elicit "thoughtful responses to a story's particular characters and situations" (Plecha, p. 105). Using the stories of "Jack and the Beanstalk," "The Sleeping Beauty," and "The Strange Case of Dr. Jekyll and Mr. Hyde" as examples, Plecha gives the following questions as illustrations: "Why does Jack go up the beanstalk the third time?" (p. 107); "Does Beauty love the Beast because of his fine qualities, or because he needs her?"; "Why is Mr. Hyde able to destroy Dr. Jekyll?" (p. 105).

These questions do not and *should not* have one right answer. They can generate a wide variety of responses, each supportable by the text. *This* is what critical thinking is all about.

As we attempt to generate "fundamental questions of meaning," we should bear in mind that our first objective is to come up with *one* fundamental question that, like Plecha's examples, may be asked of the whole story. Then we can generate other questions that relate to this fundamental question—and these, too, will have more than one answer.

As our students respond to our questions through discussion and writing, they are going to examine and re-examine the story frequently. This *re*reading is critical because it helps students view the text and construct a meaning from several different points of view. They must *justify* their developing understanding by reference to the text, and they will expand their own understanding and interpretation through hearing about those of other students. Along the way, as necessary, *we* will be asking—and re-asking—our fundamental questions for the students to respond to.

Here are some hints for beginning planned inquiry.

■ Many teachers wish to try it out for the first time with a story rather than with a chapter book. After the students' initial reading of and responding to the story, we pose our question(s). This will involve their rereading the story, followed by more discussion.

■ It is often more effective for the students and more comfortable for us if we begin these fundamental questions in a *read-aloud* format, using a core selection with the whole class, before trying it with smaller groups. This will also, of course, model in a whole-class format the type and nature of questions and thinking that are possible in responding to fiction. We can, for example, think aloud as we look for evidence to support an idea we have.

How do we prepare for this intensive inquiry? First, we must read the story or book ourselves. As we read, we jot down our own ideas and our own questions about the characters and about the situations in which they are involved: what intrigues, provokes, or puzzles us? Questions that we are still asking ourselves after finishing the book probably are "fundamental" ones worth posing to our students. Ideally, we would read the book a second time; other fundamental questions might emerge, but those that first occurred to us are probably good ones to use with our class. By using such questions, we will be genuinely engaging ourselves, along with the students, in trying to find answers. Most important, we will be setting up our students, inevitably, to think for themselves (because we *don't* have the answers). It is very helpful initially to do this type of preparation with another teacher or interested adult. We can discuss with each other the questions each of us has generated and determine how "fundamental" they are—and in the process enjoy, understand, and appreciate the selection all the more.

Writing in Response to Reading   Asking students to respond in writing to something they have read allows them to take a variety of stances toward the narrative, thus understanding not only the narrative but the world beyond it more profoundly. We should not wear out the value of encouraging students to respond through writing to what they are reading; but if well balanced, such responses can definitely deepen and elaborate awareness and understanding. Thus, writing in response to reading holds an important place in the "intensive" literacy experience we want students to engage in. (See Figure 6.4 for the overall "fit" of writing within this instructional scheme.)

Although written response activities can work well in numerous different formats, we will focus in this section on response journals. These journals are an extension of the ones students are encouraged to write in every day. Response journals can come to play a very significant role in helping students interpret and reflect on their reading.

There are a number of ways to get students writing in journals at the beginning of the year. We may start with prompts, but our primary purpose is to get the children writing; they may in fact write about whatever they wish. We should model writing in a journal for our students; the overhead projector is good for this. That way, they will see that this is a free-form expression of their thoughts, apart from expectations of "correctness" and all that it connotes.

As students become used to writing in their journals (usually it doesn't take long), we introduce the idea of responding to their *reading* in journals. In fact, throughout their reading, students should be encouraged to respond to it in writing. Their writing will not only reveal and provide support for perspectives offered in discussion but will allow different levels and types of response that may not emerge in the discussion setting (Barone, 1989).

When *we* respond to the students' responses, the journals become "dialogue" journals. Some teachers attempt to respond to every student every day, but this can be pretty demanding. Most teachers who respond on a regular basis try to respond to each child *at least* once a week. As we react to the students' responses in their reading journals, we may pose any of the types of questions we talked about in the earlier section "Asking Good Questions," or we may respond in other ways that are genuine. For each student, we should try to respond about whatever interests us; it isn't necessary to spend a lot of time on this. Our responses, as Nancie Atwell put it, should affirm, challenge, and extend (1987). In the following entry, for example, a third-grader named Jenny is responding to Beverly Cleary's *Dear Mr. Henshaw*. Leigh, the main character, was dealing with his parents' divorce. Note how Jenny's teacher, Ann Urie, *affirms* the experience Jenny has shared:

> I just love this book.
> I'm pretending to be leigh.
> last night dad called and
> told me he got merid. He asked
> me if it was ok. I said
> NO in a loud foice and started
> cring. then I felt I had
> to say somthing but I could
> not think of anything but the
> word NO then I thout of
> sorry so I said sorry and
> then Dad hung up on me. then
> I had to talk with
> mom so I did
> I told her all about it
> I asked her what to do she said call
> him tomorow so I
> did and said I am
> really sorry then I hung up. It's a
> cool book.

> Jenny,
>   I can tell this came straight
> from your heart.
>   Mrs. U.

Look back on pages 269–270 at the list of "generic" questions we can ask students orally about their reading. Those would be excellent to explore in response journals as well.

Occasionally, when students first get into a book, their responses will indicate they really aren't "picking up" on a lot of the information that is there. This usually will change later on, but we can help such students with gentle queries about *process* as we respond to their responses. For example, in response to a child who does not seem to be constructing a mental image of a setting anywhere near what the author intended, we might query: "Are you sure? Did you read the description of _____?"

We may also include, from time to time, queries about the *strategies* students are employing in their reading: "Were there any particular reading strategies that you had to use?" [This would include figuring out words: "What did you do when you suddenly realized you didn't know what was going on? How did you fix it up?"] We may also pose questions such as "How would you sell this book to someone else? Have you told anyone about it?"

In their response journals, children may also prepare for the next session of a small-group literature circle. The journal would be an excellent place to respond to questions you may have asked at the previous session. Responses should capture the ideas of the students so that the journal may serve as a "prompt," if necessary, during discussion. Children's "preparations" may include any number of activities: for example, Diane Barone had her students draw a cluster based on "secrets" before they read, in Roald Dahl's *Danny the Champion of the World,* the chapter in which Danny's father's "deep dark secret" was revealed (Barone, 1990).

Another excellent idea is to have the students write a brief summary of what they have read for that day's discussion. They can then write down whatever personal associations they may have had with this bit of reading, and they can conclude by noting what they think is the most important part of the reading, and why. In the discussion group, they will share these observations and justifications.

Students may also write *after* meeting with their discussion groups. This is an excellent way to reflect on what they learned and realized after hearing others' responses to the reading. For example, in the following response to *Island of the Blue Dolphins* (in which a Native American girl is stranded on an island for many years and has to fend for herself), fifth-grader Jennifer reveals what she learned after meeting with her discussion group that day:

> Oh, whoa. I never realized she sometimes went *naked.* That gives me a whole
> different perspective of her. Now when I think of Karana she seems totally
> different. I wish no one had said "naked." I liked her better before that.
> Oh, well. We all have to make adjustments, Right?

When students are comfortable writing in their response journals and are well into the mode of discussing their reading informally or in planned inquiry, a technique suggested by Caplan (1984) will be very effective. Take a sentence from a chapter or two that the students have read and ask them to find in what they have read evidence that supports the statement. They don't have to *copy* the "evidence"—they can just describe it in their own words. For example, third-graders could support the following statement from the chapter "Seat Work" in *Ramona the Pest* (Cleary, 1968, pp. 72–73). Ramona is a kindergartner in this story.

> When Miss Binney handed each member of the class a strip of cardboard
> with his name printed on it, anyone could see that a girl named Ramona was
> going to have to work harder than a girl named Ann or a boy named Joe.

The writing can go in the other direction as well: *before* reading a chapter, give students its first sentence and suggest that they write the first paragraph or two of the chapter as the author might write it; this would be an excellent accompaniment to your discussions about *style.* Consider the possibilities after students have been reading Beverly Cleary books, particularly those focused on an individual such as Henry Huggins, Ramona, Ralph the Mouse, or Leigh Botts. For example, try the following, again from *Ramona the Pest* (p. 128):

> "When the morning kindergarten cut jack-o-lanterns from orange paper
> and pasted them on the windows so that the light shone through the eye and
> mouth holes, Ramona knew that at last Halloween was not far away."

It is also helpful to model different "stems" for getting students' responses under way (Barone, 1992; Routman, 1991). Here are some that work quite nicely:

"That reminds me of . . ."
"I was confused . . ."
"I was wondering . . ."
"I disagree . . ."

Later on, we can encourage students to share their response journals with their classmates, writing responses back to each other. For example, consider the following exchanges between two fifth-grade students:

Dear Mr. Henshaw

I don't like how Leigh Botts
was so nice in the beginning
and so mean and rude in
the end. But it is true
that writing so many letters
would be hard
and sending all the letters
sure would cost a lot of
money for stamps.
       —Matthew

You have good thinking!
I don't like the story either.
       —Nicholas

I didn't say I didn't like the story
I just didn't like that part.
       —Matthew

Some teachers involve the home as well; parents are encouraged to respond to their own child's response. Of course, this is an excellent way to get parents to read the same book their child is reading. Parent and child can discuss meaningfully what *they* are reading. My own experience shows that parents are likely to write quite a bit in a response; they are excited because it is like having discovered a brand new way of communicating with their child—and, of course, they have. For example, issues of sibling rivalry can be addressed effectively in response to Judy Blume's *The Pain and the Great One*. How to deal with the awkwardness and sadness of having a friend who is dying is sensitively handled in Eve Bunting's *The Empty Window*.

The following literature expansion activities will complement the intensive reading instructional experiences we have just discussed.

◆ DEVELOPING YOUR INSTRUCTIONAL TOOLKIT

There are a number of ways we can help children become more explicitly aware of the structure or grammar of stories.

Retellings. We often need to model retellings for some students (Morrow, 1989). We include the main character, the setting, the problem the main character had, how he or she attempted to solve the problem, and how the story ended.

For example, after reading *The Story of Ferdinand* (Leaf, 1936) to a group of children, we could model our retelling as follows:

> So, boys and girls, our story was about Ferdinand the bull. He lived in Spain. All the other bulls ran, jumped, and butted their heads, because they wanted to be chosen for the bullfights in Madrid. But all Ferdinand wanted to do was sit just quietly and smell the flowers. When the men came to choose the most ferocious bull to go to the bullfights, Ferdinand accidentally sat on a bumblebee, got stung, and jumped all over the place. The men thought *he* was the most ferocious bull and took him to Madrid for the bullfights. And of course Ferdinand didn't want to fight, so he sat in the middle of the bullring and smelled the flowers that were in the young ladies' hair. The men who were supposed to fight Ferdinand got all upset because Ferdinand wouldn't fight them, so Ferdinand was taken back to his home. And that's where he is still, quietly sitting under his favorite cork tree and smelling the flowers.

Story Maps. For students who, for whatever reason, seem to be having difficulty understanding story structures and using information in stories to respond to questions, *story maps* may be helpful. They are beneficial for children who still seem to be "word by word" readers even though we believe they have the ability to be more fluent readers (see Chapter 5), because story maps help such children move beyond a preoccupation with words to become aware of the "big picture." Story maps provide a framework that helps students become aware of and understand the structure, elements, and interaction among elements within a story (Beck & McKeown, 1981). Story maps also guide teachers in generating questions based on a story. By more systematically guiding the sequence and type of questions, story maps allow for more direct teaching in understanding and using information in stories. It's important that the sequence of these questions follow the sequence of the story's events. Here's how we go about using story maps:

■ In a chart format, list the character(s), the setting, and a brief outline of the plot. This outline includes the beginning event and the character's (or characters') feelings in response to that event. What efforts did the character(s) make in response? What was the outcome of each attempt? What happened at the end of the story? How did the character(s) react to the ending?

■ Once we have sketched the parts of a story this way, we can generate questions to ask the students. These questions will follow the same character/setting/episode sequence as the story:

What was the setting of the story?

Who were the main character or characters?

What problem did the character(s) face? (This is usually part of the "beginning event.")

How does _____ feel about the problem? What does he/she/they decide to do about it?

What did he/she/they do? How did it turn out? What else did he/she/they do? How did that turn out?

How was the problem taken care of? (How did the story end?)

We have different options for using the story map, depending on how explicit we may need to be with different students: we may (1) need to show the map after reading a story along with the questions that directly correspond to the map, (2) show the map alone and discuss it, or (3) simply ask the questions in the order that follows the sequence of the story.

Let's apply the story map to Steven Kellogg's *The Island of the Skog,* a tale of a band of mice who escape "persecution" and sail in search of an island where they can be free. They find the "Island of the Skog," but not knowing what a "skog" is and fearing it may be a dangerous creature, they attempt to intimidate it by firing cannonballs at the island before they go ashore. The skog *is* intimidated and attempts to frighten the mice in return. A trap set by the mice attracts the skog, which turns out to be a tiny little creature who has dressed up as a terrifying monster and was trying to scare the mice away because *it* was afraid of *them.* The mice realize that "only if we'd talked to each other," all the trouble could have been avoided. Together they set up a new community for "mice and skog together."

There *are* times when, in contrast to the GRTA format, we will preview a story with students (Graves, Cooke, & LaBerge, 1983; Graves, Prenn, & Cooke, 1985). This may be done with particularly challenging stories that we want students to read because of the deeper questions and considerations these stories

Figure 6.6
Story Map for Island of the Skog

SETTING Neighborhood/Ship/ Island	CHARACTERS Bouncer/Jenny
BEGINNING EVENT	Not Safe
RESPONSE	Tired, want freedom Fight, find island
ATTEMPT/ OUTCOME	Set sail Sail toward North Pole, then turn around
ATTEMPT/ OUTCOME	Sail toward skog Fire cannon at island to scare skog Land on skog
ATTEMPT/ OUTCOME	Find enormous footprint, build trap Next morning, trap empty and boat gone
ATTEMPT/ OUTCOME	Jenny: Build another trap Trap works but skog "comes apart" — was a scared little animal
ENDING	Mice and skog build village, live together

raise. The challenge in the stories comes not from their being at students' "frustration" levels, but from the unfamiliarity of the topic, setting, style, language, or complexity of the plot structure.

The essence of a preview is this: We begin by providing an analogy or tie-in between the students' lives and backgrounds and the story. This is followed by a synopsis or gist of the story, including a description of the plot, the characters, and if necessary, the setting. We do *not,* however, give away the ending.

Awareness of Elements of Narration. We teach about each element by introducing its features; examining it in stories and exploring how writers develop it; and discussing how it helps us understand a story, and ourselves, more fully. As an example, let's explore how *characterization* might be examined: We brainstorm with students the ways in which authors develop characters. Out of such brainstorming we guide them toward realizing that characters may be described through their appearance, what they do or how they behave, what they say and what others say about them, and how they think. After reading *Molly's Pilgrim* (Cohen, 1985), for example, we may list or cluster information from the story around each of these criteria:

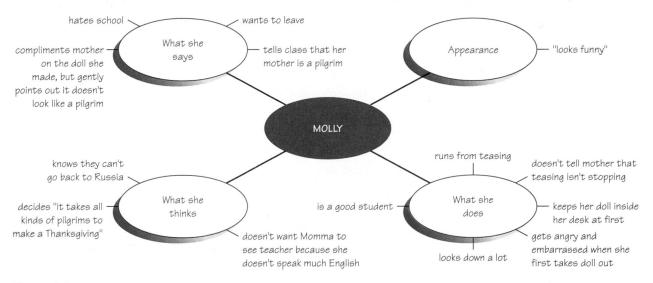

Figure 6.7
Developing Characterization: Molly in Molly's Pilgrim

■ Different small groups can explore the development of different elements in a core text. One group can track the different types of conflict; another, the use of idiomatic expressions; another, the development of characters, and so forth.

■ Compare and contrast the ways in which elements are developed in the medium of television and in the medium of the book. After we have explored a particular story element—say, *characterization*—we can have students observe and analyze how that element is developed in television "stories."

■ Compare and contrast story elements across stories that all students have read. Have different groups prepare a grid and then fill in each cell. Afterward, they can compare their grids.

All these activities for teaching different elements help define, highlight, and teach. We should keep a proper perspective on their use, however. They should not become the main focus of our instruction. Rather, we should keep in mind that our primary emphasis should be on natural, authentic engagements with aspects of narrative elements: Most of our discussions will draw upon students' developing underlying knowledge of elements, and many of our questions will reflect different elements (see the discussion of "Exemplar Questions for Narratives").

Explore an Author. Compare and contrast an author's works. Do all of them focus on the same general time and place? On the same theme(s)? Does *style* of this writer's books ever vary? Are there features common to every book (for example, adults playing a minor role; siblings working together or always at odds)?

Read and consider an author's *dedications* as affording insight. Usually dedications are straightforward ("To G.P. and R.N."), but sometimes there is a separate story behind the dedication. For example, Richard Peck dedicates his powerful book *A Day No Pigs Would Die* (1968) in this way:

*"To my father, Haven Peck . . .
A quiet and gentle man
whose work was killing pigs"*

And Theodore Taylor dedicates *The Cay*

*"To Dr. King's Dream, which
can only come true if the
very young know and understand."*

The dedication is dated April, 1968—the month in which Martin Luther King, Jr., was assassinated.

Readers Theatre. Readers Theatre (Sloyer, 1982) is a type of activity that teachers have used for many years with wonderful results. Students "perform" a text for an audience through oral reading, not through acting it out. All the preparation that goes into this performance is excellent for facilitating *thinking* about the reading. Students decide how the text will be partitioned into segments for different individuals or groups to read, and they decide whether a single individual or a small group will read each segment.

Students may establish "clubs" in the classroom that represent special reading interests; these may develop into *writing* clubs as well: a ghost stories club, a poetry club, a Beverly Cleary or a Leo Leonni club, and so forth.

Listening to Literature. In addition to making tapes of good books, it's worthwhile to keep an eye out for the excellent *recordings* of books that are available; most educational publishing companies offer these. Encourage the school media specialist to stock as many recordings as possible. Nothing can compare, for example, to hearing James Earl Jones read Virginia Hamilton's *The People Could Fly* (1985), a gripping and emotional tale of escape from slavery.

Still and all, we shouldn't forget the potential of allowing *our students* to record selections. As they experience literature, talk about interpretations, and cast a story in Readers Theatre format, they'll learn a lot about voice and reading with expression—about the *drama* conveyed through oral reading. With sufficient rehearsal, they can produce excellent tapes.

Involve students themselves in building up the classroom and school libraries. First and foremost, the monthly book clubs through which kids can get paperback books at low prices offer "bonus points" for numbers of books ordered. Let students know that these points can be applied toward ordering additional books, free of charge, for the class. Second, encourage parents directly through the class newsletter, and indirectly through the students, to donate any appropriate old books they have at home.

"Visual" Literacy. This is an area that has generated lots of interest in recent years. Visual literacy refers to learning how to look at illustrations and learning how the illustrations interact with the text to create a story (Madura, 1994). We begin by exploring how books are illustrated. For young children especially, good illustrations provide "talking points" for elaborating their concepts in general and their understanding of a story in particular. Children of all ages can learn about the different media in which illustrators work: watercolors, pastels, pencil, scissor art, papier mâché, and so forth (see the Insert tracing children's writing, reading, and art). These questions may help get you on your way:

Why has the illustrator chosen watercolors (or oils, or pencil) to illustrate the story? If more than one medium is used, what do you think the reasons are for using one medium for some pictures, and another medium for others?

What parts of the story has the illustrator chosen to illustrate, and why?

What do illustrations show that text doesn't? For example, in Don and Audrey Wood's *The Little Mouse, the Red Ripe Strawberry, and THE BIG HUNGRY BEAR,* what gives us a sense that the mouse thinks the bear may be near?

What characteristic features of a particular artist can you identify? How does he or she draw people? animals? objects?

How do artists express "point of view" in a story? For example, the text can present a point of view from one perspective, while the *illustrations* express a different point of view. The point of view of the narrator in Chris Van Allsburg's *Two Bad Ants* (1989) is omniscient, while the illustrations depict an "ant's-eye" perspective or view.

Along with learning about visual literacy, students should have opportunities to express through different media and projects their responses to their reading. They can, for instance,

Sketch a favorite scene.

Create a different cover for the book.

Take a chapter with few or no illustrations, decide which parts should be illustrated, and create those illustrations.

Make a mural illustrating the events in a book:
   Partition the book into twelve important sections and illustrate each—a subtle way of facilitating students' thinking about important themes, aspects

of plot, main ideas, and so forth. [Suggestion courtesy of Diane Olds, teacher of a combined fourth/fifth/sixth-grade classroom]

As we immerse *ourselves* in children's books, it will be downright impossible for us not to attend to what the artists are doing. We will find illustrations that will do nothing less than stagger us with their phenomenal power, depth, color, angles, and perspective. They will affect children at least as consequentially. And we will find that illustrations can be a magnet to those children who are more reluctant readers—they at least are holding, examining, and *valuing* books.

Extensive reading

Throughout this chapter, I have been referring to *extensive reading*. At this juncture, before we turn our attention more directly to writing, it may be helpful to reiterate the nature and value of extensive reading.

Extensive reading is the reading students do for pure enjoyment. We know that we provide time for this type of reading each day and that students will base their selections on their interests. We are demonstrating that we value students' choices. They are stakeholders in their own reading; they *own* it. The benefits of allowing and encouraging extensive reading include sustaining students' motivation to read, extending and expanding their interests, developing fluency, and expanding vocabulary. Skills and strategies are refined and become almost automatic in a very comfortable context—usually a text that is easy for the student, or skills and strategies are applied more deliberately, if the text is a challenging one that the student genuinely wants to explore. Children get better at reading *by* reading, by spending "time in the saddle" (Bear, 1991), and this is what extensive reading allows.

The literacy and learning environment we create in our classrooms provides a rich foundation for students' reading interests and explorations. In addition, we can generate interest through booktalks about selections that appear in the book clubs' monthly offerings. Over time, we'll discover that we have read many of those offerings and can comment on them casually to the students when we pass out the order forms.

Kids' Favorite Books: Children's Choices is a unique source of help for selecting books for the library center in our classroom. Published by the International Reading Association and the Children's Book Council, this is an ongoing publication based on the preferences of 10,000 children aged 5–13. It's easily the most comprehensive ongoing survey of students' reading interests.

I would like to be explicit about one aspect of extensive reading that, ironically, might otherwise go unnoticed (see Figure 6.2). A student immersed in a text that is being read recreationally may find herself reading it *intensively:* for whatever reason, a book pulls her deeply into it. She may discover that she is exploring that book from a critical perspective; she may realize she is exploring "fundamental questions of meaning." It is wonderful when we see this happening, for it suggests that such students have truly been empowered through literacy. Most of our students will not spend their lives in formal classrooms; will they be able to experience this empowerment elsewhere? That, of course, is our ultimate goal.

Value of Rereading—from Fluency to Deeper Insights

So often I hear the following lament: a teacher who wanted all his students to read a certain book for the *first* time *this* year in *his* class is dismayed when he learns that several of his students have already read it. This should not be a problem; given the type of reading environment we've been describing, it's a blessing. Good books can be read *innumerable* times. Especially where children are concerned, when they reread *this* year a book that they first read last year, they will have a significantly different or deeper response to it.

Forgive me if to illustrate this point, I share a "home movie" with you. Of our three children the youngest, our daughter, has been the most avid—no, *compulsive*—reader. She even reads in the bathtub and is invariably losing track of time there as she loses herself in a book. One night after her bath— she'd been reading Theodore Taylor's *The Cay* for the third or fourth time— she told me, "Every time I get to the part where Timothy dies, I get a sinking feeling in my stomach." Timothy, an elderly black sailor who remains physically and mentally strong up to his death, is one of her favorite characters in all that she has read. She went on to say, though, that she feels she *knows* him a little better after each reading of *The Cay*. Next year, when she is thirteen and reads this book yet again, she will love Timothy even more and see the book through yet another set of lenses.

In comparison to the deep emotions and understandings that our daughter's rereading of *The Cay* may engender, the notion of *fluency* may seem a little dry. Nevertheless, it is important to mention it here. Fluency, of course, is critical to meaningful reading. With successive rereadings, students' familiarity with a text supports their developing skills and concepts—particularly if the students were first "stretched" by the language and concepts in the text.

Reading a lot of books is wonderful; but students must also have the opportunity, as we have seen, to reflect on *some* books and *re*read them if they wish. Some books may be read recreationally, then intensively, then recreationally once again—though subsequent readings of a book once read intensively will always be "deeper" than the normal recreational-type read. This is how *The Cay* worked for our daughter.

It is not only the number of books we read that is important; it is also the nature of the experiences we have with them. ■

Constructing meaning through writing

As we saw earlier, writing in response to the reading that one is doing is a powerful way of involving oneself more intimately in the world of the narrative. In other words, writing can help us deepen and intensify our understanding of something we have read.

Here we will explore another angle of the relationship between writing and reading: the act of writing itself can help readers understand more about the process of meaning construction. These processes tend to be more deliberate and conscious in writing than in reading. Thus, the metacognitive stance that writers assume can help make readers more perceptive, knowledgeable, and self-aware.

Using Writing to Learn About Reading Through *writing,* children come to understand more deeply the process of *reading.* As we have said, children learn to write like readers and to read like writers (see, for example, Hansen, 1987). We make students aware of this integral relationship by helping them realize that the questions we ask before, during, and after their *reading* are very often the same questions we ask them before, during, and after their *writing*—questions that, as we now know, they will come to internalize.

In the type of classroom we are envisioning, many children will naturally want to compose their own stories. But unless we help the process at opportune points along the way, their efforts often will not get beyond the stage where they are simply describing action—the "what happens" phase. They won't be exploring and developing any of the elements that truly flesh out a story. Recall how this can occur with their reading as well: students are not nearly as likely to get beyond the "what happened" response to their reading unless we guide them into deeper waters.

Over the years, several outstanding teachers of writing have helped us understand how we can help children along in this process of developing as writers (Calkins, 1983, 1986; Graves, 1989; Nathan, Temple, Juntenen, & Temple, 1989). In so doing, they have aided us in keeping the proper perspective: our primary objective is not necessarily to turn out future Ernest Hemingways and Toni Morrisons (although such writers may be more likely to develop in these kinds of classrooms). Rather, our primary objective is to use story *writing,* as we did story *reading,* to help our students understand more deeply themselves, their world, and the meaning of their actions within that world.

While writing and discussing their writing, children come to understand more deeply the process of reading and how to develop story elements in their own writing.

Collaborative Stories   When we begin to involve students more deliberately in constructing their own narrative worlds through writing, we often find it useful to compose group *collaborative stories* (Graves, 1989; Tompkins, 1994). We do this initially when children are developing a sense of plot structure, and we do it when they are exploring the other elements of narrative.

The way we conduct this collaborative effort is akin to a brainstorming process. Following is a brief vignette of such a session I conducted with a group of third graders. I set up three columns labeled *Character, Setting,* and *Problem:*

> "Okay, kids, let's get our creative juices flowing so we can get into some story writing. Who might make a good character for a story we could write? . . . Pippi Longstocking? Okay, let's write her down. Now, where could our story be taking place? Las Vegas? Okay. . . . Now, what road block or problem might Pippi run into in Las Vegas? She runs out of money?" . . .

Then it's back to another possible character, setting, and problem. This process can be more of a free-form one; if kids propose more than one character, setting, or problem at a time, that's fine. In fact, this is quite likely to occur as they get the feel of the brainstorming. There may well be some silliness as we get into this, and that too is okay—but the improbability of some combinations of elements will more likely tickle students' creativity as much as their funnybone.

We can, then, flesh out possible beginnings, middles, and ends. We may ask the children questions along the way, and that generates more possibilities. Figure 6.8 shows the chart I generated with the third-graders.

Recall from our discussion earlier in this chapter that as students investigate a specific element in their *reading,* we can discuss its features and help them apply this awareness in their *writing.* The *writing* will now help flesh out that awareness and understanding.

Individual Stories   We realize how the group collaborative composition helps students understand and appreciate the "basics" of story writing. We will usually need to continue support as they develop their abilities to compose somewhat more original narratives.

Although we want the motivation for children's stories to come from within, many children—even after being involved in group collaborative stories—

CHARACTER	SETTING	PROBLEM/OUTCOME
Pippi Longstocking	Las Vegas	Running Out of Money
Pooh	Civil War	Chicken Pox
Alex	Media Center	Escaping Animals
Mrs. Avilla (teacher)	Circus	Drought
Shaquille O'Neal		Hunger

Figure 6.8
Chart of Possibilities for a Story

initially will rely on external prompts to get the creative juices flowing. As we discuss *leads* in stories they are reading—how the beginning "begins"—you can have on hand some one- and two-sentence leads that are "grabbers" and can get them going. For younger children they should be simple, such as "Down the road came . . ." and "The crash woke me up. . . ." For older students, leads such as these can work well: "There was no reason why I shouldn't have been able to go . . ."; "We were in orbit when Captain Biggs announced that communications with Earth were totally cut off. . . ." The same goes for *endings*. We can talk about the last lines of several different stories the students have read: How, precisely, have the authors worded them? What effect were they meant to have? This examination will then begin to transfer to endings that the students write for their own stories.

To facilitate students' story writing and keep it going, Graves (1989) suggests some general questioning guidelines. When a student seems to be drifting in focus or asks for help, we ask, "What's it about?" If he or she launches into a retelling, we may say, "Remember, you don't have to tell me the whole story up to this point; just tell me who the main character is and what problem that person is facing." Often we have to model this: we remind the student how we summarize or tell the main point or theme of a story when we are reading—in our literature response groups, for example. We can do the same with our own writing as teachers. For example, we explain that a story *we* are reading (or writing) is about "a boy who loses the ring his grandfather gave him, and how he's going to try to find it." Our short-and-simple question "What's it about?" usually helps the student identify the *theme* of his or her story. This lets the student refocus, and if the writing is getting sluggish, get back on track, pursuing new avenues of possibility.

To develop *characters,* Graves suggests, we can ask first what their *names* are. Often children write very general stories with the "good guys" (nameless) as the main characters. But putting a *name* on a character begins the process of developing the story, going beyond the straight description of action sequences with little logical connection among them. Then we can probe for specifics about the main character and discuss plot possibilities. What does he do? Why does he do the things he does—what are his *motives* (what *motivates* him)? Where did he come from? How much of a role does the *setting* play in influencing him? (Older students, by the way, love skimming through a "naming the baby" book in order to select a name; they enjoy reading what the names mean and often choose a name on the basis of its meaning. Teachers who keep a telephone book in their classrooms find that their students will use it as a source of last names for their characters.)

This interplay between character and plot development is important and exciting. Characters need a *purpose* established for what they do. As Graves also points out, many of the "good guy/bad guy" violence-ridden stories we get from children result from a lack of understanding, or thinking through, of the reasons why characters do what they do. There is no connection between pushing a button and disintegrating the bad guys (you do it because they're bad, and they're trying to kill you); and then it's "on to the next killing" (Graves, 1989, p. 40).

Collaborative to Individual and Back Again   Children will attempt to use in their own stories the conventions of writing in general, and narratives in particular, that they notice in their reading. We encourage this, of course, because it will present us with opportunities to teach appropriate minilessons along the way: for example, the use of quotation marks and indentation in dialogue; the purpose of flashbacks and the way they are handled; changing a narrative's point of view—and on and on.

As children grow in their abilities to compose better-developed stories, we encourage them to keep a "writing notebook" (it can be a section of their response journals, if we wish to control the number of notebooks the children are using). Tell the children that as ideas occur, they may jot them down. As they remember things that have happened to them, they should jot them down. As they encounter striking phrases or descriptions in their reading, they'll want to jot *these* down. All this information—impressions, turns of phrases, ideas— becomes a "treasure" that continually renews young writers as it reminds them of possibilities.

MEANING MAKERS: You, the Student

A Perspective on Writing

Just as we read along with our students during Sustained Silent Reading, we should *write* at least part of the time during writing workshops. We'll compose a story while our students are composing theirs; we may compose a paper for a graduate course, or a report that is part of our thematic unit (see Chapter 7 and Chapter 9). When we write, we set an example and send a message that we value writing; we also are likely to be more empathetic teachers of writing, as the following observation from Temple, Nathan, Temple, and Burris (1992) describes:

> Teachers who write are the best conference partners in the world because they respect their children's efforts. It's that simple. When it seems as though a piece is breaking down, a teacher who writes is more apt to ask herself, "What's this writer doing that's new?" instead of thinking, "This piece is impossible!"
>
> All of this—knowing that modeling is important, feeling vulnerable, and understanding the difficulty inherent in getting your paper to say what you mean—adds up to an honest workshop environment where writing takes the shape of the craft it is meant to be. (p. 248)

READING POETRY

Just as stories do, *poetry* resonates with a deep-seated construct in our psyches. Poetry is tied closely, of course, to rhythm; think of the lyrics in songs. Kids who say they "hate poetry" don't realize how much they love it through the songs they enjoy, the jump-rope jingles they recite, and the word games they often inadvertently play. Although *how* the language in a poem sounds is of course important, poems also move in ways that go far beyond the "sounds." Poems evoke images, feelings, and reactions. They are enduring literary forms because they can capture so much in so few words.

We readily recall types if not actual terms. In poetry, there are the formalists and the free-verse poets. *Formalists* write poems according to specific forms and structures: definite rhyme schemes, or patterns; a definite meter or rhythm of stressed and unstressed syllables ("beats") within each line; certain numbers of lines in stanzas; and so on. Then there is *free verse,* which doesn't usually rhyme and even looks like a bunch of sentences—the type of poetry that probably startled most of us when we first encountered it. Free verse often startles our students as well: "You mean, *this* is poetry, too?" Yes, it surely is; and many students think differently about poetry when they realize this. Other students will prefer the predictability of the well-known forms. This is why we provide opportunities to read and write both types in the classroom.

Georgia Heard is a free-verse poet and a teacher of poetry—especially of how to write it. Her book *For the Good of the Earth and Sun: Teaching Poetry* (1989) is excellent and quite enjoyable. For some time, I've taken particular pleasure in her description of where poems come from; it is a "demystifying" description and one that elementary students understand (cited in Calkins, 1986, p. 298):

> Feelings are the source of a poem, but you can't just write the feelings onto paper. Instead of trying to tell the reader my feelings, I go back in my mind's eye and locate the feeling in specific, concrete things that we see and hear. I get a picture in my mind then re-create that picture so the reader can feel what I felt.

All too often we are pulled away from the lure of poetry in a broader sense. Partly because of its capturing "so much," we have been intimidated in our experiences with poetry. As with the Great Books, we had teachers who told us such-and-such a poem was great because it was written by Shelley or Tennyson or Whitman or Elizabeth Barrett Browning, who were all great poets—and we had to understand the many levels of meaning, the symbolism, the historical context, and so on. Those teachers started at the wrong end of things. They weren't sure how best to "teach" a poem, so they did what *their* teachers had done: tried to talk about a poem's meaning, tried to get us to take the poem apart and figure out what the poet was "trying to say."

We already know that we shouldn't set out to "teach" characterization or theme, for example, before immersing our students in lots of reading. Only *afterward* will we casually talk about these elements, in a read-aloud context. The same approach applies to exploring poetry. *Immerse* your students in lots of it, read a lot of it, sing a lot of it, dance to a lot of it. Students will begin trying their hand at writing it. Such natural contexts give our students a "feel" for what poetry is and what it can do—without our having uttered one word about "symbolism."

Reading poetry aloud to children

First we have to read a lot of children's poetry *ourselves;* the list in Chapter 9 (see p. 441) will more than get you started. The poems that *we* most enjoy, and that are appropriate for our students, are some of the ones we should share with them.

We need to *practice* reading the poems we are going to share. It may be a little tough at first, but we often need to work at getting beyond the "sing-songiness" of rhyming poems. A poem is likely to have rhythm and rhyme; but if we are controlled totally by them, the poem can wind up sounding almost limp. The subject of the poem should help prevent this: for example, Jack Prelutsky's *Tyrannosaurus Was a Beast* offers a humorous, lighthearted, and downright delightful collection of poems about different types of dinosaurs. The reader's voice should sound light and humorous too. In Murphy's *The Last Dinosaur,* a collection of dinosaur poems, there are some that are light; but others, such as the *poem* "The Last Dinosaur," have a somber tone and are deeply moving. Again, the teacher's voice should put across this mood.

Each day during our read-aloud time, we might share at least one poem with the children. As we develop thematic units (see Chapter 9), our major topics and themes will suggest particular poems that we can share.

Students reading and responding to poetry

We should have lots of poetry books in our library corner; but an excellent tactic is to have a pile of poetry books on each cluster of desks as the children come in one morning. Simply let them rummage through the books, enjoying them however they wish. This is a good way to hook the students, without even whispering a word about poetry. Later on, as we explore different forms of poetry, we will of course have lots of examples of those forms available for the students to read (see below).

Sandy Madura, a primary-grades teacher, observes, "I always read poetry *aloud* and encourage my students to do the same when they're reading poetry on their own. I ask them to always look first to see how the words are arranged on the page. Ask 'what's the best way to read this? What do I need to look for?' "

Students should be given plenty of opportunities to respond in their journals to the poetry they are reading. We may model a response we have had, or we may simply allow the students to respond however they wish. Both approaches work.

Learning different forms

As we noted above, you'll have all types of poetry available for your students, but you'll be wise to avoid much discussion about the *structure* of these types until the students clearly enjoy poetry. The forms that educators have tradition-ally shared with elementary students are *haiku, cinquaines,* and *diamantes* (Stewig, 1984; Templeton, 1991). We are often delightfully surprised, though, to realize that kids not only are pleased with reading other forms such as *sonnets;* they also like trying to write those forms as well.

The *patterns* of various forms usually first influence children's poetry writing; later, they will appreciate learning the specifics of the forms. Notice the influence of Beverly McLoughland's "How to Talk to Your Snowman" on second-grader Kelly's poem:

How to Talk to Your Snowman	*How to Talk to a Gila Monster*
Use words that are pleasing, Like: *freezing* *And snow,* *Iceberg and igloo* *And blizzard and blow,* *Try: Arctic, Antarctic,* *Say: shiver and shake,* *But whatever you never say,* *Never say: bake.*	*Use words that he likes* *so he doesn't bite* *Like: bugs* *and water and* *black and red* *and bird and rain* *Try: Arazona and* *Navada say: Talk and walk* *and call her her name* *but don't say "bite"*

Here are two children's poems modeled after Judith Viorst's "If I Were in Charge of the World":

If I Were in Charge of the Ocean

If I were in charge of
the ocean
I'd cancel plution
killing whales
killing dolfins and maybe
trash in the water.

If I were in charge of
the ocean
There would be less plution
Healthy fish, and
Anybody who plutted I'd hang.

If I Were in Charge of the People

If I were in charge of the
people I'd cancel school,
sunday nights, shorts, and
also vegtabales.

If I were in charge of the
people there would be a better earth
and lower
prices.

When children are creating their own poems, on occasion they will get stuck. Georgia Heard suggests this tactic: When you get stuck, pretend you've just rushed into the room to tell your best friend about your idea—blurt it out; what would you say? Write that down; your poem is well on its way.

Students *will* move beyond their preconceptions of poetry: flowers, love stuff, for girls, wimps, sing-songy and always has to rhyme, and so forth. This will happen first through their reading of poetry, and then through writing it. They will develop the understanding that poetry is a short way of expressing, through words, something that you feel very deeply and powerfully.

■ A CONCLUDING PERSPECTIVE

Human beings are creatures who enjoy *and* need stories. Stories help us make sense of our lives. They can be vehicles for understanding ourselves and our world in unique ways. Children develop a *schema* for stories—a set of expectations about how stories are constructed—first by listening to them. This schema is elaborated later as children read them.

Many years ago the revered children's librarian Amelia Munson noted that we have the opportunity to "set before [children] what they never knew they wanted" (cited in Peterson & Eeds, 1990, p. 10). By providing for *extensive* and *intensive* reading, we will set before our students literature experiences that will allow them the thoughts, the reflections, and the sharing that should truly enrich their lives even as it helps them *live* their lives. Through *extensive* reading, children will simply enjoy all that stories and chapter books can offer, but they will also be building reading fluency and applying their developing skills. The selected stories and chapter books that they read *intensively* will help them construct new awarenesses, understandings, and appreciation. Intensive reading best exercises and develops children's critical thinking about stories. It involves reading and *re*reading: good stories will continue to provide many different interpretations and meanings, depending on the needs and perspectives of the reader. (This explains why we can reread a story or book after several years and wonder how in the world we missed a certain message or meaning. The answer is simple: each of us is a significantly different person now.)

"Bridge" experiences are excellent ways of supporting students' active involvement with stories as the students apply their developing skills under our watchful eye. As the label implies, bridge experiences span the terrain from the strong teacher-support necessary during beginning reading to the more intensive reading experiences in which skills are exercised at the highest level, both collaboratively and individually. For example, the Guided Reading-Thinking Activity for stories is an excellent bridge to intensive reading. It actively involves students in critical reading in a social context, with the teacher at first guiding, though not constraining, the reading and discussion. Our direct teaching plays a critical role here as well. As we engage in authentic reading experiences with students, their particular skills and strategy needs become apparent. In the context of the minilesson, then, we explain, model, and observe students' application of the knowledge about reading we directly demonstrate.

Good *questions* play a seminal role in our instruction. They not only sustain critical reading and reflection; they help teach an important *process* and over time become *internalized* to guide students' critical reading. *Informal discussion* and *planned inquiry* are two ways in which we can move children into "deep," critical encounters with narratives, and this discussion and inquiry involve *us* in the process of exploring as well. We become intrigued and excited right along with the children.

We have emphasized the role of *writing* in supporting the basic process of constructing meaning. Reading and writing are reciprocal processes. When children compose in writing in response to their reading, they cannot help but reflect on and rethink what they are reading, tapping deeper aesthetic roots that in turn branch out to make other insightful connections. Their reading response journals will play an important role in this enterprise, and the stories they compose will most likely be modeled on the stories they are reading. When children compose their own narratives—when they are thinking like writers—they acquire more insight into their own *reading* as well, because they must think about their audience, a *reading* audience.

There are probably as many ways of extending children's experiences with narrative literature as there are children themselves, and this chapter has offered several such literature extension ideas. They should work well for our students and for us, and they should provide a starting point for our own developing storehouse of ideas over the years.

The reading of poetry should be an important part of our literacy environment. Poetry is a special form of writing that captures the essence of experience and of feeling. Importantly, students should experience *both* free verse and more structured forms of poetry.

Real, authentic books written by individuals who know and care about children should form the foundation for elementary students' experiences with narratives. In the next chapter, we'll explore the role of literature—and of the *textbook*—in advancing children's learning and understanding of the various content areas. Chapter 7, "Constructing Meaning in Informational Texts" will extend an important theme that has been implied throughout this chapter: we play a seminal role in helping our students learn *how* to learn.

■ BECOMING A REFLECTIVE PRACTITIONER

Beck, I., & McKeown, M. (1981). Developing questions that promote comprehension: The story map. *Language Arts, 58,* 913–918.

Since most comprehension questions often do little more than require literal recall, Beck and McKeown have suggested using the story map as a guide toward questioning techniques that promote and develop some of the deeper comprehension skills. The organization of the text is important in the construction of questions. This article is well worth the short time it would take to read it.

Eeds, M., & Wells, D. (1989). Grand conversations: An exploration of meaning construction in literature study groups. *Research in the Teaching of English, 23,* 4–29.

This is a classic example of the importance of the student's prior knowledge and personal experiences and how they can aid in building comprehension. Once again, this article points out that the student's experiences fill in the blank spots left by the author. It also illustrates the importance of having students discuss literature (and the importance of the teacher facilitating the discussion) rather than simply answering questions about it, and emphasizes how these discussions lead to better understanding and comprehension. Comprehension involves not only the written word, but also what the reader brings to the text.

Bussis, A., Chittenden, E., Amarel, M., & Klausner, E. (1985). *Inquiry into meaning: An investigation of learning to read.* Hillsdale, NJ: Lawrence Erlbaum Associates.

This book provides an excellent overview of the current theories of learning to read. The second section (pp. 59–198) takes an in-depth look at the two extremes of beginning readers: the student that runs over words to maintain momentum, and the student that gets hung up on unknown words in order to maintain accuracy. If you would like to consult a good source regarding the importance of a student's learning style, the connection between broad or narrowed attention deployment and reading, the function of phonics rules and language rhythms in reading, and the need for children to spend "time in the saddle" reading, then this book is an excellent one to consult.

Mandler, J. M., & Johnson, N. S. (1977). Remembrance of things parsed: Story structure and recall. *Cognitive Psychology, 9,* 111–151.

Perhaps an often overlooked aspect of reading is the actual *structure* of the stories being read by students. In what has become a classic article, Mandler and Johnson look at this component to reading and the importance it plays in the ability of someone to recall a piece of literature in a sequential and accurate manner. Interestingly enough, story length was found to play a small role in recall as compared to the role played by the actual structure of the story.

■ REFERENCES

Atwell, N. (1987). *In the middle.* Upper Montclair, NJ: Boynton/Cook.

Au, K. (1993). *Literacy instruction in multicultural settings.* Fort Worth, TX: Harcourt Brace Jovanovich.

Barone, D. (1989). *Young children's written responses to literature: Exploring the relationship between written response and orthographic knowledge.* Unpublished doctoral dissertation, University of Nevada, Reno.

Barone, D. (1990). The written responses of young children: Beyond comprehension to story understanding. *New Advocate, 3,* 49–56.

Barone, D. (1992). "That reminds me of": Using dialogue journals with young students. In C. Temple & P. Collins (Eds.), *Stories and readers: New perspectives on literature in the elementary classroom* (pp. 85–102). Norwood, MA: Christopher-Gordon.

Bear, D. (1991). "Learning to fasten the seat of my union suit without looking around": The synchrony of literacy development. *Theory into Practice, 3,* 149–157.

Bear, D., & Invernizzi, M. (1984). Student directed reading groups. *Journal of Reading, 28,* 248–252.

Beck, I., & McKeown, M. (1981). Developing questions that promote comprehension: The story map. *Language Arts, 58,* 913–918.

Brown, A., Campione, J., & Day, J. (1981). Learning to learn: On training students to learn from texts. *Educational Researcher, 10,* 14–21.

Bussis, A., Chittenden, E., Amarel, M., & Klausner, E. (1985). *Inquiry into Meaning: An investigation of learning to read.* Hillsdale, NJ: Lawrence Erlbaum Associates.

California State Department of Education (1986). *Recommended readings in literature: Kindergarten through Grade Eight.*

Calkins, Lucy (1983). *Lessons from a child: On the teaching and learning of writing.* Exeter, NH: Heinemann.

Calkins, Lucy (1986). *The art of teaching writing.* Portsmouth, NH: Heinemann.

Cambourne, B. (1987). *Natural learning and literacy education.* Sydney, Australia: Ashton Scholastic.

Campbell, J. (1968). *The hero with a thousand faces* (2nd ed.). Princeton, NJ: Princeton University Press.

Caplan, R. (1984). *Writers in training: A guide to developing a composition program for language arts teachers.* Palo Alto, CA: Dale Seymour.

Cazden, C. (1988). *Classroom discourse.* Portsmouth, NH: Heinemann.

Davidson, J., & Wilkerson, B. (1988). *Directed reading-thinking activities.* Monroe, NY: Trillium Press.

Durkin, D. (1981). Reading comprehension instruction in five basal reader series. *Reading Research Quarterly, 16,* 515–544.

Gee, J. (1989) The narrativization of experience in the oral style. *Journal of Education, 171,* 75–96.

Gill, J., & Bear, D. (1988). No book, whole book, and chapter DRTAs. *Journal of Reading, 31,* 444–449.

Graves, D. (1989). *Experiment with fiction.* Portsmouth, NH: Heinemann.

Graves, M., Cooke, C., & LaBerge, M. (1983). Effects of previewing difficult short stories on low ability junior high school students' comprehension, recall, and attitudes. *Reading Research Quarterly, 18,* 262–276.

Graves, M., Prenn, M., & Cooke, C. (1985). The coming attraction: Previewing short stories. *Journal of Reading, 28,* 594–598.

Hansen, J. (1987). *When writers read.* Portsmouth, NH: Heinemann.

Heard, G. (1989). *For the good of the earth and sun: Teaching poetry.* Portsmouth, NH: Heinemann.

Heath, S. B. (1983). *Ways with words.* Cambridge, England: Cambridge University Press.

Henderson, E. (1981). *Learning to read and spell: The child's knowledge of words.* DeKalb, IL: Northern Illinois University Press.

Hepler, S. (1992). Picking our way to literacy in the classroom community. In C. Temple & P. Collins (Eds.), *Stories and readers: New perspectives on literature in the elementary classroom* (pp. 67–83). Norwood, MA: Christopher-Gordon.

Holdaway, D. (1986). Developmental model for language learning. In M. Sampson (Ed.), *The pursuit of literacy: Early reading and writing.* Dubuque, IA: Kendall/Hunt.

Irwin, J. (1991). *Teaching reading comprehension processes.* (2nd ed.) Englewood Cliffs, NJ: Prentice Hall.

Kittredge, W. (1992). The best that can be: The politics of storytelling. *Halcyon: A Journal of the Humanities, 14,* 1–16.

Lovell, J. (1992). Reader-response theory in the elementary classroom. In C. Temple & P. Collins (Eds.), *Stories and readers: New perspectives on literature in the elementary classroom* (pp. 15–31). Norwood, MA: Christopher-Gordon.

Lukens, R. (1990). *A critical handbook of children's literature* (4th ed.). Glenview, IL: Scott, Foresman/Little, Brown.

Madura, S. (1994). The line and texture of aesthetic response: Primary children study authors and illustrators. Manuscript submitted for publication.

Mandler, J. (1984). *Stories, scripts, and scenes: Aspects of a schema theory.* Hillsdale, NJ: Lawrence Erlbaum Associates.

Mandler, J., & Johnson, M. (1977). Remembrance of things parsed: Story structure and recall. *Cognitive Psychology, 9,* 111–151.

Moffett, J., & Wagner, B. (1991). *Student-centered language arts, K–12.* Portsmouth, NH: Boynton/Cook and Heinemann.

Morrow, L. (1989). *Developing literacy in the early years: Helping children read and write.* Englewood Cliffs, NJ: Prentice-Hall.

Nathan, R., Temple, F., Juntenen, K., & Temple, C. (1989). *Classroom strategies that work: An elementary teacher's guide to process writing.* Portsmouth, NH: Heinemann.

Pearson, P. D. (1984). Direct explicit teaching of reading comprehension. In G. Duffy, L. Roehler, & J. Mason (Eds.), *Comprehension instruction.* New York: Longman.

Pearson, P. D., & Johnson, D. (1978). *Teaching reading comprehension.* New York: Holt, Rinehart, and Winston.

Peterson, R., & Eeds, M. (1990). *Grand conversations.* Portsmouth, NH: Heinemann.

Plecha, J. (1992). The Great Books method of interpretive reading and discussion. In C. Temple & P. Collins (Eds.), *Stories and readers: New perspectives on literature in the elementary classroom* (pp. 103–114). Norwood, MA: Christopher-Gordon.

Purves, A., & Monson, D. (1984). *Experiencing children's literature.* Glenview, IL: Scott, Foresman.

Raphael, T. (1986). Teaching question-answer relationships revisited. *Reading Teacher, 40,* 516–522.

Raphael, T., & Pearson, P. D. (1982). *The effects of metacognitive awareness training on children's question-answering behavior* (Tech. Rep. No. 238). Urbana–Champaign: University of Illinois Center for the Study of Reading.

Rosenblatt, L. (1983). *Literature as exploration* (4th ed.). New York: Modern Language Association.

Routman, R. (1991). *Invitations: Changing as teachers and learners K–12.* Portsmouth, NH: Heinemann.

Samway, K., Whand, G., Cade, C., Gamil, M., Lubandina, M., & Phommachanh, K. (1991). Reading the skeleton, the heart, and the brain of a book: Students' perspectives on literature study circles. *Reading Teacher, 45,* 196–205.

Sleeter, C., & Grant, C. (1994). *Making choices for multicultural education: Five approaches to race, class, and gender* (2nd ed.). New York: Merrill.

Sloyer, S. (1982). *Readers Theatre: Story dramatization in the classroom.* Urbana, IL: National Council of Teachers of English.

Smith, F. (1988). *Understanding reading* (4th ed.). Hillsdale, NJ: Lawrence Erlbaum Associates.

Stein, N., & Glenn, C. (1977). An analysis of story comprehension in elementary school children. In R. O. Freedle (Ed.), *Multidisciplinary perspectives in discourse comprehension.* Hillsdale, NJ: Ablex.

Stewig, J. (1984). *Exploring language arts in the elementary classroom.* New York: Holt, Rinehart & Winston.

Temple, C., Nathan, R., Temple, F., & Burris, N. (1993). *The beginnings of writing* (3rd ed.). New York: HarperCollins.

Templeton, S. (1991). *Teaching the integrated language arts.* Boston: Houghton Mifflin.

Templeton, S., Cain, C., and Miller, J. (1981). Reconceptualizing readability: The relationship between surface and underlying structure analyses in predicting the difficulty of basal reading stories. *Journal of Educational Research, 74,* 382–387.

Thorndyke, P. W. (1977). Cognitive structures in comprehension and memory of narrative discourse. *Cognitive Psychology, 9,* 77–110.

Tompkins, G. (1994), Teaching writing (2nd ed.). New York: Merrill.

Watson, D., & Davis, S. (1988). Readers and texts in a fifth-grade classroom. In B. Nelms (ed.), *Literature in the classroom: Readers, texts, and contents* (pp. 59–67).

Urbana, IL: National Council of Teachers of English.

Weber, R., & Shake, M. (1988). Teachers' rejoinders to students' responses in reading lessons. *Journal of Reading Behavior, 52,* 421–445.

Zarrillo, J. (1991). Theory becomes practice: Aesthetic teaching with literature. *New Advocate, 4,* 221–234.

Children's Literature Cited

Babbitt, N. (1975). *Tuck everlasting.* Farrar, Straus, and Giroux.

Cleary, B. (1968). *Ramona the pest.* William Morrow.

Cohen, B. (1990). *Molly's pilgrim.* Bantam.

Hamilton, V. (1985). *The people could fly: American black folktales.* Alfred A. Knopf.

Jeffers, S. (1991). *Brother Eagle, Sister Sky.* Dial.

Leaf, M. (1936). *The story of Ferdinand.* Puffin.

LeGuin, U. (1988). *Catwings.* Orchard Books.

O'Dell, S. (1970). *Sing down the moon.* Houghton Mifflin.

Peck, R. (1968). *A day no pigs would die.* Knopf.

Rylant, C. (1985) *Every living thing.* Bradbury.

Soto, G. (1990). *Baseball in April.* Harcourt.

Speare, E. G. (1958). *The witch of Blackbird Pond.* Houghton Mifflin.

Van Allsburg, C. (1989). *Two bad ants.* Houghton Mifflin.

Yolen, J. (1990) *The Devil's arithmetic.* Viking Penguin.

CHAPTER SEVEN

CONSTRUCTING MEANING IN INFORMATIONAL TEXTS

FOCUS

■ *Distinguish between learning* information *and "learning* how *to learn."*

■ *How is the structure of* informational *texts different from the structure of* narrative *texts? What are the implications of this difference, for your teaching and for students' learning?*

■ *What is the role of* textbooks *in the different subject-matter areas?*

■ *How can informational trade books support and extend students' learning at all grade levels?*

■ *Why is it important to give equal attention to what happens before, during, and after students read informational texts? What strategies can you use to help students learn what to do before, during, and after their reading of informational texts?*

■ *How can discussion facilitate students' learning from informational texts? How can the discussion groups be structured?*

■ *How can you facilitate students' internalization of questioning as they read informational texts? How can questioning help them relate prior knowledge to the text being read?*

■ *What study strategies can be applied in "reading to remember"?*

■ *How can* writing *informational compositions facilitate students'* reading *of them?*

The process of learning how to learn—to formulate questions, read, and find an area of knowledge unique to yourself—eludes a majority of students over a lifetime.

Donald Graves, Investigate Nonfiction

Donald Graves frames one of our most fundamental missions as teachers. For decades, it seems, we have been trying to teach children the process of learning through *textbooks*. Textbooks defined what "learning" was and they defined the content to be learned. When textbooks seemed dull and were challenging to read—and because of the way so many teachers used them—many students "drifted away" after a while, never to return. The process began in the elementary grades and continued through high school. Most students, as Graves laments, never really *did* learn how to learn (1989, p. 90).

Students must learn how to read informational texts, but the genre is wide and rich, including but extending far beyond textbooks. Not only can textbooks themselves be made to "come alive"; there are many, many informational books and formats out there that are *not* textbooks. As we immerse our students in informational texts, we should never forget that we're engaging them in these texts so that they can learn and apply the content and ideas to a world beyond the books—in other words, so that they can *learn how to learn.*

In years past, many educators have distinguished between reading instruction in the *primary* grades and reading instruction in the *intermediate* grades, in terms of "learning to read" versus "reading to learn." The reasoning behind this distinction is easy enough to see—children develop the necessary literacy skills in the early grades and are able to apply them in the intermediate grades. We risk ignoring two important issues, however, if we interpret that distinction too literally. First, children *do* "read to learn" in the primary grades; we've already seen that this is always their underlying goal or purpose and can be the critical motivator in helping many children develop an interest in reading. Second, although students in the intermediate grades are reading more widely and can use reading as a critical reading tool, most of them still need specific instruction in when and how to do this. In this very important sense, "learning to read" is a *continuing* process, and as Graves suggests, plays a vital part in learning how to *learn.*

The "learning to read/reading to learn" distinction suggests another fundamental truth that we should bear in mind: while attention to meaning can and should be part of the instructional picture early on, young children need the *tools* that will enable them to focus on meaning independently in their own reading. This is why there is, for example, more emphasis on *words* and their structure in the primary years; "tools" are honed through natural development and with practice so that students become more proficient by the intermediate grades. In addition, because of their nature, very many informational materials encountered in the intermediate years (where much of the "reading to learn" occurs) *do* require more practice, ability, and skill. So there is a solid rationale for exploring them in more depth in the intermediate years, a time of students' rapid and significant growth in cognitive potential and vocabulary learning. Teaching students about these texts will be a crucial part of their overall immersion in and use of informational materials.

All our instruction, though, rests on the most fundamental point of all: If our students are reading and writing widely in the pursuit of questions *they* are interested in, they will be learning a lot along the way about the structure and strategies involved with informational texts. While reading in informational texts covers a lot of terrain, this reading should be, as much as possible, in the service of *learning* and of learning *how* to learn.

OVERVIEW OF CONSTRUCTING MEANING IN INFORMATIONAL TEXTS

Goals and purposes

The *main goal* toward which our instruction is oriented is that students be able to read and learn from informational texts *independently* (see Figure 7.1). A *subsidiary goal*—one that tells us if students are making progress toward our main goal—is that students be able to learn specific content material that meets a specific purpose in a particular text at a particular time.

Two specific *instructional purposes* are directed toward these goals:

1. Students must learn *about* materials written in informational formats.
2. Students must learn to use effective learning/thinking/reading strategies and activities in order to learn *from* informational materials, and they must learn how to use study skills to retain and remember from their reading of expository materials.

Each of these highly important instructional purposes will have its own major section in this chapter. "Understanding and Defining Informational Texts" (page 309) explores the format of information presented in different written texts, while "Learning How to Learn from Informational Texts" explores the "how to" of constructing and holding on to this information.

Here it should be helpful to pick up once again a distinction I made in Chapter 6: we are concerned with both the *process* and the *product* of reading informational texts. As applied to informational literacy, this represents a distinction between learning *how* to learn specific facts and content in general (the *process*) versus recalling these facts and content (the *product*). I'd like to elaborate a bit on this distinction:

- Our own main goal of being able to read and learn effectively from informational material reflects *process*—how we interact with informational texts. This main goal also represents our objective of helping students *learn how to learn*—and literacy skills and informational texts are important *tools* in this process.
- A subsidiary goal reflects *product,* the specific result of the process's having been applied to a specific informational text. This goal represents our objective of helping students *learn content* from informational texts.

Figure 7.1
Expository Reading Instruction: An Overview of Goals and Instructional Purposes

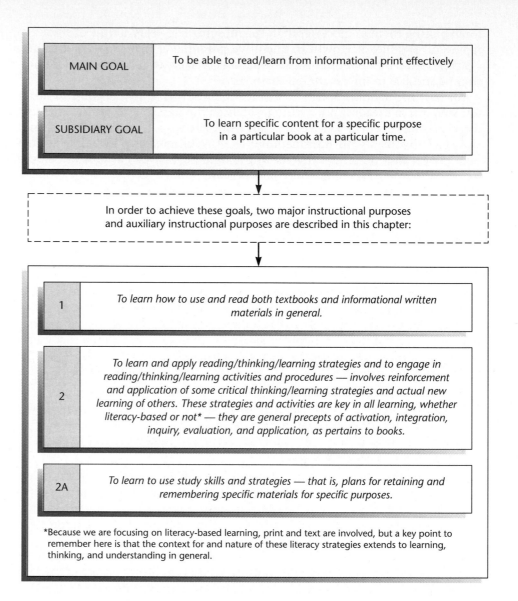

| MAIN GOAL | To be able to read/learn from informational print effectively |

| SUBSIDIARY GOAL | To learn specific content for a specific purpose in a particular book at a particular time. |

In order to achieve these goals, two major instructional purposes and auxiliary instructional purposes are described in this chapter:

| 1 | *To learn how to use and read both textbooks and informational written materials in general.* |

| 2 | *To learn and apply reading/thinking/learning strategies and to engage in reading/thinking/learning activities and procedures — involves reinforcement and application of some critical thinking/learning strategies and actual new learning of others. These strategies and activities are key in all learning, whether literacy-based or not* — they are general precepts of activation, integration, inquiry, evaluation, and application, as pertains to books.* |

| 2A | *To learn to use study skills and strategies — that is, plans for retaining and remembering specific materials for specific purposes.* |

*Because we are focusing on literacy-based learning, print and text are involved, but a key point to remember here is that the context for and nature of these literacy strategies extends to learning, thinking, and understanding in general.

MEANING MAKERS: You, the Reader and You, the Classroom Teacher

Learning Content or Learning How to Learn?

Henry James once observed, "What one knows is, in youth, of little moment; they know enough who know how to learn." His point is well taken. For a very long time in education, there has been a debate about the parts versus the whole, the product versus the process. We touched on that debate earlier in this text, most specifically in Chapter 2 when we looked at different models of reading and the types of instruction each implied. We will visit it again in Chapter 10 when we have a brief look at the history of reading instruction in North America. The debate concerns us, as teachers of informational literacy, because of our emphasis on using literacy as a "tool"; by its very nature, this metaphor implies an emphasis on *process*. This is why our *main* goal, as we've been discussing, is directed toward *process*, and the *subsidiary* goal is directed toward *product*.

It is necessary to know about and at least be acquainted with certain facts, of course, because such topic knowledge underlies our understanding of various disciplines and indeed of our world more generally. When the instructional balance tips too far in the direction of facts—the *product*—at the expense of process, however, then students are in effect forced to spend an inordinate amount of time on the least effective learning strategy of all: brute memorization. When this occurs, there is a very unfortunate loss of the appreciation if not the love of learning, and of the motivation that comes with it. Many argue that students get inherent satisfaction when they struggle to memorize a lot of information for a test, and that the very struggle takes on motivational value when they get a good grade on the test: they will memorize hard for the next test, and so forth. But what are students *really learning* in this process? Is any love of learning involved? Any love of the subject being studied? Is an exclusive reliance on this memorization or "cramming" process going to serve them well in the workplace? We know enough about short-term and long-term effects of learning to state that such an approach is the *least* effective way to learn specific facts and content (the *product*) and is an inherently defective *process*. Facts *are* important, but when most of us need specific facts, we need to have a strategy or process; that is, we need to know where to find the facts, because we can't carry everything in our heads.

When students know *how* to learn, they have a sense of ownership, of having a real stake in their own learning and their own expanding horizons. This sense comes not only from exploring content that is interesting (or rendered interesting by an effective teacher) but from the sense of enablement, downright *empowerment,* that students develop when they are shown strategies and "stances" for dealing with informational texts. The students realize that *they* are in control, rather than the subject or a textbook. They can learn how to "sample," to skim through, to get a sense of whether a particular text will provide what they need. And as we'll explore at points throughout this text, the consequences of this empowerment, as students navigate information networks and software on computers, are exciting and significant. ▪

Instructional experiences

Our basic instructional flow for informational literacy follows the same "guidance-to-release-of-control" format I presented in Chapter 6 when we discussed narrative reading. Embedded within a classroom environment in which students are immersed in purposeful and meaningful reading, instruction flows from your direct teaching/demonstrations/guidance/questioning through texts, on the one hand, to students' internalization of this instruction, on the other. But remember that this *is* a flow, so the instructional experiences that address the *process* and *product* of informational literacy often are interrelated. In the context of your demonstrating a particular strategy, for example, you will be modeling the process of asking appropriate questions so that this process and the *types* of questions become internalized, and at the same time you may be asking students to focus on finding and remembering certain facts.

In this section, we will look briefly at each type of instructional experience; and throughout this chapter, the nature of each type will be fleshed out comprehensively.

Instruction in the Primary Grades   Although, as I have already indicated, our predominant emphasis in this chapter will be on intermediate students, it will be worthwhile to first examine briefly how informational text can be embedded in a larger instructional context and discussed at the *primary* level. There will be more coverage of informational texts at the primary level in Chapter 9. Moreover, many of the basic tenets covered here in Chapter 7 certainly apply to the primary grades as well.

First, though, let's establish an important perspective. As we already know, children in the early grades are inherently curious. ("Where do stars come from? Why are all these worms on the sidewalk after it rains? How do space-shuttle astronauts use the bathroom?") Moreover, they have the drive to find things out. We help direct that drive by providing the right physical and social environment (we addressed this in Chapter 4 and will revisit it in Chapter 9). Before we go on, however, I must make a point about the role of textbooks at the primary grades: You will find textbooks helpful, and some second-graders and most third-graders can benefit from a discussion about how they're set up. *However,* it is a good idea to avoid getting overly analytical about how textbooks are set up and how kids should read them; in other words, don't require the kids to think about *how* they're going about this reading. Merely talk about the important features of the text; analysis and strategies will come later, in the intermediate grades.

Why shouldn't you get analytical with the younger children you teach? The reason is that from a developmental perspective, students are in either the "beginning reading" or the "transition" phase. Recall from Chapter 2 that they are not yet fluent readers, and effective teaching about and reading of textbooks really depends on readers who are more fluent rather than less.

So simply let most primary students "revel" in informational texts, enjoying them and using them to fit their own purposes. Have lots and lots of these texts around—for Sustained Silent Reading and for the projects the children will be doing. In other words, we should avoid getting too "metacognitive" about informational texts until the intermediate grades. In Chapter 9, we'll look at how you can prepare and teach integrated, theme-based units in the primary grades. For now, let's sketch a brief portrait of effective reading/writing/

discussion interactions between informational books and children in the primary grades.

Let's suppose that in your second-grade classroom, you have planned a two-week unit called "Your Body." You will be doing the following:

- Gathering lots of informational books
- Reading some of these books aloud to the children
- Setting up these books as resources available for children's browsing
- Having two health-care workers come in to talk with the children
- Using a life-sized plastic demonstration model of the upper body and head
- Showing several filmstrips
- Having the children trace each other's outlines on butcher paper
- Having the children cut out colored construction-paper organs to be pasted in the appropriate places within their body outlines
- Dissecting a beefheart (honest—it's a sure winner!)
- Asking the children to write in their journals their reactions to the various activities
- Discussing children's responses and observations and encouraging further reading

As you can see, an underlying theme will run throughout all of your projects related to the body. Children will be asking questions, and you will be engaging them in discussing ways to generate hypotheses and search for answers. Let's examine a few of these activities in greater detail.

Read-Alouds Some informational picture books may be read with discussion and commentary, and others may be read straightforwardly with little comment. The criterion for deciding, however, is not the book but your class. How much will your students discuss as the book is read? How much background knowledge do they have? (How much will they "invent" on the spot?!) One of your read-alouds could be *The Skeleton Inside You,* by Philip Balestrino (illustrated by True Kelley), which begins, "On Halloween I wore a skeleton costume. I used to think skeletons were made up just to scare people. Now I know that skeletons are real. They are not scary. I would not be me without a skeleton. You would not be you."

A book that may occasion some discussion, because of both content and excellent illustrations and diagrams, is *The Human Body and How It Works,* by Giovanni Caselli. From the first section, "The Body Machine," kids are engaged. Different areas of the body are cleverly labeled: the brain is "Your central control room"; the section labeled "Sending blood around" is about the heart; "Your body's transportation system" describes blood, arteries, and veins. And the potentially giggle-guaranteed discussion about waste and where it goes is handled rather cleverly.

Preparing for the First Health-Care Worker Visit Having some basic information under their belts, the children will brainstorm questions they'd like to ask the health-care worker. This is an excellent opportunity to talk about preparing for *interviews;* you will have tied this in, by the way, with children interviewing each other and then interviewing someone at home (see "Writing as a Means of Learning from Informational Text", p. 359).

Journal Writing, Sharing, and Further Reading   After the visit, you'll have the children write in their journals what they remember. Because they were ready with genuine questions prior to the visit, they will all recall at least one interesting point. Afterward, share these observations in discussion; other questions may come up, which the children can pursue with the next visitor *and* through sources you have made available.

You have established a read-write-share-discuss cycle here (Avery, 1987; Calkins, 1991). As children talk about their reading and write in their journals about their ideas, you will be asking "How do you know this? Why is it important?" (Avery, 1987, p. 613). Toward the end of your "Your Body" unit, you can ask the children to read through their journal entries and then write a little piece about the body, telling about the most important idea they had or about the most interesting information they learned (*The Important Book,* by Margaret Wise Brown, is excellent for modeling the literary style that might be most appropriate). This brief composition will be written with a definite audience in mind—fellow students, probably, but perhaps parents as well, and even the health-care workers (who will be delighted with how much additional information your students pulled together and made sense of).

Beginning in the primary grades, therefore, children will be engaged in learning, and in reading informational texts, with a definite *purpose*. Thanks to you, they will also see reading and writing as important tools. There is no finer motivation than this, and it should begin early.

Instruction in the Intermediate Grades

Direct Teaching   In the last chapter, we explored direct teaching in some depth. Having laid the foundation for direct teaching in that chapter, let's move immediately to looking at the contexts and rationale for the direct teaching you will be doing in informational texts.

Again, for many years too many teachers assumed that because students had "learned how to read," they could automatically read informational texts—textbooks in particular. This assumption included the belief that students just had to apply themselves more or pay more attention as they read in order to "get" the information in the text. As a consequence, students were not only having difficulty "getting" information from texts, they were developing lifelong *negative* attitudes toward textbooks and other informational texts.

In informational reading, most students will require some type of direct and deliberate guidance in both process and product. We will demonstrate; we will walk students through texts as necessary; and we will model how to locate, examine, and use informational texts, depending on different purposes. Often one demonstration will be enough for a particular text and task; at other times we will need to walk through the steps of the direct teaching format several times before we and the students realize we can release the control to them, "dismantle the scaffolding," because the skill or strategy is now well constructed and secure.

Guided Reading   We will soon explore in considerable depth the structure of informational texts. They are not narratives, and we usually need to address this difference head-on with students. This is why guided reading is so important with informational materials. Even when students have been immersed in informational texts in the primary grades and enjoy them, as intermediate students they will need guidance in how to select, read, and use these texts more deliberately. You will be their best guide to this type of knowledge.

Internalization of Knowledge and Strategies   As intermediate students engage in different types of informational reading, we try to ensure that they'll independently apply the knowledge and strategies we have been deliberately modeling and through which we have been guiding them. These opportunities exist in the context of purposeful questions and projects the students will be pursuing. The internalization will occur through lots of "time in the saddle" with informational reading and tasks.

Relationship of Questioning to the Instructional Flow   Questioning is an important constant throughout all our different instructional experiences. We help students become independent questioners in their own reading: help them learn how to ask questions, answer questions, and use questions as important independent learning tools. There is an art to asking good questions, and we'll attempt to make questioning "artists" of the students we instruct. Figure 7.2 shows the way effective questioning grows out of a number of experiences; students come to feel "ownership" of the process of questioning. And with experience, many of these question types can become "automated" and be at work as students read and reflect on informational texts.

UNDERSTANDING AND DEFINING INFORMATIONAL TEXTS

Informational texts come in many different formats and styles. They include many kinds of trade books as well as textbooks and a range of other specialized informational texts: reference books, brochures, advertisements, phone books, and even bus schedules, to name just a few. How do these fit into children's learning in the elementary grades? In the first major section below, we will examine several different informational-text formats and will highlight specific lists of books for specific content areas.

A hallmark of informational texts is their internal organizing structures and features, which differ from those of stories. There is usually a great deal "going on" in informational texts, and students need to be taught how to find their way through it. Otherwise, they are quite likely to pick up a textbook or other type of informational text and read it just as they would read a story—from beginning to end. So in the second major section below, we will examine the structures, concept loads, and pedagogical features of certain informational texts.

Our third major section will deal with the topic of readability, an important concept that influences our exploration of texts and of the prior knowledge of our students.

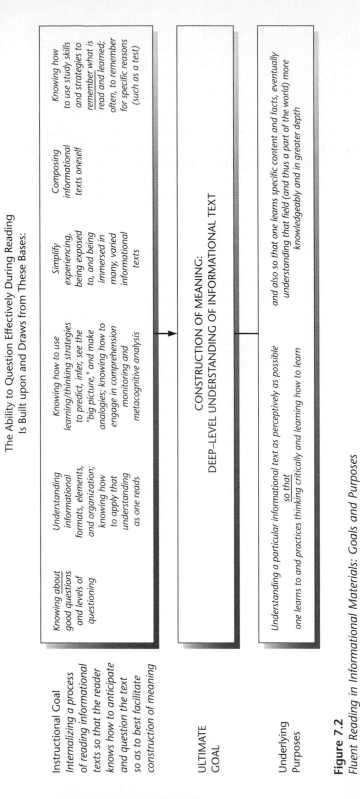

Figure 7.2
Fluent Reading in Informational Materials: Goals and Purposes

Formats

Textbooks   Think about it—when *you* pick up a textbook, for example, do you skim through, glancing at the diagrams and perhaps examining them briefly? Or do you skip the diagrams and want to get on with the reading? Do you *ever* look at the diagrams? Do you feel you probably *should* read introductory and summary sections or paragraphs—but tend to avoid doing it? Just how *do* you go about "reading" informational text?

We have two main responsibilities in teaching our students about textbooks. First, we help them understand *how* textbooks are organized—their format and the way they organize information. Second, we will help them understand how to *use* textbooks and relate the information they contain to the broader learning context.

In the type of classroom we would like to establish, textbooks will be only one of the information sources for our students. Still, we have the responsibility of making sure the children we teach really understand how textbooks work. They'll surely have teachers later on who will place a *lot* of emphasis on the textbook—who will tell them, "Read Chapter 14 because we will have a test on it on Friday."

Moore and his colleagues (1986) offer a "freeway" metaphor for explaining the role of textbooks, a metaphor that many students can understand readily: Like a freeway, a textbook can take you very rapidly through a major area. If you *really* want to examine the landscape, though, you have to get off the freeway and onto a side road, where you can slow down and examine things more closely before getting back on the freeway and zipping off to other topics. This is one very important reason why we bring in all kinds of information sources for our students; they can always see and appreciate more of the country if they can get onto side roads, those *other* avenues offered by informational trade books and other information sources. Let's briefly consider some of these sources.

Informational Trade Books   As mentioned earlier, the designation *trade book* simply refers to any books that are not school textbooks. A trade book is published by the trade division of a publishing house, rather than by its school division, or published by a company that produces only trade books. Picture books and nonfiction trade books breathe life into various subject areas. They allow students the opportunity to take off in specific realms of interest. Picture books for both primary and intermediate levels *do* have accompanying text, but the illustrations are their most obvious feature. They are a marvelous means of catching students' attention and interesting them in many, many topics.

To give yourself a taste of the possibilities offered by nonfiction tradebooks, refer to Figure 7.3. Marilyn Burns's delightful and engaging *The I Hate Mathematics! Book,* illustrated by Martha Hairston, has become a classic since it was first published in 1975. It demonstrates to children that math is much, much more than the laborious computational tasks they usually associate with it. David Macaulay's *The Way Things Work* is a masterpiece of scientific description and explanation. It presents straightforward text interspersed with a humorous, tongue-in-cheek, ongoing narrative that delightfully underscores major scien-

Figure 7.3
Examples of Informational Trade Books

tific concepts—from levers to holograms to computer chips—through the adventures and exploits of mammoths (and all this *is* hard to visualize, much less appreciate, until you see and read the book!).

Books for Specific Content Areas   Let's look briefly at the nature of the different domains in the elementary curriculum. At the conclusion of our discussion of these domains, I will offer some representative trade books, organized by specific content areas, that develop concepts and understandings in those areas. Note that picture books are indicated in brackets. Most of the books listed, by the way, have also been published in paperbacks that not only are less expensive but often are available through children's book clubs (such as Scholastic, Troll, Trophy, or Trumpet) that you will be using in your class.

Social Studies   The area of "social studies" comprises a broad array of emphases or subjects—history and geography, government, sociology—all having to do with relationships among people, in the past or at the present time. Social studies include learning about noteworthy individuals *and* about the "human-

Distinguishing Fictional from Nonfictional Texts

Even at the primary grade levels, most students at least *tacitly* grasp the difference between fiction—usually stories—and nonfiction. But by talking about these differences with them, we can help them bring this "feel" to a conscious level. Begin by exploring the difference between fantasy and reality. Compare and contrast an obvious fantasy with a real-life story: the titles may offer clues, and usually the language will offer some also. Of course the content—what is going on in each story—will likewise be apparent.

The next instructional step is to explore two texts, one fictional and one factual, about the same topic. Read each of them aloud to the students, showing with your voice how the sound and substance of the texts differ. Discuss how the two pieces are alike and how they are different. Discuss the different purposes authors may have for writing a fictional or a nonfictional piece. Discuss ways in which the two texts *look* different. Talk about the kinds of books in which you would find articles—informational or nonfictional pieces—and the kinds of books in which you would find stories (Goodman & Burke, 1980).

LEARNING IN CONTEXT: Children become aware of the differences between fictional and nonfictional texts by *experiencing* them first, then stepping back to think explicitly about the differences.

ness" of these individuals. As Milton Meltzer, noted writer of historical books for young people, has written:

> After all, what is history but the coherent story of the lives of people of the past? And not just of the empire builders, but people very much like themselves . . . young readers find those timeless constants which all persons and societies share: sorrow and happiness, success and defeat, effort and reward, effort and failure, love and hatred, guilt, shame, pride, compassion, cruelty, justice, injustice, birth, death. Everywhere you look, no matter what the time or place, you find these great fixed elements. (1993, pp. 28–29)

Getting involved in social studies means examining our beliefs about people and groups and our relationships with them. As Hyde and Bizar observe, often children's understandings "may be deeply and firmly rooted in *feelings* and not particularly grounded in accurate information" (1989, p. 166, emphasis added). This can result in *stereotyping* and *simplifications* (Gardner, 1991). Your selection of informational trade books and your students' immersion in them will ensure that accurate information is provided. Don't forget the role of *stories* in providing this information; when studying different *continents,* for example, children can be shown how the different *cultures* of those continents are revealed through their own stories. Textbooks simply cannot represent and develop adequately many complex issues and fascinating information the way informational trade books can.

Science   The domains of science are incredibly broad: physics, chemistry, biology, astronomy, and each of these is subdivided into more specific areas. In the elementary grades, our first objective is to help children develop a particular way of *observing,* and of *thinking about* what they observe. (These skills can also become part of their approach to writing narratives and informational pieces). Our second objective is to help children develop a basic understanding about fundamental processes at work in the natural world. Of course, in attempting to achieve these objectives, we also help students acquire or construct a fair amount of information that has grown out of centuries of scientific investigation. Students at *all* ages entertain a number of *mis*conceptions about scientific phenomena. For example, even most middle-grade students still believe that the differences among seasons has to do with how far the earth is from the sun—it's farther away, they think, during the winter than during the summer. This belief persists despite their ability to answer correctly a question about the angle at which sunlight reaches the earth.

Your direct and nondirective teaching of science will of course be addressing the two main objectives I've just mentioned and will help students reconcile their "intuitive" understandings about how the natural world works with the understandings that scientific inquiry has produced. But much of the groundwork and motivation for investigating scientific phenomena can be established through the informational trade books your students will explore.

Mathematics   As "The Rabbit and the Mathematicians" points out on p. 311, mathematics has two domains: *theoretical,* or "pure," and *applied.* Applied mathematics—the focus of our instruction in the elementary grades—has to do with using mathematics to explain, understand, and deal with the physical world. We usually begin with the concrete and move toward the abstract. For example, presenting the terms and the definitions of the *associative, commutative,* and *distributive* properties should come well *after* students have explored concrete examples of these properties. (And it should go without saying that *why* an understanding of these properties is important and how they can be applied in real life should also be addressed). You will find that the trade books about math recommended on page 318 develop mathematical concepts in an engaging, concrete-to-abstract fashion.

Art and Music   We have always given short shrift to art and music in our elementary schools. This is hardly the place, of course, to explore the reasons for and the consequences of this shortcoming. I do wish to point out, however, that you will have innumerable opportunities to involve your students in art and music as these domains relate to, support, and enrich the children's reading experiences and your thematic units (see Chapter 9).

Art and music are "alternative" ways of knowing, of comprehending, and of understanding our world. They tap intuitive, nonlinguistic recesses in our minds and souls. Therefore, they very powerfully bring the affective component to the construction of our cognitive schemata. Musical intelligence appears to be a unique form of intelligence, as Gardner has pointed out (see Chapter 2), and art incorporates the spatial and the bodily/kinesthetic intelligences.

Having said all this, it might seem just a trifle ironic to return to *books* as a means of exploring art and music. The books recommended on pages 318–319, however, are just a sample of those that can help children think about, appreciate, and even try these modes of expression. There is considerable overlap in age-appropriateness among the books; for this reason, I have not separated that category into primary and intermediate, as I did with the other content areas.

BUILDING YOUR KNOWLEDGE BASE
Books for Specific Content Areas

Social Studies

Primary

Adler, D. A. (1989). *A picture book of Martin Luther King, Jr.* Holiday.

Bahr, A. C. (1986). *It's OK to say no: A book for parents and children to read together.* Grosset & Dunlap.

Bernstein, J. E., & Gullo, S. V. (1977). *When people die.* Dutton.

Costabel, E. D. (1988). *The Jews of New Amsterdam.* Atheneum.

Fritz, J. (1973). *Will you sign here, John Hancock?* Coward.

Girard, L. W. (1985). *Who is a stranger and what should I do?* Whitman. [Picture book.]

Haskins, J. S. (1975). *The picture life of Malcolm X.* Watts.

Knowlton, J. (1985). *Maps and globes.* Crowell.

Rosenberg, M. (1984). *Being adopted.* Lothrop.

Spier, P. (1987). *We the people: The Constitution of the United States of America.* Doubleday.

Tobias, T. (1975). *Arthur Mitchell.* Crowell.

Turner, D. (1986). *The man-made wonders of the world.* Dillon Press/International Picture Library.

Intermediate

Abells, C. B. (1986). *The children we remember.* New York: Greenwillow.

Ashabranner, B. (1988). *Always to remember: The story of the Vietnam Veterans' Memorial.* Dodd, Mead.

Asimov, I. (1965). *The Greeks: A great adventure.* Houghton Mifflin.

Ballard, R. D. (1988). *Exploring the Titanic.* Scholastic/Madison.

Banfield, S. (1989). *The rights of man, the reign of terror.* Lippincott.

Finkelstein, N. (1989). *The other 1492: Jewish settlement in the New World.* Scribners.

Fisher, L. E. (1988). *Pyramid of the sun, pyramid of the moon*. Macmillan.

Freedman, R. (1980). *Immigrant kids*. Dutton.

Highwater, J. (1978). *Many smokes, many moons: A chronology of American Indian history*. Lippincott.

Gardner, R. A. (1971). *The boys and girls book about divorce*. Bantam.

Kaufman, C., & Kaufman, G. (1988). *Hotel boy*. Atheneum. [Homelessness.]

Knowlton, J. (1988). *Geography from A to Z: A picture history*. Crowell. [Picture book.]

LeShan, E. (1984). *Grandparents: A special kind of love*. Macmillan.

Levy, E. (1987). *. . . If you were there when they signed the Constitution*. Scholastic.

Lindstrom, A. J. (1980). *Sojourner Truth: Slave, abolitionist, fighter for women's rights*. Messner.

Mango, K. N. (1984). *Mapmaking*. Mesner.

Meltzer, M. (1987). *The American revolutionaries: A history in their own words*. Crowell.

Meltzer, M. (1990). *The Bill of Rights: How we got it and what it means*. Harper-Collins.

Turner, G. T. (1989). *Take a walk in their shoes*. Cobblehill.

Weitzman, D. (1975). *My backyard history book*. Little, Brown.

Stanley, F. (1991). *The last princess: The story of Princess Ka'iulani of Hawaii*. Four Winds.

Science

Primary

Aliki. (1981). *Digging up dinosaurs*. Crowell.

Aliki. (1979). *Mummies made in Egypt*. Crowell.

Baker, J. (1987). *Where the forest meets the sea*. Greenwillow. [Picture book.]

Anno, M. (1985). *Anno's sundial*. Philomel. [A pop-up book.]

Asimov, I. (1987). *How did we find out about sunshine?* Walker.

Berger, M. (1986). *Germs make me sick*. Harper.

Branley, F. M. (1985). *Mysteries of outer space*. Dutton.

Branley, F. M. (1986). *What makes day and night*. Crowell.

Branley, F. M. (1988). *Tornado alert*. Crowell. [Picture book.]

Carle, E. (1969). *The very hungry caterpillar*. Putnam. [Picture book.]

Carrick, D. (1986). *Milk*. Greenwillow. [Picture book.]

Cherry, L. (1990). *The kapok tree*. Harcourt. [Picture book.]

Cole, J. (1987). *Evolution*. Crowell.

Cole, J. (1987). *The magic school bus inside the earth*. Scholastic. [Picture book.]

Gibbons, G. (1988). *Sunken treasure*. Crowell. [Picture book. Gibbons has done many other excellent nonfiction picture books.]

Gibbons, G. (1987). *Weather forecasting.* Four Winds.

Heller, R. (1981). *Chickens aren't the only ones.* Grossett & Dunlap. [Picture book.]

Hirschi, R. (1987). *What is a bird?* Walker. [Picture book.]

Jeunesse, G., & deBourgoing. *The ladybug and other insects* and other books in the "First Discovery" series. Scholastic.

Parsons, A. (1990). *Amazing spiders.* Knopf. [Picture book. This excellent book is in a series that includes snakes, birds, and mammals.]

Patent, D. H. (1980). *The lives of spiders.* Holiday.

Patent, D. H. (1987). *Dolphins and porpoises.* Holiday.

Patterson, F. (1985). *Koko's kitten.* Scholastic. [Picture book. Koko, a gorilla, learns sign language.]

Peters, L. W. (1988). *The sun, the wind, and the rain.* Holt. [Picture book.]

Pigdon, K., & Woolley, M. (1989). *Earthworms.* Modern Curriculum. [Picture book.]

Ride, S. (1986). *To space and back.* Lothrop.

Siebert, D. (1988). *Mojave.* Crowell.

Simon, S. (1988). *Volcanoes.* Morrow.

Simon, S. (1979). *Animal fact/animal fable.* Crown. [Picture book.]

Simon, S. (1985). *Meet the computer.* New York: Crown. [Picture book.]

"Zoo" Books. Scholastic. [Each book focuses on a specific animal.]

Intermediate

Asimov, I. (1987). *How did we find out about the brain?* Walker.

Dolan, E. F. (1985). *Great mysteries of the ice and snow.* Dodd, Mead.

Elting, M. (1986). *The Macmillan book of the human body.* Macmillan.

Gallant, R. (1986). *The Macmillan book of astronomy.* Macmillan.

George, J. C. (1984). *One day in the Alpine tundra.* Crowell.

Giblin, J. C. (1986). *Milk: The fight for purity.* Crowell.

Giblin, J. C. (1990). *The riddle of the Rosetta stone: Key to ancient Egypt.* Crowell.

Grillone, L., & Gennaro, J. (1978). *Small things close up.* Crown.

Hoffman, S. M. (1985). *What's under that rock?* Atheneum.

Johnson, E. (1985). *People, love, sex, and families: Answers to questions that preteens ask.* Walker.

Johnson, S. A. (1985). *Bats.* Lerner.

Johnson, S. A. (1985). *Wolf pack: Tracking wolves in the wild.* Lerner.

Kohl, J., & Kohl, H. (1977). *View from the oak: The private worlds of other creatures.* Sierra Club/Scribner's.

Lauber, P. (1986). *Volcano: The eruption and healing of Mount St. Helens.* Bradbury.

Maurer, R. (1985). *The NOVA space explorer's guide: Where to go and what to see*. Potter.

McLaughlin, M. (1986). *Earthworms, dirt, and rotten leaves: An exploration in ecology*. Atheneum.

Patent, D. H. (1985). *Thoroughbred horses*. Holiday.

Reed, D. C. (1986). *Sevengill: the shark and me*. Knopf.

Sattler, R. (1988). *Hominids: A look back at our ancestors*. Lothrop.

Settel, J., & Baggett, N. (1985). *Why does my nose run? (and other questions kids ask about their bodies)*. Atheneum.

Mathematics

Primary

Adler, I., & Irving, R. (1969). *Sets and numbers for the very young*. John Day.

Anno, M. (1987). *Anno's math games*. Philomel.

Carle, E. (1974). *My very first book of shapes*. Crowell.

Dennis, J. R. (1971). *Fractions are parts of things*. Crowell.

Emberly, B. (1966). *One wide river to cross*. Prentice.

Feelings, M. (1971). *Moja means one: The Swahili counting book*. Dial.

Mahy, M. (1987). *17 kings and 42 elephants*. Dial.

Schwartz, D. M. (1985). *How much is a million?* Lothrop.

Tompert, A. (1990). *Grandfather Tang's story*. Crown.

Wildsmith, B. (1965). *Brian Wildsmith's one, two, threes*. Watts.

Wong, H. H., & Vessel, M. F. (1969). *My ladybug*. Addison-Wesley.

[See also Marilyn Burns's *Math and literature (K–3)*. (1992). Math Solutions Publications.]

Intermediate

Asimov, I. (1973). *How did we find out about numbers?* Walker and Company.

Burns, M. (1992). *Math for smarty pants: Or who says mathematicians have little pig eyes*. Little, Brown.

Burns, M. (1975). *The I hate mathematics book*. Little, Brown.

Nozaki, A. (1985). *Anno's hat tricks*. Philomel. [Illustrated by Mitsumasa Anno.]

St. John, G. (1975). *How to count like a Martian*. Watch.

Art

Aliki. (1986). *How a book is made*. Harper.

Arnosky, J. (1982). *Drawing from nature*. Lothrop.

Bjork, C. (1985). *Linnea in Monet's garden*. R&S.

Brown, L. K., & Brown, M. (1986). *Visiting the art museum*. Dutton.

Fine, J. (1979). *I carve stone*. Crowell.

Fischer, L. E. (1982). *Alphabet art: Thirteen ABC's from around the world*. Four Winds. [Picture book.]

Goffstein, M. B. (1983). *Lives of the artists*. Harper.

Graham, A. (1976). *Fossils, ferns and fish scales: A handbook of art and nature projects*. Four Winds.

Irvine, J. (1987). *How to make pop-ups*. Morrow.

Nygren, T. (1988). *The red thread*. Farrar. [Picture book.]

Ventura, P. (1984). *Great painters*. Putnam.

Zaidenberg, A. (1971). *How to draw and compose pictures*. Harper.

Music

Arnold, C. (1985). *Music lessons for Alex*. Clarion. [Picture book.]

Berliner, D. C. (1961). *All about the orchestra and what it plays*. Random House.

Bierhorst, J. (1979). *A cry from the earth: Music of the North American Indians*. Four Winds.

Fox, D., & Marks, C. (1987). *Go in and out the window: An illustrated songbook for young people*. Metropolitan Museum of Art/Holt.

Haskins, J. (1987). *Black music in America*. Crowell.

Hawkinson, J., & Faulhaber, M. (1969). *Music and instruments for children to make*. Niles, IL: Whitman.

Kuskin, K. (1982). *The Philharmonic gets dressed*. Harper.

Paxton, A. K. (1986). *Making music*. Atheneum. [Picture book.]

Previn, A. (1983). *André Previn's guide to the orchestra*. Putnam.

Terkel, S. (1975). *Giants of jazz*. Crowell.

Newspapers and Magazines   These very common types of informational materials usually should be a staple of our classrooms. Let's discuss each type in turn.

Newspapers are an excellent vehicle for applying the different skills and strategies you have been teaching (Cheyney, 1984). They deal with the students' communities and are as current as printed material can get. Because of this they usually are inherently interesting to late-primary and intermediate students, and therefore motivational.

Main idea/topic and supporting-detail instruction can be given and reinforced through a newspaper. Students examine how a headline is developed by successive paragraphs in the story or article (telling *who, what, where, when*, and often *why* and *how*). Different informational patterns such as cause/effect, collection/sequence, problem/solution, and so forth are also evident and can be identified and discussed (see below). Locational skills can be applied on a small scale as students use the index to locate, for example, weather reports and entertainment information.

As we'll soon explore, *manipulative language* can be identified and discussed as it occurs in the newspaper. Newspapers provide excellent contexts for distinguishing fact from opinion (see below): facts are usually presented, without opinions being expressed, in news stories. Opinion, as well as manipulative language, is clearly evident in advertisements. Opinion also is expressed through editorials and letters to the editor, as well as in columns in various sections of the paper.

Students often want to write and publish their own newspaper, so their explorations of the structure and character of a regular newspaper can transfer to their own creative efforts. Of course, reading skills are being reinforced as students think about *how* different features of the newspaper are written. Figure 7.4 shows part of a newspaper that a multi-age fourth/fifth/sixth-grade class published; these versions of the *Boston Observer* and the *Philadelphia Inquirer* were part of their unit on Revolutionary America.

Magazines are almost as current as newspapers but also are *visually* more engaging. Many magazines are published for elementary students, and most include coverage of topics that are of keen interest to them and can fit quite effectively into the curriculum (Stoll, 1994). Following is a partial list.

BUILDING YOUR KNOWLEDGE BASE

Newspapers and Magazines for Students

Audubon Adventures
> 613 Riversville Road
> Greenwich, CT 06831
> [A newspaper focused on the environment and ecology.]

Cobblestone
> 28 Main Street
> Peterborough, NH 03458
> [The focus is history for intermediate students.]

Sports Illustrated for Kids
> P.O. Box 830606
> Birmingham, AL 35282-9487

3-2-1 Contact
> E = MC Square
> P.O. Box 51177
> Boulder, CO 80322-1177
> [Explores the same themes as the Children's Television Workshop program of the same name—primarily science-related, but interesting mathematics themes also are explored.]

National Geographic World
> 8925 Leesburg Pike
> Vienna, VA 22184

Owl Magazine
> P.O. Box 11314
> Des Moines, IA 50340
> [Addresses many different issues of general interest to elementary-age students.]

BOSTON OBSERVER

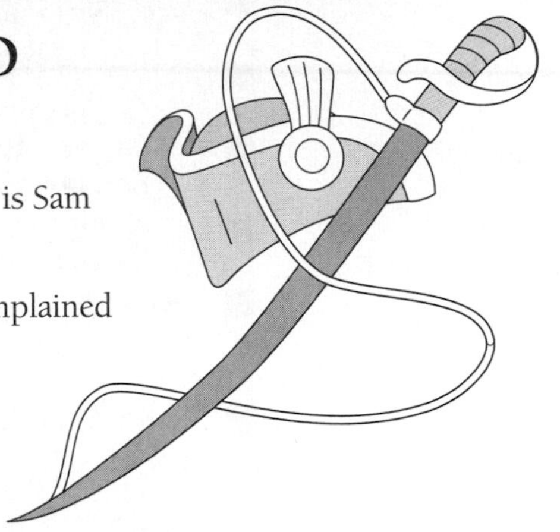

TAX BOYCOTTED: TEA DUMPED

December 16, 1773   Boston

All the English tea has been dumped into the harbor. With me is Sam Adams, politician, and anti-English spokesperson.

"The plan was followed better than expected. Many people complained about the tea tax, but we did something about it!" he said.

The rampage started when Sam Adams said, "This meeting can do no more to save the country."

That was the signal for hundreds of "Indians" to overtake the tea boats. Now all of the tea rests safely on the bottom of Boston Harbor.

PENNSYLVANIA GAZETTE

THE BILL OF RIGHTS

Philadelphia, Pennsylvania   December 15, 1791

The Bill of Rights have been ratified. It is the first ten amendments to the Constitution. Amendments change the Constitution. The first shows that congress may not take away peoples rights. Number two says we may have guns. Number three says in peace time government may not force citizens into taking soldiers into their homes. Number four says people or homes may not be searched without reason. Number five says people in court can't be forced to give evidence about themselves and they can't be tried again for the same crime. Number six says people charged in serious crimes have the right for a speedy trial. Number seven says in most cases there is a right to a jury trial. Number eight says punishment may not be cruel and unusual. Number nine and ten say if the Constitution does not give a certain right to the United States and doesn't forbid the states to have that right, the state may have the right.

Now, with the Bill of Rights ratified, Rhode Island and North Carolina will be officially a part of the new country.

Figure 7.4
Class Version of the Boston Observer *and the* Philadelphia Inquirer

Ranger Rick
> 1412 16th Street NW
> Washington, D.C. 20036-2266

Kids Discover
> P.O. Box 54206
> Boulder, CO 80323-4206

Because of their representation of contemporary cultures, both newspapers and magazines are an excellent means of helping students who are new arrivals to the country and whose native language is not English to learn about their new home as they acquire competence in English as a second language (Olivares, 1993).

MEANING MAKERS: You, the Reader

Detecting Manipulative Language

All of us need to understand *how* language can be used on us. In everything from commercials to politics to public policy, language can be used to manipulate. In fact, such use of language—once referred to as "propaganda"—is now increasingly referred to as the "manipulative arts." Most of your intermediate students are capable of learning about manipulative language. The beginning awareness of it lies in distinguishing fact from opinion. Once students grasp this basic understanding, they can explore and be intrigued by how language is used to persuade them to think in certain ways and to do certain things.

Fact vs. Opinion. The best way of deciding which a statement is expressing, fact or opinion, is to *test* the statement. Can you *check* its truth or falsity? Let's try some clearcut examples:

> A ChippieChoc candy bar weighs two ounces.
>
> ChippieChoc candy bars are yummier than BigSticky candy bars.
>
> BigSticky candy bars are manufactured in Duluth, Minnesota.
>
> Duluth, Minnesota, is more fun to live in than Tucson, Arizona.
>
> More ChippieChoc candy bars are sold in Tucson, Arizona, than in Duluth, Minnesota.

Statements such as these, because they really *are* clearcut, are good to begin with in exploring "fact versus opinion" with intermediate students. You can discuss with them how each of these statements could be tested or checked out. Is "yummy," for example, something that can be weighed or measured? Not really. . . . And how about "fun"? How can you really determine to everyone's agreement whether a place is "more fun" than another place? How can you measure "funness"? On the other hand, you *can* test how much a ChippieChoc candy bar weighs, and you can verify whether BigStickies are manufactured in Duluth.

Techniques of Language Manipulation. Language, in conjunction with certain situations and individuals, can indeed be employed to influence us in subtle ways. It is extremely important that students be aware of this and that they learn about and identify different manipulative techniques. "Propaganda," as it most often is called, often works at cross-purposes with critical, reflective thinking.

Students in the upper elementary grades can learn to identify and analyze different categories or types of manipulative techniques. Frequently there is overlap among these categories. What is paramount is that students be aware that language can be used to influence opinion and judgments. And by being aware, they are in a much better position to make decisions for themselves. Following are descriptions of four types of manipulative techniques. Although there are more categories of propaganda than these (Templeton, 1991), these four are the ones to which upper elementary students can relate most concretely and which most often are used on them.

Bandwagon. This technique appeals to students' natural and sometimes desperate desire to be accepted and to belong. They don't want to be left behind while the bandwagon moves on, with everyone on board having a wonderful and exciting time. The message is something like this: *"Everyone* is wearing this particular brand of jeans or that particular brand of athletic shoes. If you don't have them, you'll really be left out!"

Positive Association. This technique is quite simple: bring together whatever you want to sell and someone or something that is attractive and desirable to your audience. Beer commercials are perhaps the best example: on the beach or in the ski lodge, extraordinarily beautiful young people are obviously having an incredibly good time amidst coolers of ice-cold beer; young men and women gaze intently, seductively, at each other from behind a can or glass of beer. The implication is that there is a cause/effect relationship: if you drink this brand of beer, you can be in this picture! Of course these commercials are aimed at a segment of the population that the beer companies believe wants to party seriously. The associations are extremely positive, and the voice-over really doesn't have to say much—indeed, it's usually nonexistent.

Testimonial. This is a classic technique. A well-known personality endorses a particular product. Because So-and-So eats a particular cereal, wears a particular watch, or subscribes to a particular long-distance phone company, *we* are supposed to want to do likewise, so as to be more like that person. And just maybe, *we* will grow up to be famous basketball players or actors, too! In addition, there is often the appeal of *trust.* A particular individual, for whatever reason, seems especially trustworthy to us; so if he or she in turn trusts a particular product, we may do so as well.

Deck-Stacking. This is a very common and *very* subtle technique. The information you are given is indeed true—but you aren't given *all* the information: "You can lose up to forty pounds in two weeks on our SlimJim diet." Well, yes; but the ad does *not* mention that people who have lost that much weight not only were on the SlimJim diet but worked out in a gym for an average of four hours a day.

In contemporary society there is an increasingly somber yet compelling reason why we need to help elementary students understand manipulation through language and situation. Remember, manipulation is not only in the advertising world; children will be exposed to it in *social* situations as well. It is a reality that today's children are required to make certain choices that previous generations rarely or never had to make at the same age, and they are required to make these decisions earlier than we might wish. In the intermediate grades, for example, many children are having to make decisions about sexual activity and about drugs. By helping your students to analyze the logic (or lack of it) underlying manipulative techniques, you will provide them with invaluable or even lifesaving skills. You will help them see beyond the superficial, make-believe, fantasy world promised not only in ads but in many real-life encounters as well.

So while we explore commercials and advertisements, we should help students understand how similar techniques may be used on them in certain social situations. We can discuss these situations in the classroom and, for instance, as part of substance-abuse prevention and sex education programs— which often become more direct in the intermediate grades. ▪

Organization, elements, and features in informational texts

It's time to explore in more depth how informational texts may be organized, as well as some of the important elements and features of these texts. We'll first consider the overall manner in which informational texts are structured, then look at some of the most common paragraph patterns employed by the writers of informational texts. We will also examine particular challenges posed by heavy concept loads and conclude by exploring special aids and features. As we go along, I will provide examples of how to teach directly an awareness of some of these elements and organization.

Overall Structure   Whereas in stories the structure of the plot provides an organization of "what's happening," most informational texts are not so familiarly organized. (Although these are exceptions and not the rule, it is interesting to note that *some* informational texts do employ a type of narrative structure. Especially within social studies textbooks we find structures such as "Mislovich gets up in the city of Dubrovnik every morning and goes to buy milk, bread, and other foodstuffs . . . ," and we follow young Mislovich through a day in this coastal city on the Adriatic, and so forth.) Generally speaking, though the purpose of an informational book's title or of its chapter titles may be clear to students, other functions of the structure may not be: the relationship among headings, subheadings, and content—and how all these relate back to the topic represented by the book or chapter title. We usually need to teach directly the relationships among topic, main idea, and supporting details or information.

(Incidentally, students' understanding of these relationships is what will under-lie the logic behind their *outlines,* which we will discuss later in the chapter.)

Main ideas, of course, summarize pertinent surrounding information, which may be contained within a paragraph or a larger chunk of text. They may be explicitly stated or they may be implied—that is, the reader may have to infer them. A beginning understanding of "main idea" comes about when children realize that not all information is equal: some of it clearly is more important than the rest. This "big idea" notion can be used in relation to parts of the informational texts the students are reading. Chapter titles express the "biggest" ideas; headings and subheadings, supporting ideas. These supporting ideas, in turn, express the main ideas of the paragraphs that follow them. Main ideas can occur at all levels, from paragraphs on up. It is often helpful to start students' work with structure at the paragraph level—as we will see in the following activities.

Here are some ideas for introducing the concept of main idea:

DEVELOPING YOUR INSTRUCTIONAL TOOLKIT

1. Talk about situations in which the students might need to give a one-sentence summary. They won't have time to give all the facts and details, just the gist—and this will be the "main idea."

2. Provide examples of paragraphs, each of which has its main idea explicitly stated and also contains two or three supporting sentences. Talk about how you recognize the main idea, often expressed in a *topic sentence* if the context is a paragraph. Here are a sample paragraph and discussion:

   Plants create their own food. Unlike animals, who take in food and break it down, plants "build up" their nourishment. They do this through a complicated process called photosynthesis.

   "Okay; let's look at this paragraph to find its topic sentence or figure out its main idea. I ask myself, 'Are these three sentences all equal, or does one of them tell me something about the *whole* paragraph?' I read that plants are different from animals in the way they get their nourishment, and that's an important and interesting fact, I realize. I also read that there's a name for this process—*photosynthesis.* This, too, is important, but what are these two inter-esting and important sentences really telling me about? Actually, they're both about the first sentence: *Plants create their own food.* This is the most important statement, the 'big picture' statement, and the other sentences provide support-ing information or *details* about it.

   "Let's mess this paragraph up a little bit. Suppose we put the first sentence *last?* Would that mean it isn't a 'big picture,' most-important sentence any-more? Of course not! It *still* is.

   "So you'll usually find a topic sentence—the 'main idea' of a paragraph—at the beginning or the end of a paragraph. Sometimes writers put it first and then flesh it out with more information; sometimes they choose to build up to it, giving the supporting details first and then summing them up with the topic sentence."

3. You should offer a couple more examples, talk them through, and then allow the *students* to read and determine the topic sentences in two or three additional paragraphs. The students should discuss the reasons for their choices, and you'll have the opportunity to provide feedback. If you wish, you can send them off on their own to analyze paragraphs they choose from their books and then return to discuss them with the group.

As we noted earlier, not all main ideas are explicitly stated. You will need to talk about determining a main idea when all the sentences in a paragraph seem equal in importance:

"Sometimes the main idea is only *hinted at* in a paragraph. You may read and reread a paragraph but still think all the sentences seem equally important. When this happens, you have to figure out just what it is that these sentences are talking about. What's the 'big idea' that unites them and makes them go together? Let's take this paragraph as an example:

Runny noses flush out invading viruses. Coughs and sneezes blast them away. Fever heats the body too hot for bacteria. Pus is the corpses of cells that died while engulfing and digesting invaders. (Stein, 1986, p. 129)

"Pretty thrilling stuff, isn't it? Okay, let's see what the 'big idea' is here. We've got the body doing a number of things, all of which are involved with symptoms of being sick, it seems. But why is the body acting in these ways? From words like *invading* and *blasting away,* I get the sense that we've got quite a fight going on here! It appears that the body does these things to protect itself—to keep infections from *really* getting out of hand! And that might be the main idea—the body reacts in these different ways because it is combatting infection and disease; *it is protecting itself.* Each of the sentences in the paragraph gives a specific detail that supports that main idea."

Once again, after discussing another couple of examples in which the main idea is implied, you'll monitor the students' attempts to determine the main idea in paragraphs you provide for them.

Underlying Structures and Patterns In addition to the topic/main ideas/supporting details organization that most informational texts follow, there are various underlying structures or patterns that writers use in constructing their informational texts (Meyer & Freedle, 1984; Richgels, McGee, Lomax, & Sheard, 1987). These different patterns set up and develop the information in different ways. As we'll see a little later, students' ability to construct the meaning of informational texts and to understand those texts may be enhanced *if* they are aware of these ways of organizing texts (see, for example, Armbruster, Anderson, & Ostertag, 1989; Ohlausen & Roller, 1988).

Of the many different patterns that researchers have identified, these four seem to be most prevalent: *collection, cause/effect, problem/solution,* and *comparison/contrast.* Quite often there are specific words, called *signal words* or *clue words,* that indicate these patterns. The following paragraphs illustrate each type of pattern.

Collection: "Geologists have found clues that the continents moved. The first clue is the shape of the continents. . . . A second clue comes from

rocks. The geologists compared the rocks on different continents . . ." (*Holt Science,* 1986, Grade 4, p. 29)

The *collection pattern* simply groups pieces of information together. Often the grouping will be done in a *sequential* manner; and the signal words *first, next,* and *finally,* for example, will cue readers to the sequence (*first,* you do this; *next,* you do that . . .). Occasionally this pattern is referred to as a *description pattern*.

Cause/Effect: "These earliest Americans did not stay in just one place. For a time they would live where hunting was good. If the animals roamed, the hunters would follow them. If many animals died or were killed off, the hunters would move on to look for new animals." (*The United States Yesterday and Today,* 1988, Grade 5, pp. 55–56)

As well as grouping information in a "collection" pattern and sequencing that information, the *cause/effect* pattern provides clear causal links among the topics. These links are usually signaled by words or phrases such as *a result of, therefore, because, caused by,* and sometimes *if* or *then.* In the above excerpt, *If* is the single signal word, and *then* is implied: "*If* the animals roamed . . . the hunters would follow"; "*If* the animals died . . . the hunters would move on."

Problem/Solution: "Less than two weeks after his inauguration, [Lincoln] faced his first crisis. Fort Sumter, at the entrance to Charleston harbor in South Carolina, still flew the Union flag. The state's governor was demanding that the fort be given up.

"On March 15, Lincoln learned that Sumter was running out of supplies . . . the president has pledged to defend federal property in the South. Sumter has become a symbol of Northern determination, and Lincoln had to make a decision. If he sent supplies, he risked an armed attack and war. If he didn't, the fort could not hold out for long. . . .

"Finally the president acted. On April 6 he notified the South Carolina governor that a supply fleet was about to sail for Charleston. As the Union ships approached the city on the morning of April 12, rebel cannons ringing the harbor opened fire on Fort Sumter. . . ." (Freedman, 1993, p. 72)

Problem/solution patterns often contain the words *problem* and *solution;* and often other words are used, such as *question* or, as in this excerpt, *crisis.* Such a term lets the reader know the seriousness of the situation and expect to read about attempts to meet and resolve the crisis or problem.

Comparison/Contrast: "Mt. St. Helens is an exploding volcano. When it erupts, rocks and ash are tossed into the air. . . . Not all volcanoes explode like Mt. St. Helens. Mauna Loa erupts quietly." (*Holt Science,* pp. 22–23)

The *comparison/contrast* pattern notes similarities and differences among topics. Signal words are *similar, both, like, same as*—and *unlike, different from, on the other hand, not all.*

You will find it very helpful to draw on your knowledge of these patterns when particular students are experiencing difficulty in figuring out the "coherence" among sentences and ideas, or the overall links between main ideas and supporting details. Research suggests that many students can benefit from your teaching about these patterns in the fifth and sixth grades. As with all other aspects of learning about and analyzing texts, though, you should not attempt to teach about these patterns if your students are not ready; they must be reading fluently and at a good rate, and be familiar with the basic organization of textbooks and other informational texts.

Once students understand the concepts of "main idea" and "supporting details," as discussed in the preceding section, they can benefit from instruction in text patterns. This instruction will reinforce their overall understanding of how informational text is organized, which in turn increases their comprehension. Significantly, *writing* can reinforce this understanding as students come to produce increasingly coherent and well structured informational compositions.

While there are many avenues you can take to the goal of helping students understand these text patterns, one of the most effective is suggested by Armbruster, Anderson, and Ostertag (1989). They have offered a fairly structured technique that, for each pattern you wish to teach, you can introduce and monitor with the students over several days.

Let's illustrate instruction in the problem/solution pattern by taking a look at Barbara Milchak's classroom (see Classroom in Action on next page).

Concept Load   Informational texts are meant to inform, to impart information. Readers pick them up expecting to "get" information from them. We already know, however, that what readers can learn from texts depends in very large part on their prior information about the topic and how the "new" information or concepts are related to this "known" information. Informational books have to achieve an effective balance, therefore, between new and known concepts—and the vocabulary that represents them—as well as effectively *relate* new concepts to known ones.

To convey new concepts and the vocabulary that represents them, and to do so effectively, authors of textbooks for different grade levels must keep in mind the students with whom they are communicating. What do most students at a particular grade level already know in a very general sense about the topic? What concepts—and therefore vocabulary—are likely to be unfamiliar or unknown to them? How many examples and how much explanation will be necessary, to provide an adequate understanding of the new concepts—to relate this *new* information to *known* information? These considerations help determine the concept load of a textbook or other informational book.

Pedagogical Aids and Features   You're already an expert of sorts on textbooks, in that you've had much experience with them during your education over the years. You may recall one or two—perhaps more—that really seemed to work well for you. There are a probably a number of reasons why this was so, but one of the most obvious is the way in which the text attempted to facilitate your reading and learning through pedagogical aids and features. Such features and aids include the familiar table of contents, the index, and the glossary. They also include chapter headings, feature boxes, "marginalia" (important terms and/or information printed in the margin), and graphic aids such as diagrams, graphic organizers or overviews, graphs, and illustrations. We will

"Kids, you will be learning about one way the authors of these texts organize their main ideas and supporting details. It's called a *problem/solution* pattern. Let's look at an example of one from the book *Dinosaur;* it's about plant eaters":

> *Eating a diet of plants causes animals many more problems than eating meat. Plants are made of tough materials like cellulose and woody lignin and need to be broken down before digestion can take place in the animal's stomach. Plant-eating dinosaurs coped with their diet in a variety of ways: the sauropods did not chew at all, but simply swallowed raked-in vegetation. This passed directly to the stomach and was ground up by deliberately swallowed gastroliths, or "gizzard stones," or was fermented by bacteria, as in a cow's stomach. The hadrosaurs, or duckbilled dinosaurs, had special teeth which ground and chopped their food before they swallowed it. Ceratopsians tackled tough plants with their extra-strong jaws and scissor-like teeth.* [From *Dinosaur,* p. 26; this is one of the texts in the "Eyewitness Books" series of science trade books]

"What's the main problem here?" Barbara Milchak guides the discussion just like the "main idea" discussion (above); she helps the students realize that the *most* important issue or idea—the *problem*—is stated right at the beginning, in the sentence that includes the word *problems:* It is tougher to eat plants than to eat meat.

Barbara's next question has to do with the steps that were taken to solve this problem: "How do these plant-eating dinosaurs solve this problem?" She also explores the *results* of those actions—were they successful? for only a short time? for quite some time? (Armbruster, Anderson, and Ostertag, 1989, p. 133).

Using this passage or another in which she goes through these same questions again, Barbara writes in a "frame" what the problem is, what actions were taken, and the results.

Armbruster and her colleagues suggest that at this point, teachers can provide guidelines for *writing* a summary of problem/solution passages:

> Sentence 1 tells who had a problem and what the problem is.
>
> Sentence 2 tells what action was taken to try to solve the problem.
>
> Sentence 3 tells what happened as a result of the action taken.
> _____ had a problem because _____. Therefore, _____.
> As a result, _____.

look more closely at these aids and features later in our discussion. Many of them of course are also found in informational trade books.

At the beginning of the school year, it is important to find out how well your students understand how *textbooks* are organized and used. Prepare a series of tasks that will directly probe their knowledge (Bader, 1980; Lipson & Wixson, 1990). These tasks will help you determine whether the students recognize and use the important parts of a textbook and whether they understand the use of graphic aids.

You can administer these tasks to the class as a whole or to smaller groups. My preference is to do it in a smaller group, simply because that way, a teacher can observe better and perhaps do a bit of on-the-spot probing to find out what the students might accomplish with a little help. Give them specific information to locate and have them indicate *where* they found the information. Ask them to locate, turn to, and interpret specific information from different graphic aids.

We often find that students need to consider explicitly the differences between textbooks and other informational texts and *narratives*. *Format* is important, so you should explain why texts are laid out as they are. Point out marginal notes, definitions, different type sizes, different-colored headings and subheadings, and so forth. In the primary grades, we show the children the most significant parts of a book; there is, naturally, some carry-over from storybook reading and discussion, but even these three features may look a little different in an informational text: *title page, author,* and *table of contents*. With experience, children will learn about the publisher and place of publication; the *copyright page* and whatever information on it that may be of interest. Beginning in third grade for many children and fourth grade for most, "walk-throughs" of the important features of textbooks are truly useful. They serve to remind the students of the basic features of textbooks, and they extend this knowledge to other important features such as the *index* and the *glossary*.

Readability

Have you ever wondered how publishers can state that such-and-such a textbook is "written at the third-grade (or second-grade, or fifth-grade) level"? This claim is based on what educators term *readability*. Simply put, *readability* refers to the "ease of understanding" of printed material (Klare, 1984), and it is most commonly expressed in terms of *grade level*. Readability formulas estimate or "predict" the ease of understanding of texts. Educators have also developed ways to *measure* directly the ease of understanding, by trying a text out on students. We will examine each process below.

Estimating Readability with Formulas   Traditionally, readability has been determined according to two criteria: (1) the frequency and type of words used and (2) the length and type of sentences. *Readability formulas* were developed in which number and types of words and sentences were counted and evaluated, yielding a grade level for the text. One drawback of books based on readability formulas, however, is the "writing to the formula" phenomenon. In the past, this practice resulted in stilted language in texts. They didn't sound *real;* they didn't have the ring of natural language. Another issue regarding these formulas was that of how easy or difficult they were to use. Over the years, therefore, as different readability formulas have been developed, there has been a trade-off between ease of use and the inclusion of enough factors to determine more validly the difficulty level of the text. It is easier to sample a few factors than a lot, and it is easier to perform simple mathematical operations on those factors than on more complex ones. Those formulas that were easier and less time-consuming to use were less valid; those that were more difficult and *more* time-consuming to use were more valid.

The formula most familiar to reading educators and teachers is the Fry Readability Estimate (1977), and it isn't really a formula *per se*. It looks at word difficulty and sentence length—factors that the original readability researchers were looking at decades ago (Gray & Leary, 1935). The assumptions of the Fry Readability Estimate are that (1) words of more than one syllable are more difficult to decode and understand, and (2) longer sentences are more difficult to comprehend. The procedure is straightforward: Select three 100-word passages, one each from the beginning, middle, and end of a selection; then tally the number of syllables per passage and the number of sentences per passage and average across the three passages. Next, enter a graph in which you plot these averaged numbers against each other and come up with a grade level (see Figure 7.5). Just as you would predict, if there are a lot of polysyllabic words and only a few sentences, the text is rated as more difficult. It would have a higher readability level expressed in terms of grade level.

Let's say a teacher is planning on using Russell Freedman's *Buffalo Hunt* (1988) in a fifth-grade unit on Native Americans. A children's literature anthology suggests that the readability level is sixth grade and above, and the teacher's hunch is that the book would be at a middle-grade readability level—comfortable reading for some of her students, but more challenging for most. To be certain, however, she applies the Fry Readability Estimate to the book.

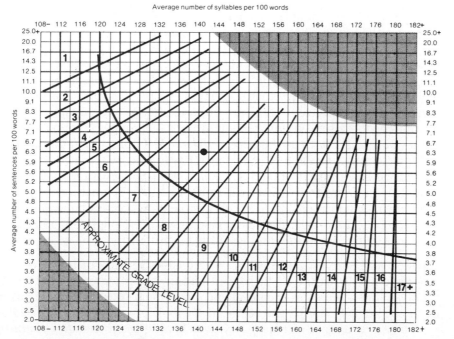

Figure 7.5
Fry Readability Graph

She selects 100-word passages from pages 1, 22, and 48, and averages across them:

Passage One—   6.6 sentences   157 syllables

Passage Two—   5.3 sentences   145 syllables

Passage Three—   5.8 sentences   134 syllables

Average no. of sentences = 5.9   Average no. of syllables = 145

When the teacher plots the average number of sentences and the average number of syllables on the Fry graph, she discovers that *Buffalo Hunt* is on an eighth-grade level. Wondering if this is a bit high, she samples another passage (actually, the more 100-word samples that are taken, the more valid the estimate). She adds this to the original three passages, averages for all four passages, and finds the estimate now at seventh-grade level. Her original hunch about middle-grade readability level is confirmed.

This same teacher applied the Fry Readability Estimate to the fifth-grade American history textbook adopted by her district (*The United States Today and Yesterday,* 1988). To her surprise, it came out at seventh-grade level:

Passage One (p. 54)—   9.1 sentences   153 syllables

Passage Two (p. 350)—   6.5 sentences   151 syllables

Passage Three (p. 546)—   7.5 sentences   141 syllables

Average no. of sentences = 7.7   Average no. of syllables = 148

While the average number of sentences, 7.7, is well within the appropriate range for the intermediate grades, the average number of syllables, 148, is on the high side. It occurred to the teacher that the syllable count might be high because of the number of *names* in these passages and, of course, throughout the text; proper nouns—names of people and places—frequently are polysyllabic. The teacher reasoned that the text would be "readable" for most of her students if she (1) pretaught the most important names and (2) did a minilesson on not spending time trying to "sound out" or pronounce other unfamiliar names but simply noting whether they were places or things and moving on.

More recently, research in readability has looked at some additional text-related variables, but these are at the *macrostructure* level rather than at the sentence- and word-level (Zakaluk & Samuels, 1988). The nature of the higher-order organization is considered; for example, how clearly the major ideas are related to one another. As we've discussed, if a text is poorly organized at this level, the ease of understanding is affected significantly.

"Trying Out" Books with Students   Three effective ways of trying out books we would like to use are (1) by administering what is termed a *cloze procedure,* (2) observing students as they evaluate a text, and (3) observing a student as he or she actually reads a text. Let's briefly look at each of these procedures.

You can determine whether a textbook is at least on students' *instructional* level (see Chapter 4) by preparing a *cloze* passage (Taylor, 1953; Pikulski & Tobin,

Current Views on Readability

Given all that we've said about matching children with the right books, and given all that we now know about factors affecting the understanding of what is read, does it strike you as odd that anyone would want to talk about "readability" in the absence of real live students? The notion of trying to determine the difficulty level of a text in the absence of children may seem quite unrealistic. *However,* it is realistic to expect that publishers will probably continue to use readability formulas to attempt to determine the general difficulty levels of their texts, trying to ensure that the texts are at least "in the ball park" in terms of appropriateness for students at particular grade levels. In part, this is because they are often expected to do this by educators who adopt subject-matter textbooks for their school or school district. Many educators will continue to ask publishers, "How have you determined that this text is appropriate for most second-graders [or fourth- or sixth-graders]?" Publishers' responses will continue to include reference to readability formulas as well as important additional criteria (such as trying chapters out on a wide range of students).

More "traditional" readability formulas have considered only the text, not the reader; and besides, as we've just acknowledged, aren't students supposed to be reading *authentic* narrative and informational *literature* anyway? Authors of authentic literature usually do not have formulas in mind when they write. Rather, they have a sense of children at different ages and this guides their style, their choice of words, and how they address their subject.

The current perspective on readability reflects the more recent conceptions of the reading process. Traditionally, readability was considered exclusively from a *text*-oriented perspective. More recently, the *reader* is considered in research on readability. "Readability" now reflects the *interactive* perspective; so *reader-related* factors such as prior knowledge, interest, and motivation are taken into account.

Knowing what readability refers to and knowing about its limitations, what should be your perspective, as a teacher, on readability? If we interpret "ease of understanding" broadly, then in a sense you are always thinking about readability as you make decisions about books to share and as you bring particular students together with particular texts. If we take readability in its narrower sense, as specifying the "grade level of a text," we should be cautious. It may indeed be helpful to have a general sense of the difficulty of a text in terms of its grade level, but we should also look at other factors, with our students in mind. We should consider our students' backgrounds, both general and specific, and their reading competence. And we need to remember that a textbook is but one of many learning resources in our classroom.

LEARNING IN CONTEXT: **Readability depends on many factors, and the appropriate determination of the readability of a text calls upon knowledge of the text, of students, and of the purposes to which the text will be put.**

1982). The word *cloze* comes from *closure,* the psychological phenomenon in which we tend to "fill in" what is not there. Applied to texts, the cloze procedure allows students to fill in a blank with the word they believe the author used.

For upper elementary students, you should select a 300-word passage from about the middle of the textbook. Type the passage, leaving the first and the last sentence intact but replacing every *fifth* word (beginning with the second sentence) with a blank space. Then make copies and ask your students to write in each blank the exact word they believe the author used—only one word per blank. The cloze procedure will give you the average readability level of this textbook for your class. In other words, is the book too difficult, about right, or far too easy? You may also wish to rehearse this procedure with the students first, using other passages, so that they are clear on the procedure.

Following is the first part of a cloze passage that a fifth-grade teacher constructed from the students' English text (Haley-James & Stewig, 1990):

> When you write a paragraph, be sure that your sentences are in an order that makes sense. This is especially important ＿＿＿ a paragraph of instructions. ＿＿＿ would happen if you ＿＿＿ giving instructions for baking ＿＿＿ muffins and did not ＿＿＿ the correct order? Filling ＿＿＿ muffin tin with batter ＿＿＿ comes before putting the ＿＿＿ in the oven.
>
> When ＿＿＿ write a paragraph of ＿＿＿, begin by telling what ＿＿＿ or materials, if any, ＿＿＿ needed. After that, use ＿＿＿ words such as *first,* ＿＿＿, *next,* and *finally* to ＿＿＿ make the sequence, or ＿＿＿, clear. Order words are ＿＿＿, but not every sentence ＿＿＿ one. . . .

[Now, if you're curious, here are the deleted words; *for, What, were, bran, use, the, certainly, tin, you, instructions, equipment, are, order, then, help, order, useful, needs.*]

In determining the readability of that passage—and therefore of the textbook—for your students, count as correct *only* exact replacements. This may seem unfair, *but* the criteria for determining readability have been adjusted for this. Average your students' scores to get the general appropriateness of this textbook for your class. If the average score is above 60%, then the text is *independent* level; 40%–60%, *instructional;* below 40%, *frustrational.* (I'll talk later about what to do with a frustration-level textbook.) While this cloze procedure is not necessarily valid for determining whether a particular student can handle a text, it is a reasonably valid measure of a text's appropriateness for a whole class (Vaughan & Estes, 1986).

Another effective means of determining whether a text will "work" with your students is simply to break them into small groups and have each group look through the text. Ask them to evaluate it: What do they like about it? Dislike? Is it well-written and clearly understandable? What about the features— the illustrations, photographs, diagrams, and so forth? Listen in on their observations and comments—they will provide excellent insights for you. This type of informal evaluation by students can valuably complement the narrower "readability" determination that measures such as the cloze procedure provide.

As I suggested in Chapter 4, and as we'll consider in some depth in Chapter 11, we can obtain a lot of information about the suitability of a text by listening to particular students read from it and noting how comfortable they seem to be with it. Sitting next to the student, have him or her begin reading to you from the first page of a chapter in the text; assess the student's fluency, how often he or she "miscues" on a word and whether and how often the student self-corrects these miscues. After two or three paragraphs are read, ask the student to tell you in his or her own words what the reading was about. Ask one or two questions based on what the student read; if he or she isn't certain of the answer, see if he or she is able to read back over the passage to locate the answer. This type of informal one-to-one assessment can be extremely helpful to you.

LEARNING HOW TO LEARN FROM INFORMATIONAL TEXTS

We have looked closely at the nature of informational texts. We are ready to explore the ways in which we can facilitate students' learning *how* to learn from them. I have partitioned our consideration of this important topic into four areas, each of which will be addressed in a separate section.

We will begin at the broadest level, looking at what students may do *before, during,* and *after* their engagements with informational texts. It is important to conceptualize these engagements in terms of the reading/thinking strategies and activities that will lead toward students' *independent* application of these competencies, and this internalization lies at the heart of our overriding instructional goals for reading informational texts. Next, we will look at *discussion formats,* which are deliberately set up to facilitate students' participation as part of a community of learners. The fundamental nature of discussion entails partner and group thinking and questioning. Discussion, too, leads to internalization of a learning/thinking process, but one significantly different from those presented in the previous section and focused more directly upon reading. *Questioning*—which we will examine next—is, of course, a central mechanism throughout all the strategies and activities we are discussing; types of questions that may be asked of informational texts and the process of asking good questions also become internalized. Finally, I will address *study skills.* While related to reading and thinking strategies, study skills have the additional characteristic of helping students *remember* specific information that they have read. Study skills are a critical aspect of learning to learn, and most intermediate students can benefit from learning about them.

"Before, during, and after" reading/thinking strategies and activities

As we discuss effective procedures for helping students connect their reading with their learning in content areas, keep in mind that these strategies all share some very important features:

They help students *before* their reading and learning by activating prior knowledge. These strategies will help students access prior knowledge, determine what they know about a topic and what they don't know, and help them identify what they would *like* to know.

They facilitate the construction of meaning *during* reading. These strategies will help students realize how to fit incoming information with what they already know and distinguish between relevant and irrelevant information.

They ensure that new information will be integrated with prior knowledge to increase understanding and retention *after* the reading. These strategies will help students understand how to reflect on the new information, realize how their existing understanding probably has changed, apply this new information to a broader context, and identify what they still need to find out.

Vaughan and Estes (1986) describe "before, during, and after" reading in terms of "anticipation," "realization," and "contemplation." They and others have pointed out that although the middle part, realization, is important, we usually spend far too little time on *anticipating* the reading and on *contemplating* what was read.

The professional literature is brimming with articles on all kinds of techniques for learning from informational texts. These techniques are referred to in a kind of shorthand: for example, SQ3R, KWL, REAP, PANORAMA, GIST, PORPE, PReP, and on and on. If you try to keep many of them in mind, you will probably wind up feeling as if you're drowning in alphabet soup. I don't point this out in order to diminish in any way the effectiveness of these procedures. Rather, I'd like to assure you that they all contain tried-and-true elements of learning from informational text. None of them is totally "brand new," offering success light years beyond any other technique. And you will probably continue to see other variations appear on the scene throughout your career.

Now let's look at some procedures that represent our best current applications of what we know about what students should do before, during, and after their reading in informational texts, and how this reading can facilitate learning. The procedures work equally well, by the way, with textbooks and with "trade" informational texts.

Activating Interest and Knowledge with Read-Alouds   You will be able to lay the foundation for enriching prior knowledge and for motivating and captivating your students through a very simple strategy: bring in lots of trade books that have to do with what the children are going to be studying. Make the books available for the children to browse through for a few days before you do anything more formally. Read several to the class.

Here's just a sampling of the types and groupings of informational trade books that can introduce different topics or units of study; Chapter 9 will provide a much broader "menu" of possibilities.

■ In a unit on nutrition, for intermediate students, share Isaac Asimov's *How Did We Find Out About Vitamins?* For primary students, pair Judith Seixas' *Vitamins: What They Are, What They Do* and *Junk Food: What It Is, What It Does.*
■ For a geology unit, try Patricia Lauber's *Volcano: The Eruption and Healing of Mount Saint Helens* and, Sara Stein's *The Evolution Book,* the sections ad-

dressing volcanic eruptions. Younger children will enjoy Faith McNulty's *How to Dig a Hole to the Other Side of the World.*

■ Plants, trees, and the life cycle may be set up for primary-grade children by introducing Ruth Heller's *The Reason for a Flower* and *Plants That Never Ever Bloom.*

■ Ancient Egypt is explored through Lila Perl's extremely engaging *Mummies, Tombs, and Treasure: Secrets of Ancient Egypt* (which includes fascinating photographs of several mummies—including the legendary Tutankhamen). Share *In Search of Tutankhamen,* by Piero Ventura and Gian Paolo Ceserani, and *Tales Mummies Tell,* by Patricia Lauber.

Narrative read-alouds are also a means of arousing interest and activating prior knowledge for a unit of content area study. Good chapter books or stories about people, times, events, and so forth provide a direct line to students' real and imagined worlds:

■ In a unit in which you want to help children explore the concept of number and relative size, for example, share the classic *Millions of Cats,* by Wanda Gag.

■ For a unit on Ancient Egypt, read parts of Zilpha Snyder's *The Egypt Game.*

■ Sheila Burnford's *The Incredible Journey* is a natural for animal study.

■ Try Esther Forbes's *Johnny Tremain* or the Colliers' *My Brother Sam Is Dead* for an American Revolution unit.

■ For a geology unit on the earth's crust and tectonic plates, read the chapter in Laurence Yep's *Dragonwings* that vividly describes Moon Shadow's experiences during and after the 1906 San Francisco earthquake.

■ The life cycle may be ushered into your classroom with Victoria Wirth's *Whisper from the Woods* (1991), enchantingly and movingly illustrated by A. Scott Banfill.

Guided Reading-Thinking Activity

The Standard Expository Guided Reading-Thinking Activity The underlying concept of the expository GRTA is to help students learn the *process* of reading textbooks so that they can more efficiently *learn* from textbooks. The expository GRTA can be adjusted to apply to informational *trade* texts, too; but you'll probably need to spend much more time demonstrating the technique with textbooks—because, as we know, most students *perceive* textbooks as more boring, difficult, and cumbersome texts.

Once students understand the *process* of reading textbooks, you can focus more on helping them *learn* from the textbook. But you should avoid expecting that your students are going to learn the process *and* be able to pick up and retain all kinds of information in the beginning. That's why I emphasize *process* first, *learning* from text second, when you first introduce this strategy.

Your pitch to the students should address both, though. Explain that they are going to be learning a technique that will help them pick up more information from the textbook and retain it longer. The basic steps are to preview, then to predict/read/confirm in each section of the chapter—and finally to *reflect* on the content of the whole chapter:

1. Explain to the students *why* you are going to help them learn this strategy. They will get more out of their reading and remember it longer.
2. *Preview* the chapter; because there's a lot more information in a textbook chapter than in a fiction chapter book, previewing tells students what's coming up. The preview includes attention to *questions* at the beginning of the chapter; headings and subheadings, illustrations and diagrams; and a reading of the chapter summary.
3. Now read the chapter one section at a time, making predictions about the information to be found in that section. After reading, check and confirm the predictions against the information found.
4. When the chapter is completed, help the students review and *reflect* on the information. Restate the main points and important supporting information. (When you first introduce informational GRTAs, remember that you shouldn't expect the students to provide at this point anything near a "comprehensive" summary; remember, your main focus is at first on the *process*.) In closing, tell the students that they should always approach their first reading of an important textbook chapter this way. Mention also that you will be practicing this procedure often throughout the year so that *they* will be sure to use it on their own.

You should know that, at first, the informational GRTA will take *longer* than the old-fashioned way of reading, which is to start on the first page of a chapter and slog through to the end. In the long run, though, students will become more adept at the procedure. In fact, they usually wind up spending no more time than they would have in the old way of reading and rereading the chapter, while remembering and recalling more information. As Bear and McIntosh note, although the GRTA is "introduced and practiced in the classroom setting, *the goal is for students to incorporate these techniques into their repertoire of independent . . . strategies*" (1990, p. 385, emphasis added). For this reason, the GRTA format for textbooks is a powerful technique. There are several variations on this basic format, most of which facilitate more systematic *studying,* and we will look at them later in this chapter.

"No Book" and "Table of Contents" Adaptations Gill and Bear (1988) and Bear and McIntosh (1990) discuss some variations on the GRTA concept that are particularly effective "before" students plunge into textbook reading.

The "No Book" GRTA works this way: First, working in pairs, the students list everything they can think of that could be in a book on this particular topic. Next, they arrange this information into groups. Third, they decide on a label for each group—in effect, a "chapter title"—and sequence these labels as a table of contents.

The last step in the No Book GRTA is, I would suggest, an optional one: the students write the book! Of course, this product would not be lengthy. The step really is meant to grab the students' attention; then they can write what really are *summaries* of each section or chapter. You can see, however, how this would *really* probe their prior knowledge and put it to work.

The "Table of Contents" GRTA works in the following way. With textbook in hand and working individually, students first read the title of each chapter and write down what they think will be presented in that chapter. Second, they read any subheadings listed for each chapter. They ask themselves: "What do I *know* I know about this topic? What do I *think* I know? What do I want to find out? What do I expect to find out in this chapter?" (Bear & McIntosh, 1990, p. 386, emphasis added). They write down this information in brief phrases or sentences. In the final step, students can compare their tables of contents with one another.

The "PreReading Plan" (PReP)   The Prereading Plan, or PReP, is really an umbrella for many types of prereading activities (Langer, 1981; Templeton, 1991). The PReP works equally well with short or long reading selections, before small units of study or large ones.

The PReP gives you a *general* feel for the "known" information your students possess, which in turn helps you figure out the type and amount of "new" information you can reasonably expect them to absorb. Knowing this, you can select and adjust materials and activities appropriately. The PReP also acts as a means of motivating your students as it helps them become aware of what they already know about a topic. Here are the steps:

1. Before meeting with the students, determine what major concepts or ideas they will be reading about.
2. When you're together with the students, stand at the chalkboard, chart, or overhead projector. For each major concept you have identified, ask the question "What comes to mind when you think of _____"? and write down their responses.
3. After you've finished generating associations, you may ask the students *why* they made certain associations: "What made you think of _____ ?" "Why do you think that _____?" "What else might go with this?" Encourage the students to query one another as well; in fact, they will probably take over this function for you! An optional procedure at this point is to *categorize* responses (Vaughan and Estes, 1986). Ask the students how the responses might be categorized, but be prepared to take the lead at first and suggest the initial categories.
4. In this final step, you will ask the students if they have any additional ideas that could be added or if they wish to change any of their original ideas.

Langer suggests that you now may analyze the responses that different students made, to determine who knows a lot, a little, or virtually nothing about the topic and the important related concepts. This is the second major part of her PReP. Your purpose in doing this would be to tailor your subsequent activities and materials appropriately to each student. While this is a laudable objective, it may mean attempting to "fine tune" your instruction a little too much. It is also putting a lot of weight on the degree to which your students felt comfortable contributing during this initial phase.

I think the best aspect of the PReP is its tapping into the knowledge base of your students and getting their thinking in gear and in focus before moving into the reading or the unit you will be exploring. Even those students who do not contribute are at least exposed to the discussion, so their cognitive gears are beginning to turn as well.

"K-W-L" Procedure   Like the PReP, the *K-W-L* procedure accesses students' prior knowledge about a topic and helps you determine how much they already know about that topic (Ogle, 1986). In contrast to the PReP, however, K-W-L is a procedure that takes students on through the reading and reflection phases as well. It also helps them become aware of their options as learners: what can they do, for example, if a specific book or textbook does *not* answer their questions?

"K-W-L" stands for what we *K*now, what we *W*ant to know or learn, and what we *L*earned (often included in this last step is what we didn't find out but may still need to learn):

1. *What We Know:* Similar to the PReP, this step involves brainstorming about what students think they know concerning the topic they will be reading about. As you write down the students' responses, you may also query them about how they know what they know, where they found out about it, and so forth. Then you and the students will categorize these responses.

2. *What We Want to Learn:* During the first step, students' interests are usually aroused. In this second step, you will help them perceive these interests as purposes for reading. You can do this as a whole class or with a small group, and you can encourage each student to formulate his or her *own* questions.

3. *What We Learned* (and what we still need to learn): After reading the selection, students will write down what new information they have acquired. They will also note any questions that remain unanswered. This aspect of the procedure helps them understand that often there may be a difference between what they would like to learn and what the selection's author chose to include. They can then understand the necessity of looking elsewhere—to other texts and sources. Often this is a good opportunity to pose some of the "exemplar"-type questions that work for informational texts in general (see page 348).

As an example, Figure 7.6 shows a completed K-W-L diagram based on a lesson on sharks that was conducted with fourth-grade students.

Figure 7.6
Completed K-W-L Diagram

SHARKS		
WHAT WE KNOW	WHAT WE WANT TO KNOW	WHAT WE LEARNED
Some are big.	Do whale sharks eat people?	Sharks lived before the dinosaurs.
Live in salt water	Did sharks live with the dinosaurs?	There are 300 kinds of sharks.
Eat other sharks and fish	How many kinds of sharks are there?	Sharks breathe through gills.
Little brains	How big do sharks get?	
Lots of different kinds		
Always get new teeth		

COLUMN A WHAT I ALREADY KNEW	COLUMN B WHAT I KNOW NOW	COLUMN C WHAT I DON'T KNOW
kangaroos Australia a continent koala bears southern hemisphere possums	animals with a pouch dry climate spiny anteater and duck-billed platypus special class of animals: monotremes egg-laying mammals kangaroo babies = joeys kangaroo herd = mob	carnivores why few predators in Australia? is a predator a carnivore?

ANSWER TO THE PURPOSE QUESTION: Marsupials are different from other animals in the following ways: They raise their young in a pouch. Most live in Australia or New Guinea. They are very small at birth, crawl from the birth canal to the mother's pouch, attach to the mother's milk gland, and develop into maturity in the pouch.

Figure 7.7
*Example of a "What-I-Know"
Worksheet*

What-I-Know (W-I-K) Textbook Comprehension Monitoring Similar to the K-W-L strategy, this strategy focuses on students' *textbook* reading. As with other such strategies, you will probably want to model it first for your students. Because W-I-K works best when students already have a basic understanding of the structure or organization of textbooks, it is an excellent strategy to use after the Guided Reading-Thinking Activity has been introduced.

Before reading a textbook chapter, distribute W-I-K worksheets to students (a completed worksheet is shown in Figure 7.7). Before they read, have them list what they already know about the general topic, in Column A. Then, at the bottom of the sheet, have them write a *purpose* for reading the chapter. Next, *as* they read, they should enter in Column B information that is new to them and that is relevant to their purpose. Also, as they read they can enter any information they find confusing, as well as questions that occur to them. After they have finished reading, they can organize and summarize the information relevant to their purpose for reading at the bottom of the sheet as well.

◤◢◣ DEVELOPING YOUR INSTRUCTIONAL TOOLKIT

Many of the activities and questions in which you involve students before, during, and after reading are addressed in their journals, which they always have at their sides. Because the students' responses are not produced on loose sheets of paper—to be turned in, forgotten about, and then lost when returned—but are *with* the students continually, there is a genuine "ownership" quality to these responses and activities. They are an ongoing, on*growing* permanent record.

Using them to record *predictions* and *summaries* throughout reading and learning are powerful activities. Some further specific examples of tasks students can address in their journals follow. Each can be augmented by *discussion* with partners or groups.

■ Turn back to "Meaning Makers: Learning Logs" in Chapter 1 (p. 14). The "what" items work just as well for elementary students as for you, and they apply equally to fictional and nonfictional reading and writing.

■ Present key terms and phrases to the students before the reading and ask them to arrange them into one or two journal sentences. After doing this individually, students can compare sentences with a partner. For example, these words and phrases would work well before students read about the causes of World War II:

world trade
competition
armies and navies
United States
staying neutral

■ Present students with situations that have complicating factors. Before reading a chapter on the Ice Age, for instance, students might respond in their journals to the following paragraph:

You are a Cro-Magnon man or woman in what is now central Europe. Your family has always lived in the same area, but each winter seems to be colder than the last. Your clan believes it is time to move to a warmer area before the next winter comes. You believe the hunting will be good for at least another season and wish to stay. Also, your young son has been ill, and you do not feel he can survive the move. You want to agree with the group and do what they wish, but you really want to stay. How will you present your argument to the group? How might they try to convince you to move *now*?

■ Once students understand the procedure and purpose of the K-W-L strategy, they can keep K-W-L diagrams in their journals.

■ "No-Book" and "Table of Contents" GRTAs can be entered in the journals.

■ For *social studies,* students can respond to certain current events—what do they think of the military dictatorship in a particular country? How might they help relieve a famine in Somalia? Should a nuclear dump be allowed in their state if the federal government gives the state a lot of money?

■ For *science,* journals become excellent repositories for *observation,* both short- and long-term. Students record changes in phenomena they are observing, from the growth of a plant to the path of the moon. Graphs may be sketched and kept. "Prediction" works well here, as students write what they think might happen in an experiment before conducting it.

■ "Clusters" or "semantic maps" may be sketched prior to reading, then added to as new information is encountered during the reading.

■ As upper elementary students learn about particular study techniques such as notetaking and outlining (see below), their journals will be an excellent "home" for these efforts.

A final word: Just as with the use of journals when we discussed them in Chapter 6, you may need to model certain of these responses. In "observing," for example, you would write on a transparency in relation to an experiment; another tactic is to keep your journal open on your desk and invite students to have a look.

Graphic Organizers   Graphic organizers are visual displays or representations of important concepts in a unit of study or in a chapter textbook. Traditionally, they have been used *prior to* moving into reading or study; a graphic organizer *before* reading is usually teacher-generated. It can give your students a "visual mnemonic" for the organization of and relationships among the major concepts they will be exploring. Insofar as helping students organize and remember information, however, they are excellent if students develop them during or *after* their reading and study.

Graphic organizers can serve an *ongoing* function throughout a unit of study. In her third-grade classroom, Sandy Madura introduces a graphic organizer before the students explore their "Dinosaur" unit, discusses it with them, and uses it as an ongoing "organizer":

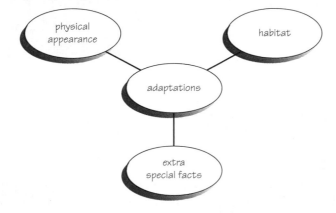

As the students read and discuss, each of them is also collecting information about a particular dinosaur for a report (an initial art project involved each student drawing a large picture of his or her dinosaur; these were then mounted on a bulletin board until the report was ready for publication). These reports will be a visual representation with accompanying text (see Figure 7.8), arranged and presented on a large poster. As the students collect their information, they record the facts about their dinosaur on strips of paper, which Sandy then tacks onto their dinosaurs on the bulletin board. When the students are ready to put together their poster reports, they each organize their strips under the headings represented in the graphic organizer. Next, students compose paragraphs in their journals or learning logs, using the information collected for each category. The last step is the transcription of these paragraphs into their final published form and their arrangement on the poster paper together with their large dinosaur picture and smaller illustrations.

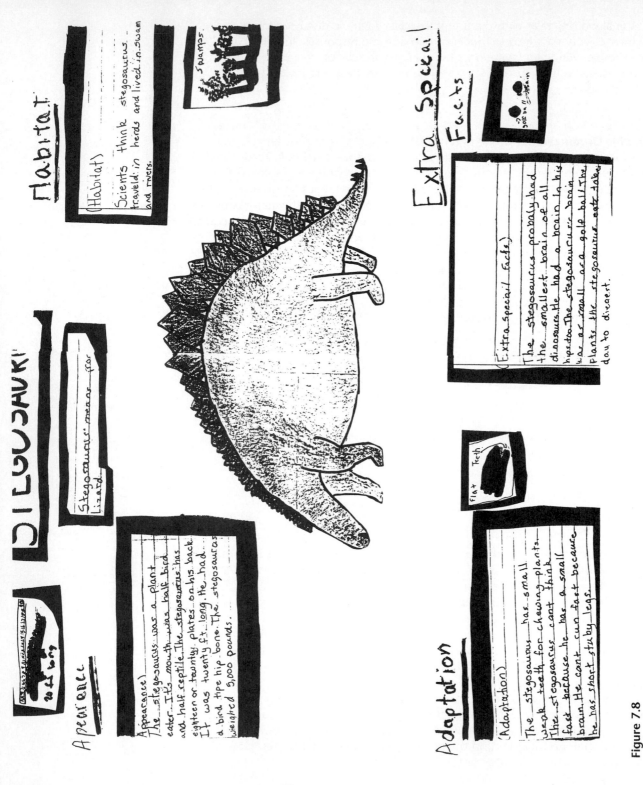

DINOSAUR!

Habitat

(Habitat)
Scients think stegosaurus traveled in herds and lived in swam and rivers.

swamps

Apearence

Stegosaurus means for Lizard.

(Apearance)
The stegosaurus was a plant eater. It's mouth was half bird and half reptile. The stegosaurus has eighteen or twenty plates on his back. It was twenty ft. long. He had a bird type hip bone. The stegosaurus weighed 5,000 pounds.

Extra Speciail Facts

(Extra speciail facts)
The stegosaurus probaly had the smallest brain of all dinosaurs. He had a brain in his hips too. The stegosaurus brain was as small as a golf ball. The plants the stegosaurus eats take day to diraest.

Adaptation

Flat Teeth

(Adaptation)
The stegosaurus has small weak teeth for chewing plants. The stegosaurus cant think fast because he has a small brain. He cant run fast because he has short stuby legs.

Figure 7.8
Third-Grader's "Poster Report" Developed Around Graphic Organizer

A graphic organizer *after* reading is usually student-generated. The procedure is simple: Give partners or small groups a set of 3 × 5 cards, each of which has an important concept from the reading and unit of study written on it. The students are to arrange these to form a graphic organizer, record it in their learning logs, and then share it with other students. This process will not only help students reflect on important information and manipulate major concepts—as they look at the efforts of other students, it will help them see alternative means of representing the information. Truly, critical thinking is going on in this kind of activity.

One last note about graphic organizers: In Chapter 8, we'll explore vocabulary development in the context of new units of study and new textbook material, but you've probably already realized that graphic organizers are also excellent for introducing and following up on new vocabulary terms as well.

Discussion formats

Approaching a Chapter Collaboratively Break the class into three or more groups. Assign each group a section of a chapter to be read. Give each group questions that tap the major ideas presented in that particular section. These questions should call for critical thinking, requiring the students to analyze and synthesize information. Students read their questions prior to the text-reading, then read the text; finally, they discuss possible responses. The class can reconvene as a whole after each group has read its chapter section and responded to the questions; each group will then present its findings. This is an excellent way for students to get an overview of the chapter prior to reading the entire chapter themselves. Questions and responses can be written down and copies made for each student to keep—a permanent overview and global study sheet if the unit includes an exam later on.

This technique works especially well for chapters that are *not* well organized according to the criteria for textbook evaluation discussed above—but which nevertheless include important information and ideas.

Following are some sample questions given to three different groups in an intermediate class and based on different sections of a history textbook chapter.

Group 1

By the time war was declared on Germany, Hitler had already taken over several other countries. Why had he been allowed to do so? Was Hitler surprised when World War II broke out?

Group 2

Why didn't the United States want to get involved in World War II? Was the United States involved "unofficially" in the war before the attack on Pearl Harbor?

Group 3

The Soviet Union was communistic. Why, then, were the United States and the Soviet Union on the same side in World War II? How were the governments of Nazi Germany and the Soviet Union alike?

When Students "Can't Read" the Textbook

A common lament among teachers is that many students "can't read" the textbook. Now that we have examined how to determine just how readable a textbook is in terms of its conceptual complexity and overall organization, how can you accommodate these students?

First of all, remember to put textbooks into proper perspective. They are not the sole source of your curriculum in the different subject-matter areas. You will have many other sources of information on hand, including (of course!) trade books.

Second, if the textbook is at certain students' frustrational level, there are adjustments you can make for chapter segments you believe are worth addressing:

■ Have the important segments taped so that students can listen to them. Be sure to include at the beginning, and interspersed throughout, any important questions you wish the students to keep in mind as they listen to the tape.

■ "Buddy read": Students for whom the textbook is at least on their instructional level can read to less-proficient students. Together the students can discuss questions you provide.

■ After listening to the text, students should write down in their learning logs the important points they remember—in particular, their responses to the questions you posed. When students are not comfortable with writing, encourage them to get down at least a few words or phrases that represent important ideas.

■ If some students' reading and writing development is far behind that of their peers, you may have them *dictate* the important points, and another student or an adult volunteer can write them down. If, for whatever reason, dictation cannot be taken immediately, have the student dictate into a cassette recorder and transcribe it later for his or her learning log.

■ Always remember, of course, that students who cannot read the textbook can *still* be involved in any prereading and follow-up discussions.

All these adaptations are particularly effective with students who are learning English as a second language and are not in a bilingual education program in which they receive subject-matter instruction in their first language. Listening to the second language in the context of meaningful discussions provides a rich context for important terms to be acquired. Encouraging such students to write in journals whatever they can—in English as well as in their first language—will usually capture the important terminology and underlying concepts. Because many ESL students may have considerable first-language knowledge of a topic, writing in their native language keeps their learning moving along with that of their English-speaking peers.

LEARNING IN CONTEXT: Students who are struggling readers should have the same degree of access to textbooks as more proficient readers, and they should be equally involved in discussion about the concepts addressed in the reading.

Jigsaw In this format, students work in groups, each working to become an "expert" in a particular area of study (Slavin, 1986; Tierney, Readence, & Dishner, 1990). They in turn will teach others what they themselves have learned. The technique works best for intermediate students. Your work first involves some preparation.

First, partition a chapter to be read, just as for the preceding discussion activity. Prepare for each section an "expert sheet" that lists the pages that will be read, includes questions, and lists what "expert" group they will be working with.

Second, you'll write two questions on each section, for a quiz. These questions will be higher-level ones, requiring students to put together, analyze, and synthesize information. Third, assign students to heterogeneous groups.

Now you're ready to present the procedure to your class and get under way. On day one, explain how the "jigsaw" format works, then allow students time to read their respective sections of the material. On the second day, students will meet with the "experts" from the other teams who are responsible for the same section of the chapter as they are. When they meet with experts from other teams, they will discuss the questions on their sheets, determine that they all understand the material well enough to respond to the questions, and then return to their respective teams, ready to teach their teammates. On day three, students meet with their own teams and report. The cooperation is important because each student realizes that he or she is responsible for material on which everyone else will be quizzed.

Questioning and informational texts

We explored "questioning" in some depth in the last chapter, focusing primarily on narrative texts. Earlier in this chapter, in our discussion of the goals and purposes of fluent reading in *informational* materials (see also Figure 7.2), I emphasized the importance of questioning. It's time to revisit "questioning" explicitly in the context of informational texts and to offer "exemplar" questions for informational texts. In addition, I would like to present a more directed framework for discussing the relationship between product questions based on informational texts and the types of understanding and thinking involved in answering them. Throughout this section runs the message that we can lead students toward the *internalization* of effective questions and effective strategies for responding to different types of questions.

In a nutshell, appropriate questions help students with both the *product* and the *process* of reading informational texts. The questions help students reflect on the *information* they have read (Hammond, 1988) and on *how* they have processed that information (Irwin, 1991).

Exemplar Questions for Informational Texts In Figure 7.9 I present a few basic, "exemplar" questions that work well in helping students acquire information—the *product*—and in helping them learn how to learn more generally—the *process*.

Let's consider "on-line" questioning for a moment. In our ongoing interaction with our students regarding their reading, we often find that we need to "interweave" product and process questions. For example, if a student is uncertain as to how to infer the answer to a "product" question, we ask a "process"

QUESTIONS FOCUSED ON PRODUCT	QUESTIONS FOCUSED ON PROCESS
* Did you find the answers to your questions? * What answers do you still need to find out? * What else did you learn that you didn't know before? * What was the most surprising or interesting thing you learned? * What have you learned by reading this that you didn't know before? (As a last question, this is usually more comprehensive than "What else did you learn that you didn't know?")	**"Microstructure" Level** * Did you understand the links between words (he, she, they, it, for example) and between sentences? * Were there any words that were used in a different way? **"Macrostructure" Level** * How do you know if a particular sentence contains the main idea? * How do you figure out the main idea if the text doesn't come out and state it for you? * What part of this made it hard for you to understand?

Figure 7.9
Exemplar Questions for Informational Texts

question that will help us identify the source of the student's difficulty. We may then conduct a brief minilesson in which we model the appropriate skill or strategy and then guide the student toward understanding on his or her own. I'd like to make an important point here. Research has established fairly well the value of questions that tap higher-order thinking on the learning and application of information: analyzing, synthesizing, and evaluating the information. If your students seem to be experiencing difficulty in responding to higher-level questions, however, you may find that by dropping back to the literal—or "right there"—level, you can determine where the difficulty lies. Especially in informational texts, some students may not be picking up enough of the facts to be *able* to respond to the higher-level questions. Students who seem to be reading appropriate texts but who are having persistent problems in recalling details, or in relating those details to each other and to the students' own prior knowledge, can benefit from your instructing them in Question/Answer Relationships and through "ReQuest" and "Reciprocal Teaching" (see below).

Question/Answer Relationships In the last chapter, we discussed the direct teaching involved in helping students understand and apply knowledge of Question/Answer Relationships in narrative texts. Now let's explore QARs again, in the context of informational texts.

Again, this is an excellent way to demonstrate directly to students *how* the text, the reader, and the question can come together to create appropriate meaning. You will find that the terminology and the demonstration can apply across different contexts in which you are teaching about comprehension. For

Darla Ketchum used the following passage to walk her fifth-grade students through a demonstration of how to use these different sources of information and of the thinking the reader engages in.

> It was an August day in the year 1958. Across the North Pole—the northernmost point on our planet, Earth, icy winds howled. Stretching to the horizon in all directions was a mass of colorless, broken, and heaved-up ice—the Polar Ice Pack. It formed an almost solid covering for the surface of the water. It was made up of pieces of ice, called floes, some several feet across, others much more than a mile. Now and then there were leads or spaces between the floes and a few stretches of open water. In most places the ice was ten or fifteen feet thick, but at times it extended as far as 90 feet below the surface.
>
> On this Saturday morning, about 400 feet below the surface of the ocean, a U.S. submarine, the Nautilus, steamed steadily northward. Her captain was Commander William R. Anderson. Together with his crew of 116 men, he was taking part in one of the most thrilling adventures upon which any sailor had ever embarked.
>
> Below the Nautilus were the floor of the Arctic Ocean and the towering cliffs of the undersea mountains. Forming an almost solid roof above her head was the ice pack. Her streamlined hull was painted with a special dark gray paint. She resembled an enormous shark as she steamed steadily northward through the dark waters.

The passage was shown on an overhead transparency. After the students read it, Darla presented questions, one at a time, and discussed the relationship between each question and the passage. Her sequence moved from the "right there" on up through the "on my own."

The first question was "Who was the captain of the *Nautilus?*" With the students, Darla skimmed back over the passage until the answer, "Commander William R. Anderson," was found. Darla pointed out how the answer to the question is *right there*—the text actually *says* the captain of the *Nautilus* was Commander William R. Anderson.

She next presented the question "Does the Polar Ice Pack have the same thickness in different places?" She modeled how she looks over the text, and when she came to the words *Polar Ice Pack* paid close attention. She read the next few sentences aloud. When she came to the sentence *In most places the ice was ten or fifteen feet thick, but at times it extended as far as 90 feet below the surface,* she talked about how she knew that the ice pack does *not* have the same thickness everywhere because the text says it can be anywhere from ten or fifteen to as much as 90 feet thick: "Boys and girls, does anyone see where the passage actually *says* 'The Polar Ice Pack did not have the same thickness'? Nope! So I have to take the information that is given and *put it together* to answer our question."

Darla told her students that whether an "In My Head" response is "author and me" or "on my own" all depends on the individual student and his or her prior knowledge. She modeled this aspect as she discussed these two types of "in my head" understandings:

"Was the *Nautilus* close to the ocean floor?" While the passage does not say or imply that the *Nautilus* was close to the ocean floor, it *does* state that the *Nautilus* was 400 feet below the surface. *If* the reader can supply the rest of the information that is needed—specifically, how deep the ocean is at the North Pole—this is an "author and me" question: by combining information from the text with information already in the reader's head, the question can be answered.

"If sailors have claustrophobia, does the Navy assign them to submarines?" This is an "on my own" question, because there is *no* information in the passage to suggest an answer. Darla explained this type of question/answer relationship this way: "*No* information that would answer this question is stated in the passage. There is no information I can 'put together' to answer the question, either—the author simply has not said or hinted at *anything* having to do with claustrophobia! So I would need to go somewhere else to find the answer, *or* I might be able to answer it anyway—even without reading the passage! This would be because I already know something about what submarines are like, and that nuclear subs in particular often stay submerged for weeks on end. This kind of a response is an 'on my own' response."

example, when you are involving your students in practice tests to get ready for the annual testing in your school district, you may demonstrate how the wording of a question can guide the students to the appropriate answer.

Knowledge about questions and about how to question will infuse all the strategies you will help your students internalize. The strategies will always require your students to think explicitly about what is new, what is known, and how this information relates to them as learners. In almost all the activities and strategies you teach, questions are posed before, during, and after the reading.

Synthesizing Questioning with Strategies That Support Students Who Need More "On-Line" Help   After you have taught about questions, texts, and relationships between them and the reader, you may still have one or more students who for whatever reason are experiencing difficulty in dealing with informational texts. The two "on-line" procedures I'll present here, ReQuest and Reciprocal Teaching, help you teach more directly to a student's needs because you are both modeling and responding to what the student is doing right at that moment.

ReQuest   This procedure involves a back-and-forth question/answer format between teacher and students (Manzo, 1969). It is very effective with students who are focusing more on individual words when they read, rather than on ideas and meaning. Here's how it works:

1. You determine how big a "chunk" of text will be read by the students. Start modestly—usually with just a single paragraph. Everyone reads this chunk silently.
2. Afterward, you ask the students one question. You may ask those who respond correctly *how* they determined the answer.

3. Read another paragraph or chunk of text. *This* time, after you finish, have the students ask *you* a question.
4. The format proceeds this way, back and forth between teacher and students asking and answering questions. Whenever necessary, the process of determining the answer is explained.

A distinct benefit of reciprocal questioning is the *modeling of questioning* you can provide. Although you may begin with easy questions, your questions will usually tap more than the "literal" or "right there" level; they should require students to pull information together. This is an excellent technique for teaching awareness of the traditional "main idea/supporting details" skill; your question may be a simply worded "What is the most important thing being talked about in this paragraph?" with the follow-up "How do you know?" In time, students begin to pick up on the types of questions you are asking and to model their questions on yours.

Reciprocal Teaching   Quite close to reciprocal questioning in objective and technique, reciprocal *teaching* involves a close interaction between teacher and students (Palincsar & Brown, 1983, 1989; Pearson, 1984; Pearson & Gallagher, 1984). It is an excellent extension of ReQuest in that it goes beyond the scope of ReQuest to pull together "questioning" with other important skills in the same instructional context, thereby helping students learn how to orchestrate them all most effectively. It is intended for use with students who need additional specific help in monitoring and in being in control of their own reading.

Based on larger chunks of text than we use for ReQuest, reciprocal teaching involves the modeling of *questioning, summarizing, clarifying,* and *predicting.* It provides a supportive scaffold as it gradually releases control of the process to the students:

1. Work with a small group. Have students read a portion of a chapter silently. When they finish, ask two or three questions based on the passage. If students are uncertain about any answer, model how to determine the response.

2. Provide a brief oral summary. "Think aloud" as you do this, saying such things as "Pulling this information together, I'd like to *summarize* or tell what the main points of this section are. . . ."

3. Ask if anyone needs something to be made *clearer:* is there anything students are uncertain about or do not understand at this point? If so, retrace your explanatory steps for them; using different words or phrases in your modeling is likely to be helpful.

4. Just as in a Guided Reading-Thinking Activity, the foundation is laid for *predictions* about information and ideas that may be encountered in the next section to be read.

Gradually, different students can take over your guiding role—with you still there to provide support, encouragement, and feedback as necessary. Your "gradual release of control" to them may involve occasionally stepping in to help the student "teacher" construct a summary, or to help clarify an aspect for another student. What you remain involved in during any one session, and how rapidly you pass along control of the interaction, always depends on the students' understanding of the different skills involved. It is an excellent opportunity for you to monitor "on-line" your students' development in an authentic interaction with an informational text.

Study skills: reading to remember

Study skills involve deliberate efforts to remember and apply information with an eye toward specific tasks that will require that knowledge and application. Of course there is overlap between such a definition and reading in informational texts in general. The main distinction between study skills and other types of critical reading in informational texts is a practical one: study skills are applied when there is a body of information "out there" in texts or lectures that students know they will be expected to learn—whether for a test or more voluntarily, because they *desire* to learn it for a project they are working on.

I'll put myself on the firing line here to offer an example. There were probably chunks of information in Chapter 2, for example, that were not intrinsically interesting to you: short-term memory, macrostructure and microstructure, and so forth—yet your professor may have required you to "learn" this information. Her or his objective, and mine, is to help you establish some familiarity with the underlying processes of reading, to lay a foundation for later information. Your *immediate* task, however, was quite clear: you were probably going to be *tested* on that material! So you may have employed certain study skills to remember the information long enough to do well on a specific task—the test—in which you would apply it. Other information in this textbook may be of more intrinsic interest to you, and you find yourself remembering it without so much deliberate effort.

Learning can be a lot more fun than we think, but it may not *always* be fun, and students will not always be able to get excited about everything they are expected to learn. Study skills help us in these kinds of situations.

It's important to be clear with our students about the reality of learning. Very, very few individuals can remember *everything* they read. We remember what is important, and we remember what we deliberately set out to remember. And as for those details we don't remember, we realize that we know how to find them later on, if we need them. *This* is the realistic and effective perspective on learning—in discussions, lectures, and reading.

Focusing   Perhaps now more than ever, when information is exploding all around our students, they must understand *how* to access the information they need. They have to learn focusing or "locational" skills (as they are often called) in order to know how to home in on what they need—to determine what resource is likely to have the information it's necessary for them to get. The ability to focus requires that students have a definite goal in mind, and on the basis of this goal, know what type of information they need. They will refer to particular informational trade books, encyclopedias, almanacs, atlases, perhaps dictionaries, and phone books (which even include simple first-aid information). And they should know how to use a card catalogue and a computerized cataloguing system. Learning about computerized systems will naturally tie in, by the way, with students' use of the telecommunications potential of computers and the information available in many software and CD/ROM packages (for example, *National Geographic Kids Network;* see also Chapter 10). In the past, these skills have rarely been taught directly, especially with regard to determining what information is relevant once the appropriate source has been accessed (Guthrie and Mosenthal, 1987). Students will need to remember both the information they access and *how* to remember, as well.

So many of your "focusing" minilessons will help your students learn and understand what to do when the reading gets tough and they've got to step back and figure out a plan of attack. In many cases, by the way, the first step might be to *speed up* to get an overall sense of what's happening. *Then* they can go back and engage the appropriate "fix-up" strategy (Atwell, 1987; Smith, 1988).

Reference Skills   Among the most important *focusing* skills are *reference skills*—such activities as learning to use an informational text's table of contents or index (see page 339). Many third-graders and most fourth-graders are capable of this type of hierarchical thinking. These skills will usually need to be revisited throughout the year. After discussing the index, for example, suggest headings or entries under which particular information could be found—and check on it. Discuss how some headings or entries might be more pertinent than others; then, check the actual index.

We then move beyond the single text, to introduce and teach about almanacs, encyclopedias, and so forth. While these have been on hand all along in the classroom, we directly discuss the structure and purpose of each and which different kinds of information can be accessed. For each type of reference text, we can brainstorm possible headings for the specific information we are looking for, and then check. Often we discover that we need to teach about the common abbreviations that are used in such texts, as well.

Once students have focused in on the particular text they need, they often need to skim or scan to find the specific piece of information they are after. We should model skimming and scanning for them, because they are also helpful skills for other kinds of reading besides "focus" reading.

Skimming and Scanning   First, let's have definitions. *Skimming* is the rapid type of reading we do to get an overall feel for material—for example, to determine whether our idea about an encyclopedia article's being most appropriate for our purpose is correct. Skimming helps us decide if we *do* need to read a selection more deliberately and deeply. *Scanning,* on the other hand, is what we do when we are looking for a specific bit of information; we know the question and want to find the answer.

Demonstrating both skills for students is done best by working from a piece of text that all the students or a smaller group of students can see, such as a transparency on the overhead projector. Next, involve the students in scanning a selection for answers to specific questions you provide—start with "right there" kinds of responses.

"Graphical" Literacy—Reading Maps, Graphs, and Diagrams

Maps, graphs, and diagrams constitute a particular kind of literacy. There are often additional symbol systems involved: In the case of maps, a *key* provides the clues—if students learn that there is in fact a key. Graphs also have "keys" of a sort, so that the type and unit of measurement is clear. Diagrams usually correspond more directly than maps and graphs to what they represent: A cutaway diagram of the heart, for example, will show more than a surface photograph, of course, but it will also illustrate the parts, their function, and the direction of the flow of blood. "Walking through" a diagram with students, discussing the step-by-step sequence of information—keeping in mind the overall organization of the diagram—is an important instructional objective.

When you first introduce and discuss maps, graphs, and diagrams, relate them to the real world. Before discussing maps in a book, create a map of the classroom—then of the playground, then of the neighborhood. When you begin graphing, start with a bar graph format and have the children graph something that is concrete—determining the number of students in class with blue eyes, for example, or brown eyes, gray eyes, hazel eyes. Students will be able to see immediately the visual representation of quantity.

When introducing *diagrams,* tie them directly to whatever they represent. A simple electric motor can be disassembled, the parts discussed, and a rough diagram drawn. When studying the body, obtain a beef brain (remember the beef *heart* earlier in this chapter?!) and discuss its parts in relation to a well-structured diagram such as the one in *Blood and Guts: A Working Guide to Your Own Insides* (Allison, 1976).

After your students are aware of the function of maps, graphs, and diagrams, you can examine them as they occur in textbooks and in trade informational books. You will need to underscore their importance as well as the need for students to examine them during their preview of a section of an informational text. Usually, of course, the tendency is to ignore them (a strategy not unknown among adult readers). Eventually, students will come to realize the importance of these graphic representations in helping them construct an overview of a section before reading, as well as in helping them grasp and retain important concepts addressed in the text.

Reinking (1986) described the "Graphic Information Lesson," an effective and motivating procedure for helping students move beyond simply learning *how* to read graphically-displayed information, to learning to interpret and make judgments about graphic aids. He stressed the importance of helping students see the relationships among the graphs, the text, and the students' background information. In this respect, Reinking's procedure is similar to the procedure for helping students understand Question/Answer Relationships. In effect, teachers help students understand the differences between information that is graphically displayed and information that the reader can infer from such a display, together with the information in the text and perhaps some background information. Students are also led to the understanding of how to make judgments about the usefulness of graphic aids: are these aids simply repeating information in the text, elaborating and clarifying it, or providing additional information that is not discussed in the text?

Using a graph from a social studies text as an example (see Figure 7.10), the teacher discusses the following with a group of students:

- the map represents the Old South and the new Cotton Kingdom; this distinction is explained in the text
- the closeness of the dots indicates that more cotton was being grown
- the Mason-Dixon line, while not discussed in the present chapter, was discussed in an earlier chapter
- the greater number of dots close to rivers suggests that the rivers were used to transport goods efficiently

The first two observations are based directly on the map. The first and third observations require explanations found in the text; the last observation goes "beyond" the map and the text. By making this type of observation, the teacher can help the students become aware of how they can apply information presented in graphics to extend more fully their understanding.

Reinking goes on to describe how, first, the teacher and then later the students can make "pseudographs" that present information based on a text,

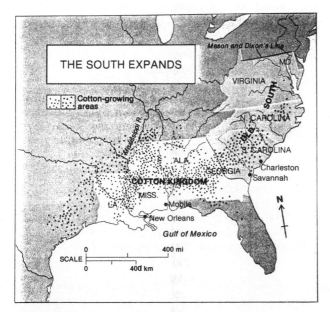

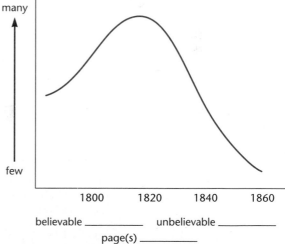

Figure 7.10
Textbook Map and Teacher's "Pseudograph"

but which may or may not be "believable." For example, as part of the unit on the American South, a teacher asked the students to judge the pseudograph presented in Figure 7.10. Note that students have to indicate the pages in the text that support their judgment. Working in small groups, as students prepare pseudographs to be shared with other students, their understanding of the text and the topic as well as of graphic aids is effectively developed. ∎

Note-Taking, Summarizing, and Outlining

Developing a "Sense" for Note-Taking   In her third-grade classroom, Donna Maxim (1990) helps her students develop a sense for notetaking as she guides them toward skill and independence in notetaking, through the following steps.

1. After listening to the teacher read aloud a chapter from an engaging informational book, as a class the students list what they remember from the text—whales, for example; which do they remember hearing about, and what information about each do they recall?

2. The next day, and each subsequent day, after another chapter from the book is read, each student writes in his or her own journal those facts that he or she recalls. In addition, students may write questions they have about the overall topic or about a specific whale: what in the book made them curious, wishing to find out more? These daily entries can lead to other reading, as well as provide discussion topics.

3. Students are ready to take notes from their own reading. As Maxim pointed out, up to this point they have built up their confidence and their skill as note-takers through *listening*. Students now choose an informational book or magazine that they believe will provide information about their topic. On the basis of the book's title and what they see on the front cover, they list questions they believe might be answered in the book. Then they read for several minutes—*without* taking any notes yet. Afterward—*without* looking back at the book—they write in their journals any answers they have found. This is not easy for many students; they want to copy the information directly out of the informational text. After a few sessions like this, though, they become much more confident. What Donna Maxim notes about the success of her third-graders should be applicable to older students as well:

> Through activities such as these, I teach my students how to listen to, read for, and respond to information. They learn how to recognize important facts, use more than one resource to verify information, take meaningful notes, and record facts quickly and easily. Instead of copying someone else's words, they are beginning to see themselves as researchers who take notes. The chances are good that they will not become victims of the plagiarism syndrome.

I would like here to underscore two important points about this approach. First, students develop confidence in their ability to select and recall important information from informational texts; second, because of this confidence, they do not fall into the "copying" mode that yields compositions that are in large part plagiarized or at least are not written in the students' own voices.

Note-Taking Based on Independent Reading It is inevitable that students will want to make notes *while* they are reading (after all, that's what most of us do when *we* study or do research). So we should, at an appropriate time, model for students how they can go about doing this. Incidentally, the strategy we model is the same one that most older students, including adults, find most beneficial. This instruction is appropriate when students understand the structure of informational texts and the relationship between main ideas and subordinate ideas. I suggest that you introduce and model it in a two-step process (Routman, 1991; Vaughan & Estes, 1986). Below is a summary of that process:

Step One: Use a well-structured textbook or informational trade book. Copy the first page of a chapter on the left-hand side of a transparency and leave the right-hand side blank (see Figure 7.11). Display the transparency on an overhead projector, then "think aloud" while you read the passage orally; underline important information and phrases, explaining your reasoning. Then, on the blank right-hand side of the transparency, you will make notes based on that information. Next, give pairs of students part of an article or chapter and a blank transparency; they will do what you

TREASURES IN THE EARTH

In the stones of the Earth is a kind of museum. Like the art museum, the museum of the Earth has many beautiful and sometimes mysterious works. These works are <u>the remains of plants and animals that lived millions of years ago</u>. To the average person, this <u>fossil record</u> looks complex. The stories held within the fossils seem hard to understand. However, to the trained observer the stories are clear and interesting. The fossils tell of an <u>Earth far different from the one we know today</u>. It is in a museum of natural history that we begin our search for an understanding of early life.

> Fossils are plants and animals that lived millions of years ago
>
> Earth was very different millions of years ago

UNCOVERING DINOSAUR FOSSILS

Today we have many remains to study, from the smallest plants to the largest animals to walk on Earth — <u>the dinosaurs</u>. You have probably seen elephants in a zoo. Elephants are very large, but the dinosaurs were much larger. <u>The largest dinosaur may have weighed 100 tons</u>, as much as a whole herd of elephants. <u>About 65 million years ago the dinosaurs died</u> out. They <u>became</u> extinct.

> Dinosaurs were the largest animals to walk on earth Largest dinosaur 100 tons 65 million years ago became extinct

Figure 7.11
Think-Aloud During Note-Taking

have modeled and what they have experienced. Afterward, each pair shares their transparency with a group or with the whole class, and you as well as their classmates offer feedback.

Step Two: This strategy for note-taking is particularly helpful in preparing students for both essay and multiple-choice tests (Vaughan and Estes, 1986; Pauk, 1974). Using a transparency of a blank page from *your* journal, explain to the students, "On the left-hand side of the page, I am going to write down the headings (or the main ideas); and across from them, on the right-hand side of the page, I'm going to write down the important supporting ideas." Then, for studying later on, students can cover one side of their own journal pages: Looking only at the main-idea side, they can practice recalling the information that supports those main ideas; then they can check themselves. When they cover the main-idea side of the page, seeing only the supporting ideas, they can recall the main ideas.

Note-Taking Based on Lectures Taking notes while listening to lectures is demanding. You can provide a solid learning context for your students by integrating your teaching about note-taking with "minilectures" and with your teaching about outlines. Introduce these strategies by informing the students that the skills you will be exploring with them will help them remember more information, will help them do better when they take tests, and *definitely* will help them with strategies for learning.

Lecture on important points that will be addressed in the reading or in an overall unit of study. Keep the lecture short; five to ten minutes, with demonstrations if necessary, is an appropriate length. It's worth bearing in mind that you'll be helping your students hone their *listening* abilities as well.

The first step in teaching about outlines is to have a simple outline clearly displayed on a transparency or on the chalkboard. Keep *closely* to this outline as you talk. No note-taking is necessary.

The second step involves your lecturing on another day and from an outline, but do not include certain points in the outline—*students* will fill in the points that they believe will fit.

From here on, but only for those students who are comfortable with the second step, you can include less and less information in your outline. An excellent way to help students check to see whether they are getting down the important points you have *not* listed on your outline is to show them your *complete* outline on the overhead projector, after the lecture. In pairs, they can compare their notes in the outline format with yours.

You may need to reassure your students that their notes are "skeletal" forms of the information, that they need not compose entire sentences but may use single words and phrases. Be sure to point out to them that these outlines/ notes are excellent study guides as well. By introducing and developing students' abilities to outline this way, you are *avoiding* the usual consequences of outlining, such as students' catching on quickly to copying down the headings and sub-headings of a chapter, but failing to think about the chapter's organization while doing so.

CONSTRUCTING MEANING THROUGH WRITING

When children compose *stories,* as we saw in the last chapter, they have a unique, active opportunity to learn about the structure and dynamics of how stories work. And on another level, they are learning much about themselves and their world. When children compose *informational* kinds of texts, they can gain the same kind of understanding of how expository text works, and they can also learn much about their world and about themselves. Writing as a part of reading and in response to reading informational texts powerfully reinforces children's concepts and understandings.

Writing as a means of understanding what informational texts are about

Composing expository texts—reports, descriptions, instructions, and so forth—gives students a unique, active grasp of the nature of informational text and how it works. In other words, students can gain a sense of "ownership" of formats and what formats allow them to do—really, all the types of information we described earlier in the section "Understanding and Defining Informational Texts." For example, Kelsey gains a genuine appreciation of the organizing role that headings and separate sections play in informational text when she is pulling together information from her interview with her grandfather which will be published in the school newspaper—she decides to organize the text according to her grandfather's childhood and his adult life, first as a parent, and then as a grandparent. Matthew discovers how a written description of the daily progress of the seedlings he has planted can complement the diagram he has drawn of their appearance—his text explores more about *why* these changes are occurring while his drawing represents more about *what* is changing.

Writing as a means of learning from informational texts

As students become motivated to pursue and learn about topics that matter to them, perhaps as part of an integrated unit (see Chapter 9), they will also come to understand the excitement about a topic that writers and illustrators of informational trade books convey. These individuals are *researchers,* and students can come to think of themselves as being researchers, too (Atwell, 1990; Macrorie, 1988).

Just as with informational *reading,* with informational *writing* we need to focus as much on *process* as on *product.* And with informational reading and writing in particular, we want to help children understand just how valuable a tool writing actually is. There are so many times when, as Lucy Calkins has put it, a writer is "not writing to produce but, instead, to think" (1986, p. 262).

So we know children are writing to learn: writing in journals or logs, writing as they engage in discussion, and of course writing as they compose more structured informational texts on their own. There is a process here, too, of moving from the concrete and immediate toward the more removed or abstract. Often we inadvertently frustrate students' efforts to write informational compositions, because we expect too much too soon. We have tried to teach them how to "write a report," for example, at the same time as we tried to teach them about reference materials, bibliographic format, and a bundle of other specific skills.

What we need to do instead is take time to help students learn the process of observing and thinking about matters that are concrete, that are in their immediate lives and experience. Then we can guide them along the road toward abstracting. When students have a stake in what they are writing about, they often will *read* more widely about their topic. This reading is usually intense and focused. Students should read, *write* about what they read, and then read some more. This will help the thoughts seep in and the insights develop. Once the writing is underway, you and your students can help sustain the effort through sharing and questioning and returning to the draft. As Calkins has expressed it, students ". . . shuttle between studying their topic and teaching others what they were learning" (Calkins, 1986, p. 282). She goes on to point out that the process "is one of collecting, connecting, and then collecting again; of shifting between learning, teaching, and learning. It is in this way that students develop the expertise from which they will write."

There are a number of ways in which we can move students comfortably into composing informational pieces at the same time as they experience such texts through their reading. These can be very effective for guiding them into an understanding of themselves as researchers.

Observing, Noting, and Recording   Before our students put pencil or pen to the informational paper, we should help them "learn how to look"—to *observe* (Graves, 1989). This is the essence of beginning to understand how things work and the processes that guide natural events. For instance, we ask our students

Two sixth graders observe pampas grass—learning how to look is the essence of beginning to understand how things work.

to "just look" and then write down in their journals what they see over the period of a few minutes. This is the beginning of stepping back, of taking an objective stance. They can then quite literally "compare notes" with one another—what did they see and hear during the last five or ten minutes?

It is a good idea to allow students plenty of time to "mess around" with their information before launching "formally" into the enterprise of writing a piece. We encourage them to write in their journals or learning logs—Lucy Calkins (1991) has referred to these as "writer's notebooks." As students record information, they can organize and reorganize it, drawing diagrams, sketches, making outlines, and so forth.

Interviewing   Rather than jumping into books for information and models, students can explore information sources that are more concrete and firsthand: Parents, grandparents, and neighbors are good beginning subjects. Students can learn more quickly how to gather, organize, and present information because it is firsthand. And since it is of interest to them personally, it is motivating. Good starter questions are: What was it like in the "old days"? What did you do for entertainment? What did you like to read?

Many teachers find that it is helpful to model an interview for the students first. They select a particular student to interview—with that student's permission—in front of a small group or the whole class. The teacher prepares a list of questions to ask the student about the project he or she is working on. After the interview, the students work in pairs, practicing writing questions about their topics and then interviewing each other. The whole class can follow up these practice interviews by generating a list of the "do's and don'ts" of

Students often benefit from interviewing people they know because doing so is motivating and it allows them to explore information sources that are concrete and firsthand.

■ ■ ■ ■ ■

**CLASSROOM
IN ACTION**

*Second-Graders
Research and Write
About the Day They
Were Born*

Using Debra Frasier's *On the Day You Were Born* (1991) as a focus, each second- and third-grader in a multi-age classroom wrote a book about his or her own birth. Frasier's book is an engaging combination of an almost poetic narrative describing different features of the earth "on the day you were born" (see Figure 7.12) with concise information about important elements that emerged in the narrative.

At the end of the book, after the narrative is concluded, Frasier presents a straightforward and interesting discussion of several striking images in the narrative; for example, "Earth . . . spinning" includes information about the earth's rotation on its *axis,* how fast the earth rotates, and so forth; "gravity's strong pull" describes weight and the effects of the sun, the moon, and the earth.

Here's how interaction with this book facilitated research and a delightful type of informational text for each student:

1. The book was read aloud on several days. Discussion included attention to Frasier's use of *paper collage* and how she chose to illustrate her text.
2. The students discussed what they would like to know about the day each of *them* was born and what their births were like. The teacher led them to the realization that they could interview their parents, so a list of possible questions was brainstormed (see Figure 7.13).
3. Each student decided which questions to ask his or her parents, and these were included in a letter that the teacher had written and duplicated to be sent home.

On the day you were born
the round planet Earth
turned toward your morning sky,
whirling past darkness,
spinning the night into light.

Figure 7.12
Pages from On the Day You Were Born

interviewing. A simple report will be the final result; it can be shared with the class and with the "live" sources of the information.

Composing and Using Letters Letters are informational texts that when sent to an audience outside the immediate school environment are a little more

Figure 7.13
Brainstormed List

How long did it take for me to be born?

Where did you live?

Where was I born?

What was the weather like?

What were you doing?

Were any relatives visiting?

What was going on in the world?

Did you save anything from that day?

What did I look like?

How did you react?

Was I sick when I was born?

4. Students organized and wrote the information from their parents' responses in their journals (children who were adopted as babies learned about the day their adoptive parents first got to see them—usually the same day that the parents brought them home).

5. The teacher talked with the students about deciding how much "text" to put on a page in their books and how to decide what to illustrate on the facing page. A "dummy book" was written first, in which the students tried out their text allotments and illustrations.

6. A final, published copy of each student's book was prepared, and the students gave the completed books to their parents as presents.

In Figure 7.14 we see Hannah's journal entry and part of her completed book.

The teacher was not concerned about students' taking what their parents said and writing it down almost verbatim; at this point, her objective was to give the children a sense of how to go about gathering and organizing information. This project was a good transition to learning how to take notes from printed sources and put that information in their own words.

■ ■ ■ ■ ■
CLASSROOM IN ACTION

Continued

abstract. Students can be encouraged to ask about something they're interested in or to complain about something. For example, a class of fifth-graders wrote letters to the local newspaper, saying how much more they enjoyed their new literature-based reading program than the traditional basal program they had been using. Their motivation for writing was a campaign by some parents who were concerned that questionable values might be promoted by the types of stories the children would be reading. Purposes such as these help students understand that the best way to effectively communicate through letters—in this case, reaching a much broader audience—is to care deeply about your topic, organize your information well, and present it in a considerate fashion.

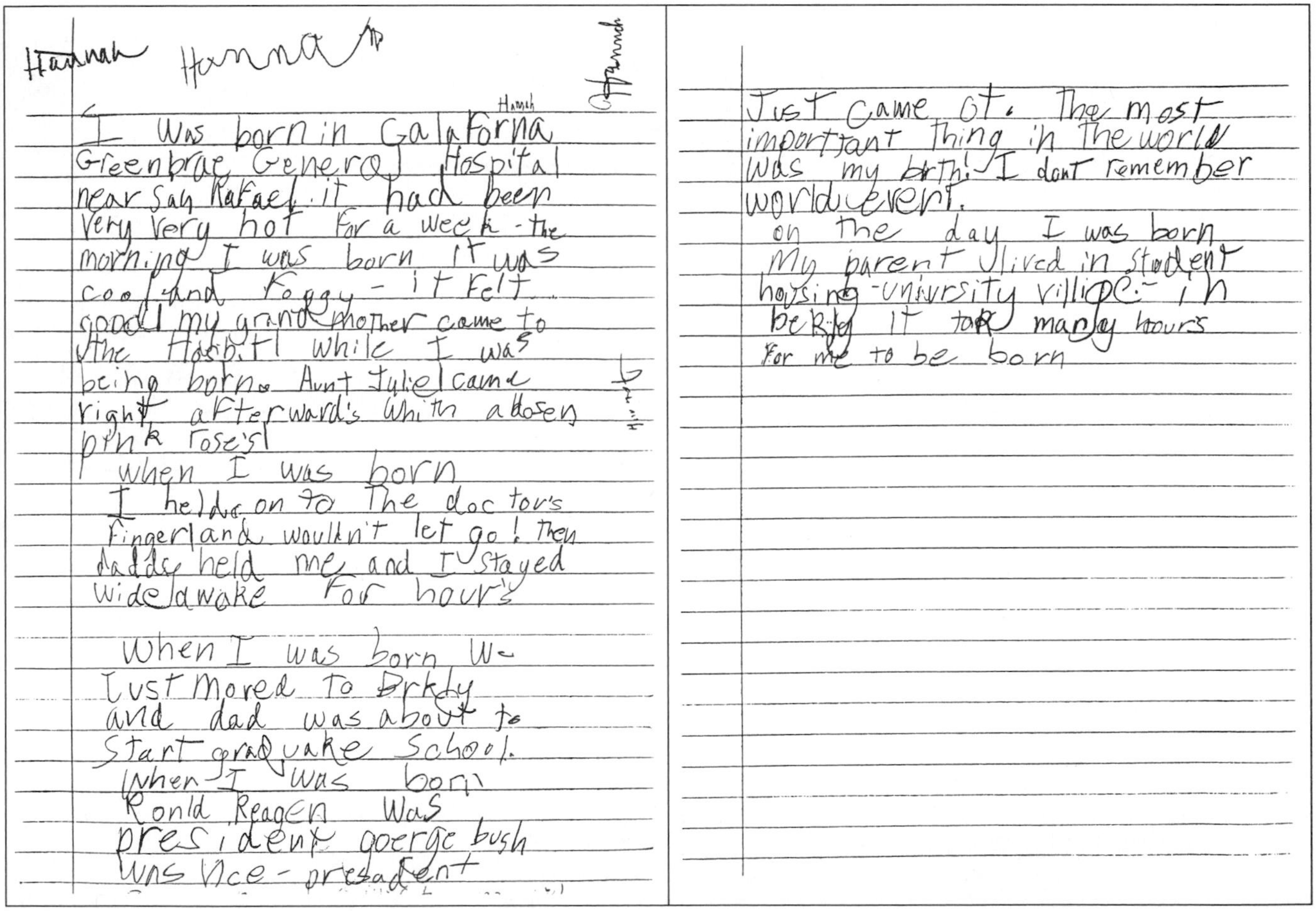

Hannah   Hannah

I was born in Galaforna
Greenbrae General Hospital
near San Rafael. it had been
very very hot for a week - the
morning I was born it was
cool and foggy - it felt
good. my grandmother came to
the Hospital while I was
being born. Aunt Julie came
right afterward's whith a dosen
pink rose's

When I was born
I held on to the doctor's
finger and wouldn't let go! Then
daddy held me and I stayed
wide awake for hours

When I was born we
just moved to Brkly
and dad was about to
start graduate school.
When I was born
Ronld Reagen was
president goerge bush
was vice - president

Just came of. The most
important thing in the world
was my brth. I dont remember
world event.
on the day I was born
my parent lived in student
housing - university villige. in
berkly it took many hours
for me to be born

Figure 7.14
Hannah's Journal Entry and Part of Her Completed Book

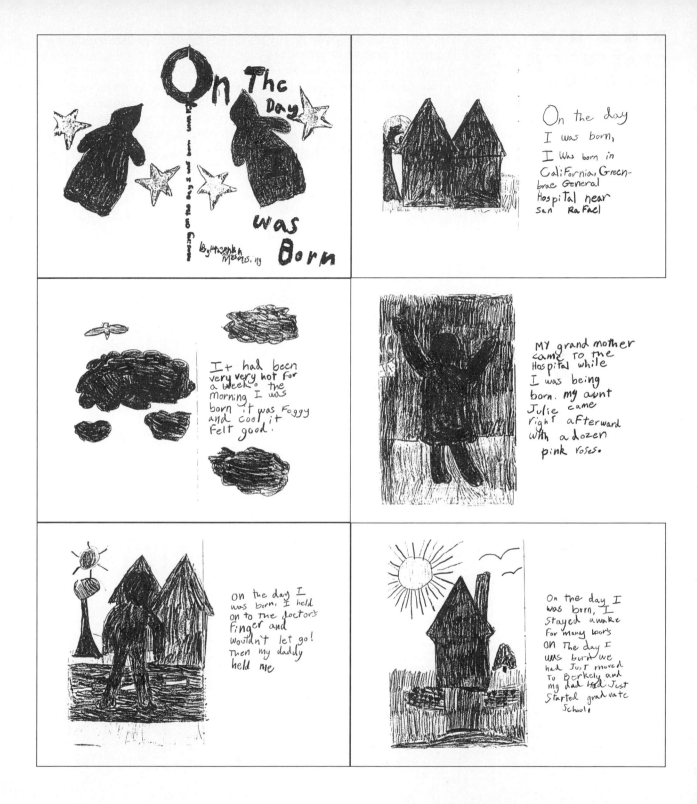

On The Day was Born

By Hannah Meares-ing

On the day I was born,

I Was born in California, Greenbrae General Hospital near San Rafael

It had been very very hot for a week. the morning I was born it was foggy and cool it felt good.

MY grandmother came to the Hospital while I was being born. my aunt Julie came right afterward with a dozen pink roses.

On the day I was born, I held on to the doctor's finger and wouldn't let go! Then my daddy held me

On the day I was born, I stayed awake for many hours On the day I was born we had just moved To Berkely and my dad had just started graduate school.

■ ■ ■ ■ ■

**CLASSROOM
IN ACTION**

*Fifth-Graders Put
Themselves into
History*

■ ■ ■ ■ ■

As part of a unit in her American history fifth-grade curriculum, Barbara Milchak handed out the "Gold Rush" sheet presented in Figure 7.15. Each student kept an ongoing log of his or her journey, and Barbara responded along the way. She has found that this format is an excellent, "real-world" means for students to integrate their developing knowledge about a topic with information and skills that arise from other content areas, such as math and science.

To give you a sense of how students respond to this format, I've included the very first and last entries from Josh's rather extensive log.

Figure 7.15
*"Gold Rush" Sheet and
Sample Log Entries*

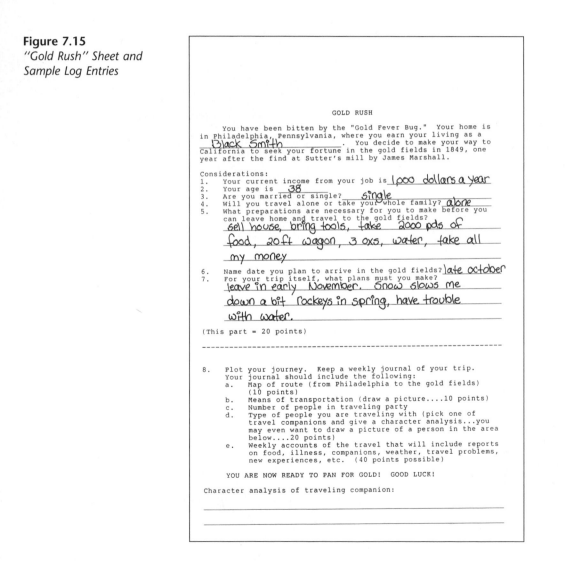

GOLD RUSH

You have been bitten by the "Gold Fever Bug." Your home is in Philadelphia, Pennsylvania, where you earn your living as a _Black Smith_ . You decide to make your way to California to seek your fortune in the gold fields in 1849, one year after the find at Sutter's mill by James Marshall.

Considerations:
1. Your current income from your job is _1,000 dollars a year_
2. Your age is _38_
3. Are you married or single? _single_
4. Will you travel alone or take your whole family? _alone_
5. What preparations are necessary for you to make before you can leave home and travel to the gold fields?
   sell house, bring tools, take 2000 pds of food, 20ft wagon, 3 oxs, water, take all my money
6. Name date you plan to arrive in the gold fields? _late october_
7. For your trip itself, what plans must you make?
   leave in early November. Snow slows me down a bit rockeys in spring, have trouble with water.

(This part = 20 points)

----

8. Plot your journey. Keep a weekly journal of your trip. Your journal should include the following:
   a. Map of route (from Philadelphia to the gold fields) (10 points)
   b. Means of transportation (draw a picture....10 points)
   c. Number of people in traveling party
   d. Type of people you are traveling with (pick one of travel companions and give a character analysis...you may even want to draw a picture of a person in the area below....20 points)
   e. Weekly accounts of the travel that will include reports on food, illness, companions, weather, travel problems, new experiences, etc. (40 points possible)

   YOU ARE NOW READY TO PAN FOR GOLD! GOOD LUCK!

Character analysis of traveling companion:

_____

_____

Getting Started with the Writing   The question or topic students explore should be a manageable one. It may spin out from something they already know a little about and *care* about—this develops into what we call the "student as expert" notion. We usually need to help children with this process of discovering what they know, and what they want to find out in relation to what they know, and we may need to model any or all of the following as prewriting activities (Graves, 1989):

1. Making a web
2. Writing a list
3. Drawing a picture

Then we can help students ask questions based on one part of the original web or idea—help them choose just a part of their information and then write about

November 8, 1849
I'm now leaving, I have some second thoughts about leaving Phily.
   Fortunely I had a wagon and ox. That saved me money. It's a cool day with a sharp breeze. It's over cast, and a black cloud is moving toids my town. I'm leaving my life, the only company I'll have now is Barrett, Webster, and Clifton my oxs. Right before I left I bought a mule, I haven't named her yet but I'm sure I will.
   I'm worried I will be going on my own, I wish I could have found a wagon train. I couldn't afford a train ticket so I'll be traveling by wagon. All I can afford 's propel raft rides.

November 25, 1849
   I'v been making good time, on the 10th I hoped a barg across the Mississippi river. It's still cool and a 1/2 inch of snow fell. That was on the 20th. It didn't alect my proformance at all. I rested in Mephis. and on the 23rd I

June 21, 1850
I slowly coming out of the 'Utah mountains. Theres lots of water, the cold slimy rocks are giving my wagon havock!
   I let molly graze there are two reasons for this, one, when the wagon would slide molly would be draged behind it, two, I felt bad for her.
   I had the worst, most dousting meal ever! I shot a cyote and decided to cut of the hind quaits and BBQ them. Back east we had no Cyots!, I didn't know what they tasted like!
   As I drawl over the golden coals waching the flesh darken, I dreamed of the red meat tumbling down my hungry throat,

that part to a particular audience. Each question may be put on a separate piece of paper or page in the learning log—it becomes a *main idea,* and information pertaining to it can be listed on that page.

■ A CONCLUDING PERSPECTIVE

Informational books constitute a very large genre, one that extends far beyond the traditional subject-matter textbook. Informational *trade* books should form a large part of your subject-matter and theme-based studies, and a number of excellent trade books in the domains of social studies, science, mathematics, art, and music have been listed in this chapter on pages 568–580.

A good deal of your instruction will help your students understand the *process* of how to go about exploring and learning—formulating and hypothesizing answers to questions posed before, during, and after reading. The process begins with the students' immersion in books that present information in engaging and enjoyable formats. You then will help them understand *how* informational texts are organized and how they can use this knowledge of structure to facilitate their learning and retention.

When you help students access prior knowledge before reading, check themselves periodically during reading, and reflect afterward on what they have read, you are helping them internalize a process of approaching any learning task, particularly one involving reading. Helping your students this way is a gradual process, culminating in the intermediate grades in the beginnings of systematic study skills.

The chapter concluded with a brief discussion of how to move your students into informational *writing.* You begin quite informally and move gradually toward more polished compositions. Keep in mind, though, that writing has also been addressed throughout this chapter, underscoring its importance in helping students understand and compose informational text.

You are in possession of the knowledge and the tools to help your students learn *how* to learn. Remember that on their own, most will not learn how to learn. They will need you to point the way and to guide them on their journey. In doing this, you will give them an invaluable gift.

■ BECOMING A REFLECTIVE PRACTITIONER

Armbruster, B, Anderson, T., & Ostertag, J. (1989). Teaching text structure to improve reading and writing. *Reading Teacher, 43,* 130–137.
   If you are in need of or are interested in a format to teach students methods of manipulating information in order to increase comprehension of content area texts, then this article is well worth the time that would be spent reading it. The authors lay it out plainly and simply for you; even though they are primarily concerned with problem/solution text structure, they also give guidelines for using texts that are compare/contrast, sequence, and cause/effect structured. The information in this article has practical application to the everyday classroom.

Guthrie, J., & Mosenthal, P. (1987). Literacy is multidimensional: Locating information and reading comprehension. *Educational Psychologist, 22,* 279–297.

Studies show that adults spend more time reading to locate information than for any other purpose. Yet the skill or process of locating information is rarely broached by texts or taught by teachers, even though these skills are essential for success in school. Guthrie and Mosenthal examine the place of information location in the scheme of reading comprehension, and how the different components of comprehension overlap and interact during the reading process, and also how they differ.

Irwin, W. (1991). *Teaching reading comprehension processes* (2nd ed.). Englewood Cliffs, NJ: Prentice-Hall.

This book synthesizes a considerable amount of research investigating the different aspects of processing that are involved in reading comprehension. But it also goes a step farther and gives good, helpful suggestions for improving and enhancing students' comprehension. A lot of these suggestions are already known to many teachers: it's just that Irwin finally puts this information into a written, organized form. This book is a terrific resource for the classroom teacher.

Meyer, B., & Freedle, R. (1984). Effects of discourse types on recall. *American Educational Research Journal, 21,* 121–143.

This article explores the importance of the structure or organization of written work and how this organization impacts the ability of students to recall information. Not only does the structure of text have an effect on what is recalled after reading a selection, but it also has an effect on recall when listening tasks are performed. Meyer and Freedle suggest that the comparative structure is the most effective in aiding recall. (See the Richgels article)

Palincsar, A., & Brown, D. (1986). Interactive teaching to promote independent learning from text. *The Reading Teacher, 39,* 771–777.

Effective ways to engage students in discussions about text (or literature) are continually being sought. Palincsar and Brown offer the concept of *reciprocal teaching* as an effective means of stimulating students to discuss and interact with the text, other students, and the teacher in order to improve the students' comprehension. This method of teaching, in which the teacher and students take turns being the teacher, not only can be used with expository text, but with narrative as well. It works with students as young as first graders (the teacher reads to the students) and it enables the students to monitor their own reading and their own comprehension.

Richgels, D., McGee, L., Lomax, R., & Sheard, C. (1987). Awareness of four text structures: Effects on recall of expository text. *Reading Research Quarterly, 22,* 177–196.

This study takes a look at the influence of a student's awareness or prior knowledge of text structure on recall and recognizing the structure of text. In addition, the study investigated the extension of this knowledge to writing and talking. Richgels et al. also examined the extent to which a student's use of a particular text structure depends upon the student's familiarity with that structure. It is interesting to see how this study agrees with and differs from the Meyer and Freedle (1984) study. If you are interested in the structure of text and its influence on recall, then these two articles are a must.

■ REFERENCES

Armbruster, B., Anderson, T., & Ostertag, J. (1989). Teaching text structure to improve reading and writing. *Reading Teacher, 43,* 130–137.

Avery, C. (1987). First grade thinkers becoming literate. *Language Arts, 64,* 611–618.

Atwell, N. (1987). *In the middle: Writing, reading, and learning with adolescents.* Upper Montclair, NJ: Boynton/Cook.

Atwell, N. (Ed.). (1990). *Coming to know: Writing to learn in the intermediate grades.* Portsmouth, NH: Heinemann.

Bader, L. (1980). *Reading diagnosis and remediation in classroom and clinic.* New York: Macmillan.

Bear, D., & McIntosh, M. (1990). Directed Reading-Thinking Activities: Four activities to promote thinking and study habits in social studies. *Social Education, 54,* 385–388.

Calkins, L. (1986). *The art of teaching writing.* Portsmouth, NH: Heinemann.

Calkins, L. (1991). *Living between the lines.* Portsmouth, NH: Heinemann.

Cheyney, A. (1984). *Teaching reading skills through the newspaper.* Newark, DE: International Reading Association.

Fry, E. (1977). Fry's readability graph: Clarifications, validity, and extension to Level 17. *Journal of Reading, 21,* 249.

Gardner, H. (1991). *The unschooled mind.* New York: Basic Books.

Gill, J., & Bear, D. (1988). No book, whole book, and chapter DRTAs. *Journal of Reading, 31,* 444–449.

Goodman, Y., & Burke, C. (1980). *Reading strategies: Focus on comprehension.* New York: Holt, Rinehart, and Winston.

Graves, D. (1989). *Investigate nonfiction.* Portsmouth, NH: Heinemann.

Gray, W., & Leary, B. (1935). *What makes a book readable?* Chicago: University of Chicago Press.

Guthrie, J., & Mosenthal, P. (1987). Literacy is multidimensional: Locating information and reading comprehension. *Educational Psychologist, 22,* 279–297.

Haley-James, S., & Stewig, J. (1990). *Houghton Mifflin English.* Boston: Houghton Mifflin Company.

Hammond, D. (1988, March). *Guidelines for asking questions.* Paper presented at the meeting of the Sierra Nevada chapter of the International Reading Association, Reno, Nevada.

Hyde, A., & Bizar, M. (1989). *Thinking in context.* New York: Longman.

Irwin, J. (1991). *Teaching reading comprehension processes* (2nd ed.). Englewood Cliffs, NJ: Prentice-Hall.

Klare, G. (1984). Readability. In P. D. Pearson, R. Barr, M. L. Kamil, & P. Mosenthal (Eds.), *Handbook of reading research* (Vol. 1). White Plains, NY: Longman.

Langer, J. A. (1981). From theory to practice: A prereading plan. *Journal of Reading, 25,* 152–156.

Lipson, M., & Wixson, K. (1990). *Assessment and instruction of reading disability.* New York: HarperCollins.

Macrorie, K. (1988). *The I-search paper* (Revised edition of *Searching Writing*). Portsmouth, NH: Boynton/Cook.

Manzo, A. (1969). The ReQuest procedure. *Journal of Reading, 2,* 123–126.

Maxim, D. (1990). Beginning researchers. In N. Atwell (Ed.), *Coming to know: Writing to learn in the intermediate grades* (pp. 3–16). Portsmouth, NH: Heinemann.

Meltzer, M. (1993). Voices from the past. In M. O. Tunnell & R. Ammon (Eds.), *The history of ourselves: Teaching history through children's literature* (pp. 27–30). Portsmouth, NH: Heinemann.

Meyer, B., & Freedle, R. (1984). Effects of discourse types on recall. *American Educational Research Journal, 21,* 121–143.

Moore, D., Moore, S., Cunningham, P., & Cunningham, J. (1986). *Developing readers and writers in the content areas.* New York: Longman.

National Geographic Society. *National Geographic Kids Network.*

Ogle, D. (1986). K-W-L: A teaching model that develops active reading of expository text. *Reading Teacher, 39,* 564–570.

Ohlausen, M., & Roller, C. (1988). The operation of text structure and content schemata in isolation and in interaction. *Reading Research Quarterly, 23,* 70–88.

Olivares, R. (1993). *Using the newspaper to teach ESL learners.* Newark, DE: International Reading Association.

Palincsar, A., & Brown, A. (1983). *Reciprocal teaching of comprehension monitoring activities* (Tech. Rep. No. 269). Urbana, IL: University of Illinois, Center for the Study of Reading.

Palincsar, A., & Brown, A. (1989). Discourse as a mechanism for acquiring process and knowledge. Paper presented at the American Educational Research Association, March, San Francisco, California.

Pauk, W. (1974). *How to study in college.* Boston: Houghton Mifflin.

Pearson, P. D. (1984). Direct explicit teaching of reading comprehension. In G. Duffy, L. Roehler, & J. Mason (Eds.), *Comprehension instruction.* New York: Longman.

Pearson, P. D., & Gallagher, M. (1983). The instruction of reading comprehension. *Contemporary Educational Psychology, 8,* 317–344.

Pikulski, J., & Tobin, A. (1982). The cloze procedure as an informal assessment technique. In J. Pikulski & T. Shanahan (Eds.), *Approaches to the informal evaluation of reading.* Newark, DE: International Reading Association.

Reinking, D. (1986). Integrating graphic aids into content area instruction: The graphic information lesson. *Journal of Reading, 30,* 146–151.

Richgels, D., McGee, L., Lomax, R., & Sheard, C. (1987). Awareness of four text structures: Effects on recall of expository text. *Reading Research Quarterly, 22,* 177–196.

Routman, R. (1991). *Invitations: Changing as teachers and learners K–12.* Portsmouth, NH: Heinemann.

Slavin, R. (1986). *Using student team learning* (3rd ed.). Baltimore: Johns Hopkins University Press, Center for Research on Elementary and Middle Schools.

Smith, F. (1988). *Understanding reading* (4th ed.). Hillsdale, NJ: Lawrence Erlbaum Associates.

Stoll, D. (Ed.) (1994). *Magazines for kids and teens.* Newark, DE: International Reading Association.

Taylor, W. (1953). Cloze procedure: A new tool for measuring readability. *Journalism Quarterly, 30,* 415–433.

Templeton, S. (1991). *Teaching the integrated language arts.* Boston: Houghton Mifflin.

Tierney, R., Readence, J., & Dishner, E. (1990). *Reading strategies and practices* (3rd ed.). Boston: Allyn & Bacon.

Vaughan, J., & Estes, T. (1986). *Reading and reasoning beyond the primary grades.* Boston: Allyn and Bacon.

Zakaluk, B., and Samuels, S. (Eds.). (1988). *Readability: Its past, present, and future.* Newark, DE: International Reading Association.

Children's Literature Cited

Allison, L. (1976). *Blood and Guts: A working guide to your own insides.* Boston: Little, Brown.

Brown, M. (1949). *The important book.* New York: Harper.

Burns, M. (1975). *The I hate mathematics! book.* Boston: Little, Brown.

Frasier, D. (1991). *On the day you were born.* New York: Trumpet Club.

Freedman, R. (1988). *Buffalo hunt.* Boston: Houghton Mifflin.

Freedman, R. (1993). *Lincoln: A photobiography.* Boston: Houghton Mifflin.

Macaulay, D. (1988). *The way things work.* Boston: Houghton Mifflin.

Perl, L. (1987). *Mummies, tombs, and treasure: Secrets of ancient Egypt.* Clarion.

Spier, P. (1980). *People.* Doubleday.

Stein, S. (1986). *The evolution book.* New York: Workman.

Wirth, V. (1991). *Whisper from the woods.*

CHAPTER EIGHT

WORD STUDY AND VOCABULARY DEVELOPMENT IN CONTEXT

FOCUS

■ *Why is the examination of words in the intermediate grades beneficial for authentic reading?*

■ *What are the instructional goals of word knowledge and vocabulary instruction at the intermediate grades?*

■ *How are word-analysis strategies at the intermediate grade level different from those at the primary grade level, and why?*

■ *How does the structure of words provide clues to their meaning and their spelling?*

■ *How can we demonstrate for students the ways in which* morphemes *combine to form English words?*

■ *What is the role of* context *in word identification in the intermediate grades?*

■ *How can we help students expand and connect word meanings? What is the value of this knowledge?*

■ *When is it necessary to teach word meanings directly? How can we best do this?*

■ *How is students' word knowledge applied in their writing?*

WHAT DOES "KNOWING" A WORD REALLY MEAN?

PRINCIPLES OF VOCABULARY DEVELOPMENT AND INSTRUCTION

Goals and Principles • Overall Contexts for Vocabulary Learning • THE CLASSROOM IN ACTION: Establishing the Context for Meaningful Vocabulary Development

HELPING STUDENTS BECOME STRATEGIC WORD-LEARNERS

An Overall Strategy for Determining the Meaning of Unknown Words • Structural Analysis: Helping Students Learn About Word Structure and How Words Work • CLASSROOM IN ACTION—Fifth/Sixth Grade: Teaching About Greek and Latin Roots • MAKING CONNECTIONS: The Relationship Between Vocabulary and Spelling—The "Spelling/Meaning Connection" • A Developmental Sequence of the Word Structure Elements to Be Learned • MEANING MAKERS: The Reader: Other Word Structure/ Meaning Clues • Helping Students Use Context Effectively • CLASSROOM IN ACTION: Context and Structural Analysis Working Together • The Role of the Dictionary

HELPING STUDENTS EXPAND AND CONNECT WORD MEANINGS

Purposes of Instruction in Word Enrichment • Developing Connotative Meanings • MAKING CONNECTIONS: Words from Mythology • Exploring Parallel Relationships Among Words • MAKING CONNECTIONS: Literature and Wordplay • Exploring Categorical Relationships Among Words • BUILDING YOUR KNOWLEDGE BASE: Words and Their "Semantic Biographies" • DEVELOPING YOUR INSTRUCTIONAL TOOLKIT • BUILDING YOUR KNOWLEDGE BASE: Books About Word Structure

HELPING STUDENTS LEARN SPECIFIC VOCABULARY

Instructional Goals of Direct Teaching of Terms • Teaching Vocabulary in Narratives • Teaching Vocabulary in the Different Content Areas • CLASSROOM IN ACTION: Preteaching Terms in a Science Lesson

APPLYING WORD KNOWLEDGE IN COMPOSITION

A CONCLUDING PERSPECTIVE

BECOMING A REFLECTIVE PRACTITIONER

REFERENCES

Words repay the attention they are accorded.

Joseph Shipley

One good word is worth a thousand pictures.

Eric Sevareid

These two quotes capture the potency and the importance of words. And if students are to develop their reading *and* writing abilities fully, they must understand what words are made of and what words can do. There is a sequence as well as a bit of serendipity in helping students learn about words. You'll be demonstrating word structure and making connections among words for them. And while, of course, you'll plan for deliberate instruction and demonstration, you will notice those teachable moments when a word reveals its semantic biography, when a meaning "family" invites closer acquaintance, and when a turn of phrase appears to cause ripples along a student's spine. Finally, you will be modeling how students can apply their knowledge about words to developing strategies they can use to determine the identity of unfamiliar words.

You have just finished reading two chapters in which the focus was on how well students can construct meaning in both narrative and informational texts. For decades, research has demonstrated that the single most powerful indicator of students' ability to comprehend or construct meaning as they read is their *vocabulary* knowledge (Anderson & Freebody, 1981; Beck & McKeown, 1990). The reason for this is that the number of words children know and understand represents their *conceptual* knowledge, which in turn depends on their *experiences*—how many they were in number, how deeply they were felt, how much the children have thought and talked about them. So discussing vocabulary knowledge is another way of talking about students' *prior knowledge* and the richness of their *schemata*—which serves as an indicator of how well they're going to be able to read. In turn, when we help students develop vocabulary through elaborating and extending their concepts, we cannot help but contribute to their development as readers.

You may be wondering, though, why it is even necessary to address vocabulary directly, when we know that experience, prior knowledge, wide reading, and discussion contribute to its development. Several researchers have suggested, in fact, that students build their vocabularies primarily through wide reading (for example, Nagy & Anderson, 1984; Nagy, 1989) and really do not benefit nearly as much from direct instruction in vocabulary. Other researchers have suggested that while wide reading is absolutely essential, students still need appropriate direct instruction in vocabulary and in the powerful clues to meaning that lie in the *structure* of words (Beck & McKeown, 1991; White, Power, & White, 1989). The key word here is *appropriate,* for here we do not have an either/or issue—wide reading *or* extensive vocabulary instruction. Rather, it is an issue of building on direct and indirect experiences in such a way that the relatively small amount of direct instruction we do will effectively complement students' wide reading, writing, and learning. When we help students refine their strategies for analyzing unknown words during their reading, we are in effect reinforcing the important roles of context and word structure.

Proficient readers need to understand the *structure* of words. Printed words are the visible keys to the concepts underlying the surface of print. If students understand the nature and use of these keys, they will be able to (1) *access* their own knowledge and schemata more efficiently and (2) *explore* and *expand* this knowledge base more effectively. For these two reasons, students must continue to develop their understanding of the *structure* of words, and they have to learn *strategies* for determining the identity or the meaning of an unfamiliar word in their reading.

WHAT DOES "KNOWING" A WORD REALLY MEAN?

Determining precisely what it means to "know" a word is difficult, since we have varying degrees of familiarity with words (Baumann & Kameenui, 1991; Beck & McKeown, 1991). Knowing the "meaning" of a word is not an all-or-nothing affair, for "meaning" is a fuzzy, personalized phenomenon. Let's consider some examples. We may be very comfortable with our understanding of the word *dog;* our rich underlying concept for this word is based on our many experiences with dogs. Our concept for *dog* includes all kinds of attributes or features such as appearance (size, color, length of hair), behavior, smell, and so on. Our underlying concept for *ozone,* however, may not be nearly as fleshed out; we can read the word, we've heard it a lot, and we may figure that it's some type of gas and that a lot of it encircles the earth. We know that it's supposed to protect the earth, though we may know nothing about its properties. Upon seeing the word *polemical,* we realize we may have run across it before, but the concept it represents may be very vague. And as for *eleemosynary*—most of us would probably say we'd never seen it before, and we wouldn't link the word to any underlying concept.

The conceptual underpinnings for any word that you "know" usually include not only a literal meaning but a network of associations as well. We can all agree that the word *school* refers to or "means" a place where instruction occurs, but we may each have different associations. One person associates *school* with sunny classrooms, good friends, and exciting, motivating teachers; another person may associate the same word with shadowy, dull green hallways and fear, frustration, and loneliness. This distinction between "literal" meaning and "associative" meaning is represented by the terms *denotation* and *connotation.* The word *school* usually *denotes* a place where instruction occurs; depending on our experiences, it *connotes* either positive associations or negative ones.

All our lives we will be learning new words, while at the same time the concepts underlying these words—representing their denotative and their connotative meanings—will continue to grow. The five-year-old's conceptual underpinnings for the word *mother,* for example, will be much, much more elaborate forty years from now, when that child is forty-five.

As teachers, we are especially aware of the relationship between words and meaning—between "keys" and whatever underlying concepts they unlock and reveal to us. Many times your students will have the necessary concepts to grasp a new term, so your goal is to help them access and relate these concepts in such a way that they will understand where and how the new term fits. At other times the necessary conceptual framework for a new word may not be in place, so your goal is more challenging: to facilitate the construction or development of that framework and then teach the "label."

It is easy to set the stage for our exploration of teaching children about words and meanings. In fact, it already has been set in the preceding chapters: First, a wide range of experiences should be provided in and out of the classroom, providing the context for appropriate and meaningful language use. Second, increasing the volume and nature of students' reading will establish the best context in which words can be explored. In your classroom, because your students will be reading and writing extensively and intensively and discussing what is read and written, this context will be rich and engaging.

PRINCIPLES OF VOCABULARY DEVELOPMENT AND INSTRUCTION

Goals and principles

This chapter follows a sequence and an organization focusing on our three overall goals for students' word knowledge and our underlying instructional means of achieving these goals. Figure 8.1 presents these major goals and their supporting instructional purposes.

The structure of words and the meaning of words interact in predictable and powerful ways, so part of our responsibility is to foster awareness of this fact. Beginning in the intermediate grades, most students have the *potential* for developing and applying such awareness. Just as with learning how to learn, though, this awareness eludes all too many of our students throughout their entire lives. We *can* turn the situation around for them, however; and in this chapter, we'll find out how, through addressing the goals that are listed in Figure 8.1.

Though wide reading is absolutely necessary, for most students it is not sufficient for developing strong word-analysis strategies or active and sustained vocabulary growth (Beck, McKeown, & Omanson, 1987; Beck & McKeown, 1991; Blachowicz & Lee, 1991; Just & Carpenter, 1987; Stahl & Fairbanks, 1986). Moreover, learning new vocabulary is not a process in which students simply add on new words, one at a time, much as beads are slipped onto a string. We do not build our vocabularies solely by trying to memorize the meaning of new words we meet in our reading or by studying lists of unrelated words. Almost every new word learned should be related or tied in some fashion to words and concepts already known. Like keys, new words extend our understanding by opening doors to other rooms in our conceptual dwellings.

GOALS FOR STUDENTS' LEARNING

1   To become independent word "solvers" and learners.

2   To develop a lively interest in words and a general attitude of inquiry about words.

3   To develop an expanded/expanding body of known words in terms of:
a) denotative and connotative meanings
b) perceived interconnections among words.

In order to achieve the above goals for learning, we as teachers can help students through the following:

INSTRUCTIONAL GOALS

1   Teach structural analysis (morphemic analysis and syllabication), active involvement with context, proper use of dictionary **and** how and when to put all of this to use — that is, a *strategy* for implementing this knowledge.

2   Teach word nuances, variations, and relationships — connotations and connections — so that students *actively* use this enriched knowledge of words while developing and enhancing an attitude of genuine interest in words.

3   Teach some selected terms, especially those of specific subject areas/disciplines, so that students can better comprehend the subject area, write about it, and *learn* about it.

4   Emphasize application and enchancement of word knowledge through *writing*.

Figure 8.1
Overview of Goals for Word Knowledge and Vocabulary Instruction

At the intermediate grades, the following principles should guide our instruction:

■ Students should have many exposures to words in meaningful contexts: contexts both in and out of connected text.

■ A concrete-to-more-abstract sequence of word elements (affixes, bases, and word roots) may be followed, and the ways in which these elements combine should be taught.

■ Students' prior knowledge should be tapped; this is especially important in learning the specialized vocabulary of various content areas.

■ Students should be actively involved in exploring words; they will thus be much more likely to develop positive attitudes toward words and learning about them.

Overall contexts for vocabulary learning

Let's now examine our instructional context from the perspective of students' vocabulary learning. Students' awareness of words, of language, and of new concepts develops best in the classroom in which the following things take place:

■ Students are reading *intensively* and *extensively* in both assigned and student-selected texts.

■ Teachers are sharing and modeling interesting uses of language and new words through *read-alouds.*

■ Students are actively *conversing about, discussing,* their reading and learning experiences; much vocabulary springs from and is used in these contexts.

■ Teachers involve students in *direct, hands-on experiences* in which the students explore theme- or content-related concepts—*and* in which teachers help students relate these experiences to their existing knowledge about the subject and their existing knowledge about words.

■ Teachers and students are open to those unplanned *"teachable moments"* when a situation, whether or not it springs from a text, allows a word or pattern to be highlighted and briefly discussed.

It's apparent that our contexts include whole-class, small-group, and one-to-one interactions. At times we're quite structured, at other times not; sometimes our lesson is embedded in a particular story or informational text we're all reading; at other times we pull words together from a number of different sources in order to explore a particular structural/meaning pattern. For example, let's recall our discussion in Chapter 6 addressing the importance of bringing together students who are reading at approximately the same level to engage in Guided Reading-Thinking Activities. That would also be an excellent opportunity to involve the students in word study and vocabulary activities, if time permits. You will know much about the nature of their word knowledge from your initial assessment (see Chapter 4). But the important point here, as you may recall from Chapter 2, is that these students will usually have similar degrees of word knowledge, so this is an excellent context in which to explore words effectively and efficiently.

The following vignette gives a flavor for the context and the principles of effective instruction in vocabulary—and I hope it will whet your appetite for the possibilities that appropriate and engaging vocabulary instruction offers. It is based on direct experience and oral language.

In a unit exploring insects and spiders, Damon Palmer has set up the following situation in which his students will compare and contrast the two groups. He has placed two transparent containers where the students can easily observe them—one containing a couple of insects, the other a couple of spiders.

Palmer: These little creatures are alike in many ways, but they are also different. What are some ways in which they are alike?
Student: They're creepy!
Palmer: Why do you think so?
Student: Because they can bite you, and they feel gross if they crawl on you.
Palmer: In what *other* ways are all of these little creatures alike?
Student: They're small and have lots of legs.
Palmer: How many legs do they have?
Student: Lots of 'em!
Palmer: That's interesting, Tim. Did you count how many legs they have?
Student: Oh, ten or a dozen or so.
Palmer: Let's count them again and see. Tim, you count how many legs each of these critters has (pointing to the insects) and Larry, you count how many legs a spider has.
Student: These guys each got six legs!
Student: Hey, you know what? Spiders have *eight* legs!
Palmer: That's very interesting. . . . These insects have six legs, and the spiders have eight legs. You know, that's an important difference between these (pointing to insects) and *these* (pointing to spiders). Actually, did you know that spiders are *not* insects? Scientists group them separately from insects. Although they look a lot like insects—they're small and they have many legs—there are some other differences we should notice.
Look at the spiders' bodies really carefully—not the legs, just the bodies. Now look at the insects' bodies. How are they different?
Student: Insects seem to have more parts to their bodies than spiders do.
Palmer: Good observation, Larry! How many parts or *segments* do you see in an insect's body? [Three] How many in the spider's? [Two] Both insects and spiders have an *abdomen* (points to lower part of the body), but the spider has its head and chest together in this second part or *segment.* The insect has these two other segments, the head and the *thorax* or chest.

In this context, Damon Palmer could proceed to discuss *antennae* (insects have them, spiders don't) and the different types of legs or *appendages.* The essence of the defining and "fleshing out" of each term lies in the process of comparison and contrast, of *relating* one feature or group of features to another. Damon Palmer could ask the children whether they have an abdomen and a thorax and to locate each. The same can be done for *appendages* and *antennae*.

In this initial guided exploration using oral language, note how the teacher introduced new terms such as *segment* and *thorax*—a solid experiential base had been established; then he used familiar terms to help define the new ones.

An excellent follow-up would be to have students sketch the parts of insects and spiders in their learning logs and then label the parts with the new terms. Alternatively, Damon could provide line drawings of an insect and a spider and ask the students to label the parts. Both types of *application* of this new word knowledge reinforces students' learning of the fundamental conceptual distinctions even as it drives home an understanding of the words that label these distinctions.

Once these general conceptual distinctions have been established and the new terms made familiar, students can learn finer distinctions *within* each concept. For example, in their learning logs students could analyze and write about likenesses and differences between the *appendages* of a particular insect and a particular spider—a grasshopper, say, and a common garden spider. This type of exploration literally establishes in the students' conceptual framework more connections that support the learning of and memory for new terms.

■ ■ ■ ■ ■

HELPING STUDENTS BECOME STRATEGIC WORD-LEARNERS

An overall strategy for determining the meaning of unknown words

There are two types of "unknown" words that students in the intermediate grades and beyond will encounter in texts: (1) words that are in the students' everyday speaking/listening vocabularies but that are not immediately recognized in print and (2) words that are *not* in students' speaking/listening vocabularies and which therefore are totally unfamiliar. In this section we will discuss a strategy that prepares students for addressing both types.

Shift in Emphasis: Primary to Intermediate Grades' Word Learning   In the primary grades—the beginning-reading phase and much of the transitional-reading phase—students' main word-analysis challenge is to decode those words that are in their everyday listening/speaking vocabularies. They simply know far more words orally than they can recognize in print, and their strategy is to apply word-analysis skills that will yield at least an approximate pronunciation. Together with the context, this approximation will reveal a word's identity. In the intermediate grades—with students moving out of the transitional phase and into the mature or proficient phase, in which the words in print they encounter far surpass their oral vocabularies—our emphasis in word identification shifts more toward determining the probable meaning of words that are brand new. While context continues to play an important role in this process, structural patterns within words come to play a significant part as well. The strategy we help students learn will address both (1) figuring out words in text, and (2) the growth of students' vocabulary as they encounter new words in their reading.

The more students learn about words, and the more they apply their word knowledge in context, the more *automatic* their process of analysis becomes. Recall how at the earlier, beginning stages of learning to read, children *consciously* attend to letters and sounds—but do not remain at this level. Their advancing letter/sound knowledge comes to underlie the automatic and efficient identification of many words as they read. So, too, will intermediate students' advancing knowledge of larger structural elements within words underlie their automatic and efficient word identification as they read.

The Strategy in Operation   As you introduce elements of word structure and help your students understand them, you will also be demonstrating how this information can become part of their strategies.

First and foremost, as with all our reading instruction, we want to keep in mind that strategies for determining the meaning of unknown words work efficiently only if readers are reading at their *instructional* or *independent* levels. When students are attempting to read at their *frustration* level—when at least one word in every ten is unknown—they do not have sufficient written word knowledge to support efficient reading, and therefore efficient word analysis, in that text.

The strategy I'm about to recommend will work well when students are reading at an appropriate level. We need next to remind them that there are two types of situations they will encounter: (1) a word not immediately identified may turn out to be in their speaking/listening vocabularies, or (2) an unidentifiable word may be a word they have not heard of before. Following is a description of *strategic* word analysis that is appropriate for intermediate students:

1. Your first step is to skip the word and keep reading. The word may be defined soon in the text (particularly if the text is a textbook), or the *context* may suggest or show the meaning. If context does not help, then you will soon find out if the word is a really important one. You'll know this if you're having real difficulty understanding what the text seems to be talking about.

2. If the unknown word does seem to be important, go back to it and use a *context* plus *structural analysis* strategy. The context often is sufficient to give you a "feel" for the meaning of the word, but to get a more precise idea of the meaning, you often will need to apply structural analysis skills:

First, look for any base words, prefixes, and suffixes you may know; then combine their meanings to see if you get a meaning that makes sense in this particular context.

Second, apply a "sounding out" strategy. Divide the word into syllable units; then blend these together to see if you get a word that sounds close to, or the same as, one you already know. (It is not necessary to come up with the *exact* pronunciation; when you get close, you are likely to be reminded of the word.)

3. If the word is still resisting your efforts, this may be one of those times when asking a classmate or the teacher, or going to the dictionary, is a must.

4. Try this meaning in the context of your reading. If you have looked the word up in the dictionary and found that it has more than one meaning, you will need to check which meaning fits the context where you had trouble with the word.

Proficient readers—who of course are very proficient at word identification—get to *be* proficient in part through explicitly learning the strategy I've just presented. And that's why I strongly recommend that you teach this strategy according to the sequence of steps presented here. You should know that much debate has occurred over the years regarding whether we should even encourage students to try to "sound out" long words when we know that emphasizing meaningful word elements is so productive. Still, you should be reassured that *both* types of knowledge—*sounding out* through syllabication and phonics, and *morphemic analysis*—can be most helpful to the reader in the context of meaning-ful reading. Proficient readers, in fact, apply these steps almost simultaneously, and often the brain may "pop out" a tentative pronunciation of a word before the reader has consciously attempted a morphemic analysis. If the word is already known, fine. If not, we will deliberately try a morphemic analysis.

The importance of teaching the strategy to students lies in the fact that it encourages them to be *flexible,* prepared to try *both* morphemic and "sounding out" analyses. What we want to avoid is students' relying *exclusively* on one type of analysis: contextual analysis, sounding out, or morphemic analysis. Rather, we want to give them a strategy that helps them engage all their word knowledge when appropriate. Our strategy is flexible, allowing students options they're aware they have. We can demonstrate to them, and they can reassure themselves, that when they are *really thinking* about what they are reading, what they know about words will usually be of great help to them when they need to apply this analysis strategy.

Where does students' knowledge of structural elements come from? As we will explore in the next section, it comes in large part from *your* direct demonstrations about word elements such as prefixes, suffixes, and roots—what they are, what they mean, and how they combine to create words' meanings.

Structural analysis: helping students learn about word structure and how words work

Traditionally, educators have said that when students' word knowledge is ready to encompass more than phonics, they are ready to learn *structural analysis* skills. *Structural analysis* is the term you will see used most frequently to refer to the type of word analysis required in learning about and analyzing words of more than one syllable. It is an umbrella term for the strategies readers apply when they encounter an unrecognizable word of two or more syllables. Their strategies can lead either to (1) the eventual "sounding out" or decoding of the word to determine if it is in their speaking/listening vocabularies or to (2) a decision about its approximate meaning, if it's a word they haven't heard before.

For readers in the late transitional-reading phase and on into the early mature or proficient phase, psychologists believe that at some level the brain is trying to "sound out" these types of unknown words as well as analyzing the meaning elements. As we just saw above, there often is interaction between these two processes.

Syllabication: Putting Its Usefulness in Perspective In speech, a *syllable* is a combination of consonant and vowel sounds. In reading, a knowledge of *syllabication*—identifying syllables in order to identify a polysyllabic word via sounding it out—involves detecting particular combinations of consonant and vowel letters in a word of more than one syllable. As part of a strategy for word identification, there are two syllabication generalizations that seem useful to teach (Adams, 1990; Henderson, 1990):

■ *When a single consonant occurs between two vowels, divide the word between the first vowel and the consonant;* then pronounce each syllable and blend together. For example, *fever* = fe + ver; *trading* = tra + ding; *before* = be + fore. In each case, because students know that a single vowel at the end of a syllable usually is long, they can sound out the first syllable, blend it with the second, and recognize the word. When a long vowel does not result in a recognizable word, they can try a *short* vowel sound—as in *cabin, damage,* and *limit.*

■ *When vowel letters are separated by two or more consonant letters, divide the word after the first consonant;* then blend the syllables together: For example, *basket* = bas + ket; *tattle* = tat + tle; *supper* = sup + per. Students already have learned that a vowel followed by a consonant is usually short, so now they can sound out the first syllable and then blend the syllables together.

In the past, we probably allowed syllabication too great a place in our instruction—we simply spent too much time on this strategy. Why is syllabication not as important as we once thought? First of all, part of our efforts had matters turned around—we tried to teach generalizations like "If the first vowel is short, divide the word after the following consonant." But *why* were we teaching syllabication in the first place? For sounding out unknown words—so if the student already *knew* that the first vowel was short, he or she wouldn't need to figure out the syllables! In other words, much of the instruction was a waste of time insofar as a word-analysis strategy was concerned. Second, as we've already noted, by the time students have sufficient word knowledge to apply this strategy, they are reading materials in which most of the unknown words will *remain* unknown if they are sounded out—they won't be in the students' listening/speaking vocabularies. The bottom line, then, is that students may find that a knowledge of the two generalizations presented here is helpful on occasion in determining the identity of some words. Knowledge of other "rules" about how to divide words into syllables can be learned either on the go, without explicit instruction, or as students examine carefully the *spelling* of polysyllabic words (Adams, 1990; Templeton, 1991).

Morphemic Analysis: What Are Morphemes and How Do They Form Words? As students continue to read widely over the years, most of the unfamiliar words they encounter will be ones they have never heard before, so of course a "decoding" analysis is of no help. This is why *morphemic* analysis—looking for the smallest units of meaning (*morphemes*) within the word and then seeing how those units fit together—becomes so powerful as students grow in the mature or proficient phase. It not only becomes *the* most important aspect of structural analysis for figuring out unknown words during reading, it also becomes a potential tool for developing and expanding students' general vocabulary and for improving their spelling.

In a rich literacy environment, rather than seeing a polysyllabic word as an unanalyzable whole or as merely a collection of syllables, students will begin to "see" (that is, their brains will "pick up") groups of letters that stand for *morphemes* rather than just units of sound. The more familiar they are with the *visual* representation of meaning in words—just as they were familiar with the visual representation of sound at the previous developmental levels—the more efficient their reading will be and the more rapidly their vocabularies will grow.

One of the most powerful understandings you can help your students develop is that of *how* types of word elements—affixes and roots—combine to create words and the specific meanings of those words. The foundations for this understanding are laid in the primary grades when students learn about adding inflectional endings to words—learn the effects that past tense and plural endings have on base words, for example. But also, during these early years, children are learning certain words that contain other suffixes and prefixes. Later, in third grade for some students and fourth grade for most, we can begin helping students learn to analyze these words in order to discover just how the word elements work together.

Exploring these combinatorial aspects of word elements will support one of your strategies for dealing with unknown words in context. Just and Carpenter (1987) make the point that while the meaning of some of these elements may be a little fuzzy when we examine the elements in frequently occurring words, their meaning is *much* more consistent in words that occur less frequently—and these are precisely the words that readers are not as likely to know and therefore need to analyze structurally. This type of exploration will also help students become aware of the *logic* underlying combinatorial principles; this awareness will help advance word knowledge so that reading and writing are more efficient.

Important Morphemes and Morpheme Combinations Let's set the instructional stage. It is necessary for us to demonstrate, to model, to show explicitly to students how words are constructed from morphemes—these smallest units of meaning—and it is necessary for us to demonstrate the *process* by which such words are analyzed. Toward this end, I'll first discuss the nature of morphemes.

A *morpheme* can be a single word such as *bag, struggle,* or *view*. Linguists call morphemes that can occur by themselves *free* morphemes. As we've already noted, morphemes can also be a *part* of a word, as is the case of *pre-* and *-ing* in the word *previewing*. *Pre-* and *-ing* are examples of what linguists call *bound* morphemes—they occur only when attached to or "bound" to other morphemes. In the word *previewing,* then, there are three morphemes—the two bound morphemes and the free morpheme *view.*

Here's a quick test: how many morphemes does *rerun* contain? Two—one bound morpheme, *re-,* and one free morpheme, *run.* Do you use the terms *free morpheme* and *bound morpheme* with elementary students? Usually not. You will, however, be using terms that are good labels for free and bound morphemes: *compound words, prefixes, suffixes,* and *roots.* Let's examine each of these in turn.

Compound Words   Compound words are formed by combining individual words in order to better describe or refer to a single characteristic, individual, or thing. Compound words can be formed in a number of ways: for example, *bulldog* (noun + noun), *whirlpool* (verb + noun), and *popcorn* (verb + noun).

Prefixes and Suffixes   Collectively, prefixes and suffixes are referred to as *affixes;* they are bound morphemes that are "fixed to" other morphemes. Prefixes are "fixed" in front; suffixes (such as *-ed, -es, -ment,* or *-ation*) are "fixed" after. Affixes modify the meaning of the morphemes to which they're attached. For instance, in the noun *unicycle,* the Latin prefix *uni-,* meaning "one," modifies *cycle,* the free morpheme to which it is attached. In the verb *disappear,* the Latin prefix *dis-,* meaning "not," modifies *appear,* the free morpheme to which it is attached. In the adjective *courageous,* the suffix *-ous,* meaning "having" or "possessing," modifies the free morpheme *courage.*

When you first introduce the concept of prefixes and their effect on the root to which they're attached, a deliberate, explicit walk-through will be important. Before further understanding of word structure can develop, students should have a good understanding of what a "root" is and how simple prefixes and suffixes can affect it. In addition, for several prefixes there will be a number of *counter*examples that you should point out, so that students do not always expect *in-,* for example, to be a prefix (you can refer to *India* and *inches*).

There are two main kinds of suffixes:

1. *Inflectional* suffixes (such as *-ed, -ing,* and plural endings such as *-s*) change the tense or number but not the grammatical role of a word.

2. *Derivational* suffixes (such as *-ment, -al,* and *-ity*) *do* change the grammatical role of a word (*-al* changes *nation,* a noun, to an adjective; *-ity* changes *serene,* an adjective, to a noun).

Roots: Base Words   What prefixes and suffixes are "fixed to" is called a *root.* The first type of root we discuss with students is referred to as a *base word* (sometimes referred to as a *root word*). A base word is a recognizable word, a *free* morpheme, which is left after the prefixes and suffixes are stripped away. *Run,* for example, is the base word of *rerun; judge* is the base word of *prejudge.*

Roots: Greek and Latin Forms   If you take away prefixes and suffixes and are left not with a base word, but with what appears to be another bound morpheme, you probably have found the Greek or Latin word root. These "bound morphemes" are very important elements: although they usually cannot stand alone as a base word, they are still the word part that stands for the core meaning of the word in which they occur. Some examples from Greek are *chron* ("time," as in *chronology*) and *tele* ("distant, far" as in *television*); examples from Latin are *dict* ("say," as in *dictation*) and *fract* ("break," as in *fracture*). Although technically there are different terms for referring to roots that come from Greek and to roots that come from Latin, we will use the common term *root* to refer to both because it is what you and your students will find used most prevalently. If you or your students *are* interested in learning these other terms and exploring words on a deeper level, I would suggest *Words: Integrated Decoding and Spelling Instruction Based on Word Origin and Word Structure* by Henry (1990), *Words Their Way: A Developmental Approach to Phonics, Spelling, and Vocabulary, K–8,* by Bear et al. (in press), and *Techniques of Teaching Vocabulary* by Dale, O'Rourke, and Bamman (1971).

Should your students memorize a lot of Greek and Latin roots and their meanings? No; certainly not during the elementary years. You should help them understand, though, that these roots are very important elements within words; as students continue to develop their reading and writing vocabularies, this awareness will underlie their understanding about words. In addition, much of the vocabulary of specific disciplines (see page 391) is built on Greek and Latin roots, so a budding knowledge of the most commonly occurring examples will provide valuable prior knowledge for learning new concepts and terms.

It's time to see how this knowledge is applied. First, I will present a sequence for the process of morphemically analyzing a word; this sequence is an elaboration of Step 2 in our strategy above (page 383) in which morphemic analysis is applied. We should model this process for students frequently:

- If there is a prefix, remove it first; if there is a suffix, remove it next (if more than one suffix, remove the last one first).
- Think of the possible meaning of the base word or word root; then put the suffix back and think about the resulting meaning.
- Finally, put the prefix back, think about its effect on the rest of the word, and check the meaning in context.

For example, notice how the following words are analyzed:

unparalleled	disapproval	restlessness
paralleled	approval	restless
parallel	approve	rest
parelleled	approval	restless
unparalleled	disapproval	restlessness

This sequence is not sure-fire in all instances—sometimes the analysis works better if the suffix is removed first—but it works often enough to recommend for a first try, while reminding the students to be flexible.

A Developmental Sequence of the Word Structure Elements to Be Learned   The examination of most types of structural, morphemic elements we have been discussing involves a logical and a developmental sequence. The *structure* of very many words is important to understand, because as you explore the word elements that make up a particular word, you will be pointing out to your students that these elements are part of ever so many *other* words. The immediate benefit will be that this knowledge will be extremely helpful to students when they are reading and encounter unknown terms. The long-range benefit will

Let's look at how Etta Sims, a fifth/sixth grade teacher, walks students through an understanding of some Greek and Latin roots:

"We've been reading about the Greeks and enjoying some of their myths. This morning, let's play around with some interesting word parts that come from the Greek language.

"Let's start by looking at this word [points to *photograph*]. We all know what a photograph is, right? Let's take the word apart—we've got the element *photo* and the element *graph.* To the ancient Greeks, *photo* meant 'light' and *graph* meant 'write.' Now, just what does this have to do with taking a picture?" [She engages the students in a brief discussion; they realize that literally, the light that is let in when someone snaps a picture "writes" on the film.]

"Okay; let's try another word. Let's look at *telephone.* What do you think the two *meaning* elements in this word are? Right! *Tele* and *phone.* Now, any ideas about what each element might mean? Can you think of any other word that has one of these parts? Ah, yes! *Television!* What type of 'vision' is 'tele'? [She engages students in another brief discussion, which leads to their realizing that *tele* has to do with "far away" and "distant."] Okay! So, looking at *telephone* again and knowing that *tele* means 'distant' what exactly *is* distant?"

The discussion continues in this way. While Ms. Sims is initially straightforward about the meanings of *photo* and *graph,* she eases the students into the process more and more, encouraging and guiding them to consider what different Greek word parts might mean.

As an immediate follow-up to this lesson, Ms. Sims involves the students in combining the following forms in as many different ways as possible and speculating about the meaning of each resulting word.

tele	phon
micro	photo
scope	graph
meter	chron

Now let's look at Ms. Sims's introduction of *Latin* roots:

"Many of the Greek roots found their way into the *Latin* language, which was spoken by the Romans. As the Roman Empire grew, it came to include Greece. In addition to including Greek roots, the Latin language provided many roots of its own. Knowing about just a few of them will help you figure out many unfamiliar words in your reading.

"When we talk about *audiovisual* equipment, what do we mean? We know what *visual* means, but what about *audio*? [Engages students in brief discussion.] Good; it has to do with hearing. Now, what about the underlined word in this sentence?

The doctor said that Jeremy has auditory *problems.*

"This has something to do with *hearing,* doesn't it? In the words *audio* and *auditory,* there is a Latin word root, *aud,* which comes from a Latin word that means . . . what? Right! It has to do with *hearing.*

■ ■ ■ ■ ■

CLASSROOM
IN ACTION

*Fifth/Sixth Grade:
Teaching About Greek
and Latin Roots*

"Here are some other words that have the *aud* root [writing on the chalk-board]: *audience, audition,* and *auditorium.* Can you get a 'feel' for how these words have come to mean what they do? For example, what does an *audience* do? An audience *hears* what is going on. An *audition* is a tryout performance for someone who literally *hears* you, and an *auditorium* is a place in which we *hear* a concert or a play, for example. Over time, these words have grown in meaning. Audiences do more than simply hear; activities not mainly involved with hearing go on in an auditorium; and so on. Originally, though, each of these words had a meaning that was narrower."

be a solid foundation in exploring words and their structure as the students move into the middle and secondary grades. In Table 8.1, I present a general sequence I suggest you follow; the table includes specific elements that illustrate each category.

Notice that in general, this sequence moves from the concrete elements to more abstract ones (Nagy, Diadikoy, & Anderson, 1993; Templeton, 1992). We begin with compound words because we can introduce the idea of first partitioning, then reassembling, a word according to its meaningful constituents, yet still be dealing with *words*—free morphemes. Simple prefixes are addressed next because although they are not words but bound morphemes, their meaning is straightforward, and their effect on base words is usually clear.

As with our overall sequence, Greek and Latin elements are sequenced according to the abstractness of their meaning, from concrete to more abstract. For example, Greek forms such as *phon* ("sound"), *auto* ("self"), and *graph* ("writing") are introduced before Latin roots, because the Greek forms' meaning is more obvious and straightforward. Also, because their meaning *is* so straight-

■ TABLE 8.1   Morphemic Elements That May Be Examined in the Intermediate Grades

Fourth-Grade Level

Simple Prefixes + Base

un-	*not*	*un*lock
dis-	*not*	*dis*pleased
non-	*not*	*non*fiction
in-	*not*	*in*active
re-	*again, back*	*re*apply
mis-	*bad, wrong, incorrect*	*mis*lead, *mis*inform

Base + Simple Suffixes

-ion/-tion/	*state of, characterized by*	perfec*tion*, examin*ation*
-ation/ition	*action*	compe*tition*
-able/-ible	*capable of, like*	lik*able*, incred*ible*
-ous	*having*	courage*ous*

TABLE 8.1   Continued

Spelling/Meaning Relationships
(Introduce the following patterns at this grade level and follow through at subsequent grade levels with additional examples.)

Vowel Patterns: Long-to-Short	crime	nation
	criminal	national
Consonant Patterns: Silent-Sounded	sign	crumb
	signature	crumble
Consonant Patterns: Sound Changes	electric	magic
	electricity	magician
Vowel Patterns: Stressed-to-Unstressed	compose	mental
	composition	mentality

Fifth-Grade Level and Beyond:

More Simple Prefixes + Base

uni-	*one*	*uni*cycle
bi-	*two*	*bi*cycle
tri-	*three*	*tri*angle
en-, em-	*make*	*en*able, *em*power
pre-	*before*	*pre*view
de-	*opposite of*	*de*salt
inter-	*between, among*	*inter*national
con-, com-	*with*	*con*struct ("build *with*"), *com*press ("force *with*")
trans-	*across, over*	*trans*port ("carry *across*")
anti-	*against*	*anti*pollution, *anti*freeze
dis-	*opposite*	*dis*union

Base + Simple Suffixes

-al	*having to do with*	coast*al*
-ness	*condition*	prompt*ness*
-ity	*condition*	prosper*ity*
-ment	*action, process of*	govern*ment*
-ful	*full of, like*	grace*ful*
-less	*without*	shame*less*
-logy	*study of*	bio*logy*

Greek Roots			*Latin Roots*		
graph	*write*	*tele*graph	spec	*look*	in*spec*t
micro	*small*	*micro*scope	vid/vis	*see*	*vid*eo/*vis*ion
photo	*light*	*photo*graph	aud	*hear*	*aud*itory
bio	*life*	*bio*logy	tract	*pull*	*tract*or
tele	*distant*	*tele*graph	rupt	*break*	inter*rupt*
hydro	*water*	*hydro*electric	struct	*build*	con*struct*
phon	*sound*	tele*phon*e	port	*carry*	trans*port*
scop	*watch*	peri*scop*e	dict	*say*	*dict*ation
bio	*life*	*bio*logy	fract	*break*	*fract*ure
auto	*self*	*auto*graph			

The Relationship Between Vocabulary and Spelling

Words that share the same roots belong, in general, to the same meaning "family" and are *related* to one another. Not only is an awareness of this fact useful to vocabulary development; it can help with students' learning *spelling* as well. This is why spelling development in the intermediate grades can occur as part of vocabulary development—and vice versa.

The *"spelling/meaning connection"* can be stated this way: *Words that are related in meaning are often related in spelling as well, despite changes in sound* (Chomsky, 1970; Templeton, 1983, 1991). Here is how the spelling/meaning connection can be explored, beginning in the upper elementary grades:

■ First, we help students become aware of spelling/meaning patterns:

(a) We begin with straightforward long-to-short vowel changes, such as *ignite-ignition* and *humane-humanity,* in which a long vowel in the base word changes to a short vowel in the related word, but the same (vowel) letter is used to spell both vowel sounds.

(b) We also point out how consonants can change pronunciation in related words but be spelled the same. For example, students realize that a so-called "silent" consonant in one word can be "sounded" in a related word. Note the italicized consonants in the following word pairs:

colum*n*	resi*g*n	mus*c*le
colum*n*ist	resi*g*nation	mus*c*ular

■ Next, we demonstrate how an awareness of the spelling/meaning connection can become a *strategy* students can use when they are uncertain about the spelling of a word. We tell the students, "Try to think of a word that is *related* in meaning and in spelling to the one you're trying to spell; such a word may provide the needed clue." An appropriate pattern to introduce for this purpose is the spelling of the *schwa,* or least-stressed, vowel sound in words such as *harmony, inspiration,* and *genetic.* This spelling is clarified by pairing these words with related words in which the corresponding vowel sound is clear and the spelling obvious:

harm*o*ny	insp*i*ration	g*e*netic
harm*o*nious	insp*i*re	g*e*ne

LEARNING IN CONTEXT: **Awareness of the relationship between spelling and meaning will support three related literacy activities: students' reading, their vocabulary development, and their spelling knowledge.**

forward, the way in which they combine is more understandable. Because Latin forms are usually more abstract *and*—depending on the word in which they occur—because their meaning can be "fuzzier" than Greek forms' meaning, they are presented a little later: *spect* ("look"); *scrib* ("write"), *rupt* ("break"; "burst"). Like Greek and Latin word roots, Greek and Latin prefixes and suffixes are sequenced according to the abstractness of their meaning.

Although I have suggested that this exploration of word structure elements begin in earnest at the fourth-grade level for most students, bear in mind that of course some children at a particular grade level will be exploring them before most of the others and that some will be exploring them later on in their development.

MEANING MAKERS: The Reader

Other Word Structure/Meaning Clues

I would like to present here three additional examples of interesting structural/meaning features of words—words that have resulted from "clipping" and from "blending," and words that are considered homophones and homographs. These are features that students often enjoy exploring and that ultimately also contribute to vocabulary growth and more meaningful reading.

"Clipping" Words. Consider, for example, the following word pairs in which the first word has been "clipped" to create the second word:

> advertisement/ad, laboratory/lab, graduate/grad, caravan/van, periwig/wig, intercommunicational system/intercom

These words, too, are clipped, but with a twist:

> bookmaker/bookie, moving picture/movie, cabman/cabbie

"Blending" Parts of Words. You may be surprised to realize how many "blended" words there are in the language; they are created by taking parts of different words and blending them:

> smoke + fog = smog   breakfast + lunch = brunch
> chuckle + snort = chortle

Students may first explore this phenomenon by examining advertisements. Copywriters are famous for creating new terms to catch the eye and ear—as in *swim + sensation = swimsation.*

The process of blending also explains *acronyms,* words created by combining letters from a series of words:

RADAR (radio detecting and ranging)

LASER (light amplification by stimulated emission of radiation)

NOW (National Organization for Women)

NABISCO (National Biscuit Company)

SONAR (sound navigation ranging)

Students delight in creating their own blended words. The "Sniglets" books by Rich Hall raise blending to a hilarious art, and students love them, particularly after learning about Greek and Latin roots and affixes. A sniglet is "any word that doesn't appear in the dictionary, but should." These books also get kids to interconnect concepts in new ways, and they reinforce awareness and understanding of morphemic analysis and the processes of word creation. Here are just a few examples (Hall, 1984):

rovalert (ro'val urt): The system whereby one dog can quickly establish an entire neighborhood network of barking. (p. 69)

memnants (mem'nents): The chipped or broken "*m&m's*" at the bottom of the bag.

detruncus (de trunk'us): The embarrassing phenomenon of losing one's bathing shorts while diving into a swimming pool.

disconfect (dis kon fekt'): To sterilize the piece of candy you dropped on the floor by blowing on it, somehow assuming this will "remove" all the germs.

Homophones and Homographs. Homophones are words that sound the same but are spelled differently; for example, *tail* and *tale*. *Homographs* are words that are spelled the same but usually pronounced differently, such as *tear* ("watery drop" versus "rip in material"). *Homonyms* are words that are spelled and pronounced the same but that differ in meaning; for instance, *flap* ("piece of material left hanging out" versus "mild disturbance or disagreement").

Do be forewarned, though, that the three words are used incorrectly almost as often as correctly. The most common mistake is the use of the term *homonym* for *homophone*. Our best way of dealing with this state of affairs with students is simply to be consistent in our own use of the terms.

There are many more homophones than homographs in English, so you can point out to students that homophones are spelled differently *because they mean different things*. If students conceptualize homophones in this manner, they will view them as interesting, rather than as examples of the "strange" spelling of English.

Fred Gwynne has written and illustrated several books that humorously portray homophones, homographs, and homonyms. See, for example, *Sixteen Hand Horse, A Chocolate Moose for Dinner,* and *The King Who Rained*. ■

Helping students use context effectively

When we help students refine their strategies for analyzing unknown words *during* their reading, we are in effect reinforcing the important and complementary roles of context and structural analysis. It is helpful to point out to students that authors will use new terms and then provide contextual support for these terms. This is frequently done by textbook authors, and authors of informational trade books who are sensitive to their audience will do this, too. Following are common ways in which authors provide contextual support:

Direct definition or explanation: The words *is* and *means* usually are clues to this type of support; for example, "Some 50 million years ago, the land mammal moved into the sea, and these first whales were called archaeocetes, which means ancient whales." (D'Vincent, 1992)

Restatements: These are often signaled by *or, that is,* and *in other words;* for example, "*Shahtis,* or scrolls, were among the first objects stolen from the pyramids to be sold on the open market."

Comparisons or *contrasts:* An example would be "Patricia's *ecstacy* could be compared to the joy someone feels when she's won a hard race."

Substitute words: These refer to synonyms and antonyms; for example, "Getting angry only *exacerbates* the problem; all it does is worsen the situation."

Summary: A number of previous, familiar concepts are summarized by the unfamiliar word; for example, ". . . Brontosaurus bones are filled with holes too small to see. The rainwater seeps into these holes. The water evaporates. But the minerals in the water stay and harden in the bones. Little by little what once was bone turns into stone. The bones of the Brontosaurus are now stone *fossils.*" (McMullan, 1989, p. 8)

Tone or *mood:* The way in which a situation is described, usually subjectively, can provide sufficient clues for the meaning of an unfamiliar word. For example, "When Dorrie first opened the door the stench was overpowering. Obviously the room hadn't been cleaned in years. Mold and decay were everywhere. Dorrie couldn't wait to leave. She had never experienced such a feeling of *revulsion.*"

We know that we need to demonstrate for students *how* contextual cues can benefit them, and we need to help them understand when context will not necessarily be helpful. The type of modeling and guidance the following "Classroom in Action" feature illustrates is a powerful demonstration for students. This type of awareness and knowledge is generalizable to ever so many words and how they work; this sensitivity to supportive context and word structure can be the engine that drives vocabulary development in the intermediate grades—and beyond.

The role of the dictionary

For decades, well-meaning teachers have advised students that when they're reading along and run into an unknown word, they should look it up in the dictionary. Unfortunately, this is quite a counterproductive strategy. Such a major interruption dams the flow of the stream of meaning at the same time as it discourages positive attitudes toward the dictionary. (Occasionally people will tell you that they always look up a word as they're reading, but I suspect that in most cases the habit developed well after they'd become fluent, comfortable readers.)

This is not to say, of course, that the dictionary is not an incredible treasury of information about words—it is. Our reasons for when and how to consult it are many and varied. As we've already seen in our strategy (p. 383), there *may* in fact be a time when everything depends on determining the meaning of a single word: other parts of our strategy have not seemed to work, and we can't stand the suspense anymore, so we look it up. But this is relatively rare.

The fact of the matter is that unless we already *know* something about the word we're looking up, the dictionary may not be of much help at all! Students must have some familiarity with the conceptual framework or schema underlying a new term, or the definition(s) will not make sense, because definitions

Here's how fifth-grade teacher Carmen Ortiz modeled this strategy for her students:

"Let's see how context and what we know about the structure of words can help us with two new words in this passage:

Every fish, reptile, amphibian, bird, and mammal has a row of bones in its back, usually called the spine or spinal column. This is the feature that groups them together as vertebrates (animals with backbones or vertebrae), distinguishing them from invertebrates such as insects and worms. (Parker, 1988, p. 40)

[Pointing to *vertebrates*] "Does the passage give us a clue to this word? . . . Right; it explains that vertebrates are living things that have a backbone. How about this word [pointing to *invertebrates*]? Yes, the passage gives us examples of invertebrates—insects and worms. But what is it about them that makes them very *different from* vertebrates? The passage doesn't tell us; but now that we know that *vertebrate* means "having a backbone," what about an *in*vertebrate? Is there a clue in the structure of the word? Right! The prefix *in-* probably means 'not'; so *invertebrate* means '*not* having a backbone.'

"Of course, there are a lot of other differences between mammals and fish on the one hand and insects and worms on the other. Whether or not creatures have a backbone, however, is a *very* important distinction that scientists make."

■ ■ ■ ■ ■

usually use other words that are associated with whatever word students are looking up.

In addition to yielding a word's meaning that students can't guess, or providing a check on the "best-guess" meaning of such a word, dictionaries can be of considerable benefit in these areas:

1. They reinforce the interest in and attitudes toward words that you are modeling.
2. They provide excellent etymological information. Even dictionaries published explicitly for upper elementary students include some of this type of information (still, however, it is very helpful to have in your classroom an "adult" unabridged dictionary that includes etymological information for most entries).
3. Because entry words are listed alphabetically, students will often find words that are *related* to a word they are looking up. This, in fact, is a little technique we share with them when they're exploring meaning families: scan before and after the target word to find other, related words—especially in the unabridged dictionary.
4. The *usage notes* in dictionaries explain subtle though important differences between words. These differences not only indicate the appropriateness of one word over another in a particular context; they also represent more elaborate underlying conceptual distinctions.

5. They provide convenient phonetic respellings for every word and *pronunciation guides* (on every other page) that will yield the appropriate pronunciation of any unfamiliar word.

Figure 8.2 presents part of a page from a dictionary intended for intermediate-grade students. Note the pronunciation guide at lower left; note also the separate boxes taken from other pages in the dictionary. These boxes represent consistent features that appear throughout this dictionary—word histories, a "vocabulary builder" that illustrates combinatorial features of word elements (morphemes), and synonyms and antonyms. Note how the examples given for the synonyms follow a continuum of "intensity." After discussing any of these topics—etymology, how word elements combine, or synonyms and antonyms—you could refer the students to the dictionary for reinforcement and illustrations.

HELPING STUDENTS EXPAND AND CONNECT WORD MEANINGS

The second major goal we presented at the beginning of this chapter is that of developing a lively interest in words and a general attitude of inquiry about them. We will engage students in looking at the power of words' connotations and at the marvelous interconnections among words.

Purposes of instruction in word enrichment

What are the benefits of developing such interest in and such awareness of words? First, our fundamental purpose in developing students' awareness of connotative meanings and of the relationships and connections among words is to have this awareness lead to *deepened, enriched understandings in the students' reading.* Students can apply this knowledge *as* they read. It operates at both an underlying, tacit level and a metacognitive, conscious level. It complements students' developing abilities to apply morphemic analysis when they encounter unfamiliar words. A secondary purpose is to show students that *all* this information—morphemic analysis and expanding word knowledge—stems from a rich interconnectedness among words; instead of learning each new word as a discrete item, students become aware of how one word leads to another. A third purpose is to create an active interest in words—an attitude of inquiry and playfulness about their meanings and patterns.

Wolf and Heath (1992) observed that ". . . figurative language, used in exploratory ways, equips every reader for the processes of cognitive and emotional discovery" (p. 2). What is true for figurative language—one of the types of enriched word knowledge we will be discussing here—is true for much of our exploration of the myriad ways in which words work.

Developing connotative meanings

Connotation goes beyond telling us directly what something or someone is or does; it helps us *live* it through emotions and physical sensations that are

matrimony *noun* The condition of being married; marriage.
mat·ri·mo·ny (măt′rə mō′nē) ◊ *noun*

matron *noun* **1.** A married woman. **2.** A woman official in a public institution, such as a hospital.
ma·tron (mā′trən) ◊ *noun, plural* **matrons**

matter *noun* **1.** Something that takes up space and has weight. **2.** Substance or content; material: *The flood was the subject matter of the newscast.* **3.** A subject of interest or concern: *I refuse to discuss the matter.* **4.** A problem; difficulty: *What's the matter with you?* **5.** Something written or printed.
◊ *verb* To be important: *We tried to pretend that it didn't matter.*
mat·ter (măt′ər) ◊ *noun, plural* **matters**
◊ *verb* **mattered, mattering**

matter-of-fact *adjective* Concerned with or conforming just to the facts: *They gave a matter-of-fact answer to the question.*
mat·ter-of-fact (măt′ər əv făkt′) ◊ *adjective*

mattress *noun* A pad of heavy cloth filled with soft material that is used on or as a bed.
mat·tress (măt′rĭs) ◊ *noun, plural* **mattresses**

mature *adjective* **1.** Fully grown or developed: *The plant blooms when it is mature.* **2.** Of or like an adult: *You are very mature for your age.*
◊ *verb* To grow up or develop fully.
ma·ture (mə tŏŏr′ *or* mə tyŏŏr′) ◊ *adjective* **maturer, maturest** ◊ *verb* **matured, maturing**

SYNONYMS

mature, adult, grown-up
Thanking your uncle for the gift without being asked was a *mature* thing to do. *Adult* education programs offer courses in computer science. Sometimes my little sister acts in a very *grown-up* way.
Antonyms: *childish, immature*

ă	pat	ĭ	pit	oi	oil	th	bath
ā	pay	ī	ride	ŏŏ	book	*th*	bathe
â	care	î	fierce	ŏŏ	boot	ə	ago, item
ä	father	ŏ	pot	ou	out		pencil
ĕ	pet	ō	go	ŭ	cut		atom
ē	be	ô	paw, for	û	fur		circus

HISTORY • novel[1], novel[2]

Novel[1] and **novel**[2] both go back to a Latin word that meant "new." But **novel**[2] came to English by way of Italian, where it was used to describe a "new" form of short story.

SYNONYMS

intense, fierce, furious, violent
The *intense* heat from the fireplace soon warmed us. It was impossible to make any headway against the *fierce* blizzard. The *furious* storm raged all night, and in the morning we found many trees knocked down. The *violent* tornado leveled all the buildings on Main Street.

Figure 8.2
Sample Dictionary Entries

aroused. When Cynthia Rylant, in her book *Appalachia: The Voices of Sleeping Birds,* describes the houses that miners lived in and writes that "you could draw a face with your finger because *coal dust had settled on their walls like snow"* and explains why the people "had this feeling of mystery about the rest of the world they couldn't see because *mountains came up so close to them and blocked their view like a person standing in a doorway,"* she is suggesting a visual, emotional, and physical world for us, pulling us into a deeper understanding and *feeling* about this region and the people who live there. When Gary Soto writes about a struggling mother and daughter in Fresno and their "dented Chevy Nova" that "gobbled up almost one hundred dollars in repairs" (1990, p. 78), intermediate and middle-grade readers realize the consequences of this situation much more than if Soto had simply written, "The repairs cost one hundred dollars."

Figurative Language   Figurative language uses what are broadly termed *figures of speech,* to express a speaker's or writer's meaning more appropriately and precisely. When we engage students in examining figurative language, we not only help them elaborate and extend the meaning they make as they read and write, we also give them a vocabulary for referring to and discussing this underlying meaning and the words that represent it. The most common figures of speech are *idioms* or idiomatic expressions, *similes* and *metaphors,* and *personification.*

Idioms   Many expressions and phrases have, over the years, moved beyond their original literal meaning and now connote something else: for example, *flying off the handle, letting the cat out of the bag, throwing the book* at someone, or saying someone is *over a barrel.* These are called either *idiomatic expressions* or just plain *idioms,* and each has its own unique and peculiar meaning. Students are often intrigued to learn the origins of idiomatic expressions, because each expression once referred to a very concrete situation.

An excellent book to introduce the concept of idioms is Marvin Terban's *In a Pickle and Other Funny Idioms* (1983). The book explains each common idiom by giving a straightforward definition followed by a brief history of *how* the expression came to be. Each idiom and its explanation are accompanied by a picture showing the *literal* meaning of the expression—which is quite a kick in itself. The *Amelia Bedelia* books are an excellent introduction to the concept of idioms, and characters who interpret idioms literally figure prominently in Sylvia Cassedy's *Lucie Babbidge's House* (1989; fantasy) and Vivian Vande Velde's *A Well-Timed Enchantment* (1990; fantasy). Idiomatic expressions, needless to say, are a challenge for ESL students, so your explicit attention to their needs is well worth the effort (Hayes, Bahruth, & Kessler, 1991).

Personification   Personification occurs when animals or inanimate objects are described in human terms, as if they were alive. Consider, for example, Jane Yolen's description in *Dinosaur Dances* (1990) of a *breeze* playing music as dinosaurs disco-danced:

> *They swayed to all the measures*
> *Of the prehistoric breeze*
> *As it played its early music on*
> *The carboniferous trees.*

Usually, students first become aware of personification through animal stories such as Arnold Lobel's "Frog and Toad" books, but there is more of fantasy than reality in the personification of these creatures. However, animals can be described very realistically, yet still have human perceptions and feelings attributed to them, as in Sheila Burnford's *The Incredible Journey. Fables,* of course, are a type of genre that relies primarily on personification.

Similes and Metaphors   A *simile* is an *explicit* comparison that is usually identified by the words *like* or *as*. Laurence Yep, in *The Rainbow People,* writes of limestone rocks "like big white pine cones" (1989, p. 180). After sharing several examples such as Yep's, we can introduce the term *simile* to our students by writing the word *similar* below *simile* and involve the students in discussing what they think is going on here. Discuss *why* we use similes and how they affect the meaning that is made. You will find the Woods' book *Quick as a Cricket* (1982) an excellent introduction to the idea of similes.

Metaphors are comparisons that are not introduced by words such as *like* or *as*. Once you and your students get to thinking about it, you'll find that metaphors are just about everywhere. Consider this example in Ursula LeGuin's *A Wizard of Earthsea* (1968): "As they came onto the hillside they thought of how the roots of it were deep, deeper than the sea, reaching down even to the old, blind, secret fires at the world's core" (p. 59). The hillside does not *literally* have "roots," of course, but LeGuin's metaphorical use of this word connotes a more precise and effective impression than if she had written literally about the dirt and geological strata underneath the hill.

How the Meaning of Words Changes   Language does change. There is no way to stem the tides of change, even if we wanted to—and there have indeed been people throughout the ages who've attempted to preserve a certain form of English that they thought was the proper form. The part of English that appears to change most markedly is its vocabulary. Most *colloquial* or slang terms come in and out of favor quickly, but some stay. In addition, new words are created to represent new ideas and new creations, while old words are applied to newer developments. Just think for a moment about words the computer field has given us. Some are new: *floppies, cursor, videodisc, RAM/ROM, megabyte, hard drive.* Some are old, with a new meaning: *bug, mouse, virus,* and *chip.*

Some changes in word meaning have come about slowly, literally over the course of centuries. Students do need to become aware of the processes by which words are formed and their meanings evolve. This knowledge certainly will reinforce their developing understanding of word structure in terms of affixes and roots. It will help them understand more fully the meanings suggested by words and quite often will alert them to the fine yet important distinctions among words in the same conceptual domain. It will also help them understand terms they will encounter throughout their lives in texts whose language is dated: Mark Twain's books, for instance, or Charles Dickens's. They'll be less likely to be thrown by the odd-seeming use of a familiar term.

Once any word exists, it can change. Meanings evolve over time. These meanings can become narrowed, as in the case of *girl,* which once referred to *any* child, regardless of gender. Meanings can become broader and more

Words from Mythology

Greek mythology provides quite an array of words whose stories kids usually find fascinating. Students often find that knowing the origins of a few terms from the myths enriches the meaning and understanding of these words and helps them understand the rich resources that have fed the English language. To give yourself the flavor of some of those terms, consider the following two examples:

Echo. Echo was a young woman who the gods felt talked far too much, so she was punished by being restricted to just repeating the last few words that were spoken to her. She was in love with Narcissus—the young man who fell in love with himself when he saw his own reflection in a pool. After his death, Echo grieved so much that eventually, all that remained of her was her voice.

Tantalize. Tantalus had been to Mount Olympus and dined there with the gods. He brought back some of their food and drink, however, and shared it with friends. This displeased the gods, so he was punished by being made to stand up to his neck in water—which receded whenever he tried to drink. Food was close by as well, but when Tantalus stretched to eat it, it moved away. This was his eter-nal fate. From his name we now have the word *tantalize,* which means teasing or tormenting someone by keeping something close by but out of reach.

Have a few mythology anthologies on hand in the classroom for your intermediate students. You may find the following particularly helpful:

Isaac Asimov (1961). *Words from the Myths.* Houghton Mifflin; [the most readable and most interesting resource of this kind.]

D'Aulaire, I., & D'Aulaire, E. (1980). *D'Aulaires' Book of Greek Myths.* Doubleday. [Of interest to third-graders and up; upper intermediate reading level.]

Fisher, L. (1984). *The Olympians: Great Gods and Goddesses of Ancient Greece.* Holiday. [Of interest to third-graders and up; third grade reading level.]

Gates, D. (1974). *Two Queens of Heaven: Aphrodite and Demeter.* Viking. [Of interest to fourth-graders and up; upper intermediate reading level.]

Kingsley, Charles (1980). *The Heroes.* Mayflower. [Of interest to third-graders and up; intermediate reading level.]

LEARNING IN CONTEXT: **The stories behind many present-day words that come from myths and legends help students remember the meanings of the terms as well as their spellings.**

generalized, or they can be elevated to a more "respected" level. Meanings can "degenerate"; *monster,* for example, once meant anything that was marvelous, but in recent centuries it has been used for something grotesque, terrible, or evil. Meanings can become *extended,* and as they do so, connotative language evolves. For example, words such as *salty* and *cold* have come to refer to or connote not only qualities of inanimate objects but aspects of people's personalities as well.

A lively book about English and how it has changed is Janet Klausner's *Talk*

About English: How Words Travel and Change (1990). See also Susan Sperling's books; for example, *Murfles and Wink-a-peeps* (1985).

Exploring parallel relationships among words

There is an infinite number of ways in which words and their underlying concepts can be related, interconnected, categorized. In this section and the next, we will explore the most productive ways, keeping in mind that by engaging our students in examining these relationships, we are supporting their vocabulary growth and the rich cognitive and affective frameworks that underlie meaningful reading.

Exploring *parallel* relationships among words with students offers some fairly straightforward ways of manipulating and reflecting on words and their underlying concepts. We can begin with antonyms and then explore synonyms, because antonyms are easier to understand—words that represent obvious opposites. Synonyms require attention to finer gradations of meaning among words, so we'll address them somewhat later.

Antonyms The concept of *antonyms* can be introduced quite easily by asking students to state the opposite idea that comes to mind when you say a word—for example, *hot, open, good, windy,* and so forth. Different types of "antonymic" relationships can be explored by requiring students to identify the antonym in a group of words (Dale, O'Rourke, & Bamman, 1971):

Good/bad

1. goodness   decency   corruption   honesty
2. mischievous   blameless   wicked   bad

Cowardly/courageous

1. cowardice   boldness   bravery   courage
2. timid   bashful   fearful   gallant

Thoughtful/thoughtless

1. careful   cautious   foolish   watchful
2. simple   thoughtful   silly   brainless

You can relate your prefix and suffix study to antonym study quite nicely by having students apply to base words the different affixes that have been studied. For example: worth/worth*less,* hopeful/hope*less;* active/*in*active, polite/*im*polite.

Synonyms By attending to *synonyms,* we help students differentiate among concepts and schemata as well as extend these to newer domains. This is because the synonyms for a particular word don't mean *exactly* the same thing—language doesn't work this way. There are subtle differences among the words in a group of synonyms, and learning these differences can elaborate and expand students' conceptual frameworks. Learning these differences can also help students think of more precise, appropriate, and *effective* words when speaking and writing.

After students have played around with antonyms for some time, you can follow this progression of synonym study:

1. Brainstorm associations based on a particular high-frequency word, such as *love* or *happy. Happy,* for example, will probably yield *joy, smile, glad, excited,* and *laughing,* among others. (*You* will know that some of the brainstormed words are synonyms and others aren't, but that's not important at this point.) After you've listed several associations, involve the students in discussing the meaning of these words and what the words have to do with *happy*. This is the first step along the way to really understanding synonymic relationships—to becoming aware of similarities and differences.

2. Remind students that they can think of the other, similar, words when they are writing and need to find just the right word or simply need to avoid a word that is overworked. Remind them also that writers have purposes in using certain words and not others, and that this will affect the meaning that the students make when they are reading.

3. After engaging in steps 1 and 2 which develop your students' awareness of synonymic relationships, you can introduce the term *synonym* and then explore words that require the students to make finer and finer distinctions among words that are considered synonyms. For example, discuss the words *promise, pledge,* and *vow,* and examine sentences from the students' reading in which these words are used to tease out the fine shades of meaning. This will be an ongoing process that may occur during literature response discussions and writing conferences.

MAKING CONNECTIONS

Literature and Wordplay

There are a few classics of children's literature through which *wordplay* is a thread that runs throughout. Lewis Carroll's *Alice in Wonderland* and *Through the Looking-Glass* are probably the best-known examples. A more contemporary classic is Norton Juster's *The Phantom Tollbooth* (1961), delightfully illustrated by Jules Pfeiffer; while some intermediate students delight in reading it on their own, it enjoys a broader appeal with most students when you share it as a read-aloud—because you can signal with your voice many of the plays on words. The main character in the book, a boy named Milo, passes through a tollbooth and emerges in a make-believe land that includes places called Dictionopolis, Sea of Knowledge, Mountains of Ignorance, and Foothills of Confusion. Like Carroll, Norton Juster plays with connotation, with all the types of figurative language, and so on. In fact, *The Phantom Tollbooth* can be a ready resource of examples of wordplay.

LEARNING IN CONTEXT: **Literature can be used to highlight different types of words and language use and to engage students in wordplay in delightful and humorous ways.**

Amanda Walsh's *The Mysterious Hubbub* (1990) is a marvelous, playful book that works wonderfully as a read-aloud and as Readers Theatre. Synonyms are the focus and provide excellent opportunities for expanding vocabularies.

Exploring categorical relationships among words

In addition to parallel relationships among words, there are *categorical* relationships in which words can be grouped according to "family" and according to topic, function, and subordinate/superordinate relationships. These types of categorical relationships help students appreciate the myriad connections among words and the concepts they represent.

Word "Families": Their Indo-European Ancestral Roots   You can help your students understand, appreciate, and *use* knowledge about many, many words through exploring relationships within word families. As we have been seeing, there are many ways in which words can be related. Exploring familial relationships and tracing their origins will facilitate students' awareness and appreciation of words, including the evolution and change of meanings over time. Fascinating familial links that intermediate students can explore are those that have developed from the *Indo-European* language.

Indo-European was a language spoken approximately seven thousand years ago by a people who probably lived in the Balkans in what is now Eastern Europe. Over time, they migrated in different groups to different areas. This resulted in their single language's eventually giving rise to a large family of languages, the "Indo-European" family. Over half the world's population speaks a language that can trace its roots back to Indo-European.

The way that Indo-European roots are spelled often does not appear close to the spelling of English words. This is because scholars use letters to stand for the original sounds in Indo-European, and these sounds have changed over thousands of years in different languages; in English, just a trace of these sounds remains. Still, there is enough similarity to allow students to get a sense of the original sounds and understand how English words originated in Indo-European.

Here are some examples of IE roots that occur in a large number of English words:

Fleu, meaning "move like water," is the ancestor of such words as *fleet, flee, flood, float, flow,* and *fly.*

Ghel, meaning "shine," yields such words as *gleam, glossy, glimmer, glow,* and *glint.*

Medhyo, meaning "middle," has given us *medium, middle, midst, media, intermediate,* and *Mediterranean.*

When your students explore several Indo-European roots and the words that belong to the "family" of each, they can understand how the nature of concrete objects and actions becomes extended to emotions and states of mind. For example, when three objects are arranged in a line, it is clear which one is in the *middle* (from *medhyo*); *media,* on the other hand, represents a more abstract understanding of "middle"—newspapers, radio commentaries, and television programs are "in the middle," between us and the events they report or portray. The word *flow* (from *fleu*), can refer to the easily observable movement of water as well as to the more abstract notion of the flow or movement of ideas.

This extension or "stretching" of meaning is a general process that occurs in all languages; it happened, for example, with Latin roots (think of *"spect"* as it functions in *spect*acles—the older word for "eyeglasses"—and in circum-*spect;* the meaning stretched from the concrete to the more abstract).

Exploring the Indo-European origins of words also helps students appreciate how particular *sounds* are used in words to suggest certain emotions and meanings. This awareness can extend to their appreciation of why writers select certain words and thus to students' own selection of appropriate words in their own writing. To illustrate, think for a moment about some words that come from the Indo-European word *ghel* ("shine"). *Glow, gleam,* and *glimmer* all have smooth-sounding *m*'s and *w*'s that suggest soft lights. The words *glisten* and *glitter* have "sharper" *s* and *t* sounds and describe a livelier light that sparkles and dances (Robinson, 1989).

BUILDING YOUR KNOWLEDGE BASE
Words and Their "Semantic Biographies"

C. S. Lewis, author of the "Chronicles of Narnia" series and one of the most knowledgeable wordsmiths of the English language, can probably best help us appreciate how words have evolved and how important this evolution is. Lewis wrote of the value of readers' having a sense of the "semantic biography" of a word. As applied to intermediate students, this does not mean that they should have an explicit knowledge of the etymological paths of large numbers of words. Rather, Lewis's statement suggests that students may have a "sense" of the notion that each word (and the elements that make it up) has a story behind it, telling why the word has come to mean what it does. This sense may enrich the totality of meaning that students construct as they read and thus their private, tacit responses, tapping deeper affective and cognitive roots. You will find that the following books, although only a sampling, provide excellent information about and examples of many fascinating "semantic biographies":

Asimov, Isaac. *Words of science, and the history behind them* (1959) and *Words on the map* (1962). Boston: Houghton Mifflin. [Events and individuals have generated many fascinating words over the years.]

Terban, Marvin. (1988) *Guppies in tuxedos: Funny eponyms.* New York: Clarion. ["Eponyms" are names that have become words in the language. Usually they were names of people *(boycott),* but sometimes they were places *(bikini).*]

Sarnoff, Jane, & Ruffins, Reynold (1981). *Words: A book about the origins of everyday words and phrases.* New York: Scribner's. [This is a good "first" book in etymology, with short, interesting histories of a number of words. It gives students a sense of how meanings have evolved and changed.]

Grouping Words Topically, Functionally, and Hierarchically   As we help students develop their perceptions of different relationships among words, we are expanding their vocabulary and their word knowledge, and often we help them think more critically—noticing relationships they had not seen before. These relationships can be described as *topical, functional,* or *hierarchical. Topical* relationships can be quite general and include words (concepts) that have to do with a topic; for example, *cleats* and *bat* have no obvious, direct relationship until they are placed under the topic of "baseball." *Functional* relationships organize words according to roles they may serve; for example, *hammer, nail,* and *saw* are related because of their common functions as tools. *Hierarchical* relationships organize words according to their level of generality; for example, *university* would be an all-encompassing concept, followed by *college, department, course,* and *student.*

In this section, we will look at a number of activities that engage students in thinking critically as they manipulate words and their underlying concepts topically, functionally, and hierarchically. First, we will consider the broad and important activity of "word sorts," then examine, more briefly, several other ways in which you can facilitate your students' word-categorization work.

Word Sorts   Word sorts, or word-categorization activities, involve students in comparing and contrasting words according to a number of different structural and semantic features (Barnes, 1989; Henderson, 1990; Moore, Moore, Cunningham, & Cunningham, 1986). When we discussed word sorts for students at the primary grade levels (see Chapter 6), we were looking at "structure" in terms of how individual letters or patterns of letters mapped to sound. For upper elementary students, "structure" corresponds to *meaning* units—the students will be sorting words according to morphemes: affixes and roots. They will also continue to sort words according to *semantic* criteria not based on specific word elements. Sometimes you will provide these criteria—a "closed" semantic sort—and at other times, the students will declare the criteria—an "open" semantic sort.

Here are some general guidelines that should help you in arranging word sorts for your students:

■ When the students begin sorting words according to a particular type of morpheme, start modestly. For example, in a closed sort format, have them sort words according to two or three prefixes. Use prefixes that are attached to *base words;* do not include Latin or Greek roots yet. When the students *are* examining such elements and are sorting words according to their common root, begin with words in which your affixes and word roots are fairly concrete.

■ The sequence of elements according to which the students will sort words will parallel your instruction about these elements. For example, after talking about the roots *-spect-* and *-vis-*, students will have the opportunity to sort words that include these roots. As you move through a sequence of specific elements, you can add words to be sorted that include previously studied elements (just as you recycled vowel patterns for sorting at the primary level).

■ In general, when students do word sorts—whether individually or in pairs—have them write down both the meaning of the common morpheme for each group *and* something about the category of the words in general. For example, one student wrote, "*Pre-* means 'before' and all of these words have to do with actions and doing things." It is not important for the students to come up with "dictionary-like" descriptions. Rather, your objective is to get them to think, talk, and write *explicitly* about what is going on in each category of words.

■ Keep the upper limit of words to be sorted at first to 15–20. As students become comfortable with and adept at sorting, the number of words can be increased.

■ Whereas we keep to known words in our sorts with primary students, it is fine (and desirable) to use a few *un*known words in sorts at the intermediate level—*especially* when you are doing sorts based on morphemic elements. This inclusion will reinforce students' attention to using morphemic elements in attempting the identification of unknown words in their reading. For example, examine the following sort in which the student sorted the words according to whether they had the word roots *-spect-* or *-aud-*:

auditorium	spectator
audible	inspection
auditory	spectacle
inaudible	circumspect
audition	spectacular
audiovisual	

For each category, the teacher included an unknown word: *inaudible* and *circumspect*. He anticipated, though, that students would be able to figure out the meaning on the basis of knowledge of the root and prefix of each word.

In addition to developing understanding of word elements and how they combine (see above), *word sorts* can be used to reinforce understandings of terms associated with a particular unit of study in a discipline or content area. New terms that have been introduced can be included along with known words that also relate to the topic in some fashion. Because so many words in science, mathematics, social studies, and geography have been created by combining word elements, students will have innumerable opportunities to sort these words structurally by common affix, base, or word root. There also will be limitless possibilities for other types of categorization. You might have students sort according to country, area, or language of origin, or you might draw from this "starter" list of possibilities:

■ Which words do you think came from myths and legends?
■ Which words are older? newer?
■ Which words are "naming" words? "action" words? "describing" words? (Notice how the teacher can deal with the inevitable issue of teaching *parts of speech* this way!)

- Which words can be used in a number of subjects? Which are limited to one subject?
- Which words can represent more than one meaning?

◼◼◼◼ DEVELOPING YOUR INSTRUCTIONAL TOOLKIT

Developing Awareness of Word Relationships

The following techniques work well in developing and reinforcing students' understanding of conceptual and structural relationships among words. They all involve discussion and critical thinking, but vary enough to involve students in looking at words and word features from a variety of perspectives.

1. *Graphic Organizer:* As we hinted in Chapter 7, the *graphic organizer* is an excellent way to introduce terms while at the same time showing relationships among them—and it will be an excellent reinforcing activity as well (see next page). Moreover, in preparing a graphic organizer for a specific chapter, you may in fact discover that *you* appreciate more clearly how the students might come to understand the relationships among the concepts about to be presented.

   First, select the most important concepts and the terms that represent them. Then arrange the words in a graphic to make the relationships among them visually apparent. Let's suppose, for example, that you are going to be teaching a unit on rocks and minerals. On the next page is a graphic organizer that displays relationships among the three major types of rocks—metamorphic, igneous, and sedimentary—and includes specific examples of each type.

   On page 414 we'll present a classroom example in which the teacher introduces and uses this graphic organizer.

2. *Word Web:* Based on a particular Latin or Greek word root in one of your important vocabulary terms, a word web illustrates how many related words share that root. Initially, *you* will need to construct most of a word web—to model how it works—so that your students will understand its function.

   Figure 8.4 is a word web for the root *-cred-;* the teacher has written each term and discussed its meaning. She engages the students in discussing how *-cred-* functions in each word and how each word is part of the same meaning "family." On another occasion, the teacher will start the word web but will encourage the students to contribute words they believe have the same root. She accepts every contribution, and afterward each word is considered in turn to see if it "fits."

3. *Semantic Map:* In recent years the cluster technique has been a popular means of helping students think about what they know. It has been adapted as an effective way to present new terms. In vocabulary instruction it is called a *semantic map,* a map that visually represents the semantic or meaning connections among terms related to a central idea or topic (Heimlich & Pittelman, 1986; Nagy, 1989). The semantic map fits nicely within the concept of the PReP, because like the "associative" aspect of the PReP, semantic maps get students thinking about their prior knowledge of a topic. You can then add new terms to the map that is created.

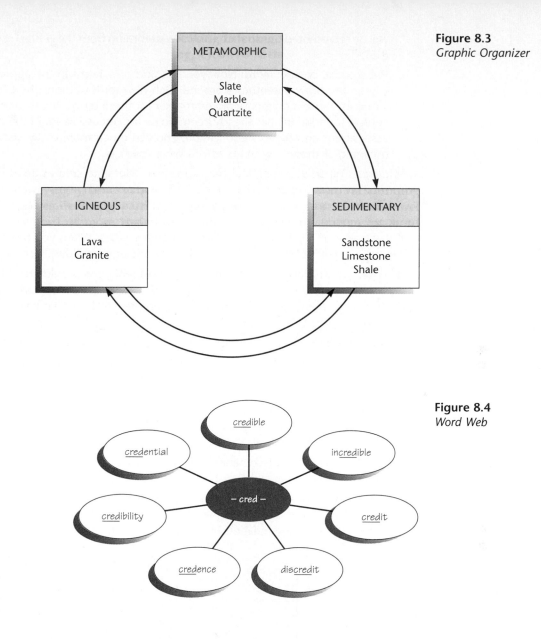

Figure 8.3
Graphic Organizer

METAMORPHIC

Slate
Marble
Quartzite

IGNEOUS

Lava
Granite

SEDIMENTARY

Sandstone
Limestone
Shale

Figure 8.4
Word Web

credible

credential

incredible

credibility

– cred –

credit

credence

discredit

Let's say you're going to build a semantic map around "clouds," one of the major topics in your fourth-grade unit on weather. Here are the steps you'll use:

a. *Brainstorm:* Have the students brainstorm words that come to mind when they think of "clouds." Write these words on an overhead transparency, on the chalkboard, or on a chart.

b. *Categorize:* On a separate large sheet of paper, draw an oval in the middle with the word *clouds* written in it. Then discuss with the students how the associated words might be grouped into specific categories; these categories will be represented by separate branches stemming from the center (see Figure 8.5).

   c. *Presentation of New Terms:* Now you can add new terms in the appropriate categories; draw parentheses around each new term to highlight it for the students or use a different-colored marker for these terms. Because the "conceptual foundation" has already been laid by the discussion about the *students'* associations and their categorization, you can much more easily discuss the meaning of these new terms as you write them.

4. *Analogies:* When you complete the expression "Hot is to cold as good is to _____," you have expressed an *analogy*. Analogies build on our awareness and understanding of synonyms and antonyms and of figurative language. They usually require more cognitive connections to be made, however, so they are not introduced directly until the late elementary years. When you believe some of your students can benefit from and enjoy analogies, follow these steps:

   a. When you first introduce analogies to your students, you should present simple, straightforward examples of the "hot is to cold as good is to bad" variety. Talk about the type of relationship between the words in each pair and about how the pairs relate to each other.

   b. After this format is introduced and discussed, present analogies in which one word is omitted and several possible words for completing the analogy are offered. This is the basic analogical challenge. For example, *sun* is to *day* as *moon* is to _____ (noon, night, stars).

   c. After students understand the nature of the task, present analogies *without* possible choices: *fork* is to *eat* as *pen* is to _____. This is also an appropriate point at which to present the usual form for analogies: *fork : eat :: pen : _____.*

   d. Later still, vary the placement of the omitted word: *guitar : _____ :: hammer : tool.*

Several types of analogical relationships have been identified, and after a fair amount of work with analogies, you may find that some of your students want to explore them. These relationships represent the higher-order thinking that

Figure 8.5
Semantic Map

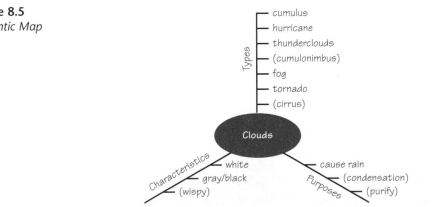

will help students identify the nature of the relationship within the analogy, which will in turn help them identify the appropriate word. Here are the different types of relationships and examples of each:

a. *Characteristics*   rock : hard :: pudding :: soft
b. *Part/Whole*   finger : hand :: wheel : bicycle
c. *Whole/Part*   book : page :: table : leg
d. *Location*   cook : kitchen :: teacher : classroom
e. *Action/Object*   kick : ball :: scrub : floor
f. *Agent/Action* or *Agent/Object*   writer : book :: architect : blueprint
g. *Class* or *synonym*   poor : poverty :: rich : wealth
h. *Familial*   grandfather : grandson :: grandmother : granddaughter
i. *Grammatical*   serene : serenity :: divine : divinity
j. *Temporal* or *sequential*   eighth : fourth :: tenth : fifth
k. *Antonyms*   nice : mean :: pleasant : unpleasant

Note applicability to previous learning: after comparing and contrasting authors, for example, present analogies such as the following:

Langston Hughes : poem :: E. L. Konigsburg : _____.

Byrd Baylor : _____ :: Jean Craighead George : Alaska.

Wilson Rawls : drama :: Judy Blume : _____.

You'll find that these books provide excellent examples as well as effectively introducing the concept: Diot's *Better, Best, Bestest* (1977) and Roman's *Bigger and Smaller* (1971).

BUILDING YOUR KNOWLEDGE BASE

Books About Word Structure

The following books are excellent sources both for specific morphemic elements and for words that contain these elements:

Bear, D., Invernizzi, M., & Templeton, S. (in press). *Words their way: A developmental approach to phonics, spelling, and vocabulary, K–8*. Columbus, OH: Merrill/Prentice-Hall.

Fry, E., Fountoukidis, D., & Polk, J. (1985). *The new reading teacher's book of lists*. Englewood Cliffs, NJ: Prentice-Hall.

Henry, M. (1990). *Words: Integrated decoding and spelling instruction based on word origin and word structure*. Los Gatos, CA: Lex Press.

Templeton, S. (1991). *Teaching the integrated language arts*. Boston: Houghton Mifflin.

Toomey, M. (1989). *Morph-aid: A source of roots, prefixes and suffixes*. Cincinnati, OH: Circuit.

HELPING STUDENTS LEARN SPECIFIC VOCABULARY

Instructional goals of direct teaching of terms

We know that the most productive type of word learning occurs as students read and encounter new words and as we help them perceive structural and semantic relationships among "families" of words. There are times, though, when it is necessary to introduce and teach some new terms directly. Understanding that real learning will best occur if connections can be made between the new and the known, we try to make this type of teaching as beneficial as we can.

Our teaching of new terms can have a ripple effect beyond those specific words. If we do it best, we are ensuring that our instruction will have at least the following three benefits:

1. Simply having more words available helps students learn other words and helps them with constructing meaning on an overall basis. It strengthens their knowledge base, reinforces their tools for reading and learning new words, and demonstrates that one word and one concept lead to the next.
2. The direct instruction itself, if done thoughtfully and "strategically," can act as a model for students in their own word work.
3. Like everything else about work with words, direct instruction can act as a circle-widener in a general way: heightening interest, awareness, connections, motivations, attitude of inquiry.

Teaching vocabulary in narratives

Recall from Chapter 6 that new words occurring in students' story reading usually are *not* pretaught. Because most of the time there will not be many of these in any one story, we want the students to apply their word-analysis skills *in context* if an unknown word is important enough to figure out. As we also noted in Chapter 6, we should preteach a word if the word "is crucial to the overall understanding of the story *and* there is little if any support from context *and* you are fairly certain that the students' word knowledge is not sufficient for figuring the word out" (p. 258). The ways in which you can preteach such terms are the same as for terms in content-area reading (see next section).

After a story is read and discussed, however—as in a Guided Reading-Thinking Activity—talk about any new words the students encountered. Discuss any strategies they applied to figure out an unknown word. Return to the place in the story where the word occurred and discuss the context surrounding the new word. An excellent follow-up is to place new terms in a story map (see Chapter 6) and then discuss them in the context of the major parts of the story. By putting into a story-map diagram words about which students are uncertain when they first read the story, you can effectively reinforce those words' meanings through discussion, teacher questioning, and the rereading of the sentences that contain the words (Blachowicz & Lee, 1991).

Remember that because your students will be reading extensively and intensively, they *will* be encountering many new words on their own. Discuss how they can remember many of these by entering them in their *word study notebooks* (see above) and trying them out in conversation and in their writing. While you will not be teaching this new vocabulary directly, of course, you *should* be clear with your students about how they can acquire new words on their own in their reading.

Teaching vocabulary in the different content areas

This section is necessarily (and noticeably) lengthier than the section on teaching vocabulary in narratives. This is because more attention to vocabulary is necessary in the disciplines or content areas. More new terms pop up in expository texts than do in narratives, and these new terms often represent major concepts central to the main topic(s). Because of this, vocabulary is an integral part of your overall instruction in the content areas. Please do keep in mind, though, that many techniques presented in this section for developing and reinforcing the meaning of new words, may be used for important new words that arise out of your students' reading of narratives as well.

Knowledge of specific vocabulary terms gives your students a handle on the subject area or discipline, a language for discussing what is going on in that discipline and for learning in that discipline. Working with vocabulary terms provides perhaps the most direct manipulation of underlying concepts, particularly if these concepts are not very concrete. These concepts, these terms, these *words* enrich the schemata that your students bring to bear on their reading and writing in these areas—relating directly to comprehension and to composition.

When you are moving into a new unit or area of study with your students, selection and presentation of new vocabulary is usually a critical part of your initial activities. It is part of the "setting the stage" process in which you are accessing your students' prior knowledge about the concepts to be explored, as you develop their interest and motivation.

Selecting Terms to Teach   What are the major concepts you wish to address? What terms represent those concepts? These two questions should guide your selection of terms to teach. A textbook will of course highlight a number of new terms, but this should not dictate your decision—you may select fewer terms or in some cases, more. It is better to have a short list that the students will really learn than a long one that will force them into rote memorization—and subsequent rapid forgetting.

For the sake of motivation and interest, also include a few terms that you *know* may be of particular interest to your students, even if these are not representative of major concepts. For example, *repulsive* and *earwig* would engage a class of fourth-graders studying insects. While these terms may not represent major concepts, they tap into the sorts of things that transfix (and repulse!) fourth-graders. And they will actually provide a more secure conceptual framework on which the other terms will depend. (Earwigs, by the way, are indeed repulsive-looking insects that folklore says work their way into the ear canal and burrow into, then dine on, the brain. They've gotten an undeserved reputation. They *do* enjoy dining on flowers and plants.)

Here's a concluding perspective to our discussion about the *initial* presentation of new vocabulary terms: Well-organized textbooks usually have examples of preparatory lessons for introducing important content vocabulary and often present examples of how certain words were created from word elements. For example, *pangea,* often used in science and geography texts, is an excellent illustration. Created from the Greek forms *pan* ("all") and *gea* ("earth"), the term refers to the first continent on earth—which eventually broke up, the sections drifting apart to form separate continents. But when textbook lessons and examples are sparse or inappropriate, *you* will need to plan the lesson— always bearing in mind the importance of accessing your students' prior knowledge first.

■ ■ ■ ■ ■

CLASSROOM IN ACTION

Preteaching Terms in a Science Lesson

Lorie Reithaller has just begun a geology and geography unit of study with her fifth-grade class. Some of the important terms she has selected are *tectonic plates, fault,* and *crust.* Before she presents the terms, she needs to prepare the conceptual groundwork. As we saw in Chapter 7, this can be done in any number of ways. The most common approach is through the PreReading Plan format (PReP) in which concepts are accessed and extended through discussion. Another way is by doing a *read-aloud* with an engaging informational trade book on the topic you're going to be addressing.

Ms. Reithaller has in fact set the stage this way, and she also has planned to show a filmstrip and a film. These will include pictures of the 1906 San Francisco earthquake; the Anchorage, Alaska, earthquake of 1964; the 1971 and 1994 Los Angeles earthquakes; the San Francisco quake in 1989; the eruptions of Mount St. Helens in Washington in 1981 and Mount Pinatubo in the Philippines in 1991. She then shows a map of the "ring of fire" that represents the junctures of tectonic plates along which earthquakes and volcanic eruptions so often occur. She points out how we are in effect floating on the surface of the earth, its *crust,* and says that this crust is made up or constructed of sections called *tectonic plates.* People who are close to the places where these plates come together or overlap, she explains, are more likely to experience quakes and/or eruptions.

By now, this teacher has accessed her students' concepts of earthquakes and volcanoes and has related the new concept—*tectonic plates*—to this prior knowledge. The students are ready to move on and speculate *why* volcanoes and earthquakes are more likely to occur at these junctures.

Later in the same unit, Ms. Reithaller uses a *graphic organizer* (the one on page 404) to present other new terms: "We're going to be looking into a few new words in this unit. In order to understand the unit, it's especially important for you to know these words. This diagram should be a real help to you for learning them. [Distributes a copy of the organizer to each student.]

"Learning the meaning of new words can often be more difficult than it needs to be because we try to learn them one at a time. We don't see the *connections* among them. If you can see how they are related to one another, you'll usually remember their definitions a lot better.

"On your diagram you see the names of the three different groups of rocks [pointing]: *metamorphic, igneous,* and *sedimentary.* Under each name, you'll see the names of some types of rocks in each group. All the rocks on earth can be classified in one or another of these groups. The arrows connecting these three different groups have a purpose. Why do you suppose, for example, there is an arrow from *sedimentary* to *metamorphic?* [The understanding here is that "one group comes from another or changes into another."]

"When we study this unit, we'll see how these changes can occur. Remembering how these words are related will help you do two things. First, you'll remember their meaning better. Second, you'll learn and remember more from the unit."

Ms. Reithaller continues: "A rock doesn't stay the same for all time. It changes over millions of years. As we'll see, it can start as *lava* from a volcano—an extremely hot, fiery liquid. All *igneous* rocks begin as extremely hot substances. The lava cools down, and over time [tracing along arrow] becomes worn down and broken up into sediment, which then recombines with other worn-down rocks in forming *sedimentary* rocks. These rocks can then be changed over time *again* [tracing along arrow toward *metamorphosis*], eventually becoming *metamorphic* rocks.

"This cycle [tracing along the arrows from *igneous* to *sedimentary* to *metamorphic*] is a very common way for rocks to change. You'll notice that the other arrows show some other directions in which changes can occur. Remember the arrows, though—they'll help you keep in mind the *cycle* of changes."

Note how Ms. Reithaller uses the new terms in conjunction with pointing to the graphic organizer, to indicate and establish the relationships among the concepts.

In the next step, Ms. Reithaller points out briefly where the word for each group of rocks came from (this includes attention to the *structure* of the words) and discusses related words. For example:

> *Igneous* comes from a Greek word meaning "fire" and is related to the words *ignite* and *ignition.*
>
> *Sedimentary* comes from the Greek word meaning "settle" and is related to *sediment.* (As students become involved in the unit, their basic understanding of how particles settle in layers and eventually form this type of rock will be elaborated.)
>
> *Metamorphic* comes from the Greek word meaning "change." Most of the time, igneous or sedimentary rocks that have undergone intense heat and pressure are *changed* or *metamorphosed* in their form and structure. Ms. Reithaller's students have already learned about *metabolism* in a unit on the body, for example, so she points out how *meta-* signals the meaning "change" in this word as well: in order to function, the body needs to change substances through chemical processes.

In addition to using the techniques just described to teach new terms, Ms. Reithaller also uses the new words in a number of different *written* contexts that involve her students in making significant semantic discriminations (Beck, McKeown, & Omanson, 1987). It is far more effective to have students consider a well-written context in which new terms appear than to have them make upsentences using the new words (unless, of course, they are trying out the words in their *own* creative writing).

APPLYING WORD KNOWLEDGE IN COMPOSITION

When they are reading widely and exploring words and their uses at the same time, we see many students spontaneously using new words, expressions, and figurative language in their writing. While students' compositions can be enriched and more effective because of the words they use, writing in turn affords students opportunities to exercise and apply their word knowledge. This application yields benefits for their reading as well.

We help students apply their word knowledge in writing through a number of minilessons and individual conferences, and as a result of *our* modeling, we see our students interacting among themselves in the same vein:

■ What is the most *precise* word that would work in a particular context? As student(s) explain what they mean in this particular context, we can suggest other words they may know, as well as use the opportunity to share with them a *new* word that may work.

■ We may also use this opportunity to model the effective use of the *thesaurus*. When students have used a particular word that represents their intended meaning, they are "primed" to consider other possible words, and *this* is the best time for turning to a thesaurus. Remind students that so-called "synonyms" do not mean *exactly* the same thing and that therefore a thesaurus entry will help them move in on the most precise meaning they intend. Always keep the usefulness of the thesaurus in a broader perspective, though: share with students the realization that while a thesaurus will be very helpful, over the long term their own wide reading will yield the words, meanings, and varied contexts that provide the knowledge base from which they will learn to select just the "right" word as they are drafting or revising.

■ Remind students that they can apply their expanding knowledge of the "spelling/meaning connection" as they are composing or revising. For instance, suggest to the student who has misspelled *competition* as *compatition* that she should think of a related word *(compete);* use the opportunity to teach the related word *solemnity* to the student who has misspelled *solemn* as *solem*.

■ A handy companion to learning about words is the *word study notebook.* It can be a separate spiral notebook or a section at the back of students' writing journals. One part of the notebook is set up in alphabetical order, and students can write down truly interesting new words that they encounter in their reading, along with a brief statement of what a word means. Suggest that they write the sentence in which they found the word as well, though this is optional and we don't want it to get in the way of their entering new words. Another suggestion is that they write any other words they can think of that share the same base word or word root and are therefore related in spelling and meaning (see "The Relationship Between Vocabulary and Spelling—The "Spelling/Meaning Connection" on p. 392). On occasion, students can share one of their truly interesting new words with a small group or the whole class; more about this in a moment.

A second part of the word study notebook can be the place where students develop different categories of words. For example: words with interesting stems;

words that share a particular prefix; homophones; eponyms; words related to a particular discipline; and so on. The types and number of category lists will change as students discover more about words.

■ A CONCLUDING PERSPECTIVE

Words live their real lives in context. Yet students can fully understand and appreciate these lives only if they understand how words are structured and how this structure reflects underlying concepts. This type of knowledge will also underlie students' rapid and efficient identification of words during reading.

Our responsibility as teachers is to help students develop strategies they can use in their reading when it is necessary to identify an unknown word. These strategies will become richer as students learn more about the structure of words. They will learn about this structure through our direct demonstrations and our guidance of their explorations of words. They will learn how affixes and roots combine to represent meanings within single words and among related words in meaning "families."

We as teachers also play a significant role in identifying the important concepts our students will explore in the different disciplines or content areas. These concepts are often represented by new terms or by familiar terms used in new ways, so we will also be helping students learn the concepts and the terms.

I would like to conclude with what I feel is an extremely important point about our facilitation of students' knowledge about words: *Keep word study fun.* Even if you do not consider yourself a "wordsmith" right now, I hope that the strategies we have discussed in this chapter and the resources referred to will encourage you in your own exploration of words. Talk about interesting words with your students; share interesting words you've come across in your reading and perhaps other words that share important features and meanings with these words; comment about interesting and engaging words that come up in your read-alouds. If you become just a *little* more intrigued by what words are and what they can do, you will find that your interest and even excitement will carry over into your teaching as you guide students in *their* explorations.

■ BECOMING A REFLECTIVE PRACTITIONER

Beck, I., & McKeown, M. (1991). Conditions of vocabulary acquisition. In R. Barr, M. Kamil, P. Mosenthal, & P. D. Pearson (Eds.), *Handbook of reading research: Volume II* (pp. 789–814). New York: Longman.
  This review of research takes a look at the complexity of vocabulary growth and its role in reading comprehension. One of the major problems with measuring vocabulary size is being able to define what vocabulary *is*. Once that is established, then the question of acquisition can be addressed. The authors look at vocabulary growth from context and from vocabulary instruction; they found that learning from context does occur but that it isn't as influential as vocabulary instruction—particularly if the instruction (1) allows for adequate time for practice, (2) includes information about the word(s) and (3) involves activities that require processing of information about

the word(s). Vocabulary growth *was* found to have a positive effect upon reading comprehension.

Chomsky, C. (1970). Reading, writing, and phonology. *Harvard Educational Review, 40,* 287–309.

This seminal article discusses the relationship between the spelling and the sound of words, and explains why most of the "irregular" spelling patterns we encounter really aren't that irregular; they are *predictable* in nature. These relationships manifest themselves in skilled readers and carry over into other areas of literacy. Importantly, they manifest themselves in expressing the *meaning* of words—what this chapter has referred to as the *spelling-meaning* connection.

Nagy, W., & Anderson, R. (1984). How many words are there in printed school English? *Reading Research Quarterly, 19,* 304–330.

Conservatively, a typical third-grade student might encounter up to 100,000 words of text in a school year, and a seventh-grade student might encounter as many as 1,000,000 words of text in a year. Obviously, direct instruction doesn't account for all of the new words that students will come across, so this article speculates on some of the additional ways that students cope with new vocabulary. It would seem that the study of word families and the morphology of words has a tremendous impact on the acquisition of new words and enables students to learn new words on their own. This is a landmark article concerning vocabulary and its development within the school setting.

Stahl, S. & Fairbanks, M. (1986). The effects of vocabulary instruction: A model-based meta-analysis. *Review of Educational Research, 56,* 72–110.

Stahl and Fairbanks take a detailed look at the importance of vocabulary instruction on reading comprehension and vocabulary acquisition. Their findings indicate not only that vocabulary instruction does benefit comprehension, but that the amount of time spent on vocabulary instruction is as important a factor in gaining knowledge of new words as is the method of instruction used. The middle section—the "Results" section of the research—is rather technical, but the information as a whole is very worthwhile and the time spent reading this article should be well spent.

Templeton, S. (1991). Teaching and learning the English spelling system: Reconceptualizing method and purpose. *Elementary School Journal, 92,* 185–201.

A case is made for the revamping of most spelling programs in use. This article argues that the memorization/workbook mentality of traditional spelling programs does little to enable students to utilize the meanings, structure, and patterns of words to be successful at spelling, writing, and reading. Spelling instruction should focus on students working with words for which they are developmentally ready and which should be at their instructional level, as opposed to their frustration level, as so often is the case. This article offers a solid introduction to the developmental approach to spelling and its implications for instruction.

■ REFERENCES

Adams, M. (1990). *Beginning to read.* Cambridge, MA: MIT Press.

Anderson, R., & Freebody, P. (1981). Vocabulary knowledge. In J. Guthrie (Ed.), *Comprehension and teaching: Research reviews* (pp. 77–117). Newark, DE: International Reading Association.

Barnes, W. (1989). Word sorting: The cultivation of rules for spelling in English. *Reading Psychology, 10,* 293–307.

Baumann, J. & Kameenui, E. (1991). Research on vocabulary instruction: Ode to

Voltaire. In J. Flood, J. Jensen, D. Lapp, & J. Squire (Eds.), *Handbook of research on teaching the English language arts* (pp. 604–632). New York: Macmillan.

Bear, D., Invernizzi, M., & Templeton, S. (in press). *Words their way: A developmental approach to phonics, spelling, and vocabulary, K–8*. Columbus, OH: Merrill/Prentice-Hall.

Beck, I., & McKeown, M. (1991). Conditions of vocabulary acquisition. In R. Barr, M. Kamil, P. Mosenthal, & P. D. Pearson (Eds.), *Handbook of reading research* (Vol. 2, pp. 89–814). White Plains, NY: Longman.

Beck, I., McKeown, M., & Omanson, R. (1987). The effects and uses of diverse vocabulary instructional techniques. In M. McKeown & M. Curtis (Eds.), *The nature of vocabulary acquisition* (pp. 147–163). Hillsdale, NJ: Lawrence Erlbaum.

Blachowicz, C., & Lee, J. (1991). Vocabulary development in the whole literacy classroom. *Reading Teacher, 45,* 188–195.

Chomsky, C. (1970). Reading, writing, and phonology. *Harvard Educational Review, 40,* 287–309.

Dale, E., O'Rourke, J., & Bamman, H. (1971). *Techniques of teaching vocabulary*. Palo Alto, CA: Field Educational Publications.

Hall, R. (1984). *Sniglets*. Collier Books.

Hayes, C., Bahruth, R., & Kessler, C. (1991). *Literacy con carino*. Portsmouth, NH: Heinemann.

Heimlich, J., & Pittelman, S. (1986). *Semantic mapping: Classroom applications*. Newark, DE: International Reading Association.

Henderson, E. (1990). *Teaching spelling* (2nd ed.). Boston: Houghton Mifflin.

Henry, M. (1990). *Words: Integrated decoding and spelling instruction based on word origin and word structure*. Los Gatos, CA: Lex Press.

Just, M., & Carpenter, P. (1987). *The psychology of reading and language comprehension*. Boston: Allyn & Bacon.

Moore, D., Moore, S., Cunningham, P., & Cunningham, J. (1986). *Developing readers and writers in the content areas*. New York: Longman.

Nagy, W. (1989). *Teaching vocabulary to improve reading comprehension*. Joint publication of the National Council of Teachers of English and the International Reading Association. Newark, DE: International Reading Association. Urbana, IL: National Council of Teachers of English.

Nagy, W., & Anderson, R. (1984). How many words are there in printed school English? *Reading Research Quarterly, 19,* 304–330.

Nagy, W., Diadikoy, I., & Anderson, R. (1993). The acquisition of morphology: Learning the contribution of suffixes to the meanings of derivatives. *Journal of Reading Behavior, 25,* 155–170.

Robinson, S. (1989). *Origins: Vol. 1. Bringing words to life; Vol. 2. The word families*. New York: Teachers and Writers Collaborative.

Stahl, S., & Fairbanks, M. (1986). The effects of vocabulary instruction: A model-based meta-analysis. *Review of Educational Research, 56,* 72–110.

Templeton, S. (1983). Using the spelling/meaning connection to develop word knowledge in older students. *Journal of Reading, 27,* 1, 8–14.

Templeton, S. (1991). Teaching and learning the English spelling system: Reconceptualizing method and purpose. *Elementary School Journal, 92,* 185–201.

Templeton, S. (1992). Theory, nature, and pedagogy of higher-order orthographic development in older students. In S. Templeton & D. Bear (Eds.), *Development of orthographic knowledge and the foundations of literacy: A memorial Festschrift for Edmund H. Henderson.* Hillsdale, NJ: Lawrence Erlbaum Associates.

White, T., Power, M., & White, S. (1989). Morphological analysis: Implications for teaching and understanding vocabulary growth. *Reading Research Quarterly, 24,* 3, 283–304.

Wolf, S., & Heath, S. (1992). *The braid of literature.* Cambridge, MA: Harvard University Press.

Children's Literature Cited

Carroll, L. (1982). *Alice's adventures in Wonderland, Through the looking-glass, and The hunting of the snark.* Chatto, Bodley Head & Jonathan Cape.

Diot, A. (1977). *Better, best, bestest.* Harlan Quist.

Burnford, S. (1960). *The incredible journey.* Little, Brown.

D'Vincent, C. (1992). *The whale family book.* Picture Book Studio.

Gwynne, F. (1980). *Sixteen hand horse.* Windmill Books.

Gwynne, F. (1980). *The King who rained.* Prentice-Hall.

Juster, N. (1961). *The phantom tollbooth.* Random House.

LeGuin, U. (1968). *A Wizard of Earthsea.* Parnassus.

Lewis, C. S. (1950–1956). The "Narnia" Chronicles. New York: Macmillan.

Lobel, A. "Frog and Toad" series. Harper & Row.

McMullan, K. (1989). *Dinosaur hunters.* Random House.

Parker, S. (1988). *Skeleton.* New York: Knopf.

Roman, R. (1971). *Bigger and smaller.* Crowell.

Rylant, C. (1991). Appalachia: The voices of sleeping birds. Harcourt.

Soto, G. (1990). *Baseball in April.* Harcourt.

Walsh, A. (1990). *The mysterious hubbub.*

Wood, D., & Wood, A. (1982). *Quick as a cricket.* Child's Play.

Yep, L. (1989). *The rainbow people.* Harper Trophy.

Yolen, J. (1990). *Dinosaur dances.* Philomel.

CHAPTER NINE

DEVELOPING THEMATIC UNITS: BRINGING INTEGRATED INSTRUCTION, LITERATURE, AND DIVERSITY TOGETHER

FOCUS

■ *How do thematic units interconnect reading, writing, and other areas of the elementary curriculum?*

■ *What are the major categories of children's literature? What are the distinguishing characteristics of each category?*

■ *How do many experienced teachers suggest you "move into" thematic units?*

■ *Describe and explain the rationale for the process of developing thematic units.*

■ *Why is "multiculturalism" such an important foundation for your literacy and thematic-unit instruction?*

■ *How can you help your students become aware of—and appreciate—cultural diversity?*

> *[Whole language instruction] brings back into the foreground . . . curriculum as integrative and inquiry centered. Furthermore, it integrates development of language, thinking, and content into a dual curriculum in which knowledge is built at the same time as thought and language are built.*
>
> *Kenneth Goodman*

Writing for the journal *Language Arts* in 1992, Kenneth Goodman discussed the philosophy of whole language instruction exactly one hundred years after John Dewey stated that the role of education is to bring "people and their ideas and beliefs together, in such ways as will lessen friction and instability, and introduce deeper sympathy and wider understanding." The challenge and the promise of meaningful integration of reading and writing with the elementary curriculum and with the "real world" have excited educators for a very long time. Equally exciting is the potential for this integration to occur in a classroom environment that will lead, as Dewey observed, to "deeper sympathy and wider understanding"—a fundamental goal in our multicultural society. We have not just recently become a multicultural society—we always have been one (Takaki, 1993)—and Dewey was reminding educators of the positive implications of this fact almost a century ago.

Beginning with Chapter 4 in this book, we have spun quite a number of instructional threads as we focused on elementary students and classrooms. We've seen how we can set up a classroom and what we can engage students in within that classroom. It is now time to pull these threads together in ways that result in the kinds of instruction Dewey and Goodman describe. This is the fundamental purpose of this chapter: I will help you picture the whole process of putting an authentic reading/integrated literacy approach into action—how it is conceptualized, planned, organized, and realized. And throughout this chapter, I will be addressing the issue of *your* progression as a teacher, encouraging and supporting your own evolution so that you'll feel fairly comfortable moving toward designing and orchestrating instruction focused on themes.

We will approach our all-important goal by considering in depth these three major topics: (1) the reasons and rationales for using thematic units as an organizational framework; (2) selecting good children's literature to provide a "best fit" within a thematic unit; and (3) the way to become a thematic-unit teacher.

First, however, let's take a quick inventory of those threads we have spun up to this point.

We know that we need to provide students with opportunities for *extensive* and *intensive* reading in lots of narrative and informational texts. We know that we usually need to provide *guidance* in their particular purposes for reading. In other words, we know we need to help them understand the *tool* of reading and how it can be applied. We have observed how the tool of reading is applied for "aesthetic" purposes—for enjoyment and for coming to understand oneself more deeply—and we have explored how the tool of reading is applied in the pursuit of knowledge.

Throughout the elementary, middle, and secondary school years, this pursuit of knowledge has commonly occurred within the domains labeled "Science," "Mathematics," "Social Studies," and so on. We will be serving our students better if we move away from thinking about "curriculum" as something "out there," dry and removed, and start thinking about it as something through which students feel invited to explore issues and questions with which they can identify. And once they begin to explore, they will inevitably grow beyond themselves. As I have been emphasizing, this is a goal you can realistically attain—probably not all at once, but gradually. This belief guides the progression I'll be suggesting to you later in this chapter, when we explore thematic teaching.

While I have suggested, throughout this book, different literature to support different aspects of your instruction, this chapter will address directly the issue of *selecting* good children's literature. We'll address it early in the chapter because effective thematic teaching builds from a familiarity with the types of literature available and from an awareness of how, when, and why to select more effective, engaging, and appropriate books.

When we accept the centrality of a strong multicultural orientation in our classrooms, we see that the most comprehensive and authentic way of exploring diversity is (1) to share the literature of diverse cultures, and (2) to learn about and understand those aspects that are unique to each culture and those that are common to all—that unite us all as human beings.

I'd like to share the following perspective with you, so eloquently expressed by Heath and Mangiola (1991, p. 17):

> Schooling should provide such a range of ways of seeing, knowing, thinking, and being that it will be equally challenging to all students and teachers to imagine other possibilities, take risks with learning, and transcend the boundaries of the immediacy of personal experience. Let us then not think of students of diverse backgrounds as bringing "differences" to school, but instead as offering classrooms "expansions" of background knowledge and ways of using language.

As this proposal affirms, and as we've noted earlier, children from diverse backgrounds offer possibilities and potential, rather than problems and perplexities. Ours is not only an increasingly multicultural society; it is increasingly *diverse* as well. This diversity represents a number of facets, including the necessity for a "global perspective" that is the result of an "interdependence among all nations" (Bennett, 1990). Many educators emphasize that diversity also includes attention to groups that for reasons other than their ethnic or racial identities are often kept outside the mainstream; for example, the homeless, the physically challenged, and lesbians and gays (Shannon, 1992).

REASONS AND RATIONALES FOR USING THEMATIC-UNIT TEACHING

A great deal of emphasis is being placed today on employing *thematic units* in our instruction (see, for example, Harste, Short, & Burke, 1989; Moss, 1992; Walmsley, 1994). Through thematic teaching we are able to *unify* most effectively the use of real literature, integrated instruction, and multicultural awareness.

In conventional elementary classrooms the students often do not perceive, much less understand, the connections between reading and writing and the applications of reading and writing—nor do they often see the connection between what happens in one subject area and what happens in another or the relationship between literacy and those subject areas. Teaching and learning through a *thematic* format allows your students to see the connections among different areas and information. They see how literature relates to content, and they see how the *tools* of literacy can be applied in the exploration of content. Thematically based instruction and learning are motivating to students and afford *all* of you—teacher as well as students—the opportunity to be part of a real community of learners (see, for instance, Gamberg, Kwak, Hustings, & Altheim, 1988; Harste, Short, & Burke, 1989; Newkirk & Atwell, 1988; Pappas, Kiefer, & Levstik, 1990). It allows important interconnections among reading and the other language arts. Because a good portion of instruction and learning is organized thematically, the *language* and the *schemas* that support the children's learning are being used continually.

In its essence, *thematic teaching* organizes instruction and learning around a central *theme* (or *topic*—the two terms are often used interchangeably). The theme is "the core . . . it defines what is to be the center of attention" (Gamberg, p. 10). This allows students to understand *how* acquiring new information and using the tool of literacy can relate to their own lives and beyond—to their community and to their world. As we will discuss in this chapter, themes may be narrow in scope or broad. Some examples would be, say, an author, a genre, volcanoes, your state's history, art collage, journeys, building a play structure for the playground. And as we'll see below, it is important to know that whatever the theme, possibilities for multicultural connections and emphases always exist.

The *scope* of thematic units can stretch along a continuum, from a single topic that is part of one area of instruction all the way to a totally cross-curricular format in which *all* instructional goals and content are organized around the theme. When we begin, we usually start at the narrower end of this continuum, with a theme that clearly integrates literature and the language arts. Over time, we can grow into addressing themes that have a broader focus and involve exploration through other areas of the curriculum.

Opportunities for emphasizing good literature

Our overview of children's literature in this chapter, together with the titles presented earlier in this text, underscore the availability and the wonderful possibilities of literature throughout the school years. Thematic units afford

Meaningful integration of the language arts with one another and with the content areas is no longer missing in classrooms such as this one where sixth graders are discussing their writing projects.

you innumerable opportunities for incorporating literature in all your teaching. And as we explore the multicultural context of the classroom, we'll be observing that by including multicultural literature in the curriculum, we give children from nondominant cultures a sense of *themselves* in what they read. While there certainly are "universals" of human experience that children can find in books reflecting the dominant culture, the immediate identification with the here-and-now world of the character or characters in a book that are from the child's *own* experience is undeniably a fundamental, critical opportunity we should not be denying any child. Yet how could it be otherwise? We know that children construct meaning initially out of their *own* experiences within their own cultural contexts. Therefore, our wish to make the acquisition of literacy and knowledge more comfortable and meaningful for them can be realized *only* if much of our instruction reflects the literature and customs of our children's own backgrounds.

Opportunities for emphasizing integrated instruction

Traditionally, reading and the other language arts were taught as discrete skills, at separate times of the school day. Subject areas were also taught at separate times, and application of the language arts to content areas was seldom explicitly made. What was missing was the meaningful *integration* of the language arts with one another and, in turn, their meaningful integration with and application to the content areas. Through thematic instruction, integration appears to occur almost naturally, though the teacher's guiding hand behind the scenes causes this "natural" feeling to develop.

As mentioned above, a good plan to follow is to begin with a narrower focus—a unit integrating the language arts—and move over time into units that connect topics across the curriculum. When using the unit with the narrower focus, your teaching in math and science, for example, may occur at other times during the day and may be addressing concepts that are not directly related to your literature/language-arts-based thematic unit. By the time you are implementing a full-fledged across-the-curriculum unit, all your instruction may be integrated. Later in the chapter, you will discover how to progress from a relatively narrow language-arts thematic unit to a more expansive integrated thematic unit. This progression will take time.

You will also need to keep in mind that although virtually *any* topic or theme can be addressed either modestly or more expansively, some topics lend themselves quite beautifully to the language arts focus and need not be expanded any further. Part of your progression as a teacher will involve learning to make such judgments comfortably and integrating your instruction accordingly.

I think you'll discover that you already have a lot of the necessary concepts for grasping the "how-to's" of putting a thematic unit together. The overall scheme of core works, extended works, and "recreational" works, and the accompanying ideas of "intensive" and "extensive" reading that we first examined in Chapter 6, apply to thematic-unit teaching as well as to your other instruction. As a refresher, Figure 9.1 presents the underlying scheme for the reading and instruction that will be organized in a thematic unit.

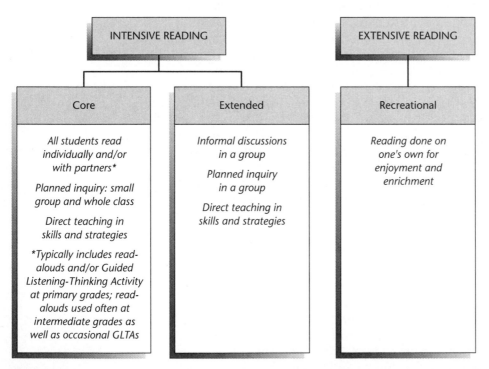

Figure 9.1
Underlying Scheme for a Literature-Based Thematic Unit

When you read different educators' descriptions of the literature that is used in thematic units, you will find small differences among terms and definitions. For example, what *I* refer to as "extensive" reading, another writer may call "independent." Don't be thrown off course by these apparent differences; just focus on the underlying organization. In just about every instance, you will see the same message with the same emphases:

■ There are texts that you read *to* and *with* all your students and that the students read on their own or with a partner; these are the *core* texts that everyone in the class will experience.
■ There are texts that students read *with* you, either exclusively or in combination with prior reading and preparation for group discussion; these texts usually allow you to teach certain skills and strategies as well; these books are *extended* works that relate to the theme represented by the core text.
■ There are texts that students are reading on their own—*recreational* texts.

Recall from Chapter 4 that even before the children first arrive, you identify important general concepts to be addressed during the school year. When you move into thematic units, you are applying the same basic planning process, although *now* you know much more about your students. For each unit you plan to construct, think about the following:

■ *What* important concepts and understandings you will be helping the students develop and *why* these concepts and understandings are important: do they lead to more critical thinking and more problem-solving?
■ *How* these concepts and understandings can be developed: what activities and experiences can you provide to facilitate this development?
■ What *skills and strategies* you will be developing.

I'd like to mention some key points before finishing this discussion. The illustrative webs and lesson plans that are presented at the end of the chapter are quite comprehensive. This is because I would like you to get a real feel for the "what" and "how" of constructing units, as well as a strong sense of their content and of how the units "play out" over several days. The examples also represent the depth of the thinking, planning, and reflective process involved in the units' development. You probably will not always write plans that are as specific and precise as the lesson plans here; as you gain more teaching experience, you may develop a shorthand way of planning and writing your units, and that's fine. Initially, however, a high degree of precision pays off, and chances are that you probably will be expected to develop teaching plans at least this specific in your student teaching practicum!

Opportunities for emphasizing diversity and multiculturalism

The term *multicultural* usually refers to groups "outside the socio-political mainstream" of the nation (Bishop, 1992, p. 40). The terms *dominant* and *"nondominant"* often are used as well to mark this distinction between mainstream and diverse cultures (Crawford, 1992). In Chapter 1, I first described the complex issues involved with helping students from nondominant cultures learn about the dominant culture while including and preserving important aspects of their own culture. As we recognize important commonalities in humanity and in human experience, we will also come to understand that there are features of our experiences that will be more meaningful to particular groups.

While the term *at-risk* can be used to describe many and various children, it is often applied to students who are not from the dominant culture. While this helps focus public attention on their needs, it certainly does not have a positive connotation. Unfortunately, the use of the term can lead to self-fulfilling prophecies. Erickson (1991) cites the comment of a second-grade teacher regarding an "at-risk" girl: "Why do I bother to get her to finish (her work)? She'll be a hooker by the time she's fifteen." The goal of changing perceptions and attitudes is a daunting one, but at least those of us in the classroom can begin by using terms that reflect the *promise* and contributions of nondominant cultures.

Part of our role as thoughtful practitioners is to understand the development of our multicultural society. As a society, our awareness of and sensitivity to diverse groups and cultures is interesting and revealing. We have gone from ignoring groups that were not a part of the mainstream to acknowledging the injustices they suffered, but there is still another level that we are just beginning to acknowledge. Ronald Takaki captures this level in his book *A Different Mirror* (1993). It is time, Takaki suggests, to see ourselves in a *different* mirror of history than the one into which we have always gazed, the one that exclusively represents a European-American perspective on the development of a nation: we have *always* been multicultural, and where we are now as a society is the result of *all* the cultures interacting with one another. Takaki is pointing out something that too often is overlooked when we *do* acknowledge the many cultures in our society: members of nondominant cultures in American society "have been *actors* in history, not merely *victims* of discrimination and exploitation" (p. 14, emphasis added).

The relationship between the dominant culture and nondominant cultures is not one-way. You will be helping your students from the mainstream culture understand nondominant cultures as well. This is the big difference between thinking of culturally diverse children as "lacking" what they need in order to succeed in the dominant American culture, and thinking of *all* children as needing to understand not only their own culture but the cultures of others. In this spirit, Heath and Mangiola offer another excellent observation:

> Our intention here is not to urge teachers to teach in special ways to students whose everyday cultural and linguistic habits differ from those of the classroom. Instead, we want to urge teachers . . . to expand the ways of thinking, knowing, and expressing knowledge of all students through incorporating many cultural tendencies. (1991, p. 37)

I would like to suggest a framework for incorporating aspects of multiculturalism within the context of thematic teaching (see Figure 9.2).

First, we can think of an "osmosis" perspective in which an awareness of multiculturalism permeates both the selection of literature for a particular theme

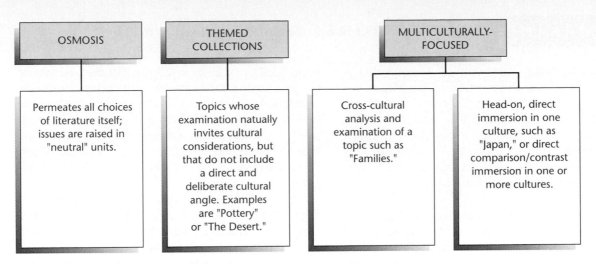

Figure 9.2
Various Means of Building Multicultural Awareness into Thematic-Unit Teaching

and the issues that will be addressed. This perspective best expresses what we are working toward: while it may not be explicitly highlighted, there is a natural, unstilted, and authentic infusion of multicultural aspects throughout our instruction and learning. This happens when you collect books on a particular topic. For example, if you are searching for narrative and informational texts about trees, you will quite naturally come across a variety of books from a variety of cultures.

Second, we can develop themed "collections" or text "sets" of literature in which the theme or topic naturally invites specific cultural considerations but does not specifically examine the similarities and differences among different cultural perspectives (Short, 1989; Smolkin, forthcoming). Smolkin, for example, has developed a "pottery" unit in which pottery is explored in different cultural and historical settings; biographies of noted potters are included as well as a number of books on how to create pottery. Another example of such a "themed collection" would be "The Desert" (see below), in which different cultures are alluded to along with other aspects of the theme—in the case of the desert, for example, different types of deserts, animals, and plant life, along with the different desert cultures.

Third, we can develop units that clearly are multiculturally focused and through which multicultural issues are forthrightly addressed—intensively investigating a specific cultural group or groups within the context of the theme. For example, themes such as "old world/new world," "equality," "conflict," "generations," and "the family" are just a few examples in which different cultural perspectives are explicitly emphasized (Tchudi & Tchudi, 1991, p. 79). In addition, a major cultural group may be the focus—the Japanese, for example, in the context of a unit on Japan. Yet despite its excellent perspective, this type of unit does have the most potential for misuse—it may be the *only* time that "multiculturalism" is addressed, and it may come across in a "contrived" con-

Ours is a remarkably multicultural society: this is the reality as well as the promise of America as we approach the year 2000. Implications of this fact touch every aspect of our teaching, and that is why I have emphasized multicultural awareness throughout this book and am about to illustrate, in this chapter, how multicultural threads can be woven through your thematic teaching in many different ways.

There is another reality, however, and we need to acknowledge that it exists. At this time in our history, discussions of multicultural awareness are often couched in such terms as "political correctness," as if this attention were a passing fad. It is not. In addition, discussion is often couched in terms of "us" as compared with "them"; one often hears observations like "Now don't get me wrong; I'm not prejudiced or racist or anything like that, but those people coming into our country today aren't like immigrants in the past. People today don't come looking for work; they come looking for a handout. . . ." And so on. Of course, exactly the same attitudes were expressed a century and more ago about Eastern European, Irish, and Chinese immigrants.

The fact that we often hear comments (and worse) expressing ignorance, insensitivity, or outright contempt for certain cultures other than one's own reflects human nature's less appealing side. As teachers, however, we often encounter these perceptions as they are reflected through a few or even many of the children in our classrooms. Through literacy learning and literacy experiences, we can address these biases and then move beyond them.

LEARNING IN CONTEXT: **Children can be shown how to move beyond biases if they are asked to function within a classroom that sensitively encourages the awareness and the appreciation of many different cultural heritages.**

text. As we have noted before, this is where "Black History Month" is often considered—and then neglected for the remainder of the year. These explicit multicultural units can be very well done, and they *should* be done, but our awareness of multiculturalism should not end with them.

Later in this chapter, I would like to share with you examples of the development and realization of thematic units in which these different ways of developing multicultural awareness are accomplished.

SELECTING GOOD CHILDREN'S LITERATURE

In Chapter 4, we looked briefly at criteria for selecting literature to have in your classroom when you get the school year under way. Now we'll look at book selection from a *thematic* perspective. What guidelines and criteria should you keep in mind when you go to the school or community library?

General guidelines for selection of books

We will discuss specific ideas for book selection throughout this chapter, but you should find the following *general* guidelines helpful when choosing books for your thematic focus.

- When you first try a thematic unit, include some books that elaborate on one or two particular aspects of the theme—books appropriate for smaller interest groups to explore (see below).
- Try to find books from each major genre: stories, informational books (primary students love "pop-up" informational books), poetry, and so on.
- Choose books that represent a range of cultural perspectives (we'll explore criteria for this below).
- Select books that represent a range of readability levels (see Chapter 7); because your students will be at different points along the developmental literacy continuum, you should have available some books that everyone can read with relative ease.
- Keep students' interests in mind: these include particular topics that may be part of a larger theme, as well as particular authors that students enjoy.

There are a number of magazines, journals, and books that have in many ways done a lot of the planning for themes, as well as recommending appropriate books for each theme. These publications can be an excellent starting point, but you will almost always need to make some adaptations. First of all, you may find that many of the suggested books are unavailable when you need them, so you'll need to locate additional titles. Second, you will probably need to pick and choose which concepts or activities suggested in the publications are indeed appropriate for your students. Third, you will need to incorporate the interests of your students as you adjust the unit. By this time, you may feel that you could have gone ahead with the planning and organization on your own, right from the start—but this is precisely the fundamental point: use these publications as excellent resources for ideas and books, but never be lulled into the expectation that you can simply "unpack" a theme from them and engage your students without significant additional thought and preparation.

Guidelines for assembling multicultural literature

We all are subject to holding stereotypical beliefs about various groups of people. We all recognize *blatant* stereotyping, but stereotyping can be subtle as well. It is the subtle type for which *we* need to be on the lookout and which we need to make sure our students recognize. While the notion of "stereotype" usually has a negative connotation, our beliefs can be just as erroneously positive as they can be negative: for example, we may romanticize one group and have paternalistic feelings about another. We also want to be alert for possible misinformation that may be presented when an author who is not a member of a particular group expresses his or her own perspective on that group.

I'd like to share with you some cautions about selecting books for thematic units, so I'll mention what we may as well call "pitfalls to avoid," since we *can* inadvertently create problems farther down the road.

First and foremost, you should be familiar with any books you select for thematic instruction. If you gather a good number of books on a particular theme, with the hope of being able to use most if not all of them, be sure to go through any you haven't read. Second, think about *how* related the books are to your theme: that is, will you be "forcing" a connection? Sometimes this happens when a teacher is having a difficult time trying to find enough books to support a theme. If, for example, you've chosen "the history and building of kites" as your topic, a book that briefly mentions a child's receiving a kite for his birthday might be a bit of a stretch. Third, what about the *quality* of the books? This is by nature almost a subjective judgment on your part; but as you read about authentic literature in this text, and as you read widely in children's literature, you will develop a strong sense of quality and appropriateness. While there are literally thousands of excellent books for children, there also are a lot of books that have not been written and produced with quality in mind. It is appropriate, of course, to talk with students about how to evaluate the appropriateness and usefulness of a book, so that they can judge independently whether or not a book will meet their needs, but we can do this without necessarily having a number of less-than-the-best books in our classroom libraries. Fourth, as we'll explore below, we should be sensitive to the accuracy of books—fictional or informational. "Accuracy" applies not only to *content* but also to the representation of individuals and groups. Many, many books published over the years contain inaccurate portrayals of the nature and the contributions of members of nondominant cultures, and we don't wish to perpetuate or contribute to such inaccuracies.

LEARNING IN CONTEXT: **The criteria for choosing books for thematic units are those of appropriateness, quality, and both social and factual accuracy.**

In this section, I'll suggest features to look for in determining the appropriateness of particular books that represent different cultures. This does *not* mean that you should avoid any book that does not "pass the test." You can involve students in contrasting some of the more authentic texts with ones that are less so—for example, a text expressing the "European" perspective on the importance of Columbus could be contrasted with one offering the Native American view. Many of the conflicting ideas may be unresolvable. The important point, however, is the *awareness* of different perspectives, the critical examination of different perspectives, and the attempt—whenever possible—to find information that just might provide some resolution.

The following guidelines and criteria are synthesized from a number of sources in the area of children's literature in general and multicultural literature in particular. They should help you be sensitive to cultural authenticity in general and to determine the cultural authenticity of a particular selection (Council on Interracial Books for Children; Harris, 1993; Norton, 1991):

- All types of people from all over the world should be represented. They should be portrayed in different roles, living conditions, and occupations.
- Include biographies of individuals who are heroes and heroines in their respective cultures.
- Counteract stereotypical perceptions: for example, Mexican-Americans as migrant workers, African-Americans as living in poverty-stricken inner-city neighborhoods, Native Americans as important only in a historical context (Bishop, 1992).
- Provide different perspectives on important events: for example, the Mexican perspective on the American takeover of Mexican lands (now the southwestern United States); the Japanese-American perspective on the internment of Japanese-Americans during World War II; the Native American perspective on the encounter between their world and that of Columbus.

When evaluating any book for cultural authenticity, you will need to consider the following questions:

- What is the author's point of view toward non-Western peoples? What type of language is used to describe individuals?
- Are people who are not Caucasians portrayed as leaders, or always as followers? Are they fully developed as characters or are they one-dimensional stereotypes? Is their language authentic in terms of the setting of the story?
- Are illustrations accurate—or stereotypical?
- What effect might the book have on a child's self-esteem? A good test is to think about whether the book contains anything that would be embarrassing or offensive if it referred to the group of which *you* consider yourself a part.

In her discussion of the nature and role of multicultural literature, Rudine Sims Bishop cites an observation by the late African-American writer James Baldwin: "Literature is indispensable to the world. . . . The world changes according to the way people see it, and if you alter, even by a millimeter, the way a person looks at reality, then you can change it" (cited in Watkins, 1979).

Bishop follows this quote by noting that *multicultural* literature can be a powerful means of influencing how children view the world and their effect on it. Multicultural literature can "change the world by making it a more equitable one" (1992, p. 51). Once again we see that the importance of multicultural literature lies not only in helping children from diverse cultures see and value themselves in books, but also in helping *all* children see and value so much more than the present boundaries of their lives.

I would like to share a personal experience regarding evaluation of cultural authenticity. In one of my undergraduate classes, we were reading Elizabeth George Speare's *The Sign of the Beaver,* a work of historical fiction in which the relationship between a European-American boy and a Native American boy plays a central role. The book is often cited as an example of an excellent work of historical fiction and was a Newbery Award Honor book. One reason I wanted my class to read and discuss it was that potentially stereotypical characterizations of Native Americans are presented, and I wished to focus both on awareness of these characterizations and on understanding why they might be offensive.

One student pointed out that she felt the following description of a dance in an Indian village would be offensive to a Native American: "A lone Indian . . . strutted and pranced in ridiculous contortions, for all the world like a clown in a village fair. The line of figures followed after him, aping him and stamping their feet. . . ." (p. 81)

A few of the other students in class declared that their classmate probably was overreacting. They believed that in the overall context of the book, this description should not offend Native Americans. The one Native American student in my class, a member of the Paiute tribe, remained silent throughout this exchange.

Shortly after this discussion, I was reading and responding to my students' journals for the class. When I read the Paiute student's journal, he referred to the controversial passage and stated that he had indeed found it quite offensive; he also explained why he had remained silent during the discussion. He wrote about the importance of dance in most Native American cultures and noted that much of it is a part of religious ritual. Speare's description struck him as particularly insensitive, bordering on sacrilege.

But this was not all the Paiute student wrote in his journal entry. He went on to point out other things that most members of other cultures are not aware of: for example, he explained the derivation of the word *squaw,* which appears often in *The Sign of the Beaver* as well as in general usage. While I was aware that it could be offensive and demeaning, I did not know its literal meaning to Native Americans. He informed me that white men had originally used the term to refer to a particular part of a Native American woman's anatomy and that later, the term was used to refer more generally to a Native American woman. (A Cherokee educator later confirmed that this student's explanation of the derivation was quite correct.)

Given what I learned from this Paiute student, I must apologize for having used the term even here, but I hope my decision to do so makes a critical point: evaluating the cultural authenticity of the literature we select and share with children is not just something to which we give lip service. Being sensitive to others' cultures and to how other cultures are portrayed in children's literature is not, as some might say, part of a passing social fad. As this Paiute student's perspective reveals so compellingly, this sensitivity runs to the heart of what we do and why we do it in our classrooms—and beyond.

LEARNING IN CONTEXT: **Within the contexts of individual cultures, actions or words may carry particular significance, and as educators we have a responsibility to be especially sensitive and respectful to all cultures.**

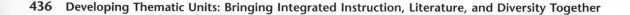

Categories of children's literature

Most children's literature experts partition the wide range of genres into seven major categories. (Note that the first of these categories, "picture books," can encompass the themes and topics of the other categories.)

Picture books

Traditional literature

Poetry

Contemporary realistic fiction

Modern fantasy

Historical fiction

Informational and biographical literature

Major children's literature texts by Norton (1991); Huck, Hepler, and Hickman (1993); and Cullinan and Galda (1994) present extensive, extremely informative discussions of these categories, and I strongly urge you to consult them. In order to assist you in selecting appropriate literature and effectively integrating it into your classroom, this section will offer a "quick reference" to these categories and to suggested books within each. Before you look over the titles and authors in this section, though, I would like to emphasize three points.

First, it is difficult to select a "representative" list because there are so many excellent authors and books we could include. Keep in mind, therefore, that this list is *by no means* exhaustive. Still, we must begin somewhere; so I present my suggestions below. Besides having read these books myself, I've checked the recommendations of highly respected children's literature experts and reviewers.

Second, most categories in this list are organized according to cultural orientation. As we have been emphasizing throughout this text, part of expanding your students' knowledge of many cultures is accomplished through exploring literature about those different cultures. While the categories titled "Picture Books," "Modern Fantasy," and "Poetry" are not set up on that basis, they do include representative books for each major cultural group.

Third, after each title listed here, I have indicated its appropriateness for preschool/primary (P), intermediate (I), or all (A) grades. As with all books, however, you should not apply these suggested levels rigidly; the make-up and needs of your class will change each academic year, and you'll want to be open to using a particular book for particular children or even a whole class. You will discover, too, that although a book may be marked for the primary grades, older children often will enjoy it just as much. I hope the lists that follow will be of real help as you explore the world of children's literature.

Picture Books   Picture books tell a story whose illustrations and text work together to provide one complete literary experience. In Chapters 3 and 5, I suggested a number of excellent picture books appropriate for young children; in this section there will be a few of those and also a number of titles appropriate for older students. (Keep in mind that picture books aren't just a genre for young children; they are for *all* ages!)

Aardema, V. (1981). *Bringing the rain to Kapiti Plain.* Dial. (A)

Adoff, A. *Hard to be six.* Lothrop. (A)

Barth, E. (1971). *The day Luis was lost.* Little, Brown. (P)

Baylor, B. (1983). *The best town in the world.* (A)

Bunting, E. (1982). *The happy funeral.* Harper. (A)

Bunting, E. (1988). *How many days to America?* Clarion. (A)

Coutant, H. & Vo-Dinh. (1974). *First snow.* Knopf. (P)

De Paola, T. (1975). *Strega Nona.* Prentice. (P)

Ehlert, L. (1990). *Feathers for lunch.* Harcourt. (P)

Feelings, M. (1974). *Jambo means hello: Swahili alphabet book.* Dial. (A)

Garza, C. (1990). *Family pictures/Cuadros de familia.* Children's Book Press. (A)

Girion, B. (1990). *Indian summer.* Scholastic. (A)

Goble, P., & Goble, D. (1978). *The girl who loved wild horses.* Bradbury Press.

Goble, P. (1989). *Iktomi and the berries.* Orchard. (A)

Goble, P. (1992). *Crow chief: A Plains Indians story.* Orchard. (A)

Greenfield, E. (1977). *Africa dream.* Crowell. (A)

Greenfield, E. (1980). *Grandmama's Joy.* Crowell. (A)

Greenfield, E. (1988). *Grandpa's face.* Philomel. (A)

Kraus, R. *Leo the late bloomer.* Windmill. (P)

Lyon, G. (1993). *Dreamplace.*

Martin, B. Jr., & Archambault, J. (1989). *Chicka chicka boom boom.* Simon & Schuster. (P)

Mayer, M. (1969). *There's a nightmare in my closet.* Dial. (P).

Ringgold, F. (1991). *Tar Beach.* New York: Crown. (A)

Rylant, C. (1985). *The relatives came.* Bradbury. (A)

San Souci, R. D. (1989). *The talking eggs.* Dial. (A)

Seuss, Dr. (1937). *And to think that I saw it on Mulberry Street.* Hale. (P)

Steig, W. (1979). *Sylvester and the magic pebble.* Windmill. (A)

Steptoe, J. (1980). *Daddy is a monster . . . sometimes.* Viking. (A)

Surat, M. (1983). *Angel child, dragon child.* Raintree. (A)

Takeshita, F. (1989). *The park bench.* Kane/Miller. [Bilingual English/Japanese]

Van Allsburg, C. (1984). *The mysteries of Harris Burdick.* Houghton Mifflin. (I)

Van Allsburg, C. (1985). *The polar express.* Houghton Mifflin. (A)

Van Allsburg, C. (1991). *The wretched stone.* Houghton Mifflin. (I)

Wiesner, D. (1988). *Free fall.* Lothrop. (I)

Wiesner, D. (1991). *Tuesday.* Clarion. (A)

Wood, A. (1984). *The napping house.* Harcourt. (A)

Yashima, T. (1955). *Crow boy.* Viking. (A)

Traditional   Traditional literature includes folktales, fables, myths, and legends. These stories have grown out of an oral tradition and have been told and retold for many, many years. They represent people's attempts to deal with both their outer and their inner worlds: real-life and imaginary experiences and explanations. The stories represent all cultures' attempts to "construct meaning" and make sense of the universal human condition—attempts that are strikingly similar. This is why comparing and contrasting folktales from different cultures, for example, opens children's eyes to the common psychological and emotional roots of humankind. Born and nurtured in the family of a culture, in different parts of the world and at different times, stories were told around the campfire and the hearth. In recent times they have been written down, often in many different versions. Their continued popularity attests to the psychological and emotional needs they address in children and in society (Bettelheim, 1976; Campbell, 1966).

Folktales include what are commonly referred to as "fairy tales" and often include elements of magic and the supernatural, as well as animals with human characteristics. *Fables* include animals as the central characters and provide an explicit moral: "A bird in the hand is worth two in the bush," for instance. *Myths* explain how things came to be: the origins of the world and of people, the causes of natural phenomena such as weather, the cycles of day and night and the seasons. *Legends* are narratives that tell of more recent events and are usually focused on real-life individuals whose deeds and exploits are embellished: the English King Arthur, the French Joan of Arc, the Hawaiian Pakaa and Ku (Brown, 1966).

African/African-American/Caribbean

Haley, G. (1970). *A story, a story.* Atheneum. (A)

Hamilton, V. (1988). *The people could fly.* Knopf. (A)

Joseph, L. (1991). *A wave in her pocket: Stories from Trinidad.* Clarion. (A)

Knutsen, B. (1990). *How the guinea fowl got her spots: A Swahili tale of friendship.* Carolrhoda. (P)

McKissack, P. (1985). *Cinderella.* Children's Press. (A)

McKissack, P. (1986). *Flossie and the fox.* Dial. (A)

McKissack, P. (1991). *A million fish . . . more or less.* Knopf. (A)

Price, L. (1990). *Aida.* Harcourt. (I)

Steptoe, J. (1987). *Mufaro's beautiful daughters.* Lothrop. (A)

Strickland, D. (Ed.) (1986). *Listen children: An anthology of Black literature.* Bantam. (A)

Asian-American (Asian Pacific American)

Belknap, J. (1973). *Felisa and the magic Tinikling bird.* Island Heritage. (A)

Brown, M. (1966). *Backbone of the king: Story of Pakaa and his son Ku.* University of Hawaii Press. (A)

Demi. (1980). *Liang and the magic paintbrush.* Holt.

Dyer, V. (1982). *The brocade slipper and other Vietnamese tales.* Addison-Wesley. (A)

Graham, G. (1970). *The beggar in the blanket and other Vietnamese tales.* Dial. (A)

Liyi, H. (1985). *The spring of butterflies and other Chinese folktales.* Lothrop. (A)

Louie, A. (1982). *Yen-Shen: A Cinderella story from China.* Philomel. (A)

Spagnoli, C. (Adapted) (1989). *Nine-in-one, grr! grr!.* Children's Book Press. [Laotian; told by Blia Xiong] (A)

Yep, L. (1989). *The rainbow people.* HarperCollins. [Chinese] (A)

Young, E. (1989). *Lon Po Po: A Red-Riding-Hood story from China.* Philomel. (A)

European-American

Brett, J. (1987). *Goldilocks and the three bears.* Dodd, Mead. (A)

Brett, J. (1989). *Beauty and the beast.* Clarion. (A)

Brown, M. (1954). *Cinderella.* Scribner's. (A)

Cauley, L. (1982). *The cock, the mouse, and the little red hen.* Putnam. (A)

Chaucer, G. (1988). *Canterbury tales.* Lothrop. [Adapted by B. Cohen] (I)

Huck, C. (1989). *Princess Furball.* Greenwillow. (A)

Magnus, E. (1984). *Old Lars.* Carolrhoda. (A)

Owen, L. (Ed.). (1981). *The complete Brothers Grimm fairy tales.* Avenel. (A)

Perrault, C. (1990). *Puss in boots.* Farrar. [Translated by M. Arthus] (A)

Sherman, J. (1988). *Vassilisa the Wise: A tale of medieval Russia.* Harcourt. (A)

Watson, R. J. (1989). *Tom Thumb.* Harcourt. (A)

Zelinsky, P. (1986). *Rumpelstiltskin.* Dutton. (A)

Hispanic-American/Latino and Caribbean

Aardema, V. (1979). *The riddle of the drum: A tale from Tizapan, Mexico.* Four Winds. (A)

Beals, C. (1970). *Stories told by the Aztecs: Before the Spaniards came.* Abelard. (I)

Belpré, P. (1973). *The rainbow-colored horse.* Warne. (I)

Bierhorst, J. (Trans.). (1984). *Spirit child: A story of the Nativity.* Morrow. (I)

Bierhorst, J. (1986). *The monkey's haircut and other stories told by the Maya.* Morrow. (I)

de Paola, T. (1980). *The lady of Guadalupe.* Holiday House. (A)

DuBois, W. (1972). *The hare and the tortoise and the tortoise and the hare: La liebre y la tortuga y la tortuga y la liebre.* Doubleday. (A)

Ehlert, L. (1992). *Moon rope.* Harcourt. (P)

Griego y Maestas, J., & Anaya, R.A. (1980). *Cuentos: Tales from the Hispanic Southwest.* Museum of New Mexico. (I)

Hinojosa, F. (1984). *The old lady who ate people.* Little, Brown. (A)

Rohmer, H., & Dornminster, W. (1987). *Mother Scorpion country.* Children's Press. (A)

Native American

Bierhorst, J. (1987). *Doctor Coyote: A Native American Aesop's fables.* Macmillan. (A)

Bruchac, J. (1985). *Iroquois stories: Heroes and heroines, monsters and magic.* Crossing Press. (A)

Carey, V. (1990). *Quail song: A Pueblo Indian tale.* Putnam. (A)

Cohen, S. (1988). *The mud pony.* Scholastic. (A)

Connolly, J. (1985). *Why the possum's tail is bare and other North American Indian nature tales.* Stemmer House. (A)

de Paola, T. (1983). *The legend of the bluebonnet.* Putnam. (A)

Esbensen, B. (1989). *Ladder to the sky.* Little, Brown. (A)

Goble, P. (1990). *Iktomi and the ducks: A Plains Indian story.* Orchard. (P)

McDermott, G. (1974). *Arrow to the sun.* Viking (A).

Norman, H. (1989). *How Glooskap outwits the Ice Giants and other tales of the Maritime Indians.* Little, Brown.

Steptoe, J. (1984). *The story of Jumping Mouse, a Native American legend.* Atheneum. (A)

Yellow Robe, R. (1979). *Tonweya and the eagles and other Dakota Indian tales.* Dial.

Poetry   As we saw in Chapter 6, there are many forms of poetry. Elementary children seem to prefer humorous poems, with familiar subjects—sometimes cast in unexpected situations. Intermediate students can appreciate the word play as well as the precision of words that are used.

Adoff, A. (1982). *All the colors of the race.* Lothrop. (A)

Adoff, A. (1973). *Black is brown is tan.* Harper. (A)

Baylor, B. (1975). *The desert is theirs.* Scribner's. (A)

Bennet, J. (1989). *Noisy poems.* Oxford. (I)

Bierhorst, J. (Ed.). (1983). *The sacred path: Spells, prayers and power songs of the American Indians.* Morrow. (A) de Gerez, T. (1981). *My song is a piece of jade: Poems of ancient Mexico in English and Spanish*. Little, Brown. (A)

Giovanni, N. (1985). *Spin a soft black song*. Farrar. (I)

Harrison, M., & Stuart-Clarke, C. (1990). *The Oxford book of story poems*. Oxford University Press. (A)

Highwater, J. (1981). *Moonsong lullaby*. Lothrop. (A)

Larrick, N. (1991). *To the moon and back: A collection of poems*. Delacorte. (P)

Merriam, E. (1989). *Chortles*. Morrow. (I)

Larrick, N. (1989). *When the dark comes dancing: A bedtime poetry book*. Philomel. (A)

Pomerantz, C. (1982). *If I had a Paka: Poems in eleven languages*. Greenwillow. (A)

Rylant, C. (1982). *When I was young in the mountains*. Dutton. (A)

Sneve, V. Driving Hawk (1989). *Dancing teepees: Poems of American Indian youth*. Holiday House. (A)

Yolen, J. (1990). *Dinosaur dances*. Putnam. (I)

Contemporary Realistic Fiction   This broad genre represents fiction cast in present or recent time. The plot, characters, and setting all are realistic in the sense that they *could* exist or occur. Realistic fiction can be the most direct mirror for elementary children; although they see themselves in all types of narratives, the characters in realistic fiction come closest to who they and their friends are in the day-to-day world—or in a different day-to-day world that the children realize *could* easily exist for them.

In recent years the range and subject matter of contemporary realistic fiction has expanded tremendously. The term *new realism* (Root, 1977) refers to subjects rarely addressed a generation ago but which are routinely addressed in books intended for younger audiences today: in addition to the usual problems associated with growing up and relating to one's peers, there are the issues of sexuality, differing family configurations, psychological/physical abuse, alcohol/substance abuse, and death. With respect to the awesome task of just growing up, good contemporary realism can facilitate students' awareness of matters involving trust, prejudice, and the shortcomings of others (so often adults) and how to put these in perspective.

African-American

Clifton, L. (1983). *Everett Anderson's goodbye*. Holt. (A)

Flournoy, V. (1985). *The patchwork quilt*. Dial. (A)

Gray, N. (1989). *A country far away*. Orchard. (A)

Greenfield, E. (1974). *Sister*. Crowell. (A)

Grifalconi, A. (1986). *The village of round and square houses*. Little, Brown. (P)

Grifalconi, A. (1990). *Osa's pride*. Little, Brown. (P)

Hansen, J. (1988). *Which way out from this place?* Walker. (A)

Heide, F., & Gilliland, J. (1991). *The day of Ahmed's secret.* Lothrop. (P)

Isadora, R. (1991). *At the crossroads.* Greenwillow. (P)

Mathis, S. (1975). *The hundred penny box.* Viking. (A)

Myers, W. (1988). *Fallen angels.* Scholastic. (I)

Myers, W. (1990). *The mouse rap.* HarperCollins. (I)

William, K. (1990). *Galimoto.* Lothrop. (P)

Asian-American (Asian Pacific American)

Chang, H. (1988). *Elaine, Mary Lewis, and the frogs.* Crown. (A)

Clark, A. (1978). *To stand against the wind.* Viking. (I)

Crew, L. (1989). *Children of the river.* Delacourt. (I)

Dunn, M., & Ardath, M. (1983). *The absolutely perfect horse.* Harper. (A)

Lee, M. (1993). *If it hadn't been for Yoon Jun.* Houghton Mifflin. (I)

Levine, E. (1989). *I hate English.* Scholastic. (P)

Paek, M. (1988). *Aekyung's dream.* Children's Press. (P)

Surat, M. (1983). *Angel child, dragon child.* Carnival/Raintree. (A)

Uchida, Y. (1983). *The best bad thing.* Atheneum. (I)

Wallace, I. (1984). *Chin Chiang and the dragon's dance.* Atheneum. (A)

Yep, L. (1979). *Sea Glass.* Harper. (I)

European-American

Aliki. (1979). *The two of them.* Greenwillow. (P)

Bauer, M. (1986). *On my honor.* Clarion. (I)

Burnett, F. (1911). *The secret garden.* (A)

Cleary, B. (1975). *Ramona the brave.* Morrow. (A)

Cohen, M. (1977). *When will I read?* Greenwillow. (P)

Fox, P. (1967). *How many miles to Babylon?* Bradbury. (I)

Hughes, S. (1983). *Alfie gives a hand.* Lothrop. (P)

Keats, E. (1981). *Regards to the man in the moon.* Four Winds. (P)

McCloskey, R. (1959). *Time of wonder.* Viking. (P)

Newman, R. (1978). *The case of the Baker Street Irregular.* Atheneum. (I)

Polacco, P. (1987). *Meteor!* Dodd, Mead. (A)

Sachs, M. (1971). *The bears' house.* Doubleday. (P)

Hispanic-American/Latino and Caribbean

Anaya, R. (1900). *The Farolitos of Christmas: A New Mexico Christmas story.* (A)

Brown, T. (1986). *Hello, amigos!* Holt. (P)

Dorros, A. (1991). *Tonight is carnaval.* Dutton. (A)

Cameron, A. (1988). *The most beautiful place in the world.* Knopf. (P)

Castaneda, O. (1991). *Among the volcanoes.* Lodestar. (I)

Cromie, W. (1970). *Steven and the green turtle.* HarperCollins. (P)

Hewett, J. (1990). *Hector lives in the United States now: The story of a Mexican-American child.* Lippincott. (A)

Hurwitz, J. (1993). *New shoes for Silvia.* Morrow. (P)

Markun, P. (1993). *The little painter of Sabana Grande.* (P)

Martel, C. (1976). *Yagua days.* Dial. (P)

Mohr, N. (1986). *Going home.* Dial. (I)

Soto, G. (1990). *Baseball in April.* Harcourt. (I)

Stanek, M. (1989). *I speak English for my mom.* Albert Whitman. (A)

Tafolla, C. (1900). *Patchwork colcha: A children's collection.* Creative Educational Enterprises. (A)

Native American

Clark, A. (1941). *In my mother's house.* Viking. (P)

Hobbs, W. (1989). *Bearstone.* Atheneum. (I)

Luenn, N. (1990). *Nessa's fish.* Atheneum. (A)

Martin, B., Jr., & Archambault, J. (1987). *Knots on a counting rope.* Holt. (A)

Miles, M. (1971). *Annie and the Old One.* Little, Brown. (A)

New Mexico People & Energy Collective. (1981). *Red ribbons for Emma.* New Seed Press. (A)

O'Dell, S. (1988). *Black Star, Bright Dawn.* Houghton Mifflin. (I)

Paulsen, G. (1988). *Dogsong.* Bradbury. (I)

Pitts, P. (1992). *Racing the sun.* HarperCollins. (I)

Sneve, V. (1974). *When thunder spoke.* Holiday House. (I)

Wheeler, B. (1986). *Where did you get your moccasins?* Pemmican Publications. (P)

Zola, M., & Dereume, A. (1983). *Nobody.* Pemmican Publications. (P)

Modern Fantasy   Much of modern fantasy is an extension of traditional literature. Many of the themes, plots, motifs, and so forth resound with the features and feelings of traditional folktales, myths, and legends. Modern fantasy, however, is created by identifiable writers. Despite the term *modern,* this genre also includes "classics" like Lewis Carroll's *Alice's Adventures in Wonderland,* Beatrix Potter's tales, E. B. White's *Charlotte's Web,* and Kenneth Grahame's *The Wind in the Willows.*

What makes fantasy work is the believability of whatever world is created in the book. If the writer has done the job well, we are quite willing to suspend our disbelief and accept his or her fantastical world. We are quite willing to accept the barnyard world with its talking animals alongside the normal workaday life of humans in E. B. White's *Charlotte's Web,* just as we accept the entirely fantastical world of Earthsea in Ursula LeGuin's *A Wizard of Earthsea.*

Works of science fiction are usually categorized under modern fantasy. While most modern fantasy relies pretty much on magic and the supernatural, in science fiction there is more "control" over what happens. There is enough science that is *real* to keep the book believable. The author helps us feel that although some of the science is impossible at the present time, it is conceivable that it may become possible soon.

Alexander, L. (1977). *The town cats and other tales.* Dutton. (I)

Alexander, L. (1978). *The first two lives of Lukas-Kasha.* Dutton. (I)

Andersen, H. C. (1974). *Hans Andersen: his classic fairy tales.* Doubleday. [Translated by E. Haugaard.] (A)

Azimov, J., & Azimov, I. (1990). *Norby and the oldest dragon.* Walker. (I)

Bond, M. (1960). *A bear called Paddington.* Houghton Mifflin. (A)

Boston, L. (1955). *The children of Green Knowe.* Harcourt. (I)

Brittain, B. (1983). *The wish giver.* Harper. (I)

Buffet, J., & Buffet, J. S. (1988). *The jolly man.* (A)

Carroll, L. (1982). *Alice's Adventures in Wonderland, Through the Looking-Glass,* and *The Hunting of the Snark.* Chatto, Bodley Head & Jonathan Cape. (A)

Cleary, B. (1982). *Ralph S. Mouse.* Morrow. (I)

Cooper, S. (1965). *Over sea, under stone.* Harcourt. (I)

Dorros, A. (1991). *Abuela.* Dutton. (P)

Gorog, J. (1990). *In a messy, messy room and other strange stories.* Philomel. (I)

Hamilton, V. (1983). *The magical adventures of pretty Pearl.* Harper. (I)

Henkes, K. (1993). *Owen.* Greenwillow. (P)

Jacques, B. (1990). *Mattimeo.* Philomel. (I)

L'Engle, M. (1962). *A wrinkle in time.* Farrar. (I)

L'Engle, M. (1978). *A swiftly tilting planet.* Farrar. (I)

Lawson, R. (1954). *The tough winter.* Viking Penguin. (A)

LeGuin, U. K. (1988). *Catwings.* Watts. (A)

Lewis, C. S. (1951–1956). The "Chronicles of Narnia" series. Macmillan. (I)

McKinley, R. (1982). *The blue sword.* Greenwillow. (I)

Milne, A. (1926). *Winnie the Pooh.* Dutton. (A)

Norton, M. (1952). *The Borrowers.* Harcourt. (A)

Potter, B. (1902). *The tale of Peter Rabbit.* Warne. (A)

Snyder, Z. (1975). *Below the root.* Atheneum. (I)

Van Allsburg, C. (1981). *Jumanji.* Houghton Mifflin. (A)

Yolen, J. (1981). *The acorn quest.* Crowell. (P)

Yolen, J. (1989). *The faery flags: Stories and poems of fantasy and the supernatural.* Orchard. (I)

Historical Fiction   Historical fiction allows children the vicarious experience of living during a time in the past. The experience seems all the more real to them because they can identify with a protagonist—a boy or girl very much like boys and girls everywhere. Although time may change, the feelings and perceptions of children *are* remarkably universal. Conflict between child and parents, concerns about growing up, spats with friends—these happened a hundred or hundreds of years ago as well. This type of identification with the main character is a powerful draw on young readers. It can immerse them in times, places, and issues they might otherwise not think about. The Colliers' *My Brother Sam Is Dead* gives a jarring and compelling perspective not only on the complexities of the American Revolution but on the awful reality of war as well. Jane Yolen's *The Devil's Arithmetic* grips the reader in the overwhelming illogic and terror of the Holocaust, in the end seeing the gas chamber through the eyes of the ten-year-old girl about to enter it.

Historical fiction is "real" in the sense that important historical figures and events are represented. Usually the main characters are fictional, though believable. If the author has been conscientious, the setting and events are as true to what we know about that slice of history as is possible.

African-American

Armstrong, W. (1969). *Sounder.* Harper. (I)

Carew, J. (1974). *The third gift.* Little, Brown. (P)

Clifton, L. (1979). *The lucky stone.* Delacorte. (I)

Keats, E. J. (1965). *John Henry: An American legend.* Pantheon. (A)

Monjo, F. N. (1970). *The drinking gourd.* Harper. (P)

Taylor, M. (1976). *Role of thunder, hear my cry.* Dial. (I)

Taylor, M. (1981). *Let the circle be unbroken.* Dial. (I)

Taylor, M. (1990). *The road to Memphis.* Dial. (I)

Turner, A. (1987). *Nettie's trip south.* Macmillan. (A)

Yarbrough, C. (1979). *Cornrows.* Coward. (P)

Yates, E. (1950). *Amos Fortune.* Dutton. (I)

Asian-American (Asian Pacific American)

Coerr, E. (1988). *Chang's paper pony.* HarperCollins. (P)

Garland, S. (1993). *The lotus seed.* Harcourt. (P)

Huynh, Q. N. (1982) *The land I lost: Adventures of a boy from Vietnam.* Harper. (I)

Lord, B. B. (1984). *In the Year of the Boar and Jackie Robinson.* Harper. (I)

Say, A. (1990) *El Chino.* Houghton Mifflin. (A)

Say, A. (1991). *The bicycle man.* Houghton Mifflin. (A)

Say, A. (1993). *Grandfather's journey.* Houghton Mifflin. (A)

Uchida, Y. (1971). *Journey to Topaz.* Scribner's. (I)

Yee, P. (1989). *Tales from Gold Mountain: Stories of the Chinese in the New World*. Macmillan. (A)

Yep, L. (1975). *Dragonwings*. New York: Harper. (I)

Yep, L. (1977). *Child of the owl*. Harper. (I)

Yep, L. (1979). *Sea glass*. Harper. (I)

European-American

Brink, C. R. (1935). *Caddie Woodlawn*. Macmillan. (I)

Dalgliesh, A. (1954). *The courage of Sarah Noble*. Scribner's. (A)

Frank, R. (1931/1986). *No hero for the Kaiser*. Lothrop. [Translated by P. Crampton.] (I)

Haley, G. (1973). *Jack Jouett's ride*. Viking. (P)

Harvey, B. (1988). *Cassie's journey: Going west in the 1860s*. Holiday. (A)

Hooks, W. (1983). *Circle of fire*. Atheneum. (I)

Lowry, L. (1989). *Number the stars*. Houghton Mifflin. (I)

MacLachlan, P. (1985). *Sarah, plain and tall*. Harper. (A)

Putnam, A. (1990). *Westering*. Lodestar/E. P. Dutton. (I)

Skurzynski, G. (1981). *Manwolf*. Houghton Mifflin. (I)

Speare, E. (1958). *The witch of Blackbird Pond*. Houghton Mifflin. (I)

Hispanic American/Latino and Caribbean

Argueta, M. (1990). *Magic dogs of the volcanoes/Los perros magicos de los volcanes*. Children's Press. (P)

Bunting, E. (1988). *How many days to America? A Thanksgiving story*. Clarion. (A)

Hamilton, V. (1985). *Junius over far*. HarperCollins. (I)

O'Dell, S. (1981). *The feathered serpent*. Houghton Mifflin. (I)

O'Dell, S. (1989). *My name is not Angelica*. Houghton Mifflin. (I)

Rohmer, J., & Rea, J. (1988). *Atariba and Niguayona: A story from the Taino people of Puerto Rico*. Children's Press.

Taylor, T. (1962). *The Maldonado miracle*. Harcourt.

Taylor, T. (1969). *The cay*. Avon. (I) [*See also* Taylor's "Prequel," *Timothy of the Cay*. (1993). Harcourt.]

Native American

Benton-Banai, E. (1979). *The Mishomis book: The voice of the Ojibway*. Indian Country Communications. (A)

Culleton, B. (1984). *April Raintree*. Pemmican. (I)

Gardiner, J. R. (1980). *Stone Fox*. HarperCollins. (A)

Goble, P. (1984). *Buffalo Woman*. Bradbury. (A).

Highwater, J. (1977). *Anpao: An American Indian odyssey*. Lippincott. (I)

Hudson, J. (1989). *Sweetgrass.* Philomel. (I)

O'Dell, S. (1960). *Island of the blue dolphins.* Houghton Mifflin. (I)

O'Dell, S. (1970). *Sing down the moon.* Houghton Mifflin. (I)

Speerstra, K. (1980). *The earthshapers.* Naturegraph. (I)

Trimble, S. (1990). *Village of blue stone.* Macmillan. (A)

Informational and Biographical. I presented fairly extensive lists for this genre in Chapter 7. I would like, however, to share with you several titles grouped here according to the particular culture each represents.

African/African-American

Adler, D. (1989). *Jackie Robinson: He was the first.* Holiday House. (I)

Adoff, A. (1970). *Malcolm X.* Crowell. (I)

Bryan, A. (1991). *All night, all day: A child's first book of African-American spirituals.* Atheneum. (A)

Greenfield, E. (1977) *Mary McLeod Bethune: Voice of black hope.* Crowell.

Hamilton, V. (1988). *Anthony Burns: The defeat and triumph of a fugitive slave.* Knopf. (I)

Lester, J. (1968). *To be a slave.* Dial. (I)

Meltzer, M. *The black Americans: A history in their own words.* Crowell. (I)

Miller, D. (1988). *Frederick Douglass and the fight for freedom.* Facts on File. (I)

Musgrove, M. (1976). *Ashanti to Zulu.* Dial. (A)

Myers, W. (1991). *Now is your time: The African American struggle for freedom.* HarperCollins. (I)

Patterson, L. (1989). *Martin Luther King, Jr., and the freedom movement.* Facts on File. (I)

Turner, G. T. (1989). *Take a walk in their shoes.* Cobblehill Books. (I)

Asian-American (Asian Pacific American)

Hamanaka, S. (1990). *The journey: Japanese Americans, racism and renewal.* Orchard. (I)

Stanley, D. (1991). *The last princess: The story of Princess Ka'iulani of Hawai'i.* Four Winds. (I)

Takashima, S. (1971). *A child in prison camp.* Morrow. (I)

Uchida, Y. (1971). *Journey to Topaz.* Scribner's. (I)

Uchida, Y. (1978). *Journey home.* Atheneum. (I)

Uchida, Y. (1991). *The invisible thread.* Messner. (I)

Yep, L. (1991). *The lost garden.* Messner. [Autobiography.] (I)

European-American

Anno, M. (1983). *Anno's USA.* Philomel. (A)

Ashabranner, B. (1987). *Into a strange land: Unaccompanied refugee youth in America.* Dodd Mead. (I)

Bunting, E. (1991). *Fly away home*. Clarion. (A)

Dionetti, M. (1991). *Coal mine peaches*. Orchard. (A)

Freedman, R. (1980). *Immigrant kids*. Dutton. (I)

Meltzer, M. (1982). *The Jewish Americans: A history in their own words*. Crowell. (I)

Spier, P. (1980). *People*. Doubleday. (A)

Hispanic-American/Latino and Caribbean

Adams, F. (1986). *El Salvador: Beauty among the ashes*. Dillon. (I)

Anderson, J. (1989). *Spanish pioneers of the Southwest*. Dutton.

Bragg, B. (1989). *The very first Thanksgiving: Pioneers on the Rio Grande*. Harbinger. (A)

Gilleis, J. (1988). *Senor Alcalde: A biography of Henry Cisneros*. Dillon Press. (I)

Gleiter, J., & Thompson, K. (1990). *Jose Marti*. Raintree. [Translated by A. Ada.] (A)

Haiti in Pictures. (1987). Learner. (A)

Hall, N., & Syverson-Stork, J. (1994). *Los pollitos dicen (The baby chicks sing)*. Little, Brown. (P)

Jacobsen, P., & Preben, (1986). *A family in Central America*. Bookwright. (A)

Lye, K. (1988). *Take a trip to Jamaica*. Watts. (P)

McKissack, P. (1985). *The Maya*. Children's Press. (P)

Meltzer, M. (1982). *The Hispanic Americans*. Crowell. (I)

Mory, J., & Dunn, W. (1989). *Famous Mexican Americans*. Dutton. (I)

Perl, L. (1983). *Pinatas and paper flowers: Holidays of the Americas in English and Spanish*. Clarion. (A)

Verheyden-Hallrad, M. (1985). *Scientist with determination, Elma Gonzales*. Equity Institute. (I)

Native American

Broker, I. (1983). *Night Flying Woman: An Ojibway narrative*. Historical Society Press. (I)

Ekoomiak, N. (1988). *Arctic memories*. Holt. [Bilingual English/Inuit.] (A)

Freedman, R. (1987). *Indian chiefs*. Holiday. (I)

Hirschfelder, A. (1986). *Happily may I walk: American Indians and Alaska natives today*. Scribner's. (I)

Hoyt-Goldsmith, D. (1990). *Totem pole*. Holiday. (A)

Hoyt-Goldsmith, D. (1991). *Pueblo storyteller*. Holiday. (A)

Katz, J. B. (Ed.). (1975). *Let me be a free man: A documentary of Indian resistance*. Lerner. (I)

Klausner, J. (1993). *Sequoyah's gift*. HarperCollins. (I)

Ortiz, S. (1988). *The people shall continue*. Children's Book Press. (A)

■ **BUILDING YOUR KNOWLEDGE BASE**

■ **Resources and Reviews**

The following guides are excellent resources for information about books. Besides providing descriptions of the books, they give information about age levels and—among other things—will help you locate appropriate titles and make connections with related books and themes.

A to zoo: Subject access to children's picture books (3rd ed.) (1989). Lima, C. W., & Lima, J. A. New York: Bowker.

Collected perspectives: Choosing and using books for the classroom (2nd ed.) (1992). H. Moir et al. (Eds.). Norwood, MA: Christopher-Gordon.

The Newbery and Caldecott awards: A guide to the medal and honor books. [Updated each year; the 1991 edition describes every book that has received each award.]

Best books for children: Preschool through the middle grades (4th ed.) (1990). Gillespie, J. T., & Naden, C. J. New York: Bowker.

Bibliography of books for children (1989). Wheaton, MD: Association for Childhood Education International.

Children's books in print. New York: Bowker. [Published annually.]

Dictionary of American children's fiction, 1960–1984. ["Books that have won significant awards."]

The elementary school library collection: A guide to books and other media (18th ed.) (1992). L. Winkel (Ed.). Williamsport, PA: Brodart.

Paperback books for children (1989). Wheaton, MD: Association for Childhood Education International.

Subject guide to children's books in print. New York: Bowker. [Published annually.]

Black authors and illustrators of children's books: A biographical dictionary (1988). Rollock, B. New York: Garland.

Something about the author autobiography series. J. Nakamura (Ed.). Detroit: [Eight volumes to date.]

Something about the author: Facts and pictures about contemporary authors and illustrators of books for young people. [Series of more than fifty volumes.] A. Commire (Ed.). Detroit: Gale.

Books in Spanish for children and young adults. (1978). Schon, J. Metuchen, NJ: Scarecrow Press.

Growing pains: Helping children deal with everyday problems through reading. (1988). Cuddigan, M. Chicago: American Library Association.

The single parent family in children's books. (1978). Herner, C. Metuchen, NJ: Scarecrow Press.

Girls are people too! A bibliography of nontraditional female roles in children's books. (1982). Newman, J. Metuchen, NJ: Scarecrow Press.

You will find a very good overview and discussion of most of these titles and additional resources for children's literature in: A. M. Pillar (1992). Resources to identify children's books. In B. E. Cullinan (Ed.), *Invitation to read: More children's literature in the reading program* (pp. 150–165). Newark, DE: International Reading Association.

BECOMING A THEMATIC TEACHER

Your progression as a thematic teacher

As a new teacher, should you expect to proceed from day one with thematically organized instruction? Here, as in other areas, I'd suggest that you ease into it. While you may have a simple organizing theme during the first week of school (remember our "friendship" focus in Chapter 4) more developed and integrated themes can wait a bit. It's important for you to first feel comfortable with your expertise in conducting and sustaining literacy activities. Then, together with your sense of organization and management of the classroom, you will get a "feel" for the promise of thematic instruction as you and your students explore and respond to books and make connections with other areas of learning.

I noted at the beginning of this chapter that themes may be quite narrow or can stretch into large undertakings that integrate learning and teaching

Many novice teachers prefer to plan simpler themes for the beginning of the year and save more complex themes for later in the year, but it is important to remember that you don't have to teach these units according to a set style.

throughout the whole day and across all the subject or content areas. The size and scope of your theme depends on your objectives, your students' needs, and—when you are a novice teacher—on your own comfort and confidence level. Throughout your career you will most likely handle both types of themes on a regular basis.

Distinguishing between thematic units with a narrower theme and those that are cross-curricular can be somewhat arbitrary in the real world of the classroom, but it is nonetheless helpful to think about thematic instruction this way. I will refer to units that are narrower in focus as "Literature/language arts" units (Routman, 1991; Walmsley, 1994; Walmsley & Walp, 1990); we'll call those that are broader in focus "across-the-curriculum" units (Harste, Short, & Burke, 1989; Pappas, Kiefer, & Levstik, 1990). It is important to remember, though, that literature and language arts are part of the larger units and that different areas of the curriculum may be reflected in the smaller units (Moss, 1990, has several excellent examples of both literature/language arts–based units and cross-curricular units).

When selecting themes, it is important to keep your students' developmental levels in mind. This is true whether you are undertaking narrow thematic units or broader ones. For younger children, emphasize *concrete* themes—themes that reflect hands-on experiences. These themes can include some that may sound abstract but with which children still have concrete experiences: "families," for example, or "homelessness." Themes that have a "tension" to them also work very well (Walmsley & Walp, 1990); for example, "brothers and sisters," "escapes and rescues," "differing points of view," or "growing and changing through relationships." A theme might be explored at different *levels;* for example, younger children can explore the lives and times of presidents or other world leaders, while older students might explore the personal side of these figures— their struggles, their families.

As you think about how you will organize instruction thematically over the next few years, you may wish to follow the lead of many experienced teachers who began their move into thematic teaching with thematically based literature/ language–arts units. Later, they expand their teaching to include other areas of the curriculum. Through these broader-based across-the-curriculum units, concepts and understandings are interconnected, *and* the roles of reading and writing as *tools* are developed and appreciated as they are applied throughout most or all the areas of the curriculum.

Many teachers comment that they found it much easier to begin with "one thing at a time"; that is, they began their teaching with literature-based reading and writing, moving later to thematic units that explored more directly connections within the language arts. They grew into their designated reading/writing or language arts time-block in the morning with (1) guided reading and literature discussions and (2) writing workshops in which the students developed their own pieces as each of them found his or her own voice. Beginning this way, and moving into thematic units a little later, allowed these novice teachers to develop their own expertise in guiding and responding to their students' reading and writing. Science, social studies, and math were taught at other times during the day—although here, too, the teachers were helping students apply content reading strategies.

As the teachers' expertise and confidence grew in facilitating reading and writing, they found themselves making conceptual connections with content areas—and these connections gave them a "feel" for how to integrate thematic units across curricular areas. For example, they could move into how the chronology of history begins to come alive and fits into their social studies curriculum through the eyes of Laura Ingalls Wilder in her *Little House* books, and through Anna's eyes in Patricia MacLachlan's *Sarah, Plain and Tall*. Through Kathryn Lasky's *The Bone Wars,* they could see how this historical perspective on life in the heartland of the country during the nineteenth century connects with the science curriculum addressing prehistoric life. Before long, the teachers realized they were *automatically* brainstorming possible connections between any book they read in the classroom and other books, curricular areas, and themes.

When you feel ready during the fall, begin introducing your literature/language arts themes. About midyear, try an across-the-curriculum theme that will stretch for anywhere from three to six weeks. This timing will give you the opportunity to prepare for the unit through your own reading and planning and your discussions with other teachers.

We have already noted that many novice teachers prefer to move from simpler to more complex themes over the course of their first or second year. This movement very often works well for the students, too. They perceive the connections within literature and the language arts, then expand their perceptions enough to see connections among all the curricular areas. Along the way, they find themselves pulling in more and more elements that will be integrated with their theme. They understand better the relationship between reading and writing, and how their writing topics evolve from the guided and independent reading that they are doing. Earlier in the year, students may need more direct guidance in *how* to work collaboratively in groups, and you will probably be engaging in more direct reading experiences with them in small groups (see Chapters 4, 5, and 6). Depending on which cultures your students come from, you may realize that you need to appear more directive and in control early in the year, then gradually guide the students toward independence (see Chapter 12). And even if some students *have* experienced this type of learning before coming to your class, you can't safely assume that they'll naturally and effectively pick right up with goal-setting and independent group work. Thus you may find that even when *you* are quite experienced and comfortable with all kinds of thematic-unit teaching, you decide to retain a progression of units on an annual basis for your students' benefit.

What is really important for you to keep in mind is that you don't *have* to teach these units according to a set style. Issues such as the following are *yours* to decide: *when* to begin units during the school year; the *scope* of your units; whether you feel more comfortable with "starting small," or with jumping right in, and so on. These issues will also depend on the background of your students; your sense of the degree to which you feel things are usually "under control" and the students able to stay involved; whether you have switched grade levels (primary to intermediate, or vice versa), and so forth. The main point is that *you* are moving comfortably toward ever-deeper integration and that you are always taking your students' needs into consideration as well.

Beware of artificial or superficial thematic units! (Routman, 1991; Walmsley & Walp, 1990) Such units disguise themselves as "thematic," but they are mere collections of activities that have to do with a particular topic. Often they are little more than occasions for busywork: Students fill out ditto sheets about a topic and assemble them in a "theme notebook" that is supposed to represent their exploration of that theme. Many commercially available "themed" units fall into this category. For example, a primary unit on frogs may include books about frogs, artwork centered on frogs, songs about frogs—but what are the objectives here? Where is the rationale for having children do these activities? While kids may exercise low-level skills in reading and writing and artwork, and so on, they are not developing deeper understandings about frogs—and indeed, such understandings *are* possible. Such units do not explore deeper ideas and relationships, they are not leading to critical thinking, and they do not give students a real stake in their own learning. A "frogs" unit that *would* accomplish those things would address concepts such as the role of frogs in the web of life, their similarities to other animals, and their benefit to us. Such a unit would help students understand major concepts such as the life cycle changes (consider the metamorphoses of frogs), and what happens during different seasons and why.

LEARNING IN CONTEXT: **The *focus* of thematic units and what children *do* in the context of thematic units must be authentic and genuine.**

MEANING MAKERS: YOU, THE STUDENT

Authenticity in Unit Construction

The illustrative thematic units on pages 457–470 are authentic in terms of focus and activities. After reading the steps involved in planning and implementing literature/language arts–based units and across-the-curriculum units, evaluate and discuss them with a colleague, keeping the following questions in mind:

- What is the logic underlying the selection and sequencing of literacy activities? How do the activities fit, in terms of perceived student need and the overall focus and flow of the unit?
- How are multicultural connections woven into the fabric of these units? (See "Opportunities for Emphasizing Diversity and Multiculturalism," page 429.) Are they infused throughout—the "osmosis" perspective? Are they "naturally" woven in through related text sets, inviting comparison/contrast? Are they "explicit," clearly focused on specific groups? ■

Planning and implementing a literature/language arts–based unit

In this section, I will first lay out the steps that may be followed in developing and teaching a literature/language arts–based unit. We'll then examine a unit that follows these steps.

1. *Identify your theme.* Your intended concepts and understandings will be narrower in scope when you first begin than later on. Your theme may be simpler in scope, perhaps more *concrete,* so that your students can clearly grasp both the theme and the interconnections you will be exploring. An excellent theme to begin with is a particular *author.* Your selection of an author or illustrator to begin a literature unit may well grow out of your students' fascination with a particular story that has been shared during read-aloud sessions several times.

2. *Brainstorm connections* after your theme is identified. The connections may include books you wish to use—books that will inform you; those to be used by you and your students in guided reading; and those that the students will be reading as part of their "recreational" reading. Other concepts will occur to you, and you may wind up keeping many of them. If your first unit is based on an author or illustrator, as is our example, the types of stories and illustrative techniques used in the books themselves will give focus to your planning.

3. *Read all the materials you will be using. Especially* when you begin developing theme units, you will feel considerably more prepared—and therefore more confident—if you have read every book you expect to use. Reading all the works of a particular author or illustrator, by the way, is not an *absolute* necessity. Even through you will be reading the core and extended texts, you may find that later on—because of all of the different books your students will be reading—there may not be time to stay on top of them all. In the beginning, though, most teachers feel vastly more prepared and more likely to experience success if they are familiar with all the texts.

4. *Determine the suitability of the books for core texts and read-alouds, extended reading, and recreational or independent reading.* When thinking about titles for *core texts,* keep in mind that you will need to be very selective about your choices. Their use in guided and directed teaching or extension activities should be pivotal to the unit of study. Since these are texts that *all* your students will be experiencing, some of your core texts will have to be available to students as a class set; others can be read aloud from a single copy.

For *extended reading,* you may find the following guidelines helpful. Select ten titles—three of them challenging, another three easy, and the balance in the middle; this will address the developmental literacy levels in your class. Obtain five to ten copies of each book, "more of longer and fewer of shorter" (Walmsley & Walp, 1990). For *recreational* titles, choose a range from the library. If you are focusing your unit on a single author, as our model teachers do in the example below, your students will enjoy having several copies of the first book the author published, copies of any that have received awards, and selections that reflect the author's growth and expanse in topics, writing style, and personal development as a writer.

If you have chosen a particular genre—say, for example, poetry—you will want to consider poems that represent a variety of styles. The poetry of Arnold Adoff, for example, sounds and feels much different from that of Shel Silverstein, Lee Bennett Hopkins, or Eloise Greenfield. The key point here is to select books within your theme that show a diversified range of readability and appeal.

5. *Look at your unit objectives and determine which curricular objectives are most important for your students.* Then slot in activities that support each of those objectives. This is where you will need to make some hard choices. Timing will not allow you to implement every idea that occurred to you during the initial brainstorming. For instance, you may have to decide on one major project out of your list of three or four possibilities. You will find that plotting out your choices in chart form will help you obtain balance in the types of activities you select (Cooper, 1993).

Once you can see the degree to which you have balanced initiating, developing, and culminating activities that are organized for individual, small-group, and whole-class work, your weekly plans will be much easier to develop.

Let's see how Sandra Madura and Teresa Mills, when they taught third grade, followed these steps in developing a unit for their students.

■ ■ ■ ■ ■

CLASSROOM IN ACTION

Primary-Grade Literature/Language Arts Unit

Ms. Madura and Ms. Mills chose Jane Yolen as a focus for an author study because of their students' frequent requests to have Yolen's *Owl Moon* read aloud to them. A "guest reader" from their state university had shared *Owl Moon* with their classes at the beginning of the school year. Since its initial reading, the story remained a favorite book for rereading. By early October, the students expressed continued interest in wanting to know more about the author. The choice for an October author study became obvious.

When Ms. Mills, a first-year teacher, and Ms. Madura, an experienced teacher, began their investigation of Jane Yolen, they went to the library and located as many books by Yolen as they could find. As they browsed through their selections, they realized they could categorize the majority of Yolen's books into four areas: family stories based on personal experience, response to nature through poetry, imaginative stories based on popular culture, and retellings or self-crafted stories based on traditional tales. As they wanted to stay with this literature unit for a four- to five-week time period, their categorization fitted their time schedule well.

Ms. Madura and Ms. Mills began with a large sheet of paper and the many books they had collected from the library. They listed their brainstorming ideas in a web format. They began with their overall objectives for the literature unit, then proceeded to list books and ideas that fell into their four categories. Figure 9.3 shows their final web for the Jane Yolen unit.

As Ms. Madura and Ms. Mills began looking more carefully at Jane Yolen's work, they realized that a portion of her work is written for older readers; therefore, not all of her books were appropriate for their third-grade students. The books the two teachers chose for their third-grade "author" theme unit on Jane Yolen are listed at the end of this example. Each book was an excellent representative of one of the four different categories they identified.

3RD GRADE OBJECTIVES

1. Gain an awareness of the different genre in which J. Yolen writes
2. Develop an awareness of the difference between "showing" writing and "telling" writing
3. Gain an understanding of how J.Y. pulls from personal experience, observation, popular culture, oral tradition, and her own imagination for story ideas
4. Gain an awareness of how J.Y. develops character, setting, voice, and plot in her stories and poems
5. Gain an understanding of metaphor and precise word choice to convey meaning

JANE YOLEN

WEEK 1
J.Y. Writes About Family

Core Texts:
Owl Moon —— Intensive and extensive reading
- GLTA
- Echo reading
- Choral reading
- Paired shared reading
- Favorite line sharing
- Content reading on owls
- Rereading – whole class, small group, individually
- KWL chart – ind. & class – J.Y.
- Text modeling of metaphor
- Summary paragraphs of owl behavior
- Mini-posters of owl info.
- Owl habitat drawing
- Owl adaptations
- Pellet dissection field notes

Character Focus:
- Background info on J.Y. as a writer – how personal experience helps mold story ideas
- Trace relationships in books – child to adults

Read-Alouds and Recreational:
Owl Moon
Grandad Bill's Song
Honkers
Letting Swift River Go
All Those Secrets of the World

Grandad Bill's Song
- Read-aloud
- Echo reading
- Readers' theatre
- Question/response format
- Interview
- Text modeling for class book, planned home inquiry, and individual books
- People drawing

WEEK 2
J.Y. Writes About Nature Through Poetry

Setting Focus:
- Natural environment animals interwoven into landscape
- Bird observations field notes

Core Texts:
Observing Nature
Read-Alouds:
Bird Watching
Ring of Earth

Daily response logs

Extended Texts:
Small Groups
Welcome to the Greenhouse
All in the Woodland Early
Bird Watch
- Echo reading
- Choral reading
- Paired reading

WEEK 3
J.Y. Writes From Her Imagination

Core Texts:
Fiction and how it's created
Read-Alouds:
1st Commander Toad
1st Piggins

Voice Focus:
- Piggins vs. Commander Toad
- Both compared to Owl Moon and Letting Swift River Go

Extended Texts:
"Commander Toad" series
- Conversion of action scenes into dramatizations

WEEK 4
J.Y. Retells and Creates Traditional Stories

Core Texts: Read-Alouds:
Wings
The Little Spotted Fish

Daily response logs

Extended Texts:
Small Groups
Sleeping Ugly – European
The Emperor and the Kite – Asian
Sky Boy – Native American

Plot Focus:
- What dialogue moves plot along
- Extend into theme

WEEK 5
Culminating Week

- Children pair for choice of book selection and response project
- Projects must include a written portion and a display or presentation

Figure 9.3
Teachers' Web for the Author Theme "Jane Yolen"

*I would like to express my sincerest appreciation and gratitude to Sandra Madura for her extensive work in developing and extending the thematic units that are presented in this chapter.   S.T.

From Ms. Madura and Ms. Mills's initial web of their author theme, they have plotted (1) appropriate *beginning, developing,* and *closing (culminating)* types of activities; and (2) the type of interaction each activity entails: *independent, partner/ small group, whole-class.* In addition, they indicate whether the activity was a self-selected, teacher-assigned, or teacher-directed one. In this case, the teachers have arranged their ideas by weekly topics. What you see in Figure 9.4 is a breakdown of their activities for the first week.

Figure 9.5 shows the first week of plans for the third-grade literature unit on Jane Yolen. You will notice that Ms. Madura and Ms. Mills's introductory week centers around the reading of two core texts, *Owl Moon* and *Granddad Bill's Song.* Notice their distribution of the various activities during each day and from one day to the next; they considered the nature of the activities and how much time they anticipated each would take. The weeks that follow will expand their students' knowledge of Jane Yolen—and of the structure and nature of the genres represented by her works—by engaging the students in reading and writing experiences with other core texts, as well as in additional work with extended and recreational texts.

Let's look again at the web in Figure 9.3. Note how the two teachers have distributed the various projects and activities over the course of the four weeks—and think about how each project or activity addresses one or more of the major learning objectives or goals the teachers have identified.

Core Texts

Bird watch. (1990). Philomel. [Illustrated by T. Lewin.]

Commander toad and the planet of the grapes. (1982). Coward. [Illustrated by B. Degan.]

Grandad Bill's song. (1994). Philomel. [Illustrated by M. Mathis.]

Owl moon. (1987). Scholastic. [Illustrated by J. Schoenherr.]

Piggins. (1987). Harcourt. [Illustrated by J. Dyer.]

The little spotted fish. (1975). Seabury. [Illustrated by F. Henstra.]

Ring of earth. (1986). Harcourt. [Illustrated by J. Wallner.]

Wings. (1991). Harcourt. [Illustrated by D. Nolan.]

Extended Texts

All in the woodland early: An ABC book. (1979). Caroline House. [Illustrated by J. Zalben.]

Bird watch. (1990). Philomel. [Illustrated by T. Lewin.]

Selections from the "Commander Toad" series.

Sky dogs. (1990). Harcourt. [Illustrated by B. Moser.]

Sleeping ugly. (1981). Coward. [Illustrated by D. Stanley.]

The emperor and the kite. (1988). Philomel. [Illustrated by E. Young.]

Welcome to the green house. (1993). Putnam. [Illustrated by L. Regan.]

INITIATING ACTIVITIES	DEVELOPING ACTIVITIES	CULMINATING ACTIVITIES
Read-aloud – Owl Moon GLTA [Wh]	Reading books by J. Yolen [I/I, P/SG, SS]	Make diagram comparing Owl Moon and Granddad Bill's Song [P/SG, Wh, TA, TD]
KWL – Pairs, then whole group, share Focus: What do we want to discover or what do we wonder about Jane Yolen? [P/SG, Wh]	Exploring point of view in Granddad Bill's Song [P/SG, TD]	Sharing of owl posters [P/SG, TA]
Begin owl poster [P/SG, TA]	Readers Theatre: Reading and sharing of core literature [P/SG, TD]	Response journal of first week with J. Yolen [I/I, TA]
Drawing of owl; focus: owl adaptations [Wh, TD]	Class book using question/response format modeled in Granddad Bill's Song [Wh, TD]	Sharing individual books [P/SG, TA]
Owl pellet dissection: Field notes and sketches of owl pellet dissection [P/SG, TD]	Reading informational books and magazines for owl facts (focus: night behavior, eating habits) [I/I, P/SG, SS, TA]	
Begin analysis of metaphor and J. Yolen's use of descriptive language [Wh, TD]	Revision of text for owl posters [I/I, P/SG, TD]	
Begin individual books modeled from Yolen's text in Owl Moon and Granddad Bill's Song [I/I, TD]	Completion of owl posters [I/I, TA]	
	Writing metaphor, using J. Yolen as model [Wh, TD]	
	Painting forest/snow landscapes to represent metaphor [I/I, TD]	
	Drawing people to complement text [I/I, TD]	

Following is the code used to indicate the type of activity:

I/I = Independent/Individual
P/SG = Partner/Small Group
Wh = Whole-Class
SS = Self-Selected
TA = Teacher-Assigned
TD = Teacher-Directed

Figure 9.4
Author Theme Unit: Jane Yolen Chart Showing Initiating, Developing, and Culminating Activities

MONDAY		TUESDAY		WEDNESDAY

WHOLE GROUP
Author: Jane Yolen – Intro
 	
CORE TEXT
<u>Owl Moon</u> – Class set
GLTA then open response
 	
SMALL GROUPS
<u>Owl Moon</u> – Planned inquiry
1. Line read by sentence – chat as go
2. Discussion: How do you feel about the girl and her father?
  What kind of relationship do they have? Find lines that show
  *Mark with sticky note special
 	
SEATWORK PAIRS
1. Browse J. Yolen books
2. List 5-6 things would like to discover about J. Yolen or wonder and why for KWL chart
3. Use zoobooks and owl info books to find out more about
  what owls do at night: use the
  following format:
  <u>Here are</u> three things an owl
 	
REGROUP BEFORE LUNCH
1. Complete KWL chart – pairs offering ideas
2. Share owl info
 	
RETURN FROM LUNCH
 	
SSR
	WHOLE GROUP
	WRITING
	Family snow image – Text modeling
	1. List 3 snow memories with family
	2. Circle one
	3. Make peronal brainstorm/guide with list
	  2 things saw
	  2 things heard
	  2 things that you touched
	  2 things that touched you
	  2 things smelled
	4. Circle the one that has the strongest memory
	5. Find a line in <u>Owl Moon</u> that is about the same "sense" you selected as your strongest memory – write it on your paper
	6. Draw a line through all distinctive J. Yolen words – leave
	  function words
	  Ex. J. Yolen – Go back to memory – pattern and change where ~~necessary.~~ ——
	  "The moon ~~was high above~~ us. It ~~seemed~~ to fit ~~exactly over the center of the clearing and the snow below it was whiter~~ than the milk in a cereal bowl."
	  Ex. The slope was long before us.
	  It seemed to stretch exactly to the forest's edge and the
	
	ART
	Forest landscapes created with colored chalk, white paper, blue paper
	Focus: Trees in winter
	Emphasize habitat – shapes and colors of trees – shapes created between trees – dip chalk in white paint where want to look snow covered – use image created in writing
	
	CLOSE DAY
	Read-Aloud: <u>Honkers</u>
		WHOLE GROUP
		<u>Owl Moon</u> – Whole group reread – added open discussion – additional thoughts – observations about language, action, problem, etc. hadn't noticed before. What makes this story appealing?
		
		SMALL GROUPS – Planned inquiry
		<u>Owl Moon</u>
		1. Choral reread
		  Then select a favorite line that shows shape/color/sound in some way – mark with sticky notes
		2. Line sharing:
		  reread several times silent share line selected and why
		3. Create new text through oral presentation of favorite line. Each child given a number card. Children read line in new numbered order. Practice several
		  times until delivery comes in continuous manner with no long pauses in between. Working for smooth transition from one line to the next for poetry feel.
		4. Select a new line and repeat process
		
		SEATWORK PAIRS
		1. Record 3 lines in double entry style that you feel J. Yolen has used an exceptional choice of words. Underline the most "stunning word." What other words could also have been used? List 3 choices. Substitute one – how has the sentence changed with the alternate word.
		2. <u>Owl Moon</u> on listening tape
		3. Zoobooks and owl info books to find out how an owl eats.
		  Format: Here is how an owl eats.
		  First _____. Next _____.
		  Then _____. Finally _____.
		
		REGROUP BEFORE LUNCH
		Check progress
			WRITING
			Family snow image continued
			1. Pair up – share and respond to image composed monday
			2. Rethink any words or phases
			3. Use story model to add a line before or after image
			4. Share with partner – get response
			5. Circle 2 words for spelling
			6. Conference with teacher for editing
			7. Final draft for display with forest habitat scene
			8. Small group final image sharing
			
			ART
			Directed drawing lesson – black line, oil pastels, white paper
			Focus: Owl on branch
			Emphasize adaptations – beak,
			
			SSR
			
			SCIENCE
			Dissect owl pellets – collect data with sketches in field note style
			
			CLOSE DAY
			Read-Aloud: <u>Letting Swift River Go</u>
				WHOLE GROUP
				Share life facts of J. Yolen
				
				CORE TEXT: <u>Granddad Bil's Song</u>
				open response – small group set – read again
				
				SMALL GROUPS – Planned inquiry
				<u>Granddad Bill's Song</u>
				1. Echo read
				2. What and how is J. Yolen sharing in this book? How did she arrange her story to give us different points of view
				3. Reread
				  Chart repetition and who's speaking (question/response format)
				
				SEATWORK PAIRS (new pairs)
				1. Prepare mini-poster – owls
				  Revision: combine info from each paragraph of night behavior/eating behavior. Prepare paragraphs using same
				  model given on Mon. & Tues. Work paragraph revisions together so each includes valuable info. shared by partner
				REGROUP BEFORE LUNCH
				1. Check KWL chart
				  Share more life facts of J. Yolen
				2. Progress check-in on owl

Figure 9.5
Author Theme: Jane Yolen First Week Lesson Plans

CLASSROOM IN ACTION

Continued

Recreational Texts

All the secrets of the world. (1991). Little, Brown. [Illustrated by L. Baker.]
Dinosaur dances. (1990). Putnam. [Illustrated by B. Degan.]
Letting swift river go. (1992). Little, Brown. [Illustrated by B. Cooney.]
Piggins and the royal wedding. (1988). Harcourt. [Illustrated by J. Dyer.]
Piggins with piggins. (1988). Harcourt. [Illustrated by J. Dyer.]

WEDNESDAY	THURSDAY		FRIDAY	
WRITING Whole class composing with question response format from <u>Granddad Bill's Song</u> for classbook 1. Brainstorm possible events that involved all of us at school that got an emotional reaction (name) from us. Select one. _____ what do you do _____? 2. *Pose lead question – list possible wordings – select one *Individually record response if you were asked – response to include 2 things 3. Share in pairs – pairs then regroup with another set – share again 4. Whole group share **SSR** **ART** Drawing people with shades of charcoal – charcoal, tan paper Focus: Faces to illustrate classbook using few strokes – clean line – light colors to highlight **WHOLE GROUP** Discussion for planned inquiry at home Focus: Compose own book of family reaction to birth, death, move, etc. – gather info. from home 1. Individual brainstorm list of possible topics – list at least three 2. Write question _____, what did you do _____? 3. Take home Record response from 2 **CLOSE DAY** Rereading of <u>Honkers</u>	**WHOLE GROUP** CORE TEXT: <u>Granddad Bill's Song</u> Reread – continued open response and discussion **SMALL GROUP** mini-readers theater 1. Choral question/ response reading – 1/2 asks question – 1/2 responds – all read 2nd page together 2. Swap roles for reading 3. Pairs read following same format 4. Group response to hearing SEATWORK PAIRS 1. Complete owl posters Arrange text on poster paper so fits with poster title, a focal **REGROUP BEFORE LUNCH** 1. Continued check-in with KWL chart 2. Pairs share posters – highlighting most interesting	**WRITING** Read classbook made Wed. Family interview – individual books 1. How did you do collecting family reaction to your chosen event? What did you need to do to get ideas down? Minilesson 2. Use of info. from homework sheet to compose 1st draft, model from a child's sheet – refer back to class book 3. Compose 1st draft – share with response partner – make any changes with partner so models pattern 4. Hold editing conference with teacher. Also discuss text placement of final draft. 5. Final drafts go in pre-made books **SSR** **ART** Focus: Snapshot drawings – colored pencils, white paper cut in photo size Small scenes that will accent memories in story. **CLOSE DAY** Rereading of <u>Letting Swift River Go</u> and life facts about J. Yolen from other sources	**WHOLE CLASS** Recap week with J. Yolen and two CORE TEXT: <u>Owl Moon</u> & <u>Granddad Bill's Song</u> Open response **PAIRS** prepare Venn diagram – regroup to create class chart – pairs contributing **SMALL GROUPS & INDIVIDUAL** Finish work 1. Any remaining owl charts 2. Complete individual books of family interview **ART** Designing individual book cover and title page Needed elements: title, author illustration Title Page: title, author, dedication, copyright **REGROUP BEFORE LUNCH** Check-in on progress	**COMPLETED BOOK SHARING AND RESPONSE** Pairs then foursomes Several to read whole class **POSTER RESPONSE** Display owl miniposters at various places around room Shared reading time of poster displays – select 3 posters to read – Complete a response slip for each – only 2 slips per poster (sticky note) On each response slip write what you liked about the poster and why – place response slip on poster – sign your name if you'd like **SSR** **JOURNAL** Response to the week What do you think of J. Yolen? What was your favorite activity this week and why? Open reaction

Planning and implementing across-the-curriculum thematic units

When you are ready to move into thematic units that incorporate some or all of the elementary curricular areas, you may build on the planning process discussed above for literature-based thematic units. With a little modification, that is the process you may follow for planning across-the-curriculum integrated thematic units as well. Let's start with the basic steps, then see how they can be applied.

1. *Select your theme, your basic learning goals, and the skills and strategies you wish to address.* This selection is based on curricular objectives as well as student interests and attitudes.
2. Just as you did in your literature/language arts–based unit, *brainstorm possible activities.* This would be a good time to begin your web.
3. *Brainstorm possible books and resources.* Do not feel that all titles have to address your theme *directly*—this will limit you too much. Include, for example, fantasy, poetry, picture books, and contemporary fiction as well as informational titles. Think about those that would work as core, extended, and recreational texts. Think about films as well as community and school support people: parents with expertise in a relevant area, business contacts, music and art teachers. Fit these into your planning web.
4. *Organize your books and activities around areas of the curriculum or your major concepts and understandings.* The usual curricular areas for the elementary grades are social studies, science/health, mathematics, music, and art. Some authorities suggest that we avoid categorizing according to the common curriculum "labels" because this may inadvertently restrict our thinking and what we do with the children (see, for example, Pappas, Kiefer, & Levstik, 1990). Their point is a good one, but don't feel guilty when you prefer to categorize according to "science," "mathematics," "social studies" and so on, if this is easier at first and helps you ensure that you are addressing the district or school curricular objectives.

Let's begin our examination of how to plan integrated across-the-curriculum units by taking a partial glimpse of how a primary-grade teacher has approached this task.

■ ■ ■ ■ ■

CLASSROOM IN ACTION

Early Phases of Planning a Primary-Grade Integrated Unit

Claudia Rossi designed a "desert" theme appropriate for the primary grades—specifically, second grade. Let's walk through the important phases of her planning process with her.

First, she selects the "desert" theme because of the keen interest of her students—they live on the edge of the high desert in northern Nevada—and because the theme allows her to explore important curricular concepts specified in the school district's curriculum guides. Ms. Rossi is a list-maker, so she generates lists before moving to a web. She has the guides close at hand as she brainstorms major areas of exploration; for example:

Ecosystems

Types of deserts

Plant and animal life

Desert cultures

Human adaptation

On the basis of this list, Ms. Rossi will generate specific learning goals or objectives; you will find them at the top of the web in Figure 9.6. Next, she

Figure 9.6
Integrated Unit: Desert Initial Web

DESERT 2nd Grade

Homogeneous groups

READING

Core Texts: used as Read-Alouds
Mojave, by Diane Siebert
Arrow to the Sun, by Gerald McDermott
Desert Giant, The World of the Saguaro Cactus, by Barbara Bash
Deserts, by Elisa Posell
Deserts, by Seymour Simon
How to Start a Day, by Byrd Baylor

All used as Read-Alouds
class sets of
1. *Arrow to the Sun*
2. *Deserts*, by E. Posell
Small Group Set:
Desert Giant

Extended Texts: small group sets
Roxaboxen, by Alice McLerran
The Warrior Maiden, by Ellen Schecter
Coyote Dreams, by Susan Nunes
This House is Made of Mud, by Ken Buchanan

Lesson Topics:
• Reading info. text – Content Guided Listening-Thinking Activity
• Identifying main idea – narrative and expository
• *Desert* as story setting
• Main characters and nature of problems in a desert setting

Recreational Texts:
Wide assortment of books – fiction, nonfiction, poetry, popups
Examples:
Happy Birthday Dear Duck, by Eve Bunting
This Place is Day, by Vicki Cobb
Creatures of the Desert World, National Geographic Popup
Amigo, by Byrd Baylor
Sand, by Angela Webb
Desert, by Lionel Bender
Quail Song, by Valerie Carey

Literature-Based Reading Series:
The Literature Experience (Houghton Mifflin)
The Tortoise and the Hare, by Janet Stevens
and grade in *Come One Come All*

ARTS

• Desert landscape drawing and painting at different times of day
• Watercolor study of the use of one color in many shades
• Desert vegetation collage

MATH

• Graphing temperature from major cities in each North American desert

day and night – highs and lows
• Compare and contrast desert areas with highest and lowest populations
• Measuring ingredients to make sandclay for relief maps

SOCIAL STUDIES

• Location of deserts on world map – map legend reading
• Location of 4 major deserts in North America
• Writing to chambers of commerce for information about each desert state
Customs and stories of cultures in U.S. deserts. Perceptions of desert animals

coyote, snakes

SCIENCE

• Rain demonstration to emphasize rainshadow – leading to understanding of desert landforms and geographic definitions
• How desert scientifically defined class sets
• Sequence of boulder to sand
• Desert as ecosystem
• Weekly topics: What is a desert
  Plants of the desert.

4 deserts in U.S. – Great Basin
  Mojave
  Sonoran
  Chuhuahuan

Everybody Needs a Rock, by Byrd Baylor

LANGUAGE ARTS

• How we read informational text compared to how we read narrative
• How poetry focuses on senses, feelings, detail
• Recording in learning log impressions of stories read and information learned
• Keep class chart of new vocabulary and interesting desert word lists
• Using question/answer relationships to focus rereadings – simplify
• Individual story writing with desert setting and desert animals as characters
• Mini-animal reports

UNIT OBJECTIVES

• Gain understanding of how physical landforms in desert are created and defined
• Gain an awareness of where deserts are located around the world
• Locate and name the deserts of North America/U.S.
• Gain an understanding of the plants and animals that live together in a desert ecosystem
• Gain an awareness of humans' experience living in the desert – past and present.
• Gain exposure to narrative, expository, and poetry texts written about the desert

OVERALL UNIT ORGANIZATION

Week 1: Defining desert/map reading and construction. Use core text balanced with recreational reading. Begin learning logs.

Week 2: Begin extended reading in small groups. Continue core text and recreational reading.
Ecosystem: plants

Week 3: Continue all texts
Ecosystem: animals

Week 4: Continue all texts
People and the desert.

Use Core Text *Deserts*, by E. Posell 1 chapter per week to fit topics balanced with extended and recreational reading; math and art projects lists more *specific* concepts, skills, and strategies from reading and language arts and from the content areas that could be addressed in this particular unit. She checks this list against the district's curriculum guides:

> **Reading and Language Arts**
> Narrative structure—for example, legends
>
> Reading informational text
>
> Oral expression and interpretation—perhaps Readers Theatre
>
> **Math/Science**
> Graphing
>
> Mapping and locating world's deserts
>
> Observation, comparison/contrast
>
> Weather systems/temperatures
>
> Plant/animal adaptation
>
> **Social Studies and Art**
> Cooking—how matter changes
>
> Painting desert landscapes—colors of the desert
>
> Uses of clay—pots, home
>
> Storytelling

Having generated this information, Ms. Rossi is ready to move from her list format to a "web" format. This helps her visualize and organize the subject-matter areas with the concepts; skills and strategies, and the projects and activities. She works out a time line and includes that in her initial web; she plans to take about four weeks for the unit. Figure 9.6 shows Ms. Rossi's planning web. It includes her overall unit objectives, a tentative weekly organization, and a breakdown of ideas by subject area.

■ ■ ■ ■ ■

In the intermediate grades "Teachers are challenged to create units that hold students' interest and, at the same time, encourage them to recognize some of the literary qualities of well-written fiction" (Monson, 1993, p. 98).

When you've become a thematic-unit teacher

As we've noted, some educators suggest that you avoid categorizing or arranging your major concepts according to the traditional labels "Social Studies," "Science," "Mathematics," and so on. They argue that this can lead to traditional, less open ways of thinking about concepts and their interconnections. Their point is very well taken. I believe, however, that *if you are aware of* these possible pitfalls, you can develop students' thinking beyond the labels while still helping

Diane Olds teaches a multigrade fourth/fifth/sixth-grade class in which there are a number of Asian-American students. Over the course of a three-year cycle, she wished to explore most of the Asian cultures. She began with a thematic unit on China and Japan.

Following the same general steps Claudia Rossi applied above, Ms. Olds generated the organizational chart you see in Figure 9.7. The list of core, extended, and recreational texts that support her unit of study is presented at the end of the unit. She chose her books very carefully and sought to balance the two sections of the unit with experiences involving the reading of chapter books, picture books, traditional stories, and informational texts. In her chart, she has included author studies in two different ways. During the days when her students will be studying China, each child will select an author to investigate for an individual project. While studying Japan, the entire class will spend time looking into the writing of one particular author. In addition, the variety of materials available to students must also support their small-group research topics. Although Diane Olds's students will be gathering information from many different sources, those available in the classroom must represent both narrative and expository text and must provide the basics for an intensive study of one particular element of Chinese or Japanese culture.

Ms. Olds's fourth-, fifth-, and sixth-grade students will need large chunks of time each day for investigating their topics of choice in cooperative small groups. While she has listed some basics that she wants all her students to experience, a great deal of her instruction will be centered around guiding her students in small groups through the process of learning how to gather information that will be shared, eventually, with the rest of the class. She has decided that each morning will be spent reading and responding to core and extended texts, with the afternoons devoted to lessons on techniques and strategies that can be applied to each group's research. These topics include interviewing, content-area reading, paragraph writing, and note-taking.

Like the other teachers featured throughout this chapter, Ms. Olds finds it helpful to group and list her activities as those that initiate, develop, or culminate each portion of this expansive unit. Below you will find a sampling of the organizing charts and daily lesson plans she has generated. Interwoven throughout the days, you will notice time set aside for read-alouds, independent writing, and word study.

Organizing a unit of this magnitude allows opportunities for the simultaneous investigation of several topics. The coming together and the sharing of that information quite naturally creates active culminating experiences for children. The young people in Diane Olds's multi-age classroom will give group presentations that demonstrate their expertise. Each will submit a written report in the format of their choice, present a group display, and organize a whole class activity.

UNIT OBJECTIVES:
- Gain an awareness of the diversity of countries and cultures that make up Asia.
- Gain an understanding of the East Asian cultures of China and Japan in the areas of Government – Philosophy – Economy – Education – The Arts – Language – Lifestyle
- Gain an understanding of the Chinese and the Japanese cultural influences in the U.S.
- Gain an understanding of the major story themes that recur in traditional Chinese and Japanese folktales
- Gain an awareness of Chinese- and Japanese-American children's authors and illustrators.

UNIT ORGANIZATION:
Day 1 – Intro to Asia
Days 2-8 – Focus on China
Days 9-10 – Culminating presentations on China
Day 11 – Transition to focus on Japan
Days 12-17 – Focus on Japan
Days 19-20 – Culminating presentations on Japan

CHINA

•• Chapterbook

READ-ALOUDS: • Selections from recreational text
•• The Rainbow People, by Laurence Yep

CORE TEXTS:
•• China's Long March, by Jean Fritz
•• Tales from Gold Mountain, by Paul Yee
• Lon Po Po, by Ed Young
• The Weaving of a Dream, by Marilee Heyer
• Yen-Chen, by Ai-Ling Louie
• The Children of China, by Matti A. Pitkonen

EXTENDED TEXTS:
•• The Starfisher, by Laurence Yep

JAPAN

READ-ALOUDS: • Selections from recreational text

CORE TEXTS:
•• Born in the Year of Courage, by Emily Crofford
• Green Willow and Other Japanese Fairy Tales, by Grace James
• Tree of Cranes, by Allen Say

Available in 5th Grade Literature → •• Sadako and the Thousand Paper Cranes, by Eleanor Coerr
Experience
H. Mifflin

EXTENDED TEXTS:
• The Funny Little Woman, by Arlene Morel
• Two Foolish Cats, by Yoshiko Uchida
• The Warrior and the Wise Man, by David Wisniewski
• The Crane Wife, by Sumiko Yagawa

Possible author and/or

Topics below to be experienced by everyone

SOCIAL STUDIES
- Great Wall of China
- Physical geography of China – diversity
- Opening of China to the west
- Women in Chinese society
- Taiwan's influence on its product production

LANGUAGE ARTS
- Compare Lon Po Po and Yen Chen to western versions
- Trace themes and motifs in traditional Chinese folktales

SCIENCE/MATH
- Tangrams (Grandfather Tang's Story, by Ann Tompert)
- Lunar calendar
- Price comparisons – wages
- Population charting and comparing
- Wildlife – panda – tiger

Topics below to be experienced by everyone

SOCIAL STUDIES
- Honoring tradition
- Involvement in WWII
- Definition of an island
- Business influences in U.S. economy
- Physical geography of Japan – how influences lifestyle

SCIENCE/MATH
- Geometry – symmetry – origami
- Money conversions
- Ocean resources – percentages
- Environmental issues
- Island weather

LANGUAGE ARTS
- Haiku – Tanka
- Traditional themes & motifs
- Traditional stories compared to modern fiction
- Language influence into English
- How art influences way of thinking and writing process

Figure 9.7
Integrated Unit: China and Japan: Two Major Asian Cultures Organizational Chart

INITIATING ACTIVITIES (Day 1)	DEVELOPING ACTIVITIES (Days 4 & 5)	CULMINATING ACTIVITIES (Day 20)
Using atlas, world map, globe to discover countries that comprise Asia [P/SG, Wh, TA, TD]	Extended reading [P/SG, TA, TD]	Research group presentations; 3 parts: written, display, activity [P/SG, SS, TA]
KWL on Asia [I/I, Wh, TA, TD]	Interview questioning [I/I, Wh, SS]	Luncheon w/Japanese restaurant owner [Wh]
Atlas, world map, globe focus for discovering facts about China specifically [P/SG, Wh, TA, TD]	Using information from an interview in text of research project [P/SG, Wh, SS, TD]	Visiting artist – Bamboo painting [I/I, Wh, TD]
Book browsing recreational texts [I/I, P/SG, SS]	Paragraph writing [I/I, P/SG, Wh, SS, TA, TD]	
Word Study: Meaning and origins of <u>atlas</u>, <u>globe</u>, <u>legend</u> [P/SG, TD]	Notetaking [I/I, P/SG, Wh, SS, TA, TD]	
Maps to find populations – averaging, calculating, distances from scale [P/SG, SS, TA, TD]	Author studies, individual and whole class [I/I, P/SG, Wh, SS, TA, TD]	
Set up research topics and groups [P/SG, Wh, SS, TA, TD]	Writing tangram stories for younger students [I/I, P/SG, Wh, SS, TA, TD]	
	Calculating foreign exchange rates [I/I, P/SG, Wh, SS, TA, TD]	

Following is the code used to indicate the type of activity:

I/I = Independent/Individual
P/SG = Partner/Small Group
Wh = Whole-Class
SS = Self-Selected
TA = Teacher-Assigned
TD = Teacher-Directed

Figure 9.8
Sample Initiating, Developing, and Culminating Activities for an Integrated Unit

9:00-9:45

CORE TEXT: Read-Aloud – <u>The Rainbow People</u>, by Laurence Yep (Chinese)
Selection – "The Rainbow People"   Open response to each
<u>Grandfather's Journey</u>, by Allen Say   then focus on setting

Intro to Asia
• Traditional tale from China
• Immigrant tale from Japan
• Asia – KWL chart – whole group and individually

9:45-10:45

ASIA AS A CONTINENT
   atlases, maps, globes – assortment – whole group and small group

• Groups of 5 – heterogeneous assigned by teacher
• From globe, world map, atlas, discover as much as you can about Asia in a
   25 minute work session – start with atlas
• Make an informal listing of as much information as you can –
   later make copies of group list for each group member
• All 5 group members must understand what's on the list
• Meet whole group to share
• Ask spokesperson from groups to share – How did you find the information
   you needed?
• Record all new information on chart
• Refer back to KWL chart – make additions or changes
• Locate and label all Asian countries on blank world map
• Back to small groups to consider: What are the implications of the diversity
   you discovered? Record in individual response logs
• Whole group – share responses
• Small groups – back to map, globe, atlas – now focus just on China and
   Japan – find 3 pieces of information on each
• Share 3 items with whole group – chart responses
• Focus now on China – small groups – locate 3 more facts – add to list
• Share whole class – add to whole group list
• Write a summary in response logs of information listed on chart.
   Use the following lead-in:
   China is one of the largest countries in Asia. From studying
   a world map, an atlas, and a globe, I can tell you that
   China . . . – location in world
                  – land size
                  – population size
                  – weather
                  – major rivers and mountains
                  – major natural resources
                  – personal thought
• Share with a partner – recheck any conflicting information
• Pairs write to each other telling partner 2 things appreciated learning
   about China after reading summary

10:45-11:15

Book browsing of recreational text in pairs – 15 minutes
• At end of 15 minutes find a book you'd like to stay with for Sustained Silent Reading time
• 15-20 minutes SSR time

11:15-12:00

SMALL GROUPS WITH TEACHER   SEATWORK PAIRS
WORD STUDY AND VOCABULARY
• Recap how used atlas, world map, and globes   • Select a Chinese folktale to read with a partner
   to find information about Asia, then China   • Pair discussions – look for dialogue that reveals
• Brainstorm, referencing back to books, any   the main character's attitudes towards others
   words that show up only in these sources: –
                  – atlas/map/globe   quote several lines in response log – give
                  – legend   personal
   possibiliti   – country names   reaction and explanation of how quote moves the
                  – population   story forward
                  – natural resources   • List 4 words from story you felt were exceptional,
                  – scale
• Focus on atlas, map, globe 1st –
   discuss how connected in meaning
• Pairs to use dictionary to share meanings:
   brainstorm any other related words – guide
   to see meaning tie-ins and word origins
• Legend: discuss how usually see meaning
   of word – stay related – new context in
   atlas and map – dictionaries to check
   meaning and related words

1:00-2:00

RETURN TO CHINA FACT SHEETS AND KWL CHARTS – reread
• Identify major areas for further study – small group research groups
• Ask students to rank order topics most interested in researching plus 3 people feel can do
   best work with
• Brainstorm ways of presenting information under guidelines – written portion – display –
   group activity due dates – groups and presentation dates to be given out Tuesday

2:00-3:00

MATH
RETURN TO MORNING GROUPS – Atlas work
• Find population of 3 cities in China
• Show – visual graph
         – average population for these 3 cities – must show and explain process for
         finding
            this information
         – calculate distance between cities using scale legend
         – write 2 story problems concerning city populations or distance in China to be

BEGIN READ-ALOUD
<u>China's Long March</u>, by Jean Fritz

Figure 9.9
Sample Lesson Plans for an Integrated Unit

9:00-9:30

SSR

9:30-10:30

EXTENDED TEXT GROUPS – Group discussions and rereading

1 Group with teacher – rotate 2 groups
2 Groups reading and writing, sharing, discussing

Starfisher
Chapter 5 – focus?
• What new things do we learn about Miss Lucy?
• How do you feel about the exchange Joan has with her mother about the
  bread money?
Chapter 6
• What do you think of Joan's experience at school?
• How is the author using the italics to express meaning in the dialogue?

Seven Chinese Brothers – 2 versions
• What do you think of the seven brothers?
• How do the versions differ?
• What similarities do you see?
• How do the illustrations change your vision of the story?

In the Year of the Boar and Jackie Robinson
Seatwork focus: consider the social interactions that go on in the
apartment building
Process: read 2 chapters – respond in log – share – discuss –
repeat process

WORD STUDY
Spelling list words – open sort – share – record in wordstudy notebook –
play game

11:30-12:00

Guest speaker: owner of local Chinese restaurant
Questions from Day 3 ready on index cards
List of topics sent to speaker:
• What made you come to this country?
• What process did you have to go through to get to the U.S. and be able
  to open a business?
• What are a few of the most important things you think we need to know
  about your culture?

12:00 – LUNCH

1:00-2:00

CORE TEXT: Read-Aloud – China's Long March, by Jean Fritz

WRITING
Grandfather Tang's Story, by Ann Tompert
• Share story
• Pass out tangrams to pairs – give free exploration time – identifiy shapes and attributes
• Put tangrams back in bags
• On overhead design an animal with overhead tangrams
• Whole class write instructions for making animal or object – focus on "direction" words and
  sequence – first, next, then, finally
• Compose a "what am I?" story for animal made with tangram
  Example: I have long white wings.
            I can be found in many city ponds.
            I am known for my graceful long neck.
            What am I?
• Write with 2nd grader as audience
• Pairs to design an animal or object
• Pairs compose building instructions and riddle story
• Try out on another pair – response
• Revise for clarity
• Design a book for 2nd grader that contains a set of paper tangrams, instructions for building
  animal or object, riddle, picture of final product, and answer to riddle bound with cover –
  options:
  cutout, pop-up, fold out, flip book

2:00 – RECESS

2:15-3:00

RESEARCH GROUPS – Minilesson Whole Class
• How to use information given by guest speaker as part of our research into Asia/Chinese culture
• Rethink questions he came with
• Model how to reference speaker in the written text
• Whole group – compose several ways to incorporate the information he gave us
• Group revision
• Break into groups

Figure 9.9
Continued

---

*Book Selection for Asia Unit: China and Japan—Two Major
Asian Cultures*

China

Core Texts
Fritz, J. (1988). *China's long march 6,000 miles of danger.* Putnam. [Illustrated
by Y. Cheng.]

Heyer, M. (1986). *The weaving of a dream.* Viking Kestrel. [Available in *The
Literature Experience,* Grade 5. Boston: Houghton Mifflin.]

■ ■ ■ ■ ■

**CLASSROOM
IN ACTION**

Continued

9:00-9:30

SSR

9:30-10:30

EXTENDED TEXT
Small group – Group discussions and rereading
1 Group with teacher – rotate 2 groups

The Funny Little Woman, by Arlene Mosel
• Oni character
• What other characters have we seen that are much like the Oni?
• How is the "trickster" motif played out in the Funny Little Woman?

Two Foolish Cats, by Yoshiko Uchida
• What kind of cat is Big Daizo? How do we know this? Find passages
• What do the cats have to teach us?
• What other circumstances parallel that of the two foolish cats?

The Warrior and the Wise Man, by David Wisniewski
• In this story what does it mean to be twins?
• Explain why it is not always best to be strong
• How do the differences in the brothers determine the plot of the story?

10:30-11:30

WHOLE CLASS – AUTHOR STUDY

Yoshiko Uchida
• Discussing the author – H. Mifflin 5th Literature Experience – Teacher's Book (TB) p.137A-138B Journal p. 57
• Reading a sample – TB p. 138B – a scene from The Magic Listening Cap

11:30-12:00

MATH –Whole class then small groups
MONEY CONVERSIONS
• Newspapers, calculators, number to Nevada Foreign Exchange
• Obtain exchange rate for yen
• Decide on what rate best for which situation when buying
• Ask for suggestions for converting exchange rates – try out
• Demonstrate actual procedure – match up to suggestions
• In pairs – make conversions for the purchase of a house, a car, groceries, clothing – record process in math logs

12:00 – LUNCH

1:00-1:45

CONTENT READING AND PARAGRAPH WRITING – Whole class
• Review of reading content material – steps to take
• Review of notetaking
• Transfer notetaking to paragraph writing
• Several choices for a strong lead sentence – continue with supporting detail
• The closing or transition
• Giving writing personal voice

1:45-2:45

RESEARCH PROJECTS – Small Groups
• Composing final portion of written section of report
• Sharing previous drafts with group members
• Revising to obtain clarity and smoothness of transitions – word choice
• Continue work on board displays or other related display

2:45-3:00

CORE TEXT: Read-Aloud – Born in the Year of Courage, by Emily Crofford

9:30-11:30

Last three groups to give research presentations
Order – Lifestyle
        – Education
        – The arts
Peer evaluation
• What information/activity from each presentation did you find the most valuable and why
• Favorite parts and why

11:30-12:00

Prepare for luncheon celebration of Japan – setup – cooking

12:00-1:00

Japanese Cuisine
Luncheon Speaker:
University professor from history department to show slides, discuss his travels in Japan and his work documenting the rise of Japanese business in the United States.

1:00-1:30

LUNCHEON CLEANUP

1:30-2:45

BAMBOO PAINTING
• Art director from private art school for children to share her experience studying art in Japan while living with a Japanese family
• As sharing personal story will instruct students in the traditional art of brush work and technique for painting with ink on rice paper
• Frame and display
• Write personal reaction to process

2:45-3:00

• Self evaluation of unit
• Focus: What activities helped you grow most as a reader and writer – explain
• What do you think was your best work during the unit and why
To continue first thing on Monday morning
• What grade do you feel you deserve on your group presentation and why

Figure 9.9
Continued

Louie, A. (1982). *Yen shen.* Philomel Books. [Illustrated by E. Young.]

Pitkanen, M. A. (1988). *The children of China.* Carolrhoda Books.

Yee, P. (1989). *Tales from gold mountain.* Macmillan. [Illustrated by Simon Ng.]

Yep, L. (1989). *The rainbow people.* HarperCollins. [Illustrated by D. Wiesner.]

Young, E. (1989). *Lon Po Po: A Red-Riding-Hood story.* Philomel Books.

Extended Texts

Bishop, C., & Wiese, K. (1938). *The five Chinese brothers.* Coward-McCann.

Demi. (1990). *The empty pot.* Trumpet Club.

Lord, B. B. (1984). *In the Year of the Boar and Jackie Robinson.* Harper. [Illustrated by M. Simont.]

Mahy, M. (1990). *The seven Chinese brothers.* Illustrated by J. and M. Tseng. Scholastic.

Yep, L. (1991). *The star fisher.* Morrow Junior Books.

Possibilities for Recreational and Support Texts

Demi. (1990). *The magic boat.* Holt.

Ferroa, P. (1991), *China.* Marshall Cavendish.

Fisher, L. (1986). *The great wall of China.* Macmillan.

Fyson, N., and Greenhill, R. (1985). *A family in China.* Lerner.

Gerstein, M. (1987). *The mountains of Tibet.* Harper.

Jacobsen, K. (1990). *China.* Children's Press.

Jacowitz, C. (1992). *The jade stone.* Holiday. [Illustrated by J. Chen.]

James, I. (1989). *China.* Franklin Watts.

Lafcadio, H. (1963). *The voice of the great bell.* Little, Brown. [Illustrated by E. Young.]

Liyi, H. (1985). *The spring of butterflies and other folktales of China's minority peoples.* Lothrop. [Illustrated by P. Aiqing and L. Zhao.]

Lobel, A. (1982). *Ming Lo moves the mountain.* Scholastic.

Miller, M. (1989). *The moon dragon.* Dial. [Illustrated by I. Deuchar.]

Mosel, A. (1968). *Tikki tikki tembo.* Holt. [Illustrated by B. Lent.]

Murphey, R. (Ed.). (1988). *China.* Gateway Press.

Pittman, H. (1986). *A grain of rice.* Hastings House.

Rau, M. (1983). *Holding up the sky: Young people in China.* Lodestar Books.

Terzi, M. (1990). *The Chinese empire.* Children's Press.

Williams, J. (1976). *Everybody knows what a dragon looks like.* [Illustrated by M. Mayer.] Four Winds.

Wolf, B. (1988). *In the year of the tiger.* Macmillan.

Young, E. (1993). *Red Thread.* Philomel Books.

Japan

Core Texts

Coerr, E. (1977). *Sadako and the thousand paper cranes.* Putnam.

Crofford, E. (1991). *Born in the year of courage.* Carolrhoda Books.

Say, A. (1991). *Tree of cranes.* Scholastic.

Say, A. (1993). *Grandfather's journey.* Boston: Houghton Mifflin.

Tames, R. (1991). *Journey through Japan.* Troll Associates.

Uchida, Y. (1983). *The best bad thing.* Atheneum.

Extended Texts

Mosel, A. (1972). *The funny little woman.* [Illustrated by B. Lent.] Dutton.

Uchida, Y. (1987). *The two foolish cats.* [Illustrated by M. Zemach.] Margaret K. McElderry Books.

Wisniewski, D. (1989). *The warrior and the wise man.* Lothrop.

Yagawa, S. (1981). *The crane wife.* [Trans. by K. Paterson.] Morrow.

Possibilities for Recreational and Support Texts

Blumberg, R. (1985). *Commodore Perry in the land of the shogun.* Lothrop.

Coates, B. (1991). *Japan.* Bookwright Press. [Photographs by J. Holmes.]

Cobb, V. (1992). *This place is crowded.* Walker. [Illustrated by B. Lavallee.]

Downer, L. (1990). *Japan.* Bookwright Press. [Illustrated by M. Walker. Photographs by P. Kristensen.]

Garrison, C. (1978). *The dream eater.* Aladdin Books. [Illustrated by D. Goode.]

Haskins, J. (1987). *Count your way through Japan.* Carolrhoda Books. [Illustrated by M. Skoro.]

Hedlund, I. (1990). *Mighty mountain and the three strong women.* Volcano Press.

Hooks, W. (1992). *Peach boy.* Bantam.

James, I. (1989). *Japan.* Franklin Watts.

Johnston, T. (1990). *The badger and the magic fan.* Scholastic. [Illustrated by Tomi dePaola.]

McDermott, G. (1975). *The stone-cutter.* Puffin Books.

Morimotot, J. (1985). *Mouse's marriage.* Puffin Books.

Morimotot, J. (1984). *The inch boy.* Puffin Books.

Paterson, K. (1990). *The tale of the mandarin ducks.* Scholastic. [Illustrated by L. and D. Dillon.]

Say, A. (1982). *The bicycle man.* Scholastic.

Shelley, R. (1990). *Japan.* Marshall Cavendish.

Snyder, D. (1988). *The boy of the three-year nap.* Houghton Mifflin. [Illustrated by A. Say.]

Stamm, C. (1962). *Three strong women.* Viking. [Illustrated by J. and M. Tseng.]

them see how the content fits into the categories that the rest of society—as well as many teachers they may have later on—understand. The labels will not be as imprisoning as we might fear.

How does this scheme fit in the classroom? First of all, it is important to remember that once you are a "thematic-unit teacher" you do not need to organize *all* your instruction around themes. Move in and out of them. Have a few weeks where your students are spending most of their time just reading independently and conferring with you about their reading—the "Reading Workshop" concept (Chapter 6). Of course, if several students are reading the same book, you can still have "intensive" reading with them in a group if you wish. You will want to meet in a group with your slower readers, so that they all can be reading a selection that is at their instructional level, allowing you to do Guided Reading-Thinking Activities and skills minilessons. It is important to keep a perspective here: your students won't always be delving intensively into literature—they need a break on occasion, just like us. Many teachers have a box of easier books on hand. These books are a great alternative, allowing the students to relax between "weightier" books (it's not unusual to find children turning to a book like *Nate the Great* after finishing one such as *Bridge to Terabithia*).

This would also be an excellent time in which to do a Writers' Workshop as well. Students may explore freely whatever themes and genres they wish, in their own writing, in sharing drafts in conferences with peers, and with you (Chapter 6). During these breaks between thematic units, content-area concepts or objectives that you are expected to address, and that may not fit into your themes easily or logically, may be addressed at other times during the day.

In summary, many teachers discover that by moving in and out of themes, they can address curriculum objectives more effectively, while giving students more opportunities to explore their own reading interests as well. And let's take the long view here: will you be using the same themes year after year? Probably not, and for all kinds of reasons. You *will* have some favorites; but each time you revisit those themes, you and your students will be changing them in many different ways. Your own knowledge base will be larger; new titles will have appeared; your students will be discovering and wanting to pursue new directions within a general theme. You will find, however, that thematic-unit teaching inevitably leads to *new* themes and is an exciting and renewing way to teach.

■ A CONCLUDING PERSPECTIVE

Harste has offered a valuable perspective on how we go about integrating our instruction within language arts and across subject-matter areas:

> By thinking through a topic, ways to invite children to explore issues occur to you. Curricular invitations should allow kids to get in touch with different dimensions of the topic. . . . Ecology isn't just a subject we want kids to learn, it's a stance or perspective on the world that we want learners to actively use as they solve problems later on. (Cited in Monson & Monson, 1994, p. 521)

In this chapter we have explored how to integrate literature and the curriculum with strategies for *inviting* students to engage in literacy experiences. While reflecting the multicultural realities of the classroom, the community, and society, the *thematic unit* represents an extremely effective context for this integration.

We have looked briefly at the various categories of literature for children, and I have offered a suggested "starter list" of titles. These books reflect a very wide range of interest and experience, and a large proportion of them reflect different cultural perspectives and backgrounds. Through thematic units, literature can be woven more integrally into your reading/writing block and then into the other areas of your curriculum. Because ours is a multicultural society, the promise that such diversity brings can first be explored and developed in the classroom. To support you as you address this, a wide range of multicultural literature has been suggested.

We have seen that there are two reasons for exploring multicultural literature throughout the elementary grades. The first is that appropriate literature can provide a familiar, reassuring context for children from diverse cultures. The second reason is that learning about other cultures through authentic portrayals in literature can help elementary children see beyond themselves and their own culture and thus acquire the beginning of *understanding*. Both personally and in terms of the larger society of which each child is a part, this understanding and growth beyond entertaining simplistic stereotypes will be essential in our increasingly interdependent society and world.

The understandings that a multicultural society potentially affords can be explored through reading and writing and through thematic units. We presented three illustrative thematic units. Beginning with a literature focus, then moving into a cross-curriculum focus, these units interrelate the language arts and interrelate concepts that underlie specific areas in the elementary curriculum. Thematic units help children see the interrelatedness of learning—they show students how strategies and knowledge are generalizable from one task or domain to another. Not coincidentally, thematic units help *us* understand this interrelatedness better. As teachers, we are part of the community of learners in our classrooms. As such, we are models of learning at the same time as we are planners and facilitators.

The challenge of being a teacher is far greater now than in years past. But the type of teaching and learning community we have been assembling throughout this text and putting into action in this chapter does not *add to* the complexity and challenge. Rather, it may well offer the best way to address these challenges.

■ BECOMING A REFLECTIVE PRACTITIONER

Goodman, K. (1992). Why whole language is today's agenda in education. *Language Arts, 69,* 354–364.

    Kenneth and Yetta Goodman are two of the most articulate and compelling spokespersons for constructivist, whole language approaches to literacy and learning—which have at their core thematically-based inquiry instruction and learning. In this article Kenneth Goodman explores the roots and precepts of the popular and influential "whole language" movement, and examines the issues involved when educators implement and sustain whole language teaching in their classrooms. For Goodman, literacy—indeed, all education—is political, and it is necessary to appreciate this fact if educators are to be successful change agents. Goodman will challenge you to think about why and how you teach, and may lead you to quite a different and compelling conception of your chosen profession.

Temple, C., & Collins, P. (Eds.) (1992). *Stories and readers: New perspectives on literature in the elementary classroom.* Norwood, MA: Christopher-Gordon.

I am recommending this interesting (and at times fascinating) volume because it brings together a number of perspectives that affect how we think about, organize, and implement thematic teaching. Contributions to the volume include perspectives on curriculum, on children's developing minds and lives, on literature, and on teaching. Some chapters are quite theoretical (the universal roots of myth and story, for example) and will take you into areas you may not have entered before, while others are quite practical, offering, for example, step-by-step guidelines for organizing and implementing literature response groups. Still others combine both stances. All contributions, however, speak to the issues involved in exploring literature in the context of thematic teaching.

Walmsley, S., & Walp, T. (1990). Integrating literature and composing into the language arts curriculum: Philosophy and practice. *Elementary School Journal, 90,* 251–274.

Sean Walmsley has been integrally involved in the movements toward literature-based reading and thematic instruction. In this article, he and Tracy Walp present the foundations for linking literature and content areas through thematic teaching. Guidelines for planning, implementing, and sustaining core, extended, and recreational texts within a thematic unit are clearly presented. The article is also of interest because the authors realistically discuss the problems and successes one New York state school district experienced as they moved away from basal readers and into literature-based, thematic instruction.

■ REFERENCES

Bennett, C. (1990). *Comprehensive multicultural education.* Boston: Allyn & Bacon.

Bettelheim, B. (1976). *The uses of enchantment: The meaning and importance of fairy tales.* New York: Alfred A. Knopf.

Bishop, R. (1992). Multicultural literature for children: Making informed choices. In V. Harris (Ed.), *Teaching multicultural literature in grades K–8* (pp. 37–53). Norwood, MA: Christopher-Gordon.

Campbell, J. (1968). *The hero with 1,000 faces* (2nd ed.). Princeton, NJ: Princeton University Press.

Cooper, J. (1993). *Literacy: Helping children construct meaning.* Boston, MA: Houghton Mifflin.

Crawford, L. (1993). *Language and literacy learning in multicultural classrooms.* Boston: Allyn and Bacon.

Cullinan, B., & Galda, L. (1994). *Literature and the child* (3rd ed.). Fort Worth, TX: Harcourt Brace Jovanovich.

Erickson, F. (1991). Introduction. In E. H. Hiebert (Ed.), *Literacy for a diverse society: Perspectives, practices, and policies.* New York: Teachers College Press.

Gamberg, R., Kwak, W., Hutchings, M., & Altheim, J. (1988). *Learning and loving it: Theme studies in the classroom.* Portsmouth, NH: Heinemann.

Goodman, K. (1992). Why whole language is today's agenda in education. *Language Arts, 69,* 354–364.

Harste, J., Short, K., & Burke, C. (1989). *Creating classrooms for authors.* Portsmouth, NH: Heinemann.

Heath, S., & Mangiola, L. (1991). *Children of promise: Literate activity in linguistically and culturally diverse classrooms.* Washington, D.C.: National Education Association.

Huck, C., Hepler, S., & Hickman, J. (1993). *Children's literature in the elementary school* (5th ed.). Forth Worth, TX: Harcourt Brace Jovanovich.

Monson, D. (1993). In B. Cullinan (Ed.), *Invitation to read: More children's literature in the reading program* (pp. 150–165). Newark, DE: International Reading Association.

Monson, R., & Monson, M. (1994). Literacy as inquiry: An interview with Jerome C. Harste. *Reading Teacher, 47,* 518–521.

Moss, J. (1990). *Focus on literature: A context for literacy learning.* Katonah, NY: Richard C. Owen.

Moss, J. (1992). Literature in the elementary classroom: Making connections and generating meaning. In C. Temple & P. Collins (Eds.), *Stories and readers: New perspectives on literature in the elementary classroom* (pp. 115–130). Norwood, MA: Christopher-Gordon.

Newkirk, T., & Atwell, N. (Eds.). (1988). *Understanding writing* (2nd ed.). Portsmouth, NH: Heinemann.

Norton, D. (1991). *Through children's eyes: An introduction to children's literature* (3rd ed.). Columbus, OH: Merrill/Macmillan.

Pappas, C., Kiefer, B., & Levstik, L. (1990). *An integrated language perspective in the elementary school.* New York: Longman.

Root, S. (1977). The new realism—some personal reflections. *Language Arts, 54,* 19–24.

Routman, R. (1991). *Invitations.* Portsmouth, NH: Heinemann.

Shannon, P. (Ed.). (1992). *Becoming political: Readings and writings in the politics of literacy education.* Portsmouth, NH: Heinemann.

Short, K., & Pierce, K. (Eds.) (1990). *Talking about books: Creating literate communities.* Portsmouth, NH: Heinemann.

Takaki, R. (1993). *A different mirror: A history of multicultural America.* Boston: Little, Brown.

Tchudi, S., & Tchudi, S. (1991). *The English/language arts handbook: Classroom strategies for teachers.* Portsmouth, NH: Boynton/Cook and Heinemann.

Walmsley, S. (1994). *Children exploring their world: Theme teaching in elementary school.* Portsmouth, NH: Heinemann.

Walmsley, S., & Walp, T. (1990). Integrating literature and composing into the language arts curriculum: Philosophy and practice. *Elementary School Journal, 90,* 251–274.

Watkins, M. (1979). James Baldwin writing and talking. *New York Times Book Review, 3,* 36–37.

Children's Literature Cited

Sharmat, M. (1977). *Nate the Great*. Dell.

Carroll, L. (1989). *Alice's adventures in Wonderland*. Philomel.

White, E. B. (1952). *Charlotte's web*. Harper & Row.

Grahame, K. (1985). *The wind in the willows*. Adama.

Lasky, K. (1988). *The bone wars*. Morrow.

LeGuin, U. K. (1968). *A wizard of Earthsea*. Houghton Mifflin.

MacLachlan, P. (1985). *Sarah, plain and tall*. Harper & Row.

Paterson, K. (1977). *Bridge to Terabithia*. Crowell.

Potter, B. (1984). *Tales of Peter Rabbit and his friends*. Chatham River Press.

Speare, E. (1983). *The sign of the beaver*. Houghton Mifflin.

Wilder, L. (1953). *Little house on the prairie*. Harper & Row.

PART THREE

MAKING CHOICES AND MEETING ALL NEEDS FOR LITERACY LEARNING

The legacy of literacy instruction is rich with methods and materials. There is much that is good in this legacy; there is much that is questionable. In this part, we take a brief look at the history of reading instruction; examine assessment in literacy and describe how you can involve your students in assessing their own growth and areas of need; and apply our examination of literacy learning and instruction for whom English is a second language, who speak a variant dialect, or who are experiencing significant difficulties in learning to read and write.

CHAPTER TEN

INSTRUCTIONAL MATERIALS IN TEACHING LITERACY

FOCUS

■ *Why is it important to know about the general historical trends in reading instruction in the United States?*

■ *Why have basal reader programs been so influential?*

■ *What are the similarities and differences between a traditional basal program and a literature-based series?*

■ *How can a basal program or a literature-based series be used to best advantage in the collaborative integrated classroom?*

■ *At the present time, what printed, computer, and multimedia materials are available for classroom use?*

*Could reading really be this simple? Could it be that reading is simply
a matter of transposing the squiggles of the writing system into the
meaning-bearing elements of the language system? And is this
transposing simply the decoding of print into speech? The answer to
these questions is so obviously "yes" that it's hard sometimes to
imagine how we—researchers and reading educators—have
managed to make things so much more complex than this.*

Charles Perfetti

Charles Perfetti, a researcher, observes that when we get right down to it,
"reading" really seems to be quite simple (1991, p. 211). Yet we know that it
takes considerable knowledge to be able to "transpose the squiggles." And
beyond *that,* there is still much to learn. Over the years, teachers have expended
much energy in searching for programs and materials that will help them offer
their students meaningful reading instruction. Unfortunately, in so doing, they
often have taken children so far away from an authentic reading context that
the process of learning to read has become overwhelmingly complex for both
teacher and children. Many teachers have mistakenly become managers of
material rather than practitioners and guides who use materials to enhance
reading instruction.

First, in this chapter, we will briefly examine reading instruction in the United
States: approaches, methodologies, philosophies, beliefs, and materials. As you'll
see, there are recurring trends that resurface over the years. These trends have
spiraled through time, expanding and developing with each new recurrence
and showing us that although very little in reading instruction is truly "new,"
each time we re-evaluate our teaching methods we enhance what has come
before. It is important to have a realistic perspective on current and future
trends in instruction and to become conversant with the vocabulary of familiar
reading terms and materials. Although methodologies come and go, the guideposts for organizing and facilitating literacy learning have remained constant.
The key is for teachers to recognize developmental benchmarks and use them
as guides for adapting instruction to the needs of each child.

Second, we'll devote a substantial amount of this chapter to examining the
nature and content of instructional materials in reading. As a professional educator, you need to know what is being used in classrooms across the country.
Although this book's approach to teaching reading does not depend on published basal reading programs, such programs *can* be a fine source of multiple
copies of stories, ideas for extension activities, and supplementary background
information on vocabulary, writing style, and literary elements. In addition,
you may find yourself teaching in a school where you'll be required to use
district-mandated materials. However you choose to use published programs
in your school, your most significant instructional resource will be *trade books;*
and while we've given them much attention already in this book, we will
comment on them again in the context of instructional materials.

Third, as we take a close look at the instructional materials that are available across the country, we will examine the workings of a "traditional" basal program and those of a literature-based series. Our focus will be on how you, as a decision-making teacher, can utilize these materials as resources in a collaborative, integrated classroom.

PERSPECTIVE ON READING INSTRUCTION: THE PART/WHOLE SPIRAL

Historically, we can trace in reading instruction recurring trends that emphasize points from quite different perspectives: either the "parts" of reading (the names and the sounds of letters) have been highlighted, or the "whole" (words, sentences, entire stories) has taken precedent. Adults often take at face value the simplicity that Perfetti observed in the quote at the beginning of this chapter: children must learn to "decode" print into speech; then the rest will follow easily. Because this decoding aspect is so obviously necessary, adults have also assumed that learning about the relationships between letters and sounds should be part-to-whole, right from the beginning. This has been a popular assumption since the Greeks invented an alphabet that represented the sounds of consonants and vowels. For centuries since that time, teaching the parts of words before expecting children to read whole words or recall entire stories has been followed in Europe and America (Mathews, 1966; Balmuth, 1982). As we saw in Chapter 2, this is still how most adults believe we should usher children into literacy. So letters and their corresponding sounds have traditionally been taught early and intensively. Eventually, children who mastered these relationships were introduced to real reading material, though the content of this material was quite different from that of today's.

From time to time throughout history, however, there has been a reaction to the part-to-whole orientation. Some educators believed that rather than drilling children in isolated letters or letter groups, and their corresponding sounds, *words* should be focused on from the beginning. Some approaches went *beyond* words to entire selections and their constituent sentences, relying on students' memory for the text as they gradually came to acquire a sight knowledge of many words; only *then* was there any examination of the component letter/sound correspondences. This "part/whole" debate continues, resurfacing each time we re-evaluate the methods and philosophy of teaching reading.

As we take a look at the origins of reading instruction and the materials that have been used to teach reading, I'd like to suggest that rather than going around and around throughout the years, we really are in an instructional *spiral*. That is, there *do* seem to be recurring trends in instructional methods; but as we continually broaden, expand, and refine those methods, we move toward more effective and more meaningful instruction. Figure 10.1 shows this spiral, and we'll consider briefly each important trend that you see represented.

In the seventeenth and eighteenth centuries in America, the materials that

Marilyn Jaeger Adams   *Beginning to Read*   1990
Phonics is important but must be balanced with a rich literacy environment where children are involved in authentic reading and writing experiences.

Jeanne Chall and The Great Debate   1967
Systematic instruction of phonics believed to be more effective in teaching children to read than a "meaning" (whole word) approach.

Rudolph Flesch   1955
Push to return to phonics instruction — teach children the sounds that the letters make and they will learn to read.

Leonard Bloomfield – Linguistic Approach   1930s
Task of reading is to learn how written language represents spoken language. Teach "regular" spelling patterns. Knowledge of individual sounds would grow out of repetitive spelling patterns. Spelling-to-sound knowledge more important than meaning.

Edward Thorndike   1900–1930s
"Father" of Educational Psychology. Developed "Principles of Learning." Sequence of instruction became more important than the child. Only what is observable is measurable.

Progress in Science, Business, and Psychology   Early 1900s
Reading material mirrored "assembly line" production. Reading instruction was broken down into a series of specific skills that were sequenced and packaged.

McGuffey Eclectic Readers   1836
First attempt to create graded reading material. Lesson structure followed a sequence: alphabet, word pronunciation, sentences. Tremendous impact on American education.

Noah Webster   Old Blue-Backed Speller   1783
Attention to letter names and memorized spelling of words in isolation; "spelling" was the key to beginning reading. Reading selections advocating contemporary American values and culture guided the reader to success.

New England Primer   1690s
Repetitive reading and recitation of morally uplifting material led to moral behavior.

Horn Book   Late 1600s
Heavy recitation of the alphabet, simple syllables, and the Lord's Prayer provided the foundation for learning to read.

Bible   1600s
Reading brought about spiritual enlightenment.

"Whole Language"   1980s–1990s
Reading is one aspect of a broader communication context that includes oral language and written language; "meaning making" is at the core; learning is a social phenomenon. The classroom is a place where talking, writing, and reading are modeled and encouraged. Children's exploration of letters and their sounds occurs naturally as children write on their own using "invented spellings."

Writing and Talking   1980s
Conversation in the classroom encouraged. Stories are discussed and modeled. Much time is devoted to having children write on their own using "invented spellings."

Psycholinguistics   1970s
Learning to read is natural and similar to learning to talk. Children learn to read through interacting with adults and other children who read and write.

Language Experience Approach   1960s
Teacher presents learning experience; children discuss and respond. Responses are written down and used as one source of beginning reading material.

"Individualized" Reading   Late 1950s–1960s
Children select literature they wish to read and discuss individually with teacher; skills taught as needed.

Basal Reader Programs   1940s
Large-scale adoption of "whole word" approach. Sight words learned first with phonics instruction introduced later.

Progressivism and Thematic Units   1930s
Encouragement of a more natural approach to beginning reading. Instruction based on children's interests.

John Dewey/Francis Parker and The New Education   1890s
Need for an integrated curriculum. Children will benefit from study of the world around them. Viewed as the "New Education." Emphasis went to the needs of the child first. Learning begins to be viewed as a discovery process.

"Sentence Method"   1880s – 1890s
The sentence is the most natural unit of meaning. Children's thoughts were written in their own words and used as the primary source of reading material.

"Whole Word" Method   1870s – 1890s
Emphasis remaining on the word and its meaning.

Horace Mann   Late 1830s
Advocate of the "word" method. Students focused on words and their meaning rather than on isolated sounds and letters. Beginning of the "part verses whole" debate.

Figure 10.1
The Part/Whole Spiral

were used to teach children to read were fairly sparse, and the actual texts that children read were "adultlike" in format and tone. The purposes for learning to read centered around spiritual enlightenment—reading the Bible.

Late in the seventeenth century the "Hornbook" and the *New England Primer* were widely used. The Hornbook was a small wooden paddle on which were inscribed the alphabet, lists of pronounceable single syllables, and the Lord's Prayer. The *New England Primer* was a printed book that included the alphabet, but with a twist: each letter was accompanied by an illustration and a short sentence, and religious overtones were always present: *A*–"In Adam's fall we sinned all"; *X*—"Xerxes the Great did die, and so shall you and I." These materials afforded sources for reading, repetition, and recitation. Children copied them and chanted them, singly and in groups, over and over.

The character and tone of reading materials changed in the nineteenth century. There were two primary reasons for this. First, there was a strong nationalistic spirit in America and a desire to distinguish American culture from the British. Second, a changing perception of children had by that time developed. Children no longer were seen as "little adults" into whose brains adult knowledge could be drilled, but as individuals whose minds and perceptions were qualitatively different from those of adults. Content shifted away from spirituality and became more oriented toward patriotic, moral conduct, reflecting contemporary American values and culture and employing language more suited to a child's development. Noah Webster played a considerable role here. His book *A Grammatical Institute of the English Language,* published in 1783 (it was known more commonly as the "Old Blue-Backed Speller"), combined beginning reading instruction with spelling instruction (Skeel & Carpenter, 1958). By sequencing words to be studied, Webster's book reflected the theory that children could learn to read words by memorizing how they were spelled. His "Blue-Backed Speller" included reading selections that centered on strong moral behavior; however, primary emphasis was first on learning the names of the letters and on spelling words in isolation.

By 1836 the first edition of the profoundly influential "McGuffey Readers" was published. William Holmes McGuffey, a professor of classics at the University of Virginia, was very interested in the teaching of reading. His singular achievement was to present reading selections that attempted to be uniformly appropriate for children across the grades (see Figure 10.2). The *McGuffey Eclectic Readers* began with structurally simple words arranged in simple sentences (for example, *The cat has a rat* and *The rat ran at Ann*) and built gradually toward more complex sentences, vocabulary, and word-analysis activities. The structure of beginning reading lessons followed a sequence: alphabet, word pronunciation, sentences, stories (Shannon, 1989). As children became more proficient readers, they moved through a series of graded reading books. The McGuffey Readers laid the foundation for the later conception of the basal reading programs that developed in the twentieth century.

Although the McGuffey Readers remained popular into the 1920s, alternate methods of instruction began to surface. In the late 1830s, Horace Mann, Superintendent of Instruction in Massachusetts, advocated what came to be called the "word" method of teaching beginning reading. Attention moved away from

Figure 10.2
Page from a McGuffey Reader

LESSON XX.

mam mä′	lär͘ge	ăṣ	pa pä′
ärmṣ	rīde	fär	bärn
bōth	Prĭn͑çe	trŏt	yo͝ur

Papa, will you let me ride with you on Prince? I will sit still in your arms.

See, mamma! We are both on Prince. How large he is!

Get up, Prince! You are not too fat to trot as far as the barn.

isolated letters and sounds and concentrated on the word and its meaning as a whole. Mann's proposals were highly controversial and began the "part versus whole" debate in reading instruction.

As the "word" method grew in popularity, and as teachers began to use it in combination with the earlier phonics approaches, later in the nineteenth century educational giants such as Francis Parker and John Dewey began to see a need to "integrate literacy instruction into elementary curricula based on children's interests, needs and inclinations; that is, to make literacy a natural consequence of children's study of their physical and social environment" (Shannon, 1989, p. 10). Thus some attention was given to a more "natural" approach, which also emphasized the "word" method. This was also a time when the "sentence" method gained some visibility. This method assumed that the *sentence* was the most logical and meaningful unit in language, so what the child expressed in his or her own words was written down by the teacher and used as the primary reading material. These more "natural" approaches were part of what came to be referred to as the "New Education," a significant reconceptualization of schooling and of schools. This movement placed primary emphasis on the needs of the child and grew out of a way of thinking that emerged from European philosophers such as Jean-Jacques Rousseau, who believed in a child's natural goodness and lively curiosity. Also accompanying this perspective was the newly emerging "science" of psychology (Cremin, 1961, 1980; Shannon, 1989).

In the last quarter of the nineteenth century, many reading programs in the form of sets of books were being published. By the twentieth century, these programs became the primary medium for delivering reading instruction. Interaction among the fields of psychology, business, and science had influenced this development (Chall, 1987; Duffy, Roehler, & Putnam, 1987). The scientific advances were primarily in the area of technology, and they supported what was happening in business: manufacturing processes were streamlined, and increased efficiency made for increased productivity. Workers were trained to perform specific tasks in very precise, sequenced ways. So, many educators thought that the principles that guided science and business could guide instruction as well. This belief was supported by the "principles of learning" that the new science of psychology was offering, in particular through the work of Edward Thorndike (1913), the "father" of educational psychology. Thorndike's "principles of learning" suggested a sequence of instruction that would lead most efficiently to the acquisition of *observable skills*. This orientation would later be called stimulus-response psychology or behavioral psychology. Individuals' *behavior* was studied to determine whether and how learning was occurring.

There was support for the theory that what worked for business would work for education, and science and psychology supported this perception. Reading instruction could be broken down into specific skills, sequenced from easy to difficult, and packaged in a format that was easily used by pupils and teachers: the basal reader. For most of the twentieth century, basal readers remained the primary means of reading instruction.

In the 1930's, the noted American linguist Leonard Bloomfield influenced the design of a type of specialized reading material, eventually published in the early 1960s when it became known as the "linguistic" approach to reading. Bloomfield believed that the job of linguistics was to describe language as it is spoken and written—to describe what is observable (1933). Unlike the psycholinguists who would follow him many years later, he believed that one cannot study the role of *thought* or *meaning* in language, because they are not observable. He contended that the task of reading, therefore, is to learn how written language represents spoken language. He knew that young children have difficulty breaking words down into individual sounds, so he bypassed this step altogether and introduced words that were "regular" in terms of spelling pattern (*rat, cat, fat,* and so on) and avoided as much as possible all "irregularly" spelled words (such as *of*). The order in which words were presented in this approach was carefully controlled.

Bloomfield assumed that children would naturally figure out individual letter/sound correspondences in words by looking at repetitive spelling patterns where the single distinguishing feature falls on the beginning consonant. Since the most important factor in a linguistic program is the spelling-to-sound knowledge, rather than meaning, a passage from a linguistic reader will sound a bit contrived: *Dan and Pam bat a ragbag. Dan took a bat and hit the ragbag. Pam took the bat and hit the bag. Nat took the bag and hid it. Pam ran and got the bag* (*Merrill Linguistic Readers,* Book A, 1966, p. 30). The influence of Bloomfield's idea about the need to control the spelling patterns in words can still be seen in many basal reading programs to this day.

Another outgrowth of psychology and science that would affect the nature and content of basal reading programs was *standardized testing.* Standardized testing became more widespread: first with respect to intelligence testing, and soon after with respect to reading (Gould, 1981). A link inevitably developed between the specific objectives listed in reading programs and what was tested by the standardized tests. A climate of *accountability* developed in which teachers believed they should stay close to the basal program so that their students would do well on the tests—and so that they themselves would be perceived to be doing their job well.

In the 1930s, in reaction in part to the systematizing of reading and of education more generally, the educational movement termed "Progressivism" fully emerged. Like the New Education of the late nineteenth century, this movement endorsed a more natural approach to beginning reading, that of basing instruction on children's interests and using their own language. This was a time when "integrated units" were in vogue: a common *theme* would unify instruction across the language arts and the elementary curriculum in science, social studies, math, and so on. The movement represented the application of many of John Dewey's ideas about education. During this time, the basal readers began to take what many educators would say was a significant turn when they came to be grounded in the "whole word" or "look-say" method; these types of basals were best exemplified by the "Dick and Jane" readers published by Scott, Foresman, and Company beginning in the 1940s.

The "look-say" method came under severe criticism in 1955 with the publication of Rudolf Flesch's book *Why Johnny Can't Read.* Flesch charged that the reason why children weren't learning to read was the schools weren't teaching phonics. With the "look-say" method, Flesch argued, children weren't learning how to sound out unknown words. This argument was bolstered a decade later with the publication of a landmark book in reading education, Jeanne Chall's *Learning to Read: The Great Debate* (1967). Chall's basic message was that early and systematic instruction in phonics, rather than a focus on word meaning, appeared to be more effective in getting children under way in reading. Flesch's book along with Chall's pushed basal reader programs into an up-front presentation of phonics.

Throughout this new controversy, there *were* small voices supporting the use of children's literature—real literature—as the primary medium for reading instruction. Like most ideas, this was not a new one (Templeton, 1990), although more educators were writing about it now than in earlier years (see, for instance, Veatch, 1959). They spoke of *individualized* reading programs, which simply meant that each child would be reading a book that interested him or her and discussing it with the teacher, while necessary skills would be taught as the need arose. The Language Experience Approach espoused by Stauffer and Allen (Allen, 1976; Stauffer, 1969) was philosophically allied with individualized reading and became increasingly popular during this time as well. During the late 1960s and early 1970s, the new field of *psycholinguistics* influenced thinking about reading instruction (Smith, 1971, 1972; Goodman, 1967; Goodman & Fleming, 1969). Literacy educators such as Frank Smith and Kenneth Goodman looked at the insights from this field and found support for the notion that learning how to read should be more "natural," more like learning how to talk, and that reading would be more likely to occur if it were *not* broken down into presumed "skills" and presented in a sequenced, step-by-step fashion. Children would learn to read by reading, and the teacher's role should be to do what might be necessary to support the child in that process. This "natural" view of education is reminiscent of the ideas of the mid-nineteenth century, when individual needs of the child were being met by using his or her own language to create reading text.

If learning to read should be more natural, then *what* is read should be more natural and engaging to children as well. During the 1970s, a move toward making literature the primary focus of instruction surfaced once again. This literature-based movement merged with two other developments in the late 1970s and early 1980s: emphasis on *writing* or composition (Calkins, 1983; Graves, 1983; Murray, 1968), and acknowledgment of the value of *talk* in the classroom (Barnes, 1976; Hymes and Cazden, 1972). There was, in other words, a realization that learning is a social phenomenon and should involve lots of conversation in response to reading and writing. Children do pick up knowledge about letters and their sounds through exposure to and practice with authentic reading and writing experiences. These combined movements came to be termed the "whole language" approach, a philosophy about teaching and learning rather than a specific method (Goodman, 1987; Altwerger, Edelsky, & Flores, 1987). Within this philosophy, "reading" is conceptualized as part of a total language-and-learning environment; reading develops and becomes refined in the course of pursuing meaningful goals.

With the growth of the whole language movement, the "phonics" controversy flared again at the beginning of the 1990s. Marilyn Jaeger Adams's book *Beginning to Read* (1990) reviewed more recent studies of beginning reading and the role of phonics knowledge in learning to read. She concluded that teaching phonics is important *but* should be done in the context of a rich literacy environment in which children are reading and writing (as they are encouraged to invent their spellings), not as an isolated and meaningless set of drills.

Now, at the end of the twentieth century, we continue our upward spiral. In our brief look back, however, it has become clear that throughout history there has been a process of refinement and expansion in reading instruction and a growing advocacy of a more meaningful, literature-based literacy environment. As we keep learning how to do a better job of integrating the parts with the whole, we are also more aware of what is *less* successful and *less* motivating with children. Today's distinctive interest in basing instruction on real literature stands on the shoulders of many educators who have gone before us. They sought and advocated a more authentic, motivating climate and approach to reading instruction. As we build on the knowledge of the past, we have the potential for developing integrated literature-based instruction in far more classrooms that ever before. We have only to focus *meaningful* attention on the "basics" that critics of reading instruction have emphasized over the years.

INSTRUCTIONAL MATERIALS: WHAT YOU CAN EXPECT TO FIND IN TODAY'S CLASSROOM

Throughout this text, I've been advocating a particular approach to teaching literacy, one that helps children construct meaning in a developmentally appropriate context, where diversity is valued and students are immersed in authentic literature. This is a place where "reading" permeates the whole classroom and the whole curriculum, for reading should not be addressed within the narrow confines of a particular set of materials. Now that we've explored almost all the foundations and applications of an approach grounded in children, literature, and learning about reading as a tool, you may wonder why I'm now devoting most of a chapter to an overview of materials.

One reason is that I strongly believe that prospective teachers need to be familiar with what is "out there" in classrooms. Just as it is important to know about trends in reading instruction over the years, it is important to be aware of prevailing materials and approaches, as well as of their advantages and drawbacks. In your teaching, you undoubtedly will work on occasion with teachers who swear by one particular approach or set of materials. The more you know about that approach or those materials, the more confident you'll be about your own approach and your own instructional decisions. You've already seen that there often is resistance to new perspectives on teaching reading. If you yourself are regarded as "new" (a common criticism of new teachers is that they are too idealistic), you can gain respect if it's clear that you are familiar with what is already being used and can acknowledge its advantages. Then you can work toward establishing perhaps a quite different reading instructional environment. A second reason for an in-depth look at materials is that if you are required to teach in a school where a set of materials must dominate, or if as a novice teacher you choose to use the framework of a published program as a guide for instruction, there will be many adaptations and modifications that you'll want to make. The information we'll discuss throughout the rest of this chapter should serve you well as an extremely important part of your knowledge base.

Basal reader programs

From what we know about reading materials in the classroom, it's evident that a teacher needs a clear understanding of a typical basal reader program and that there are three reasons why this is so:

■ Basal reader programs have defined the predominant type of reading instruction in the United States for almost a century.

■ Such programs are still much in use throughout the nation, so you may be teaching in a district that has them available or has mandated their use.

■ As we'll trace later on, a significantly different type of published program—the literature-based series—has recently evolved from the traditional basal reader program. It is helpful to look at the particulars of this evolution.

Defining the Basal   The term *basal reader program* or simply *basal* suggests that this material is the "base" or foundation of reading instruction. It is a set of books graded in difficulty level, with accompanying teacher's guides; the program is prepared by authors and publishing staffs in conjunction with reading educators in universities, in school administration, and in elementary classrooms. Traditionally, a basal reading program usually has taken one instructional focus. Some of the programs have placed much emphasis on letter/sound instruction in isolation, while others have taken a more contextualized direction. Regardless of whether or not a program features skills instruction over meaningful context, most programs include a number of ancillary materials that supplement instruction; the chief ancillary item usually is a student's workbook. Many teachers and administrators have traditionally regarded the basal as the "base" or foundation of reading instruction (Shannon, 1989; Goodman, Shannon, Freeman, & Murphy, 1988; Harste, 1989): We have already noted how basal reader programs often have been perceived as *the* core of reading instruction and must be "covered" first, before other types of reading instruction occur; for example, because of the perceived importance of the skills covered in workbook pages, teachers frequently require children to complete these assignments before being allowed to take out a library book for "free" reading.

Key Elements   Basal programs include three key elements: (1) the programs are primarily *skills-based;* (2) they are constructed according to a *controlled vocabulary;* and (3) instruction is presented primarily through the Directed Reading Activity. Let's consider each in turn.

Basal programs reflect a *"skills-based"* premise. A *scope and sequence* of skills is presented from primary grades through intermediate. Commonly, a scope and sequence includes subdivision of skills into decoding and phonics, or word analysis and vocabulary development; comprehension—literal, inferential, and critical; language and literature; and study skills. More recently, the skill strands of most basals have also incorporated literary elements such as plot, character, setting, and so forth. Under these umbrella topics, subskills are then divided. For example, the Macmillan program (Arnold et al., 1989) lists "main idea," "cause and effect," and "drawing conclusions" as subskills to be addressed under *comprehension.*

There is a clear focus at the primary levels on narratives. Beginning (to a limited degree) at the third-grade level and considerably increased at fourth grade, informational selections are included. Typically, each story or nonfiction piece is used to present or reinforce a particular subskill. The teacher is instructed to include the skill strands before, during, and after the reading experience. For example, in Silver Burdett & Ginn's World Reading Series (Clymer et al., 1989), each lesson is organized into three areas—"Vocabulary Strategies," "Guiding

Comprehension," and "Extending Skills"—each presented with a teaching sequence and referenced to accompanying practice pages. Individual stories begin with a strand titled "The Bridge," which presents the subskill objective for the story. Sample subskill objectives include predicting logical outcomes, noting details, and identifying character traits and emotions; these objectives mirror subskills presented in the scope and sequence.

Another important feature of basals is their *controlled vocabulary*. Only certain words are used, based on the criteria of frequency (how often they occur in spoken and written language) and spelling patterns (how "regular" they are—how easy to decode and learn). The assumption is that these words will be learned quickly as sight words. While vocabulary is "controlled" at all grade levels, the effects of controlled vocabulary are particularly obvious at the first-grade level and, to a degree, at the second-grade level as well. In addition, sentences are shorter at these early levels and syntactically quite simple. For these reasons, the language at these levels often strikes one as stilted and unnatural.

As the grade levels advance, vocabulary and sentence structure in the basals gradually become more difficult, more complex. Selections from children's books are included, though until recent years they were often adjusted to fit readability formulas (see below). The format according to which the teacher walks students through a selection is termed a *Directed Reading Activity* (DRA). In the DRA, the teacher presents new words or new skills prior to the reading of a selection; in reading the selection, the students are expected to be able to apply the new skills. Questions are asked during and after the reading to check whether or not the students are understanding the selection. Follow-up work reinforces the particular skills that have been taught.

One shortcoming of these "scripts" in the DRA is that although they present many questions, they do not present guidelines for appropriately *teaching* how to go about comprehending what is being read. If a teacher follows the script and a student cannot answer a question, the teacher simply asks another student. There have been few guidelines for modeling the process through which the appropriate answer can be identified (Durkin, 1981). In recent years, in response to much research in comprehension processes, guidelines and, usually, specific "scripts" for modeling have often been included in the teacher's guide.

Key Components   Traditionally, a basal reader program has had the following components:

1. *A series of graded reading books*. At the first-grade level, there are five separate books: three *preprimers* (*primer* is pronounced with a short *i*), one *primer*, and the "first reader." At the second-grade level, there are two books, each designated with a superscript: 2^1 and 2^2. Third grade continues this type of designation, 3^1 and 3^2; and at fourth grade, publishers have either two books or a single anthology. After fourth grade, most publishers uniformly have a single reader for grade five and one for grade six. Typically, this is how basals have been organized; however, the number of books per grade level may change, depending on the publisher.

2. *Teacher's Guides*. Originally an additional section at the back of a student book, the teacher's edition or teacher's guide of today is a separate volume that

organizes and systematizes reading instruction. Specific skills are comprehensively presented and reinforced. Each selection is presented via the Directed Reading Activity format just described. The teacher's guides present the scope and sequence of skills in chart form over a few pages, which enables you to see what is covered at each grade level and across all the grade levels.

Figure 10.3 shows a page from the fourth-grade teacher's edition for *Clearing Paths* of the American Readers (D. C. Heath, 1986). This page contains the introductory vocabulary, skills, and reading-and-discussing lessons that are to precede the reading of an Asian folktale called "The Seeing Stick" (p. 337). At the close of the instructions, ancillary practice pages and developing comprehension exercises are listed along with reminders about how to set purposes and predict the story's outcome.

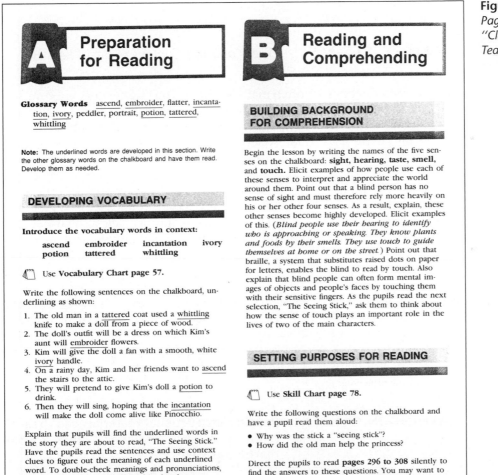

Figure 10.3
Page from American Readers: "Clearing Paths" (Grade 4) Teacher's Edition

3. *Ancillary materials.* Ancillary materials reinforce the direct instruction given by the teacher—*and* traditionally have been used for independent seatwork while the teacher works with a small group. In the early days, a single workbook accompanied the basal textbook. Programs still offer a workbook (usually called by a different name) and supplementary materials such as teacher's "resource" books with additional teaching suggestions, along with blackline masters to be photocopied for additional "practice." There is more: kits, language development programs at the kindergarten and first-grade levels, charts, manipulatives, and audiocassettes of selected stories.

Not only the content of basal programs, but the way in which teachers have been encouraged to "teach" each selection has led to dissatisfaction. It could take an entire week, sometimes longer, to get through a single story if all the activities, worksheets, workbook pages, and so on were undertaken. Originally

MAKING CONNECTIONS: *Society and the Content of Basal Readers*

The early levels of basal readers presented stories centered around the lives of Dick, Jane, Sally, Mother, Father, and the family dog and cat, Spot and Puff. These characters have become almost legendary in American culture, having been part of the experience of most young Americans on through the 1960s. Beginning in the 1960s and continuing into the 1970s and 1980s, some researchers began to examine what the content of reading programs really represented and what possible effects it could have.

The family scenario portrayed by Dick and Jane began to raise questions. In the 1960s, in the wake of the burgeoning civil rights movement, it suddenly became apparent to basal publishers that all the people in their stories were middle-class Caucasians. The rise of the Women's Movement led to a similar analysis of the basals. How were women and girls being portrayed? "Mother" was always at home—very often in the kitchen—and "Father" had a job outside the home. Problems were solved by male characters while the females looked on. The publishers' first adjustment was to include middle-class African-Americans. Inclusion of the many cultures that make up our society has become substantive over the years, so selections about influential historical figures from a variety of backgrounds are now included. In recent years, basal authors have also given much attention to other excluded groups, such as the elderly and people with handicaps. Female characters have been given an equal share of diverse, active roles.

Scholars suggest that basals were simply reflecting mainstream society. And yet we must be aware of how something as "harmless" as reading materials can in fact promote and sustain society's less than commendable values and attitudes.

LEARNING IN CONTEXT: Reading instructional materials can "teach" more than just "reading": Their *content* teaches, as well.

intended to be supportive, these components became capable of dominating the entire reading experience.

Changes in the Basal Interest and enthusiasm for introducing children to stimulating literature began to take hold throughout the 1960s and 1970s. Although basals began including trade-book stories in their reading anthologies, they did so by altering the text to fit readability formulas. This was, however, the starting point for a re-evaluation of the content and organization of the traditional basal reader. In addition, publishers responded to *Becoming a Nation of Readers* (Anderson, Hiebert, Scott, & Wilkinson, 1985), which called for a "decision-making" teacher who could emphasize basic skills while instilling a love of reading.

Change occurred as many basal reader programs began to de-emphasize subskills and focused more on constructing meaning and experiencing authentic literature. The late 1980s saw the last of the development of traditional basal materials. School districts began looking for basal reader programs that reflected a new perspective on involving children in the act of reading. It was through this process that literature-based reading series evolved.

Literature-based reading programs

How the Literature-Based Program Evolved from the Basal In the late 1980s, primarily in response to California's Reading Initiative that emphasized literature-based instruction, publishers began offering reading series that were noticeably different from the traditional basals. First and foremost, these new programs *were* literature-based. Quality selections were included *as they had been written originally,* rather than being adapted and adjusted according to readability formulas. In the literature-based series, illustrations accompanying the stories appear just as they were in the original trade book. These illustrations are an inherent part of the whole text. Even though in later years there was actually a fair amount of literature in the more traditional basals, given all the skill instruction and workbook assignments that preceded the reading, it took a long time to get to it. What may in fact be the chief distinguishing characteristics of literature-based basals are their *integration* with the other language arts and their *thematic* organization. They are, therefore, broader in focus than their predecessors.

Previously, basals had given only a nod to the other language arts. The new literature-based reading series show an obvious effort to be more substantive. You will see explicit attention given to different types of writing, to spelling, and to other areas of the elementary curriculum. Instruction is organized around thematic units with a specific focus and a "core" work that represents that theme, with suggestions for readings, projects, and activities in other subject areas. Notably, at the primary levels, narratives are balanced with informational selections; traditionally this was only done in the upper grades.

Components and Elements of the Literature-Based Program The underlying organization of literature-based reading series is very much like that of traditional basals: in most series there are the same number of books at each grade level as in the traditional basal programs. This is an acknowledgment of the expectations of the marketplace. Publishers know that if the program's look and manageability vary too greatly from what teachers have been familiar with over the years, the series may not sell. Beginning at the kindergarten level, the programs include many activities to promote language development and facilitate emergent readers and writers—the conventions of print, for example, and alphabet letters and their names.

Teacher's guides have a different look. Publishers have to walk a fine line here, too: the guides must be supportive but not organized too differently from what teachers have been used to. Remember that for many teachers a teacher's guide will be their primary resource, not only for instruction but for information about how to teach reading in a literature-based format. There is a notable shift in instruction from assigning or only partially modeling strategies to more comprehensive modeling, with suggested "think-aloud" strategies. These strategies stem from the recent research in comprehension (discussed in Chapters 2, 6, and 7). In addition, evaluation components are in most cases a closer match with what is being taught in the series.

Figure 10.4 shows a page from the Teacher's Book for *Dinosauring,* the first of two fourth-grade books in the Houghton Mifflin Literature Experience program (1993). This page shows how to use context to decipher unknown words. The lesson is presented in a think-aloud format using Dianne Snyder's retelling of the Asian folktale *The Boy of the Three-Year Nap.* The modeling segment is followed by suggestions for teacher-guided, independent, and cooperative reading. The suggestions presented on this page are open to adaptation and modification so that teachers can customize reading experiences to meet their students' needs.

■ MEANING MAKERS: YOU, THE STUDENT

Compare and Contrast Traditional Basals and Literature-Based Series

With a partner, examine the teacher's guide from a basal program published before 1986. Do the same with the guide from a literature-based series. If you wish, begin with the two lessons excerpted in this chapter. Be particularly careful to notice whether the terminology being used in a teacher's guide truly meshes with the series' actual methodology. Take some time to evaluate how each lesson is organized. As you look over the different programs, pay particular attention to differences in the tone of the language used to address the teacher, the types of activities outlined, and the nature of the ancillary materials to be used. Skim a reading selection; then refer back to the overview planning pages, considering the quality of the reading selection and how the extension activities help guide the reader to apply distinctive reading strategies to understanding the story. Together you and your partner should make some interesting discoveries. ■

Figure 10.4
Literature-Based Series

TEACHER MODELING   To model the Reading New Words Strategy for students, use the Think Aloud that follows. Have students open their Anthologies to page 17 and follow along as you read aloud the beginning of the story:

THINK ALOUD *On the banks of the river Nagara, where the long-necked . . .* Suppose I had started to read the story and I came to a word I didn't know: *c-o-r-m-o-r-a-n-t-s*. The first thing that I would do is finish reading the sentence to see if it gives me any clues about the word's meaning: *. . . fish at night, there once lived a poor widow and her son.* I can tell from the context that it is something that has a long neck and fishes, but I don't know what it is. I don't know if it is important to the story, so I'll read a little more to see if the story context can help me.

All day long the widow sewed silk kimonos for the rich ladies in town. As she worked, her head bobbed up and down, up and down, like the heads of the birds hunting for fish.

From reading this next paragraph I learn that the widow's head bobs up and down like the heads of birds hunting for fish. Using this clue and the context clues I learned from reading the first sentence, I learn that *c-o-r-m-o-r-a-n-t-s* are long-necked birds that hunt for fish.

To figure out how to pronounce it, I will look for familiar words or word parts in this unfamiliar word. I see the words *or* and *ants* in the word, and the letters *c-o-r-m* remind me of the word *corn.* I know how to pronounce *corn; c-o-r-m* is probably similar except for the *m* sound at the end. If I put all my decoding clues together I get *cormorants.* If I want to check my pronunciation, or if I remain uncertain of the meaning of the word, I can look it up in the dictionary.

RECOMMENDED WAY TO READ THE SELECTION

Teacher-Guided Reading

Based on the complexity of the story line and the vocabulary challenges, most students will have a better understanding of the story if they are guided through the first reading. Use the Teacher's Resources labeled Teacher-Guided Reading to guide students through the story.

ALTERNATIVE WAYS TO READ THE SELECTION

Independent Reading

Strong readers who are comfortable using the Reading New Words Strategy may be able to read the story independently and should be encouraged to do so.

Cooperative Reading

Proficient readers who would benefit from some support should read the story with a partner or in a small group as an alternative to teacher-guided reading.

Lynn Dennison is a second-grade teacher in her third year of teaching. Her district recently adopted a literature-based series with which she feels fairly comfortable. While her college preparation focused somewhat on integrated language arts and thematic-based instruction, she did not encounter many helpful resources or much "hands-on" guidance. At this point in her teaching career, she is happy to have a series that will help her build a repertoire of literature experiences for her students.

The literature-based series she will be using is Houghton Mifflin's *Literature Experience* (Pikulski et al., 1993). Lynn begins with the unit called "Funny Business." There are three stories in this themed unit: "The Wolf's Chicken Stew," "The Portrait," and an excerpt from *Amelia Bedelia.* The first day of the new theme, the children discuss the overall theme in their books and share particularly funny experiences they have had.

In contrast to the basal that Lynn Dennison used during her first two years of teaching, this literature-based series is set up in a "menu" format; there is no preset sequence or prescribed skill guide. Her teacher's manual provides a range of activities and strategies to choose from, in order to meet the needs of her students. For example, if certain children could benefit from a discussion of new words that appear in the first story, "The Wolf's Chicken Stew," she can draw on the section labeled "Developing Selection Vocabulary." If she feels that some children need to develop their risk-taking in making predictions, she'll look at what the sections labeled "Preview and Predict" and "Activating Prior Knowledge" have to offer. Although this year she does not have any students learning English as a second language, she sees the value of the "Language/Concept Development for ESL Students" section and includes those activities in her choices when planning her lessons.

After the whole-class discussion about humor, Lynn will work with smaller groups of children. These small groups will not necessarily be organized by reading ability, but will reflect her students' varying needs in preparation and instruction before the first story is read. Then the whole class will read and discuss the story. While suggesting that the entire story be read at the same time by all the children, the teacher's manual does offer alternatives for reading: independent reading, cooperative reading, and teacher-guided reading. Lynn also has the option of meeting with small groups of children to highlight particular portions of the text. Ideas for such discussions appear throughout the teacher's manual; the topics may or may not be the same for each group. The manual also offers suggestions for teacher read-aloud books that are appropriate for the whole class.

Some children in Lynn Dennison's class cannot read the selection on their own—the story is at their frustration level. These children can comprise a small group for teacher-guided reading of a different text, at their instructional level, with follow-up reading to be done with a "buddy"; in addition, the manual suggests additional stories and books that such students should be able to read on their own and that fit with the theme.

The seatwork that goes with the series incorporates collaborative projects and assignments and addresses writing, spelling, and oral language development. It also creates links with other curricular areas, on the basis of the theme. All these activities rely heavily on student's opinions and creativity as well as on students' need to interact and discuss their learning. Lynn likes the ways the projects and activities support her writing instruction and extend into the areas of math, science, and social studies. Although there is not always time to complete the larger project suggestions for each reading selection, she enjoys having a source for ideas when she *is* able to extend her reading themes into other areas.

As Lynn Dennison plans for each story within the thematic unit, she is able to vary her instructional techniques and custom-design her lessons for her students on the basis of the story to be read. She enjoys the freedom this type of series gives her.

■ ■ ■ ■ ■

Supplementary programs and materials

These programs and materials are meant to reinforce ongoing reading instruction rather than stand as programs in their own right. Of the total amount of money spent on reading-related instructional materials, two-thirds is spent on basals, published programs or literature series and their ancillaries. The remaining third is spent on supplemental materials (Chall & Squire, 1991). These supplemental materials primarily include, for example, workbook and skill sheet activities, additional graded books, manipulatives, cassettes, and computer software. (See your educational librarian or your reading/language arts professor about borrowing copies of catalogues from educational publishers. Browse through the catalogues to get an idea of the range and magnitude of these "supplemental" supplies.)

Often teachers purchase supplemental skills programs for phonics and comprehension instruction if they believe that there is not enough instructional support and reinforcement for these areas in the adopted basal program or literature-based series. Besides skill programs, teachers often look for "idea" books that will serve as sources of inspiration when planning units of study, writing activities, or extension projects. They also seek out audiocassettes, filmstrips, and videotapes of favorite stories. As we noted in the section on basal programs, publishers know that educators are consumers of products. We consider materials in terms of (1) how well they will work with our students and (2) how efficiently they can be used. We are also susceptible to the same enticements as anyone else. Knowing this, publishers of supplemental materials will often use current labels to name or describe their programs: *literature-based, whole language,* and *integrated* are very common descriptors at present. Some of these materials are quite good; others—despite what their labels suggest—are primarily low-level skill-and-drill.

Print Materials Increasingly, supplemental literature-based units are being published with ready-made "themes" (see Chapter 9) organized around a

Being Informed About Augmented Alphabet "Solutions" to Literacy Learning

People want their children to learn to read as easily and quickly as possible. Because this desire is so strong, many parents and educators alike may be overly impressed by commercial programs that seem to offer a surefire method for ensuring that all children learn to read. Materials using an *augmented alphabet* represent one such commercial attempt.

Programs that use an augmented alphabet assume that the most important thing for children to learn is how print represents speech. An impediment to this learning is the supposed irregularity of the match between individual letters and their sounds in conventional spelling. The programs' answer to this problem is to have a separate letter for each sound in the language. Most augmented alphabets have over forty symbols or letters. Materials are printed in this alphabet, and children learn to read using it and then "transition" into "traditional orthography." For example, in one such augmented alphabet, the "long a" sound is represented by the symbol "æ"; long "o" is "œ"; the sound at the end of *ring* is ŋ.

It would seem that a one symbol/one sound correspondence would make matters easier. In actuality, however, most children can learn the spelling-to-sound system as it actually is—and in the process, have access to a far greater number of books that they can read and that are, of course, written with conventional English spelling (Read, 1975).

At the present time, there is very little use of augmented alphabet materials in American schools. Proposals to have a more regular spelling-to-sound system continue to crop up, however. There is even a Simplified Spelling Society that once had the support of President Theodore Roosevelt. The argument these proposals raise is that a simplified system would help children learn to read and spell more easily. It is important, however, that you be aware that most children do not "learn to read" or make the transition to traditional spelling more rapidly by learning an augmented alphabet (Read, 1975), as opposed to being engaged in an integrated, literature-rich learning environment.

LEARNING IN CONTEXT: **If *we* provide the appropriate context and guidance, most children can learn conventional spelling-to-sound correspondences; "simplified" or augmented alphabets are unnecessary and can in fact stand in the way of children's access to literature.**

particular children's book. Many of these units are in fact quite good and may give you ideas for links that can be made on the basis of an individual book. A cautionary word: many of the ready-made theme books provide little more than blackline masters to be duplicated for students to complete. If you are looking for a more comprehensive discussion of how themes are organized and how they work to advance reading and writing across the curriculum, you may find books like Joy Moss's *Focus on Literature* (1990) and *The WEB (Wonderfully Exciting Books)* (1989) from Ohio State University to be more helpful. Journals and periodicals such as *The Reading Teacher, Language Arts, Instructor,* and *Book Links* serve as invaluable resources for ideas on integrating the language arts, for reviews of newly released children's literature, and for collections of successful, teacher-tested, instructional techniques.

You will also find guides for using and selecting children's literature; one of the finest on the market at this time is *Collected Perspectives,* edited by Hughes Moir, et al. (1992). This guide offers a superbly organized selection of children's books—all cross-referenced by theme, genre, grade level, and related topic. Each entry offers a description of the book, tells about additional work by the same author and other books on the same topic, and suggests discussion ideas and related projects. In addition to the ready-made theme books and the guides for using literature in the classroom, there are many resource books that present background information on children's authors and illustrators, as well as collections of literature response ideas involving puppet-making, Readers Theater, storytelling, bookmaking, and interactive writing activities and bulletin boards.

You will also find guide books for linking literature with math, science, and social studies. These materials usually highlight individual trade books or oral traditions, suggest a series of extension activities that call for experimentation and application of math and science concepts, and propose links to cultural origins and creative expression. Books of this nature include *Math and Literature,* by Marilyn Burns (1992); *Science through Children's Literature,* by Carol M. Butzow and John W. Butzow (1989); and *Keepers of the Earth,* by Michael J. Caduto and Joseph Bruchac (1989).

A number of published materials appearing in recent years have been specifically targeting the period of beginning reading. We have referred to some of them earlier in this book, specifically in Chapters 3 and 5. These materials consist primarily of predictable books that are sequenced in complexity. Unlike basal selections at beginning levels, however, these little books are engaging and lend themselves to a variety of activities and purposes. The most commonly used programs are from the *Story Box* (Wright Group), Rigby, and Scholastic. Each of these companies also publishes Big Books and oversized editions of picture books. Scholastic, in particular, now offers subscriptions to Big Book magazines: *Big Book Magazine* covers a variety of language topics often integrated with social studies themes such as the environment or Native American cultures. *Big Science* magazine presents information on topics such as light and sound, reptiles, or bones, followed by easy-to-replicate demonstrations and experiments. In addition, a wide variety of children's newspapers and other magazines are also available. Among the most popular are *Weekly Reader* and *Scholastic News, Zoobooks,* and *Ranger Rick.* I have listed several others in Chapter 7.

Teacher-Made Materials   As you work through your weekly plans, you will discover that you need certain items you will have to make yourself. In a classroom that reflects the teaching methodology set forth in this book (regardless of whether you're using a traditional basal reader, a literature-based reading series, a literature study of one author or genre, a thematic unit based solely in language arts or one that crosses into other curricular areas), you will be customizing the content and format of these series, programs, or units of study to meet your students' developmental needs. This in turn will determine the types of materials you will need to make. For example, when looking at story elements such as plot, character, or setting, you may find your lesson would be best guided by a reusable chart where you and your students can list examples from the story. Instead of making a new chart every time, you may find it advantageous to create a visually pleasing chart that you can laminate and then use over again with many different stories. The same can be true for collecting background information about authors or charting repetitive story structures and topics used by particular authors. A chart of this nature might provide areas to record the author's name and birthplace, story titles, repetitive elements, and so forth. You may also want to use enlarged pictures of specific story characters or examples of a particular illustrative technique—various watercolor brush strokes used by Ed Young might be one idea. In addition, you may want to make your own Big Book version of a classroom favorite.

When your students engage in word study activities, you will need picture cards and word cards. However, not every child will be working with the same phonics or spelling elements. Some may be focusing on beginning sounds; others may be looking at irregular vowel patterns. You will, therefore, need a supply of words and pictures to choose from, and the pictures or words you select will depend on the word sorts your students will be doing. You may want to set up word-sort packets that reinforce particular spelling patterns. For instance, one packet may ask students to sort fifteen picture cards according to the short *a* in *cat* and the short *o* in *dog;* another may use word cards and ask students to group the words by letter combinations that make the long *e* sound.

Some of the material you create will deal with the nuts and bolts of reading and writing. Suppose you need to expose your students to different types of friendly-letter formats. You and your students could collect letters from different sources and compile them in a book for easy reference. Perhaps a large number of your students are struggling to remember the more difficult contractions *won't* and *he'd.* In this case you may need to create individual flip books or quick-reference adhesive strips for their desks. You may want to make visuals that will remind students to use specific reading strategies when tackling informational texts. The whys and hows of creating teacher-made materials stem from the daily business of guiding children's learning. (And this book is also devoted to helping you become a decision-making teacher who'll know how to use any published program or set of materials to meet your students' needs.)

Traditional Audiovisual Materials   These include cassettes, filmstrips, 35 mm films, and videotapes. In the past, some audiovisual materials focused on specific subskills and complemented or extended workbook pages. Today, however, the materials available through reading programs, school libraries, and book clubs offer exceptionally well-produced readings, animated presentations, and re-creations of favorite stories and tales, as well as collaborative games that require children to apply critical thinking and other skills. In addition, there are filmstrips and videos that humorously engage children in identifying punctuation, parts of speech, and elements of style. Cassettes and videos often feature authors, artists, musicians, and other well-known public figures. Recently, companies have begun showcasing interviews with authors and illustrators, in addition

Many children love to listen to stories on tape. Such audio-visual materials offer excellent reading, animated presentations, and recreations of favorite stories and tales.

to featuring audiocassettes with authors reading their own stories. Through audiovisual materials, too, you will be able to make ties across the curriculum, particularly with science and social studies. Following are several sources of quality audiovisual materials.

BUILDING YOUR KNOWLEDGE BASE

Sources for Traditional Audiovisual Materials

Troll Instructional Materials
100 Corporate Drive
Mahwah, New Jersey 07340
1-800-526-5289

Clearvue/eav
6465 N. Avondale Avenue
Chicago, IL 6061-1996
1-800-CLEARVU

Sundance
P.O. Box 1326, Newtown Road
Littleton, MA 01460
1-800-343-8204

Listening Library
One Park Avenue
Old Greenwich, CT 06870-1727
1-800-243-4504

■ Churchill Media
  12210 Nebraska Avenue
■ Department 600
  Los Angeles, CA 90025-3600
■ 1-800-334-7830

  Scholastic Inc.
■ 2931 E. McCarty Street
  Jefferson City, MT 65101
■ 1-800-325-6149

■   ■   ■

Computers, Computer Software, and Multimedia Materials   In addition to print and audiovisual materials, an entire computer world is becoming available to educators. Many schools have either one or two computers in each classroom, or the school may have a computer lab for whole-class use. Computer education has become a standard objective in almost every school district's mandated curriculum. The potential of computer-assisted literacy education is significant.

Computers will affect the way we interact with print and the ways we think about print (Bolter, 1991; Landow, 1989; Paulson, 1989). The computer can profoundly affect texts and our ideas about reading and writing, and the social, psychological, and educational impact of computers will probably be as great as that of the printing press. With respect to literacy, therefore, you'll want to be aware of what computers can do. Let's take a quick look at the nature of computers and at how they can affect our way of teaching reading and writing.

Many schools now have one or two computers in each classroom, and the potential of computer assisted literacy is great.

- First of all, the response of a computer is just about immediate. We can see instantaneously the effects of what we do.
- Computers are increasingly user-friendly, speaking to us (sometimes literally) in conversational language.
- Computers are usually quite predictable; we know what we need to do in order to converse with them.
- Once we have learned the basics, computers allow us to connect almost immediately with whatever information we need.
- Computers increase the quality and the speed of our communication with other individuals. Through *e-mail* (electronic mail) we can send written communications to anyone around the globe who has a computer and a telephone. There are specific e-mail links for students as well—both within and outside their own countries.

Now we run up against reality. You have probably heard predictions about every student having a laptop computer and about the educational revolution this will set in motion. This probably won't happen very soon, primarily because of cost. When tight financial times strike school districts, even the purchasing of *books* is curtailed, and computers are farther down the priority list. Assuming even that computers *are* available, however, there is ongoing maintenance to be considered, as well as software that must be purchased and updated.

These problems will of course be addressed, in the long run. After all, the first books were huge objects that no one would have dreamed would someday be mass-produced and be small enough for people to read in bed or take to the beach. (Can you imagine being propped up in bed with a Gutenberg Bible?) Since we are still some years away from the resolution of the present-day problems, though, we'll focus here on how can you use computers in your day-to-day literacy instruction right now.

Wepner effectively captures the role of the computer in reading and language arts: "In other words, the computer is not an embellished drill sheet that is tacked onto a lesson; rather, the software embodies the goals of instruction" (1990, p. 15). Computers can be used to reinforce skills, to explore narratives, to link content curriculum in print and film through videodisc or "multimedia" technology, and as word processors. At present, they can reinforce, complement and extend your instruction. They can motivate simply because they are fun, as in the case of many story-writing programs. They can reinforce strategies you have modeled for students—inferring the answer to a question, for example, or determining the main idea of a paragraph. They can complement and extend experiences with literature and composition. For example, with certain graphics and "paintbrush" programs, students can embellish or create books, as they explore various ways of illustrating a text and experiment with different type faces. More software is being developed that integrates reading and language arts with content areas, allowing students greater flexibility in exploring different information and pursuing different paths.

There is also an important *research* potential in computers for students. While you will continue to need to teach the basics of locating information in the library through the card catalogue and other informational sources, in many cases these tasks are handled by computers. Your college or university library, for example, may already have all its acquisitions on-line, so that you can locate any book, journal, report, film, and so forth via a computer terminal. Many elementary schools are also organizing their holdings this way as well. If you and your students have access to telecommunication programs, there is access to individuals and resources—large data bases—going far beyond what may be found in the school media center and the city library (Rickelman & Henk, 1990).

■ BUILDING YOUR KNOWLEDGE BASE

A Starter List of Computer Software

Some computer software is very good indeed, but you will always need to balance the cost of the software with the degree of accessibility your students will have. Below is a list of software that should provide you with a starting point for reviewing program possibilities for your classroom or school:

The Children's Writing and Publishing Center. Fremont, CA: The Learning Company.

This program is a somewhat advanced word processing program that many students can learn to use themselves. It offers a wide variety of graphics that can be included in final published versions of students' compositions. It also includes specific formats for newsletters, ads, reports, letters, and so forth.

Language Experience Recorder Plus (LER+), by G. E. Mason. Gainesville, FL: Teacher Support Software.

This program provides alternatives to writing children's dictations on chart paper or in notebooks and includes a speech synthesizer that says what is typed. It also can create semantic maps, modify them, and make copies for students.

KidTalk. Long Beach, CA: First Byte Software.

This program works much like the *LER+* and is effective for recording children's dictations and for semantic mapping. It contains a speech synthesizer and can integrate your work with specific books by generating story maps.

The Literary Mapper, by G. Kuchinskas & M. C. Radencich. Gainesville, FL: Teacher Support Software.

Children can explore certain elements of narrative with this program. They can create their own retellings through writing, using print, clip art, music, and different fonts.

Magic Slate. Pleasantville, NY: Sunburst Communications.

Magic Slate offers easy word processing for students and is appropriate even for primary children. It has a feature that can generate cloze-type passages.

The Semantic Mapper, by G. Kuchinskas & M. C. Radencich. Gainesville, FL: Teacher Support Software.

This is yet another program that generates semantic maps. It can aid children in thinking through how major story concepts fit together.

Minnesota Education Computing Corporation (MECC).

MECC provides a range of programs that ask children to use their experiences with reading and math in a variety of problem-solving situations. These programs reinforce basic skills and present critical thinking scenarios in a game format.

Reading Comprehension Early Reading.

This program presents literature and folktales intended for beginning readers; it includes questions spaced periodically that facilitate prediction strategies.

Success with Reading. New York: Scholastic.

Success with Reading presents a multimedia format for encouraging children to expand their readings of core and extended texts. This program provides opportunities for rereading and for rethinking literary elements for discussion.

Super Story Tree, by G. Brackett. New York: Scholastic.

Children benefit from reprocessing information, story, elements of narrative, and other literary ingredients. These factors serve as a core of discussion in this program and reinforce the benefits of extended reading.

Hyperscreen, by G. Brackett. New York: Scholastic.

This program gives children a chance to experience the interactive nature of text that exists only in the computer. Students can explore different avenues for reading text solely on a computer screen and can work back and forth among documents, adding to and changing the text as they go.

The New Print Shop, by D. Lloyd and B. Lee. San Rafael, CA: Broderbund.

The New Print Shop gives students opportunities for creating posters, banners, cards, letterheads, and more. The choices are many for using clip art to design each of the different formats. Children enjoy the mix-and-match nature of the options available.

Superprint II: The Next Generation, by Pelican Software. New York: Scholastic.

This program offers many choices for creating classroom newspapers, posters, flyers, calendars, and banners with a variety of clip art options.

Carmen Sandiego, a series published by Broderbund.

This data base encourages students to involve themselves in the reading of many different types of texts. It presents intriguing scenarios that lead children to analyze alternatives critically when faced with a puzzling question.

The Information Connection

This data base, published by Grolier, opens opportunities for exploring books, journals, reports, and films that may not be directly available through your school library.

You can keep up on new developments and new software by following the columns that appear on a regular basis in the *Reading Teacher* or *Language Arts* magazines and in the journals *Computers in the Schools* and *The Computing Teacher.*

As you can see from the list above, computers have the potential for helping students become aware of their own *active* role in reading: readers can become partners of the author, extend their thinking, and create and change text as they work through the process of constructing meaning. The computer is, at least on the surface, more dynamic and active than the printed page, and many students may be helped toward understanding that they can play a similarly active role when interacting with the printed page.

Trade books

After having spent so much time discussing the classroom use of trade books throughout this text, it may seem superfluous to discuss them here. However, I would like to do so briefly, for two reasons:

1. To offer a reminder that along with the other materials we are discussing, trade books have been part of literature-oriented and "individualized" conceptions of reading instruction for many years.
2. To note that if trade books *are* the heart of a reading program that makes fictional and informational literature the core of the curriculum, they will be your most essential materials.

Defining Trade Books   Trade books are so named because they are published by trade publishers or by the trade division of a publishing company. A *trade*

MAKING CONNECTIONS:

Linking Up with Your Colleagues

As you explore the potential for computer use with your students, explore its potential for yourself. This will be particularly important if you are working in an outlying area where communication with other teachers and with university programs is limited. For example, the e-mail possibilities are endless. You can access all kinds of information in reading and language arts, and you can also correspond with colleagues across the nation through "bulletin board" or "forum" features. Let's say you have a question about how successful a particular theme has been

for third-graders. You can type this query into your computer; your question will appear on the bulletin board to anyone who checks this forum; and when you next check the bulletin board, you probably will have received replies from other teachers around the country. Telecommunications should be an invaluable tool for educators from here on.

One bulletin board service is Education Forum (CompuServe). This forum is partitioned into interest groups; the one that will be most immediately helpful to you is the "Language Arts" forum.

LEARNING IN CONTEXT: **Computers and their information networks expand *our* learning and communication contexts; as our use of the computer as a library tool increases, our students will also benefit.**

division publishes all fiction and informational books for children as well as adults. (An *educational division* publishes textbooks and other educational materials.) Children's trade books are, in essence, the "story" and "fact" books you and your students will read every day. As you move toward a solid literature-based foundation, you will find it helpful to have a working knowledge of the different types of trade books available. Trade books are divided into seven categories: picture books, traditional literature, poetry, contemporary realistic fiction, modern fantasy, historical fiction, and informational and biographical literature. You can review definitions and reference lists for each of these categories in Chapters 3, 5, 7, and 9.

Possible Uses for Trade Books   In the past, trade books were considered supplementary materials; they were usually purchased by the school librarian if there was extra money available. They were viewed as nonessential for the classroom; the basal was the main source of reading material. Individual *classroom* libraries were not standard in most elementary schools. In addition, although the public libraries and the bookstores had many books for children, twenty-five years ago the range and variety wasn't anything like it is today. The array, quality, and appeal of children's literature have expanded and broadened to a truly remarkable degree, as have the possibilities for using trade books in the classroom.

Trade books will be the lifeblood of your reading program and your primary source of materials for reading instruction; they will comprise both the content and the context for integrated theme units, skill instruction, vocabulary building, comprehension development, models for writing, and springboards for discussions and responses. As we saw in considerable depth in earlier chapters, they can form the foundation for much of your instruction. Their visual and literary beauty will motivate students, generating interest and inspiring reactions that will come in the form of book conversations, written responses, artwork, and extended projects.

Teachers who are working toward a more literature-based format from a basal program may at first need to try using just a few books over the course of the year. This is particularly the case at the intermediate grades, where teachers have not used "chapter books" directly as a focus for instruction. The books you select can be read aloud to an entire class, shared by students in small groups with you or with student partners; they can be read independently or used for purposes of direct instruction. As trade books of all kinds become more and more a part of your daily reading sessions, you and your students will discover innovative ways to extend your reading into other subject areas. These activities will in turn move you into a comprehensive use of trade books where they comprise the basis of your reading program.

THE DECISION-MAKING TEACHER'S RELATIONSHIP TO MATERIALS

Now that we have surveyed the materials and programs that are available, let's take a look at how you, as a decision-making teacher, can put these materials and programs to best use. As we implied in the earlier section on the history of reading instruction, there is considerable disagreement within the reading/language arts education community about the role of basal programs and literature-based series. Some educators view them as an important, necessary aspect of reading instruction because they provide a foundation; others see them as usurping the power, professional judgment, and integrity of teachers. You have seen that historically, one of the most powerful arguments for such programs was that they provided a helpful guide for teachers not extensively educated in the teaching of reading; more recently, this claim has been made for teachers who have not been well prepared in *literature*-based reading instruction. Well-constructed programs *can* still serve this function.

And now, what about *your* view? Do you need to have a program in your classroom? How you answer this question will depend upon where you see yourself in terms of your own advancement toward understanding the reading process, the developmental needs of the children you teach, and the inner workings of integrated instruction and preparation of thematic units. Your answer will also reflect the requirements of your district, and your own ability to work flexibly and creatively with all kinds of materials.

In the following three sections, we'll begin by taking a look at several ways in which you can use a basal program without compromising what you believe children need in order to "make meaning" of what they read. We'll consider, too, the expanding possibilities of working with a literature-based series and examine the value of teaching through the authentic reading/integrated literacy approach set forth in this book.

Making the basal program work for you

As you begin teaching, you may find that a well-constructed published reading program will be a comfortable, though not controlling, guide during the first few years. Almost all traditional basal reading programs present scope-and-sequence charts of the main topics and skills addressed throughout each grade level. Using these charts for quick reference can help you get a feel for the "what" and "when" of instruction for skills and strategies across the grade levels. In addition, if you take time to look over the table of contents or the planning guides in a teacher's manual, you will get an idea of what the average student in your classroom may be able to read. You may also gain background in the types of stories likely to appeal to your students, as well as information about authors whose books your students might enjoy reading more extensively.

As discussed previously, the traditional basal reader is organized in a fairly predictable, structured format that is supported by a variety of workbooks and skill sheets, many of which your students will not need to complete in order to "make meaning" in the stories they read. Keep in mind that just because your teacher's manual is set up in a particular manner, you needn't follow strict procedures prescribed by the program. In fact, you will find it more beneficial to preview the teaching suggestions, selecting only those activities you feel will meet your own students' needs. Reutzel (1985) suggests that it's worthwhile to take note of the "enrichment" activities that follow most reading selections. He finds the choices for extension to be more focused on students' active participation in developing story meaning. It is here that you will find ideas for converting stories into a play format; recipes and creative art suggestions; science experiments; tie-ins to other areas of the curriculum. Following each story, you will also find support sections for integrating reading into other subject areas. You may want to begin your planning by first reviewing these subject-area connections.

You will find that most published reading programs, regardless of their type, provide a lengthy presentation of teaching suggestions and activities to support each selection, usually more than any one teacher could possibly undertake. You needn't read the stories in their existing order, nor present all the vocabulary before reading the story, nor ask all the suggested questions. To get the most out of any basal program, you really do need to be selective—to pick and choose.

Suppose that you're a teacher using a traditional basal reader program because it is mandated by your school district, or because you feel it can provide a basic framework for you to work from. You'll probably want first of all to take a close look at the actual, authentic literature in the program. How you organize your language arts curriculum is going to determine how you'll use each story (or group of stories) for reading instruction. Your organization can, of course, change, depending on your instructional goals. Given what you now know about the essentials your students must experience in order to become skilled readers, you'll make some choices. As you review the reading content of the program, you might consider proceeding in one of the following ways:

■ *Read the stories in the order in which they appear.* However, instead of following the lesson format the program suggests, insert the instructional techniques you've been encountering in this book. For example, a traditional basal will ask you to present all or most new vocabulary before reading the selection. There may, in fact, be in a particular story several words that you know will challenge your students; however, there's an alternative: after several guided and shared readings, you might ask your students to find one or two words that intrigue or puzzle them. You may want students to reread portions of the story where the word or words appear, so that they can consider possible meanings. This discussion might lead to the dictionary, to consider alternate word meanings; you may find yourself looking more closely at how and why authors select vocabulary to convey emotions or to prepare the reader for events to come. In this way your students will have a sense of control over which words they analyze, and you will be focusing directly on what they've identified as being important to their ability to make meaning. A lesson of this kind will naturally provide practice in considering and comparing alternatives, trying out possibilities, analyzing both information from personal background and knowledge gained from the story itself, predicting logical outcomes, and identifying purposes behind word choice. A traditional basal would advise you to teach each of these skills separately, preferably using a different skill sheet for each, whereas you can double the impact of a lesson by letting your students have a say as to what they'll be studying.

■ *Use the student books as anthologies of children's literature, choosing selections according to the genre they represent.* For example, you could work with just folktales or poetry. You may find that your basal program has excellent selections of folktales from around the world. Since each of your students has a copy of the basal text, you have a built-in source of multiple copies around which you can structure several different types of small-group work. Cooperative groups of children may like investigating traditional stories from a particular country. Your basal will then serve as a springboard for students to locate similar stories in the school library. Another cooperative project might include setting up literature response groups. After several rereadings and discussions with you and their classmates, students can present story highlights to the entire class, create posters, or compose and perform radio or TV "spots" to advertise their stories, as well as keep comparison notes on the types of characters and problems that typically surface in folktales.

■ *Select several pieces that are all on the same topic but that cross genre lines.* Topics of this nature could be as complex as "getting along," "funny but embarrassing moments," "making difficult choices," or "family experiences," or as simple as "horses," "rainbows," or "songs." If on occasion you choose to teach your basal stories in this way, your students will get a taste of many different types of writing. Your reading discussions will most likely center around comparing and contrasting settings or character development. You will spend much time rereading passages that support or explain why and how a character acts in a particular way. Double-entry dialogue journals lend themselves nicely to this perspective. You and your students can select statements and actions of certain characters, to which several of you can react in writing. You may also find it advantageous to look at the difference between monologue and dialogue as you examine the ways in which characters make their decisions or handle certain situations.

■ *Integrate the stories you select into the science or social studies curriculum.* This can be done in mini-units or larger thematic units. You can read the stories in the order in which they appear, or you can earmark only those that deal with a particular content area. If you take the mini-unit tack, you might, for instance, work several days on one story that deals with snow. For extension activities, you could tie in experiments, activities, and investigations from the science and math texts: how much water content there is in a cup of snow; how much snow is typical for this time of the year; which areas in the country receive the most snow, and so forth. Another unit might include an adventure that takes a caterpillar on the journey to becoming a butterfly. A story with this focus can naturally stretch into discussions and activities about metamorphosis, life cycles, or cultural celebrations of renewal. More extensive units might cover the subjects of weather or seasonal changes for plants and animals, in which instances your students could read informational texts as well as narratives. If you are going to use your basal reader as your primary source of reading material, your topic choice will of course be far narrower than if you complement the basal selections with a variety of trade books. An extensive discussion of organizing thematic units was presented in Chapter 9.

■ *Choose selections according to writing techniques and narrative and informational structures you wish your students to model.* Since you'll be arranging time for your students to write on topics of their choice, you'll be preparing lessons that might cover strong lead sentences, descriptive words, transition sentences, dialogue, proper use of homophones or of repetitive lines, implied meaning, or realism versus fantasy. Typically, most basal reader programs' authors list a variety of individual skills they believe can be taught, illustrated, or practiced in conjunction with a chosen piece of children's literature. By checking the story overviews that precede each selection, or by locating the skills reference page(s) for all the selections in the program, you can quickly locate sources that emphasize specific writing techniques. Perhaps you've noticed that many of your students are struggling to end their stories in a logical, believable way. You might choose several basal selections that bring a problem to a convincing resolution. In addition, using previously read stories will give added purpose to rereadings. Familiarity with a story's content frees children to look more intensely at an individual element—in this case, how a problem is solved and the story brought to closure. This lesson can be presented to the whole class, or you may want to group children according to individual needs. Just reading the last five or six lines of several stories may give your students a focused look at the language used in a story's final lines. With your guidance, they will begin to observe word usage, recurring patterns, and underlying story organization.

As you become familiar with your basal reader, the district expectations for your grade level, and the developmental needs of your students, along with the teaching techniques prescribed in this text, you will be able to use your basal reader program as a resource, with you at the decision-making center.

MEANING MAKERS: You, The Reader

There Are SKILLS, and Then There Are Skills

Life in the adult world depends on our ability to perform a prescribed number of skills determined by our professional, social, and cultural environments. People who can't fulfill these requirements are not usually viewed as successful members of our society. When children come to school, their main purpose is to learn to read, write, do arithmetic, and apply reasoning in a wide range of situations; and as their teacher, it will be your responsibility to guide them. "Skills taught in isolation" are skills taught without a broader, more meaningful purpose. If children perform them in only one specific circumstance, their use is limited. Therefore, our overall goal for educating children needs to be in the meaningful as well as practical application of reading, writing, figuring (calculating), and reasoning.

When we ask students to put a group of word cards in alphabetical order, they must also understand that this skill will serve them well when they have to search for information in an encyclopedia, look up people's phone numbers in a telephone book, use an index, or use a dictionary or spelling list. In fact it is only when children undertake a task such as a research project requiring them to gather information that they truly see the broader need for specific skills such as alphabetizing, reading informational text, and note-taking. Skills begin to seem most valuable, and their purpose most clear, when they are taught for the purpose of completing a meaningful task.

The scope and sequence of any published reading program offers, as we've discussed, overview of the most important skills addressed at each grade level. Teaching with these distinctive objectives in mind, supported by the larger picture of how children can apply the specifics of, for example, letter format, inferred meaning, story structures, or word referents will help you design lessons that provide a balance between skill instruction and meaningful use of those skills. ■

Working with literature-based series

As we have discovered, a literature-based series is set up with a "menu" of choices. This organization makes the program easy to use and allows you the freedom to fit the activities and story content to your students' needs. In addition, most literature-based series have their stories arranged by related topic, focus on interdisciplinary teaching for each selection, and suggest alternatives for addressing a variety of skills. With this structure as your guide, you will be able to make meaningful links between your language arts program and your science and social studies objectives.

You're well aware, of course, that your students will represent a range of developmental levels. A well-constructed literature-based reading series will be sensitive to these differences by offering lists of books that fit the unit topic but cover a range in "readability": easy, average, and challenging. The series' selections will be geared to the average reader; however, you will discover that all readers, even the most developed, will enjoy contact with selections that cause them to stretch their skill level, as well as fall back on what they can read effortlessly. Having a "sweep" of books and story selections will help your students become wise decision-makers. A literature-based reading series can give you background in how to choose an assortment of books that will appeal to students of your grade level. However, it is both your knowledge of children's literature and the reading competence of your students that will ensure their having opportunities to reach toward more challenging material, balanced by adequate time spent in rereading familiar text.

In sum, many literature-based reading series can be used as a stepping stone for beginning to connect reading instruction to other curricular areas, or they can be used as supplementary resource material for building thematic units that extend and expand beyond teachers' manuals. As you grow and change as a decision-making teacher, whatever series you use will take a back seat to the overall organization you build into your classroom work.

Charting your own course: The role of materials within an authentic reading/integrated literacy approach

Whether you begin your teaching with a traditional basal reader program or a literature-based series, you'll probably find yourself doing what most reflective, decision-making teachers do: moving farther and farther away from the guidelines of any published program. Essentially, your attention will become so focused on surrounding your students with the elements of outstanding literature, supported by extensive writing experiences, that you won't want or need the published program's imposed structure. Ultimately, you may use program at most as a "resource" for additional ideas.

As you chart your own course and create your own reading program, you can turn to the strategies and techniques that you've been finding in this book. You should be able to provide numerous opportunities for children to interact with well-written narrative and expository literature in ways that both blend with their personal experiences and expand their background knowledge. You will be complementing these lessons with word study that calls children's attention to patterns of orthography balanced in the intermediate grades by spelling-to-meaning relationships. When you send your students back into texts for purposeful rereadings, they'll start to formulate their own questions fashioned after those they have seen you model through whole-class think-alouds and small-group discussions of plot, setting, character, and theme.

Trade books, both narrative and informational, will indeed become your primary source of reading material (Short & Pierce, 1990). To ensure that you have enough of them for your students to read, you will have to link up with other teachers, as well as with your school and local librarians. Purchasing trade books, especially multiple copies, can become expensive quickly. You can remedy this potential roadblock by asking your principal to use the money he or she would normally spend for workbooks to purchase literature "sets" for your classroom. In addition, by sending home monthly classroom book orders through companies like Trumpet Club, Scholastic, and Troll, you can earn bonus points for multiple copies of books. In this way *you* will have control over the literature and the topics around which you want your thematic units to be organized.

There will also be times throughout the year when you won't want to have one central focus: between grading periods, before vacation breaks, and (as discussed in Chapter 9) during the days after the close of a large thematic unit. You and your students just might not have the time or the concentration to begin another expansive project. During these short intervals, you can gather information or explore ideas for your next unit, or you may want to think about exposing your students to books you and they have always wanted to read, but which never seem to fit any unit in particular. These are also perfect opportunities for trying mini-units on subjects and genres you feel don't get adequate attention but that your students enjoy: poetry, plays, comedy, jokes and riddles, even idioms.

Throughout the United States, school districts reassess current series in use and often adopt new reading series and programs about every five or six years, on the average. As you accumulate teaching experience, you will most likely encounter the dismissal of old programs and the ushering in of new ones. The spiraling nature of reading philosophies and programs will undoubtedly expand and change the longer you teach. How you adapt to these changes will depend on your own knowledge of the reading process and of how we "make meaning" of text. Published reading series and programs will come and go; consequently, consistency in effective reading instruction must come from your heart—you'll have no choice but to "chart your own course."

■ A CONCLUDING PERSPECTIVE

We began this chapter with a look at the past. Not surprisingly, the methods and materials for reading instruction in America have reflected the values and perspectives of the society of the time. There are some common threads, though, that run throughout this history, and I have described them as forming an "upward spiral" that increasingly incorporates the "basics" with reading that is both authentic and purposeful.

For a good many years, a number of educators have believed that real literature should form the core of instructional practice. For a number of reasons, however, a more systematic, skills-based, bottom-up program packaged in the basal reader format and subjected to "readability" formulas eventually became the predominant mode of instruction in the twentieth century. There were "specialized" approaches to reading that emerged during this century as well: the linguistic approach; augmented alphabets—most notably, the Initial Teaching Alphabet.

As they developed, basal reader programs came to include much more guidance for the teacher in the form of the teacher's manual. In recent years these guides have contained quite specific "scripts" for teachers to use in directly teaching skills and strategies. As the basals grew to include more components, they were increasingly considered the core and foundation of reading instruction—a situation still widespread today.

You already know that American reading instruction is undergoing a profound shift from a traditional skills-based conception to a literature-based one. Literature-based instruction is becoming part of the larger integrated language arts curriculum. As many teachers move away from the "skills-based" mode, many will try to develop their instruction to make it compatible with the basal or literature-based series. Unfortunately, many are not as familiar with children's literature as they would like to be, so they may not be as confident in trusting their own judgment about selecting books for read-alouds or guiding their students' selection of books. This is often left to librarians or media specialists during the students' weekly visit to the library—often a time for the teacher to take a welcome break.

What should we make of this situation? Ultimately, all teachers should feel empowered and should be empowered to make choices confidently for and with the children they teach. Teachers *should* be reflective practitioners, rethinking their moment-to-moment interactions with children, as well as broader issues such as *why* they rely on published programs so much and what this implies for their students (Freire & Macedo, 1987). Those are our goals. But for a multitude of reasons, many teachers do not feel comfortable with moving toward what we recommend, and they will continue for the short term, at least, to rely on programs.

Although teachers ultimately should *not* feel so dependent on published materials and programs, at least the programs—as we've been seeing in this chapter—are beginning to reflect an integrated, literature-based philosophy. There are many ways to effect change, and the publishers are using one way— responding to more knowledgeable educators who are demanding change (California Reading Initiative, 1986).

There is another way to effect change. Throughout most of this text, you have been seeing how literature-based reading fits within an integrated language arts elementary curriculum. *You*, therefore, will be one of the agents of change in moving education's conception of reading instruction toward the more exciting kind. I hope I've given you a feel for the materials and programs you will most likely encounter as you enter the classroom. And ultimately, it will be your influence in managing these materials and programs that will inspire change. This will probably be a slow process because *real* change in education rarely occurs dramatically.

Literature-based series now have a stronghold on the reading market; and even though you may hear experienced teachers complain about a literature-based series' lack of sequence, inadequate presentation of skills, and overemphasis on whole-class instruction, teaching with authentic literature is here to stay. You, however, will be entering the classroom with the advantage of knowing how to design an integrated reading program as a decision-making professional. For you, published materials and programs will serve as your resources for constructing effective reading lessons—lessons planned with the developmental needs of children in mind. With your expertise, experience, and commitment, the change from the skills-based mode to the literature-based, authentic mode *will* come about.

We've also looked briefly at computers and literacy. It is hard to deny that the computer will eventually affect literacy and ideas about literacy as much as the printing press. You will undoubtedly see much of this change in your lifetime. Although for the next several years the effects of computers in your classroom will probably be modest, you should have access to computers, and you should use them in both reading and writing. Thus, in several different and significant ways, the next decades promise to be ground-breaking ones in literacy instruction, and you will be in the exciting and challenging position of experiencing it firsthand.

■ BECOMING A REFLECTIVE PRACTITIONER

Adams, M. J. (1991). A talk with Marilyn Adams. *Language arts*, 206–212.
    In this candid conversation, Adams responds to some of the feedback received concerning her book *Beginning to Read: Thinking and Learning about Print* (1990), and discusses

learning to read in general. Readers should note her concerns about letting students actively participate in their learning and the impact of sociocultural concerns on a child's ability to learn. She also addresses the relationships of writing, phonemic awareness, phonics, and knowledge/experience with print and how all of these factors play an important role in a child's acquisition of reading skills or literacy development. This article makes a wonderful epilogue—or introduction—to her book.

Altwerger, B., Edelsky, C., & Flores, B. (1987). Whole language: What's new? *The reading teacher, 41,* 144–154.

This article compares and contrasts Whole Language with other teaching methods such as the Language Experience Approach, Open Classroom, Whole Word, and the phonic approach. It is shown that Whole Language isn't a method of teaching so much as it is an attitude or view toward teaching. The purpose of Whole Language is to establish a process for constructing meaning, and this is done through *real* reading and writing, not through exercises in reading and writing. This article is probably one of the best to explain in simple, straightforward terms what Whole Language is all about.

Anderson, R., Hiebert, E., Scott, J., & Wilkinson, I. (1985). *Becoming a nation of readers.* Washington, D. C.: National Institute of Education, U. S. Department of Education.

A classic look at reading in this country as a whole, this monograph looks at what reading is, how it develops and the components involved, how to enhance or broaden reading and reading skills, and the importance of the classroom teacher in students' acquisition of reading skills. It also considers the professional development of teachers and gives a short list of recommendations that parents, teachers, and schools can utilize in order to help children learn to read. This is a book that *every* person (parent, teacher, administrator, politician) concerned with kids' learning to read should read themselves.

Chall, J. (1987). Introduction. *Elementary school journal, 87,* 243–245.

For a short, three-page paper, Chall does an excellent job of looking at basal reading programs and identifying some of the strengths and weaknesses that are associated with such programs. If you have ever considered being on or forming a textbook selection committee, this article should be required reading. This article won't give you all the answers, but it *will* raise the appropriate questions.

Goodman, K. (1967). Reading: A psycholinguistic guessing game. In H. Singer & R. Ruddell (Eds.), *Theoretical models and processes of reading.* Newark, DE: International Reading Association.

This article is the classical one to consult if you would like a description of Kenneth Goodman's theory of reading. Goodman lays out his concept of the process of reading in an eleven-step outline. He reminds us that when students make mistakes with their oral reading, these-mistakes-actually tell us what processes the student is using to gain meaning from the text. These mistakes show what the student knows, not what the student doesn't know, about reading.

Stedman, L., & Kaestle, C. (1987). Literacy and reading performance in the United States, from 1880 to the present. *Reading Research Quarterly, 22,* 8–46.

With approximately 35 million adults in this country experiencing difficulties in everyday reading tasks, this article investigates the impact of illiteracy upon American schools and society. The article addresses the problem of defining *illiteracy,* and notes that the criteria for functional literacy has grown from a fourth-grade level of education at the end of World War II to an eighth-grade (or even high school) level of education in the late seventies. Also of interest is that reading achievement has actually been fairly stable over the past 80 or 90 years.

Venezky, R. (1987). A history of the American reading textbook. *Elementary School Journal, 87,* 247–265.

This article provides excellent insight into the attitude and approach to reading (and education) in this country from the time of the Puritans to the present. This article takes texts from the hornbook and primers, to the spellers that were used for reading instruction, through Webster's influence, into the role of the McGuffey readers and more. Venezky explores the evolution of the reader and the purposes for it (for example, elocution was once an important objective of reading instruction) and how these purposes have changed and might change in the future.

■ REFERENCES

Adams, M. (1990). *Beginning to read: Thinking and learning about print.* Cambridge, MA: MIT Press.

Allen, R. (1976). *Language experiences in communication.* Boston: Houghton Mifflin.

Altwerger, B., Edelsky, C., & Flores, B. (1987). Whole language: What's new? *Reading Teacher, 41,* 144–154.

American readers (1983). Lexington, MA: D. C. Heath.

Anderson, R., Hiebert, E., Scott, J., & Wilkinson, I. (1985). *Becoming a nation of readers.* Washington, D. C.: National Institute of Education, U. S. Department of Education.

Balmuth, M. (1982). *The roots of phonics: A historical introduction.* New York: McGraw-Hill.

Barnes, D. (1976). *From communication to curriculum.* New York: Penguin Books.

Bloom, A. (1987). *The closing of the American mind.* New York: Simon and Schuster.

Bloomfield, L. (1933). *Language.* New York: Henry Holt.

Bolter, J. (1991). *Writing space: The computer, hypertext, and the history of writing.* Hillsdale, NJ: Lawrence Erlbaum Associates.

California Reading Initiative. (1986). Sacramento, CA: Department of Education.

Calkins, L. (1983). *Lessons from a child: On the teaching and learning of writing.* Exeter, NH: Heinemann.

Cazden, C., John, V., & Hymes, D. (Eds.) (1972). *Functions of language in the classroom.* New York: Teachers College Press.

Chall, J. (1967). *Learning to read: The great debate.* New York: McGraw-Hill.

Chall, J. (1987). Introduction. *Elementary School Journal, 87,* 243–245.

Chall, J., & Squire, J. (1991). The publishing industry and textbooks. In R. Barr, M. Kamil, P. Mosenthal, & P. D. Pearson (Eds.), *Handbook of reading research* (Vol. 2 pp. 120-146). New York: Longman.

Clymer, T. et al. (1989). *World of reading.* Needham, MA: Silver Burdett & Ginn.

Cremin, L. (1961). *The transformation of the school: Progressivism in American education, 1876–1957.* New York: Knopf.

Cremin, L. (1970). *American education: The colonial experience, 1607–1783.* New York: Harper & Row.

Cremin, L. (1980). *American education: The national experience, 1783–1876.* New York: Harper & Row.

Cullinan, B., & Strickland, D. (1990). Afterword. In M. Adams, *Beginning to read: Thinking and learning about print.* Cambridge, MA: MIT Press.

Duffy, G., Roehler, L., & Putnam, P. (1987). Putting the teacher in control: Basal reading textbooks and instructional decision-making. *Elementary School Journal, 87,* 357–366.

Durkin, D. (1981). Reading comprehension instruction in five basal reader series. *Reading Research Quarterly, 16,* 515–544.

Flesch, R. (1955). *Why Johnny can't read.* New York: Harper and Row.

Freire, P., & Macedo, D. (1987). *Literacy: Reading the word and the world.* South Hadley, MA: Bergin & Garvey.

Goodman, K. (1967). Reading: A psycholinguistic guessing game. In H. Singer & R. Ruddell (Eds.), *Theoretical models and processes of reading.* Newark, DE: International Reading Association.

Goodman, K. (1987). *What's whole in whole language?* Portsmouth, NH: Heinemann.

Goodman, K., Shannon, P., Freeman, Y., & Murphy, S. (1988). *Report card on basal readers.* New York: Richard C. Owen.

Goodman, K., & Smith, F. (1971). On the psycholinguistic method of teaching reading. *Elementary School Journal,* 177–181.

Goodman, K., & Fleming, J. (Eds.) (1969). *Psycholinguistics and the teaching of reading.* Newark, DE: International Reading Association.

Gould, S. (1981). *The mismeasure of man.* New York: Norton.

Graves, D. (1983). *Writing: Teachers and children at work.* Portsmouth, NH: Heinemann.

Landow, G. (1989). Hypertext in literary education, criticism, and scholarship. *Computers and the Humanities, 23,* 173–198.

Mathews, M. (1966). *Teaching to read, historically considered.* Chicago: University of Chicago Press.

Merrill Linguistic Readers (Book A). (1966). Columbus, OH: Merrill.

Monaghan, E. (1991). Family literacy in early 18th-century Boston: Cotton Mather and his children. *Reading Research Quarterly, 26,* 342–370.

Monaghan, E., & Saul, E. (1987). The reader, the scribe, the thinker: A critical look at the history of American reading and writing instruction. In T. S. Popkewitz (Ed.), *The formation of school subjects: The struggle for creating an American institution* (pp. 85–122). Philadelphia: Falmer.

Murray, D. (1968). *A writer teaches writing: A practical method of teaching composition.* Boston: Houghton Mifflin.

Paulson, W. (1989). Computers, minds, and texts: Preliminary reflections. *New Literary History, 20,* 291–303.

Perfetti, C. (1991). On the value of simple ideas in reading instruction. In S. Brady & D. Shankweiler (Eds.), *Phonological processes in literacy: A tribute to Isabelle Y. Liberman* (pp. 211–218). Hillsdale, NJ: Lawrence Erlbaum Associates.

Pikulski, J., et al. (1993). *The literature experience.* Boston: Houghton Mifflin.

Read, C. (1975). *Children's categorization of speech sounds in English.* Urbana, IL: National Council of Teachers of English.

Reutzel, D. (1985). Reconciling schema theory and the basal reading lesson. *Reading Teacher, 39,* 194–197.

Rickelman, R., & Henk, W. (1990). Telecommunications in the reading classroom. *Reading Teacher, 43,* 418–419.

Shannon, P. (1989). *Broken promises: Reading instruction in twentieth-century America.* Granby, MA: Bergin & Garvey.

Short, K., & Pierce, K. (1990). *Talking about books: Creating literate communities.* Portsmouth, NH: Heinemann.

Skeel, E., & Carpenter, E., Jr., (Eds.) (1958). *A bibliography of the writings of Noah Webster.* New York: Arno Press.

Smith, F. (1971). *Understanding reading.* New York: Holt, Rinehart, and Winston.

Smith, F. (Ed.) (1972). *Psycholinguistics and reading.* New York: Harper & Row.

Stauffer, R. (1969). *Directing reading maturity as a cognitive process.* New York: Harper & Row.

Stedman, L., & Kaestle, C. (1987). Literacy and reading performance in the United States, from 1880 to the present. *Reading Research Quarterly, 22,* 8–46.

Templeton, S. (1990). New trends in an historical perspective: Children's librarians and language arts educators. *Language Arts, 67,* 776–779.

Thorndike, E. (1913). *The elements of psychology.* New York: A.G. Seiles.

Veatch, J. (1959). *Individualizing your reading program.* New York: Putnam.

Venezky, R. (1987). A history of the American reading textbook. *Elementary School Journal, 87,* 247–265.

Weaver, C. (1988). *Reading process and practice: From socio-psycholinguistics to whole language.* Portsmouth, NH: Heinemann.

Wepner, S. (1990). Holistic computer applications in literature-based classrooms. *Reading Teacher, 44,* 12–19.

Resource Book and Children's Material References

Big Book Magazine. New York: Scholastic Inc.

Big Science. New York: Scholastic Inc.

Book Links. Aurora, IL: American Library Association.

Burns, M. (1992). *Math and literature.* White Plains, NY: Math Solutions Publications.

Butzow, C., & Butzow, J. (1989). *Science through children's literature.* Englewood, CO: Teachers Ideas Press.

Caduto, M., & Bruchac, J. (1989). *Keepers of the earth.* Golden, CO: Fulcrum, Inc.

Computers in the Schools. Binghamton, NY: Haworth Press.

Computing Teacher. Eugene, OR: International Society for Technology in Education.

Instructor. New York: Scholastic Inc.

Language Arts. Urbana, IL: National Council of Teachers of English.

Moir, H. (Ed.). (1992). *Collective perspectives* (2nd ed.). Boston: Christopher-Gordon.

Moss, J. (1990). *Focus on literature*. Katonah, New York: Richard C. Owen Publishers, Inc.

Ranger Rick. Vienna, VA: National Wildlife Federation

Reading Teacher. Newark, DL: International Reading Association.

Scholastic News. Jefferson City, MN: Scholastic, Inc.

Story Box. Bothell, WA: The Wright Group.

WEB, The. Columbus, OH: Ohio State University.

Weekly Reader. Columbus, OH: Richard J. LeBrasseur.

Zoobooks. San Diego, CA: Wildlife Education, Ltd.

CHAPTER ELEVEN

ASSESSING STUDENTS' LITERACY GROWTH IN CONTEXT

FOCUS

■ *What is* assessment *and how has its definition changed in recent years?*

■ *What are the components of* observation?

■ *What is an* informal reading inventory? *What can it tell you about a student? How can you use knowledge of informal reading inventories in your classroom?*

■ *How can you best obtain and record information about students in both* unplanned *and* planned *situations?*

■ *What is* portfolio assessment *in reading? What are your goals for portfolio assessment? How can you move toward achieving them?*

■ *What is the purpose of group standardized assessments in reading? What basic concepts underlie the scores that students obtain on these assessments? How are large-scale assessments changing to reflect more* authentic *reading tasks and purposes?*

How do you know what to teach about reading? Throughout this text, I have emphasized the importance of basing your instructional decisions on where children are *developmentally* and on how they are attempting to apply their knowledge. In this chapter, we'll address that emphasis directly and in depth. Our primary focus will be on your classroom:

■ On a day-to-day basis, how can you determine the strengths and needs of your students?
■ Over time, how will you determine and communicate your students' growth as readers and writers?

We will also look at your initial assessment of your students and explore in more depth how this information is extended throughout the year to

1. inform your ongoing instruction—help you make sure your instruction will be developmentally appropriate for each student (see Chapter 2);
2. provide documentation of each student's development;
3. involve students more directly in the assessment process as they learn how to reflect on themselves as learners growing toward independence in reading; and
4. determine grades and facilitate communication with parents.

Assessment should be tied to instruction and learning. "By observing the day-to-day interaction of teaching and responding," Marie Clay notes, ". . . rather than merely the correct responses on tests, teachers can guide the gradual build-up of effective independent strategies as a part of the young child's reading response system" (Clay, 1991, p. 312). In the same spirit, therefore, this chapter will address pulling together your instruction and students' learning, as they were discussed in Chapters 5 through 9. Toward this end, the chapter presents a firm foundation in approaches to both *informal* and *formal* assessment in reading. I will place major emphasis on informal, or *classroom-based,* assessment. Classroom-based assessment is represented primarily through your ongoing information-gathering and portfolio assessment. In this regard, Yetta Goodman noted that the assessment process "provides the most significant information if it occurs continuously and simultaneously with the experiences in which the learning is taking place" (1985, p. 10).

Because formal, standardized assessment continues to play a significant role in literacy education—it is policymakers' "test of choice"—we will briefly address the nature and purposes of these types of tests. In so doing, we will keep such tests in proper educational perspective.

A FRESH LOOK AT ASSESSMENT

Our orientation to assessment relates to the social and academic climate you expect to establish for your literacy instruction. As we'll soon discuss, this orientation may take some time to develop. Since it is a goal worth striving for, I'll describe the goal itself as well as suggest how you can move toward it.

Defining assessment

Assessment has traditionally been defined by most authorities as the administration of particular tasks in order to gather information about individuals or groups. *Evaluation* has commonly been defined as the analysis and synthesis of this information—*interpreting* it—so that decisions can be made about individuals and groups (Templeton, 1991). In literacy education at the present time, the term *assessment* is often used as an umbrella term or shorthand term that refers to *all* aspects of the assessment process, as in the "National *Assessment* of Educational Progress" and the "National Writing *Assessment*." Because in reality all assessments must be evaluated to be meaningful, and because the two acts are very intertwined in the kind of informal observational activity in which we are most interested, I will use the term *assessment* to refer to the whole process.

Topics of new interest

Assessment drives the curriculum and what we teach. It's that simple. So long as traditional standardized tests are used to determine whether or not students are learning, it is likely that instruction will be geared toward the content of those tests—and many teachers will be reluctant to establish the type of literacy and learning environment we have been exploring in this book. Thus, one of the most important if not controversial issues in literacy education as we approach the twenty-first century is that of *assessment.* For years, most educators have decried the ways in which students' progress in reading has been assessed—that is, usually in a group setting and by means of a standardized test that does not directly correspond to the types of reading materials and tasks in which students probably should be engaged on a day-to-day basis. But the public at large is not aware of this discrepancy and assumes that these tests are the best ways of measuring how well students are doing and of keeping educators accountable.

The times, however, are indeed changing. At all levels—from national to state, from the school district to your classroom—these changes are bringing about the most significantly different assessments of students' learning and literacy in decades. These assessments are more *authentic* because they reflect more closely what we now understand about the process of reading and how readers transact with texts to construct meaning. In addition, these newer assessments are beginning to reflect the results of how we should be going about the teaching of reading—assessing the kinds of thinking we engage kids in—and the consequences of that thinking when we involve them more meaningfully with texts. In the classroom, new developments in assessment are stressing the *ongoing* monitoring of students' progress and are using more authentic literacy tasks. And because they are more authentic, the tasks are more closely tied to classroom instruction.

An important part of our classroom assessment is the "portfolio" concept. *Portfolio assessment* involves *students* in determining what will be assessed. From this involvement, students learn how to evaluate *themselves* as developing readers and writers (Glazer & Brown, 1993; Tierney, Carter, & Desai, 1991). In this sense, assessment is in part a "metacognitive" process: students become aware of and think about *how* they are thinking and learning. They are also thinking about what this learning *means* to them. This demystifies assessment for students as they learn how and why they will be assessed by you and by themselves.

Because assessment *does* drive curriculum and teaching, educators hope that these changes will lead eventually to *real* change in the way we engage kids in literacy—lead to the widespread establishment of instructional climates and contexts in which students are experiencing and creating texts in ways we have encouraged throughout this book.

Purposes and settings for assessment

We have established a perspective on assessment. Let's pull together explicitly our purposes for assessing students. These overall purposes include

- initially determining strengths and areas for development in each child;
- making ongoing instructional planning decisions, including setting up groups for different purposes;
- monitoring students' learning and development, over time, and involving the students in this monitoring. Implicit in these purposes, too, is the determination of how effective *we* are in our instructional efforts.

We collect our information primarily in ongoing contexts as we observe students in their day-to-day activities, as well as in more structured contexts—as when, for example, we are gathering initial information about our students'

Ongoing classroom-based assessment occurs in several situations including teachers' one-on-one interactions with students in conferences.

abilities, interests, and attitudes, and—later on—gathering information and insights through individual reading conferences. Your ongoing, classroom-based assessment and observation will occur in a number of situations: watching students, singly or with others, as they engage in activities involving literacy; interacting with students in these contexts; interacting with students one-to-one through conferences and individual teaching; and through planned data-gathering situations—taking a "running record," conferencing about a book a student is reading, or discussing a student's assessment of his or her reading/writing portfolio.

DEFINING OBSERVATION AND INFORMAL MEASUREMENT

Observation is key to our effective classroom assessment. It is part and parcel of our goal of being teachers who are reflective meaning-makers, and it is a pivotal aspect of every assessment activity we engage in. As reflective teachers, we need to learn *how* to observe—how to really look at children through new lenses, using new tools. *Really* looking at children takes work. We have to ensure that we are really seeing and hearing what they are doing before we interpret their efforts—often with their input—and make some record of those efforts. In this section, we examine the nature of classroom observation—its components and its structure—as a key to assessment.

What does observation involve?

We need to know *what* our students are learning on a day-to-day basis and *how* they are applying what they learn. You will be making and organizing your informal observations of students' attitudes, strengths, and areas of need; you'll be describing those three factors in terms of skills, strategies, and progress (Routman, 1991). Yetta Goodman coined the term *kid-watching* (1985) to capture the spirit and the purpose of observing children and interpreting what they are doing in particular literacy contexts. As a kid-watcher, you rely on your increasing knowledge about children, language, and literacy development to tell you what to look for in any context. Perhaps this is simply another way of referring to what we've always called intuition, but it is *informed* intuition. You'll get better and better at kid-watching every day that you're in the classroom. The spirit of kid-watching also includes ongoing discussion with students about *their* perceptions of themselves as learners—of what, why, and how they are learning and what they believe they need to work on (Hansen, 1992).

It should be helpful to conceptualize classroom observation in terms of three components: watching closely, reflecting and interpreting, and recording. Let's consider each.

Watching Closely What is the child doing? This is the basic question and objective—not what you *think* the child is doing and whether it is good, bad, or indifferent. The question is simply "What is the child doing?"

It is easy to say that you should watch a child closely, but I will be the first to admit that this can in fact be quite challenging and that most of us have to work at it. We first have to step back and reflect on how *we* usually perceive what is going on, for that can affect what we are observing. We know that our brains are set up to anticipate and organize information according to our prior experiences; so when we first begin to *really* watch children closely, we have to monitor our immediate responses and conclusions to avoid responding hastily or jumping to conclusions. Part of our close observations include our own interaction with the student as we probe for clarification, explanation, or elaboration. Here are some observations teachers have made:

■ When reading with the teacher, eight-year-old Kevin stops at the end of a sentence in which he has miscued. He says, "Wait a minute . . . ," and goes back to reread the sentence and self-correct his miscue. [*Kevin is developing effective self-monitoring strategy.*]

■ Gabriella exclaims, "I see why you indent it every time someone different talks—if you didn't, it would really get confusing all lumped together!" [*Gabriella has grasped an important aspect about conventions and purposes of punctuation.*]

Recording   Our observations need to be recorded and collected. *Recording* is an important component of the observation process; it can occur along with our observations or some time after. It may also occur before, during, or after our reflections and interpretations (see next section) about what we have observed. How and in what format we record our observations depends, as we'll explore later, on our purposes and on our own style and preference. Here is how Sheena's and Brian's teachers recorded their observations:

—Noting that first-grader Sheena regularly skipped lines in her reading, her teacher recorded this observation in the journal she keeps on all her students; she also noted it during her reading conference with Sheena and recorded the observation on a special form she uses for such conferences.

—After sitting in with Brian's response group, his teacher noted that he seemed to have difficulty recalling specific details and information to support his responses to what he was reading. The teacher entered her observation in her journal (tabbed with each of her students' names).

The two observations about Brian and Sheena will require instructional attention of some type. The next two examples of recording observations illustrate documentation of the possible positive *effects* of instruction:

—An intermediate-grade teacher observes a student flipping through an informational book, pausing to look at headings and reading captions that accompany some of the illustrations. The teacher has a clipboard in hand with a pack of stick-on notes attached; she jots down the date on one note and then writes *Stacy—It looks as if you're using previewing strategy*. She later puts this note in Stacy's journal or compliments her individually, if she has the opportunity. Alternatively, she may write *Stacy is looking at headings and reading captions,* an observation that later, she will place in Stacy's reading folder and discuss with her.

—During a scheduled reading conference with a third-grade student, the teacher writes observations on a checklist he has prepared for each student: *Checks for supporting information without being prompted—"This illustrator is just like Leo Lionni. . . ."*

Reflecting and Interpreting   Once we have looked closely at a child and recorded what we have observed, we can step back to reflect on and interpret the information we have collected. While we cannot, of course, keep from interpreting what a child is doing as we are observing and recording, it is important to return to the information at a time when we can give it our undivided attention. We then are able to compare it with other information about the child, including our previous observations. We look for patterns or *trends* in behavior: what clues do they give us to how students are learning and to how they are applying their literacy knowledge? Often our reflection and interpretation leads to further observation. Following are the reflection and interpretation processes of Sheena's and Brian's teachers:

—A teacher down the hall once mentioned that Sheena might have a "tracking" problem that prevented her from consistently moving from one line to the next; that is one possible interpretation of the information. Sheena's present teacher has noted, however, that the child does not seem to have difficulty reading information that is on the chalkboard or in other parts of the environment, nor does she have difficulty with any other type of activity requiring sustained visual attention. Knowing that Sheena's developmental level should allow her to deal with simple texts *if* she is attending to meaning as she reads, the teacher suspects that something is interfering with this "meaning making"; otherwise, Sheena would realize that what she is reading doesn't make sense as she continues to skip lines.

The teacher decides to check the books Sheena has been selecting to read, and she discovers that they may in fact be at Sheena's *frustration* level. She can verify this by having Sheena read from one of the books she selected, while the teacher holds a card underneath each line, then pulls it down to reveal the following line as Sheena nears the end of the line above. When Sheena is finished, the teacher will ask her to retell what she read. This way, the teacher can check Sheena's understanding along with her word knowledge in text.

Sheena's teacher has observed a behavior, recorded the instances of it, and then formulated a hypothesis to be checked with Sheena. This example of informal, ongoing assessment yields direct and specific instructional information.

Brian's teacher reflected on *when* Brian seemed to have the problem with selecting and recalling supporting details, and it appeared to have been occurring in situations when Brian was interacting with several other students. The teacher concluded that the problem might not be with finding information *per se,* but with doing so when "the pressure was on." She then asked Brian to support his conclusions *in writing* rather than in a group context, and she found that he could in fact demonstrate the skill in this other mode. Her instructional goal for Brian has changed focus: she doesn't need to worry about *teaching* him this skill; she'll work at helping him *apply* the skill in different situations.

Developing a Sound Experiential and Knowledge Base for Making Good Observations

In the context of our discussion about *observation,* I would like to make explicit a theme I have played throughout this text regarding your progression as a teacher: experience in the classroom not only will give you confidence but will sharpen and deepen you *as* a teacher. This chapter presents the elements of effective assessment at the same time as it suggests how you can develop expertise and confidence while growing in your understanding and application of these elements. Experienced teachers apply their skills of observation as they are recording and reflecting "on-line," focused almost exclusively on a particular student or group even as—at the edge of their awareness—they continue to monitor what's going on elsewhere in the classroom.

The level of experience and expertise that supports many experienced teachers' ability to focus and to make good observations develops out of the *quality* of their time spent in the classroom. Their knowledge of literacy, of children, of the developmental nature of literacy, and so forth, affords them the opportunity to be able to step back and observe. With experience, much of their knowledge becomes almost intuitive, but at first it is usually more systematically, deliberately, and *consciously* applied. Teachers who have taught more traditionally and are now trying more classroom-based assessment find they have to work at establishing this objectivity, this detachment, and avoid jumping to conclusions.

I point this out in the hope of reassuring you. As we have already discussed, the initial challenges to novice teachers may seem at first to "get in the way" of the observing you want to be able to do. Know that if you persevere, however, you *will* gradually become aware that

—things *are* running fairly smoothly;

—the students *are* working independently and collaboratively without continual guidance from you; and therefore,

—there *are* opportunities for you to watch closely, record, reflect, and interpret.

In your initial assessments, you may feel more comfortable with more structure rather than less. In fact, most novice teachers typically move from the structure and framework of an informal reading inventory, for example, to greater comfort with informal measures based on students' self-selected books and spontaneous writing (see below). The knowledge that underlies this comfort usually grows out of administering and thinking about IRIs.

As teachers, we all need help in getting under way and making appropriate observations, so I'll present certain information-gathering procedures and means of recording information in this chapter. It is important, however, for you to realize that there are many possible ways to record and categorize information about your students' reading. As you feel more confident about your ability to observe and infer what your students are learning, you will be able to expand and elaborate the categories you are assessing. This is a crucial point because from the beginning, you will be able to make some very good observations and decisions—ones on which you will be able to base the grades that will be assigned—while knowing that you will also continue to increase your own knowledge and strategies. This is why your observation techniques and your means of recording information will always be evolving. ■

Observing: with and without measuring

Our informal classroom assessment will be based on two types of observation: those that involve some type of *measurement*—that is, they involve some form of numerical score, numerical tally, or numerical level—and those that do not. Thus far, we've been discussing primarily those types of observation that are an ongoing part of your day-to-day assessment and instruction. There are occasions, though, when a more structured, though still informal, type of observation is necessary, a type that involves measurement. Informal measurement allows you to observe students undertaking specific texts and tasks in a more structured situation that may yield more valuable information. For example, an informal reading inventory, a holistic writing assessment, and a teacher-made test all can yield very helpful initial and ongoing information about students' literacy development; also, all involve numerical scoring or measuring.

INFORMAL MEASURES

Informal reading inventory

The basic structure of an informal reading inventory (IRI) includes a graded series of word lists and a graded series of reading passages. The passages should represent both narrative and informational text. An IRI is administered one-to-one. Following the discussion (just below) of reasons for your using an IRI is a general sequence for its administration (you may refer to any number of published IRIs for more information).

Reasons for Using the IRI The informal reading inventory has been a useful tool for teachers of reading for a good many years. In a relatively brief period of time, it can yield information about a student's *word recognition* ability and *comprehension* of text, whatever *strategies* the student applies in analyzing words and addressing text, and the student's *oral reading fluency*.

There are three fundamental reasons why we will spend time discussing the informal reading inventory here:

First, administering an IRI can give you very good insight into the nature of the reading process.

Reading Levels—Definitions and Decisions

We know that reading ability is relative, and that how well a student interacts with a particular text depends on a number of factors. Perhaps this complexity explains the rather stunning estimate that 50 to 60 percent of students in the elementary grades work with inappropriate instructional materials (Shake, 1989).

How can you determine the appropriateness of reading materials? Educators have found the concept of a student's "reading levels" useful, particularly if the concept is used with caution (Betts, 1946; Stauffer, 1969; Pikulski & Shanahan, 1982; Lipson & Wixson, 1991). We addressed this issue first in Chapter 4 and then in Chapter 5, when we discussed how we can help children select reading material that is "just right" for them, as well as our purposes in encouraging them to read at their "independent" and their "instructional" levels. You should find the notion of *independent, instructional,* and *frustrational* reading levels useful in planning your direct instruction in both comprehension and word knowledge. When you reflect about your students' reading, reading levels provide a way of thinking about how well your students function *most* of the time in their reading.

When students read at their *independent* level, they know automatically just about all the words they encounter; the reading is almost effortless because meaning is "right there" for them. They do not consciously have to apply particular strategies to comprehend the text better. When students read at their *instructional* level, they are encountering some difficulty; although they comprehend approximately 70 percent of what they read, they may not know 5 to 6 percent of the words. They usually need some assistance—some *instruction*—from a knowledgeable "other," usually the teacher. This instruction may help them decide how to approach the text, or how to access the requisite prior knowledge, or how to find information they do not have but need in order to understand the text better.

When students read—or rather, *attempt* to read—at their *frustrational* level, they encounter many words they do not recognize, and they comprehend little of what they read. Unfortunately, a good many students are attempting to function at this level every day in school. We'll pursue this issue further in Chapter 12.

What role do reading levels play in the classroom? Table 11.1 on page 537 provides an overall perspective on their role, as well as criteria for determining the levels. You should urge your students to do a lot of independent-level reading; you will be engaged in helping them negotiate different texts that are on their instructional level, and you should avoid having them deal with texts that are on their frustrational level *unless* they have a keen interest in the topic and are happy to go through the text by themselves, picking up what information they can.

When making decisions about levels of books that your students are reading, the watchword is *flexibility.* Be flexible and allow the children considerable choice in the matter of selecting reading material; *however,* your direct instruction of readers usually should be at their *instructional* level—never at their frustrational level—and you'll want to make sure they are reading widely and often at their *independent* level.

LEARNING IN CONTEXT: **Awareness of the nature and characteristics of your students' individual reading levels helps you organize appropriate reading experiences.**

Second, the IRI may be particularly helpful to you in assessing the reading competency and reading levels of those children in your class who do not seem to be as far along the developmental literacy path as you would have expected.

Third, learning how to administer an informal reading inventory should help you develop skills that will be extremely helpful in your day-to-day assessment and instruction. For example, learning the types of oral reading errors or miscues, and the system for marking them, will come in handy in day-to-day observation of students' reading and in keeping a "running record" of students' progress (Clay, 1985). We will look more directly at that extension later in this chapter.

MEANING MAKERS: You, the Student

What It's Like to Read at a Frustrational Level

Imagine trying to read if every tenth word were totally unknown to you, and you were grasping very little. Imagine trying to do this type of reading day after day, while most people around you seemed to be having little difficulty with the same material. To assist you a bit with imagining, let's pretend that you've been asked to read the following bit of text, excerpted from John McPhee's *Basin and Range,* aloud to your classmates:

> As years went by, such verbal deposits would thicken. Someone developed enough effrontery to call a piece of our earth an epieugeogyncline. There were those who said interfluve when they meant between two streams, and a perfectly good word like mesopotamian would do. A cactolith, according to the American Geological Institute's *Glossary of Geology and Related Sciences,* was "a quasi-horizontal chonolith composed of anastomosing ductoliths, whose distal ends curl like a harpolith, thin like a sphenolith, or bulge discordantly like an akmolith or ethmolith." The same class of people who called one rock serpentine called another jacupirangite. Clinoptilolite, eclogite, migmatite, tincalconite, szaibelyite, pumpellyite. Meyerhofferite. The same class of people who called one rock paracelsian called another despujolsite. . . . (1981, pp. 27–28)

Well, how did you do? I wouldn't blame you if you stopped "pretending" halfway through and skipped down here to get on with some more "comfortable" reading. I'm sure you get the point, though: It's tough, isn't it? Even if you managed to pronounce those polysyllabic words as you "read aloud to your classmates," the words probably had little specific meaning for you.

We are fortunate in that we can play these kinds of games with our reading. But imagine what it's like to be a child in the elementary grades for whom this type of experience is an everyday occurrence. It is easy to understand why we lose such children after a while—why they have behavioral problems, why they have low self-esteem and, being only human, try to bolster their self-esteem by doing things that increasingly become antisocial or self-destructive. And I am *not* overdramatizing the situation.

By the way, although the excerpt you just read might suggest that the text is frustrational, if you were interested in the geology and geography of the Great Basin in the western United States, you would enjoy such a book. (And like all John McPhee's books, this one *is* most enjoyable—he's actually poking fun at the terms in the excerpt). The critical difference is that you would be struggling with the book because you *chose* to, not because your teacher required you to read it. ∎

Administering the IRI   Let's assume, for example, that you are working with a 10-year-old boy in the fourth grade. When you sit down to do an IRI, attempt to make him as comfortable as possible. Tell him that you are going to be working with him individually in order to get information that will help you help *him*. Explain briefly that he will be reading some words and then some short passages. You may have to have two sessions with the student; possible opportunities for administration—in addition to times during the reading/language arts block during the first two weeks—are before or after school, during recess or part of the lunch hour (regrettable, but sometimes these may be the only times!). If you have a session during lunch, by the way, you may want to set aside time just to eat together first—a nice icebreaker.

Word-Recognition Lists   The primary purposes of using the word lists are to gain a sense of the student's sight-word knowledge, to assess strategies for analyzing unknown words, and to determine where the student should begin reading in the graded passages.

You will test immediate word identification by very briefly exposing a word on the list—the "flash" condition. Try using two index cards in this fashion: Hold them together, just above the word you wish to expose. Slide the lower card down to expose the word for just a split second; then follow it with the upper card, covering the word again. If the student knows the word, he or she will respond immediately. If not (wait a few seconds), expose the word again by sliding the top card up. Then observe how the student tries to figure out the word—this is the "untimed" condition. You'll have a recording sheet on which to write down the student's responses. If there still is no response after several seconds, say something like, "That's a toughie—let's go on to the next one."

Observing how the student approaches the analysis of unknown words during the untimed presentation will show you whether the student follows a systematic procedure, guesses, or does a little of each. Discontinue administration of the word lists after the student falls below 75% on the flash administration.

Reading Comprehension   Next comes the comprehension portion of the IRI. These graded passages will help you determine the student's *independent, instructional,* and *frustrational* reading levels. This is done by assessing the student's comprehension through retellings and, if necessary, probing through questioning the student's oral-reading miscues. In a more specific examination of

Figure 11.1
Word Recognition in Isolation

GRADE ONE	Flash	Untimed
road	rain	rained
live	✓	
thank	think	✓
when	DK	DK
bigger	bear	✓
how	✓	
always	animals	DK
night	✓	
spring	ship	shape-shapes-shaping
today	✓	today

GRADE TWO	Flash	Untimed
our	✓	
please	✓	
myself	malicitent	DK
town	✓	
early	year	DK
send	✓	
wide	wind	DK
believe	DK	DK
quietly	quit	quenly
carefully	careful	DK

✓ = Correct   DK = Doesn't Know

the defining features we discussed on p. 534, Table 11.1 presents the characteristics and reading tasks for each level (adapted from Gillet & Temple, 1994). Ideally, you should *tape* the student's oral reading, so explain this and involve the student by having him show you how the cassette recorder works—or if he doesn't know, demonstrate. This little conversation about the recorder usually makes the student feel more at ease with the taping.

Let's go over the procedure for administering oral and silent reading passages. Begin at the student's independent reading level, which usually is determined by performance on the graded word lists. Start at the grade level at which the

TABLE 11.1 Nature and Characteristics of Reading Levels

Reading Level	Characteristics	Types of Reading Tasks
Independent: easy	■ Excellent comprehension: at least 90% ■ Excellent word recognition: at least 97% of words known ■ Rapid rate; good fluency	Recreational reading; self-selected Homework, tests, and other reading tasks to be completed individually
Instructional: comfortable	■ Good comprehension: at least 70% ■ Good word recognition: at least 90% ■ Good rate and fluency	Textbooks, basal series Guided reading activities (such as GRTAs)
Frustrational: too difficult	■ Poor comprehension: below 70% ■ Poor word recognition: below 90% ■ Slow, halting rate and fluency	No assigned reading at this level, except for occasional assessment and evaluation purposes Reading materials that the *student* chooses because of high interest

student achieved at least 90% on the *flash* administration of the graded word lists. If this did not occur at any level, begin at the lowest level reading passage, which is usually preprimer or primer (the traditional basal terminology is used in most published IRIs).

Tell the student that you would like him to read some short passages; state again that this will help you help *him*. Say that after he reads each passage, you'll ask him to tell you what happened (or to answer some questions). For each passage, provide a brief preparatory statement; for example: "Imagine what your mom would say if you brought every animal you saw home to live in your house! Please read about this nonsense zoo" (first-grade passage); or "You are about to read about a very dedicated and famous black surgeon who defied medical tradition and performed unusual surgery before the 1900s. The following information . . ." (sixth-grade passage). Both examples are from Woods & Moe (1989). For students whom we estimate to be at the late Beginning phase of development or the early Transitional phase, we alternate oral with silent reading passages. The student reads the oral passage at a particular grade level first, and after we check comprehension for that passage we ask the student to read the next passage silently. Of course, we cannot obtain information about a student's word recognition in context during silent reading, but we still are able to obtain information about their comprehension.

During the oral reading, you will be marking the errors or *miscues* on a separate page (Goodman, Watson, & Burke, 1987). The term *miscues* is preferred to *errors* because of having a more positive connotation and because *miscues* suggests not that the child was "wrong," but that he or she engaged only part of the "cueing systems" available.

There are six types of miscues to watch for and to note: omissions, insertions, substitutions, repetitions, self-corrections, and teacher assistance. Following is a description of each:

The term *omissions* refers broadly to any phrase, word, or part of a word that is left out. *Insertions* are additions to what is on the page; they also can be words or parts of words. *Substitutions* are words that are read in place of words on the page; they may be either meaningful substitutions or mispronunciations that do not make sense. For example, a meaningful substitution would be a student's reading *jet* instead of *airplane* in the following sentence: *Jerry looked up and saw the airplane in the sky.* A nonmeaningful substitution would be saying the word *ask* instead of *airplane* in the same sentence. Oftentimes the substitution *could* make sense if you stretched the situation a bit—say, if the student read *answer* instead of *airplane*. Usually, however, a pattern emerges—either the substitutions make sense or they don't, reflecting attention to the graphic appearance of the word on the page—so determining which pattern a student follows will be very useful information for you. *Repetitions* are simply any words and phrases that are repeated; *self-corrections,* of course, are not miscues but should be noted after a student has made a miscue and gone back to correct it. Often repetitions and corrections occur together: in correcting a miscue, the student rereads the phrase in which it occurred. When a student ignores punctuation, this too should be indicated; is it omitted or incorrect (as when a student continually ends declarative sentences with a rising intonation, as in a question)?

In counting the number of miscues a student makes, we count off for (a) omission of words or phrases (not for omission of punctuation), (b) insertions, (c) substitutions, and (d) providing assistance with an unknown word (*assistance* is defined as telling the child what a word is—after five seconds if the child is not attempting to identify the word, and after ten seconds if the child *is* attempting to identify it). We usually do not take off for the remaining types, although some educators disagree as to whether repetitions should be counted. I would suggest that you not count off for repetitions but that if a student is repeating excessively, you note this and check as to whether it appears to be interfering with comprehension. Woods and Moe note: "To best document patterns in a student's reading behavior, the examiner's major concern is to determine if the miscues occur consistently throughout a reading passage, and if they are the type of deviations that change the meaning of the text" (1989, p. 19). For each miscue, Lipson and Wixson (1991) suggest that you ask the following questions:

1. Is the meaning of the sentence changed by the miscue?
2. Does the miscue make sense in the context of the *whole* passage that is being read?
3. Did the student correct his or her miscue?
4. Is the miscue similar in sound and spelling to the word in the text?

These questions help guide your search for any trends or consistent pattern to the miscues. Quite often we can infer what strategies and skills children use as they read, by examining their miscues. Such miscues help you explore the degree to which children are applying their knowledge about language and about orthography, or spelling, as they read. When you are deciding if a miscue makes sense, changes the meaning, or is similar in sound and spelling to what is on the page, you are thinking about children's application of their language and print knowledge—their semantic, syntactic, and orthographic knowledge. This type of analysis of miscues is termed *qualitative assessment.* Qualitative assessment examines the nature of the miscues, the degree to which they affect the probable meaning of a passage, and what insights they may give us regarding the particular knowledge and strategies the student is using. We will examine readers' miscues qualitatively a little later.

After each passage is read, have the student retell it or respond to questions provided in the IRI. Although most IRI authors do not encourage the practice, several researchers suggest that you allow the student to "re-inspect" a passage for answers to inferential- and critical-type questions and probes. This re-inspection is more authentic in that students in a normal classroom situation usually have the opportunity to look over a passage, after reading it, in order to search for answers. If you allow a student to re-inspect the passage to determine the answer to a question he or she is uncertain about or has missed, give him credit for the response if it is correct. You can initiate a student's retelling by asking, "What is this story about?" or by saying, "Please tell me as much as you can about what you've just read."

Assessing the quality of retellings of narratives depends on your close monitoring of the student. According to Woods and Moe (1989), for example, a complete retelling should include the following:

Characters and descriptions of them

Setting (time and place)

Plot, retold according to the sequence in the passage

Summary, theme, or main idea

A retelling of an *informational* passage should include important points or ideas and the relationships among them. These retellings are usually more challenging than narrative retellings.

After the student has finished with his or her recall, you may probe further with questions derived from the student's retelling. To determine, for instance, whether the student understood more about the characters, sequence, theme, main idea, and so forth, you can phrase questions likely to cause him or her to respond. Here are a few examples:

"Please tell me more about Derek, the main character."

"After Julia fell into the ravine, what happened?"

"Describe the train that came through the town only at night."

"Why *does* heat cause this chemical reaction to take place?"

Informal reading inventories have questions that attempt to tap different aspects of comprehension abilities—literal, inferential, critical, cause/effect, sequence. Each question is labeled as to the comprehension skill it is assessing. For each passage, these IRIs also have guidelines, printed on the corresponding teacher's page, to help you determine whether the passage is at a particular student's independent, instructional, or frustrational level.

We have been talking thus far about students' comprehension during *their* reading of passages. So often, however—particularly with emergent and beginning readers and with children who have been categorized as having "reading difficulties" (see Chapter 12)—children's comprehension of text that they *hear* is significantly better than comprehension of text that they *read*. For this reason, you should obtain information about students' *listening comprehension* or, as it is sometimes called, "hearing capacity." When the student has reached frustration-level reading in both oral and silent passages, begin reading to him or her from successive passages. For example, if the child reaches frustration level at third-grade level, begin reading from a fourth-grade passage. If the child meets at least instructional-level comprehension criteria at that level, keep going until the student reaches frustrational criteria. This information about *listening comprehension* will give you a good idea of the student's *capacity* or *potential*. In other words, *if* the student's literacy development paralleled his or her cognitive development, it would correspond to his or her listening-comprehension level.

MAKING CONNECTIONS:

Putting the IRI to Use and into Perspective

I strongly encourage you to administer an entire IRI several times. As I noted above, the basics will serve you very well in your general instruction. For this reason, many novice teachers feel more comfortable at first implementing the IRI in their classrooms. When they feel more confident and experienced with gathering information in less structured but more "authentic" situations, they find they may not need the IRI. There is an analogy here that many novice teachers find useful: When they begin teaching, they often find that an informal reading inventory can be used like well-constructed literature-based basals at first. Both may be good initial guides or "tools" for instruction until teachers feel more comfortable with moving beyond and adding more and more. Many other teachers continue to use an IRI for initial assessment; with your experience as background, you will find that you should be able to gather and assess important information regardless of the type of informal assessment you use.

Informal reading inventories should be used with the realization that (as you know well by now) information about a particular child's reading development is best gained in authentic reading contexts, over a period of time. Therefore, any assessment that is made at one particular point in time, and on which instructional decisions will be made, should be used with the understanding that it will be supplemented with ongoing information collected in regular classroom literacy situations. As with other kinds of assessments I have recommended, however, and if you keep in mind the tentativeness of the information you will collect, the IRI can provide you with some good initial hypotheses about a student's general reading ability in terms of word knowledge and comprehension.

LEARNING IN CONTEXT: **The experience you gain in administering an IRI can be a bridge to gathering information more effectively in authentic literacy situations.**

Probing for Application of Word Analysis and Comprehension Strategies   After the initial IRI administration, we can glean additional information by going back and checking specific miscues and incorrectly answered questions. For example, to check the latter type of errors, have the student go back to the text passage and attempt to locate the answer. Ask him how he is looking for it; you often will find that he does not have a conscious strategy. If necessary, tell him, for example, that the answer is in *this* paragraph (and point to the paragraph). Also, if you need to, ask simplifying questions to focus the student more on the response. In other words, try to determine where the comprehension problem lies—or even that the problem is not comprehension but simply lack of sufficient word knowledge to support efficient reading.

By this point, you already will have some very good clues about the student's word knowledge. Still, check how the student approaches the oral reading miscues. In passages that are at his *instructional* level, point out an error in a passage and see whether he corrects it immediately. Often students will miss a word the first time around, but when you redirect their attention to it, they'll correct it right away. If this is not the pattern, see how the student approaches the word: does he try to analyze it as if it were in isolation or does he return to the beginning of the sentence—or to the beginning of the entire passage? If he attempts to analyze the word without returning to the beginning of the sentence, tell him to go back to where the sentence begins and see how this strategy works for him. Probe with four or five words this way.

Rate and fluency are important to note (Carver, 1989). They are an indication of how "automatically" the reader is processing print, thus being able to comprehend and reflect on the meaning that is being constructed. You can determine rate (expressed as words per minute) by dividing the number of words in the passage by the number of seconds it took the student to read the passage. Table 11.2 shows what the average rate for words per minute is at each developmental level (Bear & Barone, forthcoming).

Fluency has to do with how smoothly the student is reading aloud. Is the student reading with expression, with a natural rhythm and rate? Or is the student reading in a choppy fashion, hesitantly, in a monotone? It is not uncommon for fluency to be affected when students are reading at their frustration level, but students beyond the stages of beginning literacy should be reasonably "fluent" when reading at their instructional and independent levels.

If you wish to explore IRIs further, more in-depth discussions are provided in Barr, Sadow, and Blachowicz (1990); Baumann (1988); Gillet & Temple (1994); Kress, Johnson, & Pikulski (1987); and Stauffer, Abrams, & Pikulski (1978), as

■ TABLE 11.2 Rate of Reading as a Function of Developmental Level			
	Independent *Oral/Silent*	**Instructional** *Oral/Silent*	**Frustrational** *Oral/Silent*
Beginning	60–80/—	40–70/—	20–35/—
Transitional	80–130/90–140	70–120/70–120	40–60/40–60
Early Mature/Proficient	130–140/140–250	120–150/120–200	≤80/≤100
Later Mature/Proficient	140–160/250–500	150–160/200–250	≤100/≤120

well as in the introductory sections of several published IRIs (see, for example, Burns & Roe, 1989; Leslie & Caldwell, 1990; and Woods & Moe, 1989).

Teacher-Made IRIs In the past, some teachers have constructed their own informal reading inventories in order to ensure a closer match between the instructional materials they were using (usually a basal reading series) and their students. By constructing an IRI using the very texts to be read by the students, the teachers could be more confident that the reading instructional level they determined for each student corresponded exactly with the series.

I don't consider it really necessary for you to construct your own IRI. The time and effort usually would be better invested in thinking about the information you are able to collect from published IRIs or from your other initial and ongoing informal assessments. Should you wish to go ahead and construct your own IRI at some point, however, you will find helpful guidelines presented in Johnson, Kress, & Pikulski (1987) and Gillet & Temple (1994). Essentially, you will need to pay attention to the nature of the selections you include, the number of words in each passage to be read, and construction of questions.

Teacher-made tests

Teacher-made tests can be quite valuable, not only as a means of assessment for you but for your students' awareness of themselves as learners. It is important later in the elementary years to assess students' abilities to apply the critical-thinking competencies they are developing—to apply them in meaningful contexts *beyond* those immediate contexts. This is a part of their growing beyond themselves, beyond the here-and-now. It may sound like a rather grandiose rationale for giving teacher-made tests, but it is nevertheless true.

For example, over the course of a nine-week assessment period, you might administer two or three tests in which students are asked to respond in writing to the types of questions they have been pursuing through planned inquiry. Such an assessment demonstrates their ability to apply critical thinking to new material, to a current book they are reading; it also demonstrates their ability to organize and express this thinking.

Teacher-made tests also work well for assessing how students apply their literacy skills in expressing their understanding and application of content-area knowledge. They may be required, for example, to organize and write a description of the habitat, characteristics, and nutrition needs of a particular species living in their area.

As with all our assessments, we should be clear about the purposes for administering these types of tests, and we should be clear about our evaluation criteria as well—expectations and criteria should be discussed beforehand.

Classroom holistic assessment of writing

In this section and later in this chapter, we will consider briefly the most effective ways in which students' writing may be assessed. I would like to be explicit, however, about our rationale for assessing writing: not only do we obviously see students' growth in the critical domain of writing, but because writing is the "other side of the literacy coin," we gain important insights into the nature and types of students' *reading* as well.

I am presenting *holistic* assessment here because it offers one way in which you can quickly and informally get a feel for a student's ability to represent content and mechanics through written composition. Although holistic assessment is popularly used for large-scale writing assessments (see page 570), you can adapt the procedure for use in your classroom (Templeton, 1991; Tompkins, 1994). Used this way, it is another type of *initial* assessment that can yield important information; we will look at this classroom adaptation shortly.

Common elements according to which compositions are judged include the following (Ruth & Murphy, 1988):

Focus: How well does the paper present and maintain a theme or topic?

Organization: How well is the paper *structured*? Does it have a clear beginning, middle, and end, and do the points being made relate clearly to one another?

Support: How well are supporting details used to explain and clarify? How appropriate is the word choice?

Conventions: These include spelling and punctuation, and variety in sentence structure.

Your classroom-based holistic assessment doesn't have to be as structured as it would be if your students were being assessed as part of a large-scale district testing program; for example, you may allow the students more time or decide to let *them* select a topic. Tell them why you are asking them to write: because the information you get will help you help *them*.

You can readily see how the elements of holistic assessment—focus, organization, support, and conventions—can help you initially assess your students' writing competence. I must emphasize, however, that this is but an *initial* assessment—it is an "on demand" type of writing that, like your initial *reading* assessments, gives you an idea of the range of developmental levels in your classroom. Over the next couple of weeks, of course, you would be gathering information from a wide range of different writing activities and have many opportunities to observe *how* students are going about their writing.

We've considered how to assess students' writing holistically, and we've noted that the assessment can be adapted to the classroom. We can also examine selected compositions to determine how students are reflecting skills and strategies we have been addressing in our instruction—both writing *and* reading instruction. In the current terminology of writing assessment, these skills are examples of *primary traits*. In primary-trait assessment, you specify which particular aspects of the writing you will be assessing; in the classroom, this means that the students know which aspects they should be in control of in their writing.

In Figure 11.2, we see an example of the assessment sheet for Chanel's dinosaur "poster" report (see an example of another student's dinosaur poster report on page 344, Chapter 7). Students are assessed on primary traits for each of the categories—content, organization, mechanics, and appearance—and they

Child's Name: *Chanel*   Date: *May, 1993*

Topic: Dinosaurs

Type of Writing: Report

Scale
0 = No Connection
1 = Some Attempt But Far From Complete
2 = Reflects Basic Understanding But Not Complete/May Lack Organization
3 = Fulfills Requirements in a Fairly Well-Organized Fashion
4 = Fulfills Requirements in a Well-Organized and Consistent Fashion

SCIENCE CONTENT
Appearance:
  3-5 Facts Reported   0   1   2   ③   4
Adaptation:
  2-5 Facts Reported   0   ①   2   3   4
Habitat:
  1-3 Facts Reported   ○
Extra/Special Facts: 0   1   2   3   4
  3-5 Facts Reported   ○

                     Score ___10/16___ Grade ___B___

PARAGRAPH ORGANIZATION
Paragraphs Reflect Meaning of Heading   0   1   2   ③   4
Appearance: Gives a Mental Picture   0   1   2   ③   4
Adaptation: Explanations Provided   ○
Extra Facts: Like Facts are Grouped   0   1   2   3   4
  or Separate Facts Follow a Progression   ○

                     Score ___11/16___ Grade ___B___

LANGUAGE MECHANICS
Ideas Written in Complete Sentences   0   1   2   3   ④
Capitalization Used Appropriately   0   1   2   3   ④
Periods Used Appropriately   0   1   2   3   ④
Subjects and Verbs in Agreement   0   1   2   3   ④

                     Score ___16/16___ Grade ___A___

GENERAL APPEARANCE (Effort)
Handwriting Neat and Easy to Read   0   1   2   3   ④
Carefully Cut and Glued   0   1   2   ③   4

Overall Grade From Combined Scores   Total ___37/48___ Grade ___B___

Comments:
   Chanel –
   You've done a very nice job on your poster details – I like the nest of eggs and the layered teeth.

Figure 11.2
Primary-Trait Rating of Poster Report

know ahead of time the traits that these categories include (Templeton, 1991). As you can see in the example, this particular type of assessment also converts readily to a letter grade equivalent.

CLASSROOM-BASED OBSERVATIONS

Unplanned observations

What are some instances of unplanned observation—the attentive "kid-watching" that we spoke of earlier? These instances can occur at any time, with students and with their reading and writing; as we know, the assessment process may be going on all the time. Yet there are unplanned or unexpected moments when we notice a student's behavior in the context of a literacy or language event or see the result of students' efforts (as in their writing), and that behavior suggests an insight into what and how a student is thinking and what that student is trying out. Alert teachers will notice events like the following and reflect on what they suggest about each student's literacy development.

■ After Sustained Silent Reading, Jared comments, "This book is beginning to remind me of that other book I read—you know, the one about the frog." This is the first time that Jared has spontaneously made a connection between a previously read book and one he is reading currently. [*Jared is developing awareness of similar types of genre and styles.*]

■ Andrea suggests, "I think the way Byrd Baylor puts her lines on the page are kind of like a part of the picture." [*Andrea understands the layout and format of a text—how the illustrations and the physical placement of the print work together to convey an image and feeling.*]

Using Every Opportunity for "Kid-Watching"   As these few examples illustrate, there are many opportunities for informative observation—for kid-watching—in the classroom. Every day you spend in the classroom takes you farther along the experience/confidence/knowledge road, so that each observation you make can fit more comfortably and meaningfully in your overall schema for your students. You'll closely, carefully, observe and then—as the italicized interpretations above illustrate—interpret as best you can, reflecting on what your observation *means*. Many of these observations and interpretations occur in the ongoing course of instruction, and you adjust your responses accordingly: one-to-one chats, for example, or literature response groups in which you are involved, word study sessions, and so forth. Other opportunities occur as you are scanning the room during independent literature response group sessions, during writing time, and as you move from one group or individual to another. Often these observations not only inform your minute-to-minute instructional decisions but also may give you a broader picture of what your students are attempting to do and of how they are growing. For both specific and broader types, you can of course make mental notes; but as we've seen, it is quite often necessary and more helpful to record your observations. Such recorded observations help give an ongoing picture as well as documentation of each student's development, and they are invaluable when you are looking back over an evaluation period to summarize a student's progress (see below). These "anecdotal records" can take many forms; let's consider the most common.

Keeping Anecdotal Records   There are many ways teachers can record anecdotal observations efficiently for later reference. You may try different formats until you find the one that is most comfortable and convenient for you. For example, a spiral notebook that is tabbed for each student works well; several pages are available for notes on each. On the other hand, some teachers find it unwieldy to carry the notebook around, flipping through to find the page where they need to make an entry. Instead, they carry clipboards with stick-on notes or blank mailing labels. They can easily write their observations on these small slips and later place them in the notebook or share them with the student (Harste, Short, & Burke, 1989). Still others use checklists that include different categories with space for comments; these tend to "force" an immediate interpretation, though, whereas writing down the observation does not. Each informal observation is dated and should include information about time and place (in the context of a group; one to one at the writing center; in the reading corner while browsing for a book; and so forth). As we'll discuss in the section on portfolios, information gained through anecdotal observations can be organized by using checklists or forms.

What about the time it takes to record anecdotal observations? Since the more you do it, the easier and more efficient the process becomes, it's important to keep at it until you notice it's becoming easier. For example, for group literature discussions in which you are observing off to the side, you can make notes during the group's interaction. Later, you can examine these notes for evidence of individual students' knowledge and use of particular skills and strategies. When you are a participant, it can be distracting to try to make notes as you engage in discussion with the students. Two very effective options are to tape the discussion for transcription and analysis later on or to sit down for a few minutes immediately after the discussion and write what you remember (Paradis, Chatton, Boswell, Smith, & Yovich, 1991). But it's important to realize as well that teachers who have structured the type of literacy environment emphasized throughout this book have more opportunities for observation and keeping anecdotal records. Their students are engaged more often and longer in meaningful literacy activities and are more independent than students in a more teacher-controlled environment. Teachers in this latter type of classroom have very little time for taking anecdotal notes, and the "assessment" is not really a part of the instruction at all.

Planned observations

Planned observations are aimed at serving specific assessment purposes and goals. In these situations, you have designated times and tasks for your observations, or you have planned to examine certain aspects of the students' work. In a sense, we have already examined one important kind of planned observation—activities such as informal reading inventories and holistic writing assessments. However, these were all aimed at generating some form of numerical score or data and were concerned with *measuring*. All the planned observations defined here are purely qualitative, not quantitative. In this section, we will examine their most common categories. Your means of recording information in these planned observations, by the way, are the same as those you used for *un*planned observations.

Of Students' Participation in Learning Activities   You will become comfortable with some form of "recording device" in hand, whether it is a clipboard or a notebook. You'll be all set, in other words, for your planned observations. Some of the behaviors that reflect amount of participation include:

MAKING CONNECTIONS:

Initial Assessment of Emergent and Beginning Readers

Kindergartners' and first-graders' first day of school affords some very good opportunities for assessing reading knowledge. For kindergartners, a display of their names low on a wall will allow you to see which children can locate and identify their names in print. For first-graders, you will have taped each child's name tag to his or her desk; as they enter the classroom, you can ask them to try to find their own desks—and you'll also note which children not only find their own names but give assistance to classmates who are a little uncertain.

You may have placed a picture book on each child's desk, or you may invite them to browse in the library corner and each select a book to take back to their desks. By watching how they do this, you will get additional insight into their knowledge about books and how books are handled. How does a child hold a book—right side up or upside down? How does she try to turn the pages—awkwardly, or not at all, or with relative ease?

You will have several opportunities to obtain information about children's knowledge about print, directionality, concept of word in print, and sight-word knowledge during *shared reading experiences* of predictable texts and *group-dictated language experience charts* (see Chapter 5). Recall that concept of word in print—the ability to match word units in speech with printed word units in a line of text—is important because it means that a child may be ready to explore *and understand* the alphabetic aspect of the writing system: words are made up of individual consonant and vowel sounds, and each sound in a word can be represented by a letter.

In addition, during the first two weeks of school you will have opportunities to gather more in-depth information about each child by checking knowledge of

■ letter names;
■ the nature of the reading act—it may be either quiet or more "social," with comments to neighbors, requests for help, and so forth;
■ different types of reading material; what do they choose during independent reading or Sustained Silent Reading?

LEARNING IN CONTEXT: **The appropriate contexts and literacy experiences for emergent and beginning readers provide rich assessment opportunities for teachers.**

Degree of *engagement* with a group; does the student appear to be involved most of the time or is attention wandering or behavior disruptive?

Insightful observations in discussions.

Ability to express ideas or feelings in groups or one-to-one.

Of Students' Response Logs and Journal Entries   As you read and respond to your students' response logs and journal entries, you cannot help but see indications of growth in basic conventions as well as in the critical stance students can take toward their reading. These types of writing provide some of your best sources of information about your students' development. The response in Figure 11.3 reveals that Jennifer, a fifth-grader, has made a startling and valuable discovery during her reading of *Island of the Blue Dolphins*: "*Every once in a while, the book gives you hints about things that will happen. . . .*" What better evidence that Jennifer is pulling together information about her experience with books, what she is discovering in *this* particular book, and her own personal life experiences?

Recall that often we may provide students with questions about their reading, to be addressed in their response logs, and you can fashion these so that they'll help reveal whether students can deal with whatever type of interaction with a book you are probing: do they have the analytical or reflective abilities necessary and if so, how do they seem to apply them? For example, a fifth-grader writing in response to how Katherine Paterson concluded *A Bridge to Terabithia* observed, "I think she stopped so that she would not have to write a big chapter

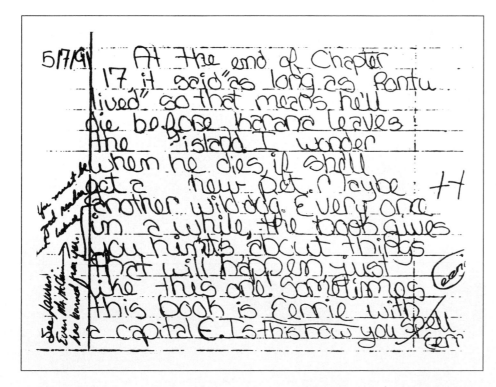

Figure 11.3
Eleven-Year-Old's Response Log Entry

book and so that she would not have to write a conclusion to *A Bridge to Terabithia*." This alerted the teacher to possibilities for exploring with certain students why authors end their books in certain ways.

Reading Conferences and One-to-One Dialogues Reading conferences are an extremely important aspect of your assessment and will provide you with opportunities to help develop your students' self-assessment abilities as well (see below). Reading conferences are one-to-one dialogues between you and each student and allow you to monitor development in both general and specific learning. During a conference, you'll discuss the book the child is presently reading, assess certain skills and knowledge, and discuss where the child plans to go next with his or her reading. Many of these aspects involve the student's *metacognitive* reflection on his or her reading. "Metacognitive" questions that we encourage students to reflect on in these conferences—though not in *every* conference—include "What do I do well?" "What do I need to work on?" and "What can you [the teacher] do to help me?" (Glazer & Brown, 1993).

The student brings his or her reading folder to the conference; this folder includes the reading response log, the book the student is presently reading, and checksheets (see below). Your conference will include:

- *Discussing a particular aspect of the book*—theme, characterization, and so forth (these aspects will usually correspond to those you have been discussing with a group of students).
- *Probing with further questions* whichever aspect you've discussed or one explored earlier in the year.

    Your conference will work best, of course, if you've read the book the child is reading, but this isn't always possible. Therefore, many of your ques-

One-on-one dialogues help develop your students' self-assessment capabilities and involve their metacognitive reflection on their reading.

tions will elicit important reflection on the student's part but also will stem from your genuine interest in the book and desire to hear about the student's reactions and thoughts. Drawing your questions from those suggested in Chapter 6 (pages 269–270) will help, and they will be ones with which students are familiar because they've been asked in response-group settings and perhaps written in response journals as well. Often you will find that simply asking the student to *retell* the major points in the book or the previous chapter is helpful.

■ *The student's reading a favorite part of the book to you* and explaining *why* he or she chose this part (you may note at this time any miscues and fix-up strategies the child uses).

■ *Talking about where the student will go from here with the reading*—specifically, in this book or, if the book will be finished soon, what book, books, or other materials he or she is planning to read, and why. (For example, a child reading science fiction about colonizing other galaxies may want to find out more about some of the concepts mentioned in the chapter books—supernovas and quasars, perhaps. You sense whether or not the student knows where to get further information.)

The reading conference may also be used to support a student having a particular problem with reading—a one-to-one "minilesson"—or one minilesson for all students with the same need.

It's a good idea to record your observations about a conference right after talking with the child, and quick notes will do. Figure 11.4 illustrates this; as you can see, four conferences have occurred with this student thus far in the school year. The record shows that other observations you make during the conference may be entered—the student's understanding and application of particular strategies, for instance.

The Qualitative Inventory of Word Knowledge   We know that it is possible to get important information about students' word knowledge from their oral reading miscues in context. You also can get considerable information from the "word recognition in isolation" portion of an informal reading inventory.

For initial information about students' *word knowledge* early in the school year, however, an easy and informative way to acquire considerable insight in a short amount of time is by administering a simple spelling assessment, one constructed so as to tap students' developmental level as well as to identify within each level specific orthographic features that students understand and features they haven't yet internalized (Gillet & Temple, 1994; Bear & Barone, forthcoming). The Qualitative Inventory of Word Knowledge presented in Figure 11.5 provides this information (Bear & Barone, 1989; Bear, Templeton, & Warner, 1991; Schlagal, 1992; Zutell, 1992).

Why does *spelling* reveal this information? A growing body of research has shown that students' spelling or encoding of words on an inventory represents their *understanding* about words and word patterns and structures (Gill, 1992; Perfetti, 1992; Templeton & Bear, 1992). Often, though, children do not apply this knowledge appropriately and effectively when they are reading and writing, so it is important that we determine what in fact they truly *know* about word

Figure 11.4
Sample Reading-Conference Log

Date	Title & Author	Comments
NAME: Jennifer		
1/23	Egypt Game Zilpha Snyder	Understands foreshadowing: "I think the author described the Professor this way so that you'd think he was the murderer — authors do that sometimes." "I don't think kids would stay interested in Egypt as long as these kids did."
2/8	Bridge to Terabithia Katherine Paterson	"Katherine Paterson didn't write a very good conclusion to this book!" Jennifer is still expecting a "happy ever after" ending and has not yet come to understand more complex, real-life types — I've tried to probe about this.
2/25	Dragonwings Laurence Yep	Exploring beyond "simpler" plots she chose at the beginning of the year. Picking up on subtleties — "I think the father's visit to the dragon didn't happen, but it made you feel it was real in some kind of other way."
3/15	Dragonwings	Taking a longer time with this book. "I like to reread so much because I love the descriptions. It's like I'm really living back then." Oral rereading of earthquake scene (pps. 154-55) really supports this — very fluent, with feeling.

patterns and structure. This way, we can provide appropriate instruction about words and can more effectively help students apply what they know, when they are reading. Even in an overview as brief as this one, you'll be able to see how this inventory can help you with initial instructional decisions. (By the way, if you're wondering right now about what *your* spelling might reveal about your word knowledge, don't be concerned: although many adults consider themselves to be "poor" spellers, they really aren't. They simply are plagued by a few words whose spelling they find troublesome, and they *can* spell correctly most words they need to use. The few errors most college-level adults do make are relatively sophisticated.)

Kevin's, Denise's, and Paul's word knowledge shows a developmental trend that we first examined in Chapter 2:

Kevin's word knowledge is *alphabetic,* characteristic of the beginning reading phase;

Denise's word knowledge is *within-word pattern,* characteristic of the early transitional phase;

Paul's is characteristic of the early mature or proficient phase.

Figure 11.5
Qualitative Inventory of Word Knowledge

	Kevin First Grade	Denise Second Grade	Paul Fifth Grade
BED	bad	bed	bed
SHIP	sep	ship	ship
DRIVE	driv	drieve	drive
BUMP	bomp	bump	bump
WHEN	wen	when	when
TRAIN	chran	trane	train
CLOSET		clozit	closet
CHASE		chase	chase
FLOAT		flote	float
BEACHES		beches	beeches
PREPARING		prepring	prepairing
POPPING		poping	popping
CATTLE		catol	cattel
CAUGHT		cot	cought
INSPECTION			inspecsion
PUNCTURE			punksher
CELLAR			celler
PLEASURE			pleasure
SQUIRREL			squirle
FORTUNATE			fortunet
CONFIDENT			confiedment
CIVILIZE			civalize
FLEXIBLE			flexable
OPPOSITION			oppasition
EMPHASIZE			imphesize

Running Records and Miscue Analysis Children about whom you need more information early in the year may be taken aside to read to you from a text that is fairly comfortable for each such child to read. When children read from a comfortable text, they can give you valuable insights into their reading strategies—how they are going about constructing meaning and recognizing words. We should avoid selections that are at students' frustrational level; they don't really give us much information at all, since the child is overwhelmed by the unknown and cannot use his or her skills and strategies efficiently.

This record of oral reading is termed a *running record* because it will be an ongoing record of oral reading throughout the year. Over this period of time, we can sample students' readings from a range of different materials. It's a very good idea to include a cassette of the child's oral reading to accompany this record. Throughout the year, this information may be gathered as part of a reading conference with an individual student. Let's look briefly at how you can gather information about students' developing reading.

Sitting where you can see the text the student is reading from, you should simply look on, ticking off the words that are read correctly and noting any of the student's miscues. We apply to each miscue the same questions we use for the informal reading inventory (see page 539). To see an illustration, examine Figure 11.6, where a sample of a second-grader's oral reading record is presented, along with a key for marking the different types of miscues. On the left-hand

Figure 11.6
Second-Grader's Oral Reading Record

Text	Teacher's Running Record of Child's Oral Reading: The Lady and the Spider, pp. 1–4
On a summer day	✓ ✓ ✓ ✓ ——— R/SC
in a lady's garden,	✓ ✓ lady/lady's ✓
a spider stood on	✓ ✓ ✓ ✓
a lettuce leaf.	✓ let-túce/lettuce /T ✓ ✓
She looked about and saw	✓ ✓ ✓ ✓ ✓
hills of green	✓ ✓ ✓
and valleys of green.	✓ vall/valleys /T ✓ ✓
Between two leaves	✓ ✓ ✓
she saw a green cave.	✓ ✓ ✓ ✓ ✓
Walking daintily	✓ daint/daintily /H /T
on her eight legs,	✓ ✓ ✓ ✓
she went inside.	✓ ✓ ✓
With the tips	✓ ✓ ✓
of her long front legs,	✓ ✓ ✓ ✓ ✓
she felt the sides and	✓ ✓ ✓ ✓ ✓ ——— R/SC
the ceiling and the floor.	✓ céi/ceiling ✓ ✓ ✓ ——— R
The cave suited her.	✓ ✓ saved/suited /suit–sc ✓
It was a leafy den	✓ ✓ ✓ ✓ ✓
just the right size	✓ ✓ ✓ ✓
to be her home.	✓ ✓ ✓ ✓

Correct reading	✓ ✓ ✓	Self-Correction	SC
Substitution	substitute/word in text	Omission	•/word in text
Asks for help	H	Insertion	inserted word/•
Tell child the word	T	Repetition	✓ R
		Repeat several words	✓ ✓ ✓ ✓ R

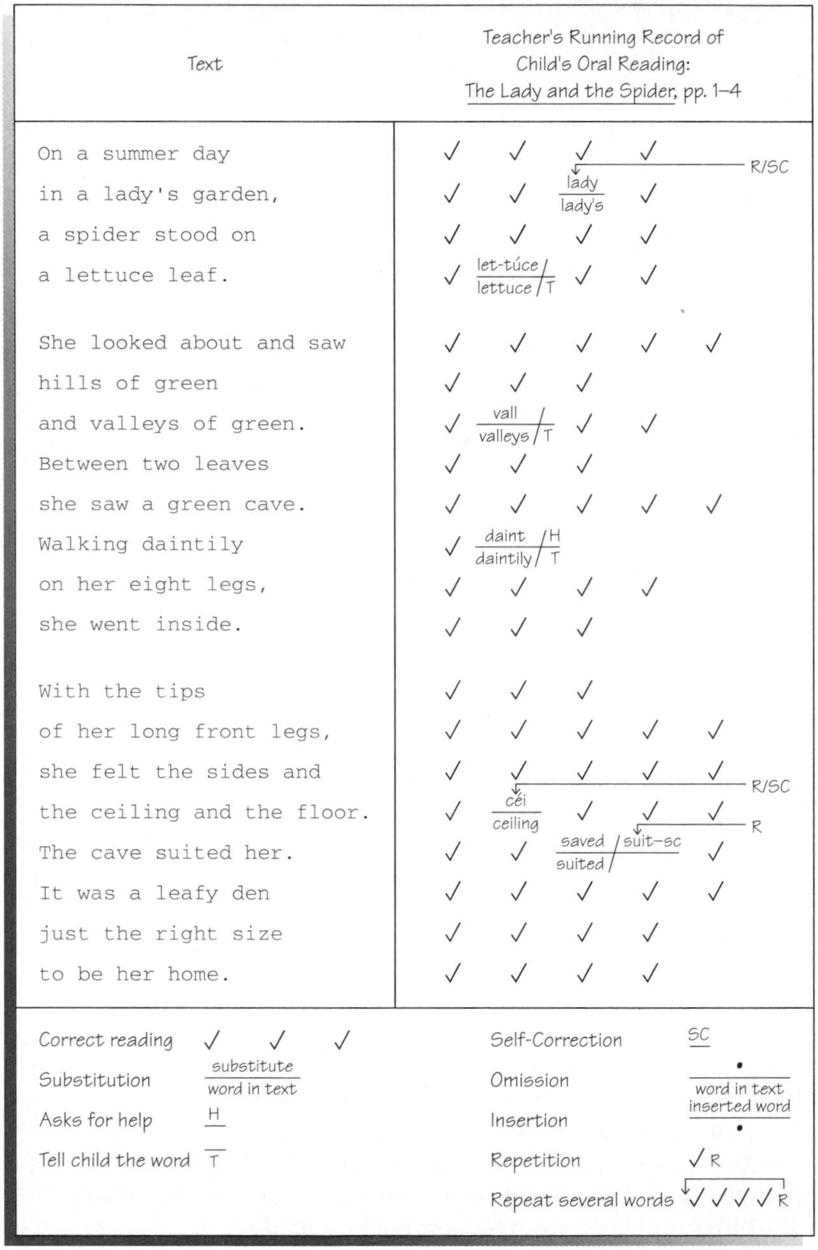

side is the text the child is reading; on the right-hand side is the teacher's record of the child's miscues.

Here is Terese's teacher's interpretation of her reading, based on these miscues:

Terese seems to be applying, appropriately, contextual skills *and* knowledge of word structure. *Lady* is corrected to *lady's* after Terese realizes that the singular form doesn't fit. The next three miscues are similar in nature. There isn't enough contextual support to narrow the possibilities for *lettuce;* Terese applies her knowledge of vowel patterns within syllables to sound out each syllable. When this does not result in a familiar word, the teacher makes the right decision to tell her the word and keep the reading comfortable. The teacher makes a note, however, to talk with Terese about what she does when she's on her own and runs into a word like *lettuce* that she can't figure out. The same situation applies to the next miscue, on *valleys.* Terese doesn't pick up on the metaphorical use of *hills* and *valleys* in the context, so she tries to sound out the word (perhaps in the first syllable based by analogy with *ball*). For the word *daintily,* Terese again tries her knowledge of vowel patterns in the absence of contextual support—this is a word she probably would not have known in oral language.

Terese uses both word and context knowledge to identify *ceiling;* she sounds out the first syllable, quickly reads the rest of the sentence, then realizes what the word has to be. The teacher notes her delight with Terese's successful merging of context and sounding-out. The miscue on *suited* is appropriate in the context to that point; when Terese reads the rest of the sentence, she realizes that *saved* no longer makes sense, so she has looked back—an excellent strategy—and sounded out the word correctly in two attempts.

Following is an example from a fifth-grader, Jerry:

Jerry's teacher observed that this student had a tendency to read rapidly and hurry through a selection. To make sure Jerry wasn't doing this only because he was reading for the teacher and perhaps feeling nervous, she watched him for a couple of weeks as he read books during SSR. In that context, he *did* seem to hurry through. What the teacher learned from this initial running record assessment was that Jerry brought to his reading a lot of background knowledge that allowed him to "fill in" gaps in the information he was not picking up from reading. Although this was a good strategy for Jerry, his teacher realized it would help him less and less once Jerry began moving through the grades and needed to read more and more informational materials. She examined the oral reading miscues that Jerry made and noted that most of them occurred with words of more than one syllable; Jerry would either substitute a similar word or mutter something to "get by," then continue with his reading. He consistently substituted *y* for *ier* at the end of words such as *heavier.* Thinking that Jerry did not know as much about word structure as his general capacity and past reading performance would suggest, the teacher compared these results with Jerry's word knowledge as revealed by the Qualitative Inventory of Word Knowledge. Sure enough, she found that he was consistently making errors in polysyllabic words. She concluded that for purposes of word study, she would begin having Jerry explore compound words and proceed from there (see Chapter 8).

Text	Teacher's Running Record of Child's Oral Reading:
You know the amount of salt in	✓ ✓ ✓ ✓ ✓ ✓ ✓
ocean water is not the same	✓ ✓ ✓ ✓ ✓ ✓
all over. How does the sun's	✓ ✓ ✓ ✓ ✓ ✓
heat cause the water in some	✓ ✓ ✓ ✓ ✓ ✓
places to be saltier? The	✓ ✓ ✓ salty/saltier ✓ ✓
more salt in the water, the	✓ ✓ ✓ ✓ ✓ ✓
heavier the water is. Heavy	heavy/heavier ✓ ✓ ✓ ✓
water sinks to the ocean	✓ ✓ ✓ ✓ ✓
bottom. When it meets less	✓ ✓ ✓ ✓ ✓
salty water, the less salty	✓ ✓ ✓ ✓ ✓
water moves over it. A	✓ ✓ ✓ ✓ ✓
circling current forms. For	circle/circling cur/current ✓ ✓
example, the water of the	✓ ✓ ✓ ✓ ✓
Mediterranean Sea is saltier	Med/Mediterranean R/T ✓ ✓ salty/saltier
than the Atlantic Ocean.	✓ ✓ At–/Atlantic ✓
Where these two bodies of	✓ ✓ ✓ ✓ ✓
water meet there is a deep	✓ ✓ ✓ ✓ ✓
current. The saltier, heavy	cur–/current ✓ salty/saltier ✓
water moves along the ocean	✓ ✓ ✓ ✓ ✓
bottom. The less salty water	✓ ✓ ✓ ✓ ✓
moves over the heavier water	✓ ✓ ✓ heavy/heavier ✓
into the Mediterranean Sea.	✓ ✓ Mediturn/Mediterranean ✓
(Holt Science, 1986, p. 29)	

Figure 11.7
Fifth-Grader's Oral Reading Record

USING A PORTFOLIO APPROACH TO EXPRESS TEACHERS' OBSERVATIONS AND STUDENTS' SELF-REFLECTIONS

''Portfolio assessment'' is a popular and exciting concept in reading and language arts. There are two ways in which educators use the term *portfolio*. First, the portfolio is a physical entity, such as a large file or folder, in which children's best representative works are kept. Indeed, many schools are moving toward using portfolios from one grade level to the next; that is, students' portfolios will accompany them through the grades. Second, we may think of a portfolio "approach" to assessment as one that emphasizes students' awareness of their own growth and development as readers, writers, and learners. In the latter case, rather than focusing simply on a place to collect work, "portfolio assessment" refers to the informed use of a range of anecdotal and direct observations, student products, and records all of which would yield a profile of students' progress and needs (Routman, 1991). Students come to be involved in the process of selecting representative work and information. "Collecting work is not unusual," note Tierney and his colleagues. "However, using the collected work for self-analysis is a unique feature of the portfolio assessment process" (1991, p. 74).

Expression, rather than collection, as the goal

This second conception is the one I would like to focus on here—the *informed* use of a range of information. *Expression* rather than merely *collection* is the goal toward which we are working. With our students, we will work toward best *expressing* what they have learned and what they can do. The portfolio will contain *products* that represent a student's finest work, but it will also contain information about the *process* that the student has been constructing over time. The defining essence or nature of the portfolio is self-expression and self-reflection, interpretation, and analysis.

The portfolio is, then, a large file folder, a loose-leaf notebook, or even an actual art portfolio packet in which growth is documented and representative work by the student is presented. Reaching the goal of what the portfolio *can* be, however, requires a process of growth for teachers as much as for students. This is why I am addressing portfolios after all the other assessment concepts—they reflect the best synthesis of *your* experience and understanding in classroom assessment. And this is why I will suggest a developmental progression toward attaining this "genuine" portfolio process in your classroom. The progression should help you conceptualize how you will initiate, sustain, and further develop a process of classroom-based assessment that will come to include your students' assessments of themselves as readers, writers, and learners.

Progression toward increasing student involvement

Our progression begins with a consideration of how *you* will pull together information about your students. Then we'll examine how your *students* can be involved in this process.

The Teacher's Reading Folder You will first need to get a handle on *your* organization of information about each child. An ongoing "reading folder" for each student will allow you to do this. This folder is not a portfolio because you, rather than the student, are setting it up. In years past, this reading folder was the sole means by which many teachers kept information about each student. As we'll see, it is now the first step toward instituting a portfolio approach in your classroom. Its contents may include:

- Running records and taped oral readings.
- Informal reading inventory forms.
- Qualitative Inventory of Word Knowledge.
- Your reading conference log.
- Checklists or forms for recording anecdotal information about students' progress (see Figure 11.8).
- A copy of the student's Reading Log (the original is stapled inside the back cover of the Response Log); the Reading Log is a record of the books the student has read and includes author, title, beginning and ending dates for reading the book, and if the student wishes, number of pages.
- Samples from the student's Response Log, word study notebook, and learning log (as we saw in Chapters 7 and 9, learning logs can include reflections on what students are learning about the process of reading and its application, as well as reflections on what they are learning in content areas).

Figure 11.8 presents sample recording forms. Under "Comments," the teacher can indicate the types of situations in which the particular skill, strategy, or knowledge was evidenced. (As we'll soon discuss, forms such as these can be appended to a grade report as well.)

The Genuine Portfolio The move from the teacher's reading folder to the student's Reading Portfolio represents a move from *your* being in control to the *student's* more active involvement. And students' understanding of their involvement will grow out of the nature and content of the discussions you have with them, individually and in groups, as you help them reflect on their strengths and on aspects they still feel they need to work on. Some educators suggest that when you feel you are comfortable in moving toward full implementation of the portfolio concept, you might introduce the most basic concept of portfolios—that of selecting and assessing one's work—by inviting older students to come to your class and discuss their portfolios in art, journalism, or some other area (Tierney, Carter, and Desai, 1991). The only possible hitch could be that students might not make the connection between a portfolio in art, for example, and a portfolio that represents their best reading (and writing; see below). You will need to be explicit about the general *purpose* of portfolios and discuss how theirs will be different from an art student's.

Routman cautioned, "There is a real danger . . . that portfolios will become collection silos—storage bins filled with data serving no useful purpose" (1991, p. 330). To avoid this occurrence, make sure your students will be involved in deciding the types of information that may be included in their portfolios, as well as the criteria for selection (Tierney, Carter, & Desai, 1991; Wolf, 1989). Remember, they will know that you have been collecting information regarding their development in their Reading Folders, and they will have had conferences with you about this information, so they will have some "background information" about possible content of their portfolios and the criteria for selecting it. With the students, generate a list of those things that might be examples of their best thinking and effort in reading, awareness of how to go about reading, and the different uses to which they apply their reading abilities.

CONSTUCTING MEANING

	SELDOM	OCCASIONALLY	ALWAYS	COMMENTS
Makes/Revises Predictions				
Recall and Use of Detail				
Ability to Infer Meaning				
Ability to Recognize or Infer Sequence and Cause/Effect				
Understands Differences Between Narrative and Expository Text				
Identifies and Understands Elements of Informational Text: ■ Main Ideas/Supporting Details ■ Fact vs. Opinion				
Appropriately Relates Text to Personal Experiences				

KNOWLEDGE
TEXT KNOWLEDGE

	SELDOM	OCCASIONALLY	ALWAYS	COMMENTS
Conventions of Punctuation				
Identifies and Understands Elements of Story: ■ Characterization ■ Setting ■ Plot ■ Theme				
Expository Text Structure ■ Table of Contents ■ Index ■ Headings/Subheadings ■ Text Patterns ■ Cause/Effect ■ Problem/Solution ■ Comparision/Contrast				
Strategies ■ Before, During, and ■ After				

KNOWLEDGE
WORD KNOWLEDGE

	SELDOM	OCCASIONALLY	ALWAYS	COMMENTS
Applies Knowledge of Contextual Cues ■ Pictures ■ Sentence ■ Beyond the Sentence (Paragraph, Overall				
Applies Knowledge of Phonic Cues ■ Beginning Consonants ■ Short Vowel Patterns ■ Consonant Blends ■ Consonant Digraphs ■ Long Vowel Patterns ■ Combines Phonic Knowledge with Context				
Applies Knowledge of Structural Analysis Cues ■ Prefixes ■ Roots: Bases ■ Suffixes ■ Roots: Latin and				
Understands Figurative Use of Words ■ Connotation ■ Idioms ■ Simile and Metaphor				

ATTITUDES AND OWNERSHIP

	SELDOM	OCCASIONALLY	ALWAYS	COMMENTS
Motivation to Read				
Persistence in Reading (Sticking with the Task)				
Takes on Challenging Reading Tasks				
Has Developed Preferences in Reading				
Able to Monitor Own Progress and Achievements				

Figure 11.8
Sample Recording Forms

While we wish students would discover and be able to articulate their own rationale for selecting items to include in their portfolios, they usually need some initial prompts from you (Hornsby, Sukarna, & Parry, 1986; Tierney, Carter, & Desai, 1991). Much of their reflection, in fact, may actually grow out of the reading conferences you have with them—those occasions when you have asked them to reflect on themselves as readers and writers. We are primarily concerned here with students' awareness of their own growth, of seeing how their expertise has changed over time, of what their individual strengths and areas of need are.

The following probes may be helpful in helping students think about their choices:

Why did they choose to include *this* particular piece?

Why did they choose one response journal entry to this piece over another entry?

What did they enjoy or remember most about this piece?

What affected them most in the piece?

How was this piece similar to or different from other pieces they have really enjoyed?

What did they learn from this selection?

And these should help facilitate their thinking about themselves as readers:

How do they determine what they will read?

What have they liked to read in the past?

What are they good at as readers?

What do they find difficult or challenging when they read?

What is their least favorite type of reading or genre? Why?

Here is a partial list of possibilities related to reading; note that some already will be a part of your reading folder for each student, and will—upon mutual agreement—simply become part of the portfolio.

■ Copies of favorite selections that have been read, with comments by the students; these may include a topic, author, or genre the student particularly enjoys.
■ Samples from reading response logs; these may include interchanges between student and teacher if the logs are used as "dialogue" journals.
■ Excerpts from selections on the Reading Log (so that, at a glance, parents and administrators can see beyond just a title and author to the nature of a selection).
■ Selections from the Learning Log, especially those that include students' "reflections" about strategies that have been learned and used.
■ Literature extension activities, which may include, for example, art, charts, or a write-up of the "dramatization" of a story.
■ Written responses to different types of story elements; these may include webs of each type, such as plot (see Chapter 6).

- Written comments from reading conferences.
- Samples from the Word Study Notebook, especially those that evidence an "Aha!" realization about the meaning or structure of a word or words; these samples may also include illustrations of new words or expressions or of figurative language.

Different information and samples may be set off by tabs in a loose-leaf notebook or by labeled divider sheets in a folder.

Let me add an important note about your progression from folders to portfolio: while, increasingly, the types of information you have included in the reading folder on each student will be kept in the portfolio, you may wish to keep reading folders for each student even when you have fully instituted a portfolio approach in your classroom. This need not violate the spirit of portfolios, either; in fact, the students should know about these and their purpose. For example, you may have quite extensive anecdotal notes on a student yet decide with the student to keep most in the folder and include in the portfolio only those notes that reflect a particular aspect of growth. District-wide standardized testing results may also be kept in the folder.

Closing Thoughts on Your Students' and Your Own Progression to Portfolios   Here, then, is the general sequence in which you will help your students become able to assess themselves productively as readers, writers, and learners. First, you provide positive feedback; second, your students will then be more comfortable with looking at *themselves* rather than comparing their progress

MAKING CONNECTIONS

The Writing Portfolio

The portfolio concept first gained popularity as a means of expressing students' growth in *writing*. Your progression toward full implementation of the "genuine" writing portfolio parallels that for the reading portfolio. You may begin by keeping representative samples of writing as well as information about students' developing writing abilities. As students discuss criteria for assessing their writing and determining what they believe are their most representative works, they increasingly take over responsibility for and ownership of the portfolio.

LEARNING IN CONTEXT: **The development of writing portfolios follows the same progression and organization as that of reading portfolios. Together, both types of portfolios can present the most authentic and comprehensive picture of students' literacy development.**

with that of *others;* third, your students will become increasingly involved in the assigning of their own grades.

In a basic, practical sense, the portfolio represents what the child is doing, and it can be a very important part of the evaluation for a specific school term. In its fullest, most developed, and most exciting sense, the portfolio can provide the opportunity for students' focus on self-assessment as well, an extremely important aspect of assessment.

OBSERVATIONS, PORTFOLIOS, AND GRADING

Traditionally, the assessment of children's progress has been reported in terms of letter grades. Over the years, other systems have been tried, but usually they have been shed in response to community confusion or dissatisfaction and traditional expectations. Like many other aspects of education, letter grades and what they mean are very deeply ingrained in the American collective consciousness. For better or for worse, they will continue to be used for quite some time, if for no other reason than because the expectations and realities of high schools and colleges depend on letter grades.

Our new orientation toward assessment, however, offers the possibility of continuing to use letter grades, but with the following criteria: (1) the nature of the students' work on which the grades are based; (2) the *students'* involvement in the assessment; and (3) better communication with parents and administrators about the nature of this work (Tierney, Carter, & Desai, 1991). In addition, many districts are moving toward revising their report cards to reflect the nature of the changing reading and writing curriculum, and letter grades are not being given in first and second grades.

Especially as your students become more and more involved in creating and maintaining their own portfolios, you may eventually "evolve" to a point where you are confident about and comfortable with their equal involvement in determining their own grades. Typically, however, *you* must in most situations assign a grade. This can be done fairly if you have been clear with your students about what will be assessed and how it will be evaluated. In other words, if you have conferenced with each student throughout the grading period, and if you have a conference with each, prior to the grade report, regarding his or her progress over the whole term, your students will clearly understand their grades and the process is, once again, demystified.

Your report card can assess reading in terms of the categories mentioned earlier: construction and interpretation of text meaning; knowledge about conventions of texts; use of strategies; attitudes; and "ownership" (Paris et al., 1992).

Figure 11.9, adapted from Routman (1991, p. 335), is an example of a reading "report card" or assessment form format. It is general enough in that it can reflect your work each term with narrative or expository text, and an attached information sheet can explain what has been focused on during the term—the *specifics* that were addressed in each grading period—as, for example, locational materials or understanding of specific genres and subtypes.

What is perhaps most important to note about this format is that it can be modified by adding to or changing categories. For example, sometimes you

NAME _____		DATE _____	
CATEGORY	CONSISTENT	INCONSISTENT	COMMENTS
Reads and Understands "Recreational" Reading Books			
Maintains Reading Log			
Completes Group Reading Assignment on Time			
Completes Reading Response Log Assignments			
Contributes Meaningfully in Literature Response Group Discussions			
Listens and Responds to Contributions of Others			
Completes Literature Extension Activities on Time			
Completes Literature Extension Activities to Best of Ability			

FINAL GRADE _____

GRADING SYSTEM

A: Consistent for 7 Out of 8 Areas   D: Consistent for 4 Out of 8 Areas

B: Consistent for 6 Out of 8 Areas   F: Inconsistent for Most Areas

C: Consistent for 5 Out of 8 Areas

Figure 11.9
Sample Report Card Format

may focus more on *strategies* that children are developing, so your categories would reflect the breakdown presented in Figure 11.8. You may wish to add a column to indicate improvement over the previous grading period.

Of course, you may have to use a set format for reporting; let's say your district's report card is more "traditional" and has the categories "Comprehension" and "Word Analysis" listed under "Reading," for example. You can still assign grades in these areas, but your supportive evidence would be provided, included with the traditional report card, on the format we've just been discussing. Several of these categories reflect comprehension, and "word analysis" assessment would be based on how well the student is applying the knowledge and strategies they are learning. And remember, let parents know on an ongoing basis what you are focusing on, and thus what their children will be assessed on. This can be done in a monthly newsletter home; when your students are composing the newsletter and writing about this aspect, their awareness and understanding of that term's grading categories and criteria are reinforced.

An advantage of periodic grading is that it requires you to take a broader look at what each student has been doing. The purpose, in other words, goes well beyond assigning grades. If you have been observing, assessing, and conferencing as you go along, both you and your students have a very good idea of what their grades will be that term. But the process of pulling all the information together toward the end of each grading period really solidifies your picture of each student and allows you the opportunity to step back and reflect more generally on their development and progress. Keep in mind, too, that an essential aspect of the "portfolio" process is the eventual involvement of the students in their own assessment—actually, their ownership of the process.

FORMAL OR "STANDARDIZED" ASSESSMENT

Some basic concepts of standardized testing

In this section we will examine both the nature of standardized assessment in reading and the major concepts that underlie it. Whether you have an additional "Tests and Measurements" course or whether the discussion here is all you may have for a while, it's important to be aware that you should become familiar with many of these concepts.

Standardized tests come in all forms, formats, and emphases. They are intended to be given to groups or to individuals; in this section, we will focus on group tests. More than likely, you have probably had the experience of taking a standardized test such as the Scholastic Assessment Test and knowing that decisions were going to be based on how well you did—decisions and conclusions that perhaps went far beyond what you believed was warranted, or even fair. Standardized assessment has developed a rather negative connotation among many educators as well as students, at the same time as it is valued by policymakers and much of the lay public.

We will always have standardized assessments in education, because we *do* need to know, in general, how well students are doing in comparison with other students. As educators, we certainly are "accountable" to a significant extent for our students' progress. The key to understanding the role of standardized assessment, therefore, is not to bemoan misuses but to work toward changing its nature and format enough to reflect our understanding of the nature, breadth, and applications of reading. As I mentioned at the beginning of the chapter, such efforts are under way, and we'll look at them soon.

For the reasons just mentioned, you will need to know about some basic concepts regarding group standardized assessment. Let's briefly consider the most important:

Does a test measure what it says it measures? If it does, we say that it is *valid* or that it has *validity*. Does the text consistently measure what it says it measures? If so, then it is *reliable* and we say it has good *reliability*.

The notion of "standard" is central to formal assessments. First of all, the *procedure* according to which a test is administered is "standardized," meaning that there is a standard or set manner in which directions are given and the test-taking organized, and there is a time limit as well. Second, the notion of "standardized" refers to comparisons of an individual student's score with those of other students who took the same test. Another way of talking about these comparisons is to say that a score is "referenced" to other students' scores. Specifically, these other students' scores come from the administration of the test in its final form before it was published and made available to the public at large. These students' scores are plotted; if enough students were included in this "standardization" or "norming" sample, as it's called, the scores then take the shape of a standard curve, which is referred to as a "bell-shaped" curve or "normal" curve (see Figure 11.10).

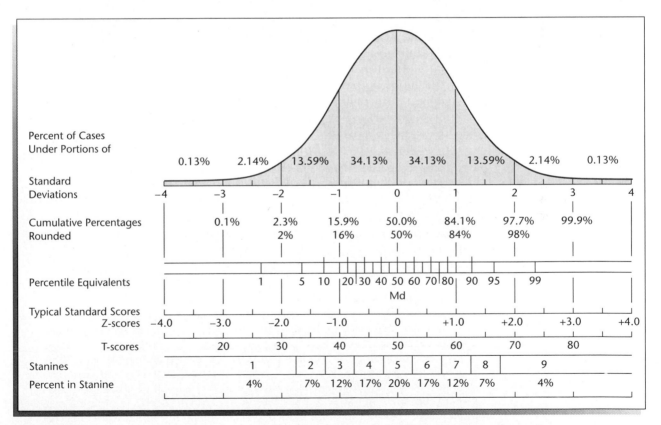

Figure 11.10
Normal Curve

It is important to keep in mind that this normal curve is based on scores of the norming sample that the test was administered to *prior to* its publication (most large-scale standardized tests are revised every few years to reflect possible changes in the characteristics and abilities of the students who are taking the test). So an individual student's score on a test is not compared with those of other students who took the test at the same time, but to the original population of students who took the test in its final stages of development. (There is an exception, however: many large school districts often contract with the test publisher to analyze test results just for that district and to report "norms" for the district.)

Some basic concepts about test performance can be described using this normal curve. Table 11.3 presents the most important.

■ TABLE 11.3   Basic Standardized Test Concepts

Mean

The average of all the scores on the test is the arithmetic mean. Note that most scores fall at the mean

---

Median

The median is the score at which half of all the scores fall above and half fall below. (On most widely used reading tests, the mean and the median are close if not identical.)

Standard Deviation

Look at Figure 11.10 again. Notice that there are percentages given; then notice that they are the same on both sides of the mean. Each segment in which a percentage is given represents what is called a standard deviation unit. The standard deviation is the term used to talk about how the scores are "spread out," or deviate, around the mean. If a test is given to enough individuals, the scores will "spread out" or deviate according to the percentages given. Most scores—68%—will be close to the mean. The remaining scores—32%—will be more spread out toward the extremes.

Standard Score (or Normal Curve Equivalent Score)

Standard scores are based on standard deviation units. For example, if a student scored at one standard deviation unit above the mean, his standard score would be $+1.0$; the student who scored one standard deviation unit below the mean would have a standard score of -1.0.

Standard scores are usually changed or transformed in a number of ways to make them more usable. Negative numbers, for example, are awkward to deal with, so they are all changed to positive numbers. The most common change involves multiplying the standard score by 10 and then adding 50 points (this transformed score is called a T-score). A score that is expressed in standard deviation units as $+1.0$, for example, becomes 60 ($1.0 \times 10 + 50$); a score expressed as -1.0 becomes 40 ($-1.0 \times 10 + 50$). A student who scores right at the mean and therefore has a standard score of 0 will have a transformed score of 50 ($0 \times 10 + 50$).

Percentile Scores

The median is the midpoint for all scores. Notice how the student who scores at the median has a percentile score of 50; this means that half the students scored below this point, and half scored at or above it. The student who scores one SD unit above the mean (standard score of 1.0; transformed or "T" score of 60) has a percentile score of 84. This means that 50% of the students below the median plus the 34% of students between the median and one SD unit above the median scored lower than this student—and 16% of the students scored above this point.

Stanine

The term *stanine* comes from the combination of two concepts: It is a score that is based on where a standard score falls on the normal curve when the curve is partitioned into nine segments. It is another way of showing where a student's score stands in relation to the scores of other students; a student with a stanine of 5 falls right in the middle of the distribution of scores; a stanine of 8 is toward the high end of the scores. (See Figure 11.10).

Grade Equivalent Score

Grade equivalent (GE) scores are one of the most frequently used scores in education. A GE score of 4.2 is read as "fourth grade second month"; 2.8 is "second grade eighth month." The actual meaning of these scores is this: the GE score stands for the average score of students in the norming sample who took the test at a particular grade level during a particular month of the year. For example: Let's say the actual or raw score that the student achieved corresponds to a GE score of 4.2; this means that the student's raw score is equal to the average raw score of all students in the norming sample who took the test in the second month of fourth grade.

Standard Error of Measurement (SEM)

If a student could theoretically take the same test over and over, without ever remembering previous administrations of the same test or learning anything new, his scores on the test could be plotted and take the shape of a normal curve. Two-thirds of those scores would fall between +1 and −1 standard deviation from the mean—just like the normal curve based on scores from many different individuals. The standard error of measurement is in effect the standard deviation for an individual student. The SEM is helpful because it defines the scores between which a student's "true" score falls. You take the actual score the student made, and by adding the SEM to and subtracting it from this actual score, you will know that two-thirds of the time, the student's score falls between those higher and lower scores.

Interpreting performance on a standardized test

After a school district administers a standardized test, a computer printout of each student's performance is provided. Most districts that administer such tests choose one that measures students' performance in several areas, not just in reading. Three widely used assessments are the *Iowa Tests of Basic Skills*, the

Stanford Achievement Test, and the *Comprehensive Test of Basic Skills* (CTBS). Figure 11.11 shows the results for a second-grade student.

This student took the CTBS in March (seventh month of second grade). The subtests that measure aspects of reading are highlighted as well as his "reading total." Note the columns of scores to the right of the subtests: NR = "Number Right"; NA = "Number Attempted"; NP = "National Percentile"; NS = "National Stanine." Let's examine a couple of the student's scores. On the Comprehension subtest he scored better than 35% of the students who took the test when it was normed, and this places him in the fourth stanine. His "Reading Total" score, which averages his performance on word analysis, vocabulary, and comprehension, places him in the sixth stanine, in the high average range. Additional information about test characteristics usually is not included on this printout, but may be found in the examiner's or technical manual for the test.

I discourage the use of results from group standardized tests in assessing individual students' development and making instructional decisions, primarily for two reasons:

1. Such tests sample only a small range of reading tasks.
2. Because reading testing occurs on only one or two days out of the entire school year, students' performances can be disproportionately affected by their physical and emotional predispositions on those particular days.

It is somewhat ironic that the primary purpose of group standardized tests— providing information about large groups of students—often is lost in our focus on the performance of *individual* students. After all, the example we've just been looking at concerns an individual student, and the scores reported invite,

Subtests	NR	NA	NP	NS	NATIONAL PERCENTILE RANK
WORD ANALYSIS	25	30	67	6	
VOCABULARY	29	32	92	8	
COMPREHENSION	24	34	35	4	
SPELLING	11	27	28	4	
LANGUAGE MECH	10	27	8	2	
LANGUAGE EXP	31	35	76	6	
MATH COMP	27	30	89	8	
MATH CONCEPTS	30	39	51	5	
SCIENCE	19	25	48	5	
SOCIAL STUDIES	15	25	34	4	
READING TOTAL	53	66	65	6	
LANGUAGE TOTAL	41	62	41	5	
MATH TOTAL	57	69	73	6	
TOTAL BATTERY	151	197	62	6	

*NR=NUMBER RIGHT NA=NO. ATTEMPTED
NP=NATIONAL %ILE NS=NAT'L STANINE

Figure 11.11
Partial Printout of Second-Grader's Performance on the Comprehensive Test of Basic Skills

if not outright encourage, comparisons between that student and others. If you discuss such results with parents, be clear about the limitations of the tests and share primarily your classroom-based assessments.

New developments in large-scale assessments

As we've already noted, large-scale assessments will always be with us. They do serve certain important purposes. We need to know, in general, whether students at the district, state, and national levels are acquiring knowledge about reading and writing—as well as about other content areas such as math, science, and social studies. Accepting this reality, as educators we work toward developing more authentic, trustworthy, *performance-based* measures (IRA/NCTE Joint Task Force on Assessment, 1994) at the same time as we work toward helping the lay public understand the purposes and the limitations of large-scale assessments.

At the close of the twentieth century, we *are* bringing large-scale assessment in reading more into line with what we know the process and the product of reading to be. The principles of the more authentic and trustworthy assessment that you will be using in your classroom are guiding assessment on a large-scale level as well. Let's see how.

Dissatisfied with the traditional standardized tests, many states have developed their own reading assessments. This is true at the national level as well. Notably, the National Assessment of Educational Progress (NAEP) has recently developed more authentic and trustworthy reading tasks (Valencia, Hiebert, & Kapinus, 1992). This is important because the NAEP tracks national and

MAKING CONNECTIONS:

How to Read the "Test" Genre

Our students know the purposes and uses of large-scale tests. Understandably, they become nervous when "test-taking" time rolls around each year. One way to alleviate their anxieties as well as prepare them for the reality of these tests is by presenting the test as another text "genre." We read stories in certain ways, and informational books in certain ways, and tests should also be read in certain ways. Tests should be examined for their features and organization, just like other genres.

You may approach tests this way with your students, even if they are at the primary grade level. Share some examples from a test similar to the one they will be taking. Discuss the similarities and differences between this type of "text" and other texts the children are reading. Help them examine the questions that accompany the passages; they may note that sometimes the questions really can't be answered on the basis of the passage. Talk about what to do when this is the case—what answer do they think the test *writers* expect?

LEARNING IN CONTEXT: Tests can be viewed as one type of text.

geographic trends and has been doing so since 1971. Every few years, the NAEP assesses fourth-, eighth-, and twelfth-grade students nationwide.

The most recent version of the NAEP assesses three types of reading: "reading for literary experiences, reading to be informed, and reading to perform a task" (Valencia, Hiebert, & Kapinus, 1992, p. 732). For each of these types of reading, four different types of questions measure initial understanding, interpretation, personal response, and critical stance. Valencia and colleagues offer the following examples for each of these types of questions, based on the "reading for literary experiences" category (1992, p. 733): An *initial response* question would be "What is the theme of this story?"; an *interpretation* question is "Why do you think the main character made the decision she did? Use information from the passage to support your answer"; a *personal response* question is "How is the character similar, or different from someone you know or have read about?"; and a *critical stance* question is "Explain how this author's use of irony contributed to the story."

The recent reading NAEP also includes actual passages from published materials. This is in contrast to most traditional reading tests, which often contain passages that are written expressly for the test and may be more contrived because of rigid adherence to readability formulas. The passages are longer, and longer time periods are allowed. A common theme extends in some cases across different types of texts—for example poem, diary, narrative.

Fluency and metacognition are also examined among five to ten percent of the fourth-grade students, and many students are assessed and interviewed on a one-on-one basis to explore (1) oral reading—including miscues and rate—and discussion of a passage; (2) the frequency and nature of their reading at school and at home; and (3) samples of their classroom work and their self-assessment. A smaller number of students is used for this information because, realistically, it could not be collected for all the students nationwide who are assessed.

Is it apparent, now, how large-scale assessment is moving toward the type of classroom-based assessment we discussed earlier in this chapter? Each of the aspects of reading just discussed in the NAEP reflects what you will be doing: assessing interaction with text; knowledge of print and text conventions; orientation/ownership; and self-assessment.

In large-scale holistic *writing* assessments, students are given a specific topic on which they are asked to write and a given amount of time in which to write. Compositions are then rated by knowledgeable evaluators on a scale of 0–4 or 0–6, with "0" being the lowest possible score. A description or "rubric" (Winograd, 1994) of the criteria for each of the numerical ratings is provided the evaluators so that the writing qualities and specifics required for each score are explicit; this is another reason, by the way, why it may be helpful to adapt holistic assessment to the classroom. Earlier in this chapter, we looked at some common elements that are judged in expository writing: *focus, organization, support,* and *conventions.* Figure 11.12 presents the compositions of two sixth-grade students who were involved in a district-wide writing assessment. The students responded to the expository prompt "What Is Your Favorite Pet?"

Matthew's paper was rated "6" by two evaluators. He has clear focus, develops

Figure 11.12
Holistic Writing Assessment Examples

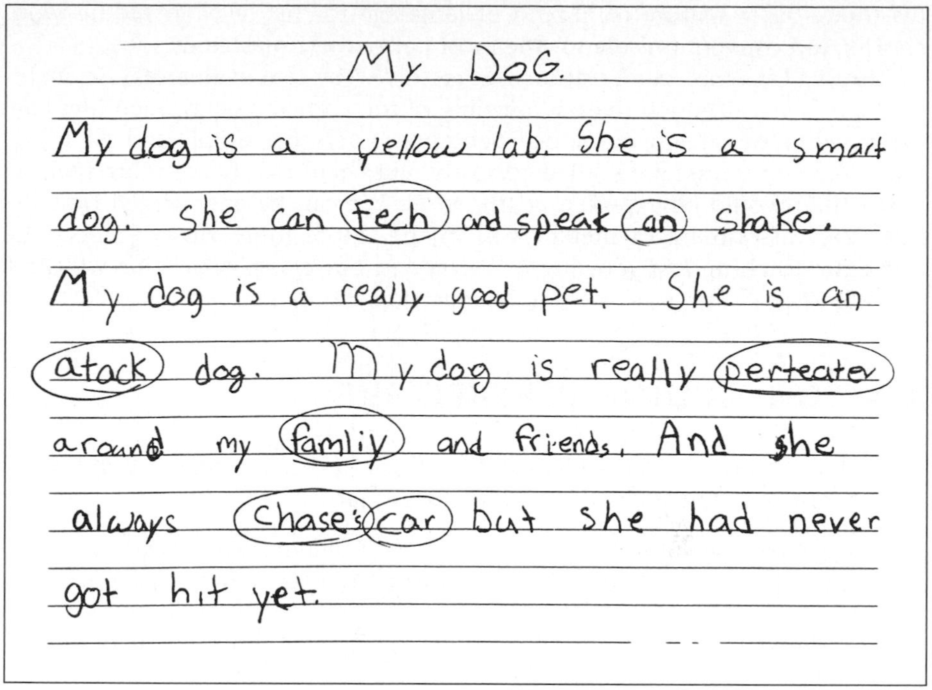

My DoG.

My dog is a yellow lab. She is a smart dog. She can (Fech) and speak (an) shake. My dog is a really good pet. She is an (atack) dog. My dog is really (perteater) around my (famliy) and friends. And she always (Chase's)(car) but she had never got hit yet.

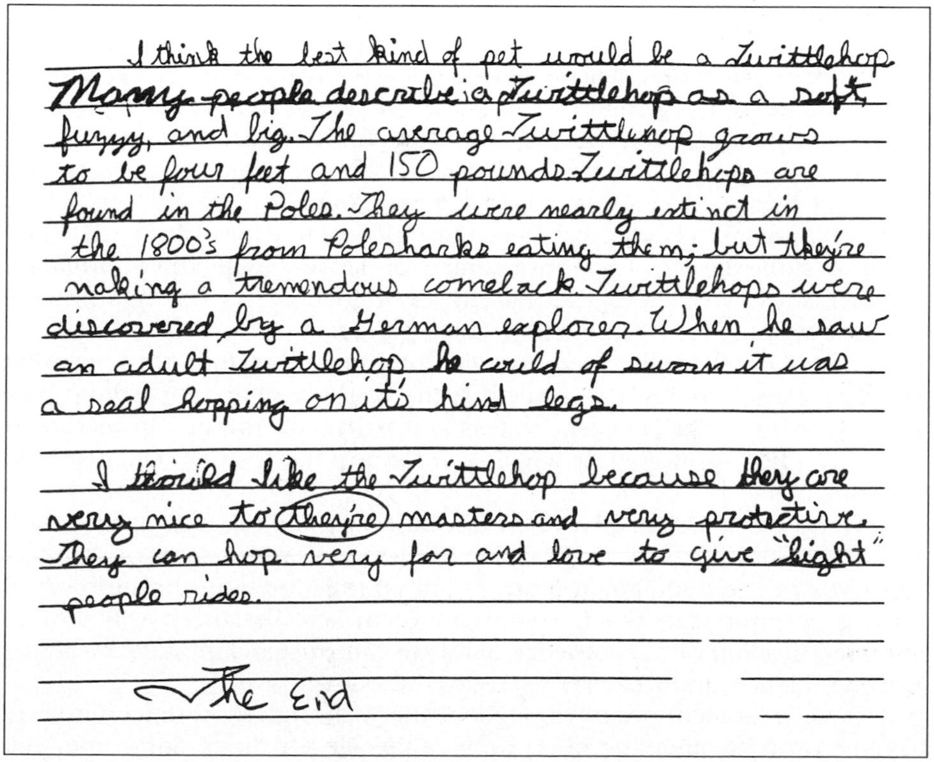

I think the best kind of pet would be a Twittlehop. ~~Many~~ people describe a Twittlehop as a soft, fuzzy, and big. The average Twittlehop grows to be four feet and 150 pounds. Twittlehops are found in the Poles. They were nearly extinct in the 1800's from Polesharks eating them; but they're making a tremendous comeback. Twittlehops were discovered by a German explorer. When he saw an adult Twittlehop he could of sworn it was a seal hopping on it's hind legs.

I would like the Twittlehop because they are very nice to (they're) masters and very protective. They can hop very far and love to give "light" people rides.

The End

his topic, has a mature command of language for his level including word choice; and conventions are for the most part clearly mastered.

Chris's "My Dog" composition was rated "3" by two evaluators. He maintained a focus, although there is a feeling of incompleteness; though ideas are expressed, none is really developed. Sentence structure is simple and the words most frequently used are spelled correctly, but there clearly are more spelling errors than would be expected at this level. We can be encouraged that the large-scale assessment of literacy will in the future more closely reflect the authentic teaching and learning of literacy in our classrooms. This will be a very significant and much-needed change from the past.

■ A CONCLUDING PERSPECTIVE

Sheila Valencia captured the goals and the spirit of our new orientation toward classroom-based and large-scale reading assessment:

> We need an assessment system that honors the alignment of instruction and assessment, so that we truly hold ourselves and our students accountable for important instructional outcomes . . . we want to communicate . . . the real literacy achievements of our students. We want to paint a more complex picture of literacy and tell a more complete story than we have been able to do with existing measures. (1990, p. 60)

Our assessment of students' reading must be authentic so that our assessment of their knowledge will guide appropriate and effective instruction. In the past, many teachers felt they had to have a specific task at a particular time to assess whether or not a child had "mastered" a skill or strategy. This was most conveniently addressed, it was presumed, by administering a standardized test. As you've seen, one of the major differences with classroom-based assessment is the fact that you can assess in an ongoing fashion. You observe and reflect about each student's knowledge about and application of the different skills and strategies along the way. There are a number of ways of pulling this information together, and as we've seen, the "pulling together" process feeds right into the process according to which you can assign grades.

Rather than relying on group standardized tests, therefore, we know that informal, classroom-based assessment is the best way of accomplishing these goals. This is true for emergent readers and writers on through to mature or proficient ones. Assessment is ongoing; it informs our instructional decisions continually.

As we first saw in Chapter 4, you will be observing and gathering information about your students beginning early in the school year. For some of your students, you will need additional, more specific information early on. The informal reading inventory can be of considerable help here because it will provide information about word knowledge, ability to construct and interpret meaning, rate and fluency, and whatever strategies the student is using.

Because assessment occurs throughout the year—indeed, throughout every day—you will be observing in all kinds of literacy situations. Sometimes you will be able to record your information on the spot; at other times you will wait until a more convenient time. Regardless, the information you will be gathering for each student will be put in your notebook, file, or portfolio for later examination, for overall assessment, and for help in partially determining the grade—if a grade must be given—for each student.

Portfolio assessment is indeed a powerful means of developing students' awareness of themselves as learners and of involving them in the organization and assessment of their growth in literacy. When students are involved this way, assessment is "demystified," and students have a clear stake in understanding and assessing how they are acquiring and applying the powerful tools of literacy.

As you evolve toward a literacy classroom environment in which the students are involved more integrally in their own assessment, at most elementary grade levels you will still need to assign grades. Students can come to play more of a role in this, too. In the meantime, the periodic "report card" time can be an opportunity to look back over the development of each of your students during that term. The grade you assign will represent both individual growth and individual progress toward involvement in the various literacy activities.

While you will be involved with informal, classroom-based assessment on a daily basis, you also will know and understand the purposes and characteristics of group standardized assessments. They can yield important information about large groups, but they cannot yield much useful specific information about your individual students. It is reassuring to know, however, that these large-scale assessments will be assessing more directly what teachers are emphasizing in their reading instruction.

We want a new perspective on assessment; we want a perspective that truly values how complex literacy is and that works *for* rather than against students' understanding and appreciation of themselves as readers and learners.

■ BECOMING A REFLECTIVE PRACTITIONER

Goodman, Y. (1985). Kidwatching: Observing children in the classroom. In A. Jaggar & M. T. Smith-Burke (Eds.). *Observing the language learner* (pp. 9–18). Urbana, IL and Newark, DE: National Council of Teachers of English and the International Reading Association.

You will find this entire edited volume to be very informative and helpful. I am suggesting Yetta Goodman's chapter in particular because "kidwatching" has become an attractive, helpful, and popular notion—though its roots, as Goodman points out, stretch far back to earlier educators and educational movements. Goodman shows *how* teachers can be effective kidwatchers and emphasizes the importance of an understanding of children and of language. This foundation will provide teachers with the knowledge base to make on-the-spot assessments of children's learning and to adjust instructional strategies accordingly.

Paris, S., Calfee, R., Filby, N., Hiebert, E., Pearson, P. D., Valencia, S., & Wolf, K. (1992). A framework for authentic literacy assessment. *The Reading Teacher, 46*, 88–98.

This article covers a lot of ground within a relatively few pages. It discusses the nature and the development of a comprehensive framework of literacy assessment for the

Kamehameha, Hawaii schools. The authors present "critical dimensions and attributes" of literacy and offer performance indicators for assessing the degree to which students manifest these attributes. The article engages the reader in a comprehensive examination of the nature of literacy and its instruction in a social context as well as in the important issues of assessment.

Tierney, R., Carter, M., & Desai, L. (1991). *Portfolio assessment in the reading-writing classroom.* Norwood, MA: Christopher-Gordon.

A number of articles and books have appeared in recent years that have addressed portfolio assessment in literacy. This book is one of the best; the authors present a comprehensive overview of the nature and scope of portfolio assessment in literacy—the promise of what it can be and the reality of moving toward that promise. It provides an excellent treatment of how to move students toward self-evaluation.

Valencia, S., Hiebert, E., & Kapinus, B. (1992). National assessment of educational progress: What do we know and what lies ahead? *The Reading Teacher, 45,* 730–734.

Valencia and her colleagues review the history of the National Assessment of Educational Progress (NAEP) and what it has shown us over the last twenty years about how well students are learning. The limitations of previous test formats are addressed, and the nature of the newest NAEP in reading is briefly explained.

■ REFERENCES

Barr, R., Sadow, M., & Blachowicz, C. (1990). *Reading diagnosis for teachers.* New York: Longman.

Baumann, J. (1988). *Reading assessment: An instructional decision-making perspective.* Columbus, OH: Merrill.

Bear, D., & Barone, D. (1989). Using children's invented spellings to group for word study and directed reading in the primary classroom. *Reading Psychology, 10,* 275–292.

Bear, D., & Barone, D. (forthcoming). *Developing literacy: An integrated approach to diagnosis and instruction.* Boston: Houghton Mifflin.

Bear, D., Templeton, S., & Warner, M. (1991). The development of a qualitative inventory of higher levels of orthographic knowledge. In J. Zutell & S. McCormick (Eds.), *Learner factors/teacher factors: Issues in literacy research and instruction* (Fortieth yearbook of the National Reading Conference) (pp. 105–110). Chicago: National Reading Conference.

Betts, E. (1946). *Foundations of reading instruction.* New York: American Book Company.

Burns, P., & Roe, B. (1993). *Informal reading inventory.* Boston: Houghton Mifflin.

Carver, R. (1989). Silent reading rates in grade equivalents, *Journal of Reading Behavior, 21,* 155–166.

Clay, M. (1985). *The early detection of reading difficulties* (3rd ed.). Portsmouth, NH: Heinemann.

Clay, M. (1991). *Becoming literate: The construction of inner control.* Auckland, New Zealand: Heinemann.

Gill, J., Jr. (1992). Development of word knowledge as it relates to reading, spelling, and instruction. *Language Arts, 69,* 444–453.

Gillet, J., & Temple, C. (1994). *Understanding reading problems* (4th ed.). New York: HarperCollins.

Glazer, S., & Brown, C. (1993). *Portfolios and beyond: Collaborative assessment in reading and writing.* Norwood, MA: Christopher-Gordon.

Goodman, Y. (1985). Kidwatching: Observing children in the classroom. In A. Jaggar & M. T. Smith-Burke (Eds.), *Observing the language learner* (pp. 9–18). Urbana, IL, and Newark, DE: National Council of Teachers of English and the International Reading Association.

Goodman, Y., Watson, D., & Burke, C. (1987). *Reading miscue inventory: Alternative procedures.* New York: Richard C. Owen.

Hansen, J. (1992). Students' evaluations bring reading and writing together. *Reading Teacher, 46,* 100–105.

Harste, J., Short, K., & Burke, C. (1989). *Creating classrooms for authors.* Portsmouth, NH: Heinemann.

Hornsby, D., Sukarna, D., & Parry, J. (1986). *Read on: A conference approach to reading.* Portsmouth, NH: Heinemann.

IRA/NCTE Joint Task Force on Assessment. (1994). *Standards for the assessment of reading and writing.* Newark, DE: International Reading Association; Urbana, IL: National Council of Teachers of English.

Johnson, M., Kress, R., & Pikulski, J. (1987). *Informal reading inventories* (2nd ed.). Newark, DE: International Reading Association.

Leslie, L., & Caldwell, J. (1990). Qualitative Reading Inventory. New York: HarperCollins.

Lipson, M., & Wixson, K. (1990). Assessment and instruction of reading disability. New York: HarperCollins.

McPhee, J. (1981). *Basin and range.* New York: Farrar, Straus, Giroux.

Paradis, E., Chatton, B., Boswell, A., Smith, M., & Yovich, S. (1991). Accountability: Assessing comprehension during literature discussion. *Reading Teacher, 45,* 8–17.

Paris, S., Calfee, R., Filby, N., Hiebert, E., Pearson, P., Valencia, S., & Wolf, K. (1992). A framework for authentic literacy assessment. *Reading Teacher, 46,* 88–98.

Perfetti, C. (1992). The representation problem in reading acquisition. In P. Gough, L. Ehri, & R. Treiman (Eds.), *Reading acquisition* (pp. 145–174). Hillsdale, NJ: Lawrence Erlbaum Associates.

Pikulski, J., & Shanahan, T. (Eds.). (1982). Approaches to the informal evaluation of reading. Newark, DE: International Reading Association.

Routman, R. (1991). *Invitations.* Portsmouth, NH: Heinemann.

Ruth, L., & Murphy, S. (1988). *Designing writing tasks for the assessment of writing.* Norwood, NJ: Ablex.

Schlagal, R. (1992). Patterns of orthographic development into the intermediate grades. In S. Templeton & D. Bear (Eds.), *Development of orthographic knowledge and the foundations of literacy: A memorial Festschrift for Edmund H. Henderson* (pp. 31–52). Hillsdale, NJ: Lawrence Erlbaum Associates.

Shake, M. (1989). Grouping and pacing with basal materials. In P. Winograd, K. Wixson, & M. Lipson (Eds.), *Improving basal reading instruction* (pp. 62–85). New York: Teachers College Press.

Stauffer, R. (1969). *Directing reading maturity as a cognitive process.* New York: Harper & Row.

Stauffer, R., Abrams, J., & Pikulski, J. (1978). *Diagnosis, correction, and prevention of reading disabilities.* New York: Harper and Row.

Templeton, S. (1991). *Teaching the integrated language arts.* Boston: Houghton Mifflin.

Templeton, S., & Bear, D. (Eds.). (1992). *Development of orthographic knowledge and the foundations of literacy: A memorial Festschrift for Edmund H. Henderson.* Hillsdale, NJ: Lawrence Erlbaum Associates.

Tierney, R., Carter, M., & Desai, L. (1991). *Portfolio assessment in the reading-writing classroom.* Norwood, MA: Christopher-Gordon.

Tompkins, G. (1994). *Teaching writing.* Columbus, OH: Merrill.

Valencia, S. (1990). Alternative assessment: Separating the wheat from the chaff. *Reading Teacher, 44,* 60–61.

Valencia, S., Hiebert, E., & Kapinus, B. (1992). National assessment of educational progress: What do we know and what lies ahead? *Reading Teacher, 45,* 730–734.

Winograd, P. (1994). Developing alternative assessments: Six problems worth solving. *Reading Teacher, 47,* 420–423.

Wolf, D. (1989). Portfolio assessment: Sampling students' work. *Educational Leadership, 46,* 35–39.

Woods, M., & Moe, A. (1989). *Analytical reading inventory.* Columbus, OH: Merrill.

Zutell, J. (1992). An integrated view of word knowledge: Correlational studies of the relationships among spelling, reading, and conceptual development. In S. Templeton & D. Bear (Eds.), *Development of orthographic knowledge and the foundations of literacy: A memorial Festschrift for Edmund H. Henderson* (pp. 213–230). Hillsdale, NJ: Lawrence Erlbaum Associates.

Following is a portrait of Jennifer, a third-grade student for whom additional information was needed after her teacher observed and gathered some information one-to-one and in small-group situations. You'll see how the teacher combined this information with the information from the informal reading inventory. Jennifer is less than a month shy of ten years of age. Figure 11.13 presents a summary of Jennifer's performance on the IRI.

Comprehension   Given Jennifer's performance on the "word recognition in isolation" lists, the teacher had her begin reading at the primer-level passages (there were no preprimer passages on this particular IRI). Jennifer was not comfortable retelling what she had read, so the teacher asked her the comprehension questions. You can see that Jennifer's comprehension on the oral passages, primer through second grade, was at the lower end of the *instructional* range. Comprehension on the primer and first-grade silent passages was somewhat better (because of less self-consciousness, the teacher sensed). The teacher discontinued having Jennifer read after completing the second-grade passages because Jennifer was clearly approaching frustrational level. To the teacher's delight, however, Jennifer's *listening* comprehension was excellent; she was at least "instructional" through the eighth grade. This is quite unusual for a third-grader and usually is an indication that a student may be talented verbally. At the very least, however, the teacher clearly affirmed Jennifer's potential for dealing with the concepts that are addressed in the third-grade curriculum and in third-grade level reading materials.

Jennifer's comprehension of the passages she read on her own showed that she was able to recall information stated factually. There were no inferential questions at the levels at which she read. She did handle inferential questions well, however, when the higher-level passages were read *to* her.

Word Knowledge   The teacher examined Jennifer's *word analysis* abilities as evidenced by her performance in "flash" and "untimed" conditions and in context on the IRI, on the Qualitative Inventory of Word Knowledge, and in her writing. Let's examine the information gained from Jennifer's invented spelling in combination with the information about her miscues in reading.

Consider Jennifer's performance on the first ten words of the Qualitative Inventory:

bed
ship
drive
bubp (bump)
whin (when)
trane (train)
closit (closet)
chasd (chased)
flote (float)
bechis (beaches)

GRADE	WORD RECOGNITION: ISOLATION		WORD RECOGNITION: CONTEXT	COMPREHENSION		
	FLASH	UNTIMED		ORAL	SILENT	LISTENING
PP	100					
P	70	90	94	60	100	
1	40	60	83	70	90	
2	40	40	89	70	40	
3			87			90
4						90
5						80
6						80
7						100
8						80
9						

NAME: Jennifer M.   AGE: 9 yrs. 11 mos.   GRADE: 3

DATE: _____

READING LEVELS:

Independent _____—_____
Instructional _____P-1_____
Frustrational _____2_____
Listening _____6+_____

Figure 11.13
IRI Summary Sheet

Jennifer's performance on the Qualitative Inventory suggests that she is at the *within-word pattern* stage of word knowledge. Does she apply this type of knowledge to the analysis of unknown words in isolation? On the word-recognition portion of the IRI, we can see that her sight-word knowledge in isolation certainly is not what we would expect for most third-graders. On both the primer and the first-grade lists, she knew only four out of ten words in the "flash" condition; given the opportunity to analyze them in the "un-timed" condition, she was able to identify only two others correctly. *She does not use her knowledge of vowel patterns to analyze the unknown words:* her attempts to analyze words in isolation were limited to using the first and sometimes the last letters and the length of the word, as clues. For example, she analyzed *road* as *rained, bigger* as *bear, wide* as *wind.*

Does she apply her within-word pattern knowledge in her reading? Figure 11.14 shows part of the qualitative analysis of her miscues in connected text.

QUALITATIVE ANALYSIS SUMMARY SHEET

FORM: _____

STUDENT: Jennifer   DATE: 9-22-94

LEVEL	# OF MISCUES	MISCUE IN CONTEXT	MEANING CHANGE	NATURE OF MISCUE
P②		The dog's name is ~~Pat.~~ (Pet)	no	Beginning/final letter sound similarity: perhaps cueing on "dog"
		The dog ~~wanted~~ (want) to eat.	no	Beginning/final similarity; omitting inflectional ending
1⑭		(Tuff) ~~was a~~ (as the) big brown bear.	yes	Examiner aid; omitted initial consonant and cued on <u>as</u>; whole word subst.
		~~He~~ (The) lived in a big park.	yes	Graphic similarity; <u>He</u> and <u>the</u>
		He liked to eat ~~honey best~~ (hungry beast) of all.	yes	Both miscues initial/final consonant similarity
		He also liked to eat ~~bread.~~ (brēd)	yes	Beginning/ending consonant similarity; vowel miscue overrides meaning
		Some people ~~were~~ (where) in the park.	yes	Overall word similarity

Figure 11.14
Qualitative Miscue Analysis

Figure 11.15
"My Bunny"

> ## My Bunny
> I got my Bunny for estar.
> He is my fevrit stuft anuml.
> He is vere stoft! my mom
> gave hem to me for estar.
> I leve he on my bed.
> and he has broun ise and
> I love him alot.

CHAPTER APPENDIX

Continued

On the basis of her miscues, it seems that *meaning* (primarily of words rather than overall sentence context) seems to override her application of within-word pattern knowledge: *Pet* instead of *Pat; hungry beast* instead of *honey best.* (At her frustrational level, second grade, her miscues were random and seldom made sense; when students are attempting to read frustrational-level material, they are not likely to apply effectively what they know about words.)

Writing Analysis   Jennifer's teacher had asked all the students to bring in something that meant a lot to them. This was used as a writing prompt after the children talked about what they had brought. Jennifer's composition shows that she is able to sustain her focus on the topic, to write descriptively, to give her readers a sense of chronology—telling us when she got her bunny— and a sense of why he means a lot to her. Her command of writing conventions reveals that she understands capitalization, basic punctuation (she even includes an exclamation point), and simple sentence patterns. There is more support here for our determination that her level of word knowledge is "within-word pattern": many sight words are spelled correctly; most short vowels are spelled conventionally; her invented spellings for long vowel and diphthong patterns reflect an understanding of the function of "silent" vowel letters—*leave*/LEVE, *brown*/BROUN, *eyes*/ISE. This supports her performance on the Qualitative Inventory—she is *applying* in her writing what she knows about words.

   In summary, Jennifer does not really have an *independent* reading level. Given her word recognition in context and comprehension percentages, her *instructional* level is clearly primer. She should also be tried, though, on first-grade level material for instructional purposes *if* she is encouraged and shown how to apply the word-analysis strategies that her level of word knowledge affords her. We would predict that with support and the confidence it brings, she would be successful at this level as well. Her *frustrational* level is second grade.

CHAPTER TWELVE

MAKING INSTRUCTION WORK FOR STUDENTS WITH SPECIAL LITERACY NEEDS

FOCUS

■ *In the context of a rich literacy environment, what adjustments should you make in facilitating the literacy growth of children who are learning English as a second language or who speak a variant dialect?*

■ *In the regular classroom, how can you accommodate the literacy instructional needs of children whose development is significantly behind that of their classmates?*

■ *What necessary adjustments must be made for children who have "primary" learning difficulties in literacy?*

> *[T]eachers need to strike a delicate balance between stepping back and giving students the space to construct their own understandings of reading and writing, and stepping in with the support they need for further growth in literacy.*
>
> Kathryn Au, Literacy Instruction in Multicultural Settings

Given the diversity of our society, children bring to school a wide range of literacy needs and talents. Teachers, therefore, must tailor their instruction to highlight their students' accomplishments, while at the same time recognizing each student's unique cultural, social, and academic differences as rich sources for understanding literacy development. Knowing exactly when and how to provide support for children who are learning English as a second language, who speak variant dialects, or who are not achieving their potential will be the focus of this chapter.

Despite teachers' efforts, a good many children do not attain the levels of literacy they are capable of reaching. Often teachers are uncertain about how to make instructional adjustments for children who are not making academic and social progress. Yet in most cases effective, developmentally appropriate instruction can pay off for children with special literacy needs.

WHO ARE STUDENTS WITH SPECIAL LITERACY NEEDS?

The goal of all of our instruction is to meet students where they are and go from there. But the groups of students we will discuss in this chapter pose particular instructional challenges that should be addressed as we facilitate their literacy learning. First, we'll look at students whose first language is not English. The challenges for them are related to learning the new language and the conventions of its use. Next, we'll consider students who speak variant dialects; their challenges have to do with usage and conventions. Finally, we'll discuss students who are not performing at the same level as their classmates.

The vast majority of children experiencing difficulty are not achieving their potential; a very small minority face limitations caused by neurophysiological or "primary" factors. In this section, I'll describe each of the three groups of students in a bit more detail. It will be helpful, as you read, to refer to Figure 12.1, which provides an overview of the different groups of students with special literacy needs.

Because literacy is a language-based phenomenon, students must understand the relationship between print and the language they hear being spoken. Many students who don't speak English may already have acquired various degrees of literacy in a first language; they already understand the "functional" aspects of literacy and many of the features of relationships between print and speech.

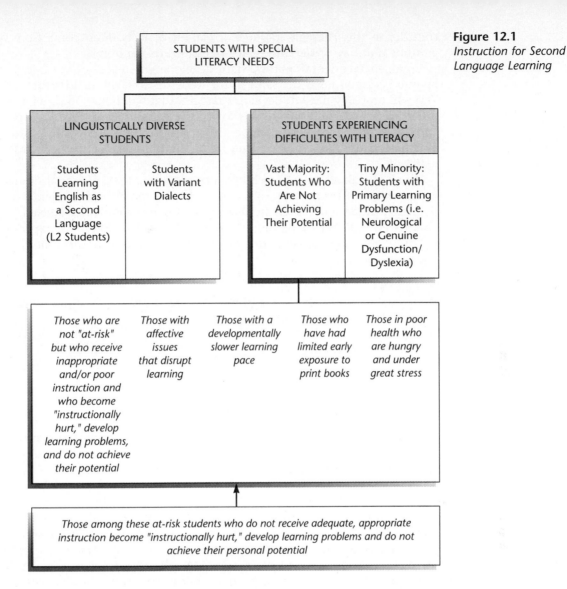

Figure 12.1
Instruction for Second Language Learning

STUDENTS WITH SPECIAL LITERACY NEEDS

LINGUISTICALLY DIVERSE STUDENTS

STUDENTS EXPERIENCING DIFFICULTIES WITH LITERACY

Students Learning English as a Second Language (L2 Students)

Students with Variant Dialects

Vast Majority: Students Who Are Not Achieving Their Potential

Tiny Minority: Students with Primary Learning Problems (i.e. Neurological or Genuine Dysfunction/ Dyslexia)

Those who are not "at-risk" but who receive inappropriate and/or poor instruction and who become "instructionally hurt," develop learning problems, and do not achieve their potential

Those with affective issues that disrupt learning

Those with a developmentally slower learning pace

Those who have had limited early exposure to print books

Those in poor health who are hungry and under great stress

Those among these at-risk students who do not receive adequate, appropriate instruction become "instructionally hurt," develop learning problems and do not achieve their personal potential

Many other such students may not be literate in their first languages, so their primary need is to develop understandings characteristic of emergent literacy.

Students who speak a variant dialect of English are very likely to have difficulty acquiring literacy if teachers prematurely stress or overemphasize speaking standard English, either before or during the learning of conventional literacy. While the standard English dialect is important to learn, students may become overloaded if we attempt to couple literacy instruction with instruction in standard usage and conventions. There is a related issue here that we will consider in this chapter: speakers of variant dialects often come from backgrounds that have different literacy traditions in the home.

Your general orientation toward the development of literacy in students from diverse backgrounds is the same as for students from the mainstream culture. You will probably need to develop strategies that will help you provide appropriate literacy-learning experiences for a great many of these students. A primary emphasis of this chapter, therefore, is to explore the foundations and nature of these strategies and see how they relate to what you already know from this textbook.

When we talk of students who are not achieving their potential, we usually mean that they do not appear to be where the majority of students are at a particular grade level; such nonachieving students are often labeled at-risk. There are a number of possible reasons why these children are experiencing difficulty; and quite often, depending on the child, some or most of them may interact:

- A slower pace of development
- Limited literacy experiences, during the preschool years, of the type that foster familiarity with stories, books, and features of print
- A mismatch of behaviors, styles, and expectations between the teacher and the student, because of different cultural backgrounds
- Issues having to do with poverty—health, hunger, exposure to drugs and violence
- Personality factors—low self-esteem, learned helplessness

It is important to realize that most of these reasons or issues are not "problems" in and of themselves but may *become* problems because of inappropriate instructional response. Unfortunately, this is quite common. And of course all these factors can affect attitude, motivation, and interest, which are crucial to the development of understandings about the nature, purposes, and functions of literacy.

If you are a kindergarten or first-grade teacher, you have the unique opportunity to address the needs of your students very early. At these beginning stages, you can give students time for growth while they participate in supportive, successful literacy experiences. In so doing, you'll be providing academic and social structure that will balance the potentially negative influences of slow development, lack of familiarity with literacy experiences, varying cultural backgrounds, and the traumas of poverty. You will be averting the damage that can come from a learning environment which requires young children to conform to the demands of a curriculum.

On the other hand, if you are a teacher at the intermediate grades, you may well encounter students who have been instructionally "hurt" at some point—or at many points—in their school experiences. These are the students for whom there has been an instructional mismatch. Throughout each academic year, children in this situation have been asked to spend the majority of their learning time with reading material and follow-up activities that are beyond their reach. The impact of this inappropriate instruction not only brings about frustration and negative attitudes about school and learning, but stagnates growth and closes off opportunities for more positive learning experiences. When these children arrive in your classroom, you'll be prepared to do your best in addressing their needs, which necessarily will involve addressing any harm that has already been done.

Along with the several groups mentioned above, you may encounter a very tiny subgroup of students experiencing difficulties because of "primary" or neurophysiological concerns. Children who fall into this category suffer from either minor or profound handicapping conditions that limit their processing of linguistic information. For the most part, they have great difficulty understanding and using printed language, verbal language, or both.

The direction you'll be taking with all students who have special literacy needs does *not* involve truly "special" techniques or unusual instruction. Instead, it will involve applying sound educational principles, choosing those strategies that are genuinely appropriate and are not aimed at a student's deficits. You will be making some specific adaptations and working as frequently as possible in individual or "attention-intensive" instructional situations. The most important of these adaptations will be discussed in the pages that follow.

MAKING INSTRUCTION WORK FOR LINGUISTICALLY DIVERSE STUDENTS

Literacy instruction for students learning English as a second language

In ever-increasing numbers, children whose first language is not English, usually referred to as "L2" (second language) students, are entering school in all regions of the nation. Accommodating L2 students in your classroom will include attention to learning English and to the conventions that accompany different types of tasks and communication exchanges. At the same time, you and your English-speaking students will be accommodating yourselves to the L2 students' customs and learning something about their languages.

Most school districts have English as a Second Language (ESL) programs or Bilingual Education programs or both. The nature and quality of these programs vary with the district. ESL programs provide initial instruction in English when students first enter a district. Some provide additional support on an occasional basis. The primary objective is to help students learn sufficient English to be successful in a regular classroom. Bilingual Education programs provide ongoing instruction in school subjects in the child's first language. The belief is that learning in the academic arena should not have to wait upon learning English as a second language. Students in bilingual education programs usually receive instruction in English as well.

Still and all, you will probably have primary responsibility for most of the academic, language, and literacy instruction for your students whose native language is other than English. Let's examine how you can get under way and sustain appropriate literacy instruction.

Your efforts may be guided helpfully by two concepts we have been describing throughout this text, and here I will introduce the terms second language educators use to label them: *affective filter* and *comprehensible input* (Krashen, 1982). For all children, new information passes through the affective filter, which represents a child's "inhibitions, motivation, [and] personality" (Richard-Amato, 1988, p. 24). The degree to which each child is able to assimilate, organize, and apply information you are providing about the second language depends on the nature of this affective filter—so once again, we see the importance of the supportive environment that encourages and values risk-taking as a learner. *Comprehensible input* refers to the modifications we make in the information we provide and in the ways in which we provide that information. Peregoy and Boyle (1993) note, "Paraphrasing, repetition of key points, reference to concrete materials, and acting out meanings are some of the ways speakers can help convey meaning and thus make language more understandable" (p. 30). When presenting new material, you can support it with gestures, pictures, and familiar structures in order to give the information a meaningful context.

Stages of L2 Acquisition   Let's begin by examining the characteristics of each stage of acquiring English as a second language. As we saw in Chapter 2, almost all children come to school with a strong competence in oral language. As learners acquire a second language, they move from nonverbal communication to single words, to combinations of two and three words, to phrases and sentences, and eventually to more complex and extended utterances. This progression has been described in terms of three broad stages through which learners of a second language pass: the *comprehension* stage, the *early speech-production* stage, and the *extended speech-production* stage (Krashen & Terrell, 1983; Richard-Amato, 1988).

The *comprehension* stage of acquiring English includes what is commonly referred to as the "silent period." L2 students listen a lot, comprehending what is going on around them through their own careful observation along with

■ TABLE 12.1   Instruction for Second Language Learning

Stage	Literacy Instructional Focus
Comprehension	■ Read-alouds ■ Patterned Dictations ■ Basic and Survival Words ■ "Key Vocabulary" Words
Early Speech-Production	■ Read-alouds ■ Dictations ■ Developing Larger Sight-Word Vocabulary ■ Beginning Word Study Activities
Extended Speech-Production	■ Dictations: Modified to follow standard English constructions; recall of content material can be dictated ■ Wider range of instructional- and independent-level materials explored ■ Transitional word study activities

assistance from the teacher and their peers. Native English speakers will "model" what is being discussed, acting out requests and responses. From such interaction, L2 students will learn simple words and phrases during this time and will respond to simple questions, usually with single words. The instructional key here to oral language learning is involvement in meaningful repetition, meaningful situations, and necessary "survival" words and phrases. Examples of "survival" words and phrases include *please, thank you, excuse me, What is this?*, and *My name is* . . . , along with words that identify objects, people, and places that students come in contact with on a daily basis: *desk, chair, pencil, coat, teacher, mother, sister, restroom, lunchroom, playground, home*. During this comprehension stage, as L2 students begin to gain some understanding of where one word ends and another begins, they often will simply repeat what they hear. You can provide additional support by setting up a classroom picture dictionary that includes labeled photographs of the places, objects, and interactions your students experience every day. The labels can feature the many languages spoken in the classroom. As the year progresses, and as your students become more proficient English-speakers, the dictionary can be expanded to include colloquial phrases and expressions as well as specific examples of academic language that you and your students use when talking about books and units of study.

Establishing *pattern* in schedule and daily routine is essential at this stage. Knowing there will be an ordered sequence to the day allows L2 students to feel a certain degree of stability because they can predict what will happen next. As the daily routine repeats, so does the language used during the transition from one activity to another. Short sentences and phrases such as *Please return to your seats, Let's gather on the carpet area, Find a partner to* . . . , or *I would like you to* . . . are heard many times within a familiar context and thus provide the L2 student with a situational structure for understanding.

During early speech-production, L2 students will gradually expand their utterances—first by simply stringing more words together, but eventually by trying out more structurally complex utterances. At this stage, speech will sound something like "Yes, lunch," "I book read," or "You come tomorrow?" There will still be many "errors" as the students try out their developing hypotheses about how English works, but development will occur more rapidly if the emphasis continues to be placed on communication and meaning than it will if the errors are highlighted and "drilled."

When L2 students are using oral English more extensively and in more complex ways, with fewer noticeable "errors," they are said to be in the *extended speech-production* phase. At this more advanced phase, students are able to fit their words together quite fluently. The meaning of what they wish to communicate will be clear, and sentence structure will be fairly close to standard conversational speech. Within extended speech-production, you will hear occasional mismatches in subject/verb agreement, be aware of missing articles or plurals, and notice confused word-meanings. When you listen to students chattering with one another, you are likely to hear statements like these: "Karen say she likes me"; "I drew some dinosaur in my journal"; "Erica's little sister tasted my pencil that's why I need to wash them." This communication is straightforward and easily understood. The inconsistencies we notice are minor; however, the flavor of the errors causes us to note nuances in meaning through word choice, subject/verb agreement, and standard use of endings. Through significant time spent in reading, writing, and talking with native speakers, L2 students eventually will develop an "ear" for the language. This means, for example, that words without correct endings simply won't "sound right" anymore. When this occurs, students will readily self-correct their errors, with increasing accuracy; in turn, this will improve their ability to understand spoken and written language as well as to be understood by others. Being able to "hear" a language like a native speaker takes much time. Therefore it's quite useful, during this final stage of second language acquisition, to focus occasional minilessons on the mechanics of standard speech.

Instructional Climate   Now, what about *your* role—and your literacy instruction at each of these stages? If you've structured your classroom environment according to the suggestions throughout this book, you have already provided at least half of what your L2 students need in order to develop competence in both English and literacy: a rich oral-language context in which children feel free to stretch and to take risks as learners.

You will be the model of the language and the standard dialect. For L2 students in the first two stages, speak slowly and use short, uncomplicated sentences as much as you can. Repeat important phrases and words. Anticipate students' possible confusion so that you'll be able to restate appropriately. But at first, limit the content of your language to the concrete here-and-now. You'll probably find it best to begin by embedding English in contexts that can be followed easily through demonstration—for example, art and physical education activities (Crawford, 1993).

How can you involve other students? The buddy system works very well here. In small groups, simple board games and card games provide excellent concrete contexts for using English and for native English-speakers' learning the language of the L2 student. Then you can move into collaborative learning groupings and peer instruction groupings, which are the predominant context for learning and working in several cultural groups.

Grouping Collaboratively   Throughout this book, we've talked about children's working collaboratively in pairs or in small groups—for example, in literature discussion groups, in jigsaw activities, and in pursuing projects as part of thematic or integrated units. Educators have referred generally to this arrangement as *cooperative learning* (Johnson, 1986; Edwards & Stoudt, 1990).

There are rules to follow so that these pursuits won't become free-for-alls, and you'll play a significant role in setting up groups and facilitating the process. Each group will be made up of children of different backgrounds, languages, genders, and degrees of ability. Diverse group composition actually increases the effectiveness of the group work (Enright & McCloskey, 1988). Students' attitudes regarding competitiveness and cooperation can change, and children come to see the value of working together. They also begin to appreciate contributions from children with whom they might otherwise interact very little (Johnson & Johnson, 1987). With regard to reading, most tasks will necessarily involve discussion about that reading, especially if each student is responsible for reading different selections and must relate the content to his or her group peers. Reading in such contexts has a definite purpose: accountability to the whole group.

Many cultures value collaboration and even have little competitiveness. The traditional American classroom in years past has emphasized competition and doing one's own work. But we've also noted that this is not the way the world works; children need to develop cooperative skills in an academic setting early on. Your students from cultures that value collaboration can be excellent models for children who have learned—and expect—the "competitive" mode. For example, Au cites research which found that many Native American students seemed to be more comfortable communicating in "small, student-run groups, indirectly supervised by the teacher" (1993, p. 109). These students quite naturally enjoyed initiating conversation with their peers and their teacher when classroom activities more closely mirrored their community events. On one particular reservation, all members of a group help plan and direct events, with each member participating to the degree he or she finds comfortable. Depending on their community patterns, you may discover that some Native American children, when they work within a classroom of diverse cultures, can be instrumental in small-group organization and collaborative decision-making.

Involving Adult Speakers of the L2 Students' Language   As much as possible, involve adult speakers of the students' first languages. Parents and grandparents are the obvious choice; but you also might invite students from the closest university, high school, or girls' or boys' organization to spend time reading and writing with your students. You might consider any senior citizens or employees of community support services or nearby businesses who you know speak a variety of languages. They can be models not only of the native language but of English as well, and this will help underscore both the importance of learning English and the value of maintaining the native language and culture. Gibbons (1993) suggests that you arrange informal social gatherings such as morning breaks or brown bag lunches for your students and classroom visitors. Once the children and the volunteers have become acquainted, you can consider having the adults work with two or three students to explain game rules or to assist with a small-group activity involving cooking, storytelling, or the reading of environmental print. When the volunteers and the children understand the workings of the classroom, you can expand adult involvement to include the publishing of bilingual classroom books, explanations of more complex math activities, and the reading aloud of stories in a child's home language. Gibbons cautions us, however, to remember that "parents or other community volunteers are not substitutes for qualified teachers . . ." (1993, p. 114). Their role in the classroom is one of support. You will find their participation in your classroom to be most beneficial if they are involved with familiar activities where students have already experienced some success. As the parents (or other volunteers) and the children become more comfortable with you, with one another, and with your classroom procedures and expectations, you can then ask the adults to help you guide your students' learning in less structured activities involving story response, small-group book discussions, or collaborative story writing.

Exploring Oral Language as a Foundation   Oral language is the foundation for understanding and learning about the literate behaviors and "power code" of the dominant culture—the "power code" being the social behavior and the language use accepted by mainstream society. As we've just seen, you can begin with the immediate and the most familiar, thus helping students learn the English language, learn about language as a tool, and learn about the uses of the tool. This foundation will support the challenging and lengthy process of students' learning about the oral and literate behaviors necessary for success in school and community environments (Cummins, 1981).

Analyzing a Discussion   Once students are moving strongly through the early speech-production stage, they can be involved in analyzing discussions. Students tape one of their group discussions, then analyze it later. For example, they would pay particular attention to these aspects:

—How well those who are knowledgeable about the topic have expressed their knowledge

—How speakers react to one another

—How group members have handled someone who was monopolizing the discussion

—How questions are asked and responded to

—How clarification of information is requested and provided.

As with all new activities, you probably would need to walk through this procedure with small groups or the whole class first. You will find it helpful to have native English-speakers participate in the discussion of the taped conversations. Listening to recorded language can be difficult at first; native English-speakers can help clarify any of the taped language that L2 students have difficulty following and understanding. They will also pick up irregularities of speech from non-native speakers—details that L2 students may not notice at first. These may include, for example, how a question is posed, word order for emphasized meaning, alternate vocabulary to make a particular point in a gentler manner.

The topics you choose to record will be important in setting the stage for the type of language used: a small-group discussion of playground behavior will have a different tone than one involving the organization of a class presentation. You will want your students listening to language from a variety of school settings, so that you can introduce them to specific language for specific purposes. Your choices will also be driven by your students' personal interests and needs. If, for example, your students are having trouble being understood and understanding others in the lunchroom, you may want to tape some exchanges between English-speaking children and the cafeteria cashier, informal table conversations, or exchanges between the lunchroom-duty teacher and children requesting help or asking permission to leave their tables.

Analyzing Interactions in the Community   When students understand and feel comfortable with the analysis of classroom and school discussions, they can expand their analyses to interactions that occur outside their daily school setting—in stores, at the post office, at a restaurant, and so forth.

These types of language analyses help students realize the functions of language as a tool, because they are considering it in actual academic and community applications. Thus, they have a real purpose for (1) examining the tool itself and (2) examining the use of the tool. This type of analysis can help students construct a strong bridge to language expressed in texts. These conversations, like those in the classroom, will reveal specific vocabulary and phrases used in particular circumstances—how to order a meal or ask for stamps, for instance. Heath and Mangiola found that second language students who had opportunities to listen to and discuss language in this manner became highly aware of "the role of language in learning" (1991, p. 32).

Helping L2 Students Learn to Read and Write   All our recommendations in Chapters 3 and 5 regarding emergent and beginning literacy environments and activities are appropriate for L2 children as well. Here I would like to point out the adjustments that need to be made for L2 children.

Comprehension Stage   *Read-alouds* help develop concepts about "storyness" in general as well as about English in particular. You should encourage story retellings whenever possible, modeling a few retellings yourself. If you select for retelling stories that come from a variety of cultural origins, your students will be exposed to numerous story patterns and eventually will be able to make detailed comparisons among them. Flannelboard characters or overhead-projector silhouette cutouts work well for retellings. They will be effective and comfortable "props" for L2 children to use when they retell favorite stories to themselves, a partner, a small group, an aide, or an adult volunteer.

Predictable pattern books are as effective for L2 speakers as for native English-speakers. The pictures usually will hold the L2 children's attention, and the children will eventually memorize much if not all of a pattern book's language. If the rhythms and rhymes can be supported by music, so much the better. Remember (from Chapter 5) that you will be modeling how reading "works" through shared reading experiences involving big books that have predictable texts; this, too, is as valuable for L2 children as for native English-speakers. Though the children will not at first understand completely, of course, they will be able through these experiences to develop concepts about literacy as well as further their development in spoken English. You are also likely to see them use the language of the predictable books in their own writing. Remember that the children can make their own predictable Big Books, an especially valuable activity for L2 children (Hayes, Bahruth, & Kessler, 1991). Figure 12.2 depicts work done by a first-grade class made up primarily of Spanish-speaking students.

This teacher used Eric Carle's rendition of *Today Is Monday* as a model to support literacy in both English and Spanish. Not only did these children look at the language used in the book; they took time to study Carle's illustrative techniques. When the project was complete, this class had a personalized version of *Today Is Monday* that everyone could read.

"Basic" and *"survival"* words are those few words that help us communicate the most fundamental of needs. They can be used to label common objects in the classroom environment; perhaps you'll write the label for each object on

Figure 12.2
First-Grade Version of Eric Carle's Today Is Monday

a card with the picture of the object on it. These cards can be presented to the L2 student and reviewed. While a number of these words eventually will be learned, you should not be overly concerned about a child's learning to read them quickly. The primary emphasis is on oral language learning at this comprehension stage. And don't forget the classroom picture dictionary: a reference book the children compose and compile themselves will make this vocabulary much more useful and meaningful.

Survival words such as WALK and DON'T WALK, EXIT, and BOYS and GIRLS can be taught through a "physical response" mode (Krashen & Terrell, 1983). In small groups or with L2 partners, native English-speakers can act out situations in which these words are highlighted. The contexts for different forms of important requests can also be highlighted: contexts such as classroom and school procedures (getting a drink, following simple directions) and forms of greeting.

Key vocabulary words can be learned even before L2 children have developed a concept of word in print in the context of learning the voice-print match (Ashton-Warner, 1963; Richard-Amato, 1988). These words of course are learned first as "whole" words but they provide powerful incentives to the students. You can set up in the classroom oral language situations that will lead to the selection of words that relate to those situations—discussions about family, friends, community, school, and classroom. You simply ask the student to choose one or two words he or she is especially interested in; then you print each on a card. Students may copy these words into their own "pictionaries" and search through books and magazines for more. Later on, these words may also become the students' first word-bank entries. These words can also be used as prompts for dramatic play when re-enacting a familiar story, for early collaborative writing or for journal entries, and for sorting and categorizing picture cards.

Early Speech-Production Stage As we've seen, *language experience* activities show a child's speech written down. Since students at this stage have a greater fluency with and command of English, they are better able to discuss situations, events, and concrete objects with you. After such discussion, you can take dictations that are a fairly direct representation of what a student has said, not yet "correcting" them according to standard English usage. Whereas at the comprehension stage, dictations were modeled on specific patterns that you introduced through oral language and print, the present dictations represent the student's developing competence with English. Not coincidentally, students usually become quite motivated by these original contributions.

You will probably want to modify your approach to the dictation schedule and the acquisition of sight words or word-bank words. For second language learners, Dixon and Nessel (1983) suggest a five-day sequence between initial dictation of a story and final harvesting of word-bank words. This five-day cycle allows for more rereading and work with each dictation as well as for more time to acquire sight words. Here are the adjustments you may make:

Day 1: Discussion; dictate story. Read the student's dictation to him or her as often as necessary and reread with the student several times. That's it for the first day.

Later, you may wish to make two copies of the dictation. One will be for the student; the other, for your ongoing assessment file. On the file copy, you will list the oral language features that you may help the student work with—not as a part of this reading instruction but at another time. For example, if the student is omitting *-ing* endings on verbs, you may plan an oral language activity that highlights this pattern.

Day 2: Have the student read the dictation silently, underlining words he or she feels are known. (Accurate self-assessment here may take several dictations to develop.) Then ask the student to read the dictation; quickly supply any word he or she may be uncertain about. Mark the student's miscues on your own copy of the dictation; this will help you keep an ongoing running record of the student's progress. In the beginning, it will also help you determine how well the student is grasping the concept of "underlining known words."

Next, present all the words sequentially in a list format (Stauffer, Abrams, & Pikulski, 1978; Dixon & Nessel, 1983). They should appear in the same order in which they do in the story, but of course the visual format has changed. Have the student read down the list; keep a record of what he or she says about having misidentified a word.

Day 3: The student again reads his or her dictations silently and underlines in a different color the words he or she considers known. Then have the student read the dictation to you. Using the copy of the story you marked on the day before, mark any miscues the student makes—also in a different color, to note progress.

In a list format, present only those words, from the preceding day's sequential word list, that the student knew. However, present them in a "scrambled" format in which they do not follow the sequential order in the story. Mark down the student's performance on this list. Again, only those words that the child can read are retained on the list.

Day 4: The student does not read the dictation but goes directly to the word list you have prepared. This too is a "scrambled" list, but it includes only the words the student correctly identified on the "Day 3" scrambled list.

Day 5: The words that were correctly identified on the "Day 4" scrambled list are now presented on cards. Those that the student still knows are placed in the student's word bank.

Keep in mind that this dictation cycle is not the only type of experience with reading that L2 students will have—it occurs in the context of the other types of experiences presented in this section. Also, you may overlap dictation cycles for different stories: on day three, for example, you may take another dictation after presenting the first "scrambled" word list for the previous dictated story.

I would suggest that you use file folders to store copies of each child's dictations. In your file you will keep your running records and prepared word lists. In the child's folder, he or she will keep all illustrated dictations that have been produced, and working word lists; the word bank remains separate. Your students will increase their reading fluency and sight-word vocabularies by multiple rereadings of familiar texts. In addition, you can return to these stories when looking at the structure of language. Gibbons (1993) suggests having children examine the structure of language in several ways. Language Experience stories can provide L2 students with readable text for these activities. She advises having children reorder word cards of known sentences, reorder sentence strips of known stories, as well as scramble together and reorder sentence strips from two different known texts. Gibbons also reminds us to consider the value of cloze activities used traditionally (every seventh word is taken out), syntactically (deletion of one type of word, such as all the verbs), semantically (removal of content words), and graphophonically (removal of some letters from particular words); all of which can be done with the children's dictated stories. This format can also be used to compose new stories from previously told stories, encouraging the L2 student to categorize the words that are missing from the passage.

Wordless books provide unique opportunities for L2 children to try out their developing competence in English. With a partner, they can relate whatever they believe to be happening in the book. Their rendering can be written down to be used as a dictation, or you can record the child's dictation on stick-on notes and ask the child to share the book with his or her original text. Students can also begin writing captions on their own or with a partner. In addition, you can ask the child to place his stick-on notes on the appropriate pages accompanied by discussion with another child. This task can also be completed as an independent or learning center activity as students move closer to the extended speech-production stage.

Word study provides opportunities for children to examine words out of context. Students at this stage are able to develop a considerable sight-word vocabulary. Just as with L1 children involved in Language Experience activities at this point, L2 students can begin exploring words through word sorts for purposes of categorizing them according to different meaning features (see Chapter 8), and learning letter/sound conventions. As their word banks grow, recall from Chapter 5 that they can be alphabetized.

Read-alouds provide a strong model for developing language skills in your young readers. Now your read-alouds will represent more complex language structures. Predictable texts with a clear "cumulative" pattern are excellent. Picture books that tap the students' interests can be shared and used as a focus for discussing the content. Keep in mind the critical role of rereadings here as well (Krashen, 1982; Wong-Fillmore, 1982). Each time that you read a familiar, enjoyable book to the students, you can propose different things for them to listen for and think about: what happened first, second, third; what was the main character's response; why didn't the other animals want to help, and so forth. Rereadings help students' comprehension and language development on both the "what happened" level and the deeper, critical level. Also, whenever possible, have texts in L2 students' first languages. Literate behaviors learned in the native language definitely are transfered to learning in the second language.

Extended Speech-Production Stage *Language Experience dictations* will continue to be excellent vehicles for reading development at this stage. One of the primary differences from dictation at the early speech-production stage is that you will be making corrections of the students' spoken-language errors in the written version of their stories. You will rewrite the stories, using conventional English patterns and vocabulary, but you will also keep a copy of the original dictation so that you and your students can make comparisons between the two versions. You can state straightforwardly what corrections you have made, without getting involved in the "rules" of the language. Students then, either orally or in writing, make corrections of the original dictation, looking at the corrected version whenever necessary. The power of this rereading of the original version lies in the student's awareness of progress with respect to learning the finer points of usage and grammar.

One other difference between dictations at the early speech-production stage and the extended speech-production stage comes when students reread their dictations. When rereading occurs, students will underline only the words they do not know, in contrast to being asked previously to underline only the words they knew they could read. With your support during rereadings, unfamiliar words will quickly become known. L2 students at this stage may also dictate content-area information that they recall through listening and hearing content-related texts read aloud by a partner or on a tape.

Early reading and writing activities include students' growing ability to read many more engaging picture books and simple chapter books independently or with minimal help. During directed lessons, you may want to select books that underscore general topics or issues such as genre, formal versus informal speech, or very specific language analysis that models common expressions of time and words used when making comparisons (Gibbons, 1993). To bring these issues to students' attention, Gibbons suggests repeated reading of books incorporating these issues, list-keeping of alternate phrases for the same idea, and the use of cloze exercises to brainstorm alternative wordings.

Students in the extended speech-production stage should continue to be encouraged to write in English as much as possible. An L1 child and an L2 child can be paired for reading and writing experiences. "Buddies" can partner-read, talk about what is being read, and respond in their journals. *You* will also want to respond to your students' journals. Setting aside time for students to share their journals with you will embellish their written responses: your discussions with them, coupled with the comments you write, will be invaluable for modeling vocabulary, spelling, sentence structure, and semantic nuances of word choice.

There may be times when you will want to direct the responses your students make in their journals about particular texts, both narrative and informational. After students have been involved in introductory discussions and background-building experiences, you can provide purpose to reading and writing tasks by giving students guide questions. As L2 students become more increasingly proficient readers and writers, the language they use to express their thoughts, verbally and in writing, will mimic less the work of their partners and the material they have just read; instead, it will begin to take on a more original flavor.

In addition, there is a growing number of books written in a variety of languages and published with L2 students in mind. Besides the increasing availability of well-known English titles translated into other languages, the development of reading programs in Spanish has been undertaken by textbook publishers. The materials in Spanish should be evaluated according to the same types of criteria that we apply to programs published in English (see Chapter 10). You'll quickly recognize that not all translated stories hold the same cultural value for all students, so you'll make a point of reviewing the content of stories in order to select those with the most relevance for the students you teach.

Along with translated materials, you will find that audiocassette recordings of stories will encourage and assist L2 students with multiple rereadings. Wordless books can also serve to inspire oral and written language. Pairs of students will enjoy creating several different descriptions and dialogues that can be shared during small-group sessions. Later, these stories can be published along with students' original illustrations.

Word study and word exploration can continue here with alphabetic features (for Beginning readers) and within-word pattern features (for Transitional readers) being studied. Continue categorization or word-sort activities, emphasizing both structure and semantic categories. These categorization activities should frequently be done in a group, so students can discuss their reasons for organizing words as well as receive direct teaching from you.

MAKING CONNECTIONS

Direct Instruction—How Much and of What Kind?

For many years educators have been sensitive to helping students from nondominant cultures acquire what they need in order to be successful and to compete on a more equal basis. Too often, however, these intentions have fallen short of the goal. Beginning in the 1960s, many educators believed the goal would be reached by breaking the task down into smaller steps and teaching each step directly and explicitly; this approach is obviously a "bottom-up" skill-driven approach. Using standardized tests as the criterion of success, this approach appeared to lead to significantly better performance by nondominant students. However, the improved performance on formal tests was not, for the most part, transfered to other contexts.

These results led other educators—from the mainstream culture themselves—to maintain that the more natural, "process" approach to reading and writing that works so well for mainstream students should work for others equally well. Educators from nondominant cultures, though, have been questioning this "one size fits all" perspective and suggest that we need an informed, effective blend of the "natural" approach and direct-instruction orientations. Reyes, speaking of literacy instruction for sec-

ond language learners, states that "more explicit instruction and culturally relevant tasks may be necessary to apply particular strategies and skills consistently, in addition to abundant opportunities for writing and reading" (1992, p. 168).

While working with children from nonmainstream cultures, let's not forget that they may expect their teachers to be direct, even authoritarian (Delpit, 1988). This does *not* mean that we need to revert to the model of the teacher as an all-knowing dispenser of information and stern disciplinarian. It does mean making very clear to our students what, why, and how we are teaching—thus making the codes and conventions of the mainstream culture explicit. While we provide lots of opportunities to read and write, we will, initially, need to play more of a role in helping children from nondominant cultures select titles and topics. We will need to teach more directly about the various types of knowledge and strategies involved in reading and writing. As nonmainstream children experience success in this context, they will gradually become comfortable with the type of risk-taking and exploration of personal interests that you want all the children you teach to be moving toward.

LEARNING IN CONTEXT: **Literacy instruction for children from nondominant cultures should balance immersion in reading and writing with direct and explicit instruction—making the nature and purposes of the tasks explicit.**

What About Attitudes in the Home?

Parents of L2 children are certainly not united on the issue of maintaining the native language. Often, first-generation immigrants wish to acquire English as quickly as possible, so they discourage their children's use of the first language; second- and third-generation Americans, however, may recognize the earlier language as a profound part of their heritage and wish to sustain it in the home and community (for example, Villanueva, 1993). You are likely to come in contact with families, however, who want to learn English to the exclusion of their first language, because they have such a strong desire to have their children assimilated into the mainstream culture. For example, one of my son's high school friends immigrated to the United States from Czechoslovakia via Germany and England. In the process, he learned both German and English exceptionally well. He was embarrassed about his language heritage, however, and wanted to blend into the American adolescent culture. My son did not realize his friend was not a native speaker of English until he visited the friend's house one day and heard the grandmother speaking a different language. The friend then "confessed" his language heritage and his incredible odyssey.

Teachers can help lift the stigma of speaking another language by integrating literacy events that draw children's families into the classroom. One way to bring a class together as a community is to have them share their home cultures. Suggestions for doing this include learning questioning techniques so that students can interview grandparents about what school was like when they were children, having students compose birth stories about themselves and their parents, then comparing the two stories for similarities and differences. You can also set aside a time every week for children to share stories about family experiences. Any of these activities will provide open, supportive opportunities for children—if they so choose—to share and talk about their home environments. It is up to you to set aside sharing and discussion time so that children can get to know one another on a personal level before they are asked to perform academic tasks.

LEARNING IN CONTEXT: The more children know about one another as members of a family community, the more easily they will bond together as a learning community.

Literacy instruction for students who speak a variant dialect

Children outside the mainstream culture whose home language is English but who speak a variant dialect may need more direct instruction and modeling, as well as discussions about aspects of language. This does not mean that there should be an entirely different or "special" program for students who speak a variant dialect—though there have been such programs in the past (see, for example, Bereiter & Engelmann, 1966). All children need to construct and interpret meaning, as well as react emotionally to their reading experiences.

We cannot lose sight of this. There may be countless ways to "hook" children on literacy, but all these ways arise from the literacy environment in your classroom: lots of talk, lots of engaging books, freedom to draw and write, and so on.

In addition, we must not lose sight of the fact that language and culture work hand in hand. One cannot be learned without the other; dialect and culture intertwine in meaning and structure. Vygotsky's notion of "mind in society" (Cole & Scribner, 1978) captures what it means to set out to learn another dialect or language. As you become aware of and sensitive to the different communication structures and patterns of the children you are teaching (Delpit, 1991; Gilyard, 1991), you will be helping your students from nondominant cultures become aware of and understand how standard American English works. As I first suggested in Chapter 1, this is not because standard American English is inherently "better" than any other dialect; but it is the dialect spoken by the members of society who traditionally hold the reins of social, political, and economic power. It is for this reason that Delpit has referred to the conventions and usage of standard English as the "code of power" (1991). If schoolchildren are to have equal access to the potential benefits this society offers, they need to know and understand how this "code" works.

Despite educators' best efforts, beginning in fourth grade many students from nondominant cultures begin to fall farther and farther behind students from the dominant culture (Chall, Jacobs, & Baldwin, 1990). It's not necessarily that a foundation hasn't been laid, but rather that we have not succeeded in helping students achieve an effective transition into the reading of expository texts or in making mainstream "power codes" explicit. If we are to succeed, it will be through maintaining the rich literacy environment established in the primary grades and by talking explicitly about standard American English, when and why we use it, and the social conventions surrounding its use. And we can start by helping students become aware of how we use language generally.

Just about all the procedures we've discussed as appropriate for L2 students are appropriate for speakers of a variant dialect as well. A variant dialect is not, of course, a different language, but because the "model" of English that we present is the standard dialect, we explicitly address its nature and its importance with variant dialect speakers. When teaching children who speak variant dialects, it becomes apparent that dialect is more than just an issue of idiom, word usage, and sentence structure: variant dialects reflect the nature of the cultures from which they come. Therefore, when we are instructing children in the use of standard American English, we also must make every effort to value and support children's home dialect by providing them with learning experiences that respect its use.

How we introduce and develop an understanding of variant dialects is important. We need to discuss the "appropriateness" of speaking in different ways, depending on the social context we are in. From this perspective, pointing out different ways of speaking does not diminish the value of the particular dialect a child may speak. We *all* speak in different ways, depending on whether we are in school, talking with friends on the phone, making an announcement at a religious service, and so on. In the primary grades, teachers needn't talk about different dialects so much as simply recognizing them while continuing to be models for standard usage most of the time. In the intermediate grades, teachers can talk more explicitly about the contexts and purposes of different ways of speaking—as can adults from a community whose native dialect may be variant, but who acquired a standard dialect in order to advance economically.

In general, the various dialects of American English are more *alike* than they are *different,* but dialects *do* differ noticeably from one another in terms of phonology, vocabulary, and syntax (see Chapter 2). If we are talking with someone who speaks a dialect different from our own, we can usually understand the message being expressed. As we have seen, however, there usually are subtle and occasionally significant differences between the cultures that are represented by different dialects. This is what we mean in part when we talk about the importance of learning the "code of power"—the implicit nuances that are a part of mainstream culture. It is important to know how to manipulate the subtleties of a language to suit a particular context.

Those aspects of dialects that are most immediately noticeable, and therefore most extensively studied, are the surface characteristics of sound and structure. Beginning in the 1960s, the dialect that has been most often studied is African-American English (Gilyard, 1991; Smitherman, 1977). Most recently, Hispanic English—a family of dialects spoken by native Spanish speakers and their descendants (Mexican-Americans, Latin Americans, and immigrants from Cuba and Puerto Rico)—has been studied closely. It may be helpful to know some of the distinctive features of each of these dialects; they will occur among students in their conversation and often will be reflected in their writing. Figure 12.3 presents several significant features from African-American English and from Chicano English, a Hispanic English dialect spoken by Mexican-Americans in the western and southwestern United States (Fromkin & Rodman, 1993; Penfield & Ornstein-Galicia, 1985).

Although there is the need to instruct children in the use of standard American English, we also must take time to celebrate language from variant dialects. During the past several years there has been an emergence of books that reflect nondominant cultures. Since we know that read-alouds are the best way, initially, to introduce children to literature, as educators we have a responsibility to share and read these books aloud with our students. How can you read in different dialects to children, though, without seeming stilted, contrived, artificial? First of all, don't feel you must try to sound exactly like a speaker of a particular dialect. Practice reading a book aloud until you feel reasonably comfortable with it. If this is not possible—and the book is one you feel should be shared—obtain a tape of the story by a speaker who represents the dialect realistically or seek out a guest from the culture represented in the book who can read and discuss the story with your students.

As books containing variant dialects become commonplace in your classroom library, discussions of how people live and speak will surface naturally. Your students will actively note the differences among stories' structure, the language used within the stories, and the illustrations used to represent the culture in which the stories originated. Open discussion of this type will encourage toler-

Common Features of African-American English

Phonological

- *L*-deletion and *r*-deletion: *toll = toe, help = hep; sore = saw, court = caught*
- Consonant-deletion at the end of words: *send = sen, mint = min*
- A *th* sound/symbol correspondence: *tooth* pronounced *toof; leather* pronounced "*lever*"

Syntactic

- Double negatives: *I ain't got no. . . . She don't eat nothing. . . .* (Double negatives abound in all dialects, however: consider *It is not unlikely that. . . .*)
- The verb *be:* In some instances it is omitted; for example, *he bad, they nice.* In other instances it is *inserted* to show habitual or ongoing behavior as opposed to what is happening right at the moment: *he be workin* (he is working and will continue to be working) versus *he workin'* (he is busy working right now).

Common Features of Chicano English

Phonological

- Vowels: Spanish has five stressed vowel sounds (as opposed to eleven in English): ē, ā, o͞o, ō, ŏ. *Bit* and *beet* are both pronounced *beet*. If Latino students have developed some literacy skills in their native language, then when first learning to read and write English, it is common to apply Spanish sound/symbol correspondences to English: *bit* is pronounced *beet, bet* may be pronounced *bait*.
- The consonant digraphs *ch* and *sh* are pronounced differently in Spanish than in English: *ch* corresponds to the "sh" sound in *ship*, so that *chicken* is pronounced *shekin; show* is pronounced *cho*.
- The initial consonant sound /th/ is pronounced as /t/: *thank = tank*
- Final-consonant omission: *part = par; clapped = clap;* third person singular as in *He thanks her,* which becomes *He tank her.*

Syntactic

- Double negatives: *I don't want any more = I don' wan' no more.*

ance and respect, as well as emphasize the genuine uniqueness of the many dialects spoken across our country.

You will find that most good books containing aspects of a dialect will probably fall within your "comfort range" for reading aloud. Virginia Hamilton's presentation of African-American folktales in *The People Could Fly* presents dialect strikingly well. Other good examples for primary children are McKissack's *Flossie and the Fox* and Haley's *A Story, a Story*. With upper elementary students, in addition to Hamilton's book you might share Giovanni's poetry in *Spin a Soft Black Song*.

Reading stories that contain variant dialects will reinforce students' awareness of the many different language styles and cultural traditions that make up the population of their classrooms and communities. Exposure to and involvement with stories and language of many different origins builds tolerance and acceptance. Only when we are able to compare and contrast differences and similarities among dialects are we able to accept and value them as a necessary part of who we are as a nation—an extraordinary mélange of sound, structure, meaning, and culture brought together through a need to communicate.

Politics, Values, and Literacy in Our Multicultural Society

I must be very straightforward about literacy instruction and what it means in a chapter of this nature. When we look at cultural diversity and failure to achieve in literacy, we should not, *cannot,* tiptoe around what are in fact issues of politics and values. So many of the reasons why children from diverse as well as mainstream or "dominant" cultures do not attain the levels of literacy we would expect, given their native competence, can be summed up in the following observation: There is a mismatch between the developmental needs of these children and the instruction they are receiving.

This is not an indictment of teachers. We know how mightily most teachers work to provide what they and others believe the children need. It is more challenging than ever before to provide what is appropriate. Rather than an indictment, this is simply a statement about the reality of the consequences of the often considerable differences between the dominant culture represented by contemporary American schools and the culture from which a child may come. We also have seen how in the past, literacy has been narrowly defined by administrators, teachers, and society as a whole—and thus how narrowly it has been taught in most schools for most of our history.

All of us must work hard not to frustrate, alienate, and lose an increasingly larger segment of students. However, if we adjust the social and literacy environments of our classrooms so that they model more closely the environments suggested in this text, we are sure to see progress from our students. That progress will come through discussion, demonstrations of the conventions of standard American English, and the building of background knowledge that is so desperately needed and desired by nondominant cultures (Delpit, 1986, 1988; Reyes, 1992). The growing language proficiency of our students will of course be an indication that what we are doing is beneficial.

LEARNING IN CONTEXT: **Politics and values have traditionally influenced our literacy instruction and narrowed our definitions of "literacy" and the "learner"; if we emphasize the *learner* and broaden the contexts for literacy instruction, more children from *all* cultures will reach higher levels of literacy.**

MAKING INSTRUCTION WORK FOR STUDENTS EXPERIENCING DIFFICULTIES

Marie Clay, eminent literacy educator, once observed, "I do not need an elaborate definition of reading difficulties. One simply takes the pupil—child, adolescent, or adult—from where he is, to somewhere else" (1979, p. 42). Her observation about taking the pupil "from where he is, to somewhere else" applies to all children, whether they are experiencing difficulties or not. And that is the point. In most cases it is the teaching, not the child, that needs to be adjusted.

In this regard, I'd like to reiterate the position I took at the outset of this chapter. The vast majority of children who experience persistent difficulty with reading do so not because they have a neurological dysfunction—they are not learning disabled, behaviorally disordered, attention-deficit disordered, or otherwise impaired. They have potential difficulties that may become problems if they experience an instructional mismatch between where they are and what the school has been attempting to do in order to move them along academically. As we have seen in several places throughout this book, children who have not had the opportunity to interact much with print, who have not been read to—who therefore do not understand much about the form and the functions of print—will likely have difficulty understanding instruction that primarily emphasizes sound/symbol correspondences. When this difficulty occurs, these children usually are not provided with the types of experiences with print that lay the foundation for understanding letter/sound correspondences. Rather, they usually are given more work focusing on letter/sound correspondences, when in fact what they need is to be read to, balanced by successful experiences in reading their own dictations and simple repetitive texts, along with opportunities to write and draw about topics important to them. Without this supportive environment that ensures their success, children with little experience with print and language will fall into a cycle of difficulty, frustration, more difficulty, and more frustration. Eventually, they may exhibit some or all of the characteristics of learning disabilities or attention-deficit disorders and become thus classified and labeled.

On the other hand, those few children who do have genuine neurophysiological problems develop learning difficulties not because they lack background with print, but rather because they can not readily process language. Even with the most appropriate instruction, these children will probably struggle to perform to grade level expectations.

In the section that follows, we will look first at ways in which you can accommodate students in your class who have not developed literacy to the degree their potential would suggest they can. We will look next at those very few children whose reading difficulties are a result of neurological dysfunctions. And finally, we will address the issue of special education as it applies to you as a classroom teacher.

Literacy instruction for students not achieving their potential

Regie Routman offers a simple yet profound perspective on working with children who are less-developed readers and writers: "Teachers who view a child as having learning abilities, as opposed to disabilities, will usually find a way to be successful in teaching the child" (1991, p. 377). Literature-based reading and writing provide a far more supportive context for students who have not developed literacy skills to the degree we would expect at a particular grade level. This is because, in part, whole-class read-alouds and discussions, which

Although most school districts have English as a Second Language Programs or Bilingual Programs, you will probably have primary responsibility for most of the academic, language, and literacy instruction for your students whose native language is not English.

are a very important component of literature-based reading, involve the less developed reader as well as the more developed one. However, in the day-to-day bustle of the classroom, it is possible to let the less able reader slide by during whole-class discussions and heterogeneous small-group interactions in which he or she may not receive enough attention from the teacher. The challenge you face as a classroom teacher will be to recognize what your less able readers can do and to place them in situations where they must use what they know about language and print to move into more challenging texts. In the end, we want them to be able to read with fluency those books that at present they rely on others to read to them.

In addition to your whole-class activities, you can address the needs of less developed readers by bringing them together for specific activities. Below, you will find some suggestions for guiding your instruction.

1. *Balance homogeneous literature-discussion sessions and Guided Reading-Thinking Activities with heterogeneous discussion groups.* In both literature discussions and GRTAs, students will be reading, discussing, and referring to selections that are comfortably on their levels. With this arrangement, you will be able to address specific needs and conduct minilessons that are particular to less developed readers. For example, a group could benefit from a "QAR" lesson based on a story they have just read in a GRTA format. Other minilessons might focus on particular aspects of dialogue, application of word knowledge in context, or identification of the main idea.

In addition, small cooperative pairs and triads will provide a setting for every group member to have a voice in presenting questions or rereading text to find support for an opinion. Children from several homogeneous groups can then be intermingled to form new heterogeneous discussion groups. You may find that homogeneous groupings work well with content-area textbook reading. For example, if you are teaching in a multigrade classroom, you may conduct a Content GRTA with the science text for your less capable readers. After several lessons of direct instruction on how to read informational material, identification of important vocabulary, and the basics of summarizing the content of the selection, these less capable readers can then pair up with classmates of varying reading abilities to guide them through the very steps they experienced with you at group time. This type of activity builds background knowledge for the less developed readers while recognizing them for the leadership role they are sometimes able to take.

2. *Do word-study activities based on the less developed readers' level of word knowledge.* While you may have students who developmentally are at the within-word pattern phase in terms of understanding word structure, you will also have those who are still functioning at the *alphabetic* or early *letter name* phase. Whatever the case may be, even if your students are not able to spell and read many words on their own, they will be able to understand the concepts underlying more advanced words. In addition to maintaining word study to fit each child's developmental needs, you'll still be able to have children suggest interesting words for discussion.

3. *Provide successful opportunities for reading grade-level materials.* Most students' listening comprehension is at least at grade level. Therefore, as much as possible, have tapes available, both in the classroom and to take home, that cover essential "reading." The tapes can include assigned readings from textbooks; be sure that important vocabulary has already been discussed in class (see Chapter 7).

For content reading material, less developed readers can dictate to you, an aide, a parent volunteer, another student, or into a cassette their recall of content material; these dictations can be transcribed, as in Language Experience activities, and become a student's own text dealing with a particular topic. These dictations may also be combined from several students in the classroom who are reading at lower levels; they will comprise alternate chapters to their companions in the actual textbook. Also, the wide range of books available in your classroom will be a definite advantage for your slower readers. As you explore a particular theme, be sure to include texts that address the theme but are comfortable for your slower readers.

4. *Take smaller steps.* To provide successful reading experiences for less developed readers, taking smaller steps does not mean the traditional breaking-down of reading into specific skills that must be addressed before "real reading" is done. The main focus needs to be on having your students get the feel of what real reading is like. Taking small steps means giving children more time and opportunity to read, write, and talk about their learning before going on to more difficult word study concepts and lengthier books with more complicated vocabulary.

5. *Develop knowledge and strategies about print.* Not only do less developed readers need knowledge about print; they need to know how to apply that

knowledge. You will be doing a lot of modeling, demonstrating how to be a strategic reader.

An important objective of your instruction is to demystify what "reading" as a process is and what printed materials are all about. This will happen as you address reading, writing, and word study with your students. Along the way, you will also assist students in developing metacognitive strategies that will help them step back and think about what they are reading and why they are reading it.

You will notice that most of these activities apply to your instruction for all students. However, they are particularly significant for less developed readers. Now, let's examine more closely the nature of the reading, word study, and writing your less able students will be doing in your classroom.

Reading The student should read material that is on his or her independent or instructional level. Unfortunately, less able readers very often spend the majority of their time attempting to read at their frustrational level and never experience the feel of reading a comfortable text that they understand and to which they are able to apply their word-analysis knowledge when necessary.

For primary students, you will need to build on predictable/patterned texts and dictations. When selecting predictable books for emergent readers, it is important to look for short, repetitive texts (the *Brown Bear, Brown Bear* type— refer back to Chapter 5). You will first need to introduce the books in a shared-reading format so that as the child attempts to read, you can chime in as necessary, carefully deciding how long to wait before providing support if the child is hesitant. Be sure to offer praise, and reasons for the praise, when a child takes a risk and applies his or her knowledge.

For example, if the child pauses before a word and you see him mouthing the beginning sound, looking at the picture and back at the text—and then successfully identifying the word, you might say softly, "Good!" and then, when the page is finished, comment "Bret, you did an excellent job of figuring that word out! You thought about the beginning, you looked at the picture for a clue—and when you looked back at the word, you got it!" Because the text is comfortable, the child's comprehension is not derailed if you allow him to apply his word knowledge when he does not immediately identify a word. Once the child has practiced reading the text to the point that he or she can do it with a great deal of fluency, you can use the story as a pattern to encourage the reader to write his own version of the text. This format will give less developed readers a model for writing stories independently. The more you encourage this supportive writing, the more successful the student will feel.

The other reading material your student has are his dictated stories (see the discussion of the Language Experience Approach in Chapter 5, pages 187–190, and above, page 597). Each dictated account may be reread as often as you and the child wish. As with L2 students, you may wish first to present isolated words in the sequence in which they occurred in the story, after which you can then present successive "scrambled" lists (see pages 595–596).

Students will also be reading books that you have helped them select—other predictable texts, picture books, and so forth—this SSR time needs to be as much a part of individual work sessions as it is a part of the regular classroom work.

Intermediate students who are at the beginning literacy phase may also enjoy predictable texts. Though most of these texts are intended for a younger audience, success in reading them becomes motivational apart from the content; these little books may be the first books the student has ever been able to read cover-to-cover. Whereas some older students may be put off by the simplicity of a predictable book like *Mrs. Wishy-Washy* where silly farm animals play in the mud, they often find the cumulative predictable texts such as *Jump, Frog, Jump* or *The Napping House* or *Bringing the Rain to Kapiti Plain* quite a bit of fun. "Building stories" like the three just mentioned repeat each additional sentence on every page following its initial introduction. Older students find challenge in trying to read the tongue-twister text fluently without error. Because of the nature of the repetition in the text, students readily understand the need for many rereadings to attain the proper flow and cadence in oral delivery. Mastery of the rhythm becomes the intrinsic reward.

Picture books that follow predictable language patterns are often motivating and interesting to the older beginning reader (see Chapter 5 for a comprehensive list). You most likely will have to spend more time looking for and selecting what you believe will be engaging titles for your students; but you will find it well worth the effort. Though the language may be simpler, the illustrations can be very engaging for the student, and your discussions about content and theme will of course be more abstract than those involving younger students.

Intermediate students in grades four through six who are at the "transitional" phase of literacy development also have the world of picture books open to them. There are so many engaging titles to choose from, far more possibilities than for the beginning reader. What are referred to as high interest/low vocabulary books are also good possibilities. A recommended list is given on page 610. The advantage of high interest/low vocabulary materials is that they address themes and topics of interest to older readers. Another advantage is that they are in fact more "readable" in terms of ease of vocabulary; this is also a disadvantage in that most of them do sound "stilted." If such books are balanced with authentic literature, I don't view the use of high interest/low vocabulary books as a limitation.

For older students who are struggling, the introduction of more readable text may help you identify some rules and practices they may have learned along the way that are interfering with their efforts at and enjoyment of reading. For example, you may notice that a less developed reader will randomly insert words for unknown words solely on the basis of the initial sound. There are many instances when we do encourage students to employ this strategy, but we do so with context in mind. If a student inserts words into the text without considering the overall meaning, you will need to redirect these habits into more useful strategies for identifying unknown words and recognizing key vocabulary. And let's not forget that continued use of dictations can provide one of the most powerful and motivating reading materials for older individuals in general—including adults.

■ **Encouraging Instructional and Independent Reading for Less Developed Readers in Grades 4–6**

■ *Books of Interest for Less-Able Readers*

■ [R = Reading Level; I = Interest Level]

■ *Moonbeam Series.* Benefic Press. [R = Preprimer–1st grade; I = 1st–6th grade] A space-traveling monkey's exploits with his human friends.

Helicopter Adventure Series. Benefic Press. [R = 1st–3rd; I = 1st–4th] Adventures; include women in strong roles.

■ *Find Out About.* Benefic Press. [R = 1st–3rd; I = 1st–6th] Science informational books exploring basic science concepts.

■ *Ready, Set, Go Books.* Children's Press. [R = 1st–3rd, I = 1st–6th] Several different topics are explored, including motorcycles and dinosaurs.

■ *A Book About.* Raintree. [R = 2nd; I = 2nd–4th] Different science topics.

New True Books. Children's Press. [R = 2nd–3rd; I = 1st–4th] Science topics.

■ *Reader's Digest Top Picks.* Random House. [R = 2nd and up; I = 3rd and up] Fiction and nonfiction selections.

■ *Inner City Series.* Benefic Press. [R = 2nd–4th; I = 2nd and up] Young people's realistic situations and problem solving.

■ *Horses and Heroines.* Benefic Press [R = 2nd–4th; I = 4th–6th]. Realistic fiction involving young women and their horses.

■ *Space Police.* Fearon Education. [R = 2nd–3rd; I = 4th and up] Science fiction that addresses realistic contemporary issues.

Sports Mysteries Series. Benefic Press. [R = 2nd–4th; I = 4th and up]. Young teens address problems in school and in sports.

■ In addition to the above series, Scholastic's *Sprint* magazine is very engaging to intermediate students [grades 4–6]. It addresses a wide range of topics.

■ ■ ■

When you are presenting new books to students, be sure to give a short "book talk" about each to whet the students' curiosity and interest. This is especially important if certain books might be perceived as only for younger students.

Send independent-reading books home to be read every night. Emphasize the importance of reading these at home and encourage parents to be supportive of this as well. This is not the kind of reading that these students usually are burdened with—the textbook, for example—but recreational reading.

With many less developed readers, you will find that their ability to construct meaning seems to be minimal. This may have to do with their conception of what reading in fact is (Johns, 1986), and you may need to find this out; the idea that reading deals with understanding may be new to them. In such cases, you may have to break into smaller segments the amount of reading that is done and discussed, and explicitly guide these readers toward strategies for locating and interpreting information.

When working with less developed readers, it will become necessary for you to actively participate in or model almost every activity you ask them to engage in. With you as an involved member of the classroom, your less developed readers will become much more comfortable with taking risks, expressing opinions, and buying into the daily literacy events that will make them better readers.

Younger and older alike, less developed students may need short book introductions to unknown texts to provide a beginning framework for understanding the story structure and anticipated outcomes (Clay, 1991). You can alter the introduction you provide, depending on the needs of your students and the nature of the text you wish them to read. If you have established yourself as a participating member of a small-group or individualized reading session, your think-aloud modeling of how to draw meaning from a text will serve as a guide for the students with whom you are working. How you think through a text to discover meaning, if modeled consistently, will eventually surface in your students' methods of interacting with text. Let's look at an example of think-aloud modeling as it occurs in a multi-age classroom.

Denise Jackson has found Don and Audrey Wood's *The Little Mouse, the Red Ripe Strawberry, and the Big Hungry Bear* particularly intriguing to students of all ages. Although the text in this book is extremely sparse, Ms. Jackson uses this story to encourage active reading from her less developed readers. The authors' careful selection of word choice and expressive illustrations prompts a variety of responses from readers of all levels. It is a text that, once introduced, will grow in interpretation with each rereading. For instance, when Ms. Jackson is working with one or two children, her initial book introduction and book think-aloud usually sounds something like this:

> Today I'd like to share with you a book about a mouse who has a problem with a bear. On the cover, the mouse has his finger up to his lips. I think this tells us that he wants us to be very quiet or that he doesn't want us to show anyone where his strawberry is. And look at that strawberry. It is easily twice the size of the mouse. If I were the bear, I'd certainly like to taste that strawberry. What do you think?

This story progresses with direct conversation going on between the reader and the mouse; yet the mouse doesn't ever answer the reader. He responds through his actions, vividly depicted through the illustrations. Ms. Jackson begins reading this story using a loose GLTA style of prediction and response, in which she adds her opinions and reasons for thinking to the questions she asks her students. Her interaction with the story blends with theirs.

> *Ms. J:* Look at the expression on this little mouse's face. He looks surprised to me. His ears are up. His eyes have a puzzled look. What do you think he's up to?

Jordan: He's hopping along with that ladder. Over at the edge of the page you can just see the strawberry. I think he's going to climb up to the strawberry. On the cover he was standing on a ladder next to the strawberry.

Alex: But where does the bear come in?

Ms. J: Well, let's read to find out.

The teacher completes a full reading of the story. At the close, she asks for thoughts from her students and offers some of her own. She goes back into the text to give examples of how she formed her opinions. Then she invites her students to choral-read the story with her, this time giving each student his or her own copy of the book. As they read together, her students begin to add comments about what they think is happening with the mouse and his interaction with the strawberry. They give details from the illustrations and ask one another questions.

Jordan: He's tried to bury the strawberry. Does the mouse really think the bear won't find it? I think bears can smell things even if they are buried. Would you try to bury it?

Alex: I don't think I'd bury the strawberry to keep it away from the bear. I know I wouldn't try to lock it up either. All those chains would probably be so heavy they would squish the strawberry anyway. Then no one would want to eat it. Come on, let's finish reading.

The talk and the reading continue through several more rereadings. With each rereading, Ms. Jackson prompts less and less and eventually chimes in only on several of the more difficult words like *disguised* and *guarding.*

As the group finishes reading, Ms. Jackson suggests that they take another look at the ways the mouse chose to hide the strawberry.

Ms. J: He's really on guard.

Alex: Look at the tacks the mouse has put all over the floor. Like the bear could really get into the little mouse's house anyway.

Ms. J: What do you think about the bear? Why don't we ever really see him? When I go back and reread how the words have us talking with the mouse, it makes me wonder if the authors haven't just *said* there was a bear, to scare the mouse.

Jordan: What would a bear be doing living in a garden?

Alex: It could be a forest. There are lots of low branches. It kind of looks like a jungle, but we don't have jungles around here. I know strawberries can grow wild. But still I think it's probably a garden. Wait a minute. Maybe *we* are the bear—the person reading the story. Maybe it's all a trick just to get the mouse to share half his strawberry with the person reading the book.

Jordan: No! I think the bear is there somewhere. Look—on this page it says, "BOOM! BOOM! BOOM! The Bear will tromp through the forest on his big, hungry feet, and SNIFF! SNIFF! SNIFF! find the strawberry. . . ."

Alex: Yeah, but why would this page say, "Share half with me"?

The low-key manner in which this teacher guides her students' reading and encourages differing interpretations of the plot by referring to the text, followed by an open-ended question to her students, offers a structured framework for increasing their comprehension. With this particular story, the simplicity of reading allows opportunities for her students to invest their energy in what is going on in the story, rather than in worrying about what the words say. Subsequent rereadings increase her students' fluency and expression.

Ms. Jackson begins each small-group session with Jordan and Alex with a rereading of a favorite story. The boys have been choosing *The Little Mouse, the Red Ripe Strawberry, and the Big Hungry Bear* for the past four days. With each new reading the boys reconsider their thoughts about the mouse's actions, how the reader becomes an active participant in the story, and who the bear really is. Their exchanges continue to be lively and inquisitive. Ms. Jackson will follow this same model when introducing a new book for these two less-developed readers. Her pattern of a brief story introduction, frequent rereadings, and open-ended questioning to redirect her students back into the text helps build her students' ability to read for meaning.

■ ■ ■ ■ ■

Word Study   This element is critical. Word study includes word-sort activities; activities in which word knowledge is applied in context; keeping a word-study notebook or log; word games such as Boggle and Perquackey; card games, and more. In general, the sequence of features the student explores should follow the developmental sequence of word knowledge (see Chapters 5 and 8).

We've already noted that less developed readers usually have spent a great deal of time in the company of phonics worksheets. They still must learn about the features of words, but we have to wean them away from the blind repetition of phonics rules coupled with inability to apply them, as well as away from their love/hate relationship with phonics (they consider phonics all-important, yet they can't stand anything having to do with phonics). We need to make words and their patterns seem interesting again—and this probably will take time. You'll contribute to the students' success if you begin by taking one step back and playing with word features they're familiar with. This will build confidence and consolidate their knowledge, thus allowing productive exploration of new features.

For example, let's consider a child who appears to have moved into the within-word pattern phase of word knowledge, who is ready to explore long vowel patterns. Such a child already knows what she finds challenging about words, so it's best to begin comparing and contrasting words according to short vowel patterns. The child will firm up and consolidate the word knowledge she's reasonably comfortable about, at the same time as she builds confidence in her present word knowledge. When you begin long-vowel word study with her, she will be much more receptive and have more of a foundation for word study.

We've talked before about the debate as to how much word study is necessary for beginning readers. The debate also occurs in the context of discussing word study for less able readers. Many educators suggest that because remedial readers have already been "over phonics-ed," we should avoid much word study with these students. Students are said to "over-rely" on phonics when they read, attempting to sound out almost every word rather than relying on context clues or similarities among words.

Although these observations are correct, the solution is not to downplay word study. In reality, less developed readers have received too much inappropriate word study. In addition, these children usually are reading frustrational-level material—so they appear to over-rely on phonics, when in fact if they were to read more comfortable texts, they would know most of the words (Stanovich, 1992; Gough, Ehri, & Treiman, 1992).

The solution is to structure word study appropriately within a literature-based context. In fact, word study may be even more critical for less developed readers (Gough, Ehri, & Treiman, 1991; Hiebert, 1992). However, it should not be emphasized at the expense of children's experiencing meaningful and enjoyable reading and writing; this is what many educators fear, and this is why they may downplay the role of word study (see, for example, Cullinan & Strickland, 1990). Structuring a language-arts block that includes read-alouds, independent reading time, instructional reading sessions, and word study activities—both guided and independent—will provide the balance for students who routinely tend to overuse their phonics skills. If we give less developed readers reading material that offers them opportunities for growth without overtaxing their abilities, they will progress, using their knowledge of phonics only where it is most appropriate.

Writing We already know that most reading-disabled students do not like reading. Usually their attitude toward writing is even more negative. Even as they've learned that "reading" is getting the words right, they've also learned that writing is getting the spelling right. It does no good to tell these children, "Just write about whatever you want to write about." Even if they believe you really mean it, and even if you tell them not to worry about the spelling, most of the time they will resist writing. Just the act of making the letters is often arduous, and they may not know how to spell a word "the way it sounds."

Why bother, then? Shouldn't we just concentrate on reading? There are two fundamental reasons why encouraging writing is important. First, children "exercise" their knowledge about print, from the word level on up. Every time they attempt to write a word, their developing word knowledge is applied in a rigorous and authentic fashion. Second, children will come to understand that their writing is a personal act that expresses who they are and represents their knowledge. This understanding takes time, but it can emerge. They must come to feel empowered through the writing process, rather than enslaved by it.

Following are some guidelines for getting writing going and sustaining it:

■ *Start with minimal task demands.* Start by requesting for example a one-line response to a short entry you have made in a journal, then comment positively and talk a little about it. Journal entries can also be lists, pictures with labels, or a two or three word comment about a sticker you have placed in the corner of the paper.

■ *Avoid negative criticism early on.* Do *not* follow up by directing the student's attention to a misspelled word you believe he should know how to spell, nor to any words written illegibly. Compliment the student on a job well done and ask him to *read to you* what he has written.

■ *Avoid focusing on trivial aspects.* You needn't call a student's attention to the fact that what he wrote is not a complete sentence or that he has used upper- and lower-case letters inappropriately. At the outset, we just want the students to get a feel of getting something down on paper.

■ *Be sure to model.* Do the type of writing in which you wish to engage the student. Your active participation in your classroom will be strongly motivational for your students, especially for those who are reluctant to write. So if, for example, the student is going to be writing in a journal, you need to have a journal, too.

■ *Write while the student is writing.* Just as when you are writing with your entire class, it is important that you write now. To avoid appearing *too* much like an "expert" when you write, you may wish to pause just a bit more than you usually do and write more slowly.

■ *Avoid lengthy, more formal, pieces of writing.* For less experienced writers, emphasis will remain for some time on just "getting the writing down." If you would like your less developed writers to compose a piece of writing of more than a few lines, consider using a familiar poem or pattern book as a framework. Books like *It Looked Like Spilt Milk* or *The First Song Ever Sung* will give your students a format for writing more than just a few words and will engage them in thoughtful discussions about word choice for conveying specific thoughts and feelings.

■ *Be supportive along the way.* When you believe the student is ready to attempt a particular type or genre of writing, allow that student to work independently, even if he or she needs to struggle a little at times. Step in to help but not to take over. You may need to act as "scribe" from time to time, or point out how many words are correctly spelled, to provide an extra boost.

Literacy instruction for students with primary learning problems

Thus far, we have been discussing problems stemming from factors outside the child—that is, in the environment—and challenges and issues caused by developmental delays. We will now look at children with what are sometimes called "primary" learning problems (Rabinovitch, 1968), those disabilities that are attributed to a dysfunction in the brain or that are so severe that they do not fit within the developmental spectrum with respect to literacy. (Incidentally, the word *primary* here has nothing to do with our other use of this term, as in *primary* grades.) Children who have primary learning problems are often labeled dyslexic. Technically, *dyslexia* refers specifically to children who have extreme difficulty in learning to read. However, severely affected readers usually have difficulty with writing, as well. *Dyslexia* is commonly used to refer to both kinds of profound literacy problems.

Dyslexia is a fearsome term, and parents are alarmed if someone suggests that their child may be dyslexic. There are a number of myths about dyslexia, perpetuated mainly by the popular media. For example, "symptoms" of dyslexia supposedly include "mirror writing" (writing right-to-left with all letters perfectly reversed) or frequent reversals of letters and words in writing. Causes of dyslexia supposedly include poor visual integration—remedied by eye exercises—or failure of the brain to "lateralize," which results in a child's not devel-

MAKING CONNECTIONS

Working with Less Developed Readers One-to-One

From time to time you may be teaching a child who needs intensive one-to-one instruction. What adjustments do you make for children who require such help?

The principles and the content of instruction for children who need one-to-one assistance are not significantly different from those that work in regular classroom situations—they are merely adjusted and made more "compact." Almost everything we've said with respect to reading in general, and about less developed readers in the classroom, also applies to working with less developed readers who need individual instruction. In the one-to-one context, however, you will have more opportunity to be sensitive to a student, to "tune in" and stay tuned in for an extended length of time. Gradually, you will become better able to determine when to ease up, when to move in, when to bear down, and when to change tasks (see, for example, Clay, 1985; Gillet & Temple, 1994; Henderson, 1981; Morris, 1992; Stauffer, Abrams, & Pikulski, 1978; Wixson & Lipson, 1990).

To begin with, you will need to be especially sensitive to and aware of any negative instructional baggage and attitudes your student may be burdened with. To avoid overtaxing his abilities, it's best to begin instruction at his independent level so that he can feel self-assured about what he does know about reading and writing.

You'll need to keep things relatively structured and predictable; this means that every day, the student needs to read, be read to, explore words, and—eventually—write. Although independent writing will be the last element to fall into place, once writing has become a regular part of your routine, your student will be finding it less and less laborious. In addition, whatever competencies the student has developed in reading should be exercised and applied to authentic texts.

As you initiate different activities and procedures, explain *why* you are doing so. For example, tell an older student that what he will be learning about reading from his dictations will help him read unfamiliar texts—his reading materials and other books he may be reading. Older students, especially, will accept new learning situations more readily if they

oping a preference for either the right or the left hand. Believing this to be the result of a "lag" in brain development, some educators in the past recommended involving the child in certain types of physical exercise, in the hope that this would develop the appropriate parts of the brain.

In his extensive work investigating severely disabled readers, Vellutino (1977; 1987) has found that among those children who consistently fall into the lowest ten percentile on measures of reading ability, there are certain persistent difficulties that children labeled dyslexic often experience. By examining these children, he and others have pretty much exploded the myths described above. They have found that severe, persistent reading difficulty is not necessarily signaled by reversals, is not strictly a visual problem, and is not remedied by certain types of physical exercises.

Rather, Vellutino and others have found that difficulties in processing oral

continued

are aware of the purpose of each lesson. For instance, picture sorting may be something your student has never done. Beginning each word study session with something like "I've noticed in your writing that you often confuse the 'ch' in *chair* for the 'sh' in *shoe*. So today I thought we might sort some picture cards that will help you understand the difference between the two sounds."

You will also find that almost every session with the student will involve a few minutes of just talking, usually at the beginning of the session. This reaffirms and develops the bond between the two of you as it allows the student to talk about whatever is on his mind.

The importance of reading to your student cannot be underestimated. You will read not only those books that he'll soon be reading on his own (the one-to-one "shared reading" context) but also books that the student could *not* read on his own. I emphasize this point because I fear that read-alouds get short shrift with many less developed readers. Although specific knowledge or skills can of course be critical, so too is the opportunity to hear what excellent literature sounds like.

You will discover that consistent successful experiences with reading, writing, and word study in a one-to-one instructional setting will provide the extra exposure and support a less developed reader needs to advance in the literacy skills. For you *and* the child, the sessions you spend together are sure to be rewarding.

LEARNING IN CONTEXT: Instruction that is effective for normally developing readers is effective for less able readers in a one-to-one context, with the added advantage of the teacher's informed judgment and support being available at every step.

language may underlie severe reading difficulties (Vellutino, 1977, 1987; Vellu-tino, Scanlon, & Tanzman, 1991; Mann, 1986; Mann & Brady, 1988; Stanovich, 1988). These difficulties may be quite subtle and at first not noticeable. For example, dyslexic individuals often have difficulty storing and retrieving infor-mation via language—in using language as a code, in other words. Specifically, this difficulty may be apparent in the length of time it takes the individual to retrieve a particular word from memory (such as the name of a particular animal) while speaking. Dyslexics also may use other words to describe the concept that the word stands for. I once assessed a young adult who could not recall the word *flag* to name the picture that I showed her. She kept shaking her head and saying, "Flapping in the breeze . . . flapping in the breeze."

Because of this type of difficulty in storing and retrieving information in a verbal mode, dyslexics have difficulty learning how print stands for oral lan-guage, and they experience difficulty in recalling the spoken representation of the printed word as they are scanning print. You can see how this condition would profoundly affect an individual's ability to read connected text with any degree of fluency or enjoyment.

This problem is also manifested in the difficulty dyslexic individuals may have in analyzing a word in terms of its component sounds. Trying to "hold" language steady as an object while taking it apart is a very abstract and challeng-ing task for such a person. We know that young children develop the ability to do it in kindergarten or first grade; for dyslexic individuals, it usually takes a lot longer to develop this ability. Indeed, progress through each developmental stage is much longer than for normal readers—and truly dyslexic individuals will rarely progress beyond the transitional phase of reading.

There is an additional problem here. The symptoms that Vellutino has identi-fied may also be characteristic of children who do not have underlying neuro-physiological problems but who have been "hurt" by inappropriate instruction. For example, when you ask such children to read aloud to you, their minds may go blank, and words that they knew a minute ago have now flown. Their nervousness and anxiety combine to "freeze" their minds. Moreover, this ten-sion actually affects their ability to focus clearly on the print; the print may seem to "jump around," blur, and even disappear momentarily. You probably experience the same feeling on occasion: in a situation where you are extremely nervous, you may have difficulty finding the appropriate words to say or in recalling information that you think you know by heart. Anxiety overrides your cognitive and language processes; this is precisely what happens to a "hurt" reader every time he is placed in a reading situation in which he must "perform."

In the classroom, how can you discriminate between the truly dyslexic child and one who is merely delayed or who has been instructionally "hurt"? If you have established an environment that encourages taking risks with learning, one that provides lots of interesting books, that does the kinds of things we have been talking about all throughout this book, you will become able, over time, to determine whether a child is truly dyslexic. The dyslexic, the instruc-tionally "hurt," and the developmentally delayed reader will all take longer to progress, but you will be far more likely to see progress occur more rapidly for the instructionally "hurt" or developmentally delayed reader than for the truly dyslexic child. Additionally, the instructionally "hurt" and developmentally delayed child will much more readily show his or her literacy skills in a comfortable pair or small-group setting. Moreover, truly dyslexic children often do not retain information about print from one day to the next. Sight words are acquired very slowly; when composing, dyslexic students usually can write just a word or two if at all. The determining difference among developmentally delayed and instructionally "hurt" children and a child who is dyslexic sometimes can become clear only through psychological and language testing provided by the school district; together with your cumulative literacy data, this intensive one-to-one assessment and evaluation will flesh out extensively a student profile much more likely to determine the root of the difficulty. Determining that a student may be truly dyslexic tells you that the prognosis for developing literacy is guarded. The road will be long, and the child will need an understanding, knowledgeable, and skillful instructional guide.

What type of instruction is required? First, you and your school reading specialist and/or resource teacher need to break the tasks down into small components, accompanied by extremely detailed demonstrations, modeling, and talk-throughs. In a few cases, you may need to teach about word structure very specifically and explicitly (see Clay, 1985; Gillet & Temple, 1994; Stauffer, Abrams, & Pikulski, 1978). Second, your overall orientation to instruction should be the same type as I have presented for the less developed reader, with adjustments as they are needed. In other words, for most dyslexic individuals the nature and content of literacy instruction is very much like that for normally developing readers but with a daily extra session of intensely structured work with familiar words and text. Your main concern for the dyslexic child will be finding material he or she can read with ease. Short dictations, along with highly repetitive text such as *Brown Bear, Brown Bear; I See; Ni Macho;* and *The Jigaree,* will provide some of the material you will need.

Help from the reading specialist or resource teacher can be invaluable, especially if he or she can provide additional practice with shared reading, modeling of text to encourage writing, and an extra dose of word study. Increased exposure to print and its conventions, as well as more time spent reading authentic texts, will increase a dyslexic student's fluency and understanding of story. If the specialist can fit into your plans by coming into the classroom to provide supplementary and complementary work with your special needs children, you will see the greatest benefit. Vellutino sums up the instructional focus:

> [Instruction] should be based on intensive one-to-one tutoring and a balanced reading program—one that makes generous use of both the holistic/meaning and the analytic . . . approaches. The training in reading should be supplemented with enrichment activities to foster language development. Such a program can help a child to develop functional and independent reading skills and so remove him or her from the disabled list. (1987, p. 41).

Related special program and special education issues

Many children who have gone through a formal evaluation process with a school psychologist will qualify for special education assistance or support programs. Many of these are provided by law and are subsidized with federal monies.

If these programs can extend and support what you are already doing in the classroom, your students will show consistent progress. Let's take a look at what these programs might be.

A number of special programs serve elementary students who need additional help in reading. For schools in lower socioeconomic neighborhoods, less developed readers may be involved in a "Chapter 1" program, the roots of which began some thirty years ago. In 1965 Congress enacted the Elementary and Secondary Education Act (ESEA), a major legislative package that directed federal dollars toward at-risk schoolchildren. Additional instruction in reading and math were foremost priorities. In 1981 the programs that had been initiated and sustained under ESEA were affected by the Education Consolidation and Improvement Act, and reading and math were addressed under Chapter 1 of the Act. The target population still was students who were developing slowly. Schools serving primarily lower socioeconomic neighborhoods have Chapter 1 programs, and each school has a "Chapter 1" teacher who works with children in need of additional support.

Children identified as being in need of special education services spend part or all of the school day in special education classrooms. They must undergo a formal evaluation by a psychologist. Special education or resource teachers attempt to address the specific needs of such students, which often include more than literacy needs.

Special Education covers a range of categories; those having to do with speech and language and learning disabilities are most relevant for literacy. The close relationship between language and reading suggests the obvious: if students are experiencing difficulty in their oral language processing, they are likely to experience difficulty in reading as well. The recent trend has been to mainstream children who qualify for special services into regular classrooms as much as possible. Currently, many school districts are also trying full inclusion of students, even those with severe emotional difficulties, in the regular classroom setting. Full inclusion, if in fact it proves to be successful and manageable for the regular classroom teacher, may eliminate many special education programs.

P.L. 94–142 (the Education for All Handicapped Children Act of 1975), P.L. 100-146 (the Developmental Disabilities and Bill of Rights Act Amendments of 1987) and P.L. 101-476 (the Individuals with Disabilities Education Act of 1990) are three of the most influential federal laws that exist to ensure that children with severely disabling conditions receive an equal-opportunity education (National Information Center for Children and Youth with Disabilities, 1991). The definition of the term *disability* acquires different interpretations, depending on which specific law is being referred to. However, Gillet and Temple (1990) describe learning-disabled students as those who show "a discrepancy between expected and actual achievement when provided with appropriate instruction . . . [have] difficulty doing tasks that others their age can do without difficulty . . . [with] problem[s] centered around some form of language use . . . [but] not otherwise handicapped by mental retardation, blindness, deafness, or the like" (p. 473).

With respect to literacy, learning disabilities are identified by examining a student's performance on a range of individual diagnostic and psychological tests. As we have already discussed in the preceding section, dyslexic children have a learning disability. However, other children also may qualify for instructional time with a special education teacher. If a significant discrepancy exists between a child's potential and his or her performance, the child may be eligible to receive additional support services. This may include children who are developmentally delayed and those who have been instructionally hurt. It is important to remember, too, that although there are federal laws guiding the placement of children in support programs, each state has the authority to interpret those laws in a manner that will best serve its school populations.

As you can well imagine, learning-disability and other special education programs are not without controversy. Both have come under fire over the last fifteen years for being convenient "dumping grounds" for children with whom regular classroom teachers had difficulty. A disproportionate number of children from nondominant cultures have been placed in special education programs; identification of these students is based on individual standardized tests often administered in situations that can be intimidating. The children do poorly on the tests—thus "qualifying" for special education—because yet once again, the classroom instruction has been inappropriate. There are, of course, many children who are genuinely handicapped, or who truly show an extreme discrepancy between their potential to learn and their daily performance, and legitimately *should* receive services, but special educators themselves are questioning whether the size of the population presently in special education classes primarily represents students who have been "labeled" and should be in regular classrooms. To help alleviate the overpopulation of special education classrooms, literacy programs offering instructional support for children who can benefit from additional one-to-one tutoring have surfaced across the country. For the past several years, the principles of good clinical practice have been applied in schools through the Reading Recovery program (Pinnel et al., 1990). Originating in New Zealand (Clay, 1985), this program couches more direct instruction in word features in a literature-based context. Reading Recovery teachers identify a child's strengths and needs and then tailor the basic read/write/word analysis principles to these specific strengths and needs. Every day, a child meets for no more than thirty minutes with the Reading Recovery teacher. During this time the child reads a new little book, rereads a little book introduced previously, is read to, and writes. Reading Recovery teachers are involved in training other teachers, so the network of expert "early intervention" teachers grows.

In conclusion, it is clear that special services are available for students with genuine special education needs. As Vellutino has shown, however, the basic instructional goals and strategies are very similar to—and in most instances identical to—those for normally developing students. We know that we need to try our very best to provide more one-to-one, appropriately paced instruction. But we have also seen that appropriately identifying these students and providing appropriate literacy instruction *in the regular classroom* can be a challenge. In most instances, additional help from a knowledgeable outside tutor or resource teacher is necessary for real growth.

■ A CONCLUDING PERSPECTIVE

Depending on where you are planning to teach—but assuredly sometime during your teaching career—you will be teaching children whose native language is not English. In addition to maintaining a supportive environment, there are some basic procedures you can follow to help your "L2" students acquire oral and written language competence. These procedures are in fact adaptations of techniques we have covered earlier in this text: Language Experience dictations and the acquisition of a sight vocabulary; word study; read-alouds; predictable or patterned books, wordless books, picture books. How you adapt these techniques and materials will depend on the L2 student's stage of acquisition: comprehension, early speech-production, or extended speech-production.

For both L2 students and students who speak a variant dialect, the codes and conventions of the standard English dialect must be made explicit. This explicitness is an important adaptation; many students from the mainstream culture have already internalized these codes and conventions and made them part of their natural response to reading and writing activities. It is only fair that we help students from nondominant cultures acquire this information as well. This can be done with sensitivity, as we can be realistic about the importance of learning about the mainstream culture and its dialect at the same time as we value students' culture at home.

For children who are struggling with learning to read and write—regardless of their cultural background—we must be explicit in our instruction. This does not mean reverting to the stultifying "skill and drill" approaches of the past, which in fact have done so much to create reading problems. Rather, we embed this explicit and direct teaching, talking, and modeling in an authentic reading and writing context, one in which struggling readers and writers begin to see the potential and the reward of exploring their worlds through print.

Literature, discussion, reading and writing as means of exploration—these recurring themes of this textbook close its concluding chapter. You really do have the opportunity to be in the forefront of a revolution in the way we guide all children into literacy. If for even a moment you doubt the significance of your efforts, consider these words from a wise young American who believed that true change *can* occur, as a consequence of the cumulative efforts of us all:

> Let no one be discouraged by the belief there is nothing one man or woman can do against the enormous array of the world's ills. . . . Few will have the greatness to bend history itself; but each of us can work to change a small portion of events . . . [we] send a tiny ripple of hope, and crossing each other from a million different centres of energy and daring those ripples build a current which can sweep down the mightiest walls of oppression and resistance.

Robert F. Kennedy, June 6, 1966
(Cited by Schlesinger, 1978, p. 803)

Be patient, take risks, and trust in the ideas you explore as you acquire competence as a teacher. You *can* persevere; you *can* be successful; and you will touch not only your students' lives but many, many other lives as well.

■ BECOMING A REFLECTIVE PRACTITIONER

Gibbons, P. (1993). *Learning to learn in a second language.* Portsmouth, NH: Heinemann.

Pauline Gibbons has packed some extremely useful information into this brief volume about teaching children who are learning English as a second language. Gibbons covers all the bases, from establishing appropriate contexts to assessing spoken language knowledge to reading and writing. She addresses those aspects of spoken and written English that may be more obscure to ESL students and offers solid recommendations for dealing with them.

Gilyard, K. (1991). *Voices of the self: A study of language competence.* Detroit: Wayne State University Press.

Keith Gilyard, a professor of English, reflects on his own experiences as a racial minority in American public schools. He describes how he negotiated the worlds of his neighborhood, the school, and eventually academia. His work teaches about the reality of dialect and literacy in a traditional classroom. One is tempted to say that Gilyard succeeded in spite of the system; his work compellingly portrays the social, emotional, and psychological pressures that are inevitably created when classrooms do not acknowledge and incorporate appropriately the cultural backgrounds of their students. For many readers, Gilyard's work may provide the first extensive and genuine insights into the experiences and the perspectives of a minority culture.

McCormick, S. (1994). A nonreader becomes a reader: A case study of literacy acquisition by a severely disabled reader. *Reading Research Quarterly, 29,* 156–176.

Sandra McCormick presents a carefully-documented case study of a boy who, after two years of schooling, knew only four words by sight. After intensive one-to-one instruction over an extended period of time, this student became a reader performing up to his potential. McCormick describes the nature of the instruction provided for this student and discusses the theoretical and practical foundations for this instruction. Notably, systematic examination of word structure as well as intensive reading of appropriate texts were key factors. This article provides an excellent examination of the many issues that touch upon reading instruction in general, and remedial instruction in particular.

Pinnel, G., Lyons, C., DeFord, D., Bryk, A., & Seltzer, M. (1994). Comparing instructional models for the literacy education of high-risk first graders. *Reading Research Quarterly, 29,* 9–39.

Gay Su Pinnell and her colleagues have been involved for a number of years in implementing the "Reading Recovery" model of remediation with at-risk children. Reading Recovery is an intensive one-to-one remedial program that has consistently shown promising results with at-risk children. In this major research study, the Reading Recovery model is compared with three other remedial instructional models. You will probably find the introductory and discussion sections of this article to be of most immediate interest; the nature and the instructional implications from such programs are described quite well. Pinnell and her colleagues suggest that the key features of successful remedial programs are the one-on-one structure and the greater involvement with text than is usually the case with other programs.

Vellutino, F. R. (1987). Dyslexia. *Scientific American, 256,* (3).

Frank Vellutino has conducted some of the most informative investigations to date into the phenomenon of dyslexia, or severe reading disability. In this relatively short article he debunks a number of myths about dyslexia, explores the nature of severe reading disability, and derives implications for instruction. If you were to read but one publication that represented our major understandings about dyslexia—what it is and what it is not—this article should be the one.

Villanueva, V. *Bootstraps* (1993). Urbana, IL: National Council of Teachers of English.

Victor Villanueva, a university English professor, writes of his experience growing up as a Latino in American schools. Through his eyes, we experience the decisions made about his education by those unfamiliar with his culture but who assumed they knew what was good for him (vocational education rather than college prep). He persisted, eventually earning his GED, and went on to earn a Ph.D. A disturbing though inspiring work, *Bootstraps* provides as well an extremely interesting analysis of the differences between the logic of academic prose and the rhetorical patterns of the Spanish language. Though not the first scholar to address this issue, Villanueva provides one of the most engaging portrayals of the educational implications of these differences.

■ REFERENCES

Ashton-Warner, S. (1963). *Teacher*. New York: Simon & Schuster.

Au, K. (1993). *Literacy instruction in multicultural settings*. Fort Worth, TX: Harcourt Brace Jovanovich.

Bereiter, C., & Engelmann, S. (1966). *Teaching disadvantaged children in the preschool*. Englewood Cliffs, NJ: Prentice-Hall.

Chall, J., & Conard, S. (1991). *Should textbooks challenge students?* New York: Teachers College Press.

Chall, J., Jacobs, V., & Baldwin, L. (1990). *The reading crisis: Why poor children fall behind*. Cambridge, MA: Harvard University Press.

Clay, M. (1979). *The early detection of reading difficulties: A diagnostic survey with recovery procedures*. Auckland, New Zealand: Heinemann.

Clay, M. (1985). *The early detection of reading difficulties* (3rd ed.). Portsmouth, NH: Heinemann.

Clay, M. (1991). Introducing a new storybook to young readers. *Reading Teacher, 45*, 264–273.

Cole, M., & Scribner, S. (1978). *Mind in society*. Cambridge, MA: Harvard University Press.

Crawford, L. (1993). *Language and literacy learning in multicultural classrooms*. Boston: Allyn and Bacon.

Cummins, J. (1981). The role of primary language development in promoting educational success for language minority students. In *Schooling and language minority students: A theoretical framework*. Los Angeles: Evaluation, Dissemination, and Assessment Center, California State University.

Delpit, L. (1986). Skills and other dilemmas of a progressive black educator. *Harvard Educational Review, 56*, 379–385.

Delpit, L. (1988). The silenced dialogue: Power and pedagogy in educating other people's children. *Harvard Educational Review, 58*, 280–298.

Dixon, C., & Nessel, D. (1983). *Language experience approach to reading (and writing): LEA for ESL*. Hayward, CA: Alemany Press.

Edwards, C., & Stout, J. (1990). Cooperative learning: The first year. *Educational Leadership, 47*(4), 38–41.

Enright, S., & McCloskey, M. (1988). *Integrating English*. Reading, MA: Addison-Wesley.

Fromkin, V., & Rodman, R. (1993). *An introduction to language* (5th ed.) Fort Worth: Harcourt Brace Jovanovich.

Gibbons, P. (1993). *Learning to learn in a second language.* Portsmouth, NH: Heinemann.

Gillet, J., & Temple, C. (1994). *Understanding reading problems: Assessment and instruction* (4th ed.). New York: HarperCollins.

Gilyard, K. (1991). *Voices of the self: A study of language competence.* Detroit: Wayne State University Press.

Gough, P., Ehri, L., & Treiman, R. (Eds.). (1992). *Reading acquisition.* Hillsdale, NJ: Lawrence Erlbaum Associates.

Hayes, C., Bahruth, R., & Kessler, C. (1991). *Literacy con carino.* Portsmouth, NH: Heinemann.

Heath, S., & Mangiola, L. (1991). *Children of promise: Literate activity in linguistically and culturally diverse classrooms.* Washington, D.C.: National Education Association.

Henderson, E. (1981). *Learning to read and spell: The child's knowledge of words.* DeKalb, IL: Northern Illinois University Press.

Hiebert, E. (Ed.). (1992). *Literacy for a diverse society: Perspectives, practices, and policies.* New York: Teachers College Press.

Johns, J. (1986). Students' perceptions of reading: Thirty years of inquiry. In D. Yaden, Jr., & S. Templeton (Eds.), *Metalinguistic awareness and beginning reading: Conceptualizing what it means to read and write* (pp. 31–40). Portsmouth, NH: Heinemann.

Johnson, D., & Johnson, R. (1986). *Learning together and alone.* Englewood Cliffs, NJ: Prentice-Hall.

Krashen, S. (1982). *Principles and practices in second language acquisition.* London: Pergamon.

Krashen, S., & Terrell, T. (1983). *The natural approach: Language acquisition in the classroom.* Oxford: Pergamon.

Lipson, M., & Wixson, K. (1990). *Assessment and instruction of reading disability.* New York: HarperCollins.

Mann, V. (1986). Why some children encounter reading problems: The contribution of difficulties with language processing and phonological sophistication of early reading disability. In J. Torgeson and B. Wong (Eds.), *Psychological and educational perspectives on learning disabilities* (pp. 133–159). Orlando, FL: Academic Press.

Mann, V., & Brady, S. (1988). Reading disability: The role of language deficiencies. *Journal of Consulting and Clinical Psychology, 56*(6), 811–816.

Morris, D. (1992). Concept of word: A pivotal understanding in the learning-to-read process. In S. Templeton & D. Bear (Eds.), *Development of orthographic knowledge and the foundations of literacy.* Hillsdale, NJ: Lawrence Erlbaum Associates.

National Information Center for Children and Youth with Disabilities. (1991). The education of children and youth with special needs: What do the laws say? *News Digest, 1,* 1–15.

Penfield, J., and Ornstein-Galicia, J. (1985). *Chicano English: An ethnic contact.* Philadelphia: John Benjamins.

Peregoy, S., & Boyle, O. (1993). *Reading, writing, and learning in ESL: A resource book for K-8 teachers.* New York: Longman.

Pinnell, G., Fried, M., & Estire, M. (1990). Reading recovery: Learning how to make a difference. *The Reading Teacher, 43,* 282–295.

Rabinovitch, R. (1986). Reading problems in children: Definitions and classifications. In A. Kenney & V. Kenney (Eds.), *Dyslexia: Diagnosis and treatment of reading disorders* (pp. 1–10). St. Louis, MO: C. V. Mosby.

Reyes, M. (1992). A process approach to literacy instruction for Spanish-speaking students: In search of a best fit. In E. Hiebert (Ed.), *Literacy for a diverse society: Perspectives, practices, and policies* (pp. 157–171). New York: Teachers College Press.

Richard-Amato, P. (1988). *Making it happen: Interaction in the second language classroom.* New York: Longman.

Routman, R. (1991). *Invitations.* Portsmouth, NH: Heinemann.

Schlesinger, A., Jr. (1978). *Robert Kennedy and his times.* Boston: Houghton Mifflin.

Smitherman, G. (1977). *Talkin' and Testifyin'.*

Stanovich, K. (1988). Explaining the differences between the dyslexic and the garden-variety poor reader: The phonological core variable-difference model. *Journal of Learning Disabilities, 21*(10), 590–604.

Stauffer, R., Abrams, J., & Pikulski, J. (1978). *Diagnosis, correction, and prevention of reading disabilities.* New York: Harper & Row.

Strickland, D., & Cullinan, B. (1990). Afterword. In M. Adams, *Beginning to read: Thinking and learning about print.* Cambridge, MA: MIT Press.

Vellutino, F. (1977). Alternative conceptualizations of dyslexia: Evidence in support of a verbal-deficit hypothesis. *Harvard Educational Review, 47*(3), 334–354.

Vellutino, F. (1987). Dyslexia. *Scientific American,* 256(3), 34–41.

Vellutino, F., Scanlon, D., & Tanzman, M. (1991). Bridging the gap between cognitive and neuropsychological conceptualizations of reading disability. *Learning and Individual Differences, 3,* 181–203.

Villanueva, V. (1993). *Bootstraps.* Urbana, IL: National Council of Teachers of English.

Wong-Fillmore, L. (1982). Language minority students and school participation: What kind of English is needed? *Journal of Education, 164,* 143–156.

NAMES CITED INDEX

Fine, J., 318
Finkelstein, N., 315
Fischel, J., 88
Fischer, L.E., 318
Fisher, L., 401, 471
Fisher, L.E., 316
Fisher, R., 180
Fitzhugh, G., 244
Flavell, J., 43
Fleming, J., 489
Flesch, R., 9, 488
Flood, J., 152
Flood, S., 152
Flores, B., 489, 518
Flournoy, V., 442
Forbes, E., 337
Fountoukidis, D., 411
Fox, D., 319
Fox, P., 443
Francis, W. N., 185
Frank, R., 247, 447
Frasier, D., 362
Freebody, P., 376
Freedle, R., 326, 369
Freedman, R., 316, 327, 331, 449
Freeman, D., 180
Freeman, Y., 491
Freire, P., 517
Freppon, P., 212
Frith, U., 68
Fritz, J., 315, 469
Fromkin, V., 40, 602
Fry, E., 185, 411
Fulwiler, T., 205
Fyson, N., 471

Gag, W., 88, 180, 246, 337
Galda, L., 88, 437
Galdone, P., 109, 246
Gallagher, M., 351
Gallant, R., 317
Gamberg, R., 426
Gambrell, 267
Gamil, M., 271
Gardiner, J.R., 447
Gardner, H., 82, 313
Gardner, R.A., 316
Garland, S., 446
Garner, R., 43
Garrison, C., 472
Garza, C., 438
Gates, D., 401
Gee, J., 242
Genishi, C., 13
Gennaro, J., 317
Gentry, J., 218

George, J.C., 246, 317
Gerstein, M., 471
Gibbons, G., 108, 316, 317
Gibbons, P., 591, 596, 598, 623
Gibbs, J., 162
Giblin, J.C., 317
Gibson, E., 94
Giff, P.R., 233
Gill, J., 257, 338, 551
Gilleis, J., 449
Gillet, J., 218, 228, 537, 542, 551, 616, 619, 620
Gilliland, J., 443
Gilyard, K., 601, 602, 623
Giovanni, N., 442, 603
Girard, L.W., 315
Girion, B., 438
Glazer, S., 528, 550
Gleiter, J., 449
Glenn, C., 242
Goble, P., 438, 441, 447
Goetz, E., 42, 44
Goffstein, M.B., 319
Goldfield, B., 89
Goodman, K., 43, 51, 74, 424, 474, 489, 491, 518
Goodman, Y., 51, 74, 118, 313, 526, 529, 538, 573
Gorey, E., 260
Gorog, J., 445
Goswami, U., 95
Gough, P., 49, 614
Gould, S., 488
Graham, A., 319
Graham, G., 440
Grahame, K., 444
Grant, C., 273
Graves, D., 302, 360, 367, 489
Graves, M., 280, 286, 287, 288
Gray, N., 442
Gray, W., 331
Greene, M., 7, 8, 24
Greenfield, E., 438, 442, 448, 456
Griego y Maestas, J. , 441
Grifalconi, A., 246, 442
Griffin, P., 5
Grillone, L., 317
Gullo, S.V., 315
Guthrie, J., 45, 353, 369
Gwynne, F., 394

Hague, K., 97
Hairston, M., 311
Haley, G., 439, 447
Haley-James, S., 334
Haley, 603

Hall, M., 90, 112, 190
Hall, N., 449
Hall, R., 393
Halliday, M., 41
Hamanaka, S., 448
Hamilton, V., 245, 282, 439, 445, 447, 448, 603
Hammond, D., 347
Hansen, J., 134, 203, 272, 286, 443, 529
Harris, 435
Harrison, L., 99
Harrison, M., 442
Harste, J., 65, 426, 452, 472, 491, 547
Harvey, B., 447
Haskins, J., 315, 319, 472
Hawkinson, J., 319
Hayes, C., 399, 593
Heald-Taylor, G., 109, 110
Heard, G., 290
Heath, S.B., 8, 19, 30, 86, 103, 273, 397, 425, 430
Hedlund, I., 472
Heide, F., 180, 260, 443
Heimlich, J., 408
Heller, R., 317, 337
Henderson, E., 69, 89, 95, 190, 193, 214, 218, 385, 406, 616
Henk, W., 506
Henkes, K., 445
Henry, M., 388, 411
Hepler, S., 271, 437
Herriman, M., 94
Hewett, J., 444
Heyer, M., 469
Hickman, J., 437
Hiebert, E., 123, 518, 562, 569, 570, 573, 574, 614
Highwater, J., 316, 442, 447
Hill, S., 162
Hill, T., 162
Hinojosa, F., 441
Hirschfelder, A., 449
Hirschi, R., 317
Hoban, F., 233
Hoban, R., 233
Hoban, T., 97, 108
Hobbs, W., 444
Hoffman, S.M., 317
Holdaway, D., 90, 96, 110, 263
Hooks, W., 447, 472
Hopkins, L.B., 456
Hornsby, D., 24, 560
Hoyt-Goldsmith, D., 449
Hubbard, W., 97
Huck, C., 437, 440
Hudson, J., 448

SUBJECT INDEX

Ability-level groups, 49, 51, 53, 152–153, 157–158
Abstract thinking, 21
Accents, 41
Achievement groups, 142, 155
Acronyms, 393
Aesthetic purpose, for reading, 45, 179, 250, 255–256, 284, 425
Affect, 39–40, 44, 58, 73
Affective filter, 44, 588
Affixes, 386–387, 406
African-American English, 603
African-American literature, 439, 442–443, 446, 448
African-American students, 273
African literature, 439, 448
Age-appropriate books, 232
Alliteration, 244
Alphabet, augmented, 500, 516
Alphabet books, 96–97
Alphabetic knowledge, 68
Alphabetic principles, 221
Alphabetic spelling, 213–215
American Readers, 493
Analogy, 410–411
Analysis, 70
Anticipation, 193
Antonyms, 402
Art, 314–315
Asian-American literature, 440, 443, 446–448
Asian thematic unit plan, 466–472
Assessment, 526
    defined, 527
    grading and, 562–564, 573
    Guided Reading-Thinking Activities and, 257, 259
    informal reading inventory and, 533–543
    observation and, 529–533, 546–556, 572
    performance-based, 569
    portfolio, 527–528, 556–562, 573
    purposes and settings for, 528–529
    qualitative, 539–540
    standardized testing and, 564–569

of writing, 543–546, 570
Association, positive, 323
At-risk children, 86–87, 430, 586
Audiovisual material, 111, 502–508, 598
Augmented alphabet, 500, 516
Authenticity, 18–20, 434–435
Authentic reading/integrated literacy approach, 5, 10–11, 515–516. *See also* Literature, authentic
Author, 455

Background, mainstream and nonmainstream, 86–87
Background knowledge. *See* Knowledge, background
Basal readers, 25, 27, 50, 141–142, 159, 488, 490–495, 510–514, 516
Base words, 383, 386–387, 406
Beginning reading. *See* Reading, beginning
Behavior, and learning, 487
Behavior norms, classroom, 163
Big Books, 111–112, 182–184, 202, 501, 593
Bilingual education, 587
Biography, 435, 437, 448–450
"Blended" words, 393
Bloomfield, Leonard, 487
Book Links, 501
Books
    immersion in, 102–103
    introduction of, 198
    parts of, 330
    sources for, 232–233
    vocabulary development and, 202
Bookshelf collection, 232
Booktalk, 271–272
Bottom-up model, 49–50, 52–53, 56, 73, 599
Bridge experiences, 256–265, 293
Bulletin boards, 137
Business principles, 487

California Reading Initiative, 495, 517
Card games, 183

Caribbean literature, 439–441, 443–444, 447, 449
Carpet area, 137
Categorical relationships, 404–408
Categorization, 193, 409–410, 599
Cause/effect pattern, 327
Chapter books, 242
Characterization, 243, 269, 281, 288
Charts
    curriculum, 141
    group-dictated experience, 113
    sound, 222, 224, 226
    story map, 279
    students' progress, 142
    thematic-unit planning and, 456
Chicano English, 603
Child development, 20
Children's literature. *See* Literature, children's
Choral reading, 114–115, 189
Classroom environment, 132–140, 179
Classroom time, 140–142, 145–150
"Clipping" words, 393
Cloze passage, 332, 334
Clusters, 342
Collaboration, 132–134, 161–163, 287, 289
Collection pattern, 326–327
Colloquialism, 400
Commonsense model, 49
Community
    integrated with classroom, 87
    involvement of, 188, 591–593
    sense of, 134, 166
Comparison and contrast, 94, 282, 327–328, 395
Composition, 416–417
Compound words, 387, 390
Comprehensible input, 588
Comprehension, 58–60, 70, 588–589
Comprehensive Test of Basic Skills, 568
Computer area, 137
Computer materials, 504–508
"Concept" books, 108–109, 187
Concept load, 328
Concept, defined, 42

"Word" method, 485–486
Wordplay, 403
Word processors, 191
Word-recognition lists, 536
Words
    awareness of, 67, 101–102, 175
    base, 383, 386, 387, 406
    blended, 393
    clipping, 393
    compound, 387, 390
    concept of, 95, 101, 548
    content, 41
    function, 41, 65, 185
    high-frequency, 185
    meaning and, 378, 400–402
    order of, 41
    reading instruction and, 64, 483,
        485–486
    relationships among, 402–408
    semantic biographies of, 405
    sight. *See* Sight vocabulary
    structure of, 43, 64
    substitute, 395

unknown, 382, 386, 488, 609
    whole, 595
Word Sorts, 228–229, 406–408, 599, 613
Word structure, 376–377, 383, 388,
        390, 392–393, 411
Word study, 111, 597, 599, 607, 613–
        615
Word study notebooks, 145, 413, 416
Word wall, 186
Word web, 408–409
Working memory, 55–58
Workplace, and reading contexts, 46
World knowledge, 40, 62, 70, 135
Writers' workshop, 155, 166, 473
Writing
    activities for, 598
    assessment of, 543–546, 570
    children's awareness of, 89–90
    children's modeling of, 119
    constructing meaning and, 285–
        289, 359–368
    facilitation of, 118–121
    forms of, 211

informational texts and, 359–368
integration with reading, 18–19, 50,
    52, 54, 63, 65–67, 176, 203–205,
    212, 275–278, 285–289, 293,
    359–368, 614–615
journals for, 121, 205–207
language development and, 68–69
Language Experience Approach to,
    120–121
metalinguistic awareness and, 95
prewriting and, 367
in response to reading, 275–278
risk-taking and, 116–118
shared book experiences and, 119–
    120
stories and, 207–211
by teachers, 289
vs. drawing, 89, 91–92
word knowledge and, 416–417
Writing center, 119
Writing portfolio, 561

Zoobook, 135, 501

CREDITS

Chapter Opener Photos: Chapter One, © Elizabeth Crews/The Image Works; **Chapter Two,** © Jean-Claude LeJeune/Stock Boston; **Chapter Three,** © Jean-Claude LeJeune/Stock Boston; **Chapter Four,** © Donna Day/ Tony Stone Images; **Chapter Five,** © Elizabeth Crews/Stock Boston; **Chapter Six,** © Bob Daemmrich; **Chapter Seven,** © Richard Hutchings/PhotoEdit; **Chapter Eight,** © Crandall/The Image Works; **Chapter Nine,** © Jerry Howard/Stock Boston; **Chapter Ten,** © Arthur Tilley/Tony Stone Images; **Chapter Eleven,** © Mug Shots/The Stock Market; **Chapter Twelve,** © Peter Beck/The Stock Market.

Figure 3.2: (three letters) From *Let's Be Friends,* by Pikulski et al., Kindergarten level, TE, © 1991 by Houghton Mifflin Company. Reprinted by permission of Houghton Mifflin Company. All rights reserved.

Figure 5.2: (Early sight words) Two illustrations with (single words of) text from *Here a Chick, There a Chick* by Bruce McMillan. © 1983 by Bruce McMillan, by permission of Lothrop, Lee & Shepard Books, a division of William Morrow & Company, Inc.

Figure 5.4: Illustration from McPhail, David, *Fix-It,* Copyright © 1994. Used with permission from Dutton Children's Books, a division of Penguin USA Inc.

Figure 5.17: (Spelling and vocabulary) From *Spelling and Vocabulary,* level 2, by Henderson et al., © 1990 by Houghton Mifflin Company. Reprinted by permission of Houghton Mifflin Company. All rights reserved.

Figure 6.1: Templeton, Shane, *Teaching the Integrated Language Arts.* Copyright © 1991 by Houghton Mifflin Company. Adapted with permission.

Figure 6.5: Illustration by Edward Gorey from *The Shrinking of Treehorn* by Florence Heide, Copyright © 1979. Used with permission from Dell Publishing Group.

Figure 7.3: (I hate mathematics) From *I Hate Mathematics Book* by Marilyn Burns. Copyright © 1975 by Yolla Bolly Press. By permission of Little, Brown and Company.

Figure 7.11 (left): (The South Expands) From *This Is America's Story* by Wilder, et al. Copyright © 1986 by Houghton Mifflin Company. Reprinted by permission of Houghton Mifflin Company. All rights reserved.

Figure 7.13: (On the day you were born) Excerpts and illustrations from *On The Day You Were Born,* copyright 1991 by Debra Frasier, reproduced by permission of Harcourt Brace & Company.

Figure 8.2: Reproduced by permission from *The American Heritage Dictionary of the English Language,* Third Edition. Copyright © 1994 by Houghton Mifflin Company.

Figure 10.3: (Preparation for reading) Excerpts from *Heath American Readers,* © 1986 by D. C. Heath & Company. Reprinted by permission.

Figure 10.4: (Developing Strategic Reading) From *Dinosauring,* level 4, by Pikulski et al., TE © 1993 by Houghton Mifflin Company. Reprinted by permission of Houghton Mifflin Company. All rights reserved.

Table 11.1: From *Understanding Reading Problems: Assessment and Instructions,* Third Edition by Jean Wallace Gillet and Charles Temple. Copyright © 1990 by Jean Wallace Gillet and Charles Temple. Reprinted by permission of HarperCollins Publishers, Inc.

Table 11.2: D. R. Bear and D. Barone, *Developing Literacy: An Integrated Approach to Diagnosis and Instruction.* Used with permission from Houghton Mifflin Company.

Figure 11.9: Figure adapted from R. Routman, *Invitations,* copyright © 1991. Used with permission from Heinemann-Boynton-Cook.

After studying many situations in which parents were reading to their children, Taylor & Strickland (1986) found that, regardless of ethnic, educational, and socioeconomic background, most parents "often expand and extend the content of the stories in natural and meaningful ways. Parents seem to sense when such expansions are necessary, or when an unembellished reading is the best way to share a particular story" (Taylor & Strickland, 1989, p. 30). The context of these story-reading experiences is usually—though not always!—a cuddly one. Bedtime is popular for booksharing, and usually more manageable for parents. Still, regardless of the time, when children want to be read to, they usually will come to the parent with a book and a demand to be read to.

Two of my children followed the scenario parents dream of. As I read to them they were usually plopped in my lap or cuddled next to me, their attention riveted on the book. They were interested, wanted to see the pictures, made comments, and asked questions about what was being read. For our middle child, however, this was decidedly not the case! He was not a "cuddler" during our reading and in fact displayed little overt interest in whatever was being read to him. I eventually learned, however, that even as he was roaming about the room, appearing to be engrossed in other activities, he was still paying a good deal of attention to what I was reading. As I sat on the floor, reading aloud, he would toddle over from time to time to have a peek at the pictures, then toddle off to get back to his blocks or whatever. I got used to this, and learned not to take it personally! So you can reassure parents who worry about their children's *not* appearing to take an interest in books that they should continue to read aloud, probably on the floor, and that very often this in itself will tempt the "active" child to come on over for a look.

Parents learn early on that children enjoy having a favorite book read to them over and over. We should indulge children in this, but also not be reluctant to introduce another book we feel they would enjoy. The advantages of reading the same book repeatedly are many. Children come to remember the story and will "read" it on their own, using pictures as clues. But we also have the opportunity to talk about what is going on in the book, from a number of different angles, and this is important, too. Remember that for young children, these stories and rhymes are like friends, and no one wishes to leave friends after only one visit!

LEARNING IN CONTEXT: As teachers, we cannot emphasize too strongly to parents the values of their reading to their children—whether their children are "cuddlers" or "wanderers" during reading time.

can be like any other type of play for very young children. At first, they don't realize that what we are saying has much to do with the book. Before long, though, we can engage the children in talk about the book. We behave as though the infant or toddler answered a question we posed, for example. In her research on reading to very young children, Ninio (1980) found that parents seemed to use three strategies or routines when sharing books with their very

From Chapter 3, page 106, the above special feature is only one example of the multiple ways this book communicates with you. See the *Special Features Table of Contents* on page xviii in the front of this book.